INDIAN COUNCIL OF HISTORICAL RESEARCH
MONOGRAPH SERIES 6

Recent Studies in Indian Archaeology

This volume contains papers contributed by senior scholars from both India and abroad who have first-hand and long-standing experience in Indian archaeology. The papers aim to synthesise existing knowledge on major topics in Indian archaeology. These topics cover prehistory, protohistory, rock art, historical and medieval archaeology, scientific studies, human skeletal biology and dating methods. While serving as comprehensive reviews on the respective topics, these essays will also fulfil the purpose of highlighting the gaps in our current knowledge and help plan further research to fill them up.

Dr. K. Paddayya is Professor of Geoarchaeology at the Deccan College, Pune. His prolonged research on the Paleolithic and Neolithic cultures of the Shorapur Doab in the Deccan, including the excavations at Hunsgi and Budihal, represents a major addition to post-Independence archaeology in India. He has published three books entitled *Investigations into the Neolithic Culture of the Shorapur Doab, South India* (Leiden, 1973); *The Acheulian Culture of the Hunsgi Valley (Peninsular India): A Settlement System Perspective* (Pune, 1982); and *New Archaeology and Aftermath: A View from Outside the Anglo-American World* (Pune, 1990) and many research papers in Indian and foreign journals.

Recent Studies in Indian Archaeology

Edited By

K. PADDAYYA

Deccan College, Pune

Munshiram Manoharlal Publishers Pvt. Ltd.

ISBN 81-215-0929-7
First published 2002

Published by

MUNSHIRAM MANOHARLAL PUBLISHERS PVT. LTD.
Post Box 5715, 54 Rani Jhansi Road, New Delhi 110 055

in association with

INDIAN COUNCIL OF HISTORICAL RESEARCH
35 Ferozeshah Road, New Delhi 110 001

Typeset, printed and published by Munshiram Manoharlal Publishers Pvt. Ltd.
Post Box 5715, 54 Rani Jhansi Road, New Delhi 110 055.

❖ Contents

❖ Preface

I would like to place on record that the original idea of bringing out this collection of essays in Indian archaeology was mooted by Professor S. Settar, Chairman of the Indian Council of Historical Research, New Delhi. This was one among the several volumes in historical and archaeological studies which Professor Settar had planned to publish on behalf of the ICHR to mark the golden jubilee of India's Independence.

Accordingly, invitations were sent to about two dozen scholars who are actively engaged in field research or laboratory studies concerning various aspects of Indian archaeology. In tune with the overall nature of the volumes planned by Professor Settar, the invited scholars were asked to prepare papers on general themes, reviewing the present status of research on the respective topics. Such reviews, it was felt, would be useful not only to students and research workers in archaeology but also to others belonging to history and related disciplines. Secondly, these papers could serve to highlight the gaps in our current knowledge and help plan further research to fill them up.

Due to other commitments some of the scholars could not accept the invitation to contribute papers. The present collection thus consists of seventeen papers which cover prehistory, protohistory, rock art, historical and medieval archaeology, scientific studies, palaeoanthropology and dating methods. I am satisfied that this is a fairly representative collection of recent studies in Indian archaeology and hope that the volume will be found useful by both students and research scholars.

Finally, I would like to place on record my gratitude to all the scholars who have readily responded to the invitation to contribute papers. Professor V.N. Misra, my senior colleague at the Deccan College, Pune, has favoured me with his valuable guidance at various stages in the preparation of this volume. Shri S.I. Amin has computer-typed the manuscripts of papers. I have received very helpful editorial assistance from Dr. Richa Jhaldiyal. I am thankful to all of them for their assistance. I deeply appreciate the faith put in me by Professor Settar as well as the complete freedom he has given me in bringing out this volume.

Pune
August 10, 1999

K. Paddayya
EDITOR

❖ Contributors

A. Tavares
Post-Doctoral Research Scholar
Department of Archaeology
Deccan College
Pune 411 006

D.P. Agrawal
Former Professor
Physical Research Laboratory
Navrangpura
Ahmedabad 380 009

G.L. Possehl
Professor of Anthropology
University of Pennsylvania
Philadelphia, Pa 19104–6394
U.S.A.

J.N. Pal
Reader
Department of Ancient History,
Culture and Archaeology
University of Allahabad
Allahabad 211 002

K. Krishnan
Reader
Department of Ancient Indian History,
Culture and Archaeology
M.S. University of Baroda
Vadodara 390 002

K. Paddayya
Professor of Geoarchaeology
Department of Archaeology
Deccan College
Pune 411 006

M.G. Yadava
Scientist
Physical Research Laboratory
Navrangpura
Ahmedabad 380 009

M.K. Dhavalikar
Former Professor of Protohistoric
and Early Historical Archaeology
Department of Archaeology
Deccan College
Pune 411 006

M.S. Mate
Former Professor of Proto-
and Ancient Indian History
Department of Archaeology
Deccan College
Pune 411 006

R. Korisettar
Professor
Department of History and Archaeology
Karnatak University
Dharwad 580 003

R.S. Pappu
Former Reader in Environmental Archaeology
Department of Archaeology
Deccan College
Pune 411 006

R.W. Dennell
Professor of Prehistory
Department of Archaeology
University of Sheffield
Sheffield S1 4ET
U.K.

S. Kusumgar.
Scientist
Physical Research Laboratory
Navrangpura
Ahmedabad 380 009

S.N. Rajaguru
Former Professor of Geoarchaeology
Department of Archaeology
Deccan College
Pune 411 006

S.R. Walimbe
Reader in Physical Anthropology
Department of Archaeology
Deccan College
Pune 411 006

Vibha Tripathi
Professor
Department of Ancient Indian History, Culture and Archaeology
Banaras Hindu University
Varanasi 221 005

V.H. Sonawane
Professor
Department of Ancient Indian History, Culture and Archaeology
M.S. University of Baroda
Vadodara 390 002

V.S. Shinde
Reader in Asian Archaeology
Department of Archaeology
Deccan College
Pune 411 006

1 ❖ The Indian Palaeolithic Since Independence: An Outsider's Assessment

R.W. DENNELL

INTRODUCTION

The legacy of British rule in India can be either lavishly praised or heavily criticised, and it is perhaps sensible to heed both viewpoints. There were undoubted benefits from the 89 years of direct British rule: a high quality civil service, good administration, relatively efficient and fair methods of collecting revenue and dispensing justice; a first-class army, and a good infrastructure of railways, communications. In archaeological terms, the British also had some reason for satisfaction. Its numbers had included outstanding antiquarians, palaeontologists and surveyors. Orientalists such as Sir William Jones rediscovered Sanskrit, and made public the richness of India's literary Sanskrit past. The mapping of India through the Great Trigonometrical Survey in the early nineteenth century was an outstanding achievement, and the accompanying topographical surveys under men like Colin Mackenzie, an eventual Surveyor-General of India, also recorded thousands of monuments (see Keay 1988). Major figures like Robert Bruce Foote and Alexander Cunningham (the first Director-General of Archaeology) put the systematic recording of India's antiquities on a professional footing; Viceroys such as Canning established the Archaeological Survey of India as early as 1861, and later, Curzon recognised that the preservation of India's antiquities was an important imperial responsibility. Palaeontologists such as Falconer and Cautley published the first monograph of the fossils of the Indian Siwaliks as early as 1845, thus making it one of the earliest on palaeontology. The first Palaeolithic implements were found by Robert Bruce Foote at Pallavaram, southern India, in 1863, only four years after the human antiquity was demonstrated in Britain and France. Officers of the Geological Survey of India such as Pilgrim in the early twentieth century were at the forefront of investigations into the Miocene to Pleistocene on a Eurasian, if not world-wide, scale. Additionally, there were scholarly giants like Sir John Marshall, who brought the Harappan civilisation to light as well as the country's Greek and Buddhist past. Although rightly castigated by Sir Mortimer Wheeler, the last British Director-General of Archaeology in India, for his obsolete recording methods, Marshall still stands as a giant in studies of world civilisation. Wheeler himself did an amazing amount of work in his brief tenure, given the restrictions of war-time, the momentum towards independence, and the increasing loss of control by the British in their final years of rule.

On the other hand, the tapestry of achievements under British rule was often flimsy and threadbare. Often, it was a case of a few remarkable individuals, who, in Wheeler's memorable phrase of Marshall, were lofty trees under which nothing grew. Too often, they were individuals without students, working in departments without the means to train successors. Although I have referred to the interwar years as the golden years of imperial scholarship (Dennell 1990), the facade does not withstand detailed inspection. Palaeolithic studies in India in the fifty years before Independence were very sparse: the main ones are a paper by Andersen (1917); Cammiade and Burkitt (1930) on south-east India, one by Todd (1939) on the Palaeolithic of the Bombay area, and of course the monograph by De Terra and Paterson (1939) on their survey of northern India in 1935, funded from Yale University. Almost all of these persons, were employed by the Government of India in administrative service. It is not an especially creditable record of imperial research.

To place this record in context, matters were not very different throughout the rest of the British Empire at the time, or for that matter in Britain itself. During the inter-war years (and indeed, long before that), most archaeological work in Britain was undertaken by amateurs such as (in Palaeolithic contexts) Hazeldine Warren, Reid Moir, Worthington Smith, and A.T. Marston. There were one or two outstanding figures in public service, such as O.G.S. Crawford in the Ordinance Survey, who pioneered air photography in archaeology, and a few university figures such as Grahame Clark (Cambridge), Gordon Childe (Edinburgh), Christopher Hawkes (Oxford) and (after 1935) and Frederick Zeuner (London). Public expenditure in the 1920–30s was always far below requirements, both at home and abroad. Indeed, given that the total university population of undergraduate and post-graduate students in the U.K. in 1939 was less than 50,000 (compared with >1 million today), it is unsurprising that so little was done both in the U.K. and abroad.

INDIAN PALAEOLITHIC STUDIES: POST-INDEPENDENCE

Before considering what Indian researchers have accomplished in Palaeolithic studies since Independence, it is worth considering two issues: the way archaeological research was organised at and after 1947, and the role of foreign collaboration.

Organisational Structures

In the nineteenth century, India acquired the same type of state-funded structures as in Britain for studying archaeology in general, and the Palaeolithic in particular. The main body was the Archaeological Survey of India (ASI), established in 1861; there was also its geological counterpart, the Geological Survey of India (GSI), and a handful of university departments whose members could claim a serious interest in the Pleistocene and Palaeolithic of India. In theory, the ASI and GSI were the national bodies ultimately responsible for documenting and investigating the archaeological and geological record of India through its field officers. The universities initially had a supporting role, the main one of which was to provide high-quality recruits for the professions and public service (including the ASI and GSI), and to undertake local research if funds permitted.

This type of dual structure has both strengths and weaknesses, whether in Britain or India. National, centrally-funded bodies such as English Heritage (or, more accurately speaking, its earlier versions) and the ASI were established to safeguard and record the national heritage. In theory, they could devote themselves wholly to recording the remains under their care, and demonstrate their commitment to those objectives through high-quality scholarship, thereby justifying public expenditure. They were also meant to be cheap: as the Viceroy, Lord Canning put it when agreeing to establish the ASI in 1861, anything more than the recording of monuments "would require an expenditure of labour and money far greater than any government of India could reasonably bestow" (Keay 1988: 81). In practice, bodies such as the ASI were always under-resourced and under-staffed, were always vulnerable to any cuts in public expenditure, and could never do more than a minimum.

In the last 50 years in both Britain and India, the relationship between national bodies such as the ASI (or its British equivalents) and the universities has changed enormously. Overall, the funding and implementation of prehistoric research has shifted decisively towards the universities. In both countries (and generally speaking, throughout most of the world), universities have become larger, more numerous, and more research-active. They often attract better funding, are usually better equipped with books and laboratories, and by their nature, are more outward looking: academics need to publish, and are more used to giving and receiving criticism. Consequently, the main discoveries, innovations and publications increasingly originate in universities rather than in national centrally-funded bodies.

Without wishing to be partisan or unduly critical of any individual or institution, the British experience of these changes may have relevance for India. In Britain, national bodies such as English Heritage and Scottish Heritage still provide the main framework for the care of national monuments, funding for the investigation of major sites (such as Boxgrove), and the legislative protection of the archaeological heritage. They also tend to work in partnership with university departments, and it is these that provide most of the expertise for excavation and post-excavation analysis. (The situation is admittedly more complex in Britain, as much rescue and contract archaeology is undertaken by excavations units, many of which are part of or affiliated to university departments; but the general principle of partnership remains.) Indian archaeology at the end of this century might benefit from closer collaboration between universities and the ASI and GSI.

The establishment of national bodies responsible for archaeology and geology had particularly unfortunate consequences on studies of the Palaeolithic in both Britain and India. From the outset, it meant that the study of the Palaeolithic and the Pleistocene was artificially separated from each other by being split between archaeology and geology. (The same divide was also reflected in many university departments, although a few such as Cambridge and Pune were important exceptions.) Even more unfortunate was the fact that neither the Palaeolithic nor the Pleistocene were seen as major priorities in their respective institutions. In a landscape so rich in monuments as India, it is unsurprising that most energies were directed to exploring and recording ancient civilisations. Likewise, the Miocene, which is so superbly represented by the Siwaliks of the northern subcontinent, overshadowed the study of the Pleistocene. Although much has been done in the last 25 years (largely through university departments) to rectify these imbalances, Palaeolithic and Pleistocene studies have tended to lag behind the study of later periods.

Foreign Involvement

In a review of what has been achieved in Palaeolithic archaeology in India since Independence, it is right and proper that the main emphasis should be on Indian researchers. Nevertheless, foreign researchers have also played a role, and that too should be acknowledged. My intention here is to place this involvement in perspective, particularly as India is sometimes criticised for being inaccessible to foreign researchers.

For many laudable reasons, India opted for self-sufficiency after Independence, and its self-reliance over the last fifty years is cause for pride and praise. The type of foreign institutes that were set up in, e.g. Turkey, Jordan, (and for a time, Iran and Iraq) and enabled foreign nationals to conduct survey and excavation under an approved permit system, and in compliance with existing Antiquities' legislation, did not occur in India. Nor did India follow the system adopted in neighbouring countries such as Pakistan, whereby a small number of permits are issued to foreigners for specific archaeological projects, in collaboration with the central government Department of Archaeology. Consequently, the number of foreign archaeologists who have undertaken or collaborated in Palaeolithic or Pleistocene research in India in recent decades has been fewer than in Pakistan, or countries such as Israel or Kenya.

It is, however, equally true that the number of foreigners participating in Indian archaeological research has actually increased since Independence, and increased greatly in the last twenty years. This point needs to be remembered, particularly by those Western researchers who contrast India unfavourably with countries like Kenya or Israel in terms of ease of access to research projects. Before Independence, very few foreigners (excluding those in state service) undertook archaeological work in India: in the arena of studies of the Palaeolithic and human evolution, the main ones were Burkitt (1930), those on the Yale Expedition of 1934–35 (Lewis at Haritalyangar, De Terra and Paterson in 1935–36), and American palaeontologists such as Barnum Brown in the 1920s, and Colbert in the 1930s. Since 1947, many more have participated: key figures from Britain were Zeuner (1950, 1951), invited to Pune by Sankalia and the ASI in 1949 to advise on geochronology; Raymond and Bridget Allchin from Cambridge, who have both taught numerous students from India, and also undertaken research in India, albeit on a small scale, over four decades (e.g. Allchin et al. 1978 on the Thar Desert). They were also instrumental in setting up the South Asian Archaeology Conferences, held biennially in Europe, the journal *South Asian Studies*, which is the main European outlet for articles on the archaeology and history of that region, and for publicising India's prehistory through text-books and syntheses (e.g. Allchin and Allchin 1982). Others have acted on a similarly independent and small scale, such as Jorge Armand (Columbia), Gudrun Corvinus (Germany), Claire Gaillard (France), Desmond Clark and Michael Petraglia (USA). If one includes geologists and environmental specialists [as is obvious from the contributors to the recent volume in honour of Rajaguru (Wadia et al. 1995)], an impressively large number of foreigners have worked in India in recent years on its Palaeolithic and Pleistocene. Moreover, and unlike the pattern before Independence, these have originated from several countries, and many have worked repeatedly in India over many years.

Post-Independence Achievements

Indian archaeologists have accomplished a great deal since 1947, especially given that India itself, with an area of 1.2 million square miles, is larger and more diverse than Scandinavia, France, Britain, Germany, Italy, Spain and former Yugoslavia. Following Sankalia's (1964) paper, there is a clear Middle Palaeolithic, and also a distinct Upper Palaeolithic (e.g. Murty 1968, Sali 1989, Sharma 1982). Although it is astonishing how recently these were recognised, it means that the basic configuration of the Indian Palaeolithic is fundamentally similar to that in S.W. Asia, East Africa and Europe. There is now an enormous literature on the Palaeolithic and Pleistocene of India, widely published in journals, monographs and syntheses. Indian scholars—often Ph.D. candidates based in Pune—have produced several excellent regional studies of the Palaeolithic industries and Pleistocene deposits. A few excavations, notably Didwana and Hunsgi, have entered the consciousness of the better informed members of the Palaeolithic community outside India. Many sites are not as well-known as they should be, such as the Acheulean site of Chirki (Corvinus 1983), and Bhimbetka, despite its wealth of artistic representations and rich sequence of occupation. Indian scholars have also frequently published their results in the leading international journals, such as the *Journal of Human Evolution* (e.g. Sankhyan 1997), *Journal of Archaeological Science* (e.g. Baskaran et al. 1986), *Current Anthropology* (e.g. Mishra 1992), *Palaeogeography, Palaeoclimatology and Palaeoecology* (e.g. Agrawal et al. 1989, Badam et al. 1986), *Quaternary Research* (e.g. Acharyya and Basu 1993) and even *Nature* (e.g. Gaur and Chopra 1984). India also has its own excellent high-quality journal, *Man and Environment*, a high-quality dating facility at the Physical Research Laboratory, Ahmedabad and a world-class archaeological research institute at Deccan College, Pune. Finally, as a sign of national and academic maturity, there are a number of Indian text-books on its own Palaeolithic and later prehistoric record (e.g. Agrawal 1982, Sankalia 1977).

Dating

Dating deserves special mention, as it remains one of the gravest problems in Indian Palaeolithic studies; it is also examined later on in greater detail. A useful beginning has been made in establishing a reliable chronological framework for the Indian Palaeolithic and Pleistocene. The establishment of radiocarbon dating facilities at the Physical Research Laboratory has been critical, but useful only for dating the final part of the Pleistocene (see Agrawal and Kusumgar 1974). At present the earliest C^{14} dates for the Upper Palaeolithic are <26 Kyr; the Middle Palaeolithic remains poorly dated, although its beginning may extend back to 150 Kyr (Misra 1995: 226). Dating earlier deposits and assemblages has proved difficult; there are good dates from Didwana of *c.* 100–200 Kyr, and ones of >350 Kyr for the earliest Acheulean (Mishra 1992).

THE IMPACT OF RECENT ACHIEVEMENTS: INDIA'S CONTEXT WITHIN WORLD PREHISTORY

What impact have these accomplishments had on studies of human evolution in a global context? Regrettably, the answer is that they have had only a marginal value. There are three main reasons: the absence of hominid fossil remains, and the way "world prehistory" has been constructed as a historical narrative by writers outside India; and problems of dating.

Palaeolithic Archaeology and Hominid Fossils

There is an insatiable public interest in human origins, especially when it concerns human fossil remains. This is particularly so in the U.S., which dominates modern palaeoanthropology. Magazines like *Time* and *Newsweek* maximise their sales if the main story is a new discovery of a fossil hominid; these discoveries are also widely reported in the international press (often on the front page), and on TV. Books on the fossil evidence for human evolution also enjoy huge sales, if well-written. What this means in practice is that sites or areas that have fossil hominids are known and widely written about; those that lack fossil hominids are ignored, however excellent the archaeological evidence might be. Sadly for archaeologists, the fossil tail wags the Palaeolithic dog. (To cite two examples: the superlative archaeological evidence from the Acheulean site of Boxgrove, U.K. was almost completely ignored until one piece of hominid leg bone was found; likewise, Dmanisi in Georgia would never have attracted the attention it has as one of the earliest sites in Asia without its hominid mandible, even though the stone tools provide unambiguous evidence for the presence of hominids.) In short, India's Palaeolithic record will remain largely ignored as long as it lacks a fossil hominid record. Sadly, the subcontinent lacks that record at present, apart from the skull-cap and clavicle from the Narmada Valley (Sankhyan 1997, Sonakia 1985). Israel affords an instructive contrast: despite its small size, it figures in almost every text-book on human evolution, largely because of the hominid remains from a small number of caves.

India in the Context of a "World Prehistory"

In the nineteenth century and well into the twentieth century, prehistory was dominated by European researchers, writing primarily for a European audience. The emphasis throughout much of the ensuing narratives was the distinction between centres of innovation, and peripheral areas to which innovations (such as the making of hand-axes, pottery, metal objects, or the invention of farming and writing) either spread in time, or not at all. Prehistory thus comprised innovators and copiers, donors and recipients. This view emphasised some areas as major innovative centres—such as East Africa for human origins, or the Near East for agriculture—and others as marginal and passive. The most extreme examples of the latter were usually Patagonia, southern Africa and Tasmania, which were widely seen as the most primitive and backward examples of humanity because of their distance at the "uttermost ends of the earth" from centres of innovation (see Gamble 1992). Essentially, the old-style world prehistory was a Europocentric view of the world, with Europe now the modern equivalent of the Near East in the Neolithic, or East Africa in the late Pliocene.

On this world-view, India was seen as marginal; regionally interesting, but nevertheless peripheral to understanding the main forces that shaped past humanity. It was a view echoed by in and outside India. For example, Sankalia (1962: 60) wrote "Archaeologists believe that India is on the periphery of culture spread. . . . The belief is probably right, but it must be said that it is also based on insufficient fieldwork done in India so far". These views were repeated more forcefully by Grahame Clark (1967: 45). Writing of the Lower Palaeolithic, he mentioned India "where the old chopping-tool and flake traditions persisted, as they appear to have done in successive stages of the Soan culture of northern India, *without contributing anything essential to the course of world prehistory*" (italics mine). After the appearance of anatomically modern humans: "From the point of view of world history, most of Africa, India and south-east Asia *were henceforth bypassed by the main agents of creative change* throughout the remainder of prehistoric times" (ibid., 47; italics mine). Thus "the greater part of the Indian subcontinent remained the *refuge of low-grade hunter-fishers*, whose microlithic flint-work stemmed from Lower Palaeolithic sources" (ibid., 180; italics mine). Likewise, the Indus civilisation, being later than but near the older civilisations of Mesopotamia were seen as secondary and derivative, the product of "stimulus-diffusion" from Sumer, arising from travellers who returned with the "idea" of urban civilisation (Daniel 1968: 117).

When put like that, there was little point in studying the Indian Palaeolithic, except to acquire knowledge of a marginal region that would remain of local importance only. This outlook may be one reason why the Indian Palaeolithic has rarely been mentioned positively in most syntheses of human evolution. Fortunately, the newer outlook exemplified by WAC, and participated in by a much wider range of scholars (gratifyingly including many from developing countries) is fostering a more inclusive view of human prehistory, and with a much reduced emphasis upon identifying core and peripheral regions.

Modern Palaeoanthropology in Eurasia

Modern palaeoanthropology offers a substantially different agenda from the older type of "world prehistory" exemplified above. Rather than trying to identify "centres" of excellence or innovation, (and neighbouring areas of backwardness), the emphasis is instead of general themes of colonisation, adaptation, and the nature of biological and cultural change. Absolutely critical to all these themes is the question of dating. We currently live in exciting times, with the advent of new dating techniques such as argon-argon and OSL, and the gradual linkage of regional, land-based chronologies for the Pleistocene that are linked to the global, deep-sea oxygen-isotope chronology. What is already emerging is that the timing of many key events in human evolution has been seriously underrepresented. This particularly applies to two of the biggest issues in current palaeoanthropology: the timing of the first colonisation of Eurasia, and the origin of modern humans. India is well placed to make a major contribution to both these issues. Before seeing how, each needs a brief review, particularly in terms of the critical issue of dating.

Dating: Palaeolithic Time-tables and Trains

Wheeler's famous utterance, that we have timetables but no trains may have been true of later prehistory, especially once radiocarbon imposed some control over sequencing and duration of various Neolithic to Iron Age periods. However, it is invalid when applied to current knowledge of the Indian Palaeolithic: the trains exist, but the time-table does not.

As an indication of how difficult it is to construct a reliable chronological framework, the Palaeolithic of southern England—far smaller than most Indian provinces, and studied more intensively than anywhere in the world—is only now beginning to acquire a reliable chronological timetable. The older, less reliable one, was derived from studies of glacial tills, river terraces, pollen cores, macro- and microfauna; the newer one is emerging through detailed, demonstrable correlations with deep sea cores, backed up with Ur/Th, OSL, TL, AMS and the emerging generation of absolute dating techniques. For earlier periods in areas such as southern Europe and East Africa, palaeomagnetism is the key, with argon-argon dating of single crystals as the key weapon if volcanic deposits are available. [Argon-argon is particularly powerful as it can not only date the earliest hominid sites, but also material less than 2,000 years old (Renne et al. 1997).] It will be these techniques that will ultimately bring clarity to the Indian Palaeolithic. Their impact on other regions is already evident in debates over the earliest hominids, and earliest modern humans, in Asia.

The Earliest Colonisation of Asia

Until only a few years ago, most opinions favoured a late colonisation of Asia, with *H. erectus* as its earliest inhabitant. Ubeidiya in Israel, dated to between 1.0–1.4 Myr (Tchernov 1989) was seen as the earliest site outside Africa. As the oldest hominid remains from Indonesia, on the eastern edge of Asia, were thought to be less than 1 Myr (e.g. Pope 1985), the implications were that India was also colonised in only the last million years.

In the last few years, there has been a remarkable change in opinion, and several now favour a much earlier timing for the earliest hominids in

Asia—perhaps as early as 1.8–2.0 Myr ago (e.g. Larick and Ciochon 1996, Tattersall 1997). The discovery of a hominid mandible and stone tools at Dmanisi, Georgia, dated to 1.8 Myr (Gabunia and Vekua 1995), and at Longgupo, China, dated to 1.9 Myr (Wanpo et al. 1995) have been especially important, as has the redating of the earliest Javan hominids to 1.6–1.8 Myr (Swisher et al. 1994). These publications have counted for far more among the palaeoanthropological community than archaeological evidence of stone artefacts but unsupported by hominid remains: for example, Riwat, Pakistan, dated to >1.9 Myr (Dennell et al. 1988), and Yiron, Israel, dated to >2.4 Myr (Ronen 1991). Nevertheless, the evidence from Riwat and Yiron point in the same direction as those sites with hominid remains.

Assuming that any one of these claims is correct, India was almost certainly occupied at roughly the same time, around 2.0–1.8 Myr. Given that the oldest archaeological dates from India have a minimum age of only 390 Kyr (Mishra 1992), India may have an archaeological record that is 1.5 Myr longer than currently demonstrated. If that is the case, there are extraordinarily exciting opportunities ahead for Indian archaeologists to investigate in the next century. The best prospects for finding very early archaeological sites probably lie in the Siwaliks of northern India, especially as these (particularly in Pakistan) have proved to be amenable to dating by palaeomagnetism and fission-track dating. I see no reason why stone artefacts (or even hominids) cannot be found in Indian Upper Siwalik deposits, extending back to and even beyond 2 million years, in the same way as they have in Pakistan and elsewhere in Asia.

If India was colonised as long as 1.8 Myr ago, and assuming that the earliest Acheulean handaxe assemblages are African and 1.4 Myr old, it follows that there has also to be a pre-Acheulean in India, as suggested by De Terra and Paterson (1939) and more recently for Pakistan by Hurcombe and Dennell (1992). What happens once Acheulean-type handaxes were used in India is less clear. One possibility is that the two traditions co-existed, in the same way that the Developed Oldowan and Acheulean continue side by side in East Africa, or handaxe and flake assemblages co-existed in much of western Europe. Another possibility is that only one tradition was involved. As an example, a strong case has been made recently (e.g. Ashton et al. 1992) for arguing that the Clactonian flake-based assemblages of southern England are simply Acheulean ones without handaxes. Either way, the Early Palaeolithic record of India is almost certainly far longer than that of Europe, covers at least as large a territory, and involves very different environments from the better known ones of East Africa and western Europe.

India has some major Acheulean localities that deserve greater attention outside India. The best known are Didwana (Gaillard et al. 1986) and Hunsgi (Paddayya 1982); others are Chirki (1983), Durkadi Nala (Armand 1983), and Paisra (Pant and Jayaswal 1991). The biggest problems lie with dating. As mentioned already, the oldest Acheulean dates are >390 Kyr; however, in Pakistan, handaxes were found embedded in conglomerates just above the Brunhes-Matuyama boundary, i.e., <780 Kyr (Rendell and Dennell 1985). It is reasonable to assume that the base of the Acheulean has yet to be found in India or Pakistan. If it began in India shortly after it first appeared in Israel, the oldest Indian Acheulean sites could turn out to be at least 1.0, if not 1.2 Myr old. Even if it is only the same age as the Acheulean in northern Europe (where it made a comparatively late appearance on the north-west fringe of Eurasia), it should be at least 500 Kyr old.

The Origin of Modern Humans

This debate is driven primarily by two related issues. The first is how to interpret the hominid fossil record of the last 100 Kyr, especially the Neanderthal specimens of Europe and Southwest Asia; the youngest *H. erectus* specimens from Java and China, and some key specimens of early anatomically-modern humans from sub-Saharan Africa. The second is the nature and timing of the Middle to Upper Palaeolithic transition, which focuses mainly on Southwest Asia and Europe. As India lacks fossil hominid evidence, it is excluded from active involvement in debates over hominid palaeontology. However, if hominid remains between 30 and 100 Kyr were ever found in India, they would be of tremendous significance, and would immediately put India right at the forefront of debate on modern human origins. Would they be like Neanderthals—generally associated with Middle Palaeolithic assemblages in Southwest Asia and Europe—or anatomically modern; if the latter, would their affinities be local, or intermediate between those of East Asia and Southwest Asia? At present, we cannot predict what they might have looked like, but meanwhile India comprises the largest single gap in the hominid record of Asia.

Leaving aside the likelihood of a chance discovery of an Upper Pleistocene hominid in India, there is still potentially an enormous amount to learn from its Middle to Upper Palaeolithic transition. At present, we understand very little about the nature and timing of that transition (or even the type of hominid(s) that caused it), the nature and meaning of any

Middle Palaeolithic variability in lithic assemblages, or the type of subsistence strategies used across India during the Upper Pleistocene. At present, the absence of clear data on these issues means that current discussions of modern human origins in Asia are seriously imbalanced. In this context, "Asia" effectively comprises Israel, China and Java: the intervening 6000 km of Central Asia, the Indian subcontinent, and mainland Southeast Asia hardly figure in the debate. Yet India is ideally placed to be a major contributor because of its size, and geographical location, and because its Middle and Upper Palaeolithic record makes it comparable to that of Southwest Asia, East Africa and Europe.

As with the current dating of the Indian Lower Palaeolithic, the present chronology for the Middle and Upper Palaeolithic in India is likely to be very compressed. The earliest prepared-core (Middle Palaeolithic or MSA) assemblages are likely to be *c.* 150–250 Kyr old, as in regions as far removed from each other as East Africa and Northwest Europe. The earliest Upper Palaeolithic assemblages are also likely to be as old as in Southwest Asia, southern Africa and western Europe; i.e., *c.* 35–40 Kyr.

These dates are likely to turn out to be an underestimate of their true age. Recent evidence from Australia offers an instructive example. There, cave profiles have been dated by C^{14}, TL and OSL, and what tends to happen is that the C^{14} dates level out around 35–40 Kyr, whereas the TL and OSL dates continue to show increasing age with depth below surface to *c.* 60 Kyr (see e.g. Nanson and Young 1987, David et al. 1997). The timing of the Middle to Upper Palaeolithic transition may thus turn out to be severely compressed in areas as well studied as Europe and Southwest Asia, as C^{14} still provides the main chronological framework. We may well find that the earliest blade assemblages in India extend beyond 30 or even beyond 40 Kyr ago, if these are systematically dated by TL and OSL, or Ar-Ar.

Summary

After a slow beginning in the first half of this century, considerable progress has been made in documenting India's Palaeolithic and Pleistocene record. India's achievements in this respect since Independence have been very impressive, and particularly so in the last 20 years. Although a large portion of India still awaits systematic exploration, there is now an impressively large and detailed literature on the Pleistocene and Palaeolithic of many parts of the subcontinent. It also has several excellent sites, and a Palaeolithic record that is likely to be much longer than that of Europe, and as long and complex as in Southwest and Southeast Asia. The fact that the Indian Palaeolithic has not yet had a major international impact can be attributed to the absence of hominid remains (with the exception of Narmada); and the paucity of reliable dates for its earliest assemblages, and later Acheulean, Middle and Upper Palaeolithic ones. All this should change in the next two decades, and Indian prehistorians can look forward to the future with a tremendous sense of excitement. The two developments most likely to revolutionise India's significance to studies of human evolution would be the discovery of hominid remains, and the application of OSL, argon-argon and palaeomagnetism to appropriate Pleistocene sequences that contain Palaeolithic remains.

REFERENCES

Acharyya, S.K., and Basu, P.K. 1993. Toba Ash on the Indian Subcontinent and its Implications for Correlation of Late Pleistocene Alluvium. *Quaternary Research* 40: 10–19.

Agrawal, D.P. 1982. *The Archaeology of India*. London and Malmo: Curzon Press (Scandinavian Institute of Asian Studies Monograph Series 46).

—et al. 1989. The Plio-Pleistocene Geologic and Climate Record of the Kashmir Valley, India: A Review and New Data. *Palaeogeography, Palaeoclimatology, Palaeoecology* 73: 267–86.

Agrawal, D.P. and Kusumgar, S. 1974. *Prehistoric Chronology and Radiocarbon Dating in India*. New Delhi: Munshiram Manoharlal Publishers.

Allchin, B. and Allchin, R. 1982. *The Rise of Civilisation in India and Pakistan*. Cambridge: Cambridge University Press.

Allchin, B., Goudie, A., and Hegde, K. 1978. *The Prehistory and Palaeogeography of the Great Indian Desert*. London: Academic Press.

Anderson, C.W. 1917. Note on Prehistoric Stone Implements Found in the Singhbhum District. *Journal of the Bihar and Orissa Research Society* 1: 14.

Armand, J. 1983. *Archaeological Excavations in Durkadi Nala: An Early Palaeolithic Pebble-Tool Workshop in Central India*. New Delhi: Munshiram Manoharlal Publishers.

Ashton, N., McNabb, J., and Parfitt, S. 1992. Choppers and the Clactonian: A reinvestigation. *Proceedings of the Prehistoric Society* 58: 22–29.

Badam, G.L., Ganjoo, R.K., and Salahuddin. 1986. Preliminary Taphonomical Studies of Some Pleistocene Fauna From the Central Narmada Valley, Madhya Pradesh, India. *Palaeogeography, Palaeoclimatology, Palaeoecology* 53: 335–48.

Baskaran, M., Marathe, A.R., Rajaguru, S.N., and Somayajulu, B.L.K. 1986. Geochronology of Palaeolithic Cultures in the Hiran Valley, Saurashtra, India. *Journal of Archaeological Science* 13 (6): 505–14.

Cammiade, L.A., and Burkitt, M.C. 1930. Fresh Light on the Stone Ages in Southeast India. *Antiquity* 4: 327–39.

Clark, J.G.D. 1967. *World Prehistory*. Cambridge: Cambridge University Press.

Corvinus, G. 1983. *The Pravara River System*, vol. 2: *The Excavations of the Acheulian Site of Chirki on Pravara, India*. Tubingen: Institut fur Urgeschichte.

David, B. et al. 1997. New Optical and Radiocarbon Dates from Ngarrabullgan Cave, A Pleistocene Archaeological Site in Australia: Implications for the Comparability of Time Clocks and for the Human Colonization of Australia. *Antiquity* 71: 183–88.

Dennell, R.W. 1990. Progressive Gradualism, Imperialism and Academic Fashion: Lower Palaeolithic Archaeology in the Twentieth Century. *Antiquity* 64: 549–58.

Dennell, R.W., Rendell, H.R., and Hailwood, E. 1988. Early Tool-making in Asia: Two Million-year-old Artefacts in Pakistan. *Antiquity* 62: 98–106.

De Terra, H., and Paterson, T.T. 1939. *Studies on the Ice Age in India and Associated Human Cultures*. Washington, D.C.: Carnegie Institution.

Gabunia, L., and Vekua, A. 1995. A Plio-Pleistocene Hominid from Dmanisi, East Georgia, Caucasus. *Nature* 375: 509–12.

Gaillard, C., Raju, D.R., Misra, V.N. and Rajaguru, S.N. 1986. Handaxe Assemblages from the Didwana Region, Thar Desert, India: A Metrical Analysis. *Proceedings of the Prehistoric Society* 52: 189–214.

Gamble, C. 1992. Archaeology, History and the Uttermost Ends of the Earth—Tasmania, Terra del Fuego and the Cape. *Antiquity* 66: 712–20.

Gaur, R., and Chopra, S.R.K. 1984. Taphonomy, Fauna, Environment and Ecology of Upper Siwaliks (Plio-Pleistocene) near Chandigarh, India. *Nature* 308: 353–55.

Hurcombe, L.M., and Dennell, R.W. 1992. A Pre-Acheulean, Lower Palaeolithic in the Pabbi Hills, Northern Pakistan? In *South Asian Archaeology 1989*, C. Jarrige, ed. Madison: Prehistory Press, pp. 133–36.

Keay, J. 1988. *India Discovered*. London: Collins.

Larick, R., and Ciochon, R.L. 1996. The African Emergence and Early Asian Dispersal of the Genus Homo. *American Scientist*, November–December 1996.

Mishra, S. 1992. The Age of the Acheulean in India: New Evidence. *Current Anthropology* 33 (3): 325–28.

Misra, V.N. 1995. Geoarchaeology of the Thar Desert, Northwest India, in *Quaternary Environments and Geoarchaeology in India: Essays in Honour of Professor S.N. Rajaguru*, S.Wadia, R. Korisettar and V.S. Kale, eds. Bangalore: Geological Society of India, pp. 210–30.

Murty, M.L.K. 1968. Blade and Burin Industries near Renigunta on the South-East Coast of India. *Proceedings of the Prehistoric Society* 34: 83–101.

Nanson, G.C., and Young, R.W. 1987. Comparison of Thermoluminesence and Radiocarbon Age-determinations from Late-Pleistocene Elluvial Deposits Near Sydney, Australia. *Quaternary Research* 27: 263–69.

Paddayya, K. 1982. *The Acheulean Culture of the Hunsgi Valley (Peninsular India): A Settlement System Perspective*. Pune: Deccan College.

Pant, P.C., and Jayaswal, V. 1991. *Paisra: the Stone Age Settlement of Bihar*. Delhi: Agam Kala Prakashan.

Pope, G.G. 1985. Taxonomy, Dating and Environment: the Palaeoecology of the Far Eastern Hominids. *Modern Quaternary Research in South East Asia* 9: 65–80.

Rendell, H., and Dennell, R.W. 1985. Dated Lower Palaeolithic Artefacts from Northern Pakistan. *Current Anthropology* 26 (5): 393.

Renne, P.R. et al. 1997. $^{40}Ar/^{39}Ar$ Dating into the Historical Realm: Calibration Against Pliny the Younger. *Science* 277: 1279–80.

Ronen, A. 1991. The Yiron-gravel Lithic Assemblage: Artefacts Older than 2.4 My in Israel. *Archaologisches Korrespondenzblatt* 21: 159–64.

Sali, S.A. 1989. *The Upper Palaeolithic and Mesolithic Cultures of Maharashtra*. Pune:

Deccan College.
Sankalia, H.D. 1962. India, in *Courses Towards Urban Life*, R.J. Braidwood and G. Willey eds. Chicago: Viking Fund Publications, pp. 60–83.
—1964. Middle Stone Age Culture in India and Pakistan. *Science* 146: 365–75.
—1977. *Prehistory of India*. New Delhi: Munshiram Manoharlal Publishers.
Sharma, M.J. 1982. *The Upper Palaeolithic Culture in India*. Delhi: Agam Kala Prakashan.
Sankhyan, A.R. 1997. Fossil Clavicle of a Middle Pleistocene Hominid from the Central Narmada Valley, India. *Journal of Human Evolution* 32: 3–16.
Sonakia, A. 1985. Skull Cap of an Early Man from the Narmada Valley Alluvium (Pleistocene) of Central India. *American Anthropologist* 87: 612–16.
Swisher III, C.C. et al. 1994. Age of the Earliest Known Hominids in Java, Indonesia. *Science* 263: 1118–21.
Tattersall, I. 1997. Out of Africa Again . . . and Again? *Scientific American* 276 (4): 46–53.
Tchernov, E. 1989. The Age of the Ubeidiya Formation. *Israel Journal of Earth Sciences* 36: 3–30.
Todd, K.R.U. 1939. Palaeolithic Industries of Bombay. *Journal of the Royal Anthropological Institute* 69: 257–72.
Wadia, S., Korisettar, R., and Kale, V.S. eds., 1995. *Quaternary Environments and Geoarchaeology in India: Essays in Honour of Professor S.N. Rajaguru*. Bangalore: Geological Society of India.
Wanpo, H. et al. 1995. Early Homo and Assoicated Artefacts from Asia. *Nature* 378–78.
Zeuner, F.E. 1950. *Stone Age and Pleistocene Chronology in Gujarat*. Pune: Deccan College.
—1951. *Prehistory in India*. Pune: Deccan College.

2 ❖ The Lower Palaeolithic Culture of India

R.S. PAPPU

THE three stages of the Palaeolithic viz, Lower, Middle and Upper, are now firmly established in the Indian subcontinent. The Lower Palaeolithic forms the earliest hominid cultural stage in India as elsewhere in the Old World. This cultural stage was variously labelled as Early Stone Age (Subbarao 1958), Series I (Cammiade and Burkitt 1930) and chopper-biface element (Ghosh 1970, 1974). It has now been finally realised that the European system of dividing the Stone Age into Palaeolithic, Mesolithic and Neolithic phases and subdividing the Palaeolithic into Lower, Middle and Upper cultural stages is more appropriate to the Indian evidence (Misra 1962, 1989a).

The Lower Palaeolithic culture comprises two distinct traditions in India: (1) the Soan represented by pebble tools and (2) the biface or handaxe-cleaver tradition. The region lying to the north of the Indo-Gangetic plain (extra-Peninsula) has mainly yielded lithic assemblages dominated by the former tool complex, while the region lying to the south of this plain i.e., Peninsular part has made known industries of the handaxe-cleaver tradition.

The Lower Palaeolithic industries of Peninsular India, as mentioned above, essentially belong to the handaxe-cleaver tradition. Two substages, viz. Abbevillian and Acheulian are further recognised in the industries. These divisions are based on typo-technology, the former exhibiting inferior workmanship and the latter displaying the refined features. The terms Abbevillian and Acheulian are derived respectively, from the sites Abbeville and St. Acheul on the river Somme in France, where lithic industries showing these typo-technological characters were first discovered. The lithic industries exhibiting similar typo-technological characters were subsequently noticed in other parts of the Old World viz., Africa, near East and India and the terms Abbevillian and Acheulian were used to describe these industries. The Lower Palaeolithic assemblages in Peninsular India are by and large dominated by tool-types showing the Acheulian characters and the Abbevillian element is rather feeble. The term Acheulian in India has been considered mainly with reference to technology and typology and this tradition has its own characteristic features.

Palaeolithic research in India is now more than 130 years old and commenced more or less simultaneously with the epoch-making discoveries regarding the antiquity and origin of man in western Europe. Robert Bruce Foote of the Geological Survey of India discovered for the first time in India on 30 May 1863 an artefact (handaxe) of Lower Palaeolithic culture in a lateritic gravel deposit at Pallavaram in Tamil Nadu (Foote 1866, 1916).

BRIEF HISTORY OF LOWER PALAEOLITHIC RESEARCH

Four broad phases could be identified in the development of Palaeolithic archaeology in India as follows: the first spanning from 1863 to 1912, the second from 1930 to 1950, the third from 1950 to 1970 and the fourth from the 1970s to the present.

First Phase

After the first discovery of Palaeolithic implements by Foote in 1863, a number of geologists of the Geological Survey of India and a few civil servants such as Ball, King, Blanford, Cockburn, Wynne, Hacket and others, reported Palaeolithic artefacts from a number of river valleys in Peninsular India (Dasgupta 1931). Among these investigators, the discoveries made by Foote occupy a prominent place. He took keen interest in the twin fields of prehistoric archaeology and Quaternary geology and carried out investigations in both these fields for more than 30 years in southern and western India. He made extensive collections of prehistoric antiquities of various ages and types. He was the first geologist in India to integrate geological and prehistoric studies and initiated the trend for close collaboration between prehistorians and geologists which continues to the present. The extensive collection of prehistoric antiquities made by him was purchased by the Madras Government Museum. He prepared a catalogue and detailed notes of these finds which were published in two volumes in 1914 and 1916 by the Museum (Foote 1914, 1916). The notes prepared by him give his views and ideas about the nature and age of antiquities, the type of associated Quaternary deposits and many varied aspects of prehistoric archaeology and Quaternary geology. The pioneering work carried out during this phase proved that the Indian subcontinent is extremely rich in prehistoric finds.

Second Phase

After Foote's work there was a void during the first two decades of the present century. Palaeolithic studies were revived in mid-thirties when Cammiade and Burkitt (1930) carried out investigations in the Kurnool region of Andhra Pradesh. They studied the surface collection of artefacts made by Cammiade in this region. The presence of four cultural stages viz., Series I to IV based on differences in typo-technology were recognised. These stages more or less coincide with the present-day division of the Stone Age into Lower, Middle and Upper Palaeolithic and Mesolithic stages. The basic framework for the Stone Age cultural sequence was thus identified some seventy years ago. This work was followed by the Yale-Cambridge expedition under the leadership of De Terra (De Terra and Paterson 1939). Explorations were undertaken by the team in the glacial tracts of the Kashmir valley, the adjacent periglacial region of the Potwar plateau, the Narmada valley in Central India and around Madras along the eastern coast. The expedition recognised a fourfold glacial succession in the Kashmir valley, a record presumed to form a parallel to that represented in the Alpine sequence in Europe. This sequence was correlated with terrace sequence found in the Potwar plateau region. The pebble tools of chopper-chopping tool tradition were recovered from these terraces in the Soan valley. The pebble tool industry was named as the Soan and was divided into Lower, Middle and Upper stages. The tools of handaxe-cleaver tradition were also noticed at a few localities. The expedition studied the Narmada valley between Hoshangabad and Narsinghpur in Madhya Pradesh. The alluvium having a total thickness of about 45 m was divided into three groups viz., Lower, Upper and Cotton Soil groups. This alluvium yielded a sequence of lithic industries of Abbevillian and Acheulian characters with a large number of mammalian fossils. The Kortallayar valley in Tamil Nadu was also studied by the expedition. The coastal region in the Kortallayar valley was latter thoroughly investigated by Krishnaswami (1938). He observed three distinct terraces and recovered from them lithic industries showing stratigraphical as well as typological evolution based on patination, staining, etc. Todd (1939) discovered a stratigraphic sequence near Bombay on the western coast in Maharashtra which yielded lithic industries ranging from the Abbevillian to the Mesolithic. Bose and Sen (1948) undertook investigations in the Mayurbhanj region of Orissa. The Lower Palaeolithic tool-bearing gravel was excavated and a lithic industry exhibiting Abevillio-Acheulian characters was recovered. Sankalia (1946) carried out investigations in the Sabarmati, Mahi, Karjan and other river valleys of north Gujarat. This study brought to light evidence of lithic industries showing Abbevillio-Acheulian characters.

Third Phase

In contrast with the limited work undertaken during the first two phases, there has been a phenomenal expansion of Palaeolithic studies in the third phase stretching between 1950 and 1970. H.D. Sankalia of the Deccan College, Pune was in the lead and organised planned explorations in the diverse geographical regions of India. These were carried out by himself, his colleagues and his Ph.D. students. Sankalia was fully aware of the contribution of geology and other physical and natural sciences in the development of Palaeolithic studies. He invited F.E. Zeuner, Professor of Environmental Archaeology at the Institute of Archaeology, London, at the suggestion of Sir Mortimer Wheeler in 1949–50. Expeditions were organised under the leadership of Zeuner to study environmental aspects of Palaeolithic and Mesolithic sites in different river valleys of the Peninsular India. A monograph was published in 1950 (Zeuner 1950) giving the preliminary findings of the expedition in Gujarat and Maharashtra. These studies laid the foundations of environmental archaeology in India.

The most significant contribution of Zeuner's work in India is the use of river deposits like gravels and silts for building up regional stratigraphic-cum-climatic sequences. The gravel-silt and humid-dry phase approach towards understanding past environment and the correlation of Stone Age cultures with these climatic phases emerged as a dominant research paradigm in Indian Palaeolithic studies during this period (Paddayya 1994). There was more emphasis on the recovery of Palaeolithic cultural material in the context of Quaternary fluvial deposits. Two or three cycles of aggradation, each beginning with gravels and ending with silts, were noticed in a number of river valleys. The deposits at the base of local aggradation cycles generally yielded Lower Palaeolithic tools. The artefacts recovered from the gravel beds are often in rolled condition, thereby indicating their transportation over considerable distance from the original place of manufacture. These are therefore secondary occurrences of cultural materials in river gravels and have limited use only in reconstructing past human lifeways.

Fourth Phase

Realising the limitations of the study of cultural material from secondary sites, prehistorians in India from the 1970s onwards began to adopt the processual approach (Paddayya 1994). Presently the emphasis in Palaeolithic research is on the discovery and systematic excavation of primary living sites as precise information for both cultural and ecological reconstruction can come only from excavated primary sites. A number of Lower Palaeolithic Acheulian sites have been discovered in recent years in primary or semi-primary contexts and have been systematically excavated. Thus there has been meaningful and significant contribution in the field of Lower Palaeolithic studies since 1970s. There has been a gradual shift in the methodology, techniques and concepts used in Palaeolithic research. The studies are now aimed at (a) recovery of homogeneous stone artefacts from excavated primary sites and their technological analysis, (b) reconstruction of the nature of hominid activities at primary sites, (c) study of strategies for the utilisation of land, water, plant and animal food resources, (d) reconstruction of the palaeoenvironment of sites and the surrounding area, and (e) dating of sites by radiometric methods. It is gratifying to note that ongoing Palaeolithic studies in India have adopted the processual approach.

An important development since 1970s concerns the application of scientific methods and techniques, particularly from earth sciences, in the field of Palaeolithic archaeology (Pappu 1995). There is at present emphasis on multidisciplinary research to resolve problems in Palaeolithic archaeology. Major recent projects undertaken during the last 2 or 3 decades involve the collaboration of specialists from both prehistory and geology. Geoarchaeologists on the faculty of Department of Archaeology at the Deccan College, Pune and from a few other universities and research institutions in India have made significant contributions to the Palaeolithic studies and attempts have been made by these geoarchaeologists to the resolution of problems pertaining to stratigraphy, palaeoenvironment, sea level changes, river behaviour, neotectonics, settlement pattern, land use pattern, site formation processes and chronology.

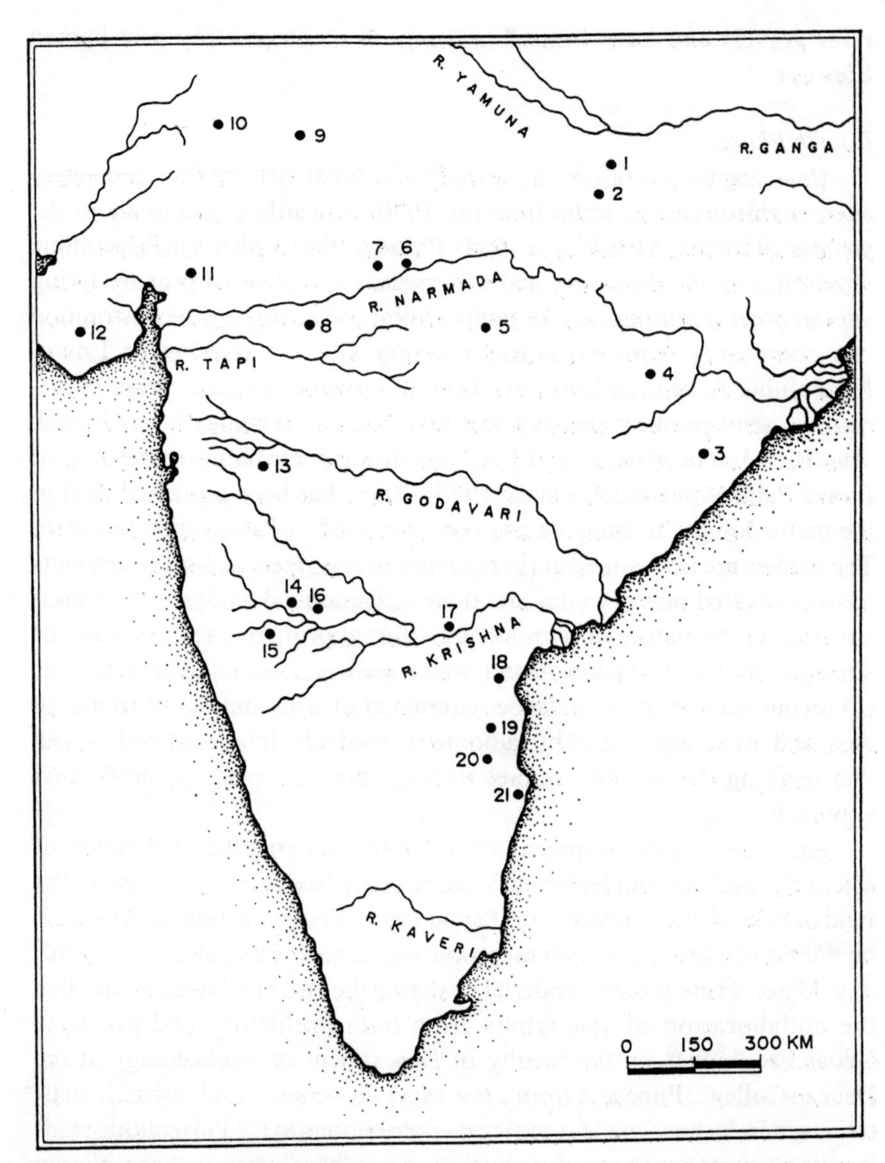

Fig. 1. Important Lower Palaeolithic sites and river valley complexes in Peninsular India: 1. Belan valley; 2. Middle Son valley; 3. Brahmani valley; 4. Singhbhum complex; 5. Mahanadi valley; 6. Central Narmada valley; 7. Raisen complex; 8. Malwa complex; 9. Berach-Banas valleys; 10. Thar Desert complex; 11. Sabarmati valley; 12. Saurashtra complex; 13. Godavari-Pravara valleys; 14. Middle Krishna valley; 15. Ghataprabha-Malaprabha valleys; 16. Hunsgi-Baichbal valleys; 17. Kurnool complex; 18. Paleru valley; 19. Gunjana valley; 20. Rallakalava valley; 21. Kortallayar valley

SALIENT CULTURAL FEATURES

Distribution

The investigations undertaken in different parts of the country during the last three to four decades have brought to light a large number of sites of the Lower Palaeolithic culture and this has substantially increased our knowledge of their distribution pattern. This cultural phase may now be said to extend practically all over the country though their density is greater in some areas than in other areas (Fig.1). The absence or sparseness of the sites in some parts of the country is due to ecological factors. The total absence of sites in the Indo-Gangetic plains is obviously due to the non-availability of rocks necessary for preparing stone artefacts. There is also the possibility that if any Acheulian sites existed there in the past, they got buried subsequently under the thick alluvium. Sites are sparse in northeast India and along the west coast and the Western Ghats due to rugged terrain, heavy rainfall and thick vegetation. Claims for the occurrence of Acheulian tools in the Garo hills in the Meghalaya region of northeast India have been made by Sharma (1997). These discoveries need to be confirmed by finding artefacts in stratified context devoid of the admixture of tools of later industries.

The Acheulian sites are thus found in varied geographic situations viz., arid to semi-arid regions like western Rajasthan, forested and hilly regions of central (Vindhyas) and eastern India (Chota Nagpur plateau), all along the east coast in the states of Orissa, Andhra Pradesh and Tamil Nadu, on river terraces in Siwalik regions of extra-Peninsula and plateau regions of the Deccan Upland, near rock exposures in central India and Karnataka, and in rock shelters and caves. The Lower Palaeolithic communities thus seem to have adapted themselves to all kinds of ecozones despite their regional differences within the basically monsoonal climate. On the basis of the presently available evidence, the Peninsular region of the Indian subcontinent happens to be one of the richest areas for the Acheulian cultural material in the Old world.

Nature of Habitats

On the basis of geomorphic settings of sites and origin of associated deposits, Acheulian sites have been classified into five groups: alluvial, coastal, slope, surface, and rock shelter and cave sites (Pappu 1985a). The first four groups fall into the category of open air sites. Cave and rock shelter sites are few in number, if not altogether lacking. The locations of sites suggest that Acheulian man lived mostly close to the river banks, sea and lake shores and in the foothill areas. Easy availability of perennial water, plant and animal foods, and raw materials for fashioning the stone artefacts were the main considerations while selecting the occupation sites.

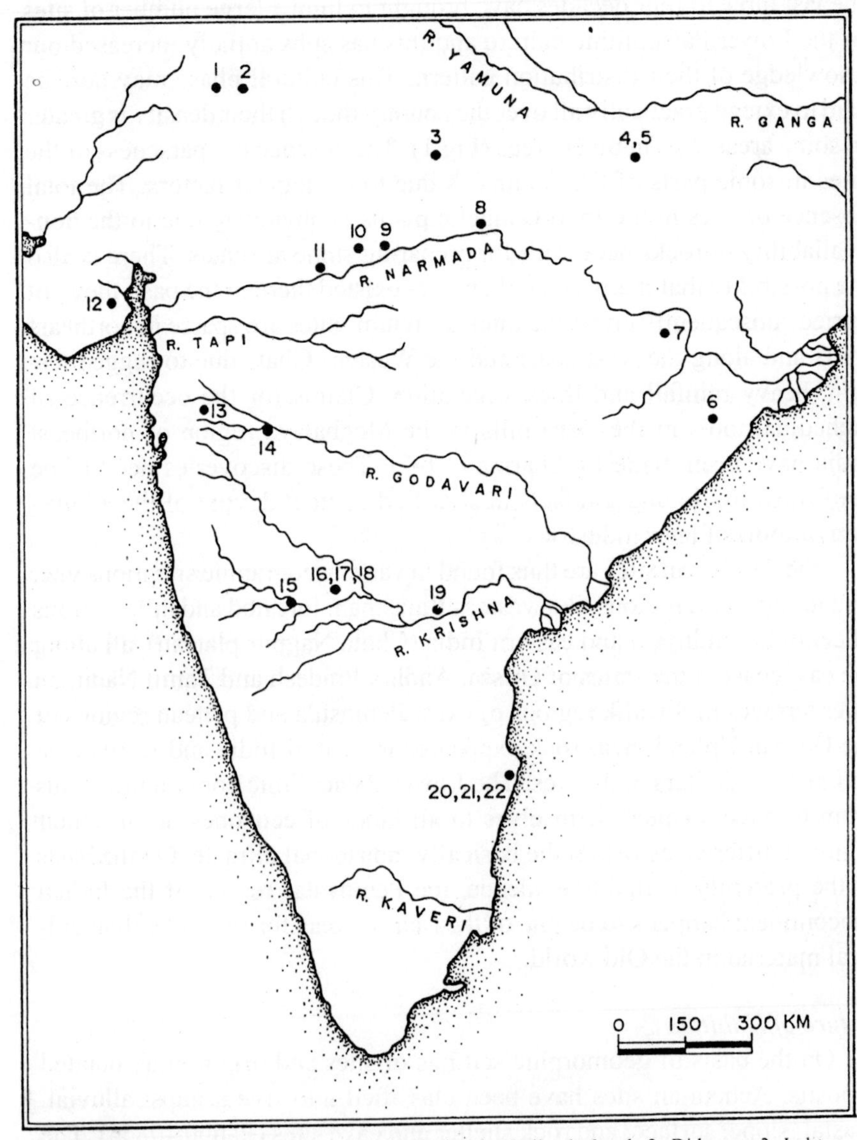

Fig. 2. Excavated Lower Palaeolithic sites in Peninsular India: 1. Jayal; 2. Didwana; 3. Lalitpur; 4. Sihawal; 5. Nakhjar Khurd; 6. Kuliana; 7. Paisra; 8. Mahadeo Piparia; 9. Adamgarh; 10. Bhimbetka; 11. Durkadi Nala; 12. Samadhiala; 13. Gangapur; 14. Chirki-on-Pravara; 15. Anagwadi; 16. Hunsgi; 17. Yediapur; 18. Isampur; 19. Nagarjunakonda; 20. Attirampakkam; 21. Vadamadurai; 22. Gudiyam

Till 1970 the majority of sites discovered were in riverine contexts. These were essentially secondary sites where tools were found embedded in gravelly deposits. It has now been realised that to obtain a comprehensive picture of the lifeways of the Acheulian communities, it is essential to have data from excavated primary sites. These sites are often sealed and undisturbed, yielding Stone Age material in undisturbed contexts. A number of such primary sites connected with occupation activities have been discovered and systematically investigated in recent years in different parts of Peninsular India (Table 1) (Fig. 2).

Open air primary occupation sites of Acheulian culture are known from Chirki-Nevasa in Maharashtra (Corvinus 1981, 1983) (Fig.3). Lalitpur in Uttar Pradesh (Singh 1965), Hunsgi and Baichbal valleys (Shorapur Doab) in Karnataka (Paddayya 1977a, b, 1979a, 1982, 1985, 1987a, b, 1989, 1991) (Fig.4), Paisra in Bihar (Pant and Jayaswal 1991) and Raisen district in Madhya Pradesh (Jacobson 1975, 1976, 1985). Semi-primary Acheulian sites in association with alluvial deposits occur at Anagawadi (Pappu 1974, 1985a, b; Pappu and Deo 1994, Deo 1991) and Khyad (Joshi 1955; Pappu 1981) in Karnataka, Gangapur (Joshi et al. 1966; Arun Kumar 1985, 1989) and Bori (Kale et al. 1986; Korisettar et al. 1989) in Maharashtra, Attirampakkam and Vadamadurai in Tamil Nadu (De Terra and Paterson 1939; Krishnaswami 1938; *IAR* 1964–65, 1966–67; Jayaswal 1985; Pappu 1996), Samadhiala (Chakrabarti 1983, 1995) in Gujarat, Belan Valley in Uttar Pradesh (Sharma 1973) and Son Valley in Madhya Pradesh (Sharma and Clark 1982, 1983) and Didwana in Rajasthan (Misra 1989b, 1995; Misra and Rajaguru 1989, Misra et al. 1982, 1988; Gaillard et al. 1983, 1985, 1986). The rock shelters and caves at Adamgarh (Joshi 1978) and Bhimbetka (Misra 1978, 1985) (Fig.5) in Madhya Pradesh and Gudiyam (*IAR* 1962–63, 1963–64) in Tamil Nadu have also provided much better evidence of occupation sites.

There is little evidence available about habitation structures or dwellings. However, a glimpse of the dwellings of these people can be had from the excavations undertaken at a few primary habitational sites. At Bhimbetka there is evidence of the construction of a wall of boulders for partitioning the interior space in one of the rock shelters during the Acheulian phase (Misra 1978, 1985). It appears that the rock shelters were occupied only seasonally, particularly in rainy season and the Acheulian groups mostly lived in the open. The open camp sites were probably provided with wind breaks. There is evidence available in support of wind breaks at Chirki and Hunsgi. At Chirki a row of boulders is observed in one of the excavated

Table 1. **List of Excavated Lower Palaeolithic Sites in Peninsular India**

S. No.	*Site Name*	*Coordinates*	*District*	*State*	*Nature of Site*	*References*
1.	Adamgarh	77°45' : 22°45'	Hoshangabad	Madhya Pradesh	Cave & Rock Shelter	Joshi 1978
2.	Anagawadi	75°40' : 1615'	Bijapur	Karnataka	Open Air	Pappu 1974
3.	Attrirampakkam	79°53' : 13°13'	Chengai-Anna	Tamil Nadu	Cave & Rock Shelter	*IAR 1964–65*
4.	Bhimbetka	77°37' : 22°50'	Raisen	Madhya Pradesh	Cave & Rock Shelter	Mishra 1978 a, b, c, 1985
5.	Chirki-Nevasa	74°54' : 19°34'	Ahmednagar	Maharashtra	Open Air	Corvinus 1981, 1983
6.	Didwana	74°35' : 27°24'	Nagaur	Rajasthan	Open Air	Mishra et al. 1982; Gaillard et al. 1983, 1985
7.	Durkadi Nala	75°36' : 22°09'	West Nimar	Madhya Pradesh	Open Air	Armand 1980, 1983, 1985
8.	Gangapur	73°48' : 20°00'	Nasik	Maharashtra	Open Air	Joshi et al. 1966; Arun kumar 1985
9.	Gudiyam	79°50' : 13°15'	Chengai-Anna	Tamil Nadu	Cave & Rockshelter	*IAR* 1962–63, 1963–64
10.	Hunsgi	76°31' : 16°27'	Gulbarga	Karnataka	Open Air	Paddayya 1976, 1977 a, b, 1979a, 1982
11.	Isampur	76°30' : 16°27'	Gulbarga	Karnataka	Open Air	Paddayya and Petraglia 1997, 1998
12.	Jayal	74°11' : 27°13'	Nagaur	Rajasthan	Open Air	Misra et al. 1980
13.	Kuliana	86°39' : 22°04'	Mayurbhanj	Orissa	Open air	Bose and Sen 1948
14.	Lalitpur	78°30' : 24°45'	Jhansi	Uttar Pradesh	Open Air	Singh 1965
15.	Mahadeo Piparia	79°16' : 23°06'	Narsingpur	Madhya Pradesh	Open Air	Supekar 1968, 1985
16.	Nagarjunakonda	79°14' : 16°31'	Guntur	Andhra Pradesh	Open Air	Subramanyam 1975
17.	Nakjhar khurd	82°13' : 24°32'	Sidhi	Madhya Pradesh	Open Air	Misra *et al* 1983
18.	Paisra	86°26' : 25°08'	Munger	Bihar	Open Air	Pant and Jayaswal 1991
19.	Samadhiala	71°41' : 21°52'	Bhavnagar	Gujarat	Open Air	Chakrabarti 1978, 1992, 1995
20.	Sihawal II	82°14' : 24°33'	Sidhi	Madhya Pradesh	Open Air	Kenoyer and Pal 1983
21.	Vadamaduarai	80°05' : 13°17'	Chengai-Anna	Tamil Nadu	Open Air	*IAR 1966–67*
22.	Yediapur	76°31' : 16°27'	Gulbarga	Karnataka	Open Air	Paddayya 1987

Fig. 3. Occupation floor, Tr. VII, Chirki-on-Pravara, Maharashtra.
After Corvinus (1983)

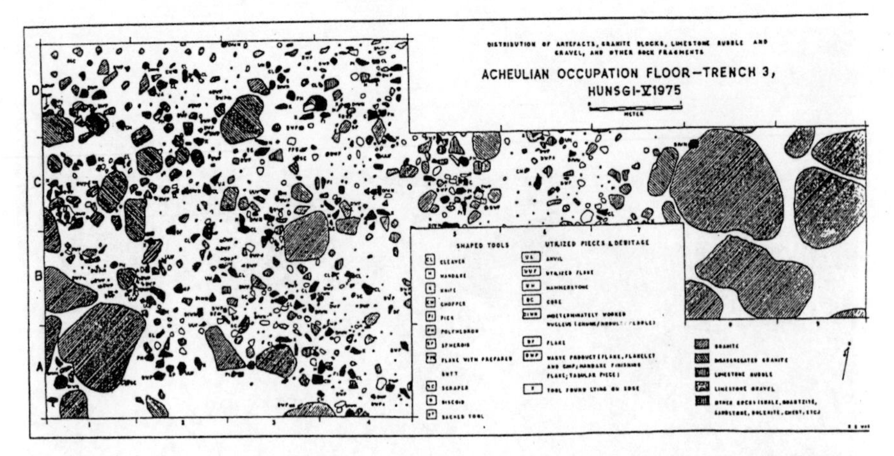

Fig. 4. Plan of occupation floor, Tr. 3, Hunsgi, Karnataka. (After Paddayya 1982)

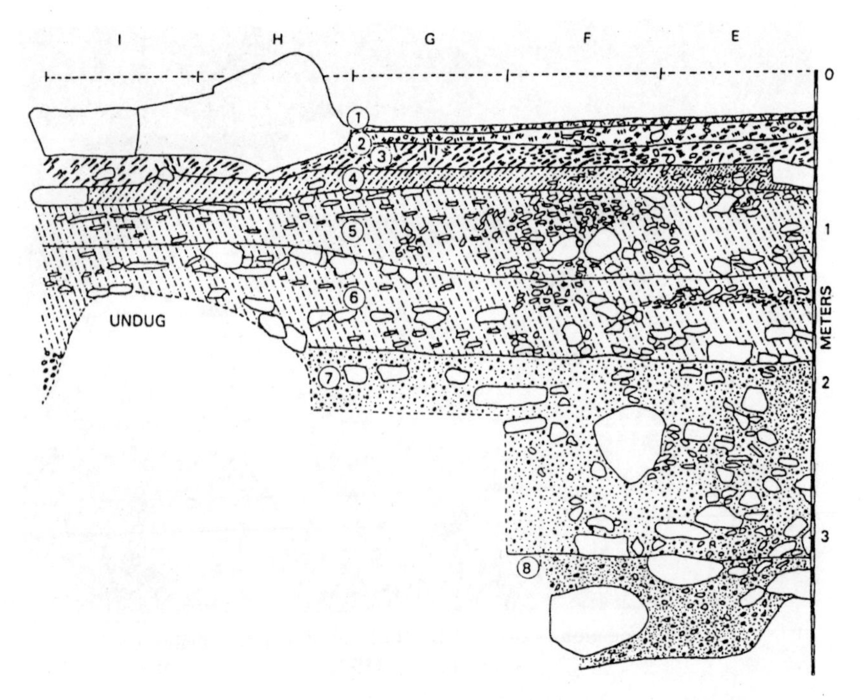

Fig. 5. Section through rock shelter III F-23, Bhimbetka, Madhya Pradesh.
(After Misra 1985)

occupation horizons (Corvinus 1983; Ansari and Pappu 1975). At Hunsgi an oval-shaped living floor is surrounded by granite boulders on all sides, some of which must have been deliberately placed by man to facilitate the construction of hut-like structures (Paddayya 1982). At Paisra the stone alignments were found associated with the Acheulian habitation floors. These alignments are mostly in straight or somewhat curved lines. Postholes were also noticed at this site. These are of three types: single postholes, in pairs, and one or two holes with some arranged stone alignments. Postholes and associated stone alignments show that small temporary structures were being constructed by the Acheulian settlers of Paisra (Pant and Jayaswal 1991). These habitational structures represent seasonal camps. The modern hunter-gatherer groups are found to return to the same locality in the same season; it is inferred that a similar mobility pattern was followed by the Acheulian groups.

Tool Types

The tool-kit of the Lower Palaeolithic culture consists of handaxes, cleavers, choppers, scrapers, discoids, points, borers, polyhedrons, spheroids, etc. Among these types handaxes and cleavers of a variety of shapes and forms dominate.

The most diagnostic tool type is the handaxe with its various subtypes. It is one of the standardised tool types and is invariably thick at one end (butt) and pointed at the other end (tip). Cleaver is the next important tool type. This is characterised by an axe-like broad cutting edge which is usually at right angles to the long axis. The other major typological forms are choppers (both unifacial and bifacial) and scrapers. On the whole the appearance of choppers and handaxes is simultaneous. Cleavers mostly appear later than choppers and handaxes. These tool types are found to occur in different proportions in the Lower Palaeolithic assemblages from different parts of the country. It is rather difficult to explain the reasons behind these differences. It is possible that tool types partially represent specific needs of the people and thus reflect adaptive mechanisms specific to various ecological zones (Ghosh 1985).

Technology

The techniques employed for making stone tools from blanks (pebbles, cores and flakes) into finished forms are basically similar to those known from Europe and other parts of the Old World. During the Lower Palaeolithic stage three main techniques were in use viz., the block-on-block, stone hammer and soft hammer or cylinder hammer. The first technique was employed to obtain large massive wide-angled flakes. A rough outline of the tool was achieved by means of heavy stone hammer technique. The desired shape of the tool was further obtained by means of light stone hammer technique. Final finishing, dressing and trimming were made by soft hammer (cylinder hammer technique). The majority of flakes were detached from the blanks by the Clactonian technique which consisted of the removal of flakes by direct percussion. A few tools suggest the use of prepared core technique (Levalloisian) in which a flake is shaped prior to its detachment from the nucleus.

Nature of Assemblages

As mentioned earlier, the Lower Palaeolithic in India comprises two distinct traditions viz., the Soan represented by pebble tools (also known as the chopper-chopping tool tradition) and biface or handaxe-cleaver tradition. The region lying to the north of the Indo-Gangetic plain (extra-Peninsula) has mainly yielded lithic assemblages dominated by the former tool complex, while the Peninsula has preserved evidence of industries of the handaxe-cleaver tradition.

However, recent investigations have shown that the tool-types of handaxe-cleaver tradition occur at a few localities in extra-Peninsula in the assemblages of the chopper-chopping tool tradition. Mohapatra (1975, 1976, 1982, 1990) has reported a large number of Acheulian sites in sub-Himalayan region. On the other hand a few assemblages devoid of tool-types of the handaxe-cleaver complex were also noticed in the Peninsular region. A few examples of this category are Nittur in Karnataka (Ansari 1970), coastal Maharashtra in Raigad and Sindhudurg districts (Joshi and Bopardikar 1972; Guzder 1980), coastal Kerala (Rajendran 1989) and coastal Andhra (Reddy et al. 1995).

A major focus of studies on the Lower Palaeolithic of the sub-Himalayan region has been to understand the Soan phenomenon in relation to the Acheulian. The Soan culture was once thought to belong to the chopper-chopping tool tradition of south-east Asia (Movius 1948).In recent years Soanian and Acheulian sites have been discovered in the sub-Himalayan tract in the Punjab, Himachal Pradesh and Uttar Pradesh: Beas—Banganga valleys (Lal 1956); Sirsa valley (Sen 1955); Markanda valley (Joshi et al. 1978) and Siwalik Frontal range (Mohapatra 1975, 1976, 1982, 1990).

There are two opinions about the position of the Soan industry. According to one view, the Soan constitutes a culture or tradition quite different from the Lower Palaeolithic Acheulian tradition of the Peninsula. Mohapatra (1976, 1985) who discovered both Soanian and Acheulian sites in the Hoshiarpur-Chandigarh sector of the Siwalik hills has argued that the Acheulian and Soanian populations inhabited two distinct types of environment, the former occupying the flat plain surfaces of the Siwalik front range and the latter the *duns* or valleys of the Himalayan flanks in the hilly region. Mohapatra (1990) considers that the Acheulian occurs in a geomorphic context which is later than that of the Soan and that the Acheulian just touched the outer fringe of the western sub-Himalayas for a short while. He has observed that Soanian tools are fashioned on water-worn cobbles and pebbles, while the Acheulian communities utilised large flakes detached from boulders for preparing bifaces. According to the second view, both the pebble-based chopper-chopping tools and handaxes-cleaver type of tools are part and parcel of a single Lower Palaeolithic handaxe-cleaver complex and there is no cultural dichotomy during the Lower Palaeolithic phase. Presently difference in raw materials and ecological settings are considered more important factors in explaining variations in the Lower Palaeolithic industries (Dennell and Rendell 1991; Jayaswal 1982).

There is no evidence so far for the presence of a pre-Acheulian cultural phase anywhere in India. Khatri (1962) earlier claimed to have discovered an industry exclusively made up of pebble tools in the lowermost red clay stratum on the Narmada at Mahadeo Piparia. He coined the term 'Mahadevian' for this pre-Acheulian industry and believed this industry to be the oldest in India comparable to the Oldowan of East Africa. The excavations undertaken subsequently by Supekar (1968, 1985) at Mahadeo Piparia conclusively proved that there was no stratigraphical basis for postulating the existence of a pebble tool substratum underlying the Acheulian handaxe-cleaver industries.

In Peninsular India at most of the Lower Palaeolithic sites, Acheulian artefacts occur in a mixed state. There is as yet no sound stratigraphical evidence to divide the Acheulian into various phases as have been recognised in Europe and Africa. Typo-technological study and metrical analysis of the Acheulian assemblages from various regions allow us to recognise two developmental phases within the Acheulian viz., Early Acheulian and Late Acheulian. The former is characterised by inferior workmanship, as revealed by deep and irregular flake scars, thick bodies and asymmetrical forms. The Late Acheulian, on the other hand, includes finer types with smoother surfaces resulting from controlled flaking and symmetrical forms.

It is to be remembered that unless these two recognised groups occur in a stratigraphical succession, they do not imply any evolutionary stages. The representative examples of the Early Acheulian tradition are Singi Talav (Didwana) in Rajasthan (Gaillard et al. 1983, 1985), Khyad (Joshi 1955), Anagawadi (Pappu 1974) and Hunsgi (Paddayya 1982) in Karnataka (Fig. 6), Chirki-Nevasa in Maharashtra (Corvinus 1981, 1983), Lalitpur in Uttar Pradesh (Singh 1965) and Mayurbhanj in Orissa (Bose and Sen 1948). The outstanding examples of the Late Acheulian tradition are Gangapur in Maharashtra (Joshi et al. 1966; Arun Kumar 1989), Rallakallava basin in Andhra Pradesh (Murty 1966), Attirampakkam and Vadamadurai in Tamil

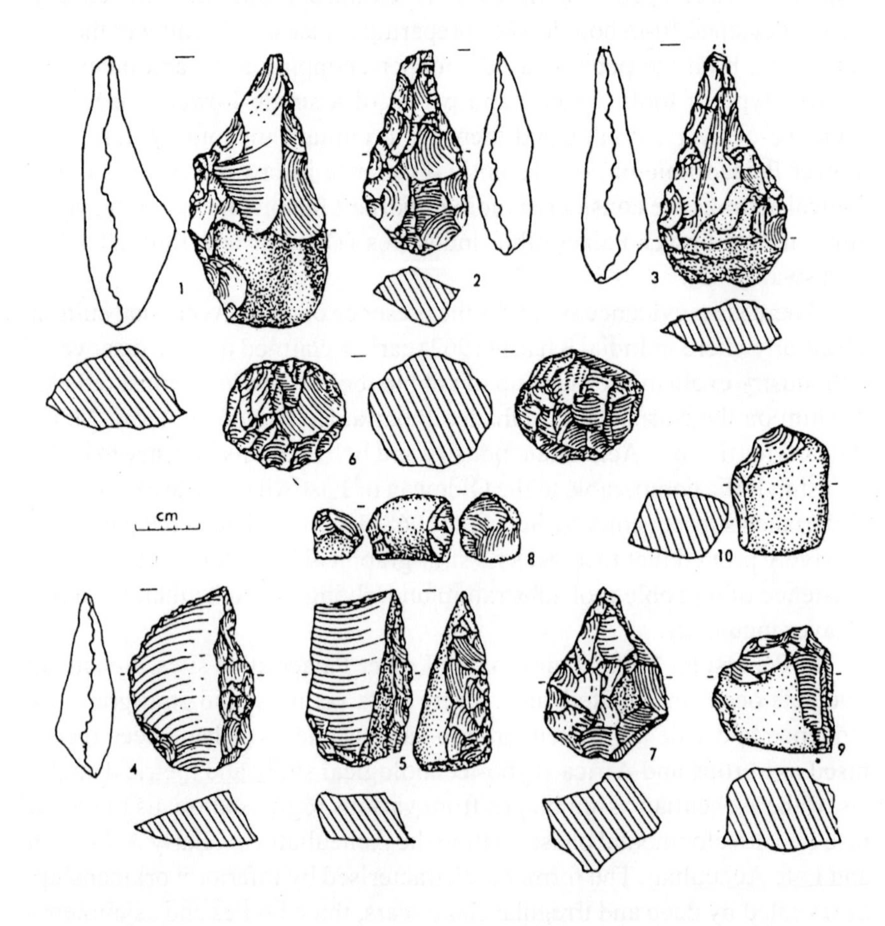

Fig. 6. Early Acheulian tools from Hunsgi, Karnataka: 1-3. handaxes; 4. knife; 5. cleaver; 6. polyhedron; 7. pick; 8. hammerstone; 9. anvil stone; 10. chopper. (After Paddayya 1982)

Nadu (*IAR* 1964–65, 1966–67, Pappu 1996), Bhimbetka (Misra 1978, 1985; Alam 1990) and Raisen complex (Jacobson 1985) in Madhya Pradesh (Fig.7) and Paleru (Madhusudhan Rao 1983) and Gunjana valleys (Raju 1988, 1989) in Andhra Pradesh.

The assemblages from Acheulian sites show differences in the proportions of the main tool-types viz., choppers, handaxes and cleavers. This is due to diversity of geographical settings and also variations in the available raw materials. Statistical and metrical analysis of the relative proportion of handaxes and cleavers undertaken at a number of Acheulian sites

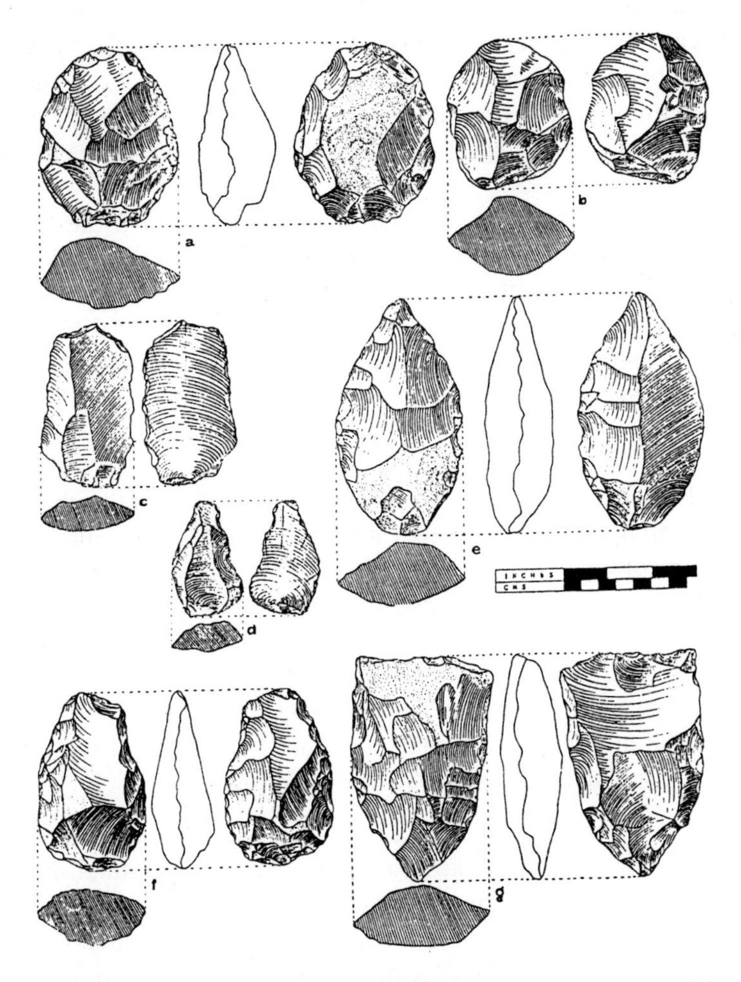

Fig. 7. Late Acheulian tools from Raisen complex, Madhya Pradesh: (a) flake knife; (b) discoidal core; (c, d) scrapers; (e) handaxe; (f, g) cleavers. (After Jacobson 1975)

(Gaillard 1995; Gaillard and Murty 1988; Gaillard et al. 1986, 1990; Joshi 1964, 1970; Joshi and Marathe 1976, 1977, 1985; Raju 1985; Madhusudhan Rao 1983; Alam 1990; Arun Kumar 1989; Ghosh and Ray 1964) show that cleaver-handaxe ratio ranges from 1:1 to 1:2. Handaxes form the dominant type even in the areas of environmental contrast. At a few sites like Adamgarh (Joshi 1978), Bhimbetka (Misra 1978, 1985) and Gangapur (Joshi et al. 1966) cleavers outnumber handaxes. Earlier it was thought that the presence of cleavers in a large number in the Acheulian assemblages reflected well-wooded country and a moist climate but the detailed study of different assemblages from excavated sites showed that this was not the case. Typologically, cleaver dominated assemblages show an advanced Acheulian cultural stage (Joshi 1970). Flake-blades are found associated with Acheulian assemblages at Bhimbetka (Misra 1982) in a fairly large number which is suggestive of the evolved character of the Acheulian assemblages.

The pebble tools (choppers) occur in a high proportion in the Acheulian assemblage at a number of sites in Peninsular India. The preponderance of pebble tools in an assemblage of handaxe-cleaver complex is to some extent related to ecological factors such as the abundance of pebbles in the river beds. Therefore the pebble tools from such regions form an integral part of handaxe-cleaver complex.

Functions of Tools

The Lower Palaeolithic phase is so far removed from the present that even the most primitive living tribes are not known to manufacture handaxe-cleaver type of tools. Comparative ethnography is, therefore, not of much help in understanding the probable use of these tool types. Their probable functions can only be speculated by their shape and form and also by making experiments with these tools. These tools were not directly useful for hunting purposes. They were perhaps employed in preparing larger weapons on wood and bone which have not survived. Some of the probable functions of the tool types may be listed as follows:

Choppers : Chopping and cutting meat and other organic materials.
Scrapers : Scraping of barks of trees and dressing of animal skins.
Handaxes : These might have served as all-purpose tools: the sharp lateral edges used for skinning and cutting animal carcasses; pointed tips for digging up roots and tubers and for opening up the bellies of animals; and the heavy butt for crushing purposes.

Cleavers : These were primarily used for cutting up meat and bone and possibly also for cutting trees.

It is possible that some of the handaxes and cleavers were not used with naked hands but were hafted in wood or bamboo handles. This is evident from the fact that on some handaxes and cleavers there are deliberately made notches which occur on either side near the butt portion.

Raw Material

The distribution of Lower Palaeolithic sites is closely related to geological formations. The Acheulian tool-makers as elsewhere in the Old World always showed a preference for quartzite as the main raw material for making artefacts because of its hardness and good flaking qualities. Quartzites are of widespread occurrence in many parts of the Indian Peninsula and form the major rock type in Vindhyan, Aravalli, Delhi, Gondawana, Cuddapah and Kaladgi formations. Therefore the classical Acheulian localities occur in those parts of the country where quartzite outcrops are found in abundance. The quartzites, being hard and resistant to weathering, form well rounded pebbles due to transportation in the media of sand and running water. Pebbles of suitable size, pebble flakes and blocks of quartzites obtained from natural outcrops were selected by Acheulian men for preparing the desired tool types.

In non-quartzite regions other rock types were preferred, e.g., hard dense basalt and dolerite in the Deccan Trap region of Maharashtra, granites in the Bundelkhand region in Uttar Pradesh and cherty limestone in the Shorapur Doab of north Karnataka.

The rarity of Acheulian sites in those parts of the Peninsula where Deccan Trap basalt outcrops is due to the non-survival of basalt tools on the surface. A plausible explanation for this phenomenon, as suggested by Mishra (1982), is that basalt which was the only rock available for tool making in this region is highly susceptible to disintegration by weathering. Thus the Acheulian sites that did not get buried under the alluvium cover soon after their use may have been totally destroyed by weathering process. The pattern seen in the distribution of sites in the Deccan Trap region therefore reflects to some extent the working of geological processes such as weathering, transport and burial rather than hominid activities. The Acheulian sites in this region are therefore preserved only in exceptional cases.

Although tools are fashioned on a variety of raw materials, on the whole they exhibit a remarkable similarity in form and technique, thereby indicating that Acheulian man handled varied raw materials with equal efficiency.

PALAEOECOLOGY AND SUBSISTENCE PATTERN

Associated Quaternary Deposits

Quaternary formations associated with Acheulian industries include glacial, fluvio-glacial, fluvial, lacustrine, fluvio-lacustrine, aeolian, littoral and colluvial deposits. In the extra-Peninsula and Indo-Gangetic plains the Quaternary deposits cover an immense area whereas in Peninsular India they have a restricted distribution. Among these deposits, sediments of fluvial origin have widespread distribution all over the country and occur in the present-day river valleys. These deposits at times contain Palaeolithic tool assemblages and have also yielded mammalian fossil remains. The stratigraphic sequence of these implementiferous deposits has been worked out for different river valleys of the country.

The glacio-fluvial deposits of Middle Pleistocene age in the Kashmir valley at Pahalgam in the Liddar valley have yielded Lower Palaeolithic implements (Sankalia 1971; Joshi et al. 1974). Fluvio-glacial deposits were also observed in the Kangra, Nalgarh and Markanda valleys of the sub-Himalayan region (Joshi et al. 1978). Thick massive fluvio-glacial cones have been developed in this region on higher terraces. This indicates that intensive fluvial activity was followed by a succession of upheavals which raised the river basins in this area producing a series of terraces. Lower Palaeolithic artefacts of pebble tool and handaxe-cleaver traditions have been found on these terraces.

The Narmada basin in Madhya Pradesh is one of the few regions in Peninsular India where well-preserved Quaternary deposits containing rich artefact assemblage and mammalian fossils occur. The trough-like nature of the central Narmada valley, formed due to tectonic disturbances in the Late Tertiary and Early Pleistocene, has favoured accumulation of vast riverine deposits of Middle and Upper Pleistocene age. The stratigraphical sequence in this region in relation to Palaeolithic industries was first worked out by De Terra and Paterson (1939) and this provided a yardstick for the Pleistocene stratigraphy and relative chronology in the Peninsula. A number of scholars in subsequent years carried out investigations in the central Narmada valley (Khatri 1961, 1962, 1966; Sen and Ghosh 1963; Supekar 1968, 1985; Armand 1980, 1983, 1985; Badam 1982; Misra et al. 1990; Joshi et al. 1978; Seamans 1981). The alluvial deposits of the Narmada

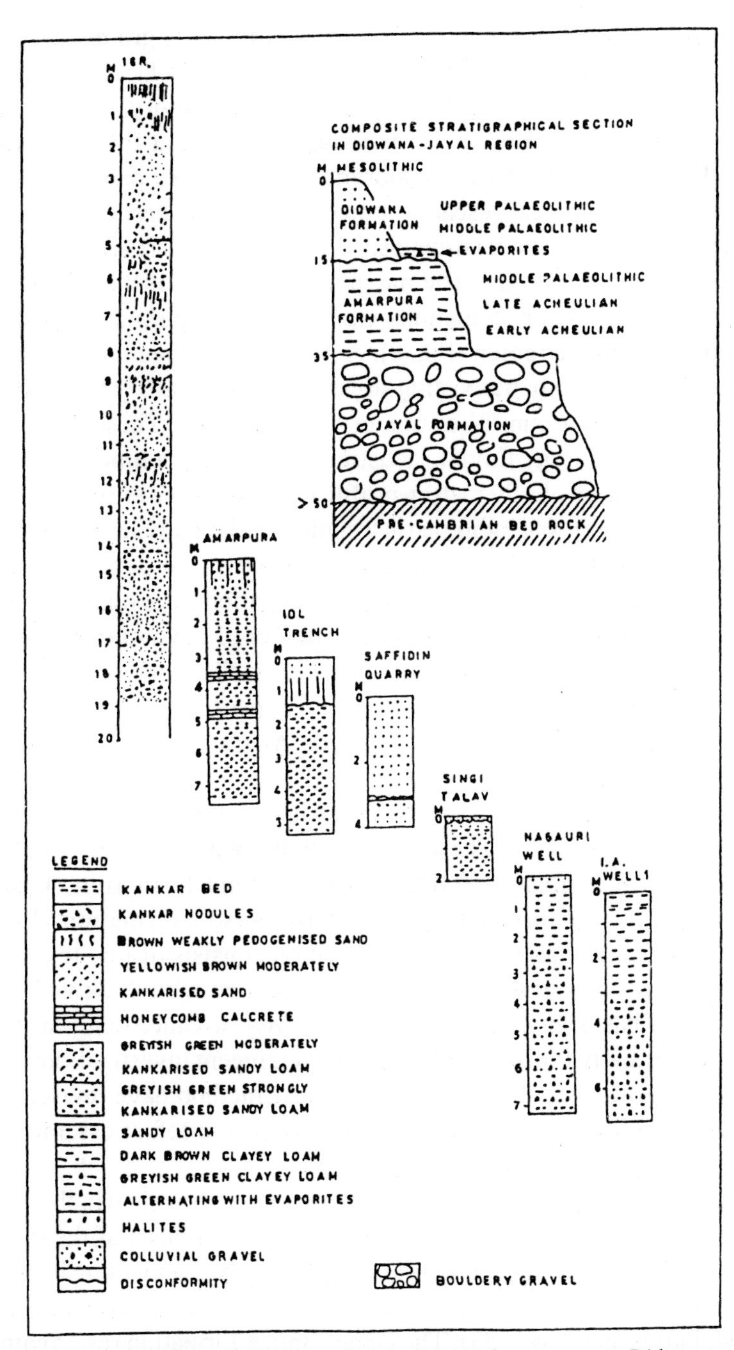

Fig. 8. Quaternary geological and archaeological sequence, at Didwana, Rajasthan. (After Misra 1995)

valley have been divided into three or more stratigraphic groups.

Between 1975 and 1985, Department of Archaeology, Deccan College, Pune in collaboration with the Physical Research Laboratory, Ahmedabad, the Central Arid Zone Research Institute, Jodhpur and the Australian National University carried out a major multi-disciplinary palaeoenvironmental and archaeological research project in the Thar desert in western Rajasthan. Quaternary surficial deposits in the Thar desert are of fluvial, aeolian and lacustrine origin. The maximum thickness of the deposits is over 100 m. Three major formations viz. Jayal, Amarpura and Didwana were reported from the region (Fig. 8). A number of Acheulian sites were discovered far away from the existing streams. Several primary Palaeolithic sites were excavated around Didwana in Nagaur district. These sites have been buried in low energy fluvial, lacustral, and aeolian sediments. In particular, the excavation of a 20 m deep profile in a fossil dune at 16 R locality and its dating by a series of radiometric techniques like Th/U series, thermoluminescence and C^{14} have provided a history of sand deposition and stabilisation of sand dunes and of human occupation of aeolian surfaces over a period of more than 200,000 years. The Acheulian hunter-gatherers camped along lakes and pools formed on the wide flood plains of shallow meandering streams. In addition they also camped on stable sand dune surfaces and extensively exposed gravel beds (Misra 1987, 1995; Misra et al. 1980, 1982; Gaillard et al. 1983, 1985).

The Quaternary formations in the Deccan upland region of Maharashtra are mainly of fluvial origin. These have been divided into Bori formation (BRF), Godavari formation (GDF), Upper Bhima formation (UBF), Chandanapuri formation (CPF) and post-Black soil formation (PBF) (Rajaguru and Korisettar 1987). Bori formation consists of fine textured, dark brown silty clays and gravels, and is associated with thick volcanic ash. The tephra has been dated by K-Ar at 1.4 Myr BP which suggests that the deposit is of Early Pleistocene age. However, recent investigations into the age of the volcanic ash by using 39Ar/40Ar method have revised the date to around 0.65 Myr BP (Korisettar 1994). The artefact assemblage from the site is Early Acheulian in character.

Godavari formation is represented by high level gravels which occur at elevations ranging from 6 to 35 m above the present beds of the rivers Krishna, Bhima, Godavari, Ghataprabha, Malaprabha and Tungabhadra and in most cases lies beyond the reach of modern flood levels (Pappu and Deo 1994; Pappu and Rao 1983). The Upper Bhima formation rests against the Godavari formation and is the most ubiquitous of all the Quaternary deposits in the Deccan upland rivers. It represents a major aggradational phase. It has a thickness of 5 to 30 m and consists of gravels, sand and silty deposits. Acheulian artefacts are generally found in a secondary context in lower unit which is made of cobbly-pebbly gravels. Fossilized bones of *Equus, Elephas* and *Bos* species are also noticed in these deposits. The chronometric dates from Yedurwadi, Didwana, Teggihalli and Nevasa are beyond the range of Th/U dating (Mishra 1992). The Chandanapuri formation is mainly represented by colluvial deposits. The post-Black soil formation is weakly calcretised dark brown sandy silt with gravel lenses. Geomorphic study of the above-mentioned fluvial sequence has facilitated the delineation of five major fluvial phases during the Late Quaternary in the Deccan upland region as follows: (1) pre-aggradational incision phase; (2) ante-Holocene aggradational phase; (3) Early Holocene rejuvenation phase; (4) Holocene alluviation phase; and (5) Late Holocene incision phase. Changes in the fluvial activity are attributed to changes in the base level, climatic changes and tectonic disturbances (Rajaguru and Kale 1985).

In the Saurashtra region of Gujarat, Acheulian tool-bearing fluvial gravels are associated with miliolite formations of marine origin. In the Hiran valley at Junagad and Umrethi, the basal bouldery pebbly gravel deposits have yielded Acheulian artefacts. Over this deposit, there is a deposit of miliolite which has been formed due to transgressive phase of the sea. This phase was followed by a rejuvenation of streams in response to lowering of the sea level. The exact cause of this phenomenon may be eustatic or tectonic or perhaps a combination of both factors. This phase was in turn followed by a major ubiquitous aggradational phase represented by fluvial gravels and silts. These gravels have yielded tools of Middle Palaeolithic industry. This terminal aggradational phase culminated in a transgressive phase represented by another miliolite formation. The miliolite from these sites have been dated by Th/U these dates suggest that the Acheulian occupation took place between 69 and 190 Kyr BP (Marathe 1981; Marathe et al. 1977).

Because of the traditional research emphasis on alluvial formations, the vast majority of known Acheulian occurrences are found in riverine settings which are essentially in secondary context. Pappu (1985a) argued that these secondary context are many times useful for providing clues about the potential existence of intact sites, inferred to be in nearby locations. Moreover, alluvial sites are also useful for reconstructing a geomorphic history and depositional environments of river valleys.

Associated Fossil Remains

Pleistocene fossiliferous localities have been observed in the Indian subcontinent for more than a century. Large and varied collections of mammalian fossils have been made from the Karewas of Kashmir, the Siwalik formations in the sub-Himalayan region in Punjab and Himachal Pradesh, the alluvia of Narmada and Mahanadi in Madhya Pradesh, Belan valley in Uttar Pradesh, Pravara, Godavari, Krishna, Ghod and Manjra valleys in Maharashtra and Hunsgi valley, Tungabhadra and Ghataprabha valley in Karnataka (Badam 1979, 1984). These faunal remains are associated with the Acheulian tools at a number of localities in the peninsular river valleys.

The Lower group of the Narmada stratigraphy which has yielded Acheulian tools contains fossil remains of *Elephas namadicus*, *Stegodon ganesa*, *Stegodon insignis*, *Bos namadicus*, *Equus namadicus, Bubalus palaeindicus*, *Cervus duvauceli, Rhinoceros unicornis, Hippopotamus palaeindicus, Leptobos frazeri, Ursus namadicus, Sus* sp., *Trionyx* sp. and *Emys* sp. In the Belan and Pravara valleys similar types of fossil remains have been found. The presence of these animals during Acheulian times indicate the existence of both forest and open grassland environments and the availability of plentiful water round the year.

Faunal studies have shown that species hitherto considered as the index for the Middle Pleistocene (*Equus namadicus* and *Bos namadicus*) in fact range from the Middle to Upper Pleistocene. Species like *Elephas maximus, Cervus duvauceli* and *Rhinoceros unicornis* range from the Upper Pleistocene to the Holocene. Only *Hexaprotodon namadicus* and *Sus namadicus* may be considered as index fossils for the Middle Pleistocene. The Upper Pleistocene is well dated by a score of C^{14} dates and contains a well defined index fossil assemblage (Badam 1979, 1988).

Associated Human Remains

A partial cranium of advanced *Homo erectus* or archaic *Homo sapiens* was discovered in 1982 in the basal gravels of the Narmada alluvium at Hathnora near Hoshangabad in Madhya Pradesh (Sonakia 1984) and a hominid clavicle was reported from the same region in 1997 (Sankhyan 1997). This is the first and so far only hominid fossil discovery reported in India. The tools of the Lower Palaeolithic Acheulian industry were also found from the same deposit. The cranium is heavily mineralised. Its position in the channel bar deposits of the Narmada and its taphonomic features indicate that the cranium was redeposited in this sediment after having been transported over some distance. The hominid fossil and the associated

Acheulian tools come from a secondary context and hence a taphonomic study is necessary to arrive at a precise chronology and palaeoenvironmental aspects of the site (Sonakia 1984; De Lumley and Sonakia 1985a, b; Badam 1989).

Subsistence Pattern

The economy of the Acheulian culture was based on hunting of animals and gathering of wild plant foods. No direct evidence is available to reconstruct the subsistence practices of the Acheulian hunter-gatherers. This is because of the poor preservation of animal and plant remains at the excavated primary sites. The organic material which is essential to understand the subsistence practices of early man have been destroyed because of the tropical nature of the climate and also acidic soil conditions.

The situation of the camp sites near the perennial streams and in the forests and grasslands provided good opportunities for hunting, fishing and gathering of plant foods. There is evidence of fossils of contemporary animals in the gravel deposits of the Narmada, Belan, Godavari, Bhima and other rivers. From this evidence it can be said that in these areas the wild elephant, the wild ox, the wild horse, the wild buffalo, deer and other animals were present in large numbers. There were also fishes, crocodiles and turtles in the rivers and in the marshy areas lived the rhino and the hippo.

No direct evidence is available to reconstruct the techniques and equipment used for hunting. The large weapons made on organic materials like wood and bone have not survived. In some cases stone artefacts like handaxes, cleavers and scrapers probably also formed part of the hunting equipment. The pointed handaxes might have served as efficient spearheads while the cleaver with sharp cutting edge could have been used for cutting the carcasses. There is little doubt that animal foods, acquired by hunting or scavenging, formed an important item of the diet of the Acheulian population.

Vegetable foods probably also formed an important part of the Acheulian diet. It has now been recognised that the meagre data available on subsistence practices of the Acheulian communities needs to be supplemented by ethnoarchaeological, ethnobotanical and ethnozoological studies. Ethnoarchaeological studies of some of the existing tribal communities like the Bushmen of South Africa have convincingly shown that they derive their subsistence mainly from plant foods (Lee 1969). Ethnobotanical investigations undertaken in some parts of India like the Hunsgi valley

(Paddayya 1979b, 1982) and Bhimbetka area (Misra et al. 1977) have revealed that the scrub jungle and deciduous vegetation tracts of Peninsular India are extremely rich in wild plant foods of various kinds like fruits, berries, tubers, roots, nuts, seeds, greens, etc. These are still being exploited extensively by tribal groups like the Gonds, the Chenchus, and the Yerukalas (Murty 1981, 1985; Nagar 1985).

Palaeoenvironment

Some idea of the past environment particularly palaeoclimate prevailing during the Acheulian times is provided by the geoarchaeological studies carried out during the last three to four decades of fluvial, aeolian, colluvial, littoral and lacustrine deposits with which the Acheulian cultural remains are associated. These studies have established that there were climatic fluctuations, sea-level changes and tectonic movements in the Indian subcontinent during the Quaternary period.

In the Deccan upland region of Maharashtra, the Quaternary deposits are mostly of fluvial origin and are found in the river valleys. Geoarchaeological studies conducted in several major river valleys of the Deccan have thrown considerable light on the behaviour of these streams in the vicinity of which Acheulian communities had located their settlements. Fluvial phases of incision and aggradation have been recognised during the Quaternary. The phases of fluvial activity were probably responses to regional climatic changes. The aggradational episodes were perhaps associated with semi-arid conditions while incision phases were related to increase in rainfall. A comparison of the east-flowing rivers with the west-flowing ones revealed an inverse correlation between the two. During the period of low sea-level there was an increase in continentality and aridity leading to aggradation on the leeward of the Western Ghats. The high sea-levels following the arid phases decreased continentality but led to increased runoff at which time the rivers began to cut down their beds (Kale and Rajaguru 1986, 1987; Rajaguru and Korisetter 1987). The above-mentioned geomorphic events indicate that climatic fluctuations were not as drastic as in Rajasthan and extra-Peninsular region. The Deccan upland region at present enjoys a tropical semi-arid monsoonal climate and more or less the same pattern of climate with minor fluctuations prevailed during the Middle and Late Pleistocene times. The prehistoric communities could very well adapt themselves to such minor environmental changes.

The evidence for major climatic changes and human response to these events during the Quaternary period comes from the present semi-arid region of western Rajasthan. There is evidence that in the present sandy plains of western Rajasthan devoid of drainage mighty, well-organised streams existed during the Early Pleistocene times. There is no evidence that man was present in this area during this period. In the subsequent Mid- and Late Quaternary times, there were intensive climatic changes and shallow streams flowing in wide floodplains deposited muds and calcareous clays in pans or shallow depressions. Acheulian artefacts in mint condition are found buried in these marly deposits at the site of the Singi Talav in the Didwana region. The evidence from Singi Talav shows that Acheulian man had adapted himself to desert environment during Mid- to Late Quaternary times. Th/U date >390 Kyr indicates an early date for the Acheulian culture. The Acheulian men camped along the pools and lakes in the flood plains (Misra 1987, 1995; Misra et al. 1982; Gaillard et al. 1983, 1985).

There were relative changes of land and sea levels during the Quaternary and there is ample evidence to show that the relationship between land and sea had fluctuated from –15 m to +50 m during the Quaternary. In recent years investigations have been undertaken on the problem of Quaternary sea-level changes in relation to Palaeolithic sites in the Saurashtra region of Gujarat (Lele 1989; Marathe 1981). Two marine transgressive phases have been identified from the occurrence of marine deposits like miliolite formations, the first at the beginning of late Middle Pleistocene about 1,70,000 yrs. BP and the second around 30,000 yrs. BP. The Acheulian tools were located at Umrethi and Junagarh sites in gravel deposits underlying first miliolite formation.

The major portion of the Indian Peninsula has been regarded as tectonically stable since post-Miocene or post-Tertiary times. Geomorphic studies undertaken in recent years in Peninsular region (Radhakrishna 1952, 1993; Vaidyanathan 1977; Rajaguru 1968, 1969) have shown that the Indian Peninsula was not as stable as is generally believed. There were tectonic disturbances of epeirogenic type during the Late Tertiary and Pleistocene times. Rajaguru's studies (1968, 1969) in the south-central Maharashtra have indicated that the aggradational and erosional phases of the rivers have been controlled by large-scale, slow tectonic movements such as positive and negative epeirogenic movements of the whole Peninsular shield. The polycylic nature of the landscape, the presence of peneplains at higher elevations, the superimposed and rejuvenated character of some of the rivers and entrenched meanders are attributed to the tectonic instability of the region. However, there is no direct evidence of tectonic activity in the form of structural displacement like folds and faults. Thus these movements have not much affected the landscape and the archaeological settlements forming part of it. This is evident from the preservation of fresh unrolled artefacts in different geomorphic settings. The landscape has remained static thereby indicating relative stability since the late Middle Pleistocene. Because of the inadequate knowledge of neo-tectonics in the region, it is rather difficult to ascertain the exact role played by tectonics in shaping varied geomorphic features.

SETTLEMENT PATTERN, ORIGINS AND CHRONOLOGY

Site Catchment Analysis (Land Use Pattern)

The explicit realisation that human groups procure resources from the regions immediately surrounding their settlements led to the introduction in the late sixties, of the analytical method of Site Catchment Analysis (Vita-Fizi and Higgs 1970). This concept is concerned with the exploitation of plant, animal and mineral resources by human groups in a particular territory. Catchment area of a site is the territory from which resources are taken to support human population and occur within a reasonable walking distance. On the basis of ethnographic data on the Kung Bushmen in Africa, two hours walking distance (10 km) has been suggested as a critical threshold for hunting-gathering economies (Lee 1969).

Over the last two decades this hypothesis has been tested with great success at a number of Acheulian sites such as Chirki-Nevasa, Anagwadi, Khyad and Hunsgi. These studies have furnished evidence for the range of movement of the Acheulian hunter-gatherers for resource exploitation and have confirmed that the resources occur within a radius of 10 km (Pappu and Deo 1994; Paddayya 1982).

Settlement Pattern

The concept of settlement pattern was first applied in archaeological studies by Willey (1953) in the Viru valley, Peru and offered a model framework for future investigations. The analysis of past settlement pattern takes into consideration the location of sites, their distribution and densities, and their relationship with ecology. In recent years this concept has been successfully applied to the study of Palaeolithic sites in India (Paddayya 1982; Pappu and Deo 1994; Deo 1991; Ray 1987; Raju 1988).

A large complex of open-air Acheulian sites was brought to light in the Hunsgi valley of North Karnataka (Paddayya 1982). A detailed investigation of the location of sites has given valuable clues about the probable annual activity cycle of the Acheulian groups and nature of their seasonal settlement systems. The Acheulian groups in the valley aggregated during dry season at spring-fed water sources in the Hunsgi stream and dispersed during wet season. It would thus emerge that wet season dispersal with attendant reliance on plant foods and small fauna and dry season aggregation characterised by large game hunting were the governing principles of the Hunsgi valley settlement system. The Acheulian groups of the Hunsgi valley practised a localised or restricted type of nomadism mostly dependent on the seasonal availability of food and water resources.

The techniques and methods of geomorphology have been used to understand the settlement pattern and man-land relationships in the Kaladgi basin in North Karnataka (Pappu and Deo 1994). The distribution of the Acheulian sites in the Ghataprabha valley of the Kaladgi basin was found to have been influenced by morphometric parameters like relief, slope and drainage density, thereby indicating their role in the location of sites. Spatial point analysis results suggest that the sites are significantly concentrated in some parts of the basin and the centrography of the basin revealed that the mean centre of the Acheulian sites is located in the lower reaches. Based on these geomorphic investigations, three distinct archaeo-geomorphic zones viz., the core zone, the marginal zone and the adverse zone, have been identified in the Ghataprabha basin.

Site Formation Processes

Past natural processes and human activity contribute to the formation of an archaeological site. The study of the diverse processes of site formation is one of the most important aspects of modern archaeological research. This study provides a basis for interpreting the duration of human occupation, the continuity or intermittence of occupation, intensity of occupation, rate of deposit formation, post-depositional alterations and the effects of erosion on the preservation of cultural remains. In India, Paddayya (1987b), Paddayya and Petraglia (1993, 1995), Petraglia (1995), Ahsan (1993), Pappu (1996), and Jhaldiyal (1997) have made an attempt to study site formation process.

Paddayya (1987b), Petraglia (1995) and Jhaldiyal (1997) made a study of site formation processes of the Acheulian sites in the Hunsgi and Baichbal basins, North Karnataka. The study was aimed to identify and evaluate the natural and cultural processes responsible for the formation of Acheulian record in the basins. The majority of the Acheulian sites in the basin are located away from the alluvial settings and occur as thin unstratified artefact horizons which are on or very close to the surface. The cultural material at these sites lies completely exposed, partially exposed or remains buried under a shallow sediment cover. The Acheulian artefacts occur in discrete clusters as isolated occurrences and as horizontally diffuse scatters in cultivated and uncultivated tracts of land.

The landscape on which Acheulian sites occur is a stable one characterised by low-energy erosional processes. The varied preservational contexts in which Acheulian sites occur indicate that the slow rates of sedimentation have played a significant role in the preservation of the Acheulian record. The contemporary contexts of occurrence of the sites are the cumulative result of the past and recent post-depositional processes. The weathering pattern analysis shows that the impact of processes on the Acheulian sites before their burial was determined by the length of exposure, topographic location and nature of substrata. Sites located on soft sediments showed excellent preservation. Examination of the assemblage composition, weathering analysis of artefacts and spatial distribution of the artefacts in some of the excavated localities showed that the colluvial processes of sedimentation were clearly responsible for creating a palimpsest deposit containing artefacts discarded during different episodes of site occupation. The study of formation processes of surface and near surface Acheulian sites shows that in the absence of a vertical view of the record, documentation of the archaeological record at a regional level gives a better and more representative understanding of the character of natural processes operative on the landscape and their impact on the archaeological record (Jhaldiyal 1997).

Origin

To understand the genesis of the Lower Palaeolithic Acheulian culture in Indian subcontinent it is necessary to know the evolutionary history of the Early Man in other parts of the Old World. There are at present two contrasting views regarding the origin of Early Man in the Old World. According to the first view, the ancestors of modern humans had their origins in Africa and from this continent they radiated to other parts of the Old World. As opposed to the view, some archaeologists have suggested polycentric origin of early human cultures.

There is now convincing evidence to show that Early Man had his origin in sub-Saharan Africa. Tremendous amount of new evidence has been brought forth in support of this in the form of hominid fossil remains. The earliest hominid type is represented by the *Australopithecines* and is dated to 5 million years before present. These were bipedal creatures but did not make any stone tools. The evidence of the earliest known chipped stone tools in the archaeological record comes from the Omo Valley in East Africa and is dated to some 2.4–3.3 million years ago. These simple tools were fashioned by the early form of *Homo* known as *Homo habilis*. This hominid had a brain larger than that of the *Australopithecines* and is significantly associated with the oldest tradition of tool-manufacture which is known as the Oldowan stage. There was the appcarance of a new hominid type known as *Homo erectus* around 1.6 / 1.5 million years ago in Africa. He had a larger stature and a brain larger than that of *Homo habilis*. The arrival of *Homo erectus* has been regarded as marking an important stage of human evolution.

By about 1.5/1.4 million years ago, a new, bifacially worked tool-kit made its appearance in Africa. This industrial complex is called the Acheulian. These stone artefacts show a significant development over the Oldowan tool-kit and continued up to 1,25,000 years BP. They are the first standardised tools to appear in the archaeological record. Around one million years ago *Homo erectus* moved out of Africa first into the Asian tropics and then later into temperate Europe. Radiation and dispersal over wide areas are characteristics of evolutionary history. The two earlier hominid types viz., *Australopithecines* and *Homo habilis* never moved out of Africa and therefore did not spread elsewhere. Sankalia (1974) and Allchin (Allchin et al. 1978) are impressed by the African parallels and have postulated that the Acheulian culture was derived from that region to India via a now submerged continental shelf or else through a land route connected by Arabia, Iran, Afghanistan and Baluchistan.

In recent years new dates are available in different parts of the Old World for the Lower Palaeolithic culture which suggest that not one but several centres of human origin are most likely. Such dates have come from Pakistan, Indonesia, Israel, Europe and Siberia (Bahn 1996). These chronometric dates range from 2.5 million to 1.2 million years BP. This has necessitated a complete revision of earlier views.

Chronology

Till recently our knowledge of the chronology of the Lower Palaeolithic Acheulian culture and its duration in India was far from satisfactory due to the absence of absolute dates. The relative dating of this cultural stage was based on palaeontological and geomorphological evidence. At times weathering of Quaternary gravels and fluorine/phosphate ratios in fossil bones were used in estimating relative age (Mishra et al. 1988; Joshi and Kshirsagar 1986). In the last ten years, a significant number of absolute dates have been obtained by use of Thorium-Uranium (Th/U), Potassium-Argon (K/Ar), and Thermoluminesence (TL) methods. A list of these dates obtained for the Acheulian sites is given in the table (Table 2).

The Acheulian in the Indian subcontinent has been dated to the beginning of the Middle Pleistocene at the site of Bori in western Maharashtra (Mishra et al. 1995; Horn et al. 1993) and at Jalalpur and Dina in the Siwalik sediments in Pakistan (Rendell and Dennell 1985). At Bori, volcanic ash associated with an Early Acheulian industry has been dated between 670–530 Kyr. At Jalalpur and Dina, Acheulian artefacts were found *in situ* in gravels just above the Bruhnes/Matuyama boundary and an age between 600–400 Kyr has been estimated for the Acheulian culture at these sites. On the basis of palaeomagnetic stratigrphy minimum dates of 190 Kyr and 66 Kyr were available on miliolite overlying gravels containing Acheulian artefacts in Saurashtra (Baskaran et al. 1986). Th/U dates at the sites of Didwana, Yedurwadi and Nevasa show that the Acheulian is beyond the range of Th/U dating i.e., >350 Kyr. In the Hunsgi and Baichbal valleys, one date is beyond the range of Th/U dating and two further dates from the same context are close to the limit of Th/U dating.

In summary, the dates from Umrethi and Adi Chadi Wao in Saurashtra are suggestive of the minimum dates for the Acheulian in India. The dates obtained from Didwana, Teggihalli, Nevasa and Yedurwadi are beyond the limit of Th/U dating method. K/Ar dating of volcanic ash at Bori suggests that the Acheulian belongs to early Middle Pleistocene. On the basis of this evidence it is clear that the Acheulian in India falls within the time span of 600 Kyr and 66 Kyr. In terms of geological time scale it covers a period from the beginning of early Middle Pleistocene to mid-Upper Pleistocene. The chronology of the Acheulian culture in India has thus been pushed backward in time. This time framework compares fairly well with the chronology of the Acheulian in other parts of the Old World.

Comparison and Correlation

In the European Palaeolithic framework the term Acheulian applies to a handaxe tradition characterised by symmetry in morphological features (Bordes 1968). In Africa the term Chelleo-Acheulian was in vogue to denote the succession of handaxe industries but at present both early and late components of handaxe industries are considered as belonging to one stage and the entire series of handaxes is now called Acheulian (Clark 1970).

Table 2. **Thorium Uranium & Potassium Argon Dates for Acheulian Sites in Peninsular India**

S.No.	Site	Material dated and its connection with Acheulian culture	Methods used	Age	References
1.	Umrethi, Saurashtra, Gujarat	Miliolite lying over Acheulian artefacts	Th/U	190,00+29,000 –22,000	Baskaran et al. 1986
2.	Adi Chadi Wao	Miliolite lying over Acheulian artefacts	Th/U	69,000+3800 –3600	Ibid.
3.	Didwana, Rajasthan	Calcrete associated with Acheulian artefacts	Th/U	>390,000	Raghavan et al. 1989
4.	Sadab, Baichbal valley, Karnataka	*Elephas* molar associated with Acheulian artefacts	Th/U	290,405+20,999 –18,186	Szabo et al. 1990
5.	Kaldevanhalli, Hunsgi valley, Karnataka	Travertine underlying rubble containing Acheulian artefacts	Th/U	174,000±35,000 166,000+15,000 –13,000	Ibid.
6.	Teggihalli, Baichbal valley	*Bos* molar associated with Acheulian artefacts	Th/U	287,333+24,169 –18,180	Ibid.
		Elephas molar associated with Acheulian artefacts		>350,000	
7.	Nevasa, Maharashtra	Calcrete associated with Acheulian artefacts	Th/U	>350,000	Atkinson et al. 1990
8.	Yedurwadi, Karnataka	Calcrete associated with Acheulian artefacts	Th/U	>350,000	Ibid.
9.	Bori, Maharashtra	Volcanic Ash associated with Acheulian artefacts	K/Ar Ar/Ar K/Ar	537,000±47,000 670,000±30,000	Horn et at. 1993 Mishra et al. 1995

(Affter Mishra 1992, 1995 b; Mishra et al. 1995, 1998)

The Acheulian industries both in Africa and Europe show typo-technological evolution viz., Early, Middle, Upper and Advanced or evolved phases. The evolution has a sound stratigraphic basis also. The time span of Acheulian culture is from 1.5 million years BP to 0.1 million years BP and from 0.6 million years BP to 0.1 million years BP respectively in Africa and Europe. As the Lower Palaeolithic culture progressed there was an increase in finely made flakes and special knapping techniques were developed to produce flakes of predetermined shape and size. A number of primary occupation sites with dwelling structures containing living floors and hominid remains have also been preserved at a number of sites in Africa and Europe. Many of the sites occur in datable contexts. In Africa, pre-Acheulian industries are associated with the hominid remains of *Australopithecines* and *Homo habilis*. The Acheulian industries occur in association with the hominid remains of *Homo erectus* both in Africa and Europe. On the basis of this evidence it has been possible to reconstruct behavioural pattern of the early hominids in Africa and Europe.

In India there is as yet no evidence for the presence of a pre-Acheulian cultural phase. There is also no sound stratigraphical evidence to divide the Acheulian into various sub-phases as in Africa and Europe. A few primary occupation sites like Chirki-Nevasa, Hunsgi, Bhimbetka and Paisra have been systematically investigated. However, there is no evidence of hominid remains at any of these excavated primary sites. At present we have evidence of only two fragmentary pieces of *Homo erectus* found in a secondary context at the site of Hathnora on the Narmada.

The Indian Acheulian industries are broadly similar to corresponding industries both in Africa and Europe. There are however certain differences which concern the sizes and shapes of tool-types and presence of certain specialized forms. Handaxes from India compare well with all European and African counterparts. The cleaver though rare in Europe is extremely common in Africa and appears rather late in the Acheulian sequence. Quartzite was commonly used both in Africa and India; this could have led to close similarities in tool types.

This review of the Lower Palaeolithic culture has brought to light various aspects of the earlier phase of human occupation in India. Significant progress has been achieved in the research on this remote phase of the human past in the country. There are no doubt a number of complex problems still awaiting resolution. Only planned research will give satisfactory solutions to these problems.

REFERENCES

Ahsan, S.M.K. 1993. A Study of Palaeolithic Site Formation Processes in Subhumid Environment of Central India with Special Reference to Samnapur Palaeolithic Site (Madhya Pradesh). Ph.D. Dissertation. Pune: University of Pune.

Alam, M.S. 1990. *Morphometric Study of the Palaeolithic Industries of Bhimbetka, Central India*. Ph.D. Dissertation. Pune: University of Pune.

Allchin, B., Goudie, A., and Hegde, K.T.M. 1978. *Prehistory and Palaeogeography of the Great Indian Desert*. London: Academic Press.

Ansari, Z.D. 1970. Pebble Tools from Nittur (Mysore State), *Indian Antiquary* 4 (1–4): 1–17.

Ansari, Z.D., and Pappu, R.S. 1975. Some Observations on the Excavation at Acheulian Site Chirki-Nevasa, District Ahmednagar, Maharashtra. *Bulletin of the Deccan College Research Institute* 35: 1–8.

Armand, J. 1980. The Middle Pleistocene Pebble Tool Site of Durkadi in Central India. *Paleorient* 5: 105–44.

—1983. *Archaeological Excavations in Durkadi Nala: An Early Palaeolithic Pebble Tool Workshop in Central India*. New Delhi: Munshiram Manoharlal Publishers.

—1985. The Emergence of the Handaxe Tradition in Asia with Special Reference to India, in *Recent Advances in Indo-Pacific Prehistory*. V.N. Misra and P. Bellwood, eds. New Delhi: Oxford & IBH Publishing Co., pp. 3–8.

Arun Kumar. 1985. Quaternary Studies of the Upper Godavari Valley. A Study in Environmental Archaeology. Ph.D. Dissertation. Pune: University of Pune.

—1989. A Metrical Analysis of Handaxes and Cleavers from the Acheulian Site at Gangapur, Nasik District, Maharashtra, *Man and Environment* 13: 49–64.

Atkinson, T.C., Rower, P.J., Powar, N.J., and Kale, V.S. 1990. Unpublished Report Submitted to the Natural Environmental Research Council (U.K.).

Badam, G.L. 1979. *Pleistocene Fauna of India*. Pune: Deccan College.

—1982. Biostratigraphy of the Central Narmada Valley—A Reappraisal, in *Indian Archaeology: New Perspectives* R.K. Sharma, ed., Delhi: Agam Kala Prakashan, pp. 38–47.

—1984. Pleistocene Faunal Succession of India, in *The Evolution of East Asian Environments,* R.O. Whyte, ed., Hong Kong: University of Hong Kong, pp. 746–75.

—1988. Quaternary Faunal Succession of India. Geological Survey of India, Special Publication 11: 277–304.

—1989. Observations on the Fossil Hominid Site at Hathnora, Madhya Pradesh, India, in *Perspectives in Human Evolution*, Ashok Sahni and Rajan Gaur, eds., Delhi: Renaissance Publishing House, pp. 153–71.

Bahn, P.G. 1996. The First Colonisation of Europe, in *The Oxford Companion to Archaeology*, B.M. Fagan, ed., Oxford: Oxford University Press, pp. 224–25.

Baskaran, M., Marathe, A.R., Rajaguru, S.N., and Somayajulu, B.L.K. 1986. Geochronology of Palaeolithic Cultures in Hiran Valley, Saurashtra, India. *Journal of Archaeological Science* 13: 505–14.

Bordes, F. 1968. *The Old Stone Age*. New York: McGraw Hill.

—1961. *Typologie du Paleolithique Ancien et Moyen*. Bordeaux: Delmas.

Bose, N.K., and Sen, D. 1948. *Excavations in Mayurbhanj*. Calcutta: Calcutta University.

Cammiade, L.A., and Burkitt, M.C. 1930. Fresh Light on the Stone Age in Southeast India. *Antiquity* 4: 327–39.

Chakrabarti, S. 1983. Acheulian Culture in Saurashtra in Relation to Pleistocene Stratigraphy: An Overview. *Journal of the Indian Anthropological Society* 18(1): 1–9.

—1995. Late Quaternary Stratigraphy and an Upper Acheulian Occupation Site in the Kalubhar Valley, Saurashtra, in *Quaternary Environments* and *Geoarchaeology of India*, S. Guzder, R. Korisettar and V.S. Kale, eds. Bangalore: Geological Society of India, pp. 277–81.

Clark, J.D. 1970. *The Prehistory of Africa*. London: Thames and Hudson.

Corvinus, G. 1981. *The Pravara River System*, vol. 1: *The Stratigraphy and Geomorphology of the Pravara River System*. Tubingen: Institute fur Urgeschichte.

—1983. *The Pravara River System*, vol. 2: *The Excavations of the Acheulian Site of Chirki on Pravara, India*. Tubingen: Institute fur Urgeschichte.

Dasgupta, R.C. 1931. Bibliography of Prehistoric Indian Antiquities. *Journal and Proceedings of Asiatic Society of Bengal* 27(1): 1–96.

De Lumely, Henry, and Sonakia, A. 1985a. Contexte Stratigraphique et Archaeologique del' Homme de la Narmada Hathnora, Madhya Pradesh Inde. *L'Anthropologie* 89(1): 3–12.

—1985b. Premiere Decouverte d'un *Homo erectus* sur le Continent Indian a Hathnora dans la Moyenne Vallee de la Narmada. *L'Anthropologie* 89(1): 13–61.

De Terra, H., and Paterson, T.T. 1939. *Studies on the Ice Age in India and Associated Human Cultures*. Washington D.C.: Carnegie Institution.

Dennell, R.W., and Rendell, H.N. 1991. De Terra and Paterson and the Soan Flake Industry: A New Perspective from the Son Valley, Northern Pakistan. *Man and Environment* 14(2): 91–100.

Deo, S.G. 1991. Geomorphic Study of Palaeolithic Settlements in the Ghataprabha Basin, Karnataka. Ph.D. Dissertation. Pune: University of Pune.

Foote, R.B. 1866. On the Occurrence of Stone Implements in the Lateritic Formations in Various Parts of Madras and North Arcot District, *Madras Journal of Literature and Science* III(2). Reprinted in 1966 in *Studies in Prehistory*, D. Sen and A.K. Ghosh, eds. Calcutta: Firma K.L. Mukhopadhaya, pp. 1–22.

—1914. *The Foote Collection of Indian Prehistoric and Protohistoric Antiquities: Catalogue Raisonne*. Chennai: Government Museum.

—1916. *The Foote Collection of Indian Prehistoric and Protohistoric Antiquities: Notes on Their Ages and Distribution*. Chennai: Government Museum.

Gaillard, C. 1995. An Early Soan Assemblage from the Siwaliks: A Comparison of Processing Sequences between this Assemblage and an Acheulian Assemblage from Rajasthan, in *Quaternary Environments and Geoarchaeology of India*, S. Wadia, R. Korisettar and V.S. Kale, eds. Bangalore: Geological Society of India, pp. 231–45.

Gaillard, C., and Murty, M.L.K. 1988. Typo-Technological Comparison of Two Acheulian Assemblages at Renigunta South India. *Man and Environment* 12: 123–33.

Gaillard, C., Misra, V.N., and Murty, M.L.K. 1990. Comparative Study of Three Series of Handaxes: One from Rajasthan and Two from Andhra Pradesh. *Bulletin of the Deccan College Research Institute* 49: 137–43.

Gaillard, C., Raju, D.R., Misra, V.N., and Rajaguru, S.N. 1983. Acheulian Occupation at Singi-Talav in the Thar Desert: A Preliminary Report on 1982 Excavation. *Man and Environment* 7: 112–30.

Gaillard, C., Misra, V.N., Rajaguru, S.N., Raju, D.R., and Raghavan, H. 1985. Acheulian Occupation at Singi-Talav in the Thar Desert: A Preliminary Report on 1981 Excavation. *Bulletin of the Deccan College Research Institute* 44: 141–52.

Gaillard, C., Raju, D.R., Misra, V.N., and Rajaguru, S.N. 1986. Handaxe Assemblages from the Didwana Region, Thar Desert, India: A Metrical Analysis. *Proceedings of the Prehistoric Society* 52: 189–14.

Ghosh, A.K. 1970. The Palaeolithic Cultures of Singhbhum. *Transactions of the American Philosophical Society* 60(1): 1–68.

—1974. Concept of Chopper/Chopping Tool Complex in India, in *Perspectives in Palaeoanthropology*, A.K. Ghosh, ed. Calcutta: Firma K.L. Mukhopadhyay, pp. 221–34.

—1985. An Attempt to Understand the Acheulian Succession in India from Spatial Distribution, in *Recent Advances in Indo-Pacific Prehistory*, V.N. Misra and P. Bellwood, eds. New Delhi: Oxford & IBH Publishing Co., pp. 29–34.

Ghosh, R., and Ray, G. 1964. A Technological Study of the Cleavers of Mayurbhanj. *Man in India* 44(1): 50–74.

Guzder, S. 1980. *Quaternary Environment and Stone Age Cultures of the Konkan, Coastal Maharashtra, India*. Pune: Deccan College.

Indian Archaeology—A Review. 1962–63, 1963–64, 1964–65, 1966–67. New Delhi: Archaeological Survey of India.

Horn, P., Muller-Sohnius, D., Storzer, D., and Zoller, L. 1993. K-Ar Fission-Track and Thermoluminescence Ages of Quaternary Volcanic Tuffs and their Bearing on Acheulian Artefacts from Bori, Kukdi Valley, Pune District, India. *Zeitschrift der Deutsheh Geologischen Gesellschaft* 144: 326–29.

Jacobson, J. 1975. Early Stone Age Habitation Sites in Eastern Malwa. *Proceedings of the American Philosophical Society* 119: 280–97.

—1976. Evidence for Prehistoric Habitation Patterns in Eastern Malwa, in *Ecological Background of South Asian Prehistory*, K.A.R. Kennedy and G. Possehl, eds. South Asia Occasional Papers and Theses, 4, Ithaca: Cornell University, pp. 1–6.

—1985. Acheulian Surface Sites in Central India, in *Recent Advances in Indo-Pacific Prehistory*, V.N. Misra and P. Bellwood, eds. New Delhi: Oxford & IBH Publishing Co., pp. 49–57.

Jayaswal, V. 1982. *Chopper-Chopping Tool Component of Palaeolithic in India*. Delhi: Agam Kala Prakashan.

—1985. The Acheulian Industry of Vadamadurai, in *Recent Advances in Indo-Pacific Prehistory*, V.N. Misra and P. Bellwood, eds. New Delhi: Oxford & IBH Publishing Co., pp. 73–76.

Jhaldiyal, R. 1997. Formation Processes of the Prehistoric Sites in the Hunsgi-Baichbal Basins, Gulbarga District, Karnataka. Ph.D. Dissertation. Pune: University of Pune.

Joshi, R.V. 1955. *Pleistocene Studies in the Malaprabha Basin*. Pune: Deccan College and Dharwar: Karnatak University.

—1964. Acheulian Succession in Central India, *Asian Perspectives* 8(1): 150–63.

—1970. Significance of Cleavers in Indian Acheulian Industries. *Archaeocivilisation* 7–8: 39–46.

—1978. *Stone Age Cultures of Central India: Report on the Excavations of Rock Shelters at Adamgarh, Madhya Pradesh*. Pune: Deccan College.

Joshi, R.V., and Bopardikar, B.P. 1972. Stone Age Cultures of Konkan, in *Archaeological Congress and Seminar Papers*, S.B. Deo, ed. Nagpur: Nagpur University, pp. 47–59.

Joshi, R.V., and Kshirsagar, A.A. 1986. *Chemical Studies of Archaeological Bones from India*. Pune: Deccan College.

Joshi, R.V., and Marathe A.R. 1976. Metrical Analysis of Handaxes from Chirki on Pravara,

W. Maharashtra, India. *Puratattva* 8: 3–12.

—1977. Correlation Analysis of Handaxes and Cleavers and the Functional Interpretation. *Bulletin of the Deccan College Research Institute* 37: 48–60.

—1985. A Comparative Study of Metrical Data on Handaxes and their Cultural Interpretations, in *Recent Advances in Indo-Pacific Prehistory*, V.N. Misra and P. Bellwood, eds. New Delhi: Oxford & IBH Publishing Co., pp. 77–79.

Joshi, R.V., Bopardikar, B.P., and Sali, S.A. 1966. Animal Fossils and Early Stone Age Tools from Gangapur on the Godavari River, Nasik District, Maharashtra State. *Current Science* 35: 144.

Joshi, R.V., Badam, G.L., and Pandey, R.P. 1978. Fresh Data on the Quaternary Animal Fossils and Stone Age Cultures from the Central Narmada Valley, India. *Asian Perspectives* 21: 164–81.

Joshi, R.V., Rajaguru, S.N., Pappu, R.S., and Bopardikar, B.P. 1974. Quaternary Glaciation and Palaeolithic Sites in the Liddar Valley (Jammu–Kashmir). *World Archaeology* 5(3): 369–79.

Joshi, R.V., Rajaguru, S.N., Badam, G.L., and Khanna, P.C. 1978. Environments and Culture of Early Man in Northwest India: A Reappraisal. *Journal of the Geological Society of India* 19(2): 83–86.

—1986. Relationship Between Sea Level and Continentality Along Western Maharashtra During the Late Quaternary. *Bulletin of the Deccan College Research Institute* 45: 67–70.

--1987. Late Quaternary Alluvial History of the Northwestern Deccan Upland Region. *Nature* 325: 612–14.

Kale, V.S., Ganjoo, R.K., Rajaguru, S.N., and Ota, S.B. 1986. Discovery of Acheulian Site at Bori, District Pune. *Bulletin of the Deccan College Research Institute* 45: 46–49.

Kenoyer, J.M., and Pal, J.N. 1983. Report on the Excavation and Analysis of an Upper Acheulian Assemblage from Sihawal II, in *Palaeoenvironment and Prehistory in the Middle Son Valley,* G.R. Sharma and J.D. Clark, eds. Allahabad: Abinash Prakashan, pp. 23–28.

Khatri, A.P. 1961. Stone Age and Pleistocene Chronology of the Narmada Valley, Central India. *Anthropos* 56: 519–30.

—1962. Mahadevian: An Oldowan Pebble Culture in India. *Asian Perspectives* 6: 186–96.

—1966. Origin and Evolution of Handaxe Culture in the Narmada Valley (Central India), in *Studies in Prehistory*, D. Sen and A.K. Ghosh, eds. Calcutta: Firma K.L. Mukhopadhyay, pp. 96–121.

Korisettar, R. 1994. Quaternary Alluvial Stratigraphy and Sedimentation in the Upper Deccan Region, Western India. *Man and Environment* 19 (1–2): 29–42.

Korisettar, R., Venkatesan, T.R., Mishra, Sheila, Rajaguru, S.N., Somayajulu, B.L.K., Tandon, S.K., Gogte, V.D., Ganjoo, R.K., and Kale, V.S. 1989. Discovery of a Tephra Bed in the Quaternary Alluvial Sediments of Pune District (Maharashtra), Peninsular India. *Current Science* 58(10): 564–67.

Krishnaswami, V.D. 1938. Environmental and Cultural Changes of Prehistoric Man Near Madras. *Journal of Madras Geographical Association* 13: 58–90.

Lal, B.B. 1956. Palaeoliths from the Beas and Banganga Valleys, Punjab. *Ancient India* 12: 58–92.

Lee, R.B. 1969. Kung Bushman Subsistence: An Input-Output Analysis, in *Environment and Cultural Behaviour*, A.P. Vadya, ed. New York: Natural History Press, pp. 47–79.

Lele, V.S. 1989. Quaternary Formations in the Bhadar Valley. *Bulletin of the Deccan College Research Institute* 47–48: 165–206.

Madhusudhan Rao, V.V. 1983. Metrical Analysis of Acheulian Tools from the Paleru Valley, Coastal Andhra, in *Rangavalli: Recent Researches in Indology*, A.V. Narasimha Murthy and B.K. Gururaj Rao, eds. Delhi: Sundeep Prakashan, pp. 11–17.

Marathe, A.R. 1981. *Geoarchaeology of the Hiran Valley, Saurashtra, India*. Pune: Deccan College.

Marathe, A.R., Rajaguru, S.N., and Lele, V.S. 1977. On the Problem of the Origin and Age of the Miliolite Rocks of the Hiran Valley, Saurashtra, Western India. *Sedimentary Geology* 19: 197–215.

Mishra, Sheila. 1982. On the Effects of Basalt Weathering on the Distribution of Lower Palaeolithic Sites in the Deccan. *Bulletin of the Deccan College Research Institute* 41: 107–15.

—1992. The Age of the Acheulian in India: New Evidence. *Current Anthropology* 33: 325–28.

—1995. Chronology of the Indian Stone Age: The Impact of Recent Absolute and Relative Dating Attempts. *Man and Environment* 20(2): 11–16.

Mishra, S., Kshirsagar, A.A., and Rajaguru, S.N. 1988. Relative Dating of the Quaternary Record from Upland Western Maharashtra, in *National Seminar on Recent Quaternary Studies in India*, N.P. Patel and N. Desai, eds. Vadodara: M.S. University of Baroda, pp. 267–78.

Mishra, S., Venkatesan, T.R., Rajaguru, S.N., and Somayajulu, B.L.K. 1995. Earliest Acheulian Industry from Peninsular India. *Current Anthropology* 36(5): 847–51.

Mishra, S., Rajaguru, S.N. and Somayajulu, B.L.K. 1998. Contribution of Geoarchaeology to Indian Human Heritage, in *The Indian Human Heritage*, B. Balasubramaniam and N. Appaji Rao, eds. Hyderabad: Universities Press, pp. 60–68.

Misra, V.D., Rana, R.S., Clark, J.D., and Blumenshine, R.J. 1983. Preliminary Excavation of Son River Section at Nakhjhar Khurd, in *Palaeoenvironments and Prehistory in the Middle Son Valley*, G.R. Sharma and J.D. Clark, eds. Allahabad: Abinash Prakashan, pp. 101–15.

Misra, V.N. 1962. Problems of Terminology in Indian Prehistory. *Eastern Anthropologist* 15(2): 113–24.

—1978. The Acheulian Industry of Rock Shelter III F-23 at Bhimbetka, Central India. *Australian Archaeology* 8: 63–106.

—1982. Evolution of Blade Element in the Stone Industries of the Rock Shelter III F-23, Bhimbetka, in *Indian Archaeology: New Perspectives*, R.K. Sharma, ed. Delhi: Agam Kala Prakashan, pp. 7–13.

—1985. The Acheulian Succession at Bhimbetka, Central India, in *Recent Advances in Indo-Pacific Prehistory*, V.N. Misra and P. Bellwood, eds. New Delhi: Oxford & IBH Publishing Co., pp. 35–48.

—1987. Evolution of the Landscape and Human Adaptations in the Thar Desert, Presidential Address (Anthropology and Archaeology Section), 74th Session of the Indian Science Congress, Bangalore.

—1989a. Stone Age India: An Ecological Perspective. *Man and Environment* 14(1): 17–64.

—1989b. Human Adaptations to Changing Landscape of the Indian Arid Zone During the Quaternary, in *Old Problems and New Perspectives in the Archaeology of South Asia*, J.M. Kenoyer, ed. Madison: University of Wisconsin, pp. 296–320.

—1995. Geoarchaeology of the Thar Desert, Northwest India, in *Quaternary Environments and Geoarchaeology of India*, S. Wadia, R. Korisetter and V.S. Kale, eds. Bangalore: Geological Society of India, pp. 210–24.

Misra, V.N., and Rajaguru, S.N. 1989. Palaeoenvironments and Prehistory of the Thar Desert, Rajasthan, India, in *South Asian Archaeology,* 1985, K. Frifelt and P. Sorensen, eds. Copenhagen: Scandinavian Institute of Asian Studies: Occasional Paper no. 4. London: Curzon Press, pp. 296–320.

Misra, V.N., Mathpal, Y., and Nagar, M. 1977. *Bhimbetka: Prehistoric Man and His Art in Central India*. Pune: Bhimbetka Souvenir Committee, Deccan College.

Misra, V.N., Rajaguru, S.N., Agrawal, D.P., Thomas, P.K., Zahid Hussain, and Dutta, P.S. 1980. Prehistory and Palaeoenvironment of Jayal, Western Rajasthan, *Man and Environment* 4: 19–31.

Misra, V.N., Rajaguru, S.N., Rajaguru, D.R., Raghavan, H., and Gaillard, C. 1982. Acheulian Occupation and Evolving Landscape Around Didwana in Thar Desert. India, *Man and Environment* 6: 72–86.

Misra, V.N., Rajaguru, S.N., and Raghavan, H. 1988. Late Pleistocene Environment and Acheulian Culture Around Didwana, Rajasthan, *Proceedings of the Indian National Science Academy* 54 A(3): 425–38.

Misra, V.N., Rajaguru, S.N., Badam, G.L., Ganjoo, R.K., and Korisettar, R. 1990. Further Research in the Narmada Valley, in *Adaptation and Other Essays*, N.C. Ghosh and S. Chakrabarti, eds. Shantiniketan: Visva Bharati Research Publication, pp. 53–60.

Mohapatra, G.C. 1975. Acheulian Element in the Soan Culture Area. *Journal of the Archaeological Society of Nippon* 80(4): 4–18.

—1976. Geotectonic Developments, Sub-Himalayan Lithic Complex and Post-Siwalik Sediments, in *Perspective in Palaeoanthropology*, A.K. Ghosh, ed. Calcutta: Firma K.L. Mukhopadhyay, pp. 31–59.

—1982. Acheulian Distribution in the Siwalik of Punjab, in *Indian Archaeology: New Perspectives*, R.K. Sharma, ed. Delhi: Agam Kala Prakashan, pp. 28–37.

—1985. The Lower Palaeolithic in India, in *Archaeological Perspectives of India Since Independence*, K.N. Dikshit, ed. New Delhi: Books & Books, pp. 1–8.

—1990. Soanian Acheulian Relationship. *Bulletin of the Deccan College Research Institute* 49: 251–60.

Movius, H.L. Jr. 1948. *Early Man and Pleistocene Stratigraphy in Southern and Eastern Asia*. Peabody Museum Paper 19.

Murty, M.L.K. 1966. Stone Age Cultures of Chittoor District. Ph.D. Dissertation. Pune: University of Pune.

—1981. Hunter-Gatherer Ecosystems and Archeological Patterns of Subsistence Behaviour on the Southeast Coast of India: An Ethnographic Model. *World Archaeology* 13(1): 47–58.

—1985. The Uses of Plant Foods by Some Hunter-Gatherer Communities in Andhra Pradesh, in *Recent Advances in Indo-Pacific Prehistory*, V.N. Misra and P. Bellwood, eds. New Delhi: Oxford & IBH Publishing Co., pp. 329–36.

Nagar, Malti. 1985. The Use of Wild Plant Foods by Aboriginal Communities in Central India, in *Recent Advances in Indo-Pacific Prehistory*, V.N. Misra and P. Bellwod, eds. New Delhi: Oxford & IBH Publishing Co., pp. 337–42.

Paddayya, K. 1977a. An Acheulian Occupation Site at Hunsgi, Peninsular India: A Summary of the Results of Two Seasons of Excavation (1975–76). *World Archaeology* 8(3): 344–55.

—1977b. The Acheulian Culture of the Hunsgi Valley (Shorapur Doab), Peninsular India. *Proceedings of the American Philosophical Society* 121: 383–406.

—1979. Excavation of a New Acheulian Occupation Site at Hunsgi. Peninsular India, *Quartar* 29–30: 139–55.

—1979. Palaeoethnography *vis-a-vis* the Stone Age Cultures of India: Some Methodological Considerations. *Bulletin of the Deccan College Postgraduate and Research Institute* 38: 63–90.

—1982. *The Acheulian Culture of Hunsgi Valley (Peninsular India): A Settlement System Perspective*. Pune: Deccan College.

—1985. Acheulian Occupation Sites and Associated Fossil Fauna from Hunsgi-Baichbal Valleys, Peninsular India. *Anthropos* 80: 653–58.

—1987a. Excavation of An Acheulian Occupation Site at Yediapur, Peninsular India, *Anthropos* 82: 610–14.

—1987b. The Place of the Study of Site Formation Processes in the Prehistoric Research in India, in *Natural Formation Processes and the Archaeological Record*, D.T. Nash and N. Petraglia, eds., Oxford: B.A.R. International Series 352, pp. 74–85.

—1989. The Acheulian Culture Localities Along the Fatehpur Nullah, Baichbal Valley, Karnataka, (Peninsular India), in *Old Problems and New Perspectives in the Archaeology of South Asia*, J.M. Kenoyer, ed. Madison: University of Wisconsin, pp. 21–28.

—1991. The Acheulian Culture of the Hunsgi-Baichbal Valleys, Peninsular India: A Processual Study. *Quartar* 41/42: 111–38.

—1994. Investigations of Man-Environment Relationships in Indian Archaeology: Some Theoretical Considerations. *Man and Environment* 19(1–2): 1–28.

—, and Petraglia, M.D. 1993. Formation Processes of Acheulian Localities in the Hunsgi and Baichbal Valleys, Peninsular India, in *Formation Processes in Archaeological Context*, P.Goldberg, D.T. Nash and M.D. Petraglia, eds. Madison: Prehistory Press, pp. 61–82.

—1995. Natural and Cultural Formation Processes of the Acheulian Sites of the Hunsgi and Baichbal Valleys, Karnataka, in *Quaternary Environments and Geoarchaeology of India*, S. Wadia, R. Korisettar and V.S. Kale, eds. Bangalore: Geological Society of India, pp. 333–51.

Pant, P.C, and Jayaswal, V. 1991. *Paisra: The Stone Age Settlement of Bihar*. Delhi: Agam Kala Prakashan.

Pappu, R.S. 1974. *Pleistocene Studies in the Upper Krishna Basin*. Pune: Deccan College.

—1981. Recent Geoarchaeological Investigations Around Badami, District Bijapur, Karnataka. *Bulletin of the Deccan College Research Institute* 40: 170–79.

—1985a. Geomorphic Setting of Acheulian Sites in Peninsular India, in *Recent Advances in Indo-Pacific Prehistory*, V.N.Misra and P. Bellwood, eds. New Delhi: Oxford & IBH Publishing Co., pp. 9–12.

—1985b. Geomorphology and Prehistoric Environments in the Ghataprabha-Malaprabha Valleys, Karnataka, in *Proceedings of Symposium on Quaternary Episodes in Western India*, S.S. Mehr, ed. Vadodara: M.S. University of Baroda, pp. 229–39.

—1995. The Contribution of the Earth Sciences to the Development of Indian Archaeology, in *Quaternary Environments and Geoarchaeology of India*, S. Wadia, R. Korisettar and V.S. Kale, eds. Bangalore: Geological Society of India, pp. 414–24.

Pappu, R.S., and Deo, S.G. 1994. *Man-Land Relationships During Palaeolithic Times in the Kaladgi Basin, Karnatak*. Pune: Deccan College.

Pappu, R.S., and Rao, J.V.P. 1983. On the Problem of Age and Origin of High Level

Gravels Around Moravkonda, Dt. Kurnool, Andhra Pradesh. *Bulletin of the Deccan College Research Institute* 42: 119–30.

Pappu, Shanti. 1996. Reinvestigation of the Prehistoric Archaeological Record in the Kortallayar Basin, Tamil Nadu. *Man and Environment* 21(1): 1–23.

Petraglia, M.D. 1995. Pursuing Site Formation Research in India, in *Quaternary Environments and Geoarchaeology of India*, S. Wadia, R. Korisettar and V.S. Kale, eds. Bangalore: Geological Society of India, pp. 446–65.

Radhakrishna, B.P. 1952. The Mysore Plateau: Its Structural and Physiographic Evolution. *Bulletin of the Mysore Geologists Association* 3: 1–56.

—1993. Neogene Uplift and Geomorphic Rejuvenation of the Indian Peninsula. *Current Science* 64(11–12): 787–93.

Raghavan, H., Rajaguru, S.N., and Misra, V.N. 1989. Radiometric Dating of a Quaternary Dune Section, Didwana, Rajasthan. *Man and Environment* 12: 19–22.

Rajaguru, S.N. 1968. Some Aspects of the Late Pleistocene Period in South Central Maharashtra, in *La Prehistorie: Problems et Tendances*, F. Bordes and D. de Sonnville Bordes, eds. Paris: CNRS, pp. 349–57.

—1969. On the Late Pleistocene of the Deccan, India. *Quaternaria* 11: 241–53.

Rajaguru, S.N., and Kale, V.S. 1985. Changes in the Fluvial Regime of Western Maharashtra Upland Rivers During Late Quaternary. *Journal of the Geological Society of India* 26(1): 16–27.

Rajaguru, S.N., and Korisettar, R. 1987. Quaternary Geomorphic Environment and Cultural Succession in Western India. *Indian Journal of Earth Sciences* 14(3–4): 349–61.

Rajendran, P. 1989. *The Prehistoric Cultures and Environments of Kerala*. New Delhi: Classical Publishing Co.

Raju, D.R. 1983. Palaeolithic Cultures and Ethnography of the Gunjana Valley, Andhra Pradesh. *Bulletin of the Indo-Pacific Prehistory Association* 3: 10–17.

—1985. Handaxe Assemblages from the Gunjana Valley, Andhra Pradesh: A Metrical Analysis. *Bulletin of the Indo-Pacific Prehistory Association* 6: 10–26.

Raju, D.R. 1988. *Stone Age Hunter-Gatherers: Ethno-Archaeology of Cuddapah Region, South-East India*. Pune: Ravish Publishers.

—1989. The Lower Palaeolithic Cultures in the Gunjana Valley on the Southeast Coast of India. *Bulletin of the Deccan College Research Institute* 47/48: 283–300.

Ray, R. 1987. *Ancient Settlement Patterns of Eastern India*. Calcutta: Pearl Publishers.

Reddy, K.T., Vijaya Prakash, P., Rath A., and Rao, C. Udhaya Bhaskar. 1995. A Pebble Tool Assemblage on the Visakhapatnam Coast. *Man and Environment* 20(1): 113–18.

Rendell, H.M., and Dennell, R.W. 1985. Dated Lower Palaeolithic Artefacts from Northern Pakistan. *Current Anthropology* 26(5): 393.

Sankalia, H.D. 1946. *Investigations into the Prehistoric Archaeology of Gujarat*. Vadodara: Baroda State.

—1971. New Evidence for Early Man in Kashmir. *Current Anthropology* 12(4–5): 558–63.

—1974. *Prehistory and Protohistory of India and Pakistan*. Pune: Deccan College.

Sankhyan, A.R. 1997. A New Human Fossil Find from the Central Narmada Basin and Its Chronology. *Current Science* 73(12): 1110–11.

Sen, D. 1955. Nalgarh Palaeolithic Culture. *Man in India* 35: 177–84.

Sen, D., and Ghosh, A.K. 1963. Lithic Culture Complex in the Pleistocene Sequence of the Narmada Valley, Central India. *Rivista di Scienze Preistoriche* 18(1–4): 3–23.

Sharma, G.R. 1973. Stone Age in the Vindhyas and the Ganga Valley, in *Radiocarbon and*

Indian Archeology, D.P. Agrawal and A. Ghosh, eds. Mumbai: Tata Institute of Fundamental Research, pp. 106–16.

Sharma, G.R., and Clark, J.D. 1982. Palaeoenvironments and Prehistory in the Middle Son Valley, Northern Madhya Pradesh. *Man and Environment* VI: 56–82.

—, eds., 1983. *Palaeoenvironment and Prehistory in the Middle Son Valley (Madhya Pradesh, North Central India).* Allahabad: Abinash Prakashan.

Sharma, T.C. 1997. Recent Advances in the Prehistory and Archaeology of North East India, in *Indian Prehistory: 1988*, V.D. Misra and J.N. Pal, eds. Allahabad: Department of Ancient History, Culture and Archaeology, University of Allahabad, pp. 82–83.

Singh, R. 1965. The Palaeolithic Industry of Northern Bundelkhand. Ph.D. Dissertation. Pune: University of Pune.

Sonakia, A. 1984. The Skull-cap of Early Man and Associated Mammalian Fauna from the Narmada Valley Alluvium Hoshangabad Area, Madhya Pradesh, India. *Records of the Geological Survey of India* 113(6): 157–72.

Subbarao, B. 1958. *The Personality of India*, sec. rev. edn. Vadodara: M.S. University of Baroda.

Subrahmanyam, R., ed., 1973. *Nagarjunakonda (1954–60),* vol. I. Memoirs of the Archaeological Survey of India, no. 75, New Delhi: Archaeological Survey of India.

Supekar, S.G. 1968. Pleistocene Stratigraphy and Prehistoric Archaeology of the Central Narmada Basin. Ph.D. Dissertation. Pune: University of Pune.

—1985. Some Observations on the Quaternary Stratigraphy of the Central Narmada Valley, in *Recent Advances in Indo-Pacific Prehistory*, V.N. Misra and P. Bellwood, eds. New Delhi: Oxford & IBH Publishing Co., pp. 19–28.

Szabo, B.J., Mckinney, C., Dalbey, T.S., and Paddayya, K. 1990. On the Age of Acheulian Culture of the Hunsgi-Baichbal Valleys, Peninsular India. *Bulletin of the Deccan College Research Institute* 50: 317–32.

Todd, K.R.U. 1939. Palaeolithic Industries of Bombay. *Journal of the Royal Anthropological Institute* 69: 257–72.

Vaidyanathan, R. 1977. Recent Advances in Geomorphic Studies of Peninsular India: A Review. *Indian Journal of Earth Sciences* (Ray Volume): 13–55.

Vita-Finzi, C., and Higgs, E.S. 1970. Prehistoric Economy in the Mount Carmel Area of Palestine: Site Catchment Analysis, *Proceedings of the Prehistoric Society* 36: 1–37.

Willey, G.R., ed. 1953. *Prehistoric Settlement Patterns in the Viru Valley, Peru.* Bulletin of the Bureau of American Ethnology. Washington D.C. no. 155.

Zeuner, F.E. 1950. *Stone Age and Pleistocene Chronology in Gujarat.* Pune: Deccan College.

3 ❖ The Mesolithic Phase in the Ganga Valley

J.N. PAL

INTRODUCTION

THERE is no need to emphasise the importance of the Gangetic plain in the development of Indian culture and civilisation as it is too obvious from literary and archaeological records. The Gangetic plain, geographically speaking, forms part of the vast Indo-Gangetic plain of north India which is the most fertile and densely populated region in the country. The archaeological investigations in different parts of the Gangetic plain have revealed a large number of sites belonging to different cultural periods. But the earliest evidence of human occupation in the form of Mesolithic settlements has been found at the junction of the upper and middle Gangetic plains, in the districts of Allahabad, Pratapgarh, Sultanpur, Jaunpur and Varanasi north of the Ganga (Fig. 1). The present paper proposes to synthesise the archaeological data of the Mesolithic phase of the Gangetic plain.

The junction region of the upper and middle Gangetic plains, having an average elevation of 91 m with a gentle slope from northwest to southeast, is drained by the Ganga and its tributaries and their feeders. The noteworthy among these rivers are the Varuna, the Sai, the Gomati and the Ghaghara. One of the distinctive geomorphological features of the area is the existence even today of numerous horseshoe lakes. Many of the rivers and nalas originate from these lakes. A large number of horseshoe lakes, representing meanders of ancient rivers, have been subsequently filled up by natural and human agencies and converted into farmlands, but their

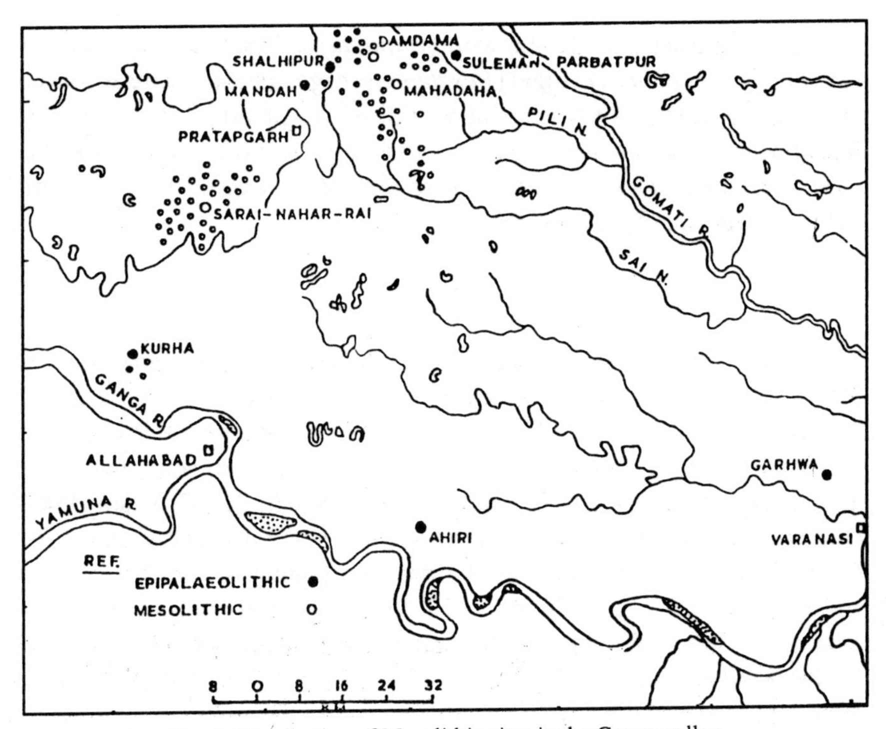

Fig. 1. Distribution of Mesolithic sites in the Ganga valley

morphology is still clear enough and allows us to identify them as extinct lakes. These perennial/seasonal lakes and rivulets attracted the ancient colonisers who established settlements on their banks and exploited terrestrial resources as well as aquatic and avian fauna.

The annual average rainfall of the area is about 1000 mm. The natural vegetation cover, on account of increasing population pressure and consequent human manipulation, has been almost completely obliterated, but the remains of typical tropical dry deciduous woodland can be seen in heavily degraded and isolated patches in the area. As indicated by pollen analysis (Gupta 1976, Pant and Pant 1980), in the past the area was covered with grassy vegetation. The small shrubs and trees which still survive in the badland ravines include dhak (*Butea menosperma*), sheesham (*Dalbergia sissoo*), siras (*Albizzia lebbek*), banyan (*Ficus glomerata*), pakar (*Ficus infectorisa*), pipal (*Ficus religiosa*), mahua (*Basia latifolia*), tamarind (*Tamarindus indica*), neem (*Azadirachta indica*), babul (*Acacia arabica*), kaitha (*Feronia elephantum*), chilbil (*Ulmus integrifolicus*), lisora (*Cordia myxa*), etc. Similarly the wild life has also been reduced to a small number of species such as the wolf (*Canis lupus*), jackal (*Canis aurus*), fox (*Ulpes bengalensis*), nilgai (*Boselephas tragocamelus*), hare and monkey. Even as late as sixty years ago wildlife was plentiful when herds of blackbuck (*Antelope cervicapara*), chital (*Axis axis*), hyena (*Hyena hyena*), porcupine (*Hystrix indica*), boar (*Sus scrofa*) could be seen commonly in the vicinity of villages.

HISTORY OF RESEARCH

The history of Stone Age archaeology in the Gangetic plain goes back to 1969–70 when the exciting discovery of a Mesolithic site at Sarai Nahar Rai (Lat. 25°48' N., Long. 81°1' E.), about 15 km southwest of Pratapgarh, was made by the archaeological team of Allahabad University under the direction of the late Prof. G.R. Sharma (*IAR, 1969–70*: 36–37, Misra 1996). During the excavation of Sarai Nahar Rai several other sites of the Mesolithic culture were brought to light in the adjoining region of Allahabad and Pratapgarh districts (Sharma 1973: 130). Though the first human skeleton of the Mesolithic people at Sarai Nahar Rai was excavated by the Anthropological Survey of India in collaboration with State Archaeology Department of Uttar Pradesh in 1970, it was the subsequent excavation of 1972 of Allahabad University in collaboration with the U.P. State Archaeology Department which yielded human skeletons, hearths, animal bones, microliths and other valuable evidence pertaining to habitation and subsistence patterns in an area of 1800 sq, m representing the ancient yellow or whitish soil, which is demarcated by the surrounding blackish compact clay of lacustrine origin. The results of the first excavation were published by G.R. Sharma and the Mesolithic lake culture of the Gangetic plain was brought to the notice of the archaeologists on a wider scale (Sharma 1973). The results of subsequent excavation of 1973–74 and further explorations leading to the discovery of additional Mesolithic sites were published by G.R. Sharma in 1975 (Sharma 1975). The major occupational deposit at the site had been washed away, leaving only the basal 6 cm thick deposit. However, excavations at the site revealed evidence of long duration settlement. Eleven human graves, one with four burials (Fig. 2), eight pit hearths, one of them preserving evidence of use in two phases, and a hut floor with post-holes are the remarkable results of these excavations.

The site of Mahadaha (Lat. 25°59' 2" N., Long. 82°11' 30" E.), situated on the western bank of a horseshoe lake at a distance of 31 km to the northeast of Pratapgarh, was brought to light in 1978 when the work was in

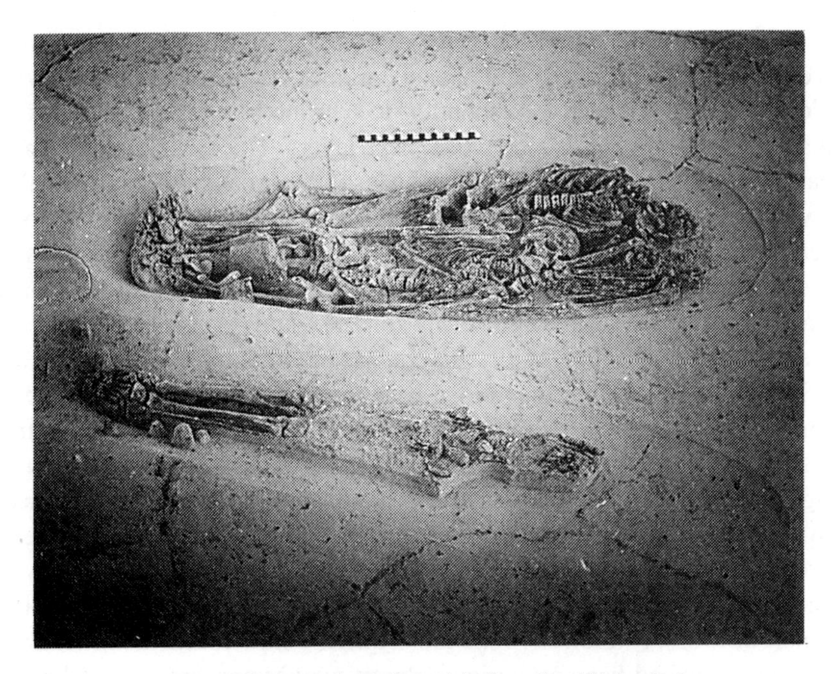

Fig. 2. Multiple and single burials from Sarai Nahar Rai

Fig. 3. General view of excavation, Mahadaha

progress to widen a canal that passed through the site. The site extends over an area of 8000 sq, m and has 60 cm thick occupation deposit divisible into four layers, each corresponding to a distinct phase. Stratigraphically there is no gap discernible between these layers. The canal has disturbed many of the skeletons, pit-hearths and Mesolithic working floors specially towards its western embankment (Fig. 3). At Mahadaha the excavations were conducted for two seasons in 1977–78 and 1978–79. In the first season three areas were excavated which were identified as (i) the habitation-cum-cemetery complex, (ii) the butchering complex, and (iii) the lake complex. The excavation report of the first season has been published (Sharma et al. 1980). In 1978–79 the excavations were done mainly in the habitation-cum-cemetery area which was under the embankment of the canal in the western part of the site. As the canal embankment was made from the earth dug out from the site itself, it contained a lot of Mesolithic cultural material. An analysis of human bones collected from the earth of the embankment revealed that they belonged to 11 individuals (Sinha 1983). The excavations in the second year were confined only to the last phase of the settlement (Pal 1985). Microliths, bone tools, querns, mullers and hammerstone fragments, rubbed haematite pieces, burnt clay lumps and animal bones

Fig. 4. Hearths, burnt floors and human burial from Damdama

were recovered from the excavations. Among the structural remains are included 35 oval or circular pit hearths, 28 human graves and several patches of burnt floors/plasters (Pal 1992b).

Damdama (Lat. 26°10' N., Long. 82°10'36" E.), extending over 8,750 sq, m area, is situated on a slightly raised ground at the confluence of two branches of Tambura nala, a tributary of Pili Nadi which discharges into the Sai river. The site is located at a distance of 5 km towards northwest of Mahadaha and was discovered in 1978 and was extensively explored in 1979 during the excavations at Mahadaha. The site was excavated continuously for seven seasons from 1982–83 to 1986–87. The preliminary report of the first two seasons (1982–83 and 1983–84) was published in 1985 (Varma et al. 1985) and preliminary reports of subsequent excavations have been published in *Indian Archaeology: A Review*. Excavations at the site brought to light 41 human graves, several pit hearths, both plastered and plain (Fig. 4) and microliths, bone objects, grinding stones, hammer-stone-cum anvils, burnt clay lumps, animal bones, etc. (Misra 1988; Pal 1992a, 1992b, 1994).

PALAEOENVIRONMENT AND MESOLITHIC CULTURE

The study of the Pleistocene and Holocene deposits of the Gangetic plain has not been done in detail by geologists. But the study of type section of the Gaṇga near Phaphamau towards north of Allahabad and its tentative correlation with that of the Belan is helpful in inferring the palaeoclimate of the area (Sharma 1975). The Ganga section of Phaphamau having a thickness of 8 to 10 m is composed of four distinct layers. The lowest is a concretionary horizon which has been tentatively equated with gravel III of the Belan. The succeeding layer is of blackish clay containing calcium nodules and small mollusk shells and is equated with the palaeosol of the Belan. The third layer is a deposit of plastic clay with calcium carbonate nodules and is associated with the artifacts of late Upper Palaeolithic and early Mesolithic cultures. The last layer is a deposit of sandy soil associated with Mesolithic artifacts. This deposit is coeval with the top aeolian formation of the Belan section.

The first colonisers of the Gangetic plain were the late Upper Palaeolithic and early Mesolithic groups. The investigations have revealed that at the fag end of terminal Pleistocene and at the beginning of early Holocene period the Stone Age man from the Vindhyas used to cross the Ganga and Yamuna rivers in the north and colonise the Gangetic plain hitherto uninhabited by man. Primarily change in climate resulting in paucity of food resource in the Vindhyas might be the reason for this migration. In the Holocene period return of moderate climate resulting in rich food resource in the Gangetic plain and population pressure in the Vindhyas forced the Stone Age man to colonise the Gangetic plain on a larger scale.

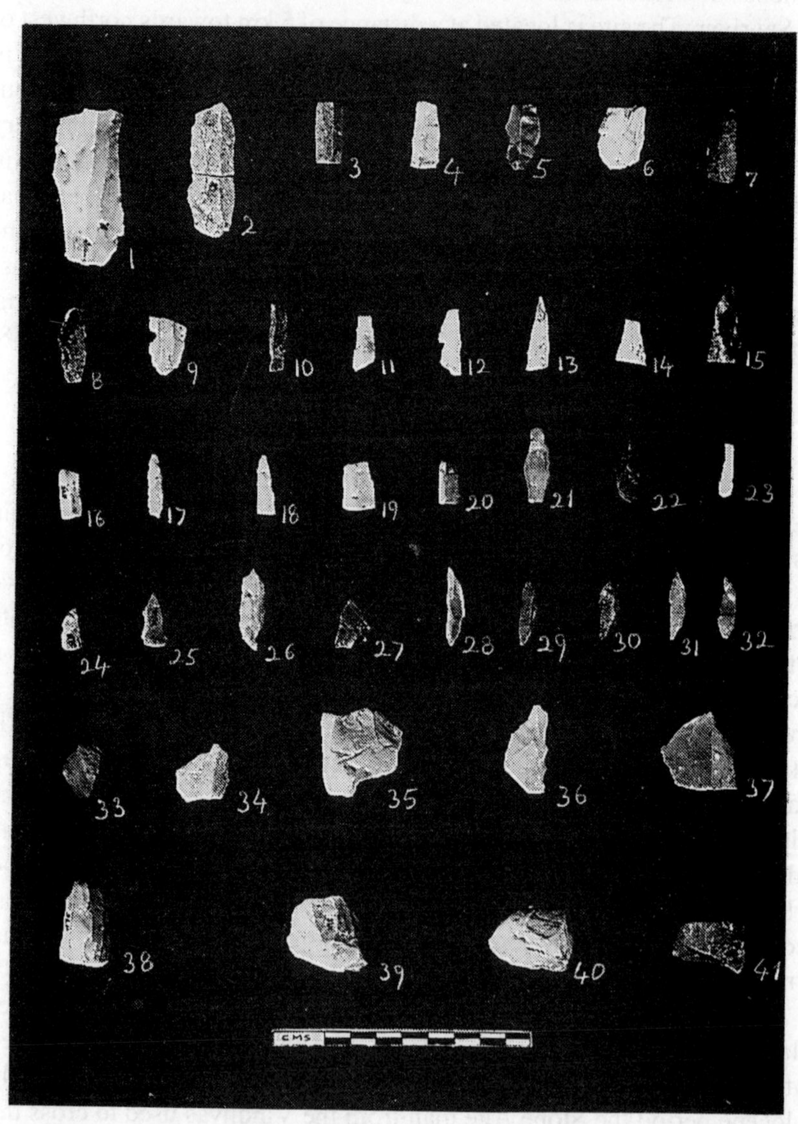

Fig. 5. Epipalaeolithic artefacts from Ganga valley

More than 200 Mesolithic sites have been discovered in the Ganga valley. On the basis of correlation of artefact-bearing levels, use of raw material for manufacturing the artifacts, state of patination and techno-typology of the artifacts, the Mesolithic culture is divisible into two phases: (i) Epipalaeolithic and (ii) Mesolithic.

The Epipalaeolithic is the earliest phase of Stone Age culture in the Ganga valley. Six sites of this phase—Mandah, Shalhipur, Suleman Parbatpur in Pratapgarh district, Kurha and Ahiri in Allahabad district and Garhwa in Varanasi district—have been located. Scatter of artifacts on hard concretionary plastic clay horizon has been found. Manufactured mainly on chert of varying shades of grey, black, red, yellow and white and occasionally on chalcedony, the modified and unmodified artifacts along with finished and utilized tools (Fig. 5) suggest that these are in primary context. The finished tools include retouched blades (1.63%), backed blades (4.65%), notches (0.15%), points/drills (1.63%), burins (0.38%), scrapers (2.01%) and lunates (1.51%). The unmodified waste is divisible into blades (10.15%), flakes (11.55%), cores (5.15%), core rejuvenating flakes (2.51%) and chips (59.30%). The artifacts are highly patinated (Pal 1984). The artefact-bearing horizon is thin and indicates that these were seasonal camp sites. The artifacts generally exposed on present surface are mostly fragmentary. No biological remains have been found from these surface sites.

The next phase is known as the Mesolithic phase. On the basis of the presence of geometric microliths at some of the sites the Mesolithic sites have been divided into two groups: (i) Mesolithic with non-geometric microliths (172 sites) and (ii) Mesolithic with geometric microliths (21 sites). The majority of sites yielding non-geometric microliths (Fig. 6), both unmodified waste (cores, flakes, blades, chips, chunks) and finished tools represent camp sites (temporary settlements).The remaining sites having thick occupational deposit with rich cultural material and biological remains represent semi-sedentary settlements of the Mesolithic people. The bones of swamp deer and hog deer found at these sites indicate several hunting seasons within a year and the occurrence of rodent remains also suggest occupation at the sites of Mahadaha and Damdama throughout the year (Chattopadhyay; 1988, Chattopadhyay and Chattopadhyay 1990). Such settlements are located generally on the banks of the ancient horseshoe lakes.

As mentioned earlier, three of the semi-sedentary settlements, viz., Sarai Nahar Rai, Mahadaha and Damdama all lying in Pratapgarh district

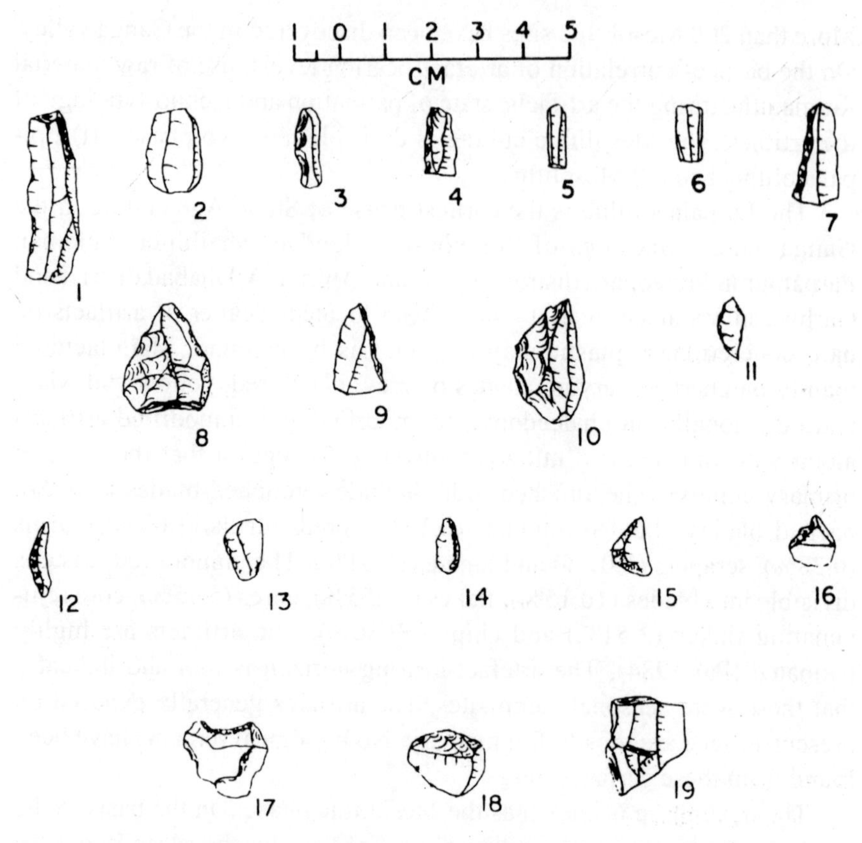

Fig. 6. Non-geometric microlithic artefacts from Ganga valley

have been excavated and have given valuable data for reconstructing various aspects of the Mesolithic culture in the Ganga valley.

Human Burials

The excavations have revealed a good number of human burials within the habitation area which throw welcome light on the mortuary practices, rituals and beliefs, dietary behaviour, palaeopathology and social structure of the people. The dead were buried, generally in the vicinity of hearths. The graves may have been associated with fire as these contained refuse material from hearths. Fire was probably regarded as a life-giving source after a person had died. These are extended human burials in shallow oblong grave pits in supine position. There are only three exceptions, one at Mahadaha and two at Damdama of crouched/flexed burials (Pal 1988). The crouched burial from Mahadaha is interesting as its right hand is on the right pelvic and left one below the left pelvic, phalanges of both the hands touching each other below the pelvic girdle. The legs are folded upward from the knee in a very unnatural position, the feet lying along the pelvic girdle. This may be the skeleton of a *sanyasi* or a punished individual (Pal 1985). There are also some exceptions of the general practice of placing the burials in supine position. A few graves at Damdama revealed the skeletons in prone or lateral position. Barring a few exceptions, the burials are oriented west to east or east to west, possibly signifying some belief regarding rising and setting of the Sun and the Moon prevailing in Mesolithic society. The multiple burials probably signify the development of strong family ties. Double and multiple burials containing pairs of male and female of about the same group may be related to each other as husband and wife. A multiple burial containing two pairs of male and female at Sarai Nahar Rai, two double burials at Mahadaha and four double burials at Damdama may be put under this category. In the double burials having a pair of male and female the female is placed on the left side of the male. In one of the double burials at Mahadaha the female was placed above the male and at Damdama an interesting double burial containing male and female placed in opposite directions has been unearthed (Pal 1988). At Damdama, in one of the double burials both individuals are male and in another grave containing three individuals two are male and one female. A few burials at Mahadaha and Damdama revealed special grave goods—ornaments made on animal bone, bone arrowheads and a triangular terracotta cake. One of the graves at Mahadaha yielded a jaw bone (mandible) of a carnivore (Pal 1992a).

Physical anthropology of the human skeletons including dental remains is an extensively investigated aspect of the Mesolithic culture of the Gangetic valley (Dutta 1984, Dutta et al. 1972; Kennedy 1984; Kennedy et al. 1986, Kennedy et al. 1992, Lukacs 1992, Lukacs and Pal 1992, Lukacs and Pal 1993, Lukacs et al. 1996). The microscopic examination of the dental remains of 51 skeletons (35 from Damdama and 16 from Mahadaha) done by Lukacs revealed features typically associated with hunting-gathering or foraging adaptation (Lukacs and Pal 1993). The dental microwear analysis of molar teeth from Mahadaha also indicates hunting-gathering subsistence pattern which includes tough, fibrous and abrasive vegetable foods and a diet reliant upon wild fauna (Paster 1992). These people along with other South Asian Mesolithic populations present a taller stature than that of the living population, have larger teeth, are skeletally robust and reveal low incidence of infectious diseases (Kennedy 1996). The Mesolithic

Fig. 7. Hearths from Damdama

Fig. 8. Plastered hearth from Mahadaha

lifeway was conducive to a relatively high standard of health and a realization of genetic growth potential for a majority of individuals (Kennedy 1997).

Hearths and Floors

Pit hearths are the most frequently found structural remains (Fig. 7). The oval or circular pit hearths are sometimes plastered with multiple clay coatings (Fig. 8). Most of the pit hearths were overfilled with burnt clay clods, charred animal bones and ash. It seems that these hearths were used for roasting the animal flesh and vegetal foods and the clay lumps put in the hearths during roasting facilitated a better roasting. Some of the plastered pits devoid of burnt clay lumps and animal bones were possibly used for storing roasted food or other food material. Burnt plastered floors made of yellow clay are found in the area surrounding the sites. Such floors were also used as fire places as is evident from their burnt red surface. The community hut floor at Sarai Nahar Rai and several floors with multiple layers at Damdama are noteworthy. Patches of such burnt plasters were also found at Mahadaha.

Stone and Bone Artefacts

As mentioned earlier, the excavated sites representing semi-sedentary settlements have revealed a good number of microliths, bone objects, grinding stones, hammerstone-cum-anvils, burnt clay lumps, charred and semi-charred animal bones, rubbed haematite pieces, ornaments made of animal bones, etc. It is interesting to note that the Mesolithic man of the Gangetic plain was dependent on the Vindhyas for raw material to manufacture microliths, sandstone and quartzite to make grinding stones and hammers and anvils, and haematite and ochre pieces to prepare pigments.

Microliths (Fig. 9) are an integral part of the tool-kit of the Gangetic Mesolithic culture, even though stone was not locally available in the plains. Microliths are made on chert, chalcedony, agate, carnelian and quartz brought from the Vindhyas. The finished tools include retouched blades, backed blades, truncated blades, scrapers, points, borers, awls, lunates, triangles and trapezes (Pal 1986).

On the basis of the preliminary microwear analysis of microliths from the Mesolithic sites of the area inferences have been made about the functions of tools, orientation of use and probable contact material on which the tool was used. The tentative results indicate that the microliths were used for scraping, sawing, cutting, drilling, incising, grooving, etc. The

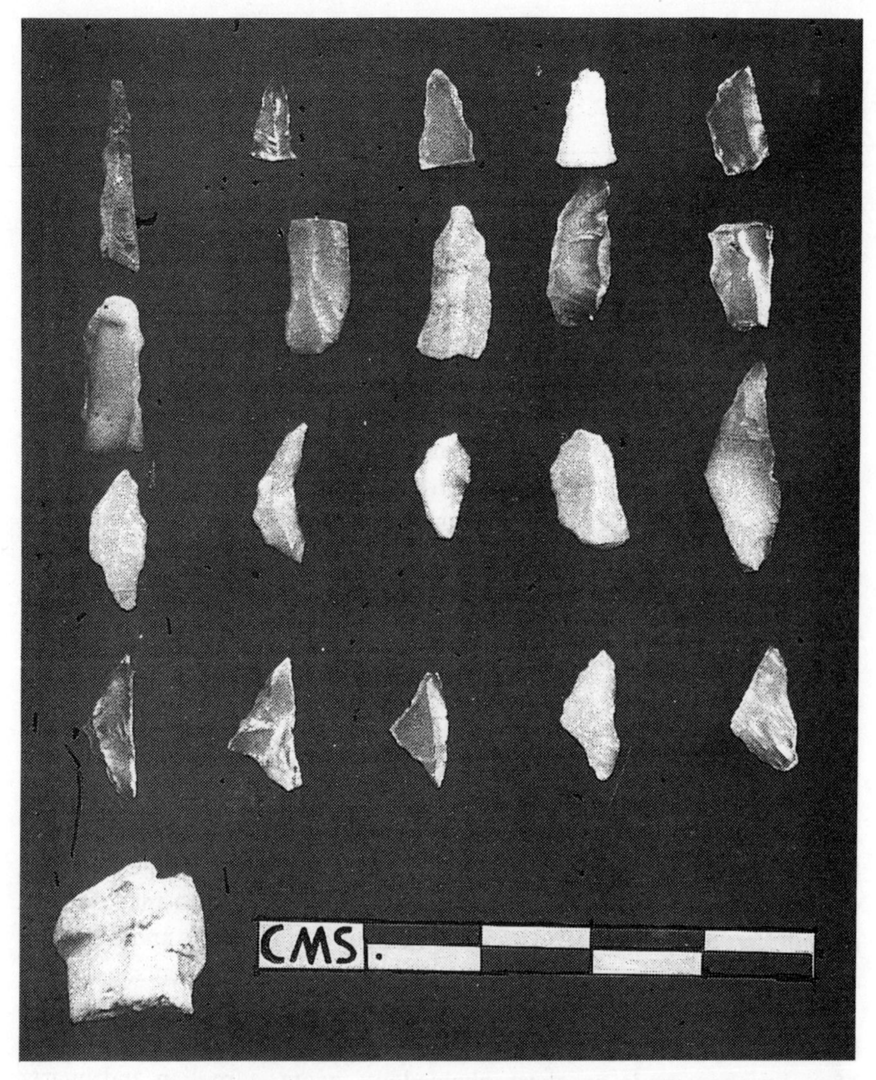

Fig. 9. Geometric microlithic artefacts from Ganga valley

use of tools as arrowheads and evidence of hafting also can be inferred on the basis of edge damage feature. Among the probable contact materials, mention may be made of hide, dry hide, meat, soft plant, green grass, green reeds, dry reeds, wood, dry wood, fresh bone, dry bone and antler. The linear arrangement of polishes also indicate similar use (Pal 1996, 1996–97).

A good number of bone tools and arrowheads (Fig.10) also formed

Fig. 10. Bone tools from Mahadaha

part of the tool-kit of the Mesolithic people. An arrowhead made on quartzite from Damdama is also noteworthy. A concave bone object with two perforations and a shining surface on which were resting two complete bone arrowheads was possibly part of a quiver used for carrying a bunch of arrowheads during hunting expedition (Pal 1992a). Among the other bone objects mention may be made of pendants, earrings (Fig. 11), flat disc-shaped beads and some other decorative objects which suggest that the Mesolithic people of the Ganga valley were fond of wearing ornaments. However, it seems that it was not a common practice, as only a few graves yielded ornaments, which possibly belonged to those individuals who enjoyed a special status in society (Pal 1994).

Subsistence

A preliminary study of the plant remains from Damdama by Kajale (1990) and Saraswat revealed several wild plant remains (wild grasses,

Fig. 11. Skeleton with a bone earring from Mahaḍaha

Fig. 12. Stone quern fragment from Mahadaha

millet-like grains, jujube and some charcoal fragments). A large number of grinding stones, querns (Fig.12) and muller-cum-anvils (Fig.13) with heavy use-marks and lustrous polished surface suggests inclusion of vegetal food (wild grains, roots, tubers, etc.) in the diet.

The Gangetic Mesolithic is extremely rich in faunal remains in the country. The identification of vertebrate and invertebrate fauna from Damdama done by Thomas and Joglekar revealed interesting evidence of the species (Thomas et al. 1995). More than 30 species of animals have been identified, comprising mammals, reptiles, birds, fishes and molluscs. The preliminary result of this analysis suggests a wide diversity of animals, birds, reptiles, gastropods and fishes. Among the most frequent animals identified are included six species of deer (Thomas et al. 1996). The species include chital (*Anix axis*), hog deer (*Axis porcinus*), blackbuck (*Antelope cervicapra*), gazelle (*Gazella sp.*), deer (*Cervis sp.*), musk deer (*Moschus moschiferus*), barking deer (*Muntiacus muntijak*), four-horned antelope (*Tetracerus quadricornis*), buffalo (*Bos babulus*), cattle (*Bos indicus*), bison (*Bos qaurus*), nilgai (*Boselephas tragocamelus*), elephant (*Elephas sp.*), rhinoceros (*Rhinoceros sp.*), porcupine (*Hystrix sp.*), wild pig (*Sus scrofa*), pygmy hog (*Sus selvanis*), etc. Among other animals mention may be made

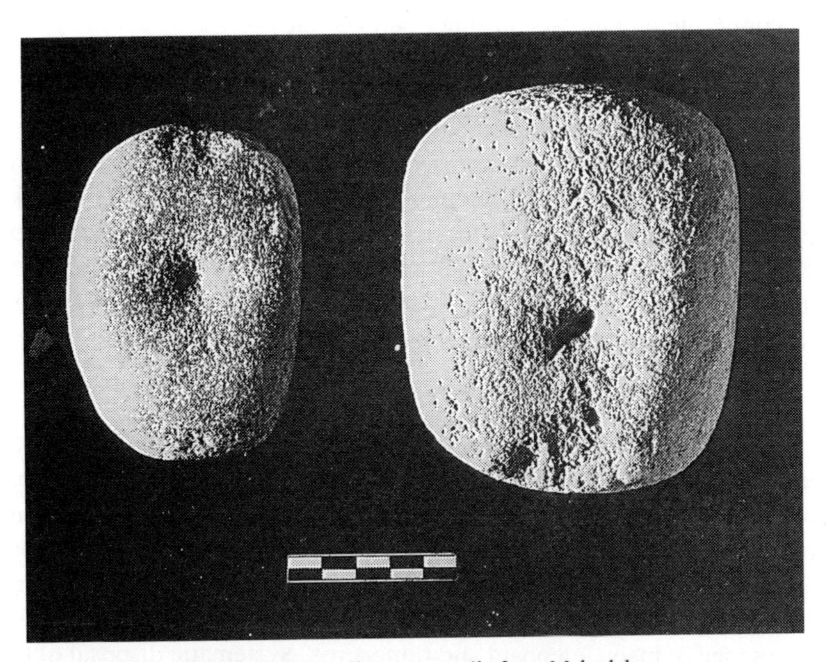

Fig. 13. Stone muller-cum-anvils from Mahadaha

of bones of carnivores like wolf (*Canis lupus*), jackal (*Canis auregus*), fox (*Vulpus bengalensis*), etc. which have cut marks indicating thereby that these were also included in the diet. The majority of animal bones are in charred and semi-charred condition suggesting thereby that roasted meat was consumed. From the evidence of grassy and shrubby vegetation and patches of *dhak* and *singhor* forest even today, we may infer that the Mesolithic people hunted wild animals and gathered edible fruits, grains and tubers from surrounding forests (Pandey 1985, 1990). The evidence of floral remains from Damdama has tentatively been analysed by Kajale (1990) and evidence for seeds of wild plants assignable to families such as chenopodiaceae, polygonaceae, portulacaceae, labiatae, etc. have been found (Kajale 1996). The prevalence of hunting and gathering economy in the Ganga valley during the Mesolithic phase is attested not only by the remains of wild animals and plants but also by the implements of stone and bone (Pal 1994).

Several haematite and ochre pieces with rubbed surfaces indicate that the Mesolithic people of the Ganga valley were preparing some kind of paintings as their counterparts in the Vindhyas. But possibly here the paintings were made on animal skins. It is also possible that the ochre was used to decorate the human face or other parts of the body as tribal people do even today on some special occasions.

The ethnoarchaeological studies of Baheliyas, Kanjars, Beriya, Musahars and other hunting-foraging communities of the Ganga valley, though now considerably modernised, have also helped in reconstructing the Mesolithic culture of the region (Nagar and Misra 1989). Tribes like the Kanjars are almost certainly the descendants of these Mesolithic hunter-gatherers and they can be assumed to be continuing some of the traditions of these prehistoric forbears in their settlement and subsistence activities, technology and material culture (Nagar and Misra 1990).

CONCLUSION

The investigation of the Mesolithic phase in the Ganga valley suggests that initially it was seasonal migration marked by temporary camp sites of the Stone Age man from the Vindhyas but subsequently it became more continuous involving the establishment of long term camps but still having close contacts with the original homeland. A moist climate is suggested by the presence of bison, elephant and rhinoceros. Systematic disposal of the dead, use of fire in pit hearths for roasting the food and use of stone equipment for food processing are some of the remarkable features of the culture. The microliths and bone tools, a variety of wild animals, birds, fishes and wild plants exploited from surrounding forests, lakes and rivulets suggest the presence of both vegetal and non-vegetal foods in the diet. The preliminary microwear analysis of microliths suggests hunting and gathering as the basis of subsistence; this inference tallies well with the results of other biocultural and archaeological studies. The physical anthropological investigations of dentition of Mesolithic population of the Ganga valley suggested the presence of heavy dietary stress indicating a pathology pattern consistent with hunting-foraging and gathering subsistence system and primitive food-processing technology (Lukacs and Pal 1992).

The chronology of the culture is still not firmly established. Two radiocarbon dates have been obtained from Sarai Nahar Rai on bone samples reading 10050 ± 110 BP and 2860 ± 120 BP. The former date seems to represent the early phase of the culture. The preliminary analysis of the thermoluminescence sample from Damdama, which is under process by A.K. Singhvi of Physical Research Laboratory, Ahmedabad, indicates an antiquity between 5000 and 7000 BP Two AMS C^{14} dates from Damdama reading 8, 865 ± 65 BP (from the earliest phase) and 8, 640 ± 65 BP (from phase VIII) suggest an early Holocene antiquity for the site (Lukacs et al. 1996). A time span of 8000 BC to 2000 BC may be proposed for the Mesolithic phase of the Ganga valley (Misra 1977, Varma 1987).

REFERENCES

Chattopadhyay, U.C. 1988. Subsistence Variability and Complex Social Formations in Prehistoric Ganga Valley: Problems and Prospects. *Man and Environment* 12: 135–52.

Chattopadhyay, I., and Chattopadhyay, U.C. 1990. The Spatial Organization of Mortuary Practices in the Mesolithic Ganga Valley, in *Adaptation and Other Essays*, N.C. Ghosh and S. Chakrabarti, eds. Shantiniketan: Visva Bharati, pp. 103–21.

Dutta, P.C. 1984. Sarai Nahar Rai Man: The First and Oldest Human Fossil Record in South Asia. *Anthropologie* 23 (1): 35–50.

Dutta, P.C., Pal, A., and Biswas, J.N. 1972. Late Stone Age Human Remains from Sarai Nahar Rai: The Earliest Skeletal Evidence of Man in India. *Bulletin of the Anthroplogical Survey of India* 21: 114–38.

Gupta, H.P. 1976. Holocene Palynology From Meander Lake in Ganga Valley, District Pratapgarh, U.P. *The Palaeobotanist* 25: 109–19.

Kajale, M.D. 1990. Some Initial Observations on Palaeobotanical Evidence for Mesolithic Plant Economy from Excavations at Damdama, District Pratapgarh, Uttar Pradesh, in *Adaptation and Other Essays*, N.C. Ghosh and S. Chakrabarti, eds. Shantiniketan: Visva Bharati, pp. 98–102.

—1996. Plant Resources and Diet Among the Mesolithic Hunters and Foragers, in *Bioarchaeology of Mesolithic India: An Integrated Approach, The Prehistory of Asia and Oceania*, Gennadii E. Afanas'ev, Serge Cleuziou, John R. Lukacs, Maurizio Tosi, eds. Colloquium XXXIII. International Union of Prehistoric and Protohistoric Sciences, Forli, Italy, pp. 251–53.

Kennedy, K.A.R. 1984. Biological Adaptations and Affinities of Mesolithic South Asians, in *The People of South Asia: The Biological Anthropology of India, Pakistan and Nepal*, J.R. Lukacs, ed. New York: Plenum Press, pp. 29–57.

—1996. Skeletal Adaptations of Mesolithic Hunter-Foragers of North India: Mahadaha and Sarai Nahar Rai Compared, in *Bioarchaeology of Mesolithic India: An Integrated Approach, The Prehistory of Asia and Oceania*, Gennadii E. Afanas'ev, Serge Cleuziou, John R. Lukacs and Maurizio Tosi, eds. Colloquium XXXIII, International Union of Prehistoric and Protohistoric Sciences, Forli, Italy, pp. 291–300.

—1997. Recent Developments in the Physical Anthropology of Prehistoric Man in India, in *Indian Prehistory: 1980*, V.D. Misra and J.N. Pal, eds. Allahabad: Department of Ancient History, Culture and Archaeology, University of Allahabad, pp. 196–202.

Kennedy, K.A.R., Lovell, N.C., and Burrow, C.B. 1986. *Mesolithic Human Remains from the Gangetic Plain: Sarai Nahar Rai*, Occasional Papers and Theses; South Asia Program. Ithaca: Cornell University, pp. 101–89.

Kennedy, K.A.R., Lukacs, J.R., Poster, R.F., Johnston, T.F., Lovell, N.C., Pal, J.N., Hemphill, B.E., and Burrow, C.B. 1992. *Human Skeletal Remains from Mahadaha: A Gangetic Mesolithic Site.* South Asia Occasional Papers and Theses, no. 11. Ithaca: Cornell University.

Lukacs, J.R. 1992. Mesolithic Hunters and Foragers of the Gangetic Plain: Summary of Current Research in Dental Anthropology. *Dental Anthropology News Letter* 6(3): 3–8.

Lukacs, J.R., and Pal, J.N. 1992. Dental Anthropology of Mesolithic Hunter-gatherers: A Preliminary Report of the Mahadaha and Sarai Nahar Rai Dentition. *Man and Environment* 17(2): 45–55.

—1993. Mesolithic Subsistence in North India: Inferences from Dental Attributes. *Current Anthropology* 34(5): 745–65.

Lukacs, J.R., Pal, J.N., and Misra, V.D. 1996. Chronology and Diet in Mesolithic North India: A Preliminary Report of New AMS C-14 Dates, d-13C Isotope Values, and their Significance, in *Bioarchaeology of Mesolithic India: An Integrated Approach, The Prehistory of Asia and Ocenia*, Gennadii E. Afanas'ev, Serge Cleuziou, John R. Lukacs, Maurizio Tosi, eds. Colloquium XXXIII, International Union of Prehistoric and Protohistoric Sciences, Forli, Italy, pp. 310–11.

Misra, V.D. 1977. *Some Aspects of Indian Archaeology*. Allahabad: Prabhat Prakashan.

—1988. Excavations at Damdama (Warikalan), Pratapgarh, Uttar Pradesh. *Bulletin of Museum of Archaeology in U.P.* 41–42: 59–64.

—1996. History and Context of Mesolithic Research at Allahabad University, Allahabad, India, in *Bioarchaeology of Mesolithic India: An Integrated Approach, The Prehistory of Asia and Oceania*, Gennadii E. Afanas'ev, Serge Cleuziou, John R. Lukacs, Maurizio Tosi, eds. Colloquium XXXIII, International Union of Prehistoric and Protohistoric Sciences, Forli, Italy, pp. 245–50.

Nagar, M., and Misra, V.N. 1989. Hunter-Gatherers in An Agrarian Setting: The Nineteenth Century Situation in the Ganga Plains. *Man and Environment* 13: 65–78.

—1990. The Kanjars—A Hunting-Gathering Community of the Ganga Valley, Uttar Pradesh.

Man and Environment 15:(2): 71–88.

Pal, J.N. 1984. Epipalaeolithic Sites in Pratapgarh District, Uttar Pradesh. *Man and Environment* 8: 31–38.

—1985. Some New Light on the Mesolithic Burial Practices of the Ganga Valley: Evidence from Mahadaha, Pratapgarh, Uttar Pradesh. *Man and Environment* 9: 28–37.

—1986. Microlithic Industry from Damdama. *Puratattva* 16: 1–5.

—1988. Mesolithic Double Burials From Recent Excavations at Damdama. *Man and Environment* 12: 115–22.

—1992a.Mesolithic Human Burials From the Gangetic Plain, North India. *Man and Environment* 17(2): 35–44.

—1992b. Burial Practices and Archaeological Recovery, in *Human Skeletal Remains from Mahadaha: A Gangetic Mesolithic Site*, K.A.R., Kennedy, et al., ed., pp. 25–60.

—1992c. Human Burial Practices at Mesolithic Damdama, in *Archaeological Perspective of Uttar Pradesh and Future Prospects*, Rakesh Tewari, ed. Lucknow: U.P. State Archaeological Organization, pp. 59–65.

—1994. Mesolithic Settlements in the Ganga Plain. *Man and Environment* 19: 91–101.

—1996. Lithic Use Wear Analysis and Subsistence Activities Among the Mesolithic People of North India, in *Bioarchaeology of Mesolithic India: An Integrated Approach, The Prehistory of Asia and Oceania*, Gennadii E. Afanas'ev, Serge Cleuziou, John R. Lukacs, Maurizio Tosi, eds. Colloquium XXXIII, International Union of Prehistoric and Protohistoric Sciences, Forli, Italy, pp. 267–77.

—1996–97. Microwear Studies of Microliths of the Mesolithic North India: Preliminary Reports on Methods and Results. *Pragdhara* 7: 1–9.

Pandey, J.N. 1985. Settlement Pattern and Life in the Mesolithic Period in Uttar Pradesh, D. Phil. Thesis. Allahabad: University of Allahabad.

—1990. Mesolithic in the Middle Ganga Valley. *Bulletin of the Deccan College Research Institute* 49: 311–16.

—1996. Burial Practices and Funeral Practices of Mesolithic India, in *Bioarchaeology of Mesolithic India: An Integrated Approach, The Prehistory of Asia and Ocenia*, Gennadii E. Afanas' ev, Serge Cleuziou, John R. Lukacs, Maurizio Tosi, eds. Colloquium XXXIII, International Union of Prehistoric and Protohistoric Sciences, Forli, Italy, pp. 279–90.

Pant, D.D., and Pant, R. 1980. Preliminary Observations on Pollen Flora of Chopani Mando (Vindhyas) and Mahadaha (Ganga Valley), in *Beginning of Agriculture*, G.R. Sharma et al., eds. Allahabad: Abinash Prakashan.

Paster, Robert F. 1992. Dietary Adaptation and Dental Microwear in Mesolithic and Chalcolithic South Asia, in *Culture, Ecology and Dental Anthropology*, J.R. Lukacs, ed. Delhi: Kamla-Raj Enterprises, pp.215–28.

Sharma, G.R. 1973. Mesolithic Lake Cultures of the Ganga Valley, India. *Proceedings of the Prehistoric Society* 39: 129–46.

Sharma, G.R. 1975. Seasonal Migrations and Mesolithic Lake Cultures of the Ganga Valley, in *K.C. Chattopadhyay Memorial Volume*. Allahabad: Department of Ancient History, Culture and Archaeology, University of Allahabad, pp. 1–20.

Sharma, G.R., Misra, V.D., and Pal, J.N. 1980. *Excavations at Mahadaha*. Allahabad: Department of Ancient History, Culture and Archaeology, University of Allahabad.

Sinha, P. 1983. Mesolithic Human Skeletal Remains from Canal Dump of Mahadaha, District Pratapgarh, Uttar Pradesh: A Case Study. *Man and Environment* 7: 147–53.

Thomas, P.K., Joglekar, P.P., Misra, V.D., Pandey, J.N., and Pal, J.N. 1995. A Preliminary

Report of the Faunal Remains from Damdama. *Man and Environment* 20: 29–36.
Thomas, P.K., Joglekar, P.P., Misra, V.D., Pandey, J.N., and Pal, J.N. 1996. Faunal Evidence For the Mesolithic Food Economy of the Gangetic Plain with Special Reference to Damdama, in *Bioarchaoelogy of Mesolithic India: An Integrated Approach, The Prehistory of Asia and Ocenia*, Gennadii E. Afanas'ev, Serge Cleuziou, John R. Lukacs, Maurizio Tosi, eds. Colloquium XXXIII, International Union of Prehistoric and Protohistoric Sciences, Forli, Italy, pp. 255–66.
Varma, R.K., Misra, V.D., Pandey, J.N., and Pal, J.N. 1985. A Preliminary Report on the Excavations at Damdama (1982-1984). *Man and Environment* 9: 45–65.

4 ❖ The Problem of Ashmounds of Southern Deccan in the Light of Recent Research

K. PADDAYYA

INTRODUCTION

THE Neolithic cultures of Kashmir, northern Vindhyas, eastern India and south India are the four major regional traditions within the Neolithic phase in India (Thapar 1965, 1974; Sundara 1985; Singh 1991: 128–42). Among these the Neolithic culture of south India is the most extensive one in terms of geographical extent (covering large parts of Karnataka, Andhra Pradesh and Tamil Nadu). It is probably also the best studied one (for general reviews, see Allchin 1960: 122–36; Paddayya 1973: chapter 7). Polished stone axes were reported for the first time in 1845 by Meadows Taylor at Lingsugur in Raichur district of Karnataka. In the second half of the last century Bruce Foote not only discovered numerous other sites from all over the study area but made a set of meaningful observations about the Neolithic way of life (Foote 1916: 17–24). In the first half of this century new sites were added to the list by the officers of the erstwhile princely states of Hyderabad and Mysore.

All these were surface sites, completely lacking in stratigraphical-chronological context. This lacuna was filled up by Mortimer Wheeler's famous excavation at Brahmagiri in 1947 (Wheeler 1948). Here the Neolithic cultural material comprising pottery, stone tools and simple copper objects, burials, etc. was found below the levels of the Iron Age Megalithic culture; the latter culture was in turn followed by levels representing the Early Historic culture. Thanks to the stimulus provided by Brahmagiri excavation a number of other sites were excavated in the subsequent decades: Sanganakallu, Maski, Piklihal, Nagarjunakonda, Tekkalakota, Hallur,

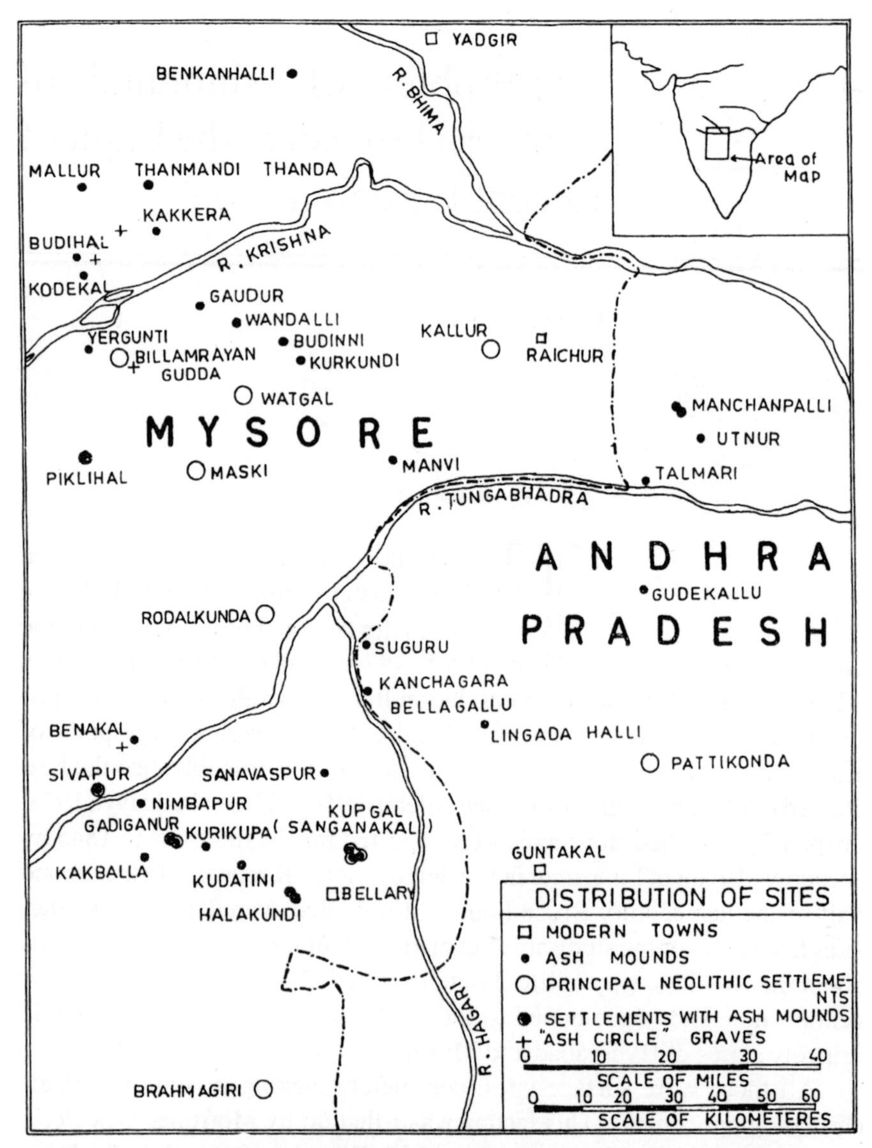

Fig. 1. Map showing important ashmounds and other Neolithic sites in the Bellary-Raichur zone and adjacent areas. (Modified after Allchin 1973)

T. Narasipur, Hemmige, Paiyampalli, Kesarapalli, Virapuram, Singanapalli, Ramapuram, Banahalli and, more recently, Watgal. In addition, several regional surveys of an intensive nature were undertaken (Nagaraja Rao 1964; Sundara 1968; 1970, Paddayya 1973; Rami Reddy 1976; Narasimhaiah 1980; David Raju 1990; Venkataka Subbaiah 1987–88, 1992). All these studies have thrown valuable light on various aspects of the Neolithic culture such as the distribution pattern of sites, intraregional diversity, dwelling structures, food economy, burial practices, ceramic and stone tool traditions, ornaments and rock art. Moreover, a large number of C^{14} dates are available now; these bracket the culture between 2500 BC and 1000 BC (Paddayya 1971).

Ashmounds constitute an important and, to some extent, problematic aspect of the south Indian Neolithic culture. There are well over a hundred sites concentrated in the region of southern Deccan, as formed by the middle reaches of the river Krishna where it is joined by its major tributaries, viz., the Tungabhadra, the Bhima, the Ghataprabha and the Malaprabha (Fig.1). In terms of present-day administrative units, the area covers the districts of Bellary, Raichur, Bijapur, Gulbarga and Belgaum in north Karnataka and Kurnool, Mahbubnagar and Anantapur districts of the Rayalaseema region of Andhra Pradesh. After providing a brief review of the various interpretations about the nature and age of this characteristic group of archaeological sites, the present paper presents the results of the author's more recent research involving both fresh explorations and a large-scale excavation at the site of Budihal in Gulbarga district. To anticipate the main conclusions of these fresh studies, ashmounds are regular Neolithic pastoral settlements and serve as an excellent example of the adaptation of a food-producing community to a landscape characterized by semi-arid climate and hilly terrain lacking in extensive tracts of land useful for plant agriculture. Budihal excavations have exposed various functionally specific activity areas within the site—cattle penning and cowdung disposal areas, human settlement area with burials and an animal butchering floor, chert workshop, and polishing grooves.

Among the protohistoric sites of the subcontinent, ashmounds are probably the first ones to be recorded by antiquarian workers (Allchin 1963: chapter 1). Colonel Colin Mackenzie, the first Surveyor General of India, discovered a few sites (including the famous ashmound at Kudatini on the Bellary-Hospet road) in the opening decade of the last century. He found these sites in the course of his tours for preparing regular topographical maps of the area covering parts of the present-day states of Karnataka and Andhra Pradesh (for details about his career and antiquarian researches, see Mackenzie 1952; Cohn 1992; Dirks 1994).Colonel Meadows Taylor (1941: 36–42) noticed a few more places in the Shorapur doab (the area formed at the confluence of the Bhima with the Krishna) in the middle of the century and even cut a trench across one of the mounds near Shahpur to expose the strata. It was however Robert Bruce Foote (1916) who, during his extensive geological surveys in South India from the 60s through the 80s of the century, not only discovered many additional ashmounds but also made very pertinent remarks about their origin and cultural context. The officers of the Geological and Archaeological Departments of the erstwhile Hyderabad State added some more sites to the list in the first half of the present century (Munn 1934, 1935, 1936; Mahadevan 1941: 160; Mukherjee 1941: 53–54). During the 60s and 70s Sundara (1971), Rami Reddy (1976) and Paddayya (1973) brought to light many additional sites in the course of their respective intensive regional surveys in the districts of Belgaum, Bijapur, Anantapur and Gulbarga.

Several widely divergent views were put forward about the origin and age of the ash deposits, which at places like Kudatini, Gaudur, Wandalli, Eachanal and Kakkera assume mound-like formations of gigantic sizes and consist of a few lakh cubic feet of sediment. Based upon the local legends and myths, early workers considered these places to be the cremation grounds of *rakshasas* or demons referred to in the epic *Mahabharata* and other ancient Hindu texts. A second set of views regarded the ash deposits as geological deposits—kankar formations, volcanic ash, limestone slag, etc. A third set of interpretations dated the sites to the medieval period and the ashes were taken to be the physical remains of mass *sati* immolations of women who had lost their husbands in the wars between the Vijayanagara rulers and Deccan Sultanates. Another class of views linked the ash deposits with industrial activity of different sorts—iron-smelting, gold-smelting, brick-making, pottery-making, etc. The view linking ash deposits with iron-smelting was originally put forward by the officers of the Nizam's Government in the 30s of the present century.

Robert Bruce Foote (1916: 90–95) put forward a totally different interpretation about their age and origin. Influenced as he was clearly by the closeness of ashmounds to the Neolithic settlements, he unhesitatingly ascribed them to the Neolithic culture. Further, the overwhelmingly pastoral character of the present-day rural life in the region and the importance still accorded by the local groups to cattle and their dung led him to the conclusion that the ashmounds represent nothing but cowdung formations burnt due to chance and carelessness of the people. The cowdung origin of the deposits was confirmed by the chemical analysis done by W.E. Smith of Presidency College, Chennai, in the last century (Foote 1916: 95) and later by F.E. Zeuner (1960).

Based upon the small excavations which Sundara (1971; 1987) and Rami Reddy (1976; 1990) carried out, respectively, at Palavoy in Anantapur district and Terdal in Bijapur district, which produced some Iron Age pottery and a few iron objects and ore/slag pieces, these scholars revived the iron-smelting theory. But the excavations conducted at Kupgal in Bellary district (Mujumdar and Rajaguru 1967) and Kodekal in Gulbarga district (Paddayya 1973: chapter 6) produced only Neolithic cultural material, thereby confirming Foote's view referred to above.

F.R. Allchin's book *The Neolithic Cattle-Keepers of South India* (1963) is surely the most important piece of research undertaken till now on this topic. Both by virtue of being a planned piece of research involving the use of regional archaeological data on ashmounds and crucial evidence obtained from Allchin's own excavation at the site of Utnur in Mahbubnagar district (Allchin 1961) and also because of Allchin's employment of ethnographic data concerning place-names having the word *Budi* (ash) and folk religious traditions pertaining to cattle and cattle-dung for supplementing archaeological evidence, this book constitutes a landmark publication in the history of Indian archaeology since Independence. Allchin fully endorsed Foote's view about the Neolithic Age of the ashmounds. Further, he interpreted them as cattle-pens and distinguished them from human settlement sites. Based upon the evidence of stockade preparations and cattle-hoof impressions found in the excavation at Utnur, he concluded that these cattle-pens underwent several stages in their formation: each stage involving levelling of the surface; preparation of stockades; cattle occupation; cow-dung accumulation and burning; and ash formation. Moreover, Allchin disagreed with Foote about the cause of cow-dung burning and insisted that, far from being accidental, the burnings were intentional and formed part of a Neolithic ash-fire cult probably for promoting the fertility of cattle herds.

Barring some occasional repetition of previous interpretations, the 80s did not produce any fresh work on this topic. With a view to ascertaining the possible scope for extending the benefits of horizontal or lateral approach (intensive, region-oriented survey and study of sites against their landscape contexts, and shift from a concern with vertical/stratigraphical understanding of archaeological deposits to a study of their horizontal relationships in ecological and functional terms), which the author had already effectively employed in the investigation of the Acheulian sites of the Hunsgi and Baichbal valleys of the Shorapur doab, to the study of ashmounds of the area he revisited in 1989 the ashmounds at Budihal and a few other places discovered by him in the 60s as a part of his doctoral research. Among other features, the most interesting finding made during these explorations concerned the occurrence of thick and extensive occupation deposit around ashmounds; this feature had escaped the attention of all previous workers. Encouraged by this new feature brought to light on account of the application of landscape approach, the author spent three seasons (1989–91) in reexploring the major ashmound sites occurring in the Shorapur doab as well as the districts of Raichur, Bellary, Mahbubnagar and Anantapur.

This landscape approach brought to light several novel features which are of crucial importance for understanding the whole problem of ashmounds (Paddayya 1993a). The following four aspects deserve special attention:

1. Concentration of ashmounds in the hilly tracts occupied by the Archaean granite-gneiss formations which support plentiful pasture but are ill-suited for agricultural purposes on account of poor, sandy soils;
2. Location of sites close to perennial water sources (large or small rivers, ephemeral nullahs with year-round water pools and natural springs;
3. Availability of large stretches of open land around ashmounds, ideally suited for purposes of human occupation;
4. And the presence of thick and extensive occupation deposit in the open area around ashmounds, yielding rich Neolithic cultural material of various kinds.

From the absence of any traces of smelting operations and cultural material datable to the Iron Age, it was clear that the ashmounds do not belong to the Iron Age and are unconnected with iron working. The pottery and other cultural material from the author's surveys left no doubt about the Neolithic Age of the sites. At the same time the author's field research clearly revealed that these sites are much more than cattle-pens where burning of cowdung deposits took place. In fact, these sites were regular pastoral settlements preserving various kinds of evidence pertaining to typical Neolithic human occupation as well. In order to place these inferences on a sound footing and gain a fresh understanding of the lifeways of these early pastoral groups, it was felt necessary to take up at least one site for detailed investigation including large-scale excavation. It was against this background that the author undertook intensive surface survey as well as excavations at the site of Budihal for seven field seasons (1990–91 to 1996–97).

Fig. 2. Map showing the location of Budihal ashmound site in relation to other archaeological sites in the vicinity

BUDIHAL SITE

The Geographical Setting

The village of Budihal (Lat.16°22" N; Long.76°23" E) lies about 110 km southwest of the district town of Gulbarga. It is situated about 1.5 km from the left bank of the Don river, a small left-bank tributary of the river Krishna. The Don originates in the adjoining Bijapur district and joins the Krishna 15 km downstream of Budihal. Several important archaeological sites such as the famous dolmens of Rajankolur discovered by Meadows Taylor, the Hanamsagar stone alignment found by Mahadevan, the ashmounds at Kodekal and Tirth, the well-known Late Chalukyan temple complex and habitation site at Hegratgi, and the medieval fort of Rayanpal are located within a radius of four to eight kilometres from Budihal (Fig. 2).

The climate of the area is semi-arid, with an average annual rainfall of about 50 cm. The meagreness and uncertain nature of the rainfall, the rugged nature of the terrain which is occupied by the Archaean granite-gneiss formations and Bhima sandstones and limestones, and the thin and sandy nature of the soil cover render the area ill-suited for dry farming; it forms part of the drought-prone Deccan belt. Jowar, bajra, groundnut and horsegram are the principal traditional crops, which depend on the south-

Fig. 3. Living cattle pastoralism at Budihal

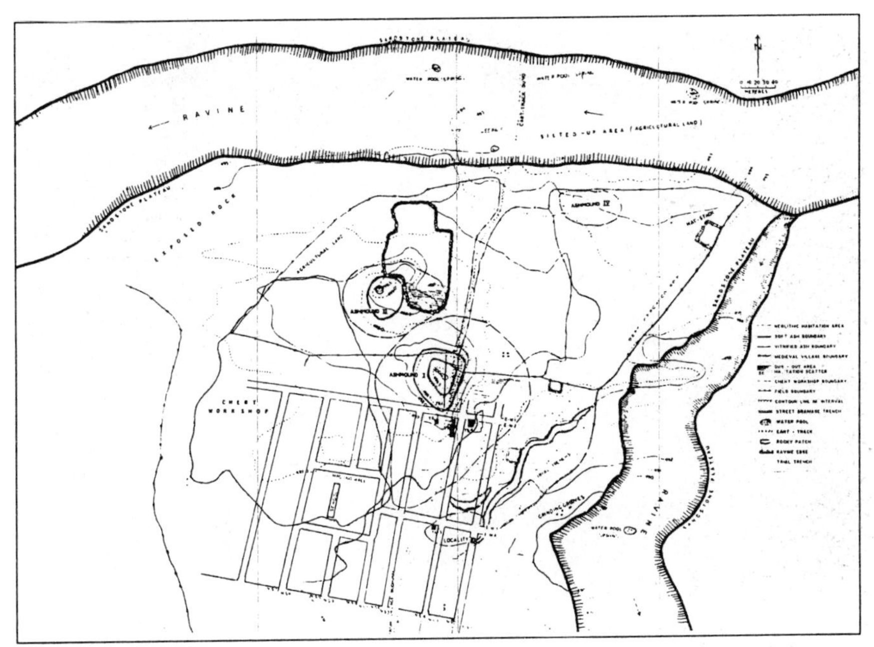

Fig. 4. Site map of Budihal showing ashmound localities (I to IV), chert workshop, grinding grooves and layout of roads of the proposed new village

west monsoon. Given this undependable nature of agriculture, it is not surprising at all that till now cattle and sheep/goat pastoralism formed an essential ingredient of the local way of life (Fig. 3). With the introduction of irrigation in recent years (as facilitated by the construction of a major dam at Narayanpur on the Krishna) and reclamation of virgin lands for farming the pastoral component of the economy is presently experiencing a downward trend.

The ashmound, lying about a kilometre north of the village, was discovered by the author in December 1965 in the course of field studies undertaken as a part of his doctoral research (Paddayya 1973: 6–7). It is situated on a sandstone plateau forming part of the Bhima series of rocks. The plateau surface is covered with stony, brown soil (15–20 cm thick) which, while being of marginal value for farming, supports a fairly thick cover of pasture. There are over 20 species of shrubs and grasses which are used for grazing cattle and sheep/goats.

The ancient site is defined on its northern and eastern sides by 15–20 m deep ravines containing perennial waterpools, which are seep-springs originating from the junction of sandstones with the underlying granite formations. It is quite certain that these pools formed a secure source of

Fig. 3. Aerial view of the ashmound site of Budihal. (1) ashmound locality I; (2) ashmound locality II; (3) ashmound locality III; (4) ashmound locality IV; (5) chert workshop; (6) grinding grooves; (7 and 8) eastern and northern ravines, respectively, with perennial waterpools. The area in the top left corner forms part of the proposed new village with layout of roads and a few buildings.

drinking water to the Neolithic inhabitants of the site. The site consists of four localities (I–IV) which are separated from one another by patches of farmland covered with brown soil. Each locality consists of ash and habitation deposits. The whole area measures 400 m north-south and 300 m east-west (Figs. 4 and 5).

A special feature of the Budihal site concerns an extensive chert workshop located immediately to the west of localities I and II. This site is spread over an area of over 4 hectares and is covered with brownish soil; it is completely devoid of greyish habitation soil and ashy deposits found on the main localities. Moreover, pottery, faunal and other cultural material are totally lacking. Instead, the whole surface is littered with a large amount of lithic material pertaining to chert blade industry. This material comprises chert nodules, fluted cores, hammerstones, simple blades, small flakes and chips. The raw material employed here was brought from the chert veins occurring in limestone formations lying at a distance of 5 or 6 km north of the site. Considering the unusually large size of the workshop and also the fact that chert debitage is found even in the habitation area, it is

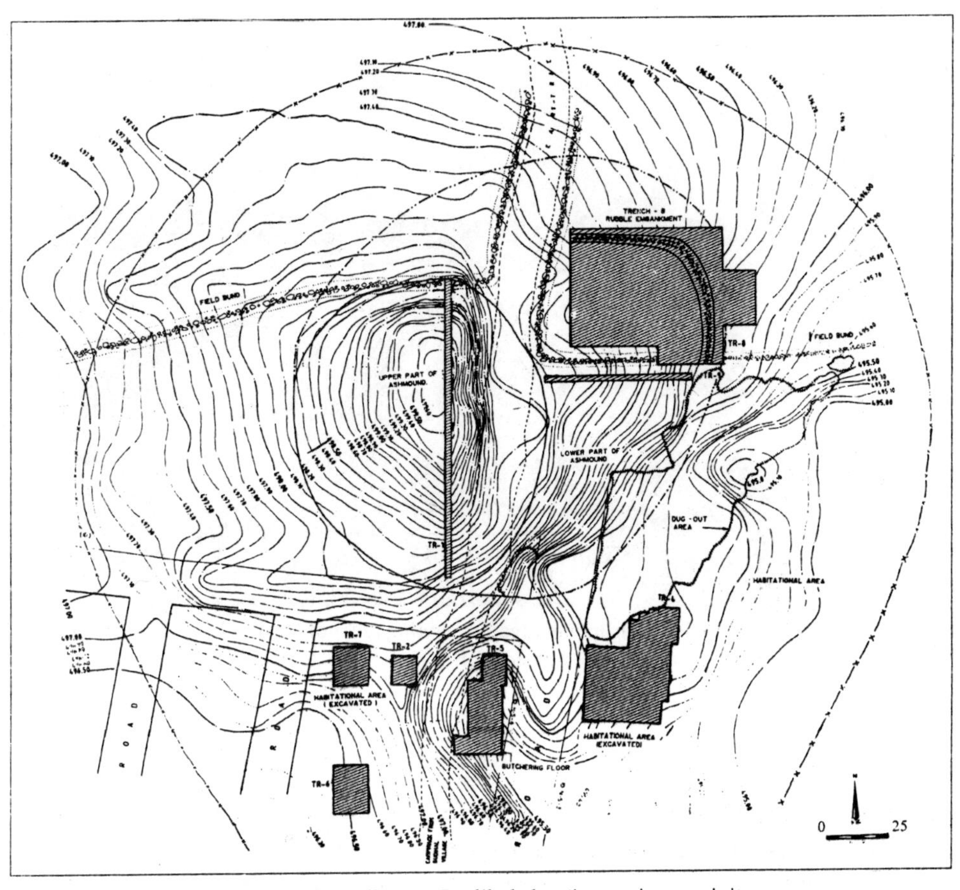

Fig. 6. Ashmound locality I at Budihal showing various activity areas

most likely that the products from the workshop were being sent to other Neolithic settlements in the Shorapur doab and probably even to sites in Raichur and Bellary districts.

Another general feature of the Budihal site worth mentioning concerns the cluster of over a dozen grinding grooves noticed on sandstone blocks forming part of the ravine on the eastern side. These grooves, obviously resulting from grinding of axes, chisels and other dolerite artefacts of the pecked and ground stone industry, take the form of oval-shaped depressions (2–5 cm deep, 20–40 cm long, and 10–20 cm broad). Such grooves were found earlier at Sanganakallu (Subbarao 1948) and other Neolithic sites.

Fig. 7. View of the lower ashmound (cattle panning area) of locality I at Budihal. The elevated patch on the left side forms part of the upper ashmound

LOCALITY I

Locality I is the major one among the four localities at Budihal (Figs. 6 and 7). It is also the best preserved one and covers a total area of 1.84 ha. In addition to its large size and relatively good state of preservation, there was an additional consideration which influenced its selection for detailed field investigations. It forms part of a large portion of the sandstone plateau surface which the State Irrigation Department acquired in 1988–89 for resettling the present village of Budihal affected by waterlogging caused by seepage of water from a major irrigation canal skirting the village. The demarcation of housing plots and lay-out of roads of the new settlement was already completed. Buildings for housing the village council, school and community temple were soon constructed on the site. The stratigraphical profiles exposed in the long ditches dug for laying roads of the proposed new village were examined and mapped in January 1991. These profiles provided valuable evidence about the extent and thickness of ash and habitation deposits (Paddayya 1993b). Based upon this initial work the author conducted large-scale excavations at the site for six seasons (1991–92 to 1996–97).

Three trenches were dug in the ashmound area—Trench 1 (60 m long and 1 m wide) in the upper ashmound and Trenches 8 (total extent: 873 m^2) and 9 (32 m long and 1 m wide) in the lower ashmound. Five trenches (Trenches 2, 4, 5, 6 and 7), covering a total area of about 550 m^2, were excavated in the human settlement area. In addition to these regular trenches, an area of 744 m^2 was excavated in the final season (1996–97). This area was located at the junction of the lower ashmound and the settlement area to its south and east. Soil quarrying by the village people had already resulted in the removal of a large volume of the Neolithic deposits. The author made use of this field situation and cleared the remaining sediment to reach the original sandstone surface. This clearance work enabled him to demarcate the boundary between the lower ashmound and settlement area and also to understand how the Neolithic settlers prepared the sandstone surface by levelling it and packing the hollows with stone rubble and soil before using it for human and cattle occupation. A total of about 50 trial pits (1 m^2) were also dug in various parts of the site to ascertain the depth of cultural and ash deposits. All these field operations led to the identification of various functionally differentiated areas within locality I (Paddayya 1995a, b).

An important aspect of excavations at Budihal was the association on a regular basis of colleagues from natural sciences. They included M.D. Kajale (archaeobotany), P.K. Thomas and P.P. Joglekar (archaeozoology), B.C. Deotare and A.A. Kshirsagar (archaeological chemistry), and Bilal R. Khrisat (geoarchaeology). Their field and laboratory studies provided a valuable complement to archaeological reconstructions.

Ashmound: Garbage Disposal and Cattle-Penning Areas

The ash deposits had a maximum thickness of 3 m and occupied a more or less central position within the locality; these covered an area of half a hectare. The stratigraphical profiles exposed in Trenches 1, 8 and 9, coupled with surface observations and chemical analyses of sediments undertaken by Deotare and Kshirsagar (1993, in press) and Khrisat (1999), clearly revealed the existence of two distinct units within this area: the flattish lower part (ash deposits measuring 1.2 m in thickness and 3000 m^2 in extent) on the east which was used for community cattle-penning and the actual mound-like formation (ash deposits measuring about 3 m in thickness and 2000 m^2 in extent) on the west resulting from the dumping and burning of cowdung cleared from the penning area.

Trench 8, located in the northern part of lower ashmound, produced

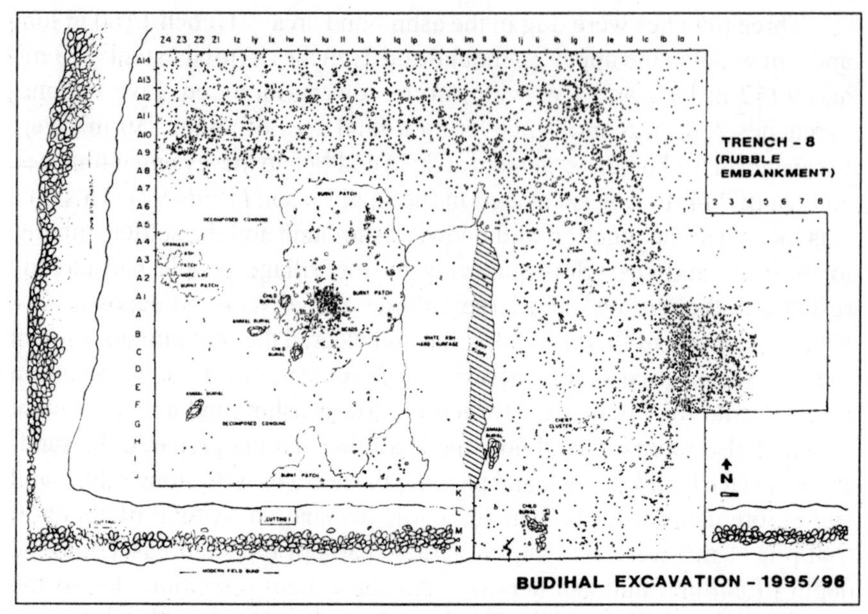

Fig. 8. Plan of rubble embankment exposed in Trench 8 of lower ashmound at locality I, Budihal

valuable evidence of structural remains pertaining to cattle penning (Paddayya 1998). This trench measured 873 m² in extent and preserved 65 cm thick sediment resting above sandstone surface. The deposit consisted of several layers/lenses of fine or granular ash, decomposed cowdung and carbonaceous matter, which represent various episodes of cattle penning, dung accumulation and clearance/burning. More important, this trench revealed that the periphery of the penning area was defined by a sandstone rubble embankment (2–2.5 m wide and 50–65 cm high) (Fig. 8). From the presence of a large quantity of carbonaceous matter (burnt plant remains) in the sediments found within the trench, it would seem that the rubble embankment was covered with a thick mass of thorny matter for strengthening the enclosure. It is important to note that such stone rubble-cum-thorn brush enclosures are still in use in the area for penning cattle as well as sheep/goats (Fig. 9).

Trench 1 was dug in the upper ashmound and exposed ash/cowdung deposits having a total thickness of about 3 m. These layers were 40 cm–1.2 m in thickness and were discontinuous in horizontal extent. They tailed off towards the ends, thereby imparting a dome-shaped appearance to the mound (Paddayya 1993b: fig. 24). If the large lumps of vitrified ash found

Fig. 9. View of a rubble-cum-thorn-bush enclosure used for cattle penning at Budihal

on the surface of the mound are any indication, it is probable that originally the deposits were thicker by a metre or so. The sediment loss was caused by ploughing and other agricultural activities of modern times. The cowdung from which these deposits were formed was cleared from the penning area to the east, heaped up in this part and burnt periodically. While these burnings may have been initiated out of practical considerations (keeping the penning area hygienic and warding off wild animals), it is possible that in the course of time they acquired ceremonial connotations (Allchin 1963: chapter 10).

Human Occupation Area

Habitation deposit was spread around the ashmound, particularly on its southern and eastern sides. The total area measured 1.34 ha in extent. The deposit had a thickness of 50 to 60 cm and rested on thin brown soil that had developed over sandstone surface. Features like the presence of sediments lying in a secondary condition close to the locality suggest that originally the deposit was thicker by at least 20–30 cm and that the top portion was stripped away due to soil erosion accelerated by ploughing and other agricultural activities of modern times.

Five trenches (Trenches 2, 4, 5, 6 and 7) were excavated during the

Fig. 10. View of round structures exposed in Trench 4 at Budihal. Several child burials were found in the lower part of the trench

Fig. 11. A present-day dwelling hut from Budihal area

Fig. 12. Infant burial in a cylindrical pot from Trench 4 at Budihal

first four field seasons (1991–92 to 1994–95). Trench 4 was a major one and covered an area of 307 m². Four layers were exposed in the excavation: layer 1 (light grey soil measuring 15–20 cm thick) representing the plough zone; layer 2 (20–25 cm thick greyish soil constituting the main Neolithic horizon; layer 3 (greyish brown soil, 5–10 cm thick) representing the basal phase of Neolithic occupation; and layer 4 representing natural soil, as formed by sandstone surface.

Structures

Layer 1 was affected to a large extent by ploughing and produced, in addition to Neolithic cultural material, a dozen instances of incomplete house floors as well as stone blocks which had obviously been displaced by the plough from their original positions in house-walls and other structural features. Layer 2 exposed ground plans of seven structures preserved in a good condition (Fig. 10). These included a platform for chert working and a storage place for pottery. The remaining five structures were meant for residential purposes and compare well with the dwellings of poorer sections of the present-day local population (Fig. 11). One of these structures was rectangular and the rest were oval on plan, measuring 3 to 4.5 m across. They had low walls (20 to 30 cm high and 30 to 40 cm wide) of

Fig. 13. View of Trench 5 at Budihal showing animal butchering floor in Trench 5 at Budihal, showing stone tools and animal bones

stone blocks packed or set in mud. Over this stable base, a conical framework of wooden sticks was raised and this was covered with grasses or reeds. The whole framework was further supported by a central vertical post fixed into the ground. Each one of these structures was provided with clay or ash flooring, a hearth, a small rubble platform to serve as a shelf for household articles, and a chipped oval-shaped limestone slab for preparing food items. Ground plans of four other structures similar to the ones described above were found in Trenches 6, 7 and 8.

Burials

A total of 13 human burials were exposed in Budihal excavation—three in the lower ashmound area and the rest in the settlement area, close to dwelling structures (Walimbe and Paddayya, in press). Among the latter class of burials seven were found in a clustered fashion in Trench 4 and the remaining four in other trenches. In four cases the dead were interred in pits and the rest were urn burials. The skeletal material is completely dominated by the sub-adult segment; some of the urn burials belong to infants aged a few months. In four cases long cylindrical pots (30–35 cm long), open at either end, were used for interring the dead (Fig. 12). In some cases pottery and chert blades were used as funerary goods. The significance of

Fig. 14. Close-up of the animal butchering floor in Trench 5 at Budihal, showing stone tools and animal bones

these burials is twofold. First, they give added support to our reinterpretation of ashmounds as regular pastoral settlements. Secondly, the preponderance of child burials is probably a reflection of the physiological stress that was being experienced by the Neolithic population.

Animal Butchering Floor

This unique facility was found at a depth of 20–22 cm below surface in Trench 5 of the settlement area. This trench lay on the southern side of the ashmound area and measured 129 m^2 in extent (Fig. 13). It is estimated that the original butchering floor measured about 250 m^2 in extent. Unfortunately, nearly half of this area has been destroyed in recent times due to soil-quarrying and road-making operations of the local people.

The following stratigraphy was exposed in this trench: layer 1 (15–20 cm thick) representing the plough zone and consisting of soft greyish soil yielding Neolithic cultural material; layer 2 (5 cm thick) consisting of faunal material; layer 3 (2–5 cm thick) made up of a rammed floor of kankar-like material; layer 4 marking natural soil (brown soil). Chemical analyses showed that the hard, kankar-like material of layer 3 consists of fine ash, clay and tiny bits of chert, pottery and charcoal, all mixed with water, spread over the brown soil and rammed well in order to obtain a hard working surface (Deotare and Kshirsagar 1995; Khrisat 1999). In the archaeological record of peninsular India this is the earliest known instance of the preparation of an artificial plaster.

Unlike other trenches dug in the settlement area, this trench (layer 2) yielded extremely meagre quantities of pottery and debitage of chert working; nor were there any remains of dwelling structures or burials. The principal cultural material consisted of chopping tools and hammerstones of dolerite and limestone, and large knife-like blades of chert (Fig. 14). What is more important, we found these artefacts in association with a large quantity of faunal material belonging to domestic cattle and, to some extent, sheep, goat and buffalo (Paddayya et al. 1995). The body parts represented included skull and jaw pieces, proximal and distal ends of long bones, ribs, vertebrae, fragments of pelvis and scapula blades, and lower extremities of limb bones (carpal and tarsal bones, metapodials and phalanges). Many of these bones bear on their surfaces taphonomic marks of chopping, splitting and cutting obviously resulting from the use of chopping tools, hammer-stones and chert blades mentioned above. All these lines of evidence clearly establish that animal butchering took place on the floor; the bone material found on it represents primary discard resulting from carcass processing.

The faunal and lithic material found on the floor consisted of several clusters, which probably represent different episodes of carcass processing. One of these clusters consisted of the lower extremities of the hind leg of cattle found in undisturbed position (Paddayya et al. 1995: fig. 9). Considering the fairly large size of the floor and the large number of bone and lithic tool clusters found on it, it is most likely that this structural facility was meant for common use on certain important (ceremonial?) occasions when several animals were butchered and the meat so obtained was shared by the whole community.

The floor was associated with a few burnt soil patches containing charcoal pieces. Also found on it were three pits (20–25 cm across and 15–20 cm deep) containing ashy soil, charcoal and burnt bone pieces. It is most likely that these features were connected with roasting and cooking of meat.

Other Important Features

Barring a small number of modern and medieval potsherds and glass bangle pieces found in the top digging levels of the deposit, the cultural material from both ashmound and settlement areas was purely Neolithic in character. It consisted of red and grey ceramic fabrics, various artefact

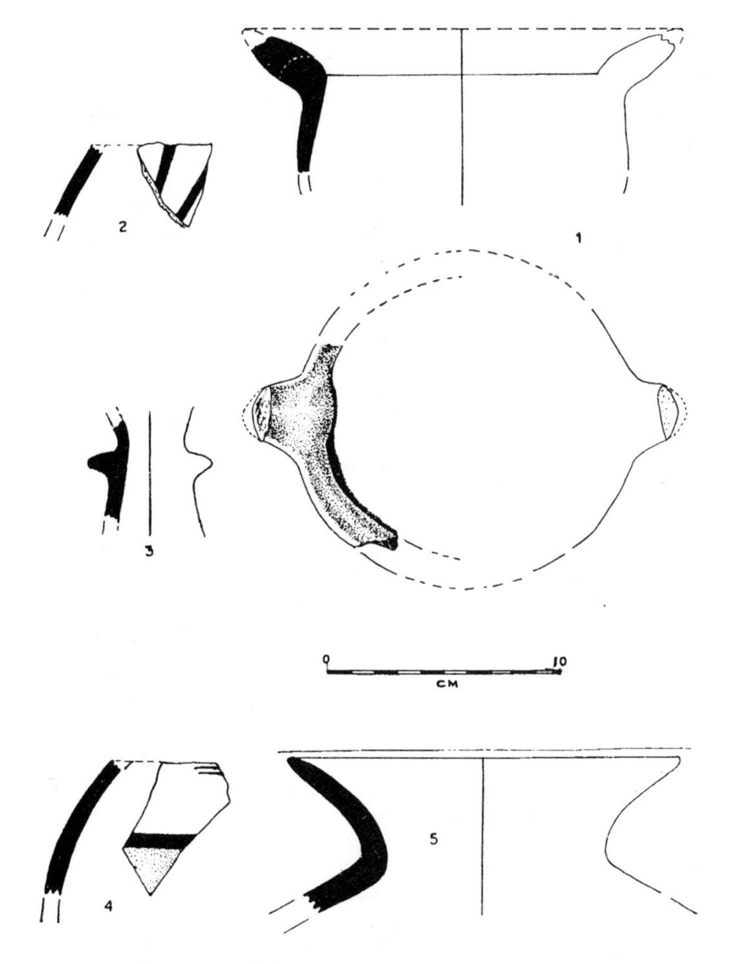

Fig. 15. Neolithic pottery from Trench 4, Budihal

types (including a large number of sandstone querns) belonging to pecked and ground stone and chert blade industries, a limited number of bone artefacts including ground axes, and ornaments comprising beads and pendants of shell, bone, terracotta and semi-precious stones (Figs. 15–17). Waste products resulting from iron-working and such other industrial processes were conspicuous by their absence. The cultural material from the site compares well with the evidence from other Neolithic sites in the Shorapur doab and other parts of north Karnataka.

Biological Remains

The excavation yielded remains of 15 species of animals. This faunal

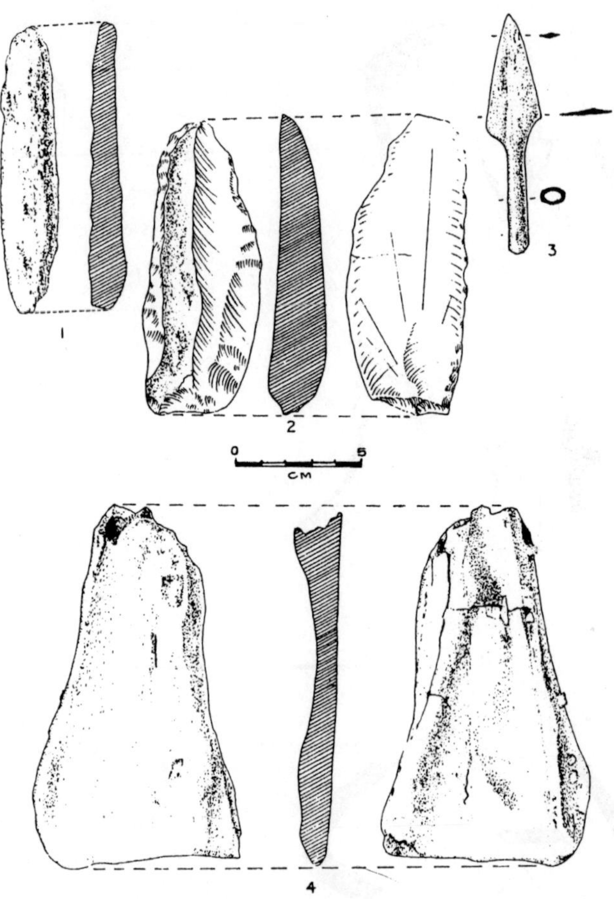

Fig. 16. Stone and bone artefacts from Trench 4 at Budihal. (1) bone scraper; (2) chert knife; (3) An iron arrow-head found on surface; (4) bone axe (medieval)

material is being studied in detail by P.K. Thomas and P.P. Joglekar. The preponderance of domestic cattle bones in the collection leaves no doubt whatever that the ancient inhabitants of Budihal were essentially relying upon cattle pastoralism and, to a lesser extent, on other domestic animals (buffalo, sheep/goat and fowl). They also exploited wild animals such as the nilgai, the blackbuck, the four-horned antelope, the monitor lizard, birds, and aquatic foods like fish, tortoise, crabs and mollusks (for a review of the faunal evidence from the south Indian Neolithic sites, see Paddayya 1975).

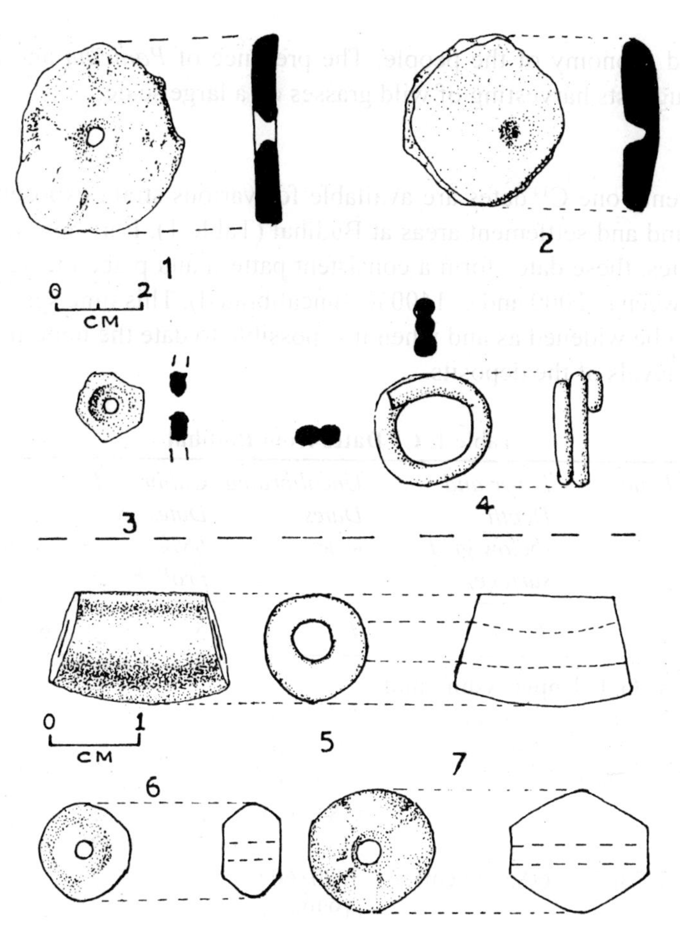

Fig. 17. Ornaments from Trench 4 at Budihal. (1–3) edge-ground potsherds, with a perforation; (4) copper ring; (5) tubular bead of chalk-like material; (6) shell bead; (7) biconical carnelian bead

M.D. Kajale carried out systematic and extensive flotation of soil samples from all the excavated trenches in order to recover plant remains. He recovered uncarbonized fruitstones of three wild species, viz., the Indian jujube, the Indian cherry and the emblic myrobalan from the ash deposits (Kajale 1996). He also recovered from the habitation deposits carbonized grains of domesticated barley, horsegram and Indian bean/haycinth bean, and graminaceous seeds (*Panicum* and *Setaria* types) and portulacaceae type of weed seeds. Considering the rugged nature of the terrain and its poor soil cover, agriculture could have played but only a subsidiary role in the food economy of the people. The presence of *Panicum* and *Setaria* seeds suggests harvesting of wild grasses on a large scale.

Dating

Twenty-one C^{14} dates are available for various strata exposed in the ashmound and settlement areas at Budihal (Table 1). Barring one or two anamolies, these dates form a consistent pattern and place the age of the site between *c.* 2000 and *c.* 1400 BC (uncalibrated). This time span is most likely to be widened as and when it is possible to date the uppermost and bottom levels of the deposits.

Table 1. **C^{14} Dates from Budihal**

S. no.	*Lab. no.*	*Layer and Depth (below grid surface)*	*Uncalibrated Dates BP/BC*	*Calibrated Dates (BC) 68% probability*	*98% probability*
1	*2*	*3*	*4*	*5*	*6*
Budihal I, Tr.1 (Upper Ashmound)					
1.	BM–2888	3(99 cm) (430 BC)	2380±60 BP 530–390	755–705	765–360
2.	GrN–19661	6(80–85 cm)	3795±30 BP (1845 BC)	2278–2226 2208–2188 2164–3142	2312–2306 2294–3134 2070–2054
3.	BM–2887	6(85–90 cm)	3880±60 BP (1930 BC)	2465–2295	2565–2540 2500–2195 2155–2145
4.	GrN–19662	9(105–110 cm)	3805±5 BP (1855 BC)	2282–2192 2162–2146	2392–2384 2336–2136 2076–2054
5.	GrN–19663	10(145–150 cm)	3795±40 BP (1845 BC)	2282–2216 2214–2186 2168–2140	2394–2384 2338–2130 2080–2046
6.	BM–2886	10(210 cm)	3810±50 BP (1860 BC)	2450–2445 2395–2385 2350–2190 2160–2145	2450–2135
Budihal-I, Tr.4 (Settlement Area)					
7.	GrN–19978	2(28 cm)	3370±40 BP (1420 BC)	1734–1722 1688–1610 1552–1536	1740–1708 1700–1588 1582–1526

1	*2*	*3*	*4*	*5*	*6*
8.	GrN–19979	2(35 cm)	3470±40 BP (1520 BC)	1874–1840 1814–1806 1780–1738 1714–1692	1880–1830 1826–1684
9.	GrN–19980	2(40 cm)	3750±35 BP (1800 BC)	2196–2154 2152–2130 2080–2046	2278–2230 2206–2036
10.	GrA–2502	2(20 cm)	3770±50 BP (1820 BC)	2278–2228 2206–2132 2078–2048	2390–2388 2334–2030 1998–1986
11.	GrA–2506	2(28 cm)	3610±50 BP (1660 BC)	2030–1998 1984–1886	2130–2080 2044–1872 1842–1812 1808–1780
12.	GrA–2504	2(30–35 cm)	3730±50 BP (1780 BC)	2194–2160 2146–2034	2280–2222 2210–1974
13.	GrA–2503	2(30–35 cm)	3900±50 BP (1950 BC)	2460–2320	2482–2266 2264–2200
14.	GrA–2484	2(37 cm)	3600±60 BP (1650 BC)	2032–1994 1988–1878 1834–1822 1794–1788	2132–2078 2048–1862 1850–1758
15.	GrA–2486	3(40–45 cm)	3830±60 BP (1880 BC)	2398–2378 2346–2190 2162–2144	2458–2134 2074–2052
16.	GrA–2487	3(40–45 cm)	3850±60 BP (1900 BC)	2450–2434 2402–2374 2354–2268 2264–2200	2464–2136
17.	GrA–2488	2(25 cm)	3600±60 BP (1650 BC)	2032–1994 1988–1878 1834–1822 1794–1788	2132–2078 2048–1862 1850–1758
Budihal-I, Tr.5 (Animal Butchering Floor)					
18.	GrN–19981	3(40 cm)	3820±45 BP (1870 BC)	2324–2192 2162–2146	2452–2430 2404–2368 2364–2136 2068–2056

1	2	3	4	5	6
19.	GrA–2483	2(10 cm)	3770±60 BP (1820 BC)	2282–2216 2212–2128 2080–2044 2044–1978	2446–2440 2440–2376 2350–2022
20.	GrA–2489	2(15–20 cm)	3810±50 BP (1860 BC)	2318–2186 2168–2140	2452–2430 2404–2368 2364–2130 2078–2046
Budihal-III (Trial pit) (Settlement Area)					
21.	GrN–19982	3(40 cm)	3810±80 BP (1860 BC)	2398–2378 2346–2134	2462–2030 1996–1986 2076–2054

CONCLUSION

The author's fresh field investigations concerning the ashmounds of lower Deccan in north Karnataka and the prolonged and large-scale excavations at Budihal constitute one among a very limited number of examples of problem-oriented research undertaken in Indian archaeology in recent decades. This work made a significant contribution towards our understanding of the problem of ashmounds. First, these sites represent a characteristic mode of adaptation on the part of the Neolithic settlers to the ecological setting of the region. The area, covered as it is mostly with granite-gneiss hills and hill-chains of the Archaean age, offers but limited scope for agricultural activities but contains vast reserves of pasture ideally suited to pastoral activity. It is the latter alternative which the Neolithic groups opted for and specialized in cattle and, to some extent, sheep/goat pastoralism. Ashmounds are an eloquent testimony to the overwhelmingly pastoral orientation of the Neolithic culture of southern Deccan.

Secondly, these fresh studies place beyond doubt Bruce Foote's views about the Neolithic Age of the ashmounds and their cowdung origin. At the same time these studies, while they support Allchin's cattle-pen hypothesis, prove that his division of the Neolithic sites of this region into habitation and cattle penning sites is untenable. It is now certain that ashmounds are full-fledged pastoral settlements. Budihal excavations exposed various functionally specific activity areas within the site. The author would like to point out here that during his visit (in January 1995) to the site of Utnur excavated by F.R. Allchin he noticed a similar twofold

Fig. 18. Cattle fair (Paramananda Jatra) at Benkanhalli in the Shorapur Doab.

division of the ashmound into an upper mound representing cowdung disposal and burning area and the lower portion where Allchin laid his trenches and obtained structural and other forms of evidence of cattle penning. The author also noticed an extensive Neolithic habitation area on the eastern side of the ashmound. The ashmound at Hulikallu in Anantapur district also produced evidence of human occupation including burials around the ash deposit (Krishna Sastry 1979).

Thirdly, a definite gradation is discernible in the sizes of ashmounds. Sites like Budihal are enormous in size and probably served as local/regional centres where periodic congregations similar to the present-day cattle fairs were held (Fig. 18). Presumably socioeconomic and other transactions were taking place at these congregations. The extensive chert workshop found at Budihal assumes a large measure of importance in this regard; some of its blade products were in all likelihood being sent to other settlements.

Fourthly, this research on the ashmounds of southern Deccan leads one to the implication that evidence of cattle penning and resultant accumulation of cowdung and ash deposits should be expected at other Neolithic-Chalcolithic sites characterized by agropastoral economy. It is gratifying to note that such deposits have been noted at sites like Inamgaon (Dhavalikar et al. 1988: 131) and other sites in northern Deccan (Sali 1987) and Balathal (Misra et al. 1995: 74) in Rajasthan.

Finally, it is by no means the case that the research on ashmounds outlined in the present paper has provided answers to all issues connected with this topic. Ashmounds do seem to hold clues for reconstructing even the sociological and ideological realms of Neolithic life. Recent attempts at redefining the concept 'Neolithic' in terms of human sentiments and motivations (Thomas 1991) and books like Hodder's *The Domestication of Europe* (1990) and Tilley's *A Phenomenology of Landscape* (1994) give rise to many possibilities of further work. There is tremendous scope too for additional geo- and bioarchaeological investigations which can place our understanding of the Neolithic pastoral adaptations of southern Deccan on a firmer and broader footing.

ACKNOWLEDGEMENTS

During my field research in the Shorapur doab covering the last three decades I have had the good fortune of receiving unstinted support and cooperation from Drs. M.S. Nagaraja Rao, A. Sundara and D.V. Devaraj, successive Directors of the Department of Archaeology and Museums, Government of Karnataka. I am grateful to all of them for their generous attitude towards me. Likewise I have received excellent support and encouragement from a wide cross-section of local people ranging from government engineers and doctors to school teachers and simple-minded village folk. I must in particular mention the cooperation extended by the Hunsgi Mandal Panchayat committee and two esteemed friends from Hunsgi, Dr. S.R. Biradar and the late Shri Basappa Amarannavar.

The large-scale and prolonged field research at Budihal would have been impossible but for the kind permission and cooperation given by the Irrigation Department of Karnataka and three landlords of Budihal (Smt. Mallamma Mulimani, Shri Saheb Gowda and Shri Siddaramappa Gowda) in whose lands the Neolithic site is situated. Grateful thanks are also due to Shri Bhimaraya Pale, Headmaster of the Primary School at Budihal, and his colleagues and his young pupils in providing us both camping accommodation in the school building and excellent company during our several seasons of excavation at Budihal. The following teachers, technical staff and students of the Department of Archaeology, Deccan College, Pune, took part in the Budihal excavation and assisted in many ways: Drs. P.K. Thomas, M.D. Kajale, B.C. Deotare, P.P. Joglekar, S.R. Walimbe, A.A.

Kshirsagar, P.S. Joshi; Messrs C.J. Padwal, N.S. Gaware, B.S. Waghmode, D.D. Phule, S. Rokade, S.S. Pradhan, V.G. Vishwasrao, D.V. Karanjkar, Vinayak Bhatawadekar, Ashok Omble and Chandrakant Shendge; S.K. Aruni, Richa Jhaldiyal, Bilal R. Khrisat, Suchi Dayal, Madhuca Geethakrishnan, P.C. Venkata Subbaiah, V. Selvakumar, S.B. Darsana and Jitu Mishra. Shri Sunil Jadhav and Shri Ravi Dhamapurkar prepared the photographs. Aerial photography of the Budihal site was carried out by Dr. A.R. Marathe; he used the low altitude aerial reconnaissance (LAAR) technique for this purpose. Dr. J. van der Plicht of the Centre for Isotope Research, Groningen University, the Netherlands, and Dr. Janet Ambers of the Research Laboratory of British Museum, London, kindly provided the C^{14} dates for Budihal charcoal samples. Shri S.I. Amin typed the manuscript.

REFERENCES

Allchin, F.R. 1960. *Piklihal Excavations*. Hyderabad: Government of Andhra Pradesh.

—1961. *Utnur Excavations*. Hyderabad: Government of Andhra Pradesh.

—1963. *Neolithic Cattle-Keepers of South India: A Study of the Deccan Ashmounds*. Cambridge: Cambridge University Press.

Cohn, Bernard S. 1992. The Transformation of Objects into Artifacts, Antiquities and Art in Nineteenth Century India, in Barbara Stone Miller, ed., *The Powers of Art: Patronage in Indian Culture*. New Delhi, Oxford University Press, pp. 301–29.

David Raju, B. 1990. The Settlement and Subsistence Pattern of the Neolithic Culture of the Lower Krishna Valley. *Man and Environment* 15(2): 45–51.

Deotare, B.C., and Kshirsagar, A.A. 1993. Ashmound at Budhihal, Karnataka: A Chemical Approach. *Bulletin of the Deccan College Research Institute* 53: 39–48.

— In press. Chemistry of Activity Areas from Neolithic Budihal, Gulbarga District, Karnataka. *Bulletin of the Deccan College Research Institute*.

Dhavalikar, M.K., Sankalia H.D., and Ansari, Z.D. 1988. *Excavations at Inamgaon*, vol. I, part 1. Pune: Deccan College.

Dirks, Nicholas B. 1994. Guiltless Spoliations: Picturesque Beauty, Colonial Knowledge, and Colin Mackenzie's Survey of India, in Catherine B. Asher and Thomas R. Metcalf, eds., *Perceptions of South Asia's Visual Past*. New Delhi: Oxford & IBH Publishing Co., pp. 211–32.

Foote, R.B. 1887. Notes on Some Recent Neolithic and Palaeolithic Finds in South India. *Journal of the Asiatic Society of Bengal* 46(2): 259–82.

—1916. *The Foote Collection of Indian Prehistoric and Protohistoric Antiquities: Notes on Their Ages and Distribution*. Chennai: Government Museum.

Hodder, I. 1990. *The Domestication of Europe*. Oxford: Basil Blackwell.

Kajale, M.D. 1996. Neolithic Plant Economy of Lower Deccan and South India, in Abstract 1: the Sections of the XIII International Congress of Prehistoric and Protohistoric *Sciences* held at Forli, Italy, 8–14 September 1996.

Khrisat, Bilal R. 1999. Geoarchaeology of the South Indian Neolithic Sites With Special

Reference to Budihal, Shorapur Doab, Karnataka. Unpublished Ph.D. thesis. Pune: University of Pune.

Mackenzie, W.C. 1952. *Colonel Colin Mackenzie: First Surveyor-General of India*. Edinburgh and London: W.R. Chambers.

Mahadevan, C. 1941, Geology of the South and Southwestern Parts of Surapur Taluk of Gulbarga District. *Journal of the Hyderabad Geological Survey* 4(1): 102–61.

Misra, V.N., Shinde, V.S., Mohanty, R.K., Dalal, Kurush, Mishra, Anup, Pandey Lalit, and Kharakwal, Jeevan. 1995. Excavations at Balathal: Their Contribution to the Chalcolithic and Iron Age Cultures of Mewar, Rajasthan. *Man and Environment* 20(1): 57–80.

Mujumdar, G.G., and Rajaguru, S.N. 1966. *Ashmound Excavations at Kupgal*. Pune: Deccan College.

Mukherjee, S.K. 1941. Geology of Parts of Surapur and Shahpur Taluks, Gulbarga District. *Journal of the Hyderabad Geological Survey* 4 (1): 9–54.

Munn, L. 1934. Prehistoric and Protohistoric Finds. *Journal of the Hyderabad Geological Survey* 2 (1): 121–35.

—1935. Prehistoric and Protohistoric Finds in the Raichur and Shorapur Districts. *Man in India* 15 (4): 225–50.

—1936. Archaeological Finds in the Eastern Portion of the Raichur Doab. *Journal of the Hyderabad Geological Survey* 3 (1): 1–82.

Nagaraja Rao, M.S. 1964. Recent Explorations in the Tungabhadra Basin: The Chalcolithic Phase. *Bulletin of the Deccan College Research Institute* 23: 55–67.

Narasimhaiah, B. 1980. *Neolithic and Megalithic Cultures in Tamil Nadu*. Delhi: Sundeep Prakashan.

Paddayya, K. 1971. Radiocarbon Dates and South Indian Neolithic Culture. *Antiquity* 45: 134–38.

—1973. *Investigations into the Neolithic Culture of the Shorapur Doab, South India*. Leiden: E.J. Brill.

—1975. The Faunal Background of the South Indian Neolithic Culture, in A.T. Clason, ed., *Archaeozoological Studies*. Amsterdam: Elsevier Publishing Company, pp. 329–34.

—1993a. The Ashmounds of South India: Fresh Evidence and Possible Implications. *Bulletin of the Deccan College Research Institute* 51–52 (1991–92): 573–626.

—1993b. Ashmounds Excavations at Budihal, Gulbarga District, Karnataka. *Man and Environment* 18(1): 57–87.

—1995a. Further Field Investigations at Budihal, Gulbarga District, Karnataka. *Bulletin of the Deccan College Research* 53 (1993): 277–322.

—1995b. New light on the Early Agropastoral Communities of South India. *Proceedings of the 19th Session of Andhra Pradesh History Congress*. Presidential Address: Ancient Andhra History and Archaeology Section, Anantapur, pp. 5–15.

—1998. Evidence of Neolithic Cattle-penning at Budihal, Gulbarga District, Karnataka. *South Asian Studies* 14: 141–53.

Paddayya, K., Thomas, P.K., and Joglekar, P.P. 1995. A Neolithic Animal Butchering Floor from Budihal, Gulbarga District, Karnataka. *Man and Environment* 20(2): 23–31.

Rami Reddy, V. 1976. *The Prehistoric and Protohistoric Cultures of Palavoy, South India, with Special Reference to the Ashmound Problem*. Hyderabad, Government of Andhra Pradesh.

—1990. Ashmounds in South India: A Review, in A. Sundara, ed., *Archaeology in Karnataka*. Mysore: Directorate of Archaeology and Museums, 85–99.

Sali, S.A. 1987. The Savalda Culture of the Deccan with Special Reference to Evidence from Daimabad, in B.M. Pande and B.D. Chattopadhyaya, eds., *Archaeology and History: Essays in Memory of Shri A. Ghosh*, vol. I, New Delhi: Agam Kala Prakashan, pp. 295–311.

Singh, Purushottam. 1991. *The Neolithic Origins*. New Delhi: Agam Kala Prakashan.

Subbarao, B. 1948. *The Stone Age Cultures of Bellary*. Pune: Deccan College.

Sundara, A. 1968. Protohistoric Sites in Bijapur District. *The Journal of the Karnatak University—Social Sciences* 4: 3-23.

—1970. Neolithic Cultural Patterns and Movements in North Mysore State. *The Journal of the Karnatak University—Social Sciences* 6: 3–13.

—1971. New Discoveries of Ashmound in North Karnataka: Their Implications, in S., Ganeshan, S. Rajan and M.D. Sampath, eds., *Professor K.A. Nilakanta Sastri Felicitation Volume*, Chennai, pp. 308–14.

—1985. Cultural Ecology of the Neolithic in India, in S.B. Deo and K. Paddayya, ed., *Recent Advances in Indian Archaeology*. Pune: Deccan College, pp. 39–57.

—1987. Studies in Ashmounds, in B.M. Pande and B.D. Chattopadhyaya, ed., *Archaeology and History: Essays in Memory of Sri A. Ghosh*. New Delhi: Agam Kala Prakashan, pp. 313–24.

Taylor, Meadows. 1941. *Megalithic Tombs and other Ancient Remains in the Deccan* (Collected papers edited by G. Yazdani). Hyderabad: Archaeological Department of Hyderabad State.

Thapar, B.K. 1965. Neolithic Problem in India, in V.N. Misra and M.S. Mate, eds., *Indian Prehistory: 1964*. Pune: Deccan College, pp. 87–112.

—1974. Problem of the Neolithic Cultures in India. *Puratattva* 7: 61–65.

Thomas, J. 1991. *Rethinking the Neolithic*. Cambridge: Cambridge University Press.

Tilley, C. *A Phenomenology of Landscape*. Oxford: Berg.

Venkata Subbaiah, P.C. 1987–88. Protohistoric Investigations in the Central Pennar Basin, Cuddapah District, Andhra Pradesh. *Puratattva* 18: 79–84.

—1992. Protohistoric Investigations in the Central Pennar Basin, Cuddaph District, Andhra Pradesh. Unpublished Ph.D. Thesis. Pune: University of Pune.

Walimbe, S.R., and Paddayya, K. In press. Human Skeletal Remains from the Neolithic Ashmound Site of Budihal, Karnataka. *Bulletin of the Deccan College Research Institute*.

Wheeler, R.E.M. 1948. Brahmagiri and Chandravalli 1947: Megalithic and Other Cultures in Mysore State. *Ancient India* 4: 180–310.

Zeuner, F.E. 1960. On the Origin of the Cinder Mounds of the Bellary District, India. *Bulletin of the Institute of Archaeology*, London, 2 (1959): 37–48.

5 ❖ The Early Harappan

G.L. POSSEHL

THE Early Harappan period was most fully defined by M.R. Mughal in his Ph.D. dissertation at the University of Pennsylvania. It was the first broadly based study of the archaeological assemblages that can be dated to *c.* 3200–2500 BC in the Greater Indus Region, and would have been the historical antecedent to the peoples of the Harappan Civilization. He consciously selected the term "Early Harappan" for this stage of cultural development: "In my opinion the term 'pre-Harappan' is misleading because it creates the impression that chronological gap exists between the 'pre-Harappan' period of the first half of the third millennium BC and the 'mature' period of the Harappan culture belonging the later half of the third millennium. The other terms, 'antecedent' and 'proto-Harappan' sometimes used in the archaeological literature are vague, remain undefined and beg questions . . . I feel that all of the material found stratified below the 'mature' Harappan at Kot Diji, Amri, Kalibangan and the pre-defense levels of Harappa and related material discovered at other sites belongs to an Early Harappan period assignable to the first half of the third millennium BC. Among these separately treated sites, having regional differences in ceramics, there are many common traits present in ceramics, stone tools and technology, terracotta objects and in architecture which also occur in the 'mature' Harappan period. The radiocarbon dates also tend to strengthen the chronological priority of Kot Dijian and related material over that of the 'mature' Harappan culture. It is therefore quite justified to call this material Early Harappan" (Mughal 1970: 5–6).

Walter A. Fairservis, Jr. independently defined the Early Harappan in his writings on the origins of the ancient cities of the Indus (Fairservis

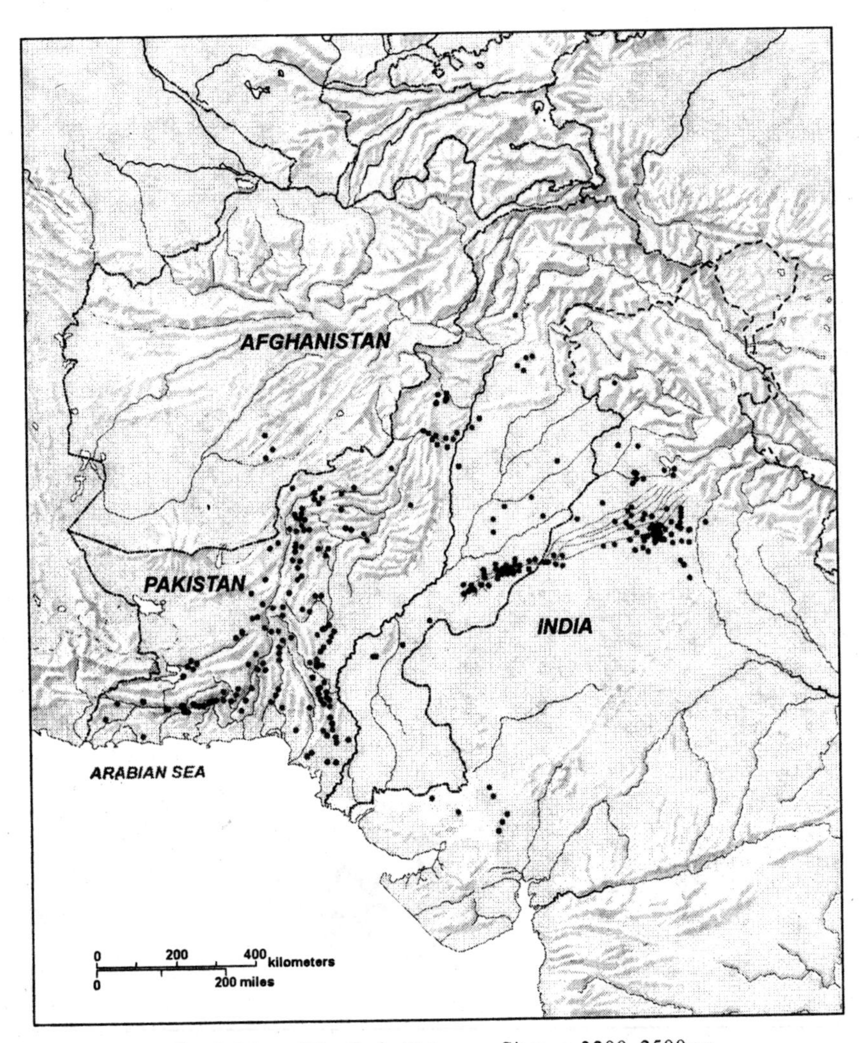

Fig. 1. Map of the Early Harappan Sites, *c.* 3200–2500 BC

1971:221). He proposed that the regional mosaic formed by assemblages from sites such as Amri, Kot Diji, Kalibangan and Nal should be considered the "Early Harappan". "By this we mean the Harappan artefact form and decoration, not the civilization" (Fairservis 1971:221). Mughal, however, is the scholar who developed the idea.

The radiocarbon chronology for the Mature and Early Harappan can be used to estimate that these periods belong principally in the third millennium BC. There is a Transitional Stage between them which was relatively short (*c.* 100 years) and is important in understanding the formation

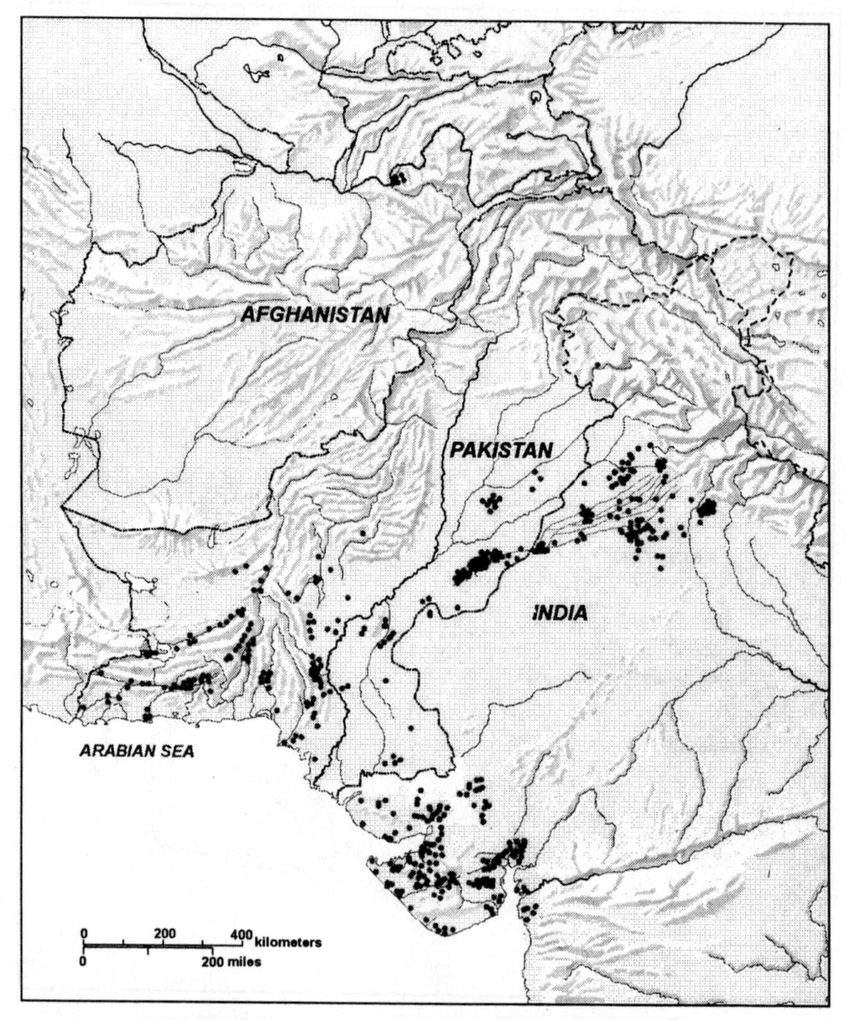

Fig. 2. Map of the Mature Harappan Sites, *c*. 2500–1500 BC

processes of the Harappan Civilization. The most recent comprehensive studies of chronology (Shaffer 1992; Possehl and Rissman 1992; Possehl 1993) estimate that these assemblages date to:

Table 1. **Chronological Data**

Mature Harappan	*c*. 3200–2600 BC
Early/Mature Harappan Transition	*c*. 2600–2500 BC
Early Harappan	*c*. 3200–2600 BC

My gazetteer of sites of the Indus Age, the period from the beginnings of the village farming community and pastoral camps to the early Iron Age in the Greater Indus Region, contains information on over 2500 archaeological sites.

Table 2. **Sites of the Early and Mature Harappan**

Archaeological Stage	*Number of Sites*	*Average Site Size in Hectares*
Mature Harappan	1019	7.25
Early Harappan	477	4.51

The overall distribution of sites belonging to the Early and Mature Harappan periods is shown in Figs. 1 and 2.

There are too few sites that can presently be assigned to the Early/Mature Harappan Transition for numbers of this kind to be meaningful. Two things emerge from these data. There is a substantial growth in the number of sites between the Early Harappan and Mature Harappan, a little over twice as many and the average size of these sites also rises rather markedly—just under twice the size. Although there is much exploration left to do in the Greater Indus Region, these figures seem to indicate that there was significant growth between the Early and Mature Harappan.

The Phases of the Early Harappan

There are four different archaeological phases that make up the Early Harappan: the Amri-Nal, Kot Diji, Damb Sadaat and Sothi-Siswal.

The Amri-Nal Phase

The Amri-Nal Phase was first defined in the writings of Walter Fairservis. The people of the Amri-Nal Phase inhabited southern Baluchistan and western Sindh, with pioneer settlements in North Gujarat. Period I at Dholavira may be associated with this phase. The ceramics of the Amri-Nal Phase are shown in Fig. 3.

The sites of the Amri-Nal Phase are found in the valley bottoms of Gedrosia and in Sindh Kohistan and the Kirthar Piedmont. There tends to be more Amri ware than Nal ceramics in Sindh and just the opposite in Gedrosia where the Nal wares predominate. These regions appear to have been bound together by the seasonal movement of agropastoralists and other itinerants. They visited the lowlands in the winter and returned to

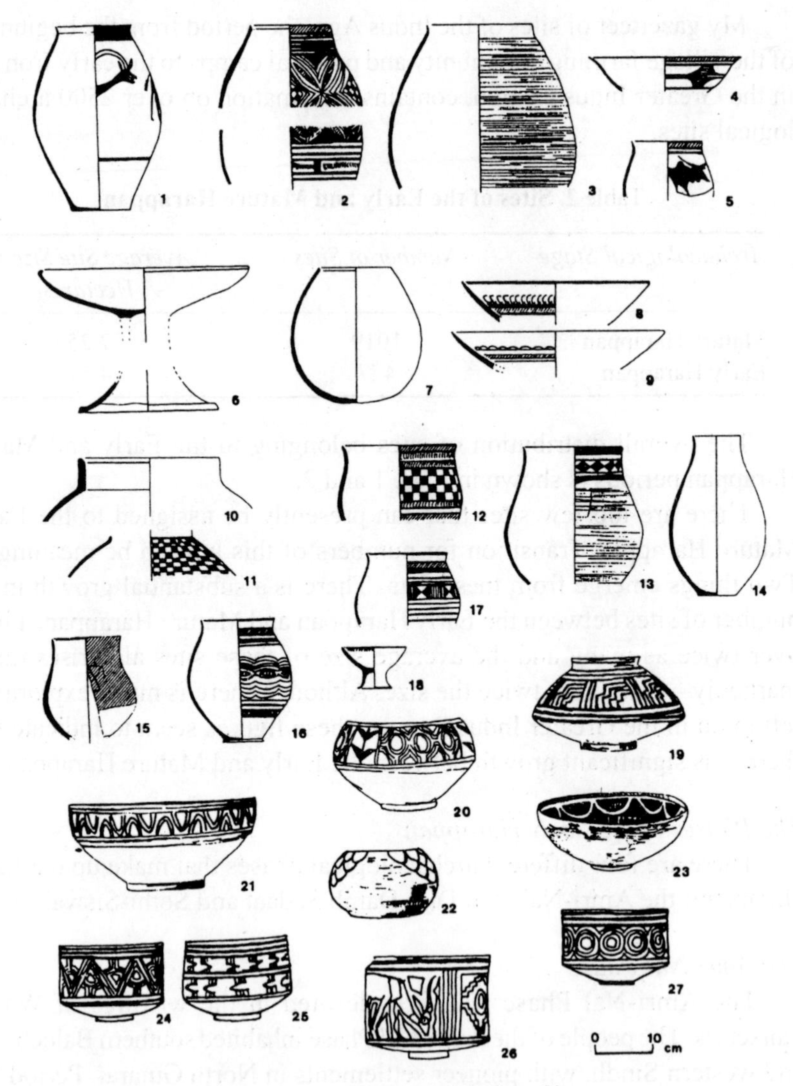

Fig. 3. Ceramics of the Amri-Nal Phase Sites

their mountain homes in the summer. Some of them began to exploit the pasture and agricultural resources of North Gujarat, as seen in places like Nagwada (Sonawane and Ajithprasad 1994) and Moti Pipli (Majumdar 1994).

The geographical distribution of Amri-Nal sites is shown in Fig. 4. Table 3 has information on site counts and size. The average size of the Amri-Nal Phase sites is below the mean of all Early Harappan sites.

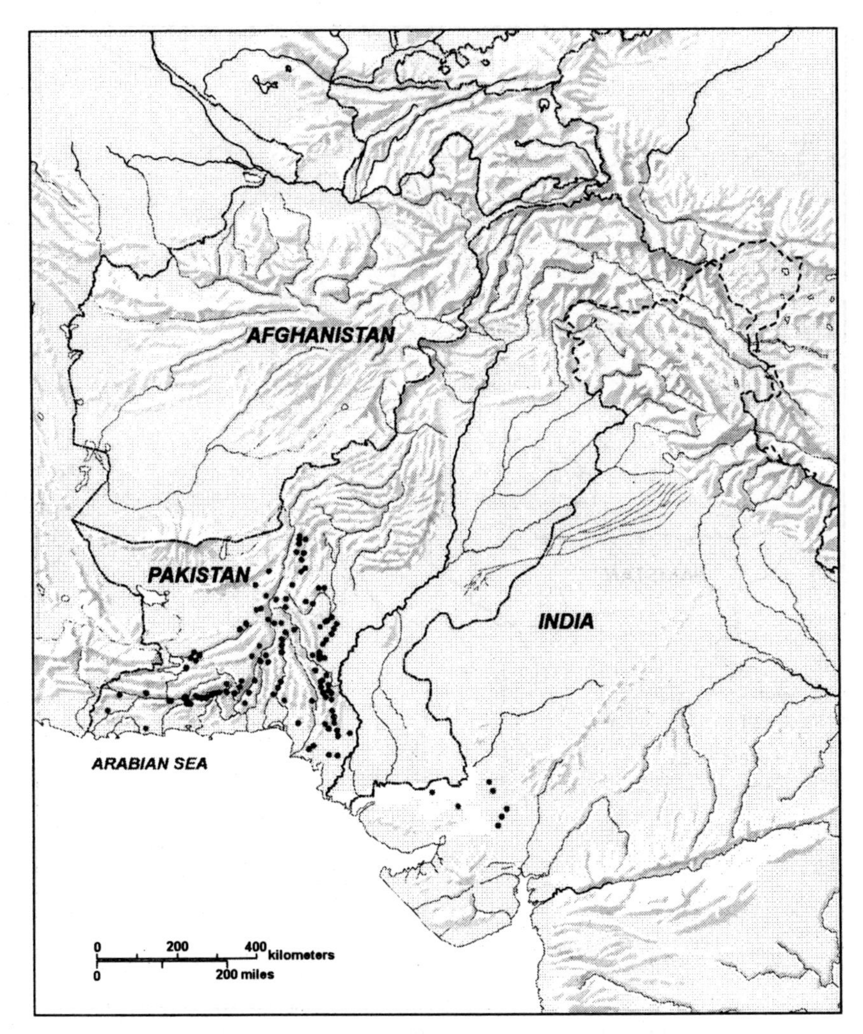

Fig. 4. Map of the Amri-Nal Phase Sites, *c.* 3200–2500 BC

Table 3. **Amri-Nal Phase**

Total Number of Sites	164
Average Site Size in Hectares	3.67
Estimated Total Settled Area in Hectares	602

There is an overlap between the Amri-Nal and the Kot Diji Phase sites in southwestern Sindh. Moreover, many of the Amri-Nal sites have some Kot Diji ceramics. These telltales indicate that there was probably rich

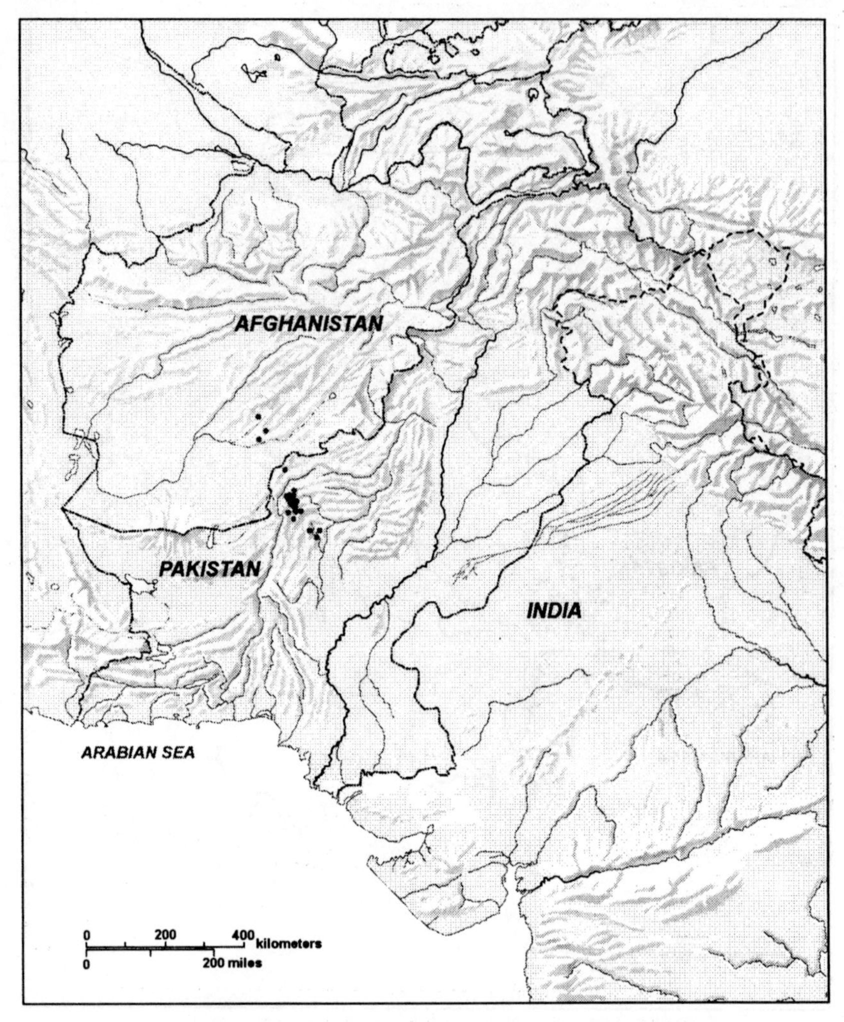

Fig. 5. Map of the Damb Sadaat Phase Sites, *c.* 3200–2500 BC

interaction between these peoples on many levels: economic, sociocultural, political.

The Damb Sadaat Phase

The Damb Sadaat Phase is found in the Quetta valley and surrounding valleys of northern Baluchistan. It is the smallest, and in some ways the most distinctive Phase of the Early Harappan. Settlement data are given in Table 4. The small average site size is striking.

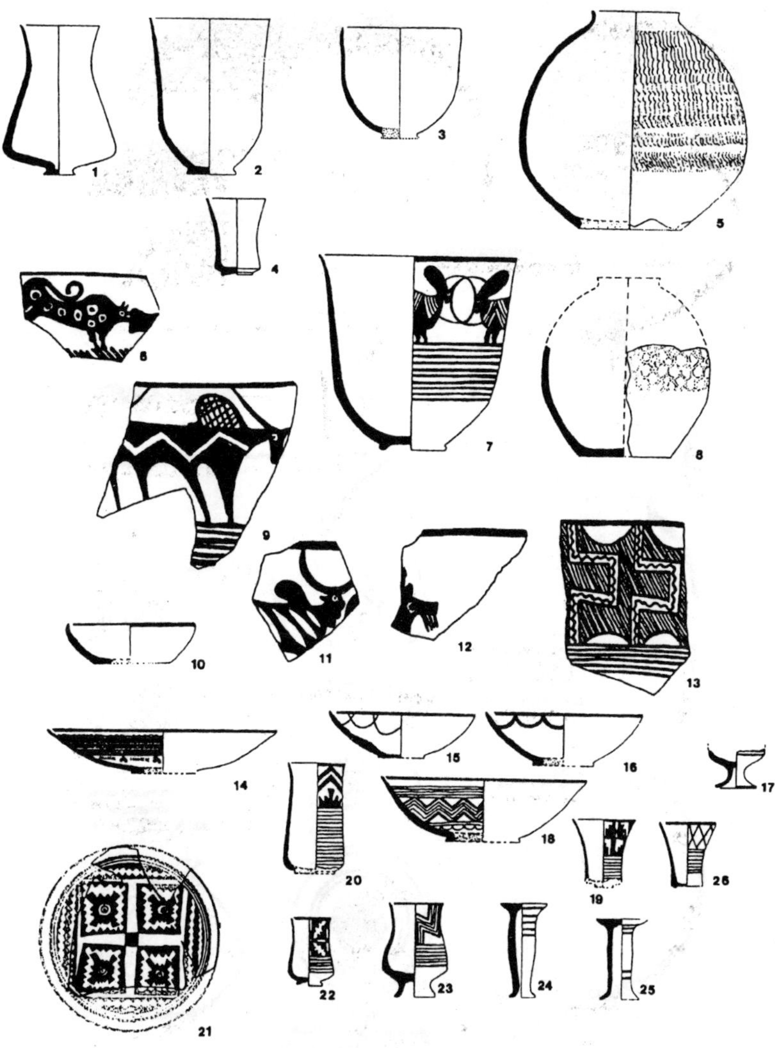

Fig. 6. Ceramics of the Damb Sadaat Phase

Table 4. **Damb Sadaat Phase**

Total Number of Sites	37
Average Site Size in Hectares	2.64
Estimated Total Settled Area in Hectares	98

The distribution of Damb Sadaat Phase sites is shown in Fig. 5 and the ceramics in Fig. 6.

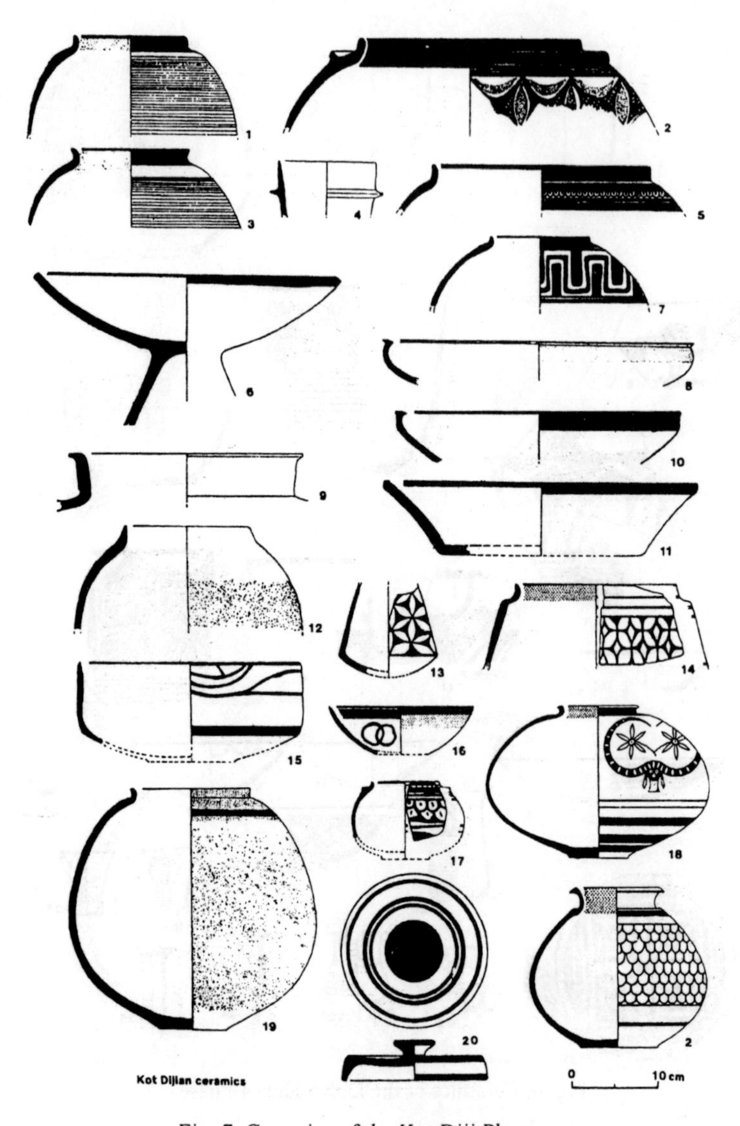

Fig. 7. Ceramics of the Kot Diji Phase

It is well-known that the ceramic motifs of the Damb Sadaat Phase are widely shared, extending into Central Asia. The valleys of Quetta and Pishin were key routes of communication between the Indus Plains and Afghanistan, and the sites of the Damb Sadaat Phase were key players in these communications.

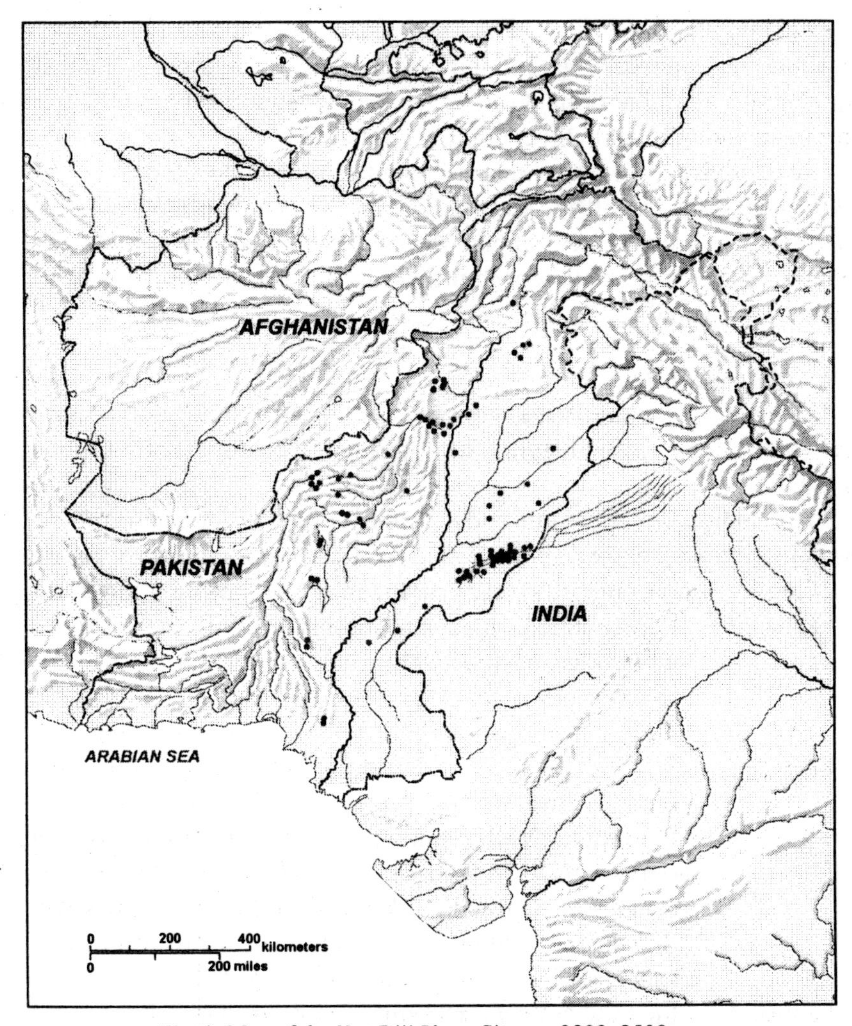

Fig. 8. Map of the Kot Diji Phase Sites, *c.* 3200–2500 BC

The Kot Diji Phase

The Kot Diji sites were a focus of Mughal's dissertation (1970). Settlement data for them are found in Table 5.

Table 5. **Kot Diji Phase**

Total Number of Sites	111
Average Site Size in Hectares	6.31
Estimated Total Settled Area in Hectares	700

Kot Diji Phase sites, on average, are the largest for the Early Harappan. This, and the relatively large number of Kot Diji sites, seem to indicate that they played an important role in the development of Indus urbanization. A selection of Kot Diji ceramics is found in Fig. 7.

Sites with Kot Diji ceramics are found as far south as the end of the Kirthar Range at a small site known as Phang. They are also in the Kirthar Piedmont, the alluvial areas of northern Sindh, the Punjab and Northwest Frontier. There is a small concentration in Cholistan, in the delta of the ancient Sarasvati (see Fig. 8).

The Sothi-Siswal Phase

There are broad similarities between Kot Diji and Sothi-Siswal ceramics as well as other assemblages. The Sothi-Siswal ceramics are illustrated in Fig. 9.

The ceramics of both Sothi and Siswal have been described in terms of the fabrics found at Kalibangan in Period I. These were originally laid out by B.K. Thapar, who identified six fabrics, which are designated A through F.

Fabric A: Poorly potted with painted designs in faint black. At times white was added. Kot Diji short-necked jars with a black band at the neck. A grooved ceramic generally called "Bhoot Ware" also occurs in the Kot Diji assemblage.

Fabric B: Rusticated lower portion and smooth upper portion of the pot. This ware closely resembles a ceramic type from the Quetta Valley known as Khojak Parallel Striated (Fairservis 1956:268; *IAR 1962–63*: 27) Kot Diji short-necked jars with a black band at the neck sometimes have this surface treatment. Periano Wet Ware in northern Baluchistan could also be classified as Fabric B.

Fabric C: Fine ware pottery with smooth outer surfaces. Slips in red, purple and plum red are present.

Fabric D: Thick sturdy ware used for storage jars, troughs and basins, The interior of Fabric D basins may be combincised. Grooved Bhoot Ware also occurs in this fabric.

Fabric E: Buff ware.

Fabric F: Grey ware (*IAR 1962-63*: 20–7)

Flange-neck jars, flat lids for pots and the globular jar with a short, vertical rim are important forms in both the Kot Diji and Sothi-Siswal assemblages.

Sothi-Siswal sites are found in Indian Punjab, Haryana and northern

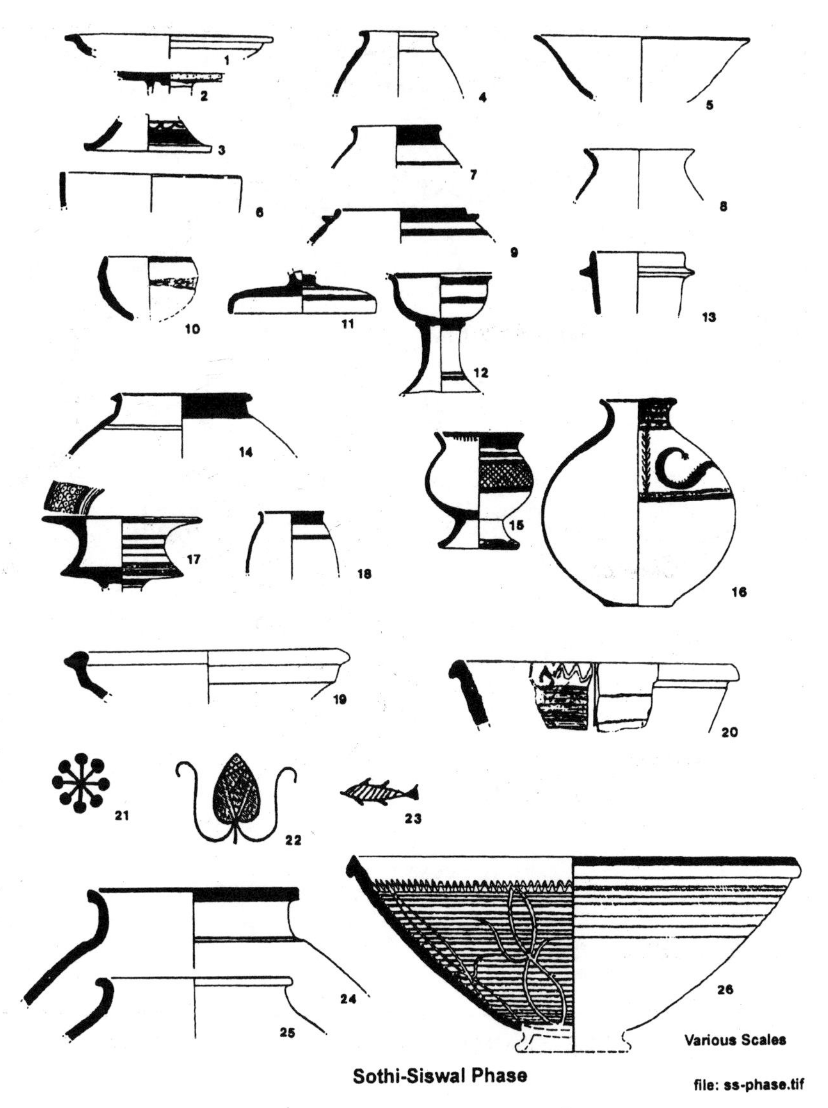

Fig. 9. Ceramics of the Sothi-Siswal Phase

Rajasthan. One Sothi-Siswal site (Navabans) is in the northern doab between the Ganga and Yamuna rivers (Fig. 10).

The boundary I have established between the Kot Diji and Sothi-Siswal sites is somewhat arbitrary. The commonalities in the ceramics have already been noted. They seem to form a continuum of variation. The ceramics of the Kot Diji sites in Sindh and the Sothi-Siswal sites in Haryana are

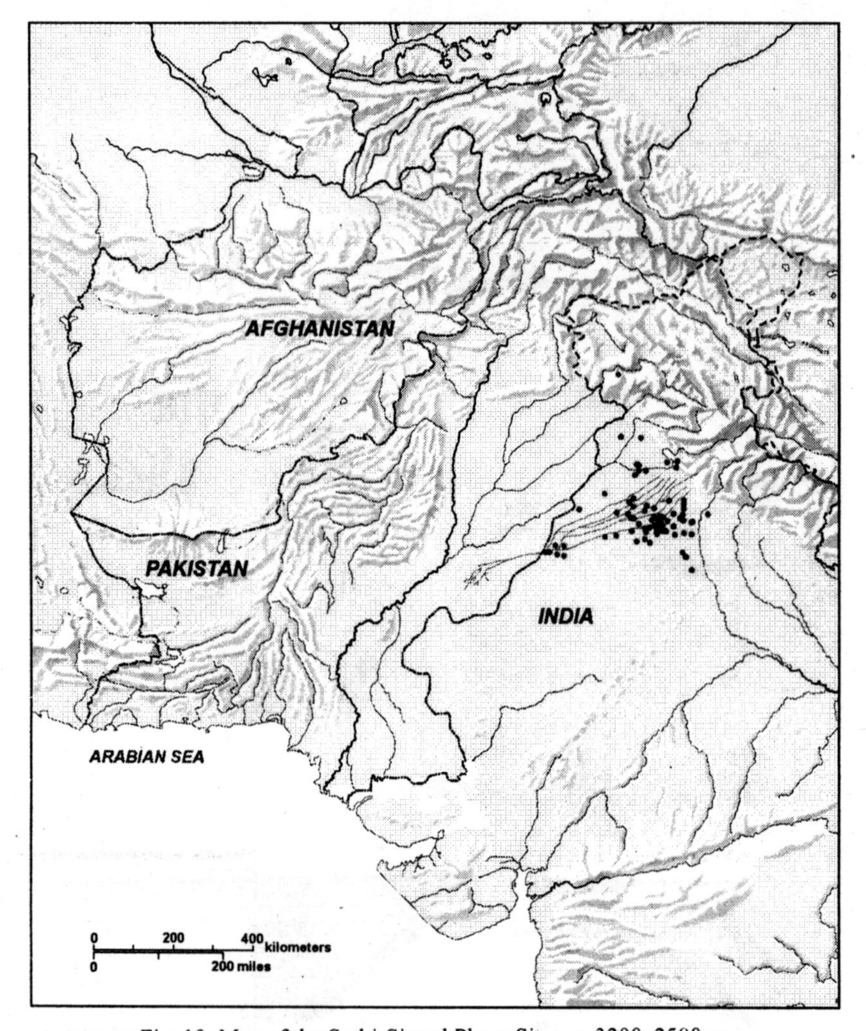

Fig. 10. Map of the Sothi-Siswal Phase Sites, *c.* 3200–2500 BC

different, but still share some features. If one looks at the ceramics from Kot Diji sites to the northeast of Kot Diji itself, they become increasingly Sothi-Siswal-like as one approaches, then passes, Kalibangan. Conversely, to begin at a place like Navabans and look at the ceramics from Sothi-Siswal sites to the southwest, they become increasingly Kot-Diji-like approaching, then passing Kalibangan. The border between the DK-G North and Sothi-Siswal sites is fuzzy but indicates strong lines of communication between the people who made and used these wares.

Settlement data on the Sothi-Siswal sites is given in Table 6. Average site size is the second highest for the Early Harappan Phases, in keeping with the close affinities to the Kot Diji assemblage.

Table 6. **Sothi-Siswal Phase**

Total Number of Sites	165
Average Site Size in Hectares	4.28
Estimated Total Settled Area in Hectares	706

The Early Harappan and Transitional Stages

The Early Harappan is remarkable in the sense that there are so few archaeological indicators of impending urbanization (Possehl 1990). The settlements are relatively small, there is little evidence for public architecture, social differentiation or craft specialization. There is no "proto" stage here for the still undeciphered Indus script, nor are there prototypes for the square stamp seals. We believe that these are features of the sociocultural systems of the Greater Indus Region that developed in the aforementioned Early/Mature Harappan Transition. This concept was first vetted in the 1980s (Possehl 1986: 96–8; 1990). It has been strongly supported by Jim Shaffer and Diane Lichtenstein (1989), who put their own stamp on the idea. A senior Indian scholar has seen the value of this period as a link, or "transition" between the Early Harappan and Mature Harappan. "There is now a complete rethinking amongst scholars on the problem of relationship between the Kot Diji or Early Indus-Saraswati culture-complex and Harappan or Mature Indus-Saraswati culture-complex. So far it was believed that the former directly developed into the latter but somewhat abruptly, but now we believe that the situation was not as simple as that there was definitely a transitional phase between the two cultural peaks. It is datable to the period between 2800 BC and 2600 BC, i.e., a time bracket of at least 200 years, may be even more" (Gupta 1996: 68). Jim Shaffer and Diane Lichtenstein have completed a review of the radiocarbon dates for the Indus Valley and Baluchistan and suggest that the Harappan Civilization is a fusion of the Bagor, Hakra and Kot Diji traditions or "ethnic groups" in the Ghaggar/Hakra Valley on the borders of India and Pakistan. This fusion ". . . appears to have been very rapid, reinforced no doubt by its own success. The earliest set of Harappan dates are from Kalibangan, in the northern Ghaggar/Hakra Valley at *c.* 2600 BC, while dates from Allahdino, Balakot and sites in Saurashtra indicate Harappan settlements were established in the southern Indus Valley by *c.* 2400 BC Possehl (1986: 96–8; Possehl and Rissman 1992) suggests a rapid origin of 150 years for the Harappan. We suggest it was even less, or 100 years, *c.* 2600–2500 BC. Within the next 100 years, the Harappan became the largest ethnic group within the Indus Valley. This rapid distribution rate was matched only by Harappan abandonment of large sections in the Indus Valley which was under way by *c.* 2000 BC, a process intensified by later hydrological changes. Whatever the Harappan group's organizational complexity, it was a cultural system promoting rapid territorial expansion" (Shaffer and Lichtenstein 1989:123).

There is some disagreement about the length of the Early/Mature Harappan Transition, but I believe that the shorter length is supported better by the radiocarbon dates available so far (Possehl 1993).

The Transitional Stage between the Early Harappan and the Mature Harappan has been found at Nausharo (Periods IC and ID), Mehrgarh (Period VIIC), Lal Shah, Gumla III, Ghazi Shah (Period II), Amri (Period II), Dholavira (Period I) and Harappa (Period II). There are also two sites in the Eastern Domain which seem to document the transition. R.S. Bisht has suggested that it is present at Banawali (Period IC) (Bisht 1982: 116; *IAR 1987–88*: 23–5). There is material from Kunal in Hissar district of Haryana that appears to be affiliated with the Transitional Stage (Khatri and Acharya 1995, in press). To the west there are other signs of emerging urbanization at Mundigak, in Subperiod IV, although the chronological considerations are immense and not clearly resolved.

The most obvious point that emerges from a synthesis of this information is that not much is known about the transition. But, at Amri II it appears most clearly in the ceramics with the beginning of what later flourishes as the Mature Harappan style. There is some burning at the end of Period II, but the significance is not understood. The Transitional Stage at Harappa has not yet been published with illustrations; however, the excavation team has discussed their material (Kenoyer 1991: 44–50) and three radiocarbon dates are available. The same is true for Ghazi Shah (Flam 1993); there has been discussion of the levels and two radiocarbon dates, but very little publication of finds from these levels. At Amri and Nausharo there is a good discussion of architecture, radiocarbon dates and the illustration of some finds, all of which support the notion that there was a continuous development of material culture that bridges the Early and Mature Harappan stages without a break in the living, cultural traditions of the times.

CONCLUSIONS

There is still much to be learned of the Early Harappan and the Early/Mature Harappan transition. What is seen today is an Early Harappan with some amount of diversity among the constituent archaeological assemblages. These peoples exploited a wide range of habitats from the mountains and valleys of Baluchistan to the alluvium of Sindh, Cholistan and Haryana. The Early/Mature Harappan Transition seems to be an archaeological environment within which will be seen the results of important sociocultural changes that led to the Harappan Civilization. The excavation of sites where this phase is represented should be considered a priority in Harappan archaeology.

REFERENCES

Bisht, R.S. 1982. Excavations at Banawali: 1974–77, in *Harappan Civilization: A Contemporary Perspective*, G.L. Possehl, ed. Delhi: Oxford & IBH Publishing Co. and American Institute of Indian Studies, pp. 113–24.

Excavations at Kalibangan, *Indian Archaeology—A Review, 1962–63*. New Delhi: Archaeological Survey of India, pp. 20–31.

Excavations at Banawali, *Indian Archaeology—A Review, 1987–88*. New Delhi: Archaeological Survey of India, pp. 21–27.

Fairservis, W.A. Jr. 1956. *Excavations in the Quetta Valley, West Pakistan*. New York: Anthropological Papers of the American Museum of Natural History, 45(2).

—1971. *The Roots of Ancient India*. New York: Macmillan.

Flam, L. 1993. Excavations at Ghazi Shah, Sindh, Pakistan, in *Harappan Civilization: A Recent Perspective*, G.L. Possehl, ed. Delhi: Oxford & IBH and American Institute of Indian Studies, sec. edn., pp. 457–67.

Gupta, S.P. 1996. *The Indus-Saraswati Civilization: Origins, Problems, Issues*. Delhi: Pratibha Prakashan.

Kenoyer, J.M. 1991. Urban Processes in the Indus Tradition: A Preliminary Model from Harappa, in *Harappan Excavation 1986–1990: A Multidisciplinary Approach to Third Millennium Urbanization*, R.H. Meadow, ed. Monographs in World Archaeology, 3, Madison: Prehistory Press, pp. 29–60.

Khatri, J.S., and Acharya, M. 1995. Kunal: A New Indus-Saraswati Site. *Puratattva* 25: 84–6.

— (in press). Kunal, in *An Encylopaedia of South Asian Archaeology*, G.L. Possehl, ed. New Delhi: Oxford & IBH Publishing Co.

Majumdar, A. 1994. Disposal of the Dead During the Chalcolithic Period of Gujarat. A Study of Harappan Burial Customs. M.A. Dissertation. Vadodara: Department of Archaeology and Ancient History, Maharaja Sayajirao University of Baroda.

Mughal, M.R. 1970. The Early Harappan Period in the Greater Indus Valley and Baluchistan. Ph.D. Dissertation. Philadelphia: Department of Anthropology, Univesity of Pennsylvania.

Possehl, G.L. 1986. *Kulli: An Exploration of Ancient Civilization in South Asia*. Durham:

Carolina Academic Press.

—1990. Revolution in the Urban Revolution: The Emergence of Indus Urbanization. *Annual Review of Anthropology* 19: 261–82.

—1993. The Date of Indus Urbanization: A Proposed Chronology for the Pre-urban and Urban Harappan Phases, in *South Asian Archaeology 1991*, A.J. Gail and G.J.R. Mevissen, eds. Stuttgart: Franz Steiner Verlag, pp. 231–49.

Possehl, G.L., and Rissman, P.C., eds., 1992. The Chronology of Prehistoric India: From Earliest Times to the Iron Age, in *Chronologies in Old World Archaeology*. R.W. Ehrich, ed., third edn., 2 vols., Chicago: University of Chicago Press, pp. 465–90 and 447–74.

Shaffer, J.G., and Lichtenstein, D.A. 1989. Ethnicity and Change in the Indus Valley Cultural Tradition, in *Old Problems and New Perspectives in South Asian Archaeology*, J.M. Kenoyer, ed. Madison: Wisconsin Archaeological Reports, 2, pp. 117–26.

Shaffer, J.G. 1992. The Indus Valley, Baluchistan and Helmand Traditions: Neolithic Through Bronze Age, in *Chronologies in Old World Archaeology*, R.W. Ehrich, ed., third edn., 2 vols. Chicago: University of Chicago Press, pp. 441–64 and 425–46.

Sonawane, V.H., and Ajithprasad, P. 1994. Harappa Culture and Gujarat. *Man and Environment* 19(1–2): 129–39.

6 ❖ The Mature Harappan

G.L. POSSEHL

THE Indus, or Harappan, Civilization[1] is now well dated by radiocarbon determinations and cross ties to Mesopotamia to the second half of the third millennium or *c.* 2500–1900 BC (Fig. 1). This is the period when northwestern India and Pakistan embraced a distinctive form of Bronze Age urbanization. It was preceded by the so-called "Early Harappan" (*c.* 3200–2600 BC) which is made up of not fewer than four regional aspects: the Amri-Nal, Kot Diji, Damb Sadaat and Sothi Siswal. The Early Harappan is discussed in greater detail elsewhere in this volume. There is now broad agreement (e.g., Possehl 1986: 96–8, 1990; Shaffer and Lichtenstein 1989; Gupta 1996: 68–100) that the Early and Mature Harappan periods are bridged by a transitional period. Some (Possehl and Shaffer and Lichtenstein) think of this as rather short (50–100 years), others make it somewhat longer (e.g., Gupta, at 200 years) but they agree that it was during this period that the distinctive features of urbanization developed in the greater Indus region.

Shaffer and Lichtenstein believe that the Indus Civilization is the fusion of the Early Harappan peoples: ". . . this fusion appears to have been very rapid, reinforced no doubt by its own success. The earliest set of Harappan dates are from Kalibangan, in the northern Ghaggar/Hakra Valley at *c.* 2600 BC; while dates from Allahdino, Balakot and sites in Saurashtra indicate Harappan settlements were established in the southern Indus Valley by *c.* 2400 BC. Possehl (1986: 96–8; Possehl and Rissman 1992) suggests a rapid origin of 150 years for the Harappan. We suggest it was even less, or 100 years, *c.* 2600–2500 BC. Within the next 100 years, the Harappan became the largest ethnic group within the Indus Valley. This rapid distri-

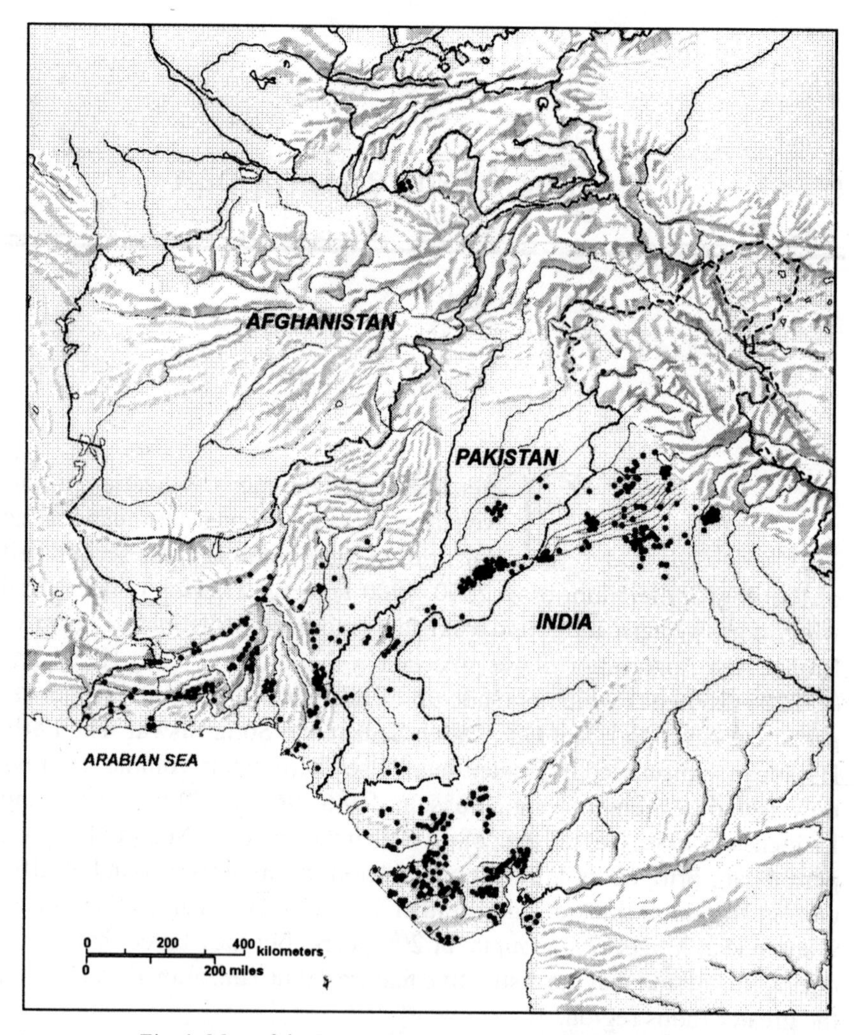

Fig. 1. Map of the Mature Harappan Sites, *c.* 2500–1900 BC

bution rate was matched only by Harappan abandonment of large sections in the Indus Valley which was under way by *c.* 2000 BC, a process intensified by later hydrological changes. Whatever the Harappan ethnic group's organizational complexity, it was a cultural system promoting rapid territorial expansion" (Shaffer and Lichtenstein 1989: 123).

Perhaps the most refreshing perspective in this book is the discussion of the Early/Mature Harappan Transition, which occupies an entire chapter (Gupta 1996: 68–100).

> "There is now a complete rethinking amongst scholars on the problem of relationship between the Kot Diji or Early Indus-Saraswati culture-complex and Harappan or Mature Indus-Saraswati culture-complex. So far it was believed that the former directly developed into the latter but somewhat abruptly, but now we believe that the situation was not as simple as that there was definitely a transitional phase between the two cultural peaks. It is datable to the period between 2800 BC and 2600 BC, i.e., a time bracket of at least 200 years, may be even more. The change over was thus not only slow and gradual but also smooth. The Transitional Phase has been clearly worked out at least at four very carefully excavated sites: Dholavira, Kot Diji, Kunal and Harappa" (Gupta 1996: 68).

The sites of Amri, Nausharo, Ghazi Shah and Banawali can be added to the list of sites where the Early/Mature Harappan Transition has been found.

The notion of a Mature Harappan thus suggests the growth and maturation of a cultural tradition that extends back to the beginnings of village farming communities and pastoral camps. Urbanization, not a state polity, is the single clearest marker of the sociocultural complexity of the Mature Harappan. Urbanization is a set of intertwined features and processes that are centered on the city as a large settlement inhabited by people organized in ranked social classes, based on craft and career specialities. Urbanization generally brings together many kinds of people, different ethnic and linguistic groups, into a sociocultural whole. In this sense the Indus Civilization was ethnically and linguistically complex. This kind of complexity is implied by the diverse "cultures" of the Early Harappan and the view expressed by Shaffer and Lichtenstein that the Mature Harappan is a "fusion" of these peoples. The peoples of the Mature Harappan knew the art of writing, engaged in long distance trade, both at sea and overland, and some of them probably lived abroad, in Mesopotamia (Parpola, Parpola and Brunswig 1977, Possehl 1994).

Trade between Mesopotamia and the Mature Harappan emerged from the study of Mesopotamia cuneiform texts, especially those from Ur. In a classic article entitled "Seafaring Merchants of Ur, " Leo Oppenheim (1954) noted that maritime trade was important to the Mesopotamian state, and the palace levied taxes on the imported copper (Oppenheim 1954: 13). The temple was also involved, as Oppenheim noted: "Travels to Telmun (Dilmun) are repeatedly mentioned in a group of tablets which come patently from the archives of the temple of the goddess Ningal and list votive offerings, incoming tithe, etc. The contexts suggest that returning sailors were wont to offer the deity in gratitude a share of their goods" (Oppenheim

1954: 7). Sailors offered the goddess Ningal small silver boats as thanks for their safety and good fortune (Oppenheim 1954: 8, fn. 8).

Most of the third millennium tablets from Mesopotamia that deal with maritime concerns in the Gulf relate to the country, or land, of Dilmum that can be shown to be the modern island of Bahrain and the adjacent Saudi Arabian coast. Two other places are prominently mentioned: the lands of Magan and Meluhha. Magan is now known to have been the vicinity of the Straits of Hormuz, and included Oman and the adjacent Iranian coast. Meluhha is then the area beyond Magan, and would have included the Makran, Indus Valley and Gujarat.

There are 76 citations to Meluhha in cuneiform documents prior to the reign of Hammurabi (Possehl 1996). The following products are mentioned:

Table 1: **Frequency of Citations of Products of Meluha in Cuneiform Texts**

A wood, Gis-ab-ba-me-luh-ha	12 attestations
Carnelian	8 attestations
A bird	8 attestations; but 5 as figurines
Mesu wood	7 attestations
Meluhhan style furniture	3 attestations
Copper	2 attestations
A ship of Meluhhan style	2 attestations
Lapis lazuli	1 attestation; but in an incantation
Pearls	1 attestation
Fresh dates	1 attestation
A dog of Meluhha	1 attestation
A cat of Meluhha	1 attestation
Gold	1 attestation

Ivory is not associated with the trade with Meluhha, although it is mentioned in connection with Dilmun. None of the texts inform us of the Mesopotamian products being sent directly to Meluhha, although there is some information on the products sent to Dilmun.

The cuneiform documents speak of trade that affected the kings of Akkad and their temples. Elites, the state and "national" institutions are involved. Archaeological research in the Gulf, and coast of the Saudi Arabian peninsula has informed us that there was another level of significant maritime activity based on subsistence fishing and trade. The subsistence activities during the third millennium have been especially well documented at sites on Ras al' Junayz and Ras al'Hadd (Cleuziou 1984, 92; Cleuziou and Tosi 1986, 1988; Cleuziou, Reade and Tosi 1989; Tosi 1986).

There is evidence for strong contacts between the Indus Civilization and Mesopotamia through the Gulf, using the maritime route. There is also good evidence that the Mature Harappans were in contact with the emerging states of northern Afghanistan and Central Asia using an overland route (Tosi 1979). The presence of the Mature Harappan site of Shortughai on the banks of the Amu Darya, documents a Mature Harappan presence there (Francfort 1989). This is, in fact, an outcome of contact between the Quetta Valley of northern Baluchistan and Central Asia that goes back at least as far as the Early Harappan. The presence of two Indus seals at Altyn Depe along with other Indus style artefacts further informs us of this relationship. But, unlike Mesopotamian artefacts, which are very scarce at Indus sites, there are Central Asian materials from Mohenjo-daro and Harappa.

There is an important conclusion emerging from this study of international trade, commerce and contact. The Harappan Civilization emerges as the eastern anchor of a network of routes, a very large interaction sphere, that included the Mesopotamian city states, the Gulf, Iranian Plateau and Central Asia. It also seems to have included a sea lane from the vicinity of the Straits of Hormuz, south to the mouth of the Red Sea, where the Indus Civilization figuratively "knocked on the back door of Dynastic Egypt". There is very little, if any, Egyptian material in prehistoric South Asia, and no Indus material in Dynastic Egypt (Dhavalikar 1993), but this route was important for the acquisition of millets by the Harappan peoples (Possehl 1986, 1997). I have come to think of this melding of peoples and economics of the second half of the third millennium BC as the "Middle Asian Interaction Sphere" (Fig. 2).

Another level of consideration is implied by the rather mechanical observation that the Indus Civilization "anchors" the eastern end of the Middle Asian Interaction Sphere. The Indus Civilization is also the easternmost expression of Bronze Age civilization in the Nile Valley-Near East-Central Asian-South Asian world region. There is nothing like it to the east, in the central and eastern Ganga Valley, or Madhya Bharat, the Deccan and South India. Travelling east one has to go to northwestern China to find glimmerings of urbanization and archaic state formation at a comparable time, and this is of an entirely different, independent cultural tradition.

There is an ecological variable that ties the ancient civilizations of the Middle Asian Interaction Sphere together. In 1961 Walter A. Fairservis,

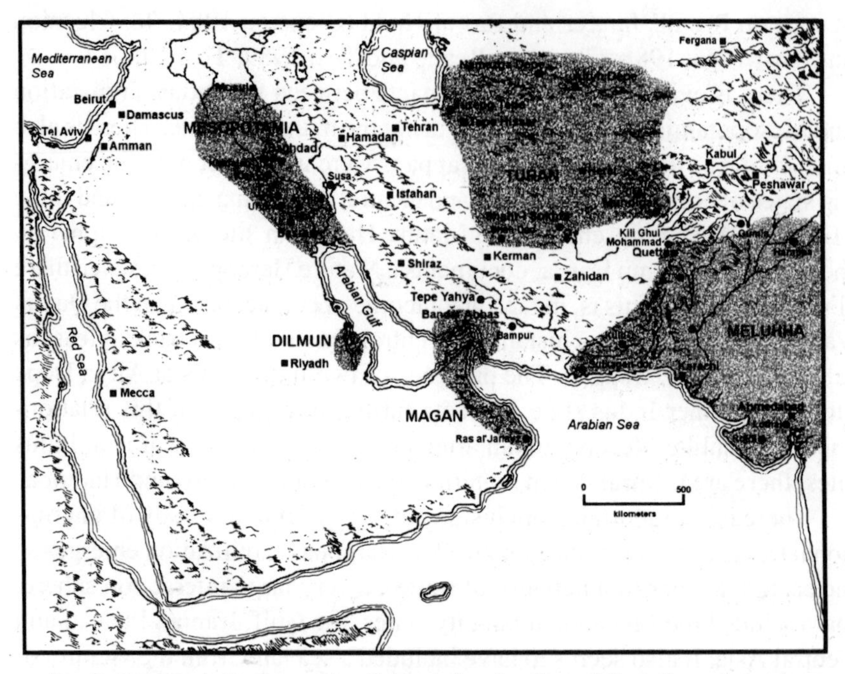

Fig. 2. 'Middle Asian Interaction Sphere' showing the melding of peoples and economies of the second half of the third millennium BC

Jr. pointed out that the Indus Civilization expanded to the limits of the wheat/barley growing zone of the subcontinent (1961: 5, 28). These are the grains that were first used as domesticated plants during the earliest phases of food production in the Nile Valley-Near East-Central Asian-South Asian region. Barley seems to have been the principal foodgrain in Sindh and the Punjab during Mature Harappan times. Wheat is known from Rojdi in Saurashtra at a comparable time. They are winter grasses that grow well under cold, damp conditions. Wild barley has been found from the Mediterranean to Baluchistan. Wheat has not been found that far east, but it might have been present. The Mature Harappan farmers used these grains everywhere and the limit of Mature Harappan sites closely approximates the modern boundaries of the wheat/barley zone of the subcontinent.

Wheat and barley were also the principal foodgrains in the other regions of the Middle Asian Interaction Sphere. This is an important, shared feature of these ancient civilizations, that rests on the observation that the eastern "anchor" of interaction also approximates the eastern limit of the zone, where wheat and barley were probably endemic, and/or could be adapted to local conditions. This observation about the natural world and the subsistence systems of humans should not be thought of as deterministic; but it does seem to be well founded in a great deal of archaeological and palaeobotanical work. Growing wheat and/or barley was a successful form of adaptation in ancient times. The people who used these plants, employed them to the limits of the niche, in the eastern, South Asian zone, at least.

I have observed that the strong ties and contacts of the Indus Civilization are to the west: the Gulf, the Iranian Plateau, Central Asia. There are also ties and contacts to the north, with the Northern Neolithic, possibly down the Ganga, and into Central India. Although further research might change this picture, today I do not believe they had the strength and intensity of the interaction with the west. The Northern Neolithic might be seen as an exception here, but these people were a near neighbour, and I do not believe that it materially changes the image of the larger picture. In the end we have third millennium urbanization, sometimes proto-urbanization, to the west of the Indus Civilization (the Nile Valley-Near East-Central Asian region) but not to the north, south or east. That is the big picture, and it is one that is formed along the contours of an environmental, or ecological variable. How did this come to be?

I am hard pressed to give a well rounded answer to this question, but I suspect that it rests firmly within the realm of culture and geography. The Indus peoples were expert managers of the wheat/barley/cattle/sheep/goat complex of domesticates. It was the basis of their livelihood and they tended to travel to places where these plants and animals survived well. They went to other places as well, to the north, south and east of the Indus Civilization, and peoples from these "other places" visited them. But, it was good sense not to imperil the fundamentals of food supply, so the tendency was for the frequency and strength of travel, and interaction to the west, toward the Iranian Plateau, Central Asia, the Gulf and Mesopotamia, where the subsistence system of the Mature Harappan peoples had common ground.

This interaction with the west would have had strong grounding in the subsistence system with the seasonal movement of animals from the mountains to the plains and back. There would have also have been a firm tie to the seasonal nature of the rainfall regime. Trade and commerce played a role, and it was probably true that the seasonal movement of pastoralists provided transpiration for trade goods, owned and purveyed by the pastoralists themselves, and/or by specialists in these fields. Tinkers, potters and other craftsmen are also frequently mobile. Travelling bards and storytellers, mendicants and simple wanderers may well have been part of this cultural scene of the third millennium. Exploiters of the sea, sailors and seafarers, also emerge from the textual and archaeological record as a significant part of the story of contacts between ancient India and the west.

The strength and intensity of interactions of the Harappan peoples with the west, and of peoples from the west with the Harappan peoples, was surely not constant, and the form or shape of the individuals and institutions that participated in them would have shifted and changed over time. But, what is beginning to emerge from the archaeological record, and to some degree the textual record of Mesopotamia, is that the third millennium, especially the second half of the third millennium, was a period of unprecedented interaction between and among the peoples of the Middle Asian Interaction Sphere, and that the Harappan Civilization was the eastern "anchor" of this institution.

NOTE

1. This ancient culture has attracted more than its share of nomenclature. When it was first discovered, Sir John Marshall referred to the materials from Mohenjo-daro and Harappa as "Indo-Sumerian Civilization" (Marshall 1924–25). In 1925–26 the term was dropped by Sir John: "And here I may say parenthetically that I shall use the term 'Indus' henceforth to designate the particular culture of the chalcolithic period which I have hitherto designated Indo-Sumerian, since the latter term is likely to imply a closer connection with Summer than now seems justified" (Marshall 1925–26: 75; see also Marshall 1926–27: 53).

Marshall attempted to make "Indus Civilization", never "Indus Valley Civilization", the standard and this was incorporated into the title of his great three volume work on Mohenjo-daro (Marshall 1931), but he was never quite successful. His colleagues in the Archaeological Survey of India, E.J.H. Mackay and M.S. Vats, saw this term as parochial since the civilization extended well beyond the confines of the Indus Valley, even if Marshall never intended a close geographical connotation for his name. Mackay preferred the notion of "Harappa Culture" taking the archaeological tradition of using the "type fossil" concept to name archaeological assemblages. This was the terminology used in Mackay's monograph on his excavations at Chanhu-daro (Mackay 1943). Marshall's disappointment in this choice of terms can be seen in a footnote appended to his preliminary report on these excavations (Mackay 1935–36: 39) that reads as follows: "This suggestion of Dr. Mackay has not found favour among other scholars, notably Sir John Marshall"—Editor.

M.S. Vats tended to follow the lead of G.R. Hunter, one of the early scholars working with the Indus script (Hunter 1929, 1932, 1934). Hunter coined the term "Proto-Indian" which was used by Vats, following his excavation at Rangpur (Vats 1934–35: 38). "Proto-Indian" is still current with some scholars, more so in Russia, and particularly with those involved with the Indus script and other iconographic topics.

I am not sure of the history of "Mature Harappan" as a term, but it is widely used in contemporary publications on this civilization. It was certainly a favourite in the writings of Walter A. Fairservis, Jr.

There is now a movement in some circles (Gupta 1993, 1996) to rename this archaeological culture the "Indus-Sarasvati Civilization". The primary justification for this shift is the very large number of Mature Harappan sites in the Cholistan Desert of Pakistan, in the ancient inland deltaic termination of the now dry Sarasvati River.

There are three reasons to resist "Indus-Sarasvati Civilization" as a term for the Indus Civilization. First, it is another parochial term, centering the Mature Harappan in a particular, and rather small, area of a vast civilization. It implies that the Harappans in Saurashtra and North Gujarat are outside the Mature Harappan, as are those in the Ganga-Yamuna Doab. And, what of the Kullis in Baluchistan, and Mature Harappan settlements like Sutkagen-dor, Miri Qalat and Sotka Koh? The second reason to resist this name change is the simple fact that there are already too many names given to this ancient culture—we only confuse matters for ourselves, but especially non-specialists, with this kind of "jockeying" and instability. Finally, the term "Indus-Sarasvati Civilization" is unacceptable to our colleagues in Pakistan. In this sense it tends to be divisive, and lead to contentiousness, which is unnecessary.

Parochialism seems to be a growing phenomenon associated with the study of the Indus Civilization. The field director of the recent excavations at Harappa has just published a book with the title *Ancient Cities of the Indus Valley Civilization* (Kenoyer 1998). This is a term that is no less narrow than "Indus-Sarasvati" and therefore not acceptable for the same reasons. Moreover, it is as unpalatable to many of our colleagues in India as "Indus-Sarasvati" is to the Pakistanis. . . .

REFERENCES

Cleuziou, S. 1984. Oman Peninsula and its Relations Eastward During Third Millennium, in *Frontiers of the Indus Civilization*, B.B. Lal and S.P. Gupta, eds. New Delhi: Books and Books, pp. 371–93.

—1992. The Oman Peninsula and the Indus Civilization: A Reassessment. *Man and Environment* 17(2): 93–103.

Cleuziou, S., and Tosi, M. 1986. Trial Excavation at Site RJ-2: The Bronze Age Mound, in *The Joint Hadd Project: Summary Report on the First Season*, S. Cleuziou and M. Tosi, eds. Rome: The Joint Hadd Project, pp. 9–25.

—1988. A Short Report on the Excavations of the Second Campaign at RJ-2, in *The Joint Hadd Project: Summary Report on the Second Season, November 1986- January 1987*, S. Cleuziou and M. Tosi, eds. Naples, pp. 11–26.

Cleuziou, S., Reade, J., and Tosi, M. 1989. *The Joint Hadd Project: Summary Report on the Third Season: October 1987-February 1988.* Rome: The Joint Hadd Project.

Dhavalikar, M.K. 1993. Early Contacts, in *India and Egypt, Influences and Interactions.* Mumbai: Marg Publications.

Fairservis, W.A. Jr. (1961). *The Harappan Civilization: New Evidence and More Theory.* New York: American Museum of Natural History, Novitates. no. 2055.

Francfort, H.P. 1989. *Fouilles de Shortughai: Recherches sur l'Asie Centrale Protohistorique.* Paris: Diffusion de Boccard.

Gupta, S.P. 1993. Longer Chronology of the Indus-Saraswati Civilization. *Puratattva* 23: 21–29.

—1996. *The Indus-Saraswati Civilization: Origins, Problems, Issues.* Delhi: Pratibha Prakashan.

Hunter, G.R. 1929. The Script of Harappa and Mohenjo-Daro and its Connection with Other Scripts. Ph.D. Dissertation, Oxford: Oxford University.

—1932. Mohenjo daro—Indus Epigraphy, *Journal of the Royal Asiatic Society of Great Britain and Ireland* 84: 466–503.

—1934. *The Script of Harappa and Mohenjo-Daro and its Connection with Other Scripts.* London: Kegan Paul, Trench, Trubner; reprint, 1993, New Delhi: Munshiram Manoharlal Publishers.

Kenoyer, J.M. 1988. *Ancient Cities of the Indus Valley Civilization.* Karachi: American Institute of Pakistan Studies and Oxford University Press.

Mackay, E.J.H. 1935–36. Excavations at Chanhu-daro, *Annual Report of the Archaeological Survey of India*, 1935–36: 38–44.

—1943. *Chanhu-daro Excavations,* 1935–36. American Oriental Series, vol. 20. New Haven: American Oriental Society.

Marshall, John. 1924–25. The Prehistoric Civilization of the Indus, Annual Report of the Archaeological Survey of India, 1924-25: 60–63.

—1925–26. Exploration, Western Circle, Mohenjo-daro, Annual Report of the Archaeological Survey of India, 1925–26: 72–98.

—1926–27. The Indus Culture, *Annual Report of the Archaeological Survey of India,* 1926–27: 51–60.

—, ed., 1931. *Mohenjo-Daro and the Indus Civilization.* 3 vols. London: Arthur Probsthain.

Oppenheim, A.L. 1954. Seafaring Merchants of Ur. *Journal of the American Oriental Society* 74: 6–17.

Parpola, S., Parpola, A., and Brunswig, R. 1977. The Meluhha Village: Evidence of Acculturation of Harappan Traders in the Late Third Millennium. *Journal of the Social and Economic History of the Orient* 20(2): 129–65.

Possehl, G.L. 1986. *Kulli: An Exploration of Ancient Civilization in South Asia.* Durham: Carolina Academic Press.

—1990. Revolution in the Urban Revolution: The Emergence of Indus Urbanization. *Annual Review of Anthropology* 19:261–82.

Possehl, G.L., and Rissman, P.C. 1992. The Chronology of Prehistoric India: From Earliest Times to the Iron Age, in *Chronologies in Old World Archaeology*, R.W. Ehrich, ed., third edn., 2 vols. Chicago: University of Chicago Press, pp. 465–90 and 447–74.

—1994. *Of Men. From Summer to Meluhha: Contributions to the Archaeology of South and West Asia in Memory of George F. Dales, Jr.*, J.M. Kenoyer, ed. Madison: Wisconsin Archaeological Reports 3, pp. 179–86.

—1996. *Meluhha. The Indian Ocean in Antiquity,* J.E. Reade, ed. London: Kegan Paul International in Association with the British Museum, pp. 133–208.

—1997. Seafaring Merchants of Meluhha, in *South Asian Archaeology 1995*, F.R. and B. Allchin, ed. New Delhi: Oxford & IBH Publishing Co., pp. 87–100.

Shaffer, J.G., and Lichtenstein, D.A. 1989. Ethnicity and Change in the Indus Valley Cultural Tradition, in *Old Problems and New Perspectives in South Asian Archaeology*, J.M. Kenoyer, ed. Madison: Wisconsin Archaeological Reports, 2, pp. 117–26.

Tosi, M. 1979. The Proto-urban Cultures of Eastern Iran and the Indus Civilization, in *South Asian Archaeology 1977*, M. Taddei, ed. Naples: Instituto Universitario Orientale, Seminario di Studi Asiatici, Series Minor 6, pp. 149–71.

—1986. Early Maritime Cultures of the Arab Gulf and the Indian Ocean, in *Bahrain Through the Ages, the Archaeology*, S.H.A.A. Khalifa and M. Rice, eds. New York: Kegan Paul International, pp. 94–107.

Vats, M.S. 1934-35. Trial Excavations at Rangpur, Limbdi State, Kathiawar, *Annual Report of the Archaeological Survey of India*, 1934–35: 34–38.

7 ❖ Harappan Civilization: Post-Urban Phase

V.H. SONAWANE

INTRODUCTION

CULTURAL transformation or change is a continuous process with varying degrees of intensity. It involves factors like human adjustments to prevailing environmental and social conditions of the region. Culture change is also multidirectional and the degree and nature of change varies in time and space. Precisely, therefore, the beginning, growth and decline of the Harappan culture, like other cultures, has been categorized into separate phases termed differently by various scholars (Rao 1963; Mughal 1970; Possehl 1977, 1980, 1984, 1993). In order to eliminate the confusion created by the indiscriminate use of the terms pre- and/or Eariy Harappan and the often misused notion of a Late Harappan, Possehl (1992a: 118) has proposed an alternative terminology for the Harappan cultural tradition using the terms pre-Urban, Urban and post-Urban phases indicating socio-cultural and technological development in various stages of the Harappan occupation. In this system too, although the Urban phase is rather well defined through type-fossils and several other settlement features, the pre-Urban and post-Urban phases are not so clearly defined. There seems to be a lack of consistency in the material relics from different sites of both the pre-Urban and post-Urban phases. Moreover, it must be noted that these three divisions are not necessarily time brackets applicable throughout the entire Harappan region (Sonawane and Ajithprasad 1994: 130).

Before going into details of the post-Urban phase, it is pertinent to note various aspects which led scholars to define the Urban phase of Harappan Civilization. These broad parameters include large size settlements, monumental architecture, long distance trade, craft specialization, class hierarchy, state organization as well as diagnostic artefacts such as Indus seals, ceramic forms like goblets, perforated cylindrical jars and jars with 'S' profiles often decorated with intricate or naturalistic painted motifs. In addition, triangular terracotta cakes, kidney shaped inlays, long chert blades of Rohri origin, etc., as suggested by Childe (1950) and Wheeler (1968: 63), are also characteristic features of the Harappan settlements associated with the Urban/Mature phase. However, with the renewed research on the above-mentioned aspects of Urban/Mature Harappan phase, it is clear that the presence or absence of these features would depend on multiple factors like location and nature of the settlements.

The entire gamut of the Harappan Civilization in its Mature phase is thought to be urbanized giving an impression that all the settlements during this phase are of urban character. In fact, in this context, it is observed that the number of small settlements representing rural aspects of the Harappan culture are far more in number than the urban centres. It is a well-known fact that urban centres cannot exist without a strong rural base. A glance at the settlement pattern reveals that even during the Mature Harappan phase, village or rural settlements existed in clusters around the primary urban settlements, thereby demonstrating a symbiotic relationship between the two (Sonawane and Mehta 1985: 38). It would therefore be far fetched to expect all the features of urbanism from any single site representing the mature cultural phase. One of the first casualties in the wake of these new studies is the concept of Harappan homogeneity. This observation is especially true when it comes to the regional diversities within the Harappan Civilization, particularly in the far flung areas of its expansion.

POST-URBAN PHASE

The very term post-Urban phase indicates that it does not mark the end of a cultural tradition but suggests the termination of an Urban phase within it as a process of localization and invariably marks the collapse of a flourishing civilization. The preceding Urban/Mature phase was, perhaps, more in line with the concept of civilization while the post-Urban phase was a poor reminder of this glorious past. This phase is identified with the archaeological assemblages which follow the cultural continuity of the earlier Urban/Mature phase but appear when the homogeneous Harappan culture declines. This phenomenon appears to be the outcome of the normal process of cultural transformation in Harappan culture and changes in the internal interaction of the society due to general economic decline. Obviously, this feature explains how, when the urban fabric of a culture disintegrates, the material culture becomes poor. It also witnessed a general decline in the civic standards and marks a devolutionary trend or stage. In fact this cultural phase represents the reversal of all the abstract criteria of urbanization as laid down by Childe (1950) and discussed by Adams (1966: 10–11). Ghosh has identified this cultural phase with those which are later than the Mature Harappan but still have affinities with it in a degenerate form (Dikshit 1981–83: 55). Dales observed that with the decline of this civilization, the sophisticated Harappan traits were watered down by mingling with the impoverished local cultures, until what was once distinctively Harappan was diluted to the point of non-existence (Dales 1966). Possehl, in the context of Gujarat, believes that the level of socio-cultural attainments which existed throughout its Mature phase was slowed down in its later stage. It was centrally less organized, less differentiated and less specialized than the Urban phase (Possehl 1980: 20). Whereas, in the light of recent studies, Shaffer considered it as a process of decentralization and localization which gave rise to regional cultural expressions rather than extinction (Shaffer 1992). This stage is the result of the breakdown of the urban fabric of the Harappa Civilization and represents a stage of readjustment by an urban system to a rural setting without losing its basic ethos (Gupta 1993: 58). Chitalwala remarks that the existence of both cognate and extraneous cultural strains which are easily identifiable and have not metamorphosed into a wholly new cultural entity, showing Harappan affinity even in its barest outlines, could be regarded as post-Urban (Chitalwala 1985: 58). On similar lines, Lal has tried to define the term Late Harappan as a culture which has transformed itself from the Mature Harappan, while losing some of the latter's traits and evolving some new ones, but still identifiable as having been derived from the latter (Lal 1997: 263).

The idea of devolution and, therefore, a post-Urban phase of the Harappan Civilization was first expressed by N.G. Majumdar in 1928 at the site of Jhukar by identifying a pottery type which was in certain ways different from the Mature Harappan. The cultural strata representing Jhukar type of pottery showed occupational and cultural continuity of the earlier Mature Harappan tradition at the site (Majumdar 1934: 154). A similar situation also prevailed at Amri, Chanhu-daro and Mohenjo-daro; however, the material culture indicating the lifestyle of the people reflected adverse economic conditions. Mackay later pointed out that the structural sdata from the late levels of Mohenjo-daro are relatively poor in comparison to the preceding levels (Mackay 1938: 06).

These observations, in turn, evoked speculations about the causes of changes towards the deterioration and end of the Harappan Civilization. Catastrophic climatic changes, floods (Marshall 1931), vagaries of the Indus river (Mackay 1938: 6), Aryan invasion (Wheeler 1947), violent tectonic uplifts in the lower reaches of the Indus resulting in the ponding of flood waters (Raikes 1964; Dales 1966; Misra 1984), an overly taxed subsistence system (Fairservis 1967), and overall decline in the international trade in the beginning of the second millennium BC were some of the proposed explanations. These explanations mainly depend upon models of diffusion and culture change to explain the deterioration and abandonment of the cities of this Civilization; however, no single cause can be isolated as a complete explanation of the process of change or end. In fact, all these theories point towards a cultural devolution rather than an abrupt end. In cultural devolution also one could observe that its rate and configuration varied from region to region, depending on a number of local factors. The discovery of a large number of post-Urban settlements spread over different parts of the entire domain of the Harappan Civilization has removed the last lingering doubts about the continuity of the Harappan tradition even after the decline of the major urban centres. The current research, thus, shows that the Harappan culture did not end abruptly as was thought before (Possehl 1980: 13).

The post-Urban phase of the Indus Civilization is an integral part of total spread of this culture beginning from the Afghan area in the extreme north to the Godavari basin in the south and from the Makaran coast in the west to western Uttar Pradesh in the east. This area comprises a large portion of the Indian subcontinent and includes Sindh, Punjab, Baluchistan, Kashmir, Haryana, Rajasthan, western Uttar Pradesh, Gujarat and northern Maharashtra. A large number of sites representing the post-Urban Harappan phase have been noted from these different regions which formed a part of the Harappan culture zone.

Gujarat

The Harappan concept, derived from the findings at major sites in the Indus valley, significantly influenced the interpretations of the discoveries in Gujarat. Initially M.G. Dikshit's (1950) and B. Subbarao's (1958) recognition of the Chalcolithic or regional phenomena at some of the Harappan settlements of Saurashtra was neglected or even opposed. Against this background, Rao in his renewed excavations at Rangpur in 1953 tried to ascertain the nature of the material relics and was able to identify the Harappan character by following the type-fossil analogy method. Nevertheless, he had also observed that much of the materials at the site was at variance with true Harappan material and stratigraphically these "sub-Indus" elements predominantly came from the upper levels (Rao 1963). Subsequently, Possehl and Raval (1989) claimed regionality of the Harappa culture after a systematic analysis of the excavated materials from Rojdi. Although some of the classic Harappan traits are found at Rojdi, the ceramic assemblage has nothing in common with classic Harappan pottery. Furthermore, the radiocarbon dates indicate that the early levels at Rojdi were contemporaneous with the Mature/Urban phase of the Harappa culture. Thus "Sorath Harappan", a regional manifestation of the Harappa culture in Gujarat as distinct from the "Sindhi Harappan" was proposed as an explanatory model. This changed drastically the traditional picture about the existence of sites in Saurashtra during the Urban Harappan phase (Possehl 1992b). Furthermore, the region of Saurashtra and the western part of north Gujarat along the eastern margin of the Little Rann of Kutch revealed sites of the pre-Urban phase showing the existence of indigenous regional Chalcolithic cultural traditions involving non-Harappan pottery types such as the pre-Prabhas ware (Dhavalikar and Possehl 1992), Padri ware (Shinde and Kar 1992), Micaceous Red ware (Rao 1985: 393–95; Herman and Krishnan 1994), Black and Red ware (Rao 1979: 24) and Anarta ware (Ajithprasad and Sonawane 1993) prior to the penetration of the Harappans in this area (Sonawane and Ajithprasad 1994: 130–36). Therefore, one has to view the development of post-Urban phase in the light of antecedent Urban and pre-Urban phases of Gujarat.

With the recent radiocarbon determinations from Rojdi (Possehl and Raval 1989: 12) and Vagad (Sonawane and Ajithprasad 1994: 133) all the reported sites of Rangpur IIB category in Saurashtra now fall in the time bracket of Urban/Mature Harappan phase. Long ago, Misra also had suggested that Rangpur IIB is part of Rangpur IIA only (1965: 45–46). Therefore, in the light of reanalysis of the excavated data, the post-Urban phase in Gujarat is now represented by Lothal B, Rangpur IIC and III, Rojdi C, Kuntasi II (Dhavalikar et al. 1996), Padri IIIB (Shinde 1992), Vagad IB and IC (Sonawane and Mehta 1985) and Dholavira stages VI and VII (Lal 1997: 137–39). The excavations carried out at Kanewal (Mehta et al. 1980), Nesadi (Mehta 1984), Ratanpura (Sonawane 1994–95: 8–9) and Oriyo Timbo (Rissman and Chitalwala 1990) also demonstrate the existence of this non-Urban phase.

It is clear from the fact that though certain forms like 'Indus goblets', beakers and 'S' shaped jars almost disappear, other characteristic ceramics, including the perforated jar, continue with slight changes in shape and decoration; however, the fabric became coarser and in painted design linear patterns became common in contrast to the diagnostic Mature Harappan naturalistic decorations. The convex-sided bowls developed a blunt or even sharp carination at the shoulder. The stud of the handled bowl which became longer at Rangpur did not undergo any change at Rojdi, where long and short handles occur at all levels. The stem part of the dish-on-stand became squat while the projected dish acquired a beaded rim. Lustrous Red ware which is actually introduced in the upper levels of Rangpur IIC became the prominent ceramic type during period III. The white painted Black and Red ware also became more conspicuous by its presence. Graffiti on pottery, some of which resemble the signs of the Harappan script also occur, reminding us of the continuity of the earlier tradition though in a reduced frequency. Although classical Reserved Slip ware totally dis-appeared, its crude variant as an imitation was found lingering at a few sites. Some elements of Jhukar pottery were also observed in the ceramic assemblage in its upper strata at Dholavira.

This transformation is not reflected in ceramics alone. Among other artefacts, long chert blades, a material that had been imported from the Sukkur Rohri hills of Sindh, Pakistan, was no longer available because of the steep fall in trade and were substituted by smaller blades of locally available chert and chalcedony. Perhaps for the same reason, the cubical chert/agate weights, so diagnostic of the Urban phase, are no longer found and replaced by truncated spherical weights of sandstone and similar material. Though terracotta beads become common, simple varieties of semi-precious stone beads and shell objects did continue to some extent because of the local availability of the required raw material. In addition, there are stray occurrences of terracotta triangular cakes, sporadic finds of stamped seals with only inscriptions and devoid of the usual animal or other figure depictions. The overall decline in the material culture of this phase is also reflected in the use of metal objects.

The deterioration in settlement pattern is also very explicit as compared to the earlier phase. The acropolis, warehouse and dockyard at Lothal were abandoned. Even the house floors were now made of brickbats collected from earlier constructions. The situation of Rangpur is not much different. The circular huts built out of bricks robbed from previous structures at Dholavira again suggest the adverse economic conditions of the people.

Stone structural remains found at Rojdi and Kuntasi and mud constructions at Prabhas Patan and Padri reflect the overall decline in the planning of settlements. The archaeological data recovered from these sites witnesses clear signs of shrinkage in the size of settlements during this cultural phase.

The other category of settlements exhibiting nondurable architectural features comprising simple round huts with wattle-and-daub walls, as seen at Kanewal, Vagad and Nesadi, are far more in number. These have been interpreted as small rural villages or dry season pastoral camps, where people were engaged in agricultural and pastoral subsistence activities. Intensive survey carried out by Possehl (1980), Bhan (1886), Chitalwala (1979), Momin (1979) and by the team of archaeologists from the M.S. University of Baroda (Ajithprasad and Sonawane 1993), particularly in Saurashtra and western part of north Gujarat, revealed that most of the sites representing Rangpur IIB (Urban phase) were continued during period IIC; however there is a marked decline in the number of settlements thereafter which are associated with Rangpur III—Lustrous Red ware sites (Bhan 1992). The recently discovered sites in north Gujarat offer a good example of the dispersed type of settlement pattern in contrast to that of linear-dendritic pattern of Saurashtra. The pattern of settlements in Saurashtra is mostly controlled by various river systems, whereas in north Gujarat it was based on locational variables of relict sand dunes associated with inter-dunal depressions forming ponds rather than rivers. Whereas the majority of Saurashtra sites are attributed to a shift in the pattern of land use from *rabi* to *kharif* crops, based on an agrarian economy (Possehl 1980: 54), north Gujarat, because of its typical ecological and environmental factors, favoured pastoral activities. The availability of excellent grassland, water, patchy appearance of thin cultural deposits and a high frequency of animal bones suggest that sites in north Gujarat may have served as temporary or seasonal camps engaged in pastoral activities (Bhan 1992: 175–79; Sonawane 1994–95: 8–10). On the other hand, only ten sites of this phase have been reported from Kutch so far. It seems that, after having served as a corridor during the Urban/Mature phase, most of the sites in Kutch were abandoned, most probably because of its inhospitable terrain and climate.

The cultural variables seen in subsistence and settlement pattern therefore show a lack of standardization and homogeneity. The small size of settlements with non-descriptive architectural pattern, reduced number of items of material culture and thin habitational deposits corroborate this assumption. Although there was certainly a decline in the material prosperity, a basic continuity of the Harappan tradition is still observed in the presence of some lingering features of the Harappan assemblage.

Maharashtra

The Gujarat Harappans played a key role in the penetration of the Harappan culture further south into Maharashtra. The interaction must have taken place in the Tapi river basin which acts as a buffer zone for the movement of human populations. The Harappans may have gone beyond the Kim estuary of south Gujarat into the central Tapi basin where about 50 sites have been discovered by Sali (1970) in Dhule district of Maharashtra; however, much of our understanding is based on the excavated data available from Daimabad, a fairly large settlement, located in the upper Godavari basin in Ahmednagar district of northern Maharashtra (Sali 1993). Daimabad is considered as the southern outpost of the Harappan culture. The available data suggests that the Harappans never occupied Maharashtra during the Urban/Mature phase.

Phase II at Daimabad represents a post-Urban Harappan occupation, sandwiched between two regional cultures named after the Savalda ware and the Buff and Cream ware. The characteristic finds were two terracotta button seals and potsherds bearing the Harappan script, a terracotta seal, a broken copper celt and a leaf-shaped gold bead reminding one undoubtedly of the Harappan cultural traits. The exposed structural remains suggest the use of mud as well as mud bricks. The moulded mud bricks used here conform to the standard Harappan 1:2:4 ratio. Although the pottery was of an inferior quality, it shows affinity with the post-Urban pre-Lustrous Red ware Saurashtra tradition. Apart from these, the chance discovery of an unstratified hoard of four massive bronzes from Daimabad is quite unique. Stylistically, they are different in execution and technique from other Harappan bronzes. Their superior quality and workmanship has posed a question regarding their antiquity. However, Dhavalikar (1993) has most convincingly argued that the hoard belongs to the post-Urban Harappan phase at Daimabad. The hoard consists of an exquisite chariot pulled by a pair of bulls, an elephant, a rhinoceros and a water buffalo with which the Harappans were quite familiar (Chitalwala 1985: 61).

Rajasthan

To assess the situation in Rajasthan, one has to depend on the data gathered from northeastern Rajasthan, a zone of Harappan domain. Except Kalibangan, not a single noteworthy site has been excavated so far. The prolonged excavations at Kalibangan did not reveal evidence of the survival of the settlement during the post-Urban phase. The reason for the abandonment of Kalibangan and, for that matter, other sites in the region by the end of Urban phase seems to be the drying up of the Ghaggar river which was the main or perhaps the only source of water supply to sustain the human populations. Fifty sites representing the post-Urban phase have however been discovered by Mughal (1990) in the adjoining Hakra area of Cholistan, in the former Bahawalpur state of Pakistan. All these sites are characterized by the Cemetery H culture. Unfortunately, none of these sites have been excavated and one is therefore not in a position to discuss the transformation from the Urban/Mature Harappan phase to the Cemetery H phase.

Haryana

In Haryana, particularly in the valleys of the Saraswati, Drishadvati, Sibi and Yamuna, the settlements representing post-Urban Harappan phase are comparatively more frequent than the Urban/Mature phase sites. There are many small to relatively large rivers in this region which form part of the Ghaggar (ancient Saraswati) system. Unlike the middle Ghaggar valley, water was not much of a problem during the Harappan times in its upper region and hence we find a good deal of evidence relating to the post-Urban Harappan phase. It was observed that most of these later sites are located away from the perennial rivers or found generally outside the flood plains of seasonal streams. The excavations carried out at Banawali (Bisht 1987), Balu (Singh and Bhan 1982), Mitathal (Bhan 1975) and Siswal (Bhan 1971–72) revealed a cultural sequence starting from pre-Urban to post-Urban through Urban phase. On the other hand, the site of Bhagwanpura (Joshi 1978) tells the story beyond the post-Urban phase, to a point of overlap between an amalgam of various trends derived through a long process of devolution from the Harappan, Baran and Kalibangan I cultures, and the Painted Grey ware culture.

To begin with at Banawali, the cultures of periods I and II are comparable with Kalibangan I and II, representing pre-Harappan and Mature Harappan periods respectively. However, period II was marked by the arrival of newcomers after desertion of the site by the Harappans. It seems that the settlement during this period was confined to the eastern periphery of the mound only and that too outside the earlier fortification. The structural remains of clay-walled houses containing clay-bins, internally plastered storage pits, fire places and *tandoors* were found within a deposit measuring about 50 cm in thickness. So far as the ceramic assemblage is concerned, all classical Harappan shapes and painted decorations are found to be absent, yet surprisingly period I pottery types continued with a slight or pronounced modification. By and large, it has shown strong genetic relationship with two distinct ceramics i.e., Kalibangan period I and the Bara pottery (Bisht 1987: 152). Likewise, none of the characteristic artefacts of the Mature Harappan period was found in the antiquities of period III except for some small pieces of baked clay which are reminiscent of the Harappan triangular terracotta cakes. Therefore, Lal (1997: 264–65) has rightly pointed out that Banawali does not give us the story of an *in situ* devolution of the Mature Harappan culture itself; instead, it presents a *fait accompli*—a culture distanced from the Mature Harappan both in time and content. Qualitatively, this last phase here, it may be noted, had no Urban insignia.

On the contrary, the evidence from Balu shows a transition from the Urban to the post-Urban phase. A clear reflection of this trend is seen in the material remains obtained from the levels of Balu C, which is post-Kalibangan II. As usual, though there were changes in the ceramics, the size of the bricks remains the same, as in Balu B. Moreover, burnt brick drains were also noticed in this phase suggesting that civic standards did not yet completely disappear.

In this regard, the Mitathal excavation offers an interesting clue. Here, period II has been divided into A and B. In period IIA not only did the elements of period I which is similar to that of Kalibangan I continue but those of typically Mature Harappan culture are also incorporated, while one could see a deterioration in the cultural equipment from period IIA to IIB. Some of the pottery shapes occur in their modified forms. The dish of dish-on-stand now has a drooping rim. Some of the vessels have a long neck that gradually flares out and ends up in a wide mouth with an everted rim and bowl-shaped lid with a central knob. Similar deterioration is also observed in the construction of poor quality mud brick structures. The terracotta biconical beads underwent typological evolution whereas toy cart wheels became comparatively thicker and smaller. The triangular terracotta cakes were replaced either by round or oblong varieties and the Harappan script survived in the form of graffiti only.

The excavation at Bhagwanpura revealed a twofold cultural sequence i.e., sub-period IA and IB (Joshi 1993). Assignable to IA were the authors of the post-Urban Harappan phase who first established their settlement over the alluvial deposit of the Saraswati. A solid, sizable mud-platform raised as a protective measure against the floods of the Saraswati harkens back to the Harappan method of planning settlements. Harappan Red ware—

plain and painted—was a predominant pottery type. The most distinctive forms are dish-on-stand with drooping rim, jars with long splayed out necks and everted rims, thin flasks, button-based goblets and cups. Among the painted designs pipal and banana leaves were very common. However, beakers and perforated jars were absent in the Harappan repertoire. The excavator also refers to a thick Grey ware as well as Baran pottery. Besides this, the possibility of Cemetery H affiliation of some pottery forms may be only superficial since the typical Cemetery H forms and painted designs have not been reported from this level. The presence of terracotta bulls, toy cart-wheels with central hubs, bangles, copper rods and pins, faience beads and bangles, beads of semi-precious stones and bone pins in the antiquities certainly points towards the continuity of the Harappan tradition. Sub-period IB witnessed further devolution in the material culture of the earlier stage leading to a point of overlap with the Painted Grey ware culture without the intrusion of iron.

Thus, the Indus culture in Haryana did not end abruptly after the Urban/ Mature phase but slowly merged with the later traditions.

Punjab

To understand the situation in Punjab one has to refer back to the advancements taking place in Harappan studies in the core region of the Harappa culture. The analysis of data from Mohenjo-daro, Jhukar, Amri and Chanhu-daro shows that the Harappan Civilization in the Sindh region developed gradually and transformed into what is known as the Jhukar culture. Similarly, fresh excavations at Harappa carried out by Dales, Meadow and Kenoyer suggest that Periods I and II relate to a Pre/Early Harappan (Pre-Urban) culture. Period III is typically Urban/Mature Harappan while period IV shows elements of transition, this time towards the Cemetery H culture, which is fully manifested in Period V. Referring to Period V, Kenoyer (1991: 56) adds: "The final occupation of the protohistoric period is characterized by Cemetery H or Late Harappan ceramics. . . ." Thus in Sindh and western Punjab, Jhukar and Cemetery H cultures are treated as the post-Urban Harappan cultures having Chanhudaro and Harappa as type sites. From the distribution of sites it appears that the Jhukar culture sites are found more in the lower Indus region while most of the Cemetery H related sites are concentrated in the Sutlej-Beas basin. In the case of Cemetery H, the repertoire of designs and the animal and floral motifs are usually encountered with the Harappan ceramic assemblage, and hence Cemetery H people culturally and racially do not seem to have been different from the Harappans (Sankalia 1974: 397).

The situation in Punjab however remains far from clear. The picture emerging from the major excavated sites such as Kotla Nihang, Bara, Ropar, Sanghol, Chandigarh, Dadheri, Kathpalon and Nagar highlight a local ceramic tradition termed the 'Baran'. Though the Harappan contact is seen in its heyday, in due course of time, the Harappan elements became feeble and the thrust of the Baran continued and finally we witness an overlap between the Baran and the succeeding Painted Grey Ware complex (Sharma 1993).

Jammu and Kashmir

Manda, located near Akhnoor on the Chenab, is recognized as the northern outpost of the Harappan culture in terms of its expansion within the boundaries of the present Indian territory. In a threefold cultural sequence of this solitary excavated site, Period IA is marked by the arrival of Harappans incorporating pre-Harappan material traits with the Urban/Mature Harappan. In Period IB, however, the pre-Harappan elements have disappeared, though sturdy Harappan Red ware continued along with Grey ware and Black Slipped ware as the ceramic tradition. In the Harappan Red ware, though jars, dishes and dish-on-stands are found in a considerable quantity, beakers and goblets are completely absent. In contrast, the ceramic shapes representing Baran and Cemetery H cultures found in the sites of Punjab and Haryana are conspicuously absent at Manda. The Grey ware does however resemble the typical Painted Grey ware. The triangular terracotta cakes are also not traced (Joshi and Madhu Bala 1993). By Period IB, therefore, the decline of the Urban/Mature Harappan elements and a 'transition' to some new cultures become very explicit here.

Uttar Pradesh

The Harappan settlements in Uttar Pradesh are confined to its western region with a heavy concentration in Saharanpur district. Most of these sites are generally located on the tributaries of the Yamuna and not on the Yamuna proper, ensuring safety against the recurring floods of the Yamuna. It seems, looking for new grounds, the Harappans penetrated further east into the Ganga-Yamuna doab sometime towards the end of the third or the beginning of the second millennium BC. Alamgirpur, Hulas and Bargaon are the three important excavated sites located immediately to the east of the Yamuna.

At Alamgirpur, out of four periods of occupation, the earliest has revealed some advanced Harappan cultural traits like the script, goblets, perforated cylindrical jars and beakers. Some pottery shapes which are distinctive of the post-Urban Harappan phase i.e., dishes of dish-on-stands with a prominent drooping rim, jars with long neck and splayed out rim do however occur. Triangular terracotta cakes, cubical dice with 1–6 markings on different faces, toy-carts, faience bangles, steatite beads, etc. are among the other distinct Harappan antiquities. Because of limited excavated area not much is known about the structural details. Besides the use of mud and mud-bricks, kiln fired bricks had also been used in the constructions. Considering the location and cultural remains of Alamgirpur, it becomes the eastern outpost of the Harappan Civilization.

Evidence from Hulas speaks of it being a typical post-Urban Harappan settlement. Although, in terms of material remains, diagnostic Mature Harappan traits such as weights, measures and seals remained absent, it did yield a sealing bearing three letters of the Harappan script without any motif. Similarly, the ceramic forms and decorations are characteristically comparable to their counterparts from sites found in the region immediately to the west of the Yamuna and classified as post-Urban/Mature Harappan. The presence of terracotta toy-cart wheels with a raised hub, terracotta cakes either oval with pointed ends or round with deep finger impressions, beads of faience, agate and carnelian (without white etching), bangles of copper, faience and terracotta suggest the continuity of Harappan tradition in its entity. At the same time, the structural remains reveal a simple form of mud-built houses. The existence of a large mud platform constructed to protect the settlement against the floods again reminds one of the Harappan planning techniques. Unlike Bhagwanpura, however, Hulas does not show any overlap with the subsequent occupation of the Painted Grey ware (Dikshit 1993).

Bargaon, unlike Alamgirpur and Hulas, is a single culture site, located further north in the doab region and seems to have been influenced by features manifest in the post-Urban Harappan settlements of the Sutlej region to its west because of its geographical location. As concern material culture, it is a poor reminder of Hulas and hence represents a later stage of the post-Urban Harappan phase having an admixture of Ochre-coloured pottery culture. As no Harappan settlement is noticed beyond the Hindon, a tributary of the Yamuna, the settlements containing Ochre-coloured pottery found in the central Ganga-Yamuna doab are free from the Harappan influence to a great extent (Dikshit 1984).

CONCLUSION

In the present state of our knowledge, based on the available radiocarbon dates from different Harappan sites, it appears that the onset of decline or deurbanization of the Harappa culture took place in the beginning of the second millennium BC (Lal 1997: 238–54). Though the causes of this decline are not yet precisely known, it is certain that each of the different regions had its own particular problems. Climatic changes, tectonic movements and shifts in hydraulic regime can be regarded as crucial factors. The post-Urban phase took different hues in different parts of its diffusion and it cannot be regarded as homogeneous. All do however share the common features of deurbanization i.e., the relative smallness of the settlements, lack of monumental buildings and the absence of long distance trade as summarized by Ghosh (1993: 383). As a result, the social fabric of the post-Urban Harappans became weak and economic conditions were geared more to meet the subsistence requirements than to gain any surplus. Because of weak political power, it witnessed a process of decentralization and localization, giving rise to regional cultural expressions. To a certain extent, this process of deurbanization can be equated with the indigenization process of Malik (1968: 120–21) and Subbarao's (1958: 151–52) idea of various cultures influencing one another.

REFERENCES

Adams, R.M. 1966. *The Evolution of Urban Society*, London.

Ajithprasad, P., and Sonawane, V.H. 1993. Harappa Culture in North Gujarat: A Regional Paradigm. Paper presented at the Conference on "The Harappans in Gujarat: Problems and Prospects". Pune: Deccan College.

Bhan, K.K. 1986. Recent Explorations in the Jamnagar District of Saurashtra. *Man and Environment* 10: 1–21.

—1989. Late Harappan Settlements of Western India, with Specific Reference to Gujarat, in *Old Problems and New Perspectives in the Archaeology of South Asia*, J.M. Kenoyer, ed. Madison: Wisconsin Archaeological Reports 2, pp. 219–43.

—1992. Late Harappan Gujarat. *The Eastern Anthropologist* 45(1–2): 173–92.

Suraj Bhan. 1971–72. Siswal: A Pre-Harappan Site in Drishadvati Valley. *Puratattva* 5: 44–46.

—1975. *Excavation at Mitathal (1968) and Other Explorations in the Sutlej-Yamuna Divide*. Kurukshetra: Kurukshetra University.

Bisht, R.S. 1987. Further Excavation at Banawali: 1983–84, in *Archaeology and History: Essays in Memory of Shri A. Ghosh*, B.M. Pande and B.D. Chattopadhyay, eds. Delhi: Agam Kala Prakashan, pp. 135–56.

Childe, V.G. 1950. The Urban Revolution. *The Town Planning Review* 21(1): 3–17.

Chitalwala, Y.M. 1979. Harappan and Post-Harappan Settlement Patterns in the Rajkot District of Saurashtra, in *Essays in Indian Proto-History*, D.P. Agrawal and D.K. Chakrabarti, eds. Delhi: B.R. Publishing Corporation, pp. 113–21.

—1985. Late Harappan Culture, in *Recent Advances in Indian Archaeology*, S.B. Deo and K. Paddayya, eds. Pune: Deccan College, pp. 57–64.

Dales, G.F. 1966. The Decline of the Harappans. *Scientific American* 214(5): 92–100.

Dhavalikar, M.K. 1993. Daimabad Bronzes, in *Harappan Civilization: A Recent Perspective,* G.L. Possehl, ed. New Delhi: Oxford & IBH Publishing Co., pp. 421–26.

Dhavalikar, M.K., and Possehl, G.L. 1992. The Pre-Harappan Period at Prabhas Patan and the Pre-Harappan Phase in Gujarat. *Man and Environment* 17(1): 72–78.

Dhavalikar, M.K., Raval, M.R., and Chitalwala, Y.M. 1996. *Kuntasi: A Harappan Emporium on West Coast*. Pune: Deccan College.

Dikshit, K.N. 1981–83. Late Harappan Cultures—A Reappraisal. *Puratattva* 13–14: 55–61.

—Late Harappan in Northern India, in *Frontiers of the Indus Civilization*, B.B. Lal and S.P. Gupta, eds. New Delhi: Books & Books, pp. 253–69.

—1993. Hulas and the Late Harappan Complex in Western Uttar Pradesh, in *Harappan Civilization: A Recent Perspective*, G.L. Possehl, ed. New Delhi: Oxford & IBH Publishing Co., pp. 399–411.

Dikshit, M.G. 1950. Excavations at Rangpur, 1947. *Bulletin of the Deccan College Research Institute* 11(1): 3–55

Fairservis, W.A. Jr. 1967. The Origin, Character and Decline of the Early Civilization. *Novitates* 2302: 1–48.

Ghosh, A. 1993. Deurbanization of the Harappan Civilization, in *Harappan Civilization: A Recent Perspective*, G.L. Possehl, ed. New Delhi: Oxford and IBH Publishing Co., pp. 381–84.

Gupta, S.P. 1993. The Late Harappan: A Study of Cultural Dynamics, in *Harappan Civilization: A Recent Perspective*, G.L. Possehl, ed. New Delhi: Oxford and IBH Publishing Co., pp. 51–59.

Herman, C.F., and Krishnan, K. 1994. Micaceous Red Ware: A Gujarat Proto-Historic Cultural Complex or Just Ceramic? in *South Asian Archaeology 1993*, Asko Parpola and Petteri Koskikallio, eds. vol. I. Helsinki: Suomalainen Tiedaekatemia, pp. 225–43.

Joshi, J.P. 1978. Interlocking of Late Harappan Culture and Painted Grey Ware Culture in the Light of Recent Excavations. *Man and Environment* 2: 98–101.

—1993. *Excavation at Bhagawanpura 1975–76*. New Delhi: Archaeological Survey of India.

Joshi, J.P. and Madhu Bala. 1993. Manda: a Harappan Site in Jammu and Kashmir, in *Harappan Civilization: A Recent Perspective*, G.L. Possehl, ed. New Delhi: Oxford & IBH Publishing Co., pp. 185–95.

Kenoyer, J.M. 1991. Urban Process in the Indus Tradition: A Preliminary Model from Harappa, in *Harappa Excavations 1986–90*, R.H. Meadow, ed. Madison: Prehistory Press, pp. 29–60.

Lal, B.B. 1997. *The Earliest Civilization of South Asia: Rise, Maturity and Decline*. New Delhi: Aryan Book International.

Mackay, E.J.H. 1938. *Further Excavations at Mohenjo-daro*. New Delhi: Government of India, reprint, 1998, New Delhi: Munshiram Manoharlal Publishers.

Majumdar, N.G. 1934. Explorations of Sind, *Memoirs of the Archaeological Survey of*

India, 48. New Delhi: Archaeological Survey of India.

Malik, S.C. 1968. *Indian Civilization: The Formative Period—A Study of Archaeology as Anthropology*. Simla: Indian Institute of Advanced Study.

Marshall, John. 1931. *Mohenjo-daro and the Indus Civilization*. London: Arthur Probsthain.

Mehta, R.N. 1984. Valabhi—A Station of Harappan Cattle-Breeders, in *Frontiers of the Indus Civilization*, B.B. Lal and S.P. Gupta, eds. New Delhi: Books & Books, pp. 227–30.

Mehta, R.N., Momin, K.N., and Shah, D.R. 1980. *Excavation at Kanewal*. Vadodara: M.S. University, Archaeology Series no. 11.

Misra, V.N. 1984. Climate, A Factor in the Rise and Fall of the Indus Civilization—Evidence from Rajasthan and Beyond, in *Frontiers of the Indus Civilization*, B.B. Lal and S.P. Gupta, eds. New Delhi: Books & Books, pp. 461–89.

Momin, K.N. 1979. Archaeology of Kheda District (Gujarat) Up to 1500 AD. Ph.D. Dissertation. Vadodara: M.S. University of Baroda.

Mughal, M.R. 1970. The Early Harappan Period in the Greater Indus Valley and Baluchistan. Ph.D. Dissertation. Philadelphia: University of Pennsylvania.

—1990. The Proto-Historic Settlement Patterns in the Cholistan Desert, in *South Asian Archaeology*, M. Taddei, ed. Rome: IsMEO, pp. 143–56.

Possehl, G.L. 1977. The End of a State and the Continuity of a Tradition: A Discussion of Late Harappan, in *Realm and Region in Traditional India*, Richard Fox, ed. New Delhi: Vikas Publishing House, pp. 234–54.

—1980. *Indus Civilization in Saurashtra*. New Delhi: B.R. Publishing Corporation.

—1984. Archaeological Terminology and the Harappan Civilization, in *Frontiers of the Indus Civilization*, B.B. Lal and S.P. Gupta, eds. New Delhi: Books & Books, pp. 27–38.

—1992a. The Harappan Civilization in Gujarat: The Sorath and Sindhi Harappans. *The Eastern Anthropologist* 45 (1–2): 117–54.

—1992b. The Harappans in Saurashtra: New Chronological Considerations. *Puratattva* 22: 25–29.

—1993. The Harappan Civilization: A Contemporary Perspective, in *Harappan Civilization: A Recent Perspective*, G.L. Possehl, ed. New Delhi: Oxford & IBH Publishing Co., pp.15–28.

Possehl, G.L., and Raval, M.H. 1989. *Harappan Civilization and Rojdi*. New Delhi: Oxford and IBH Publishing Co.

Raikes, R.C. 1964. The End of the Ancient Cities of the Indus. *American Anthropologist* 66 (2): 179–93.

Rao, S.R. 1963. Excavations at Rangpur and Other Explorations in Gujarat. *Ancient India* 18–19: 5–207.

—1979. *Lothal: A Harappan Port Town 1955–62*, vol. I. New Delhi: Archaeological Survey of India, Memoir no. 78.

—1985. *Lothal: A Harappan Port Town 1955–62*, vol. II. New Delhi: Archaeological Survey of India, Memoir no. 78.

Rissman, Paul C., and Chitalwala, Y.M. 1990. *Harappan Civilization and Oriyo Timbo*. New Delhi: Oxford & IBH Publishing Co.

Sali, S.A. 1970. The Harappan Culture as Revealed Through Surface Exploration in the Central Tapi Basin. *Journal of the Oriental Institute* 20 (2): 93–101.

—1993. The Harappans of Daimabad, in *Harappan Civilization: A Recent Perspective*, G.L. Possehl, ed. New Delhi: Oxford & IBH Publishing Co., pp. 175–84.

Sankalia, H.D. 1974. *Prehistory and Protohistory of India and Pakistan*. Pune: Deccan College.

Shaffer, J.G. 1992. The Indus Valley, Baluchistan and Helmand Traditions: Neolithic Through Bronze Age, in *Chronologies in Old World Archaeology*, vol. I. R. Ehrich, ed. Chicago: University of Chicago Press, pp. 441–64.

Sharma, Y.D. 1993. Harappan Complex on the Sutlej (India), in *Harappan Civilization: A Recent Perspective*, G.L. Possehl, ed. New Delhi: Oxford & IBH Publishing Co., pp. 141–65.

Shinde, V.S. 1992. Padri and the Indus Civilization. *South Asian Studies* 8: 55–66.

Shinde, V.S., and Kar, S.B. 1992. Padri Ware: A New Painted Ceramic Found in the Harappan Levels at Padri in Gujarat. *Man and Environment* 17 (2): 105–10.

Singh, U.V., and Bhan, S. 1982. A Note on the Excavations at Balu, District Jind (Haryana), in *Indian Archaeology: New Perspectives*, R.K. Sharma, ed. New Delhi: Agam Kala Prakashan, pp. 124–26.

Sonawane, V.H., 1994–95. Harappan Settlements of Rupen Estuary, Gujarat. *Pragdhara* 5: 1–11.

Sonawane, V.H., and Ajithprasad, P. 1994. Harappa Culture and Gujarat. *Man and Environment* 19 (1–2): 129–39.

Sonawane, V.H., and Mehta, R.N. 1985. Vagad—A Rural Harappan Settlement in Gujarat. *Man and Environment* 9: 38–44.

Subbarao, B. 1958. *The Personality of India*. Vadodara: M.S. University of Baroda, Archaeology Series no. 3.

Wheeler, R.E.M. 1947. Harappa 1946: The Defenses and Cemetery R-37. *Ancient India* 3: 58–130.

—1986. *The Indus Civilization*, third edn. Cambridge: Cambridge University Press.

8 ❖ Chalcolithic Phase in Western India (Including Central India and the Deccan Region)

V.S. SHINDE

INTRODUCTION AND A BRIEF HISTORY OF RESEARCH

WESTERN India, which includes the geographical regions of central India, the Deccan and the whole of Gujarat, is unique in India inasmuch as it is considered to be a cradle of early civilization. Central India consists of two major geographical units, namely the Malwa plateau and Chambal valley and includes the southeastern part of Rajasthan (Mewar region) which, in fact, is an extension of the Malwa plateau. On the basis of ecological variations, Gujarat is divided into two broad zones, namely Saurashtra and Kutch. The former, being rich in fertile soil and pasture land, was thickly populated. The latter area is almost a desert zone in Gujarat. The northern part of the Deccan, drained by the Tapi and several of its tributaries, was ecologically rich in resources and hence supported a large population right from the beginning of agriculture in the second millennium BC. The middle and the lower parts of the Deccan, drained by the Godavari and the Bhima respectively, are comparatively less fertile and that is why these tracts were not favoured for extensive human occupation. Major parts of these geographical units, covered by fertile black cotton soil, were occupied and intensively exploited by the early farming community, which flourished almost towards the end of the fourth millennium BC.

The archaeological research in this area was ignored for a long time and the protohistoric period was poorly understood till the late fifties of this century. This is mainly because Sir R.E.M. Wheeler and his colleagues did not cover these territories and the Archaeological Survey of India continued the same policy even after his departure in 1948. It was H.D. Sankalia and his colleagues at the Deccan College who undertook systematic and problem-oriented research and tried to fill the large blanks on the archaeological map of India. This period was termed as "The Vedic Night". After the decline of the Harappans the impression conveyed was that the cultural evolution in India reappeared only after the Greek invasion and the resultant "second urbanization" in the sixth century BC. Sankalia's "holistic" approach to Indian archaeology enabled him to observe a complete picture of Indian archaeology as it emerged from a variety of restricted excavations all over this region. As shown in his early writings (Sankalia 1974), human adaptations to the landscape persisted over time and can be clearly established through historical, cultural, geographical and ethnographic studies. Sankalia decided to concentrate in this area initially with a view to surveying the occurrence of certain painted ceramics and to establishing relative chronological positions of these ceramics. V.S. Wakankar of the Vikram University, Ujjain, joined hands with Sankalia in central India and carried out pioneering work for almost three decades. Since the accidental discovery in 1950 of the Chalcolithic site at Jorwe near Sangamner in Ahmednagar district of Maharashtra, over 300 sites of the same period have been brought to light due to a well thought and implemented research strategy. Of these several selected ones have been excavated. The vertical excavations at Prakash in Dhule district (Thapar 1967) and Nevasa in Ahmednagar district (Sankalia et al. 1960) in the Deccan and Ahar (Sankalia et al. 1969), Gilund (*IAR 1959–60*) and Kayatha (Ansari and Dhavalikar 1973) in central India have provided a complete regional cultural sequence starting from the Chalcolithic period. Most of these sites have also produced evidence of a break, both cultural as well as stratigraphical, between the protohistoric and Early Historic periods in the form of a sterile layer.

Excavations carried out in late fifties and thereafter at Maheshwar, Navdatoli, Eran, Nagada, Ahar and Kayatha in central India established a stratigraphic succession of three principal ceramic traditions labelled Ahar, Kayatha and Malwa, the first two named after their type-sites and the third after the region. The present author, however, does not agree with the division of Chalcolithic period into three cultural periods, based on just slight variation in the painted ceramic tradition. He prefers the term phase for the culture (Shinde, in press). Radiocarbon dates have shown that these ceramic traditions date to the period between 2200 and 1200 BC. Numerous excavated sites in the Deccan such as Jorwe, Nasik, Nevasa, Prakash, Bahal, Inamgaon and Daimabad have yielded four principal ceramic traditions labelled

Savalda, Late Harappan, Malwa and Jorwe. Subsequently, the present author treated minor variations in the painted ceramic traditions almost at regular intervals in the Chalcolithic period as denoting internal development within it (Shinde 1994). As a result of these excavations, it was demonstrated to the world, by the early seventies, that after the eclipse of the Harappans, large parts of central and western India were populated by the "Protohistoric Community".

Large-scale excavations carried out at sites like Navdatoli (Khargaon district, Madhya Pradesh) (Sankalia et al. 1971), Balathal (Udaipur district, Rajasthan) (Misra et al. 1995 and 1997), Inamgaon (Poona district), situated on the right bank of the river Ghod, one of the major tributaries of the Bhima (Dhavalikar et al. 1988) and Daimabad (Ahmednagar district) on the left bank of the river Pravara, the major tributary of the Godavari (Sali 1986; Shinde and Pappu 1990), have thrown light on various aspects including socio-economic organization of the Chalcolithic cultures of western India. The most significant contribution of the Inamgaon excavation is the discovery of the Late Jorwe phase (*c.* 1000-700 BC), which has bridged the gap between the Chalcolithic and Early Historic periods.

In the beginning of the third millennium BC Gujarat witnessed the rise of food-producing communities as the evidence from Lothal (Rao 1979 and 1985) and Padri (Shinde 1998a) in Saurashtra, Dholavira in Kutch (Bisht 1991) and Loteshwar in north Gujarat (Sonawane and Ajithprasad 1994) indicates. Two regional Chalcolithic painted pottery traditions appeared in Saurashtra between 1800 and 1200 BC; they have been labelled as Prabhas (1800–1200 BC) and Lustrous Red Ware cultures (1700–1200 BC).

The published literature gives the impression that archaeological research in the Deccan prior to the beginning of Inamgaon excavation[1] involved mainly vertical digging. This was the right choice of the excavation method as the primary aim then was to build a regional cultural sequence. The horizontal excavation at Inamgaon carried out between 1968 and 1982 by the Department of Archaeology, Deccan College, Pune, was a landmark in the history of Indian archaeology. Not only was this the most extensive and systematic excavation, but several scientific methods were employed in the recovery and analysis of archaeological data. The multidisciplinary approach enabled reconstruction of various aspects of economic and socio-political organization of the early farming community of the Deccan. The researchers also realized the importance of the contextual approach, propounded by Walter Taylor (1948) and Ian Hodder (1986), which was an integral part of the research methodology at Inamgaon. The evidence gathered thereby provided sufficient clues to the existence of a chiefdom society in the Deccan around the middle of second millennium BC. The most convincing evidence in this regard consisted of a site hierarchy, certain structures and burials (Dhavalikar et al. 1988). In the early eighties, the focus of research was shifted from large and rich site archaeology to small, semi-permanent site archaeology. Two sites in the Deccan, namely Kaothe in Dhule district and Walki in Poona district of Maharashtra, were subjected to systematic horizontal excavations. They have produced different evidence compared to the sedentary and bigger sites like Inamgaon and Daimabad. The excavation carried out at Kaothe during the 1983-84 season brought to light the semi-permanent nature of the site. The traces of habitation debris are spread over a very large area (more than 30 hectares) (Shinde 1985 and 1992). The site of Walki was a farmstead of Inamgaon. This fact has been established by the study of pottery by X-Ray Diffraction method (Gogte and Shinde 1994–95).

SALIENT FEATURES

Settlement Pattern

The early farming community (Chalcolithic culture) flourished in an ecological zone characterized by environmental uniformity that includes fertile black cotton soil and semi-arid climate. Culturally the various Chalcolithic phases found over this large landscape also display certain uniformity. These include painted, wheel-made ceramic traditions, a specialized blade/flake industry, restricted use of copper and subsistence based on farming, stock-raising and limited hunting. They constructed either rectangular or round mud houses. In the absence of diagnostic ceramics and chronological control, it becomes nearly impossible to distinguish the locus of any of these cultures across the entire region.

Based on palynological data from Rajasthan lake deposits, the following climatic sequence for the Holocene period has been reconstructed (Krishnamurty et al. 1981):

Before 8000 BC	Severe aridity
8000–7500 BC	Relatively Wet
7500–3000 BC	Relatively Dry
3000–1700 BC	Sudden increase in wetness
1700–1500 BC	Relatively Dry
1500–1000 BC	Relatively Wet
1000–500 BC	Arid

This climatic sequence can be made applicable to the larger semi-arid region that makes up western and central India. It is argued that these climatic fluctuations were responsible, to certain extent, for the origin of early farming communities and cultural change. It is believed that abundance of plant and animal foods to the Mesolithic hunter-gatherers around 10,000 years ago possibly led to an explosion in the population. This is evident in the sudden increase in the Mesolithic settlements all over the subcontinent. The congenial climate till about 1700 BC enabled them to flourish (Dhavalikar 1988).

The Chalcolithic people of western India located their settlements in the proximity of fertile black cotton soil and perennial supply of water. Most of the rivers in western India, being semi-perennial, the early farmers established their settlements in the river meanders. This is mainly because of certain advantages such as protection to the settlement on three sides, formation of deep pools in the meander which retains water for the whole year and the availability of water resources such as fish, crabs, shells, etc. The early farmers, particularly on the banks of the rivers Tapi and Narmada located their settlements near crossing points. Both these rivers are mighty and are crossable at selected points only. The author has noticed settlements on both the banks of such crossing points in the Tapi basin (Shinde 1998b). Extensive and intensive surveys carried out in different parts of western India during the last fifty years have brought to light nearly 200 sites in the Deccan and 185 sites in central India, including the Mewar region of Rajasthan. The Chalcolithic settlements of the Deccan have been subjected to a detailed study. It has been hypothesized that there was a heavy concentration of settlements in the Tapi basin, less in the Godavari basin and a sporadic occurrence of sites in the Bhima basin (Shinde 1986–87; Shinde 1987; Dhavalikar 1979). This may be true to some extent, but it should be borne in mind that the Tapi basin has been surveyed thoroughly (Shinde 1998b), whereas similar systematic efforts to locate sites have not been made so far in the Godavari and Bhima basins. In fact, this uneven distribution appears to be mainly due to the inadequate regional survey.

The author surveyed thoroughly 103 Chalcolithic sites from the point of view of settlement pattern studies (Shinde 1998b). The Chalcolithic people in the Tapi basin appear to have chosen suitable ecological niches where adequate resources were available. The region along both the banks of the Tapi is one of the most fertile stretches in the country, but was sparsely inhabited during the Chalcolithic period. The same phenomenon has been observed by C.D. Deshpande in the case of modern settlements. He observed that "quite contrary to the general pattern of the rivers, the Tapi discourages population concentration on its banks. Erosion and consequent badland topography prevent irrigation and intensive cultivation" (Deshpande 1948:149). The river Tapi gets flooded frequently in the monsoon season. In a flood-affected area, the general tendency of the people is to establish settlements either on the elevated older terrace, which is beyond the reach of normal flood water, or away from the river. This is one of the perennial and mighty rivers of India, which is not crossable everywhere. There are very few crossing points on this river, which were occupied by the early farmers. The banks of the Tapi are very high ranging from 15 to 20 m above the water level. It is, therefore, a very hard task to obtain water from the river for domestic use. Because of these various reasons, the Chalcolithic people located their settlements away from the Tapi in the tributary zone.

In sharp contrast, the tributaries of the Tapi were thickly populated during the Chalcolithic period. There are a number of reasons for this. Most of the tributaries originate in the Western Ghats and hence get assured supply of water throughout the region. They flow through deep and narrow valleys and therefore the flood water is hardly allowed to spill out of their channels. Naturally, the settlements along the banks are not threatened and the fertile cover of the soil does not get eroded fast. The other important reason is that the tributaries, being narrow and small, can easily be dammed. There are also numerous river meanders in the tributaries. A majority of the settlements are found located in the river meanders, obviously due to a number of advantages (Shinde 1998b, in press).

Detailed examination of the sites as well as of the ecological conditions in the Tapi basin enabled the author to identify sites of different categories. Thus, it is now clear that there were regional centres, agricultural settlements, farmsteads, herding units, factory sites or seasonal camps (established to exploit the local resources). The sites in the first category were usually found in the proximity of fertile tracts of black cotton soil and perennial sources of water. They were extensive settlements with fairly thick habitation deposits, suggesting long term occupation by a large population. Some of the large settlements like Inamgaon, Daimabad, Prakash, etc. fall in this category. The settlements that were strategically located may have served as regional centres. The other category was agricultural villages, most of which are located in the proximity of fertile arable land. Agricultural villages, being permanent settlements, are usually large in size and have a considerably thick habitation deposit. A large number of settlements in the Deccan fall in this category. In the vicinity of large-sized settlements, are found very small, seasonal settlements. According to Hole and Flannery (1967), such small-sized settlements were occupied by a group of people from large-sized villages during planting and harvesting seasons. Small sites like Walki and Gotkhil, close to Inamgaon, have been identified as farmsteads on the basis of their proximity to arable land. At the same time, their small area and very thin habitation deposits denote the temporary nature of occupation. A number of sites in the Tapi basin situated near the foothills in the vicinity of pasture land have been identified as 'herding units' occupied seasonally by a small group of people for grazing their flocks. Such sites, occupied for a short duration of time, leave behind a few potsherds and flimsy traces of habitation. Small sites like Garmal near Inamgaon, which was located close to the source of chalcedony, the chief raw material used by the early farming community to manufacture blade tools, can be identified as camps. Such sites are represented by a few potsherds and scanty habitation debris as the duration of their occupation is very short. Thus, it is clear that the Deccan witnessed the emergence of a clear-cut site hierarchy towards the beginning of the second millennium BC.

The first farmers of central India, labelled as the Kayatha culture, inhabited mostly the Chambal valley, where over fifty sites of this phase have been discovered. A majority of them are very small, less than 2 hectares in size. They are located away from the main river Chambal. The settlements of the succeeding phase (labelled Ahar) are medium-sized villages. Over 80 settlements of this phase have been discovered and majority of them are confined to the southeastern part of Rajasthan and a few in the western part of Malwa. Most of the sites are located in the valleys of the rivers Banas, Berach, Gambhiri, Kothari and their tributaries (Misra 1967). The site of Gilund, spread over an area of roughly 10 hectares, appears to be the regional centre on account of its strategic location in the centre of the basin and the size. The last Chalcolithic phase, labelled as the Malwa culture, is confined to mainly the Malwa region of central India. A vast majority of Malwa sites are small, ranging from 1 to 4 hectares in extent. The site of Navdatoli, located on the left bank of the river Narmada, is the largest known site in this region, occupying an area of about 10 hectares. This can be identified as a regional centre in this region. Various features of the central Indian Chalcolithic, in fact, became clear only after horizontal excavations at this site (Sankalia 1974).

The Prabhas culture sites discovered so far are very few[2] and they display a dispersed settlement pattern. The main focus of the culture was the southern part of Saurashtra. Besides Prabhas Patan, the type site of the culture, the other important site is Khambhodar, about 15 km east of Porbandar. The presence of Prabhas culture pottery at Rojdi in central Saurashtra, further increases the extent of this culture in Saurashtra (Dhavalikar 1997). Intensive work in Saurashtra by G.L.Possehl brought to light 127 settlements of the Lustrous Red Ware culture, most of which are located along the banks of the Ghelo and the Kalubhar in a linear pattern (Possehl 1980). Possehl has postulated a sharp decrease in population during the Rangpur period on the basis of the number of sites and their extent. Only the type site Rangpur was very large in extent. The distribution of the other Lustrous Red Ware culture sites is as follows:

Number of sites	*District*	*Number of sites*	*District*
1	Ahmedabad	8	Kheda
8	Amreli	2	Kutch
1	Banaskantha	22	Mehsana
15	Bhavnagar	23	Rajkot
35	Jamnagar	1	Surat
2	Junagarh	9	Surendranagar

From the above distribution it is clear that the Lustrous Red Ware culture was confined to the present boundary of Saurashtra, except for two sites, which are located in Kutch. In the estuary of the Rupen in north Gujarat close to the eastern margin of the Little Rann of Kutch and on either side of the narrow creek-like depression that connects the Little and the Great Rann, more than hundred Chalcolithic sites have been discovered. They have been scattered in a dispersed fashion over this region.

Origin

It should be stated that the Chalcolithic culture of western India is the best studied archaeological culture in India. However, as regards the origin of agriculture in this region, no convincing evidence has come forth. So far it was firmly believed that the Harappans in Gujarat played an important role in the origin and development of the Chalcolithic culture in western India (Shinde 1989, 1990a and 1994). This hypothesis was propounded on the basis of sudden induction of advanced technology of pottery, copper and bead manufacture in the Deccan. It was thought that these technologies were supplied to the early farmers by the Harappans who had mastered the skill and were themselves using these technologies.

The recent evidence from north Gujarat and Balathal in the Mewar region of Rajasthan suggests that the Chalcolithic community came into being much before the Harappan period. It is obvious therefore that the Harappans did not play a significant role in the origin of the Chalcolithic culture in Gujarat and central India. The beginnings of settled life in these regions go back to the beginning of the third millennium BC, as the radiocarbon dates from the sites of Loteshwar in north Gujarat and Balathal in Mewar region would indicate.[3] The Chalcolithic cultures in Mewar and north Gujarat in fact were contemporary with the Pre/Early Harappan culture of western Rajasthan and Gujarat. A small excavation carried out at Loteshwar, 17 km north-east of Shankheshwar in Mehsana district of Gujarat, has produced interesting evidence of the beginning of settled life that is earlier than the Harappan period. The Chalcolithic deposit overlies the Mesolithic material. The thin habitation deposit has revealed numerous large pits, some of which could have been even pit-dwellings; these were found filled with pottery, animal bones, clay lumps, etc. The other material equipment associated with the Chalcolithic culture includes micro steatite beads, microlithic tools and some crudely made shell bangles and beads.[4]

The excavations at Balathal (Udaipur district, Rajasthan), roughly 42 km northeast of Udaipur city, have produced evidence pertaining to the origin of the early farming community of central India (Misra et al. 1997). A considerably thick deposit at the base of the settlement (Phase A) at Balathal (around 1 metre) has produced evidence of the origin of the Chalcolithic culture and a gradual development in the ascending order. Excavation to the natural level in a limited area[5] has demonstrated a gradual growth of the settlement from a modest beginning. The people who established the settlement on the bed rock constructed only mud and wattle-and-daub structures. In one of the index trenches (HX2) at Balathal, remains of a circular hut (2 m diameter) having well made floor and plastered with cowdung were found. Some of the characteristic Chalcolithic wares such as thick and thin Red, Black-and-Red were introduced right from the beginning. However, they are coarse, thick in section, inadequately fired and the majority of vessels are handmade. Shapes such as wide-mouthed, deep carinated bowls, small narrow-mouthed jars and storage jars with beaded rim, the fossil types of the Chalcolithic phase in this region, are present right from the beginning. A gradual development is seen in these different wares in terms of technology and quality of vessels. The wares gradually became finer and reached their highest quality in the middle level.

The Reserve-slipped ware was also introduced by the pioneering settlers. Since the earliest known occurrence of this ware in the subcontinent is at Balathal, it may be inferred that the technique of its production was borrowed by the Harappans when they established a close contact with the Chalcolithic farmers of Mewar around 2400 BC. The middle levels of the Chalcolithic period (Phase B), dated to the middle of third millennium BC, have been extensively excavated. It is the people of this level who established close contacts with the Harappans in Gujarat, resulting in overall development that is visible in their structures and other material equipment.

Material Culture

Different phases identified within the Chalcolithic period in the Deccan and central India share many common items of material culture. They are characterized by painted Black on Red ceramic tradition, mud houses which are either rectangular or circular on plan, well-developed blade industry, restricted use of copper and mixed subsistence based on farming, stock raising and hunting and gathering. It is on the basis of minor variation in their painted ceramic traditions that the different phases[6] have been identified (Shinde 1989 and 1994). The chronology of the five phases identified within the Chalcolithic period of the Deccan is as follows:

Phase I	(Savalda)	2200–1800 BC
Phase II	(Late Harappan)	1800–1600 BC
Phase III	(Malwa)	1600–1400 BC
Phase IV	(Early Jorwe)	1400–1000 BC
Phase V	(Late Jorwe)	1000–700 BC

Prior to the excavations at Balathal, most of the large Chalcolithic sites produced evidence of modest-sized rectangular or circular houses with low mud walls and wattle-and-daub screen above them. Floors were made of alternate layers of silt and black clay and periodically plastered with cow dung. People occupying semi-permanent settlements like Kaothe in Dhule district and Walki in Pune district of Maharashtra, however, preferred different dwellings.

Besides rectangular and circular mud houses, the excavations at Kaothe have yielded pit-dwellings (Dhavalikar et al. 1990 and Shinde 1992). The settlement, as the evidence suggests, possibly occupied seasonally, belongs to Phase I of the Chalcolithic period in the Deccan. A number of circular pit-dwellings in clusters were exposed. Each cluster consisted of five to six dwellings. On the basis of the contents, it was possible to distinguish between pits used for dwelling/storage purposes and pits for keeping poultry. The sides and bottoms of the pit-dwellings were plastered with cow dung or lime. Kitchen facility was located either inside or outside the dwellings (Dhavalikar et al. 1990a, Shinde 1994).

Different architectural evidence of Phase IV comes from the site of Walki, located on the right bank of the Bhima river. Walki, identified as a farmstead of Inamgaon (Gogte and Shinde 1994–95), was a semi-permanent settlement, located roughly 27 km west of Inamgaon, and produced flimsy circular huts, without proper walls and well made floors. They are found in roughly circular clusters. Each cluster consisted of at least one hut each for purposes of dwelling, storage and poultry or animal (sheep/goats) shed. Shelters for animals could be identified by the analysis of the nitrogen content and the ethnographic parallels (Shinde 1991 c). Some of the clusters even consisted of possible threshing floors and silos. The cooking place in most of the cases was found outside in the open. In all 106 architectural features were uncovered in course of excavation (1985–86 and 1986–87), of which 54 belonged to the earliest phase and 52 of later phase. Seven clusters of circular huts were unearthed. A number of permanent structures (rectangular/squarish mud houses) found in the centre of the habitation, could have been inhabited by those who lived here throughout the year for the protection of farmstead (Shinde 1989, Dhavalikar et al. 1990b).

The dead persons were accorded ceremonious burial. They were buried within the habitation, either beneath the living floors or in the courtyards. No human burials were found associated with the Chalcolithic culture in central India and Gujarat. The evidence in this respect comes from the Chalcolithic sites in the Deccan. The evidence from Kaothe suggests that the first farmers (Phase I) of the Deccan buried both children and adults in an extended, supine posture in an oval pit without any burial goods (Shinde 1990, 1992). Only one adult burial has been reported from the site of Daimabad that belongs to Phase II. It was placed on a well-rammed floor, over which were mud bricks and brickbats. The grave was covered with earth and brickbats and at the top of this tumulus a stone was placed near the head (Sali 1982). In Phase III of the Deccan Chalcolithic at Daimabad only one adult skeleton without burial goods was found. However, a number of child burials of this phase have been exposed at Inamgaon and Daimabad. They are twin-urn burials, in which the urns were either of the painted pottery or of coarser grey variety. The body of the child was accommodated in the urn with the head towards north and buried in a pit. A number of pots, ornaments and tools formed part of burial furniture. This mode of child burial became popular in the succeeding Phases IV and V. Regular adult burial practice was noticed in both these phases. Usually they were buried in an extended position in north-south direction, accompanied by a number of small pottery vessels. Possibly the pots contained water and food for the deceased person, suggesting belief of the people in life after death. The feet of the dead adults were chopped off before burying possibly because of the belief that they do not walk away and turn into ghosts. This normal rule of the community was perhaps not applicable to the chief and his family as the evidence from the house that is attributed to the chief of the community would suggest. The chief and his relatives were buried in four-legged clay jars and the feet were not chopped.

We have some idea about the religious beliefs of the early farmers from the excavated sites. Some of the terracotta male and female figurines found at Nevasa, Inamgaon and Daimabad may have been worshipped as gods and goddesses. Terracotta bull figurines found at a number of excavated sites in the Deccan and central India may be taken as representation of a bull cult. The evidence of a fire altar at Navdatoli as well as of sacrificial altars and an apsidal mud-walled structure identified as a shrine at Daimabad lead us to believe that fire worship was in vogue in the Chalcolithic period (Shinde 1989, 1990).

Central Indian Chalcolithic

The excavations being carried out at Balathal in central India produced new architectural evidence from its middle level dated to *c.* 2400 BC. The site was occupied during Phase II (Ahar). However, it has yielded quite early radiocarbon dates, going back almost to the beginning of the third millennium BC. The middle phase of the Chalcolithic occupation at Balathal is the most prosperous as during this level the inhabitants established very close contacts with the Harappans. As a result some new architectural features made of stone and mud-bricks such as the outer fortification wall, fortified enclosure and complex structures were introduced by the Chalcolithic farmers at Balathal. No other Chalcolithic site in South Asia has yielded such a unique evidence.

Fortified Enclosure: This unique structural feature was constructed in the middle level of the Chalcolithic phase at Balathal. It was built over a 70 cm high platform made of mixture of clay, silt, brickbats and bricks. This method of construction was in fact introduced by the Harappans for constructing citadel parts of the settlement. The structure is roughly rectangular on plan with its longer axis along the east-west direction. It has thick walls of mud and brickbats supported on both the sides by stone courses set in mud mortar, each being 1.25 m thick. The average thickness of the wall at the top is 4.80 m and gradually broadens to 6.50 m at the base. It is because of this construction method that it has survived at places to a height of nearly 4 m. A fairly large area of this structure has been exposed in the southwestern part, where both the inner and outer stone walls (revetment) have been exposed. The ground plan of the inner side of the fortified enclosure is exposed in a number of sondages taken at different points. In the southwestern corner, there is a roughly rectangular bastion, attached perpendicular to the main outer revetment. The southern wall runs in east-west direction for a distance of 16.45 m and then takes a right angle turn to the south. After running for a distance of 9.50 m it again turns to the east for a distance of 14.30 m and joins the southeastern corner. The western wall, which is 27.40 m long, runs in north-south direction. The northern wall, which runs in straight east-west direction, is 38.35 m long. The eastern wall, however, does not run straight. It is 37.65 m long and runs in northeast-southwest direction. The eastern wall as is clear in trenches (G7–G8) is the thickest (6.80 m), whereas the average thickness of the remaining three walls is 4.80 m. The total area enclosed by the structure is roughly 500 sq m. Inside the structure at least three very well-made floor levels have been exposed suggesting that it was in use for a considerably long period. Since only a small portion inside the structure has been exposed, it is difficult to determine its exact function.

Structure Complexes: On the southern side of the settlement, a number of residential structures were exposed in the course of excavations. Four structural phases have been identified in Chalcolithic Phase B at Balathal. Only broken walls of structural phases I and IV have been exposed whereas II and III have been relatively well represented. It is structural phase II, which is the most prosperous at Balathal possibly because of the establishment of close contacts with the Harappans in Gujarat in the middle of the second millennium BC. A number of structures of this phase exposed in the course of excavations at Balathal demonstrate that a modicum of planning was adopted at the site around 2400 BC possibly as a result of their contacts with the Harappans.

Three structure-complexes of stone and mud bricks have been exposed, of which two lie on either side of the main street running in north-south direction. The third complex, close to the southern periphery of the settlement, is separated from the second complex by a small lane. The street is 4.80 m wide, three times wider than the lane (1.60 m). The complex (I) located on the eastern side of the street is the biggest amongst the three exposed so far. It consists of a number of rooms, eleven of which have been exposed so far. It is not yet fully exposed. The peripheral wall, particularly on the western side, is quite thick (average thickness 90 cm) and made of stones set in mud mortar. The rooms of varied dimension, either rectangular, square or rhomboidal in shape, were meant for storage, cooking and such other purposes. Two of the rooms (nos. 10A and 10F) have domestic hearths in them. They have been assigned to the cooking activities. Six rooms of the complex (nos. 10B, 10C, 10D, 10H and 10J) may have been used as storage. This inference is based on the size and shape of the rooms and the contents such as clay bins, storage jars and circular stone-topped clay platforms and silos. One of the rooms (10K) may have been for dwelling purposes as it has a well made floor. Room 10E of the complex can be identified as a kitchen as it contained two domestic hearths, each represented by three stones placed in a triangular fashion. By the side of these hearths were found charred bones and grey ware globular pots with soot marks on their bases. The inner walls dividing the complex into different rooms, are thin (average thickness 60) and made of stone, mud or mud bricks. This is the largest and richest complex exposed so far. It is not unlikely that it belonged to a very rich family or to someone who was quite high in the social hierarchy. The other complex (II), located on the western side of the street, is a hall-like structure, roughly squarish on plan. Its northern part is not yet exposed. The complex had stone foundation and walls of mud bricks. The eastern part of the complex had storage and cooking facility in the form of domestic hearth, saddle quern and storage pits. The function of the rest of the complex cannot be determined as it underlies the structure of later phase. The third complex located near the southern periphery of the mound consists of three structures inside the enclosure wall of mud-bricks over a stone foundation. Of the three structures, the one located on the east is a mud brick feature rectangular in shape with rounded corners. Possibly this was the kitchen of the complex as it contains a large, circular fire-place. The middle one is of stone, having walls on three sides and open on the south, possibly serving as an entrance; it appears to be a dwelling place as it had a well-made floor. The third, located immediately to the west of the middle structure, is a circular hut having sunken floor. Possibly this was the storage place of the complex. This structure-complex, the poorest of the three, possibly belonged to either a economically poor family or those whose standing was low in the social hierarchy. Architectural remains of structural Phase III exposed in the course of excavation, indicate absence of any structure complex as noticed in the second phase. On the southern side on top of the structures of Phase II were located either single or double-roomed residential structures of this phase. On the western side of the settlement were located the structures of potters. The pottery kiln found in one of the structures of this phase is rectangular on plan and is enclosed by mud or mud-brick walls. Within the kiln were noticed a number of circular clay containers of varied dimensions. One more pottery kiln found at the same place but slightly later in age (belonging to structural phase IV) suggests hereditary succession of the craft.

Outer Fortification: On the eastern periphery of the mound at Balathal an outer fortification wall made of stones set in mud mortar has been exposed partially. The wall was possibly constructed in two phases. The lower 1.15 m portion of the wall, which tapers upwards, represented the first phase, whereas the wall of the upper phase was constructed 35 cm away from the edge of the wall of the first phase. It is perfectly vertical to a height of 85 cm. On top of this stone wall was a mud brick construction, the traces of which were found at places.

None of the sites of Lustrous Red Ware culture in Saurashtra and the Chalcolithic culture of north Gujarat have been excavated horizontally and therefore there is no evidence of their architectural activities. A huge structure complex was unearthed in the Prabhas culture level at Prabhas Patan. The structure consists of a number of small squarish rooms varying in size from 1.50 to 3.50 sq m and a few rectangular rooms about 3.50 m × 1.50 m. In the absence of post-holes, the excavators have propounded that it was roofless. Considering the thickness of walls (60 cm), it is also presumed that they were not very high. In the absence of domestic hearth in the structure complex, the excavators believe that it was not a residential structure but most probably a warehouse (Dhavalikar 1997).

The evidence from Inamgaon, Daimabad, Navdatoli, Nagda, Eran and Balathal clearly demonstrates the presence of a chiefdom society in the Chalcolithic period in western India. The evidence for some of the characteristic features of a chiefdom society has been found at these sites. Features like site hierarchy, well-developed craft specialization, house and burial of a chief at Inamgaon, public architecture such as fortification, ditch, public granary and artificial irrigation channel, well-established hinterland trade network, etc. testify to the existence of a chiefdom society in the Chalcolithic period (Shinde 1991).

Ceramic Assemblage

The pottery of the Chalcolithic period is predominantly wheel-made and can be broadly divided into two varieties: fine and coarse. Their identification is based on the degree of purity of clay, surface treatment, nature of firing, vessel forms and decoration. The fine variety is made of refined and well levigated clay, has a thin and highly burnished slip on one or both surfaces and is baked at a very high temperature. Because of these features, it is sturdy, has a reddish core, looks attractive, produces a metallic sound and therefore constitutes deluxe pottery. The vessel forms in this variety mainly comprise dish and bowl, with or without a stand, in varying sizes. The coarse variety is made of unrefined clay and is poorly fired; it has a grey or black core and is mainly decorated with incised and applique designs. The vessel forms in this variety mainly comprise large globular pots of various sizes and they were used for storage and cooking.

As stated earlier, it is the painted ceramic assemblage which has enabled identification of different phases within the Chalcolithic period of western India. The ceramic assemblage associated with the north Gujarat region is referred to as Anarta pottery (Sonawane in press). Much of our understanding of this ware is based on the excavation data recovered from the sites of Nagwada and Loteshwar. The ceramic assemblage of period IB at Nagwada is dominated by four wares, namely, Gritty Red, Fine Red, Burnished Red and Burnished Grey/Black wares. The Gritty Red ware, made from coarse clay, is the most common ware. Most of the pots in this ware are either handmade or made on slow wheel. The important types in this include bowls with straight or convex sides and with slightly incurved rims, basins with a thick flaring rim and large pots. The pots are treated with red slip, over which are found painted decorations in different shades of black and red on a white or cream background, thereby producing a bichrome effect. Motifs include simple horizontal, vertical and wavy lines, latticed circles and squares and intersecting loops. The Fine Red ware is made of levigated clay containing mica particles and fired to perfect temperature. As far as shapes and surface treatment are concerned, it shares a lot of common features with the Gritty Red ware. The Burnished Red ware is painted with parallel and wavy lines using white or bluish grey pigment on a black background over red slip, while the Burnished Grey/Black ware is painted with fugitive white colour. All these fabrics have common vessel shapes and share common features of decoration, which suggests that they belong to a single pottery tradition. It has wide distribution in north Gujarat and had an independent existence prior to the Harappan culture.

The Prabhas culture is characterized by painted Prabhas ware. It is made from fine levigated clay and the vessels are treated with a pinkish or orange wash. The motifs were painted in purple or dark brown and they include simple geometric patterns such as groups of vertical and oblique strokes, wavy lines, hatched triangles and loops. Most of the painted motifs are set in panels or registers. Sub-spherical bowl with a featureless rim, sometimes slightly incurved and sharpened internally, and globular jar with an outcurved rim are the predominant types in the Prabhas ware. Other forms such as the stud-handled bowl, dish-on-stand and perforated jar, which are evidently derived from the Harappan pottery, also occur in this ware (Dhavalikar 1997).

The Lustrous Red ware is the main ware of the Rangpur culture. It is of a very fine fabric but slightly coarser compared to the Harappan painted ware. It is thin walled and treated with a bright red slip, which is highly burnished. The painted ornament is in black and the designs include vertical or oblique lines and triangles and lozenges, sometimes hatched. Animal figures too occur and include the bull, deer and even birds. The forms include a variety of bowls, many of which are carinated and some have stands. There are large storage jars with heavily beaded rims and dishes-on-stands, which are obviously derived from the Harappan, the only difference being that the dishes do not have carination, but have beaded rims. The Lustrous Red ware is associated with the Black-and-Red ware painted in white. It is similar to that associated with Phase II of the central Indian Chalcolithic (Rao 1963).

Phase I of the Chalcolithic period of central India is characterized by three types of ceramic assemblage, namely, the Kayatha ware, Painted Buff ware and Combed ware. The Kayatha ware is an extremely fine fabric and well fired and treated with chocolate slip. A close examination of pots reveals that they were made in parts and luted together. Most of the pots were provided with either ring or disc base. Over the slip, the painted patterns were executed in purple pigment. The decorations were confined to the upper half of the external surface of the pots. They include mostly linear patterns such as horizontal bands, vertical lines, short strokes, etc. The typical Indian *lota* having globular body, a constricted neck and wide, flaring mouth, bowls, high and short necked storage jars with globular profile and basins are some of the common shapes in this ware. This ware resembles the pre-Harappan Sothi ware in terms of fabric and surface treatment.

The Painted Buff ware is another important ceramic industry of Phase

I of the central Indian Chalcolithic culture. It has a thin core and fine fabric. The pots, made on fast wheel, were treated with a buff wash but sometimes the colour varies from yellowish to pinkish. The painted designs over this background are executed in black colour. They include gèometric patterns such as hatched diamonds, vertical and horizontal bands, etc. The most predominant form is represented by the Indian *lota*, with concave neck and globular body, either with or without carination. The other forms, not so common, include dish or shallow bowl and a basin (Ansari and Dhavalikar 1973).

Another ceramic associated with Phase I is the Combed ware. This is also a fine fabric pottery, made on wheel and fired to high temperature. It is devoid of slip. The sobriquet Combed Ware has been given because of the decorations on the vessels which consist of groups of incised lines executed with the help of a comb-like instrument. The most common patterns seen on this ware are horizontal wavy lines and zigzags in groups. It is represented mostly by bowls and basins. This ware is close to the pre-Harappan Fabric D of Kalibangan (Ansari and Dhavalikar 1973).

Phase II of the central Indian Chalcolithic period is characterized by the presence of four different wares, namely, Thin Red, Black-and-Red painted in white, Tan and Reserve-slipped wares. The Thin Red ware has a thin, highly burnished slip on the external surface which is generally plum red but occasionally tends to be brownish red, tan or chocolate. The inner surface is without any slip or wash and is generally greyish. The shapes in this ware mainly consist of convex-sided deep bowls of various sizes and occasionally of small globular vessels with everted rim, narrow mouth and high neck. They are decorated by a single row of punctured or incised triangles, and occasionally by single or double ridges in low relief on the shoulder. The rims of some pots were made separately and luted to the body.

The Black-and-Red ware is so named because the entire inner portion and the shoulder portion of the outer surface of the pot is black while the rest of the external surface is red. This effect is believed to have been achieved by the application of inverted firing technique. Both surfaces were treated with a slip and burnished. The pots in this ware are painted in white pigment, either inside or outside the pots. The decoration seems to have been executed after the pots were fired and therefore it tends to fade. The motifs include groups of straight or wavy lines, spirals, dots and circles. The shapes in this ware mostly comprise wide-mouthed, convex-sided bowls of varying size.

The Tan ware is of medium thickness and has a thin slip of light orange colour. Some sherds in this ware have a thick brown or chocolate coloured slip, similar to that of Kayatha ware. The principal shapes in this ware are dish, dish-on-stand and bowl-on-stand with considerable variations in size. Other shapes are large convex-sided bowls with thick rims, globular pots with either beaded or flat projecting rims and large basins with ledges on the neck. The prominent ledges may have been used to hold the vessels while the low ledges may have been purely decorative. Two sherds of the basal portions of globular pots with ring bases have been reported from the site of Balathal. A few specimens of perforated pots, similar to those used by the Harappans, have also been found. In respect of fabric and shape this ware is identical to the Harappan pottery of Gujarat though unlike the latter it lacks painted decoration.

A number of sherds of the Reserve-slipped ware have been found in the Chalcolithic levels at Balathal and comprise two types: imported and locally made imitations. The imported Reserve-slipped ware is made from a very fine paste, uniformly fired to a high temperature and treated with a dark greyish slip. The outer surface is highly burnished. The combed patterns executed on the outer surface are done carefully and meticulously as compared with the locally produced variety. The shapes in this variety cannot be discerned as only body sherds have been found. The painted decorations include a set of eight zigzag lines, a broad band of light greyish colour on the neck, a set of running loops below a horizontal line, double horizontal bands below which is a pattern resembling a serrated edge, and horizontal lines at regular intervals filled in with dots.

The imitation variety is reddish in colour and is made from a fine clay to which fine sand has been added as a tempering material. It is fired uniformly to a high temperature and therefore the core has turned brick-red in colour. It was first treated with a red wash over which a thick, dark red slip was applied. When the slip was wet various patterns were executed by scooping out the second slip possibly with a comb-like instrument. The patterns are usually found in sets or groups. Only shallow dish with a round, slightly incurved rim, cylindrical hollow stem and stand with flared sides and short, out-turned ring is found in this ware. The decoration, mainly on the inner surface, consists of closely spaced horizontal lines and sets of zigzag lines (Misra et al. 1995).

The coarse variety of pottery is represented by a thick, Bright-Slipped Red ware and a Grey ware, both of which were locally produced and primarily used for storage and cooking. These wares are made of coarse clay, are poorly fired and are mainly decorated with incised and applique designs. In the Red ware the most common forms are large narrow-mouthed and wide-mouthed globular jars, small *handi*s, and dishes-on-stand. They are treated with a highly burnished bright red slip on the upper part of the external surface. The middle part of the external surface is decorated with two or more parallel raised bands and a variety of incised designs like multiple wavy lines, chevrons, herring-bone patterns, criss-crosses and triangular incisions.

Phase III of the central Indian Chalcolithic culture is characterized by the Malwa ware, which is the most profusely decorated ware in the Chalcolithic period in India. It is either orange or buff in colour and bears painted decorations in black colour. The pottery was wheel-turned, either slow or fast. The clay used for its manufacture contains tempering materials like sand, chopped grass and husk. Belonging as it does to a coarse fabric, the pottery is not well fired. The important types include typical Indian *lota* with elongated, bulbous belly and wide flaring mouth, the concave carinated bowl and high-necked storage jars with globular body. The site of Navdatoli has produced the evidence of cup-on-stand, channel-spouted cups and pedestalled goblets. They have significant parallels in Iran and hence associated with the Aryans (Sankalia 1963). Over six hundred different motifs have been executed on the Malwa ware and they include primarily geometric designs such as triangles, lozenges and linear patterns. Besides, there are some naturalistic motifs such as animals, birds, dancing human figures and plant motifs. The finer variety of the Malwa ware found at Eran is called the Eran Fabric.

In the Grey ware there are two varieties, namely, burnished and plain. In the burnished variety the upper part of the exterior is slipped and highly burnished while the plain variety bears a slip but has no burnishing. The lower part of the outer surface of vessels in this variety is roughened by the application of sand mixed with clay and is often covered with soot, showing that the vessels were used for cooking. The most common vessel forms in both the varieties are wide-mouthed small *handi*s. The middle portion on the external surface is decorated with incised and applique designs similar to those of the burnished Red ware. The other shapes in plain grey ware are shallow hand-made *tawa*s, apparently used for making rotis or unleavened bread, and lids, sometimes with handles.

Phase I of the Deccan Chalcolithic is characterized by the Savalda ware. It is rather coarse in fabric. The core is very often gritty, showing impurities, and is also not fully oxidized due to slightly poor firing. Thin and thick varieties are found and most of the pots of the latter variety appear to have been made on a slow turn-table. The outer surface is treated with a thick slip of different shades of colour consisting of pink, chocolate and red. The characteristic types in this ware are globular pots with high necks and round bottom, globular pots with high, but very narrow necks, convex-sided bowls with featureless rims and Indian *lota*-like types. The Savalda ware is unique in the entire ceramic range of the Deccan Chalcolithic because of the variety of delicately painted motifs in black pigment. These include, besides linear and geometric patterns, figures of wild animals and birds such as elephant, wild boar, peacock, cock, snakes and aquatic creatures like fish and frogs. Even arrows, bows, swords and harpoons are depicted. All these painted motifs have been executed with great care and display the mastery of Chalcolithic artists (Shinde 1990a).

The Deccan Chalcolithic people established contact with the Harappans in Saurashtra in Phase II and hence the ceramic assemblage found in this phase bears a lot of similarity with the Harappan painted ware. The similarity is confined to the fabric. However, painted motifs and shapes in this phase are not very different from those found in the succeeding phase (III) (Shinde 1991b).

The Malwa ware found associated with Phase III in the Deccan is slightly different from that associated with Phase III of central Indian Chalcolithic culture. It is characterized by a slightly coarse fabric with a wash of pink or pale red over the exterior surface, over which the painted designs are executed in black colour. The painted designs include linear and geometric patterns and a few motifs such as the stylized bull, deer and running dog. The important types associated with the Malwa culture are the Indian *lota* with a slightly flared mouth and round, bulbous body, the concave sided carinated bowl, the globular vessel with beaded rim and the spouted jar with wide mouth, flaring rim and tubular spout (Shinde 1990b).

The Jorwe ware, so termed after the type site, is characterized by a light to dark red wash, over which painted motifs are executed in black pigment. It is made from a very fine clay and fired uniformly to a high temperature. The painted designs consist of geometric patterns such as vertical and horizontal bands, zigzag lines, spirals, diamonds, either empty or hatched, criss-cross patterns, loops, chevrons, etc. Animal motifs such as stylized deer, fish-scale patterns, cranes, human figures, either standing or dancing, occur very rarely. The diagnostic forms in the Jorwe ware are the concave-sided carinated bowl, spouted jar with a funnel mouth and globular jar with either a high or constricted neck. Other forms, which are not very common, are the chalice, goblet and bowl with a convex profile. Most of the characteristic features of the Early Jorwe ware continued in the Late Jorwe phase, but the ware became slightly inferior in quality and most of the naturalistic motifs disappeared. New forms like the bottle-necked pot and Black-and-Red ware, similar to the ones used by the Neolithic farmers of south India, were introduced (Shinde 1989).

Decline

The deterioration in the standard of living that took place towards the end of the first millennium BC is strongly believed to be due to the fluctuating climatic conditions (Shinde 1989; Dhavalikar 1988). The chemical analysis of a sterile layer found between the protohistoric and Early Historic periods at Nevasa, which was believed to have been formed around 1000 BC, revealed that it was formed under arid conditions (Mujumdar and Rajaguru 1965). As a result it was difficult for the Chalcolithic farmers to cope with the changed climatic conditions and therefore they deserted their settlements in Gujarat, central India and northern Deccan. However, they continued to live in the Bhima basin until 700 BC. Moreover, considering the fact that at Inamgaon people continued to cultivate crops such as barley, peas, and oil seeds till around 700 BC, it seems that this area was receiving the bare minimum rainfall required for growing these crops. A section of the population, which constructed clusters of round huts, could have led a semi-nomadic existence. However, the continuation from Phase IV of the construction of large, multi-room structures on the eastern part of the main habitation mound at Inamgaon suggests that half the population was leading a normal, sedentary life. Even the chiefdom social organization continued till the last phase, as the house of a chief was located in this phase at Inamgaon (Dhavalikar et al. 1988). There is a strong possibility that the Megalithic people, equipped with effective iron implements and fast moving horses, began to arrive in the Deccan around 800 BC and were responsible for the end of the Chalcolithic culture in this region. The evidence from Inamgaon suggests that most of the exposed permanent rectangular structures of the last phase were burnt down and possibly a large section of the population was massacred, which is clear from their burials. In the earlier phase the adults were ceremoniously buried underneath the house floor with utmost care and usually only one person was buried in a single pit. But in the last phase the presence of more than one skeleton in one pit, absence of burial goods in many cases, and missing limbs such as a hand or a leg or even the head of a skeleton, lead one to infer that perhaps because of large scale killing, it was difficult for the survivors to perform the last rites properly and give a ceremonious burial to each individual. Possibly the surviving people were taken away by the invaders as slaves or were absorbed by them into their society.

Concluding Remarks

The foregoing study sketched the culture process in western India from the beginning of the third millennium to the end of the second millennium BC. With the appreciably congenial climate and the formation of black cotton soil, the entire region was covered with thick vegetation and game became plentiful. This favourable condition appears to be responsible for an increase in the population and the seeds of sedentary life were sown. The Saurashtra Harappans must have played a key role in the origin and development of the early farming communities of the Deccan. The interaction must have taken place in the Tapi basin, which acts as a buffer zone for the movement of human population from north to south and vice versa. But the Chalcolithic culture at Balathal flourished due to close contacts with the Harappans. The creation by the Chalcolithic people at Balathal of monumental and complex buildings, the presence of Tan ware and Harappan-like copper objects may have been the result of such a contact.

The creation of a number of cultures is not justifiable for the simple reason that they have been identified on the basis of minor variations in the painted ceramic assemblage. Earlier, considering the insufficient data, it was not possible to challenge the interpretation offered by certain scholars, and, therefore, most of the researchers accepted this division of cultures. However, in the last two decades, enormous data on the early farming community of western India has been brought to light as a result of systematic survey and large-scale scientific excavations. A critical review of the fresh data and the new discoveries will have to be considered while offering a holistic view about the western Indian Chalcolithic culture.The obvious reasons for not accepting the creation of different cultures are the identical material equipment from the beginning to the end of the Chalcolithic Phase and the unbroken stratification within the habitation. The author, in turn, has suggested different phases within the Chalcolithic period, denoting minor changes or internal development due to various reasons such as a change in the social organization, local innovation, changes in the dietary habits of the people and cultural contact.

Most probably the fluctuating climatic conditions around 1000 BC and the Megalithic people, who began to arrive in the Deccan around 800 BC, were responsible for the decline of the Chalcolithic culture. This hypothesis is based on the evidence from the site of Inamgaon. This is certainly not sufficient for making any general statement. Despite the fact that the Chalcolithic culture of western India is the best studied, we still need evidence for understanding certain problems like the causes for its decline and disappearance around 1000 BC.

NOTES

1. Excavations at Inamgaon in Pune district of Maharashtra were carried out between 1967 and 1982 under the direction of Professor H.D. Sanakalia of the Deccan College Post-Graduate and Research Institute, Pune. Excavation activities at Inamgaon were temporarily discontinued between 1974 and 1976 as Professor Sankalia decided to work on the Chalcolithic site of Prabhas Patan in Gujarat. Excavation at Inamgaon is certainly one of the longest and largest in the history of Indian archaeology.
2. The exact number of sites of the pre-Prabhas and Prabhas Ware cultures is not known. None of the earlier explorers has given the exact number. Unfortunately, the scholars working in Gujarat have been concentrating their research on the Indus Civilisation, in which process the other cultures have not received due attention.
3. All the radiocarbon dates of the Chalcolithic culture of western India have been listed in Tables 1 and 2 at the end of the paper.
4. Excavations at the site of Loteshwar were conducted by the Department of Archaeology, M.S. University, Vadodara in 1991. I thank Professor V.H. Sonawane for supplying relevant information about the site.
5. The natural level has been reached so far at the ancient site of Balathal only in an area of 150 sq. m out of the total excavated area of roughly 1800 sq. m.
6. Different phases within the Chalcolithic period have been designated by earlier scholars as different cultural periods. For example, five phases within the Chalcolithic period in the Deccan have been designated as the Savalda, Late Harappan, Malwa, Early Jorwe and Late Jorwe cultures respectively, in chronological order. Similarly three phases within the central Indian Chalcolithic period have been frequently referred to as the Kayatha, Ahar or Banas and Malwa cultures respectively.

REFERENCES

Ansari, Z.D., and Dhavalikar, M.K. 1973. *Excavations at Kayatha*. Pune: Deccan College.

Bisht, R.S. 1991. Dholavira: A New Horizon of Indus Civilization. *Puratattva* 20: 71–82.

Deshpande, C.D. 1948. *Western India: A Regional Geography*. Dharwar: Student's Book Depot.

Dhavalikar, M.K. 1979. Early Farming Cultures of the Deccan, in D.P. Agrawal and D.K. Chakrabarti, eds., *Essays in Indian Protohistory*. New Delhi: B.R. Publishing Corporation, pp. 247–65.

—1988. *First Farmers of the Deccan*. Pune: Ravish Publishers.

—1997. *Indian Protohistory*. New Delhi: Books & Books.

Dhavalikar, M.K., Sankalia H.D., and Ansari, Z.D. 1988. *Excavations at Inamgaon*, vol. I,

parts II and I. Pune: Deccan College.
Dhavalikar, M.K., Shinde, V., and Atre, S.M. 1990a. *Excavations at Kaothe*. Pune: Deccan College.
—1990b. Small Site Archaeology: Excavations at Walki. *Bulletin of the Deccan College Research Institute* 50: 197–228.
Gogte, V.D., and Shinde, V. 1994–95. Chalcolithic Walki—The Satellite Settlement of Inamgaon: A Study by X-Ray Diffraction of Pottery. *Puratattva* 25: 62–63.
Hodder, Ian. 1986. *Reading the Past—Current Approaches to Interpretation in Archaeology*. Cambridge: Cambridge University Press.
Indian Archaeology—a Review, 1959–60. New Delhi: Archaeological Survey of India.
Krishnamurty, R.V., Agrawal, D.P., Misra, V.N., and Rajaguru, S.N. 1981. Palaeoclimatic Influences From the Behaviour of Radio-Carbon Dates of Carbonates From Sand Dunes of Rajasthan. *Proceedings of the Indian Academy of Sciences* (Earth Science) 90: 155–60.
Misra, V.N. 1967. *Pre- and Proto-history of the Berach Basin, South Rajasthan*. Pune: Deccan College.
Misra, V.N., Shinde, V., Mohanty, R.K., Dalal, Kurush, Mishra, Anup, Pandey, Lalit, and Kharakwal, Jeevan. 1995. The Excavations at Balathal: Their Contribution to the Chalcolithic and Iron Age Cultures of Mewar, Rajasthan. *Man and Environment* 20(1): 57–80.
Misra, V.N., Shinde, V., Mohanty, R.K., Pandey, Lalit, and Kharakwal, Jeevan. 1997. Excavations at Balathal, Udaipur District, Rajasthan (1995–97), with Special Reference to Chalcolithic Architecture. *Man and Environment* 22(2): 35–59.
Mujumdar, G.G., and Rajaguru, S.N. 1965. Comments on Soils as Environmental and Chronological Tools, in V.N. Misra and M.S. Mate, eds., *Indian Prehistory—1964*, Pune: Deccan College, pp. 248–53.
Rao, S.R. 1963. Excavations at Rangpur and Other Explorations in Gujarat. *Ancient India* 18–19: 5–207.
—1979 and 1985. *Lothal: A Harappan Port Town (1955–62)*, vols. I and II. New Delhi: Archaeological Survey of India.
Sali, S.A. 1982. The Harappan of Daimabad, in G.L. Possehl, ed., *Harappan Civilisation: A Contemporary Perspective*, New Delhi: Oxford & IBH Publishing Co., pp. 175–84.
—1986. *Daimabad 1976-79*. New Delhi: Archaeological Survey of India, Memoir no. 83.
Sankalia, H.D. 1963. New Light on the Indo-Iranian or Western Asiatic Relations Between 1700–1200 BC. *Artibus Asiae* 26: 312–32.
—1974. *Prehistory and Protohistory of India and Pakistan*, sec. edn., Pune: Deccan College.
Sankalia, H.D., Deo S.B., Ansari, Z.D., and Erhradt, S. 1960. *From History to Prehistory at Nevasa*. Pune: Deccan College.
Sankalia, H.D., Deo, S.B., and Ansari, Z.D. 1969. *Excavations at Ahar*. Pune: Deccan College.
—1971. *Chalcolithic Navdatoli (1957–59)*. Pune: Deccan College.
Shinde, V. 1985. Kaothe—A Late Harappan Settlement in the Central Tapi Basin. *Bulletin of the Deccan College Research Institute* 44: 173–77.
—1987. Farming in the Chalcolithic Deccan, India. *Tools and Tillage* 5(4): 214–27.
—1987–88. Land-use Pattern During Chalcolithic Phase in the Tapi Basin. *Puratattva* 18: 54–60.
—1989. New light on the Origin, Settlement System and Decline of the Jorwe Culture of

the Deccan, India. *South Asian Studies* 5: 60–72.

—1990a. Settlement Pattern of the Savalda Culture: The First Farming Community of Maharashtra. *Bulletin of Deccan College Research Institute* (*Sankalia Memorial Volume*) 49–50: 417–26.

—1990b. The Malwa Culture in Maharashtra: A Study of Settlement and Subsistence Patterns. *Man and Environment* 25 (2): 53–60.

—1991a. Craft Specialization and Social Organization in the Chalcolithic Deccan, India. *Antiquity* 65(249): 796–807.

—1991b. The Late Harappan Culture in Maharashtra: Study of Settlement and Subsistence Patterns. *South Asian Studies* 7: 91–96.

—1991c. Experimentation in Archaeology—An Ethnographic Model, in *Archeologie Experimentale,* Tome 1: Le Feu, Paris: Cetouvrage a ete publie avec la Societe des Autoroutes, pp. 22–28.

—1991–92. Settlement Archaeology of Kaothe: A Chalcolithic Site in the Tapi Basin. *Puratattva* 22: 47–52.

—1994. The Deccan Chalcolithic: A Recent Perspective. *Man and Environment* 19(1–2): 169–78.

—1998a. Pre-Harappan Padri Culture in Saurashtra: Recent Discovery from Padri. *South Asian Studies* 14: 173–82.

—1998b. *Early Settlements in the Central Tapi Basin.* New Delhi: Munshiram Manoharlal Publishers.

— (in press). Central Indian Chalcolithic Culture, in G.L.Possehl, ed., *Encyclopaedia of South Asian Archaeology*. New Delhi: Oxford & IBH Publishing Co.

Shinde, V., and Pappu, R.S. 1990. Daimabad: The Chalcolithic Regional Centre in the Godavari Basin. *Bulletin of the Deccan College Research Institute* 50: 306–16.

Sonawane, V.H., and Ajithprasad, P. 1994. Harappan Culture and Gujarat. *Man and Environment* 19(1–2): 129–39.

Taylor, Walter. 1948. *A Study of Archaeology.* New York: Memoir of the American Anthropological Association.

Thapar, B.K. 1967. Prakash 1955: A Chalcolithic Site in the Tapi Basin. *Ancient India* 20–21: 1–167.

Table 1. **Radiocarbon dates for the Western Indian Chalcolithic Sites.** (After Possehl 1993) (unpublished list)

1	*2*	*3*	*4*	*5*	*6*	*7*
Ahar	V-58	3890+100 BP	2055+105 BC	2455, 2416, 2405 cal. BC	Phase IIA bottom	Charcoal
Ahar	V-55	3825+120 BP	1990+125 BC	2993 cal. BC	Phase IIA bottom	Decayed Wicker
Ahar	V-54	3835+95 BP	2000+100 BC	2306 cal. BC	Phase IIA lower	Charcoal
Ahar	V-56	3715+95 BP	1875+100 BC	2316 cal. BC	Phase IIA middle	Charcoal
Ahar	TF-37	3165+110 BP	1310+115 BC	1436 cal. BC	Phase IIA middle	Charcoal
Ahar	V-57	3975+95 BP	2145+100 BC	2551, 2549, 2489 cal. BC	Phase IIA top	Charcoal
Ahar	TF-34	3570+135 BP	1725+115 BC	1925 cal. BC	Phase IIB	Charcoal
Ahar	TF-31	3130+105 BP	1275+110 BC	1420 cal. BC	Phase IIC	Charcoal
Ahar	TF-32	3400+105 BP	1550+100 BC	1733, 1721, 1697 cal. BC	Phase IIC	Charcoal
Balathal	PRL-1933	5770+100 BP	3800+100 BC		Phase II bottom	Charcoal
Balathal	PRL-1930	3760+110 BP	1800+100 BC		Phase II bottom	Charcoal
Balathal	PRL-1928	4550+180 BP	2700+150 BC		Phase II lower	Charcoal
Balathal	PRL-1937	3980+90 BP	2000+100 BC		Phase II middle	Charcoal
Balathal	PRL-1925	3810+170 BP	1900+150 BC		Phase II middle	Charcoal
Balathal	PRL-1846	4310+80 BP	2400+75 BC		Phase II middle	Charcoal
Balathal	PRL-1944	4300+80 BP	2350+75 BC		Phase II middle	Charcoal
Balathal	PRL-1843	4120+70 BP	2200+80 BC		Phase II middle	Charcoal
Balathal	PRL-1834	4350+70 BP	2400+80 BC		Phase II middle	Charcoal
Balathal	PRL-1835	3830+60 BP	1900+60 BC		Phase II top	Charcoal
Eran	TF-327	3280+100 BP	1430+105 BC	1570,1528 cal. BC	Phase III	Charcoal
Eran	P-526	3136+68 BP	1280+70 BC	1422 cal. BC	Phase III	Charcoal
Eran	TF-331	3355+90 BP	1505+95 BC	1675 cal. BC	Phase III	Charcoal
Eran	TF-324	3130+105 BP	1275+110 BC	142o cal. BC	Phase III	Charcoal
Eran	TF-326	2905+105 BP	1040+110 BC	1096 cal. BC	Phase III	Charcoal
Eran	P-528	2878+65 BP	1015+65 BC	1042 cal. BC	Phase III	Charcoal
Eran	TF-330	3020+100 BP	1365+105 BC	1514 cal. BC	Phase III	Charcoal

1	2	3	4	5	6	7
Eran	P-525	3193+69 BP	1340+70 BC	1469, 1485, 1455 cal. BC	Phase III	Charcoal
Eran	TF-329	3300+105 BP	1450+70 BC	1607, 1554, 1544 cal. BC	Phase III	Charcoal
Kayatha	TF-680	3850+95 BP	2015+100 BC	2334 cal. BC	Phase I	Charcoal
Kayatha	TF-779	3685+105 BP	1845+110 BC	2127, 2077, 2043 cal. BC	Phase I	Charcoal
Kayatha	TF-781	3720+105 BP	1880+110 BC	2138 cal. BC	Phase I	Charcoal
Kayatha	TF-780	3680+95 BP	1840+100 BC	2123, 2080, 2042 cal. BC	Phase I	Charcoal
Kayatha	TF-974	3485+95 BP	1640+100 BC	1873, 1840, 1816 1803, 1780 cal. BC	Phase I	Charcoal
Kayatha	TF-405	3320+100 BP	1470+105 BC	1621 cal. BC	Phase I	Charcoal
Kayatha	TF-778	3550+95 BP	1705+100 BC	1895 cal. BC	Phase I/II	Charcoal
Kayatha	TF-400	3800+105 BP	1965+110 BC	2278, 2234, 2209 cal. BC	Phase II	Charcoal
Kayatha	TF-777	3625+95 BP	1785+100 BC	2023, 1998, 1983 cal BC	Phase II	Charcoal
Kayatha	TF-678	3560+100 BP	1685+105 BC	1886 cal. BC	Phase II	Charcoal
Kayatha	TF-399	3525+100 BP	1680+105 BC	1884 cal. BC	Phase II	Charcoal
Kayatha	TF-777	3790+125 BP	1645+130 BC	1874, 1839, 1817 1801, 1781 cal. BC	Phase II	Charcoal
Kayatha	TF-776	3455+110 BP	1610+115 BC	1754 cal. BC	Phase II	Charcoal
Kayatha	TF-401	3190+105 BP	1335+110 BC	1491, 1489, 1451 cal. BC	Phase II	Charcoal
Kayatha	TF-679	3155+130 BP	1300+135 BC	1430 cal. BC	Phase II	Charcoal
Kayatha	TF-396	3575+105 BP	1730+110 BC	1931 cal. BC	Phase III	Charcoal
Kayatha	TF-398	3520+100 BP	1675+105 BC	1883 cal BC	Phae III	Charcoal
Kayatha	TF-397	3350+100 BP	1500+105 BC	1673 cal. BC	Phase III	Charcoal
Kayatha	TF-402	3240+100 BP	1385+105 BC	1519 cal. BC	Phase III	Charred seeds
Kayatha	TF-676	3160+105 BP	1305+110 BC	1433 cal. BC	Phase III	Charred seeds
Loteshwar	PRL-1564	4460±110 BP	2510±111 BC	2921 cal. BC		Charcoal
Loteshwar	PRL-1565	5050±110 BP	3110±110 BC	3698 cal. BC		Charcoal
Navdatoli	P-201	3892+128 BP	1645+130 BC	3032, 2963, 2942 cal. BC	Phase III Lower	Charcoal

1	*2*	*3*	*4*	*5*	*6*	*7*
Navdatoli	P-200	3457+127 BP	1610+130 BC	1757 cal. BC	Phase III Lower	Charcoal
Navdatoli	P-475	3455+70 BP	1610+70 BC	1754 cal. BC	Phase III Lower	Charcoal
Navdatoli	TF-59	3380+105 BP	1530+110 BC	1985 cal. BC	Phase III Lower	Charcoal
Navdatoli	P-476	4125+69 BP	2300+70 BC	2861, 2815, 2733, 2729 2694, 2681, 2664, 2632 2681 cal. BC	Phase III Middle	Charcoal
Navdatoli	P-202	3503+128 BP	1660+130 BC	1878, 1833, 1826, 1791 1789 cal. BC	Phase III Middle	Charcoal
Navdatoli	P-204	3449+127 BP	1600+130 BC	1749 cal. BC	Phase III Upper	Charcoal
Navdatoli	P-205	3294+125 BP	1445+130 BC	1602, 1559, 1536 cal. BC	Phase III Upper	Burnt Wheat
Prabhas Patan	TF-1287	4280+105 BP	2460+110 BC	2911 cal. BC	Phase I Pre-Prabhas	Shell
Prabhas Patan	PRL-90	4240+110 BP	2415+115 BC	2892 cal. BC	Phase I Pre-Prabhas	Charcoal
Prabhas Patan	PRL-92	3830+95 BP	1995+100 BC	2299 cal. BC	Phase II Prabhas	Charcoal
Prabhas Patan	TF-1286	3595+90 BP	1755+95 BC	1953 cal. BC	Phase II Prabhas	Charcoal
Prabhas Patan	TF-1284	3465+95 BP	1620+100 BC	1859, 1848, 1769 cal. BC	Phase II Prabhas	Charcoal
Prabhas Patan	PRL-91	3860+165 BP	2025+170 BC	2343 cal. BC	Phase III LRW	Charcoal
Prabhas Patan	PRL-20	3340+105 BP	1490+110 BC	1643 cal. BC	Phase III LRW	Charcoal
Prabhas Patan	PRL-19	3100+160 BP	1245+165 BC	1406 cal. BC	Phase III LRW	Charcoal

Table 2. **Radiocarbon Dates for the Deccan Chalcolithic Sites.** (After Possehl 1993) (unpublished list)

1	*2*	*3*	*4*	*5*	*6*	*7*
Apegaon	PRL-384	3520+100 BP	1675+105 BC	1883 cal. BC	Phase I	Charcoal
Apegaon	PRL-382	3450+100 BP	1605+105 BC	1749 cal., BC	Phase III	Charcoal
Apegaon	PRL-383	3450+100 BP	1605+105 BC	1749 cal. BC	Phase III	Charcoal
Chandoli	TF-43	2905+100 BP	1040+105 BC	1096 cal. BC	Phase IV	Charcoal
Chandoli	P-747	3099+185 BP	1240+195 BC	1400 cal. BC	Phase IV	Charcoal
Daimabad	PRL-429	3390+150 BP	1540+155 BC	1730,1729, 1689 cal. BC	Phase I	Charcoal
Diamabad	BS-176	3590+90 BP	1750+95 bc	1947 cal. BC	Phase I	Charcoal
Daimabad	PRL-654	3460+100 BP	1615+105BC	1851, 1850, 1761 cal. BC	Phase I	Charcoal
Daimabad	PRL-420	1410+140 BP	500+145 BC	642 cal. BC	Phase II	Charcoal
Daimabad	PRL-426	3600+150 BP	1760+155 BC	1961 cal. BC	Phase II	Charcoal
Daimabad	PRL-180	3390+100 BP	1540+105 BC	1730, 1729, 1689 cal. BC	Phase II	Charcoal
Daimabad	PRL-657	3140+100 BP	1285+105 BC	1424 cal. BC	Phase II	Charcoal
Daimabad	PRL-177	3460+100 BP	1615+105 BC	1851,1850, 1761 cal. BC	Phase between	Charcoal
Daimabad	PRL-419	2980+110 BP	1120+115 BC	1258, 1235, 1226 cal. BC	Phase between II & III	Charcoal
Diamabad	PRL-655	3490+110 BP	1645+115 BC	1875, 1838, 1818, 1800, 1872 cal BC	Phase between	Charcoal
Daimabad	BS-182	3130+90 BP	1275+95 BC	1420, cal. BC	Phase between II & III	Charcoal
Daimabad	PRL-428	3400+110 BP	1550+115 BC	1733, 1721, 1697 cal. BC	Phase between II & III	Charcoal
Daimabad	BS-181	2990+100 BP	1130+105 BC	1261, cal. BC	Phase III	Charcoal
Daimabad	PRL-412	3250+110 BP	1400+115 BC	1521, cal. BC	Phase III	Charcoal
Daimabad	PRL-411	3230+100 BP	1375+105 BC	1516, cal. BC	Phase III	Charocal
Daimabad	BS-178	2950+100 BP	1090+105 BC	1211, 1180, 1165, cal. BC	Phase IV	Charocal
Daimabad	BS-179	2970+100 BP	1110+105 BC	1255, 1240, 1221, cal. BC	Phase IV	Charocal
Daimabad	BS-656	3050+150 BP	1190+155 BC	1420, cal. BC	Phase IV	Charocal
Inamgaon	TF-1000	3230+80 BP	1375+80 BC	1516 cal. BC	Phase III	Charocal
Inamgaon	PRL-59	3210+110 BP	1355+115 BC	1512 cal. BC	Phase III	Charocal

1	*2*	*3*	*4*	*5*	*6*	*7*
Inamgaon	TF-934	3225+200 BP	1370+205 BC	1515 cal. BC	Phase III	Charocal
Inamgaon	TF-1001	3415+90 BP	1565+95 BC	1738 cal. BC	Phase III	Charocal
Inamgaon	PRL-133	3230+105 BP	1375+110 BC	1516 cal. BC	Phase III	Charocal
Inamgaon	PRL-77	3310+110 BP	1460+115 BC	1614 cal. BC	Phase III	Charocal
Inamgaon	BS-277	3078+100 BP	1220+105 BC	1393, 1332, 1328 cal. BC	Phase III	Charocal
Inamgaon	BS-263	3310+130 BP	1460+135 BC	1614 cal. BC	Phase III	Charcoal
Inamgaon	TF-997	1530+105 BP	375+110 BC	544 cal. AD	Phase IV	Charcoal
Inamgaon	PRL-78	2740+115 BP	870+120 BC	901 cal. BC	Phase IV	Charcoal
Inamgaon	PRL-76	3220+110 BP	1365+115 BC	1514 cal. BC	Phase IV	Charcoal
Inamgaon	TF-1087	3260+105 BP	1410+110 BC	1523 cal. BC	Phase IV	Charcoal
Inamgaon	BS-103	3355+105 BP	1505+110 BC	1675 cal. BC	Phase IV	Charcoal
Inamgaon	BS-468	3120+105 BP	1265+120 BC	1415 cal. BC	Phase IV	Charcoal
Inamgaon	TF-1086	3385+150 BP	1535+155 BC	1687 cal. BC	Phase IV	Charcoal
Inamgaon	TF-1085	3295+105 BP	1445+110 BC	1603, 1558, 1538 cal.	Phase IV	Charcoal
Inamgaon	BS-488	3050+100 BP	1190+105 BC	1376, 1346, 1318 cal. BC	Phase IV	Charcoal
Inamgaon	PRL-57	3050+105 BP	1190+110 BC	1376, 1346, 1318 cal. BC	Phase V	Charcoal
Inamgaon	TF-922	3260+105 BP	1410+110 BC	1523 cal. BC	Phase V	Charcoal
Inamgaon	BS-467	2740+100 BP	870+105 BC	901 cal. BC	Phase V	Charcoal
Inamgaon	BS-466	3060+120 BP	1200+125 BC	1382, 1341, 1321 cal. BC	Phase V	Charcoal
Inamgaon	BS-461	3070+100 BP	1210+105 BC	1388, 1336, 1325 cal BC	Phase V	Charcoal
Inamgaon	TF-995	1775+125 BP	120+130 BC	241 cal. AD	Phase V	Charcoal
Inamgaon	BS-923	2855+150 BP	990+155 BC	1010 cal. BC	Phase V	Charcoal
Inamgaon	BS-487	3000+100 BP	1140+105 BC	1263 cal. BC	Phase V	Charcoal
Inamgaon	TF-1235	3135+90 BP	1280+95 BC	1422 cal. BC	Phase V	Charcoal
Inamgaon	BS-462	3310+110 BP	1460+115 BC	1614 cal. BC	Phase V	Charcoal
Inamgaon	BS-501	3160+80 BP	1305+80 BC	1433 cal. BC	Phase V	Charcoal
Inamgaon	BS-500	3100+90 BP	1245+95 BC	1406 cal. BC	Phase V	Charcoal
Inamgaon	BS-486	3020+100 BP	1160+105 BC	1299, 1276, 1269 cal. BC	Phase V	Charcoal

1	2	3	4	5	6	7
Inamgaon	BS-489	3020+100 BP	1160+105 BC	1299, 1276, 1269 cal. BC	Phase V	Charcoal
Inamgaon	BS-463	2980+110 BP	1120+115 BC	1258, 1235, 1226 cal. BC	Phase V	Charcoal
Inamgaon	PRL-93	3020+105 BP	1160+110 BC	1299, 1276, 1269 cal BC	Phase V	Charcoal
Inamgaon	TF-1330	3090+100 BP	1235+100 BC	1400 cal. BC	Phase V	Charcoal
Inamgaon	PRL-94	3020+115 BP	1160+120 BC	1299, 1276, 1269 cal.	Phase V	Charcoal
Inamgaon	BS-502	3050+100 BP	1190+105 BC	1376, 1346, 1318 cal. BC	Phase V	Charcoal
Inamgaon	TF-923	2890+170 BP	1025+175 BC	1057 cal. BC	Phase V	Charcoal
Kaothe	BS-567	3870+90 BP	2035+95 BC	2451, 2433, 2392 2384, 2356 cal BC	Phase I	Charcoal
Songaon	TF-384	3415+105 BP	1565+110 BC	1738 cal. BC	Phase III	Charcoal
Songaon	TF-383	3185+100 BP	1330+105 BC	1448 cal. BC	Phase IV	Charcoal
Songaon	TF-379	3150+90 BP	1295+95 BC	1248 cal. BC	Phase IV	Charcoal
Songaon	TF-380	3230+105 BP	1375+110 BC	1516 cal. BC	Phase IV	Charcoal
Songaon	TF-382	3195+100 BP	1340+105 BC	1499, 1482 1458 cal. BC	Phase IV	Charcoal

9 ❖ The Protohistoric Cultures of the Ganga Valley

VIBHA TRIPATHI

THE Ganga valley witnessed intense human activity through the millennia. The rivers Ganga and Yamuna and their tributaries have shaped the physico-cultural personality of the land. The upper regions are climatically drier and more arid as compared to the lower parts of the plains that remained swampy and too thickly forested to facilitate human occupation till a much later period. Stone Age cultures, however, did flourish in the surrounding hilly areas. The plains, especially the upper Gangetic doab, was first colonised by a culture known as the Ochre Washed Ware or Ochre-Coloured Pottery culture (OCP). It was partially contemporaneous with the highly developed Indus Valley civilization, as found in the arid zone of the Indo-Gangetic divide. The two appear to have existed largely independent of each other in their respective ecological zones. At some stages possibly there was some interaction, the traces of which are somewhat reflected in the ceramic tradition. But by and large the OCP culture seems to emerge without any antecedents, remains a transient and flimsy culture, and disappears without much of a legacy. This may be treated as a prelude to what Sir Mortimer Wheeler designated as the "Ganges Civilization". The present discussion is confined to the protohistoric cultures of Ganga plains and includes both the OCP and Painted Grey Ware (PGW) cultures. Together, these cultures occupy a time-span of nearly two and a half millennia.

THE OCHRE-COLOURED POTTERY CULTURE

Copper hoards containing heavy copper implements in sizable numbers were discovered in the Upper Ganga plains. Several of these sites yielded

OCP from excavation. The ware was first discovered at Bisauli in Badaun district and at Rajpur Parasu in Bijnaur district, both in western Uttar Pradesh, by Lal in 1950–51 (Lal 1951: 233). The site of Bhadarabad in Hardwar district was discovered in the following year (Sharma 1961). These initial discoveries were quickly followed by the reporting of a large number of OCP sites like Ambakheri and Baragaon both in Saharanpur district (Deshpande 1965), Hastinapur in Meerut district (Lal 1954–55), Atranjikhera in Etah district (Gaur 1983), Ahichchhatra in Bareilly district (Banerjee 1969) and Lal Qila in Bulandshahar district (Gaur 1955). OCP has also been found in the neighbouring states of Haryana, Punjab and Rajasthan. There is a definite concentration of sites in Saharanpur, Muzaffarnagar, Meerut and Bulandshahar districts of western Uttar Pradesh. The OCP culture extends from Bahadarabad near Haradwar to Noh near Bharatpur in Rajasthan (a distance of 300 km. from north to south) and from Katpalon near Jullundar in the Punjab to Ahichchhatra near Bareilly in UP (a stretch of approximately 450 kms. from west to east). The upper Ganga-Yamuna doab, particularly the district of Saharanpur which accounts for as many as 80 sites, forms the focal point of distribution.

Dikshit (1973) and Suraj Bhan (1971–72: 16–21) have suggested two clear-cut divisions within the OCP culture. Agrawal (1982) discusses the OCP culture under two zones (western and eastern zones). There are also cultural specifications associated with these geographical regions. Zone A includes eastern Rajasthan, Haryana, western Uttar Pradesh with sites like Jodhpura, Siswal, Mitathal, Bara, Ambakheri and Baragaon. The region has a predominantly Harappan overtone, especially in its ceramic repertoire. Late Harappan and Cemetery H traits mixed with local features are also discernible. Zone B is the area of mid- and eastern Uttar Pradesh containing sites like Lal Qila, Atranjikhera, Hastinapur, Saipai, Jakhera and Sringaverpura. The pottery of this zone is by and large devoid of Harappan and Cemetery H influences. There is the absence of shapes like basins with beaded rim, dish-on-stand and flasks. Gaur feels that this is the genuine OCP culture (Gaur 1995). He further believes that the late Harappans came into contact with the OCP people somewhere near the western borders of Uttar Pradesh, following which a mutual borrowing of cultural traits took place.

The Ceramic

The OCP culture is predominantly characterized by a ceramic described by B.B. Lal 'as-ill fired, thick, ochre-washed and rolled' Similarly Y.D.

Sharma (1961) calls it 'red, thick and inadequately fired'. It rubs off easily. It is treated with a wash which is red in colour. The fabric of OCP ranges from fine to medium. Examples with a coarser fabric are not altogether missing. In view of the rolled nature of the ware, the striation marks are missing, thereby making it difficult to ascertain whether the pottery was wheel made. Subsequent excavations at sites like Lal Qila and Saipai yielded well-preserved pottery with a bright red surface and paintings in black or bearing incised and applique decorations. These excavations further attested to the use of wheel along with hand-made specimens. The main shapes of OCP are jars with horizontally splayed out rim (found at Saipai, Lal Qila, Ambakheri), basins with splayed out beaded rim (Ambakheri, Lal Qila), storage jars with slightly beaded rim (Ambakheri), bowl-shaped lid with central knob, ring stand (Ambakheri), bowl with everted rim (Ambakheri, Lal Qila and Atranjikhera), dish-on-stand with a drooping rim (Ambakheri and Bahadarabad), flask (Ambakheri), channel-like spout (Atranjikhera, Ahichchhatra and Saipai), and miniature pots (Jhinjhina and Ambakheri).

Most of the shapes (specially the first seven) have been noted at sites with Harappan affiliations too (Gaur 1969). The surface treatment, however, is not identical. This may possibly be due to the extraneous factors like waterlogging or wind action that have affected the OCP. The flask at Ambakheri is quite similar in shape to the one found in Late Harappan levels of Bhagwanpura in Haryana. On the basis of these affinities, archaeologists like Gaur have advocated some kind of a relationship between the Late Harappan of the Indo-Gangetic divide and the OCP of the Ganga-Yamuna doab. The presence of typical objects like terracotta cakes and terracotta humped bull along with the above-mentioned shapes is a strong indication of the survival of the Harappan traits at some of the OCP sites.

Atranjikhera, Lal Qila and Mainpuri have a variety of painted designs showing a vague affinity with the Bara ware. According to Gaur, wide, thick bands on or above the shoulders of pots are the most frequent motif; parallel bands and also parallel bands alternating with incised ribs and criss-cross or check designs on the body of the vessels are the other designs generally met with.

Suraj Bhan (1971–72: 17) underlines the fact that group A has three dominant features, viz., surviving Harappan, Cemetery H, and non-Harappan and non-Cemetery H elements (as at Ambakheri). "Group B is distinguished by preponderance of the last category of elements and is almost free from the other two categories of wares, i.e., the Harappan and

Cemetery H as at Atranjikhera, Saipai, etc." It has incised decorations. Group A pottery has close affinities with Bargaon and Alamgirpur. Hence Suraj Bhan (1971–72: 18) states that "the group A is nothing more than the Bargaon ware minus the classical Harappan shapes."

The Settlements

The OCP settlements may be grouped under two classes: single period sites and multiculture sites with OCP being the earliest culture. The sites belonging to the former group are marked by a slightly raised level of earth from the surrounding area. At Keseri the deposit is 0.5 m thick, 0.6 m at Jhinjhina and Bahadarabad and 0.92 m at Baharia. At multi-culture sites the thickness shows considerable increase: 0.69 m at Ahichchhatra, from 0.98 m to 1.50 m at Atranjikhera, 0.90 m at Noh, 1.2 m at Jodhpur, from 1 to 2.45 m at Lal Qila, and from 0.75 m to 1.5 m at Daulatpur.

In horizontal extent the OCP settlements are generally quite small and measure up to 200/300 m^2. At Atranjikhera the OCP settlement is about 300 m^2 and at Daulatpur it measures 240 × 190 m. At sites like Bahadarabad, Bisauli, Rajpur Parasu and Saipai the mounds are quite small and are now being further cut into by the expanding cultivation around them. Some of the settlements are of a relatively bigger size. Lal Qila covers an area of 632 m^2. The special status of this site is also discernible in its cultural material (Gaur 1995).

The density of OCP settlements is higher in the area of Saharanpur and Bulandshahar districts. In Sharanpur the distance between two sites is 4 to 6 km (Dikshit 1979). Gaur (1995: 215), on the basis of his explorations of Kali Nadi in Bulandshahar district, pointed out that the distances between OCP sites varies from 1 to 3 km. Thus this area seems to form the focal point of OCP culture. The settlements are generally found at distances of 5 to 8 km in other parts of Upper Ganga plains. On the basis of these data it would appear that small-sized villages were located at short distances on river banks. Many of these villages had a short life span too, as indicated by the thin deposits. Certain other sites present a slightly different picture: a large site surrounded by smaller, satellite sites.

The evidence of structures from OCP levels is very limited primarily due to the disturbed nature of deposits and also due to the small size of excavations. However, at sites like Lal Qila, Atranjikhera, Daulatpur and Jodhpura definite evidence of structures has been unearthed. Though no definite house plans could not be ascertained, it may be said that the people in the beginning were living in houses made of wattle-and-daub as shown by the finding of pieces of burnt clay-plastered with reed marks at Lal Qila, Atranjikhera and Daulatpur. The floors were made of beaten earth. At Lal Qila, in phase B a fairly extensive clay-plastered floor, reinforced with horizontally laid potsherds rammed in earth and containing postholes, has been found. At Atranjikhera pieces of burnt clay plastered with reed marks have been discovered (Gaur 1983: 22). At Daulatpur (Gaur 1995: 217) several floors have been traced out with a large number of postholes. These postholes indicate that the huts made of wattle and daub were of different types and sizes (circular, rectangular and square). At this place the evidence of mud walls has also been found. Gaur (1983: 22) thinks that at Atranjikhera the walls were first made with reeds and twigs, then covered carefully with straw and leaves, and finally they were thickly coated with mud plaster, probably on both sides, to provide strength and smooth surfaces. Rice husk and small particles of chaff were often mixed with the clay plaster. In phase II of Lal Qila a corner probably joining two walls of a room of five courses was exposed. The exact thickness of the wall could not be traced.

At places bricks were found to be laid in single courses and joined together with clay mortar. Associated with this wall a mud platform was also discovered. In phase III the debris of mud and burnt bricks was found (including a complete wedge-shaped brick measuring 29.5/21 × 7.50 cm). The dimensions of bricks vary from 27 to 30 cm in length, from 20 to 23 cm in width and from 7.5 to 10 cm in thickness. A few brickbats were also recovered at Atranjikhera (Gaur 1983: 23). Pieces of burnt bricks were also found at Daulatpur (Gaur 1995: 217). Most probably these bricks were used in making drains and bathrooms. The most significant discovery in this regard was from Jodhpura (Vijay Kumar 1977). Here in phase ID a mud brick structure was noticed. The size of bricks ranges from 18 to 30 cm in length, from 11 to 0.26 cm in breadth and from 6 to 7 cm in thickness. These bricks were laid in two courses and joined together with mud mortar. Hearths from Lal Qila, Ambakheri and Daulatpur have been reported.

Summarizing the settlement data of the OCP culture, it may be said that it was an agrarian society with a techno-cultural make-up fit enough to occupy the virgin land of the Ganga-Yamuna doab. The relatively arid climate was a favourable factor in colonization. The settlements were close to the rivers with arable land. The villages consisted of hutments built with reeds, straw and clay. It is only the site of Lal Qila that had an exceptionally large area and houses employing use of mud bricks. Baked bricks of varying sizes probably fulfilled some special functions. Lal Qila must have served as a centre of commerce or political power, as may be presumed from its large size and material culture.

One difficult question about the OCP culture concerns the source of copper for manufacturing heavy implements. On analytical grounds, Agrawal (1968) suggested Rakha mines of Bihar as a resource zone. On typological grounds Lal (1951: 32, pl. XI) suggested similarities between the celts found in hoards from the region and specimens from Bihar and Orissa. He also brought to light the contemporary use of bar celts by the Ban Ashuria tribe of Chhotanagpur area. Rajasthan is the second likely source area, with the Ganeshwar-Jodhpura copper objects showing some typological affinities with Copper Hoard objects. There is a need to work further on the subject before saying anything positive on it. What is certain is that copper had to be brought here from a distance, as there are no known deposits in the vicinity. Nevertheless the society attained a economic and social status which permitted the luxury of exchange of some precious items to procure the metal they needed.

Terracotta Objects

The people achieved a fair degree of mastery over terracotta art. Lal Qila yielded two unique female figurines (mother goddess), and at Ambakheri animal figurines (humped bull) have been found. Lal Qila also produced two modelled anthropomorphic figurines, two animal figurines, two legs of two different animals, two birds and two dogs. Besides, dabbers, sling balls, pottery discs and pendants are reported from Atranjikhera. Terracotta beads and cakes have also been reported from Ambakheri. A large member of other terracottas have also been reported from Lal Qila. These include: wheels (14 in number), bangles (27), playing balls (18), sling balls (2), clay tablets (2), gamesmen (2), crucibles (2), pottery disc, (12), stamp (1), terracotta beads (25), grinders (16), querns (29), miniature querns (3), skin rubber (1), and sharpeners (4).

Stone Objects

Stone objects of various kinds have been recovered from excavations at Atranjikhera, Ambakheri and Lal Qila. At Atranjikhera querns of sandstone (7) and dark grey quartzite pestles of sandstone and orthoquartzite, and a few indeterminate objects of sandstone have been found. A carnelian bead and saddle querns with pestles have also been reported from Ambakheri. Lal Qila excavation (Gaur 1995) has yielded a large number (114 altogether) of stone objects of various types. These include beads (4), points (1), pestles (23), grinders (16), querns (29), miniature querns (23), sharpeners (4), skinrubber (1), slingballs (2), netsinker (1), indeterminate objects (27), and pebbles (3). Most of the objects are from the middle level (70).

Bone Tools

The authors of OCP culture also used bone tools of various types. From Lal Qila 17 bone objects including arrowheads (6), styluses (4), and points (7) have been excavated.

Copper Implements

Sites like Atranjikhera, Saipai and Lal Qila yielded copper objects too. At Atranjikhera (Gaur 1983) a piece of copper and fragments of a terracotta crucible containing copper granules have been found. Two copper objects, a hooked spearhead and a harpoon have also been discovered from Saipai. From Lal Qila excavation five copper implements comprising pendants (2), and one specimen each of bead, arrowhead and broken celt have been reported.

Plant Remains

The OCP people recognized the fertility of the soil and practised agriculture. Grains of barley, paddy, gram and grass pea have been reported from Atranjikhera (Chaudhary 1983: 457–60). Barley, wheat, rice, cucurbitaceous seeds and a broken corn seed have been recovered from Lal Qila (Gaur 1995: 159).

Animal Remains

Among the animal remains pig, horse and dog are domesticated. The bones of these animals have been reported from Lal Qila. The bones of cattle have also been found at Atranjikhera and Saipai. Lal Qila excavations have yielded bone material representing animals like the Nilgai and birds.

The foregoing data provides some insight into the socio-economic life of the authors of the OCP culture. Despite its short spatial and chronological limits, the culture appears to have evolved a sound economic base. Agriculture appears to have been substantiated by animal husbandry and hunting. The large-sized storage jars indicate production on an appreciable scale. Similarly, the presence of a fairly good number of grinding stones, pestles and querns suggests sedentary life with a bias towards agricultural economy.

The OCP people were adept in the use of copper. If Copper Hoards are to be attributed to the OCP culture, not much elaboration is needed about their expertise in metal (copper) technology. The metallurgical skill, though not too well developed, involved the use of simple closed moulds for casting. Casting and annealing were practised. Generally the copper objects are of pure copper but 46% of them show arsenic alloying (Agrawal 1982: 210). This kind of alloying pattern sets the Copper Hoards apart from the Harappan metal works. This is a feature that needs special attention, particularly in view of the minor similarities between the pottery traditions of the two cultures.

Chronology and End of OCP Culture

The nature of deposit of the OCP culture is such that carbon samples useful for C^{14} dating could not be found. There are TL dates from several sites: Atranjikhera, Lal Qila, Nasirpur and Jhinjhina have given TL dates ranging from 2650 to 1180 BC. Three dates fall between 2630 and 2030 BC and five between 1780 and 1180 BC (see Table 1). Thus the culture appears to be a late contemporary of the Indus Valley civilization and continues up to the Late Harappan cultural horizon of Punjab-Haryana. We cannot therefore rule out some kind of late Harappan affiliations in pottery forms or

Table 1. **Thermoluminescence dates for sites belonging to Ochre-Coloured Pottery culture**

Site	*Sherd no.*	*T.L. Age (Years BC)*	*Mean T.L. (Years BC)*
Atranjikhera	$111b^4$	1610	1690
	$111b^5$	1170	
	$111c^1$	2280	
	$111c^2$	1250	
	$111c^3$	2130	
Lal Qila	$112a^1$	1730	1880
	$112a^2$	2030	
Jhinjhina	$113a^2$	1990	2070
	$113b^1$	1570	
	$113b^2$	2650	
Nasirpur	$114a^1$	1500	1340
	$114a^2$	1180	

design repertoire of the OCP. Yet the two traditions maintained their respective identities as is apparent from the cultural material. The late Harappan impact on ceramic tradition was confined to a restricted area comprising especially Haryana.

OCP and large hoards containing copper objects have turned up in different parts of the Ganga plains due to some accidental diggings since 1822. Outside the valleys of the rivers Ganga and Yamuna, similar implements have been found from Chhotanagpur, Orissa, Bengal and Bihar. Identical objects have been unearthed in fairly sizable number in Rajasthan too. However, the highest number of hoards are present in the Ganga-Yamuna doab and these have the most exclusive typology too. These hoards were quite enigmatic, including their cultural affiliation and authorship. However, the presence of two implements of this family at Saipai in Etawah district (Wahal 1971–74: 12; Lal 1971–72: 47) serves to clinch the issue of their authorship. These are a hooked sword and a harpoon that are identical in shape and size with the Copper Hoard typology (see Pl. II A and II B in *Puratattva* no. 5 1971–72). Without going into details on this subject it may safely be stated here that there is a fair possibility that the Copper Hoards were related to the OCP culture. The sudden disappearance of the OCP from the scene suggests a calamity or eventuality that forced people to put together their precious belongings into hoards and bury them before leaving the habitations while running for their lives. The enormous weight must have been a deterrent in carrying them along. It has been argued that the OCP came to an end due to (a) heavy flood and (b) strong wind action. A few words about these views may not be out of place here.

The end of OCP was an outcome of wind action is a hypothesis put forth by Dr. B.B. Lal (1971–72: 49–58). He had systematically analyzed soil samples determining the grain size and content from OCP sites like Ahichchhatra, Baragaon, Hastinapur, Nasirpur and Jhinjhina. He has summed up his examination stating that the OCP strata do not appear to have been deposited by water as there are neither ripple marks or are they current bedded. "In view of these considerations the deposits in question cannot be attributed to flooding and water logging" (Lal 1971–72: 55). He has argued that not all the pots show weathering. In case of waterlogging every pot would have been affected. The reasons for weathering seem to relate to wind activity caused by arid condition. The OCP suffered weathering as a result of exposure to atmosphere for a considerable amount of time. It remained in contact with moisture and soluble salts and this led to peeling of the surfaces of vessels.

Agrawal, on the other hand, attributes these surface features to water action. The pottery, in his opinion, remained submerged in water for a prolonged period. It may be concluded on the basis of the present state of knowledge that due to severe climatic conditions the OCP sites had to be deserted. The desertion was under duress forcing the inhabitants to bury their precious belongings like the heavy copper implements at safer places in the hope of future recovery. However, the conditions remained severe for a long period, as evidenced by the sterile layer intervening between PGW and OCP deposits, at most of the sites of the Ganga plains.

THE PAINTED GREY WARE CULTURE

Sir Mortimer Wheeler (1959) chose to designate the PGW culture as the Ganges Civilization, perhaps to match it with the Indus Civilization. Indeed, among the cultures of the Gangetic plains the PGW culture with its sophisticated pottery and other material attributes drew enthusiastic attention. Though first discovered during the excavations at Ahichchhatra (in Bareilly district) in the forties (Ghosh and Panigrahi 1945), the PGW culture gained real significance with excavations at Hastinapur (Lal 1954–55). Being the earliest prominent culture with flimsy traces of OCP lying underneath it at a site like Hastinapur, it got a Mahabharata affiliation (Lal 1954–55). The excavation at Hastinapur was followed by explorations and trial trenching at a large number of sites in the surrounding region. Interestingly, the PGW culture was found at sites like Indrapat, Bhaghpat, Sonepat, Tilpat, Kurukshetra, Mathura, Kampil and Raja Karan ka Qila, most of which have some connections with the Mahabharata story. On the strength of such circumstantial evidence and also taking into consideration chronological proximity, Lal put forward the hypothesis that the PGW represents the Mahabharata culture. Notwithstanding the objections and counterarguments by several scholars the hypothesis still holds ground. Additionally, there are other cultural attributes for which the PGW culture is known, viz., technological advancement as exemplified in the use of iron and glass (in this region), and a better and more organized socio-economic structure that brought the Gangetic plains to the threshold of urbanization.

The PGW culture has so far been studied with the help of vertical excavations conducted in the Ganga-Yamuna doab and the adjoining Saraswati-Drishadvati valleys. Most of the early excavations were confined to digging of small trenches; such excavations have a limited role to play. As Subbarao (1958: 2) pointed out, “Once a rough outline has emerged within the framework of a satisfactory chronology, we shall be able to revert to large scale horizontal excavations to fill in the details." Have we succeeded in our planning? Even after forty years we have carried out only a few horizontal excavations. We still have skeletons without much flesh and blood added to it. In the light of data from recently excavated sites we may take a review of the main aspects of the PGW culture.

The Ceramic

The Painted Grey Ware, as the name itself suggests, is a smooth surfaced grey coloured pottery, with the grey colour ranging from soft silvery grey to battleship grey. There is black painting, generally consisting of simple geometric designs decorating both surfaces of the pots. Clay used for this ware is of a high quality, totally devoid of degraissants. Elaborate preparation of the clay seems to have been made to ensure a fine pottery with a very thin section."The fabric is so distinctive that it is the safest criterion to distinguish it from the cruder forms to which it degenerated later" (Lal 1954–55: 32).

The pots are thrown on a fast rotating wheel for egg-shell thickness. They are returned to the wheel for a second time once they attain a leather hard condition. The walls of pots are trimmed and pared further with the help of scrapers. Some kind of smoothening emulsion was applied at this stage to obtain smooth surface with a matt finish. This technique, however, is restrictive as only open mouthed shapes could be fashioned by its application. Perhaps this is the reason for the presence of a limited variety of shapes in PGW. We generally come across bowls and dishes. However, other shapes like *lota* or miniature pots are also met with, albeit in very restricted numbers (Fig. 1).

Firing technique must have been highly evolved too, as indicated by virtually flawless finish with a uniform texture and colour of pots. The temperature in the kiln must have been high and the atmosphere reducing. Sana Ullah (1934–35: 88) attributed the colour to the presence of black ferrous oxide in the clay as the core of pottery is grey coloured too. The iron in the grey pottery was reduced to ferrous state during the firing. There are many PGW specimens having a reddish hue. A good number of such sherds were noted by the author in the collection from Ahichchhatra (Tripathi 1976: 43). Such specimens could be the outcome of oxidization or perhaps a different kind of local clay used for manufacture.

PGW has a very distinctive painting tradition. Black or deep chocolate designs adorn the grey surface of the ware. The motifs are simple and

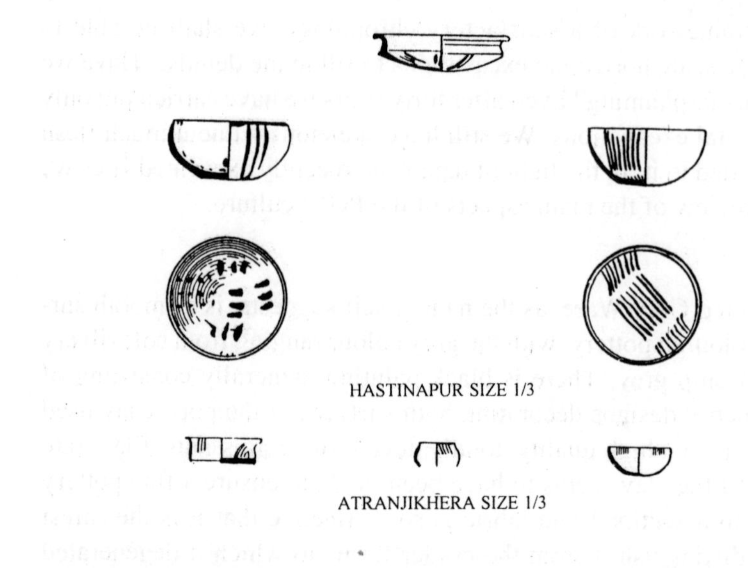

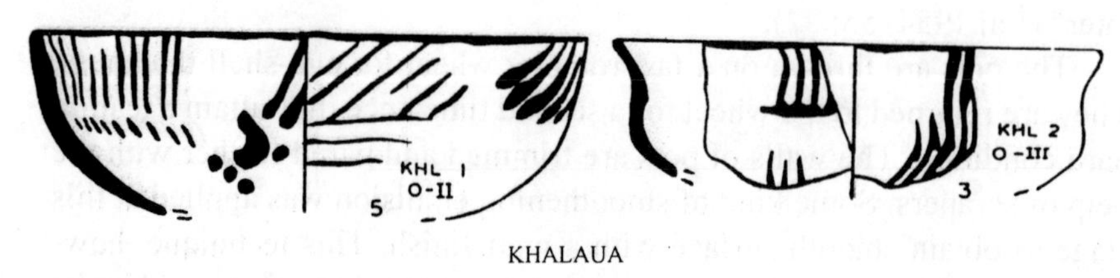

Fig. 1. Vessel forms in Painted Grey Ware

mostly geometric with multiple strokes being the most common design. Dots, dashes, circles, spirals, concentric circles, checks, swastika and sigmas are commonly executed designs. Maltese cross is found at Bhagwanpura in Haryana. Some natural designs like floral patterns and sun symbols are also present, though not very commonly (see Tripathi 1976: figs. 6–9). What is noteworthy about the paintings of this ware is that there is the use of multiple brush so as to paint several rows of the motif simultaneously. The effect is uniformity in strokes.

Incised designs are also found in this fabric but on plain grey ware. Many a time the same designs like spirals and concentric circles are repeated in stamped and incised forms of decoration. Such decorations are more commonly seen on sites of Rajasthan area. On closer observation, it seems that many of these stamped motifs appearing on several Punjab-Haryana and Rajasthan sites have been painted with black pigment on the PGW of the Gangetic doab.

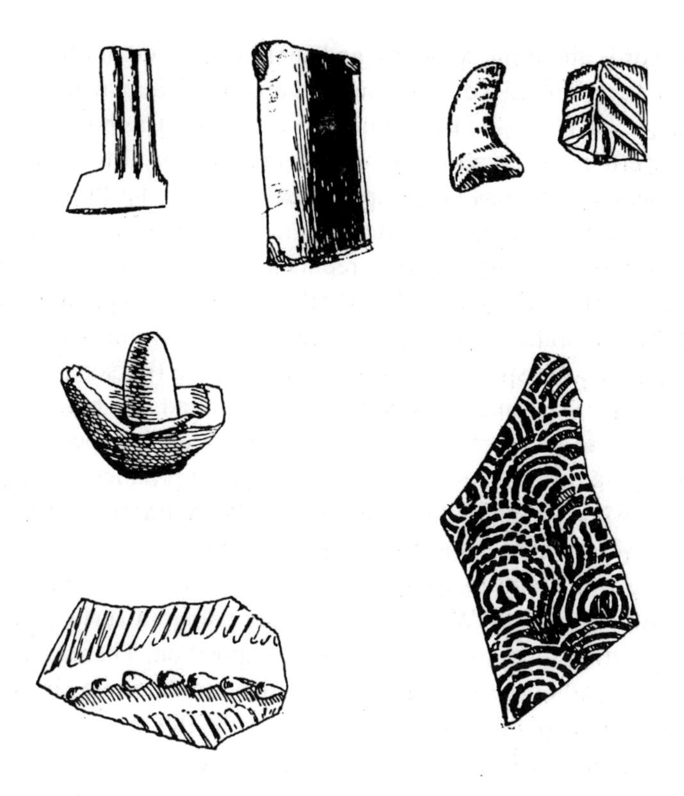

Fig. 2. Some rare shapes and designs of the Painted Grey Ware culture

Though no formal and detailed functional analysis of PGW has been undertaken, it has been suggested by Lal (1969: 5; pl. 4) that it was the table ware of its time. It represents the typical dining set of a traditional Indian kitchen, perhaps of the elite class. It has been designated as the deluxe ware of its times, for the simple reason that this pottery accounts for only a very small percentage (3–10%) of the total ceramic assemblage of its period. The other functions of the kitchen and storage were fulfilled by a variety of ceramics like plain grey ware, Black Slipped Ware (BSW), Black-and-Red Ware (BRW) and the commonest of all, Red ware. Besides bowls and dishes of the typical PGW type, jars, vases and vessels of different varieties, basins (clipped, plain and footed) and perforated jars are commonly found. Water vessels and storage jars have been produced in medium to coarse fabric. Amongst the rare types (Fig. 2) mention may be made of knobbed lids (Sardargarh, Rajasthan), stoppers (Kampil, U.P.), *lota* (Rupar) and ring base (Allahpur) (see Tripathi 1976: pl. I–V).

A few words about the scientific and analytical observations of PGW are in order here before we move on to the cultural dimensions of this period. Sana Ullah (1934–35) and Ballabh Saran (1969), as pointed above, have made certain observations about the manufacture of PGW. More recently, Hegde (1987) has taken up a close study of the PGW. He has observed that PGW bears black painting which is of the same pigment as the surface of NBP. It is difficult to agree with Hedge, as the NBP is noted for its shining surface while the PGW (both its surface and painting) has a matt finish. No laboratory examination is required to say this. However, in certain cases, e.g., the specimens from Sringaverpura (personal observation), a grey ware very similar to PGW has been found; the pigment used in painting is close in lustre to NBP. May be the late PGW period specimens showing up during the NBP period are a local product prepared by artisans, who were somehow familiar with the PGW tradition. The plain grey pottery was painted using NBP slip to produce the effect of PGW. Technically, it is difficult to separate the pigment used for painting from the surface of a typical PGW sample. Both the coloured surface and the pigment of painting seem to have the same composition. There is a possibility that some carbonaceous material was added to the same clay by the potter to prepare the pigment for painting (Tripathi 1997a: 65).

To sum up, the PGW is one of the most evolved ceramic traditions of its times and reflects the mastery that its makers achieved on pyrotechnology. Firing process was perfect, as with pyro-technologies associated with metallurgy and glass.

Distribution Pattern

The PGW is the most extensive protohistoric culture of the Indo-Gangetic doab that came up after the decline of urban centres of the Indus Valley Civilization. It expands from the Himalayan foothills, Gharinda near Attari on the Indo-Pak border in Amritsar district and Rupar in the north to the plateau region of Madhya Pradesh (up to Kayatha and Ujjain) and from the Bahawalpur state of Pakistan to Kausambi on the Yamuna near Allahabad. Earlier it was thought to have occupied only the plains but more recently the culture has been found in the hilly regions of Kumaon-Garhwal at Kashipur, Thapli, Purola (Nautiyal et al. 1996) and several other places. In time, the PGW is argued to have started in 1100 BC (or even earlier) and lasted up to 500–400 BC. Thus both in time and space the culture is fairly extensive. It is only too natural to expect that such circumstances rule out a uniform cultural pattern.

Regional Variability

On closer observation the PGW culture manifests strong regional variations (Tripathi 1976, 1990–91, 1997a, 1997b). At least four zones have been identified on the basis of finer variations in pottery and other cultural material.

Zone I includes the sites in the Cholistan region of Bahawalpur state in Pakistan covering the dried up beds of the rivers Saraswati (locally called Hakra in Pakistan) and Drishadvati. Ghosh had explored the area and conducted small-scale excavations at a few sites. The PGW sherds are quite restricted in number with a greater variation of designs. There is also a relative profusion of BRW and plain grey ware. Another distinctive feature here is that a large number of red ware sherds bear stamped and incised decorations which are quite typical of this zone.

Zone II lies in the upper reaches of the Saraswati valley. One barely finds traces of occupation of the PGW culture in the lower reaches, as this stretch is more or less dry for most of the year. The Drishadvati has only two sites (as located by Ghosh) while the Saraswati, on its eastern side, yielded 44 sites. In Haryana alone there are about 71 PGW sites, all located in the upper reaches of the river. It appears that the dwindling supply of water forced the PGW folk to move upwards in search of better land. The intervening drier region has been avoided by the settlers. There are Late Harappan sites in this area, but the PGW sites are negligible in number there. In Harayana, in the upper Saraswati basin, the PGW and late Harappan cultures have been found overlapping as at Bhagwanpura and other sites reported by Joshi (Joshi 1993). Some Late Harappan influence on the PGW culture is inevitable here.

Zone III is the mature level of the PGW culture and covers the Ganga-Yamuna doab. There is standardization in the ceramic tradition with sophistication of a high order. The structural activity is more elaborate with mud bricks instead of only use of wattle-and-daub houses. The evidence from Jakhera (Sahi 1994) and also Atranjikhera (Gaur 1983) shows improvement in settlements. There is an expansion in the size of settlements and an overall improvement in the cultural repertoire.

In Zone IV the culture shows a gradual degeneration in PGW fabric and form. The number of PGW shapes is extremely restricted as compared to Zone III. As pointed above, at Sringaverpura NBPW pigment has been used to paint the grey surface of the so-called PGW. A case of such imitation of this sophisticated deluxe ware is also discernible at Vaisali (Tripathi 1992–93). Whether to call it a PGW sherd has been questioned by the present author.

The zones also indicate a shift both in time and space. There appears to be a perpetual search for better and more fertile lands with perennial sources of water. The search culminates in the colonization of the doab. Eventually the PGW culture gives way to the NBP culture with the two ceramic traditions co-existing for some time (with the exception of Hastinapur where a cultural hiatus exists between the two).

Genesis

Sahi (1996: 107) in a recent paper on the PGW culture has tried to underline its divergent contexts in different parts of its distribution zone. At sites like Rupar and Alamgirpur (and also at Hulas) the culture is preceded by a deposit of the Harappan culture and followed by the NBP culture and gaps on both the sides. At other sites like Hastinapur, Ahichchhatra and Jhinjhina it is preceded by the OCP culture or at sites like Dher Majra by the Cemetery H culture. At Daulatpur I there is an admixture of traits of the Early Harappan, Harappan, Late Harappan, OCP and Mitathal IIB cultures. At sites like Atranjikhera, Noh, Jodhpura and Jakhera the PGW is preceded by a plain BRW deposit which is independent. Jakhera has a still earlier deposit designated at proto-PGW by Sahi. The PGW culture also has several single period sites like at Kampil, Purola, etc. It is succeeded by the NBP at Sardargarh, Sonkh, Bairat, Khalaua, Mathura, Purana Qila, Allahpur, and Kanauj. At Bhagwanpura and Dadheri, as stated earlier, the PGW culture overlaps with the Late Harappan culture. Based on his personal observation of excavations at Bhagwanpura, Sahi (1996) draws attention to certain features like (a) water-borne sterile deposit intervening between the Harappan/OCP and PGW deposits; (b) the PGW assemblage in layers 1–4 having certain late NBP pottery forms; and (c) absence of BRW. In Sahi's view, the last feature is a typically late one, as evident at Allahpur, Atranjikhera, Jakhera, Noh, and Jodhpura.

These observations are important indeed for finding the antecedent stages of the PGW culture. In Sahi's view the proto-PGW stratum at Jakhera has predominant Chalcolithic features (Sahi 1996: 113, 114). He also advocates Malwa culture influences on the PGW, especially in stroke paintings, presence of a thin grey pottery at sites like Eran, Kayatha and Besnagar which "may have been an earlier manifestation of the PGW and both might have had a genetic relationship" (ibid., 110). However, this assumption appears to be tenuous in view of the slender evidence it is based on. Lal (1954–55) drew attention to similarities with a grey ceramic found at Shahi

Tump and several other sites in areas bordering India in the northwest to prove movement of grey ceramic and an Aryan association of the PGW culture. This has hardly found acceptance among scholars so far. The tradition of grey pottery is present in a big way in the Gandhara region (Gandhara Grave culture).

Joshi (1993: 237–8) has found a plain grey pottery at Manda, 28 km northwest of Jammu on the Chenab river in the foothills of Pir Panjal Range. In sub-period IB at Manda a grey ware generally found in association with the PGW was noted. The main shapes are bowls and dishes and this pottery accounts for 7 to 19 per cent of total ceramic assemblage. The rest of the ware is burnished grey ware of Harappan affiliation. Thus an interlocking of grey ware with the late Harappan culture has been suggested by Joshi (1993: 241–42). Manda, also being the northernmost site having a grey ware, is supposed to have an important bearing on the genesis of the PGW culture. Hence scholars have accepted this route for suggesting a movement of people from the west. Thapar's (1970: 151) comments in this connection are significant: "The link of grey complex, howsoever tenuous, is reinforced *a priori* by (a) the evidence about the use of horse (*Equus caballus*) in association with the grey ware in northern Iran (Shahi Tump II and III), Swat Valley and the Gandhara region of Pakistan (Gandhara Grave Culture) and upper India (PGW levels) and (b) the association of the predominantly Mediterranean type of people with this grey ware of northern Iran and Swat Valley. With this generalization a loop is left open at this stage for other intermediate developments which future investigators may cover." This loop, however, cannot be filled up by the Chalcolithic grey ware of central India. Even today the balance appears to be titled more in favour of the western and northern influence than others. The literary evidence belonging to the time period 1000 BC–500 BC is rich. It proves beyond doubt that there was a movement of people from the Saraswati-Drishadvati region to the Ganga plains. The geochronological evidence for the drying up of the Saraswati is strong and well understood today. The archaeological data seems to favour such movements too. However, due to geographical proximity regional variants play a strong role in the transmission of cultural elements. Sahi's observations may be explained under these conditions. The area of impact is localized. Phases like the proto-PGW are restricted to a very limited area indeed. This does not seem to have a serious repercussion on the issue of genesis of the PGW culture (see Tripathi 1997: 67–70).

Chronological Perspectives

The zonal distribution is interlinked with the dispersal of the culture both in time and space. There is every probability that the sites in the Saraswati-Drishadvati valleys are earlier than those of the Ganga valley. In view of the proposed heterogeneous character of the PGW culture, its chronology cannot be uniform throughout the distribution zone. Every individual site has to be evaluated on its own merits. A site like Hastinapur which has a break between cultures may not bear the same age as the one which shows an overlap with the Late Harappan culture. Likewise, the Harappan contacts or iron association may be important factors having inevitable repercussions on chronology of the culture at the site. We may therefore propose a few distinct site categories:

1. Sites in the dried up Saraswati-Hakra bed.
2. Sites in the upper reaches of the Saraswati river having Late Harappan association as an overlap, but without any knowledge of iron.
3. Sites in the Ganga-Yamuna doab having iron.
4. Sites in the peripheral regions as at Sravasti, Kausambi, Ujjain, Kayatha, etc.

There are no radiocarbon dates from the sites of the Saraswati-Drishadvati valleys, but these sites seem to be earlier than those of the Ganga-Yamuna doab. The nature of pottery, the absence of iron and the literary evidence support an earlier time bracket for the sites of this region (see Tripathi 1990–91).

As one moves upwards on the Saraswati, one comes across the Bhagwanpura complex of sites showing an overlap of Late Harappan and Grey Ware traditions. An unpainted grey ware has been found at Manda in Jammu. Similar grey pottery has been found underlying the PGW level at Bhagwanpura also. Thus there appears to be an undercurrent of a grey ware tradition which came in contact with the Late Harappan. This was followed by the PGW in the succeeding strata.

There are no radiocarbon dates from Bhagwanpura. But TL dates (BARC, Bombay) help the excavator place the earliest period (IA) between 1700–1300 BC or even later and a date of *c.* 1400–1000 BC or a little earlier could be given to period IB (Joshi 1993: 25). However, we know that the Late Harappan pottery tradition lasts till quite late in Haryana. Therefore the PGW in this region of Haryana must have come in contact with that surviving tradition and then moved further east and north (towards Rupar and other Punjab sites).

At those sites where there is an underlying BRW cultural phase, the PGW impinges upon it. We come across this evidence at sites like Atranjikhera, Jakhera, Noh and Jodhpura. This pre-PGW culture has been dated to 1300–1100 BC by the excavator (Gaur 1983). However, there are two much younger radiocarbon dates (one of them reading 820+520 BC) from this phase of Atranjikhera which have been ignored while dealing with the chronology of this culture.

At sites like Allahpur we have another feature. There is a preponderance of BRW in the lower levels of PGW cultural horizon, though PGW is present in a small quantity. It has been designated IA on this basis (layers 14–13). By layer (12) representing IB the PGW outshines. The associated Red Ware of this sub-phase corresponds with Alamgirpur PGW phase. Without any change in frequency, fabric or form the PGW continues up to the Mauryan period. The excavator (Dikshit 1973) thinks that in view of this the PGW levels at Allahpur should be earlier than that of Hastinapur. He states that the earlier phase at the site "cannot be pushed beyond 800 BC as the ware continues up to the Mauryan levels and has a duration of approximately 400–500 years."

In any case, since PGW overlaps with NBP ware at most of the sites, the upper limit of the culture should be close to the date of beginning of NBP culture, especially at sites in western Uttar Pradesh where the culture is supposed to be later than its variant in Bihar and eastern U.P. The NBP culture is generally dated to 600–300 BC. In the PGW zone, with the exception of a few sites on the main trade caravan routes like Taxila, Sravasti and Vidisa, the NBP culture should begin around 500 BC. This also should be the date for the end of PGW culture. If this culture had a life of three to four hundred years, it should begin in 900–800 BC in the doab area. In the more westerly region it might have started somewhat earlier, say by 1000 BC. The evidence of radiocarbon dates substantiates this view (see Tripathi 1990 a, b; fig. 2). The majority of PGW sites have yielded C^{14} dates clustering around seventh to eighth centuries BC (Table 2). With the sole exception of Atranjikhera (1025+100 BC), on calibration this comes to 3136+100 BP, i.e., twelfth century BC. Since this date is an outlier, it does not warrant a serious consideration in view of a large number of dates which are centuries younger. This aspect has already been discussed at length by the author (Tripathi 1990).

Table 2. **Radiocarbon dates for Painted Grey Ware sites with iron objects**

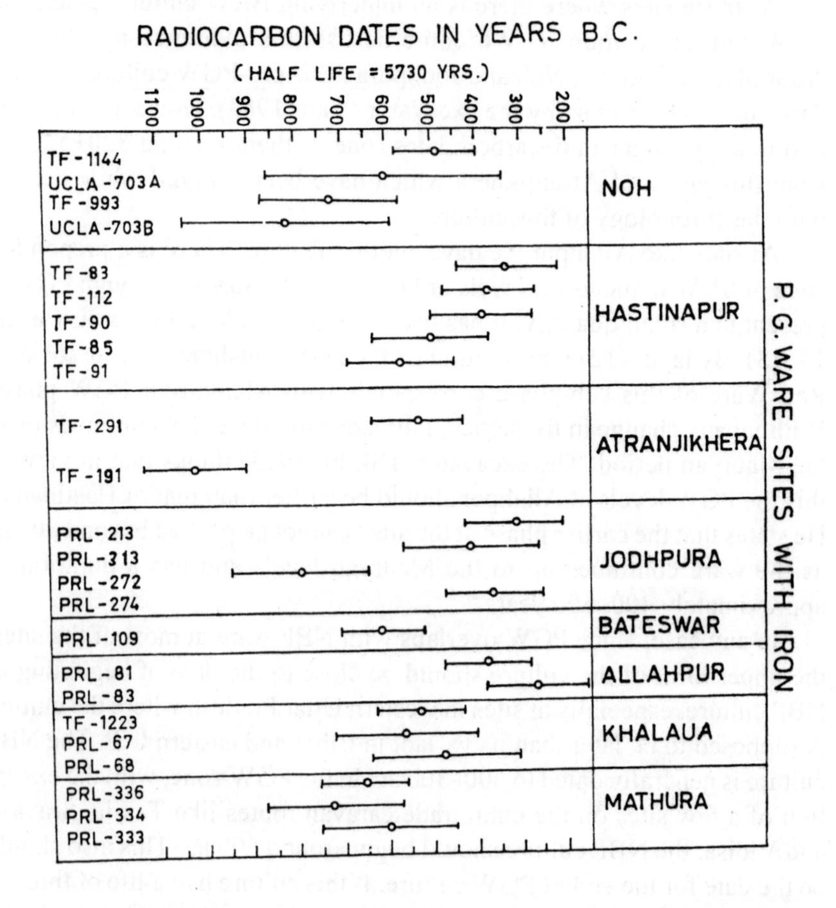

Material Culture

With relatively more extensive excavations at sites like Bhagwanpura and Jakhera, in addition to the earlier data coming from sites like Hastinapur, Alamgirpur, Ahichchhatra, Allahpur, Mathura, Kampil, Noh, and Jodhpur and from more easterly sites like Kausambi and Sravasti, the picture of PGW culture is somewhat clearer. To this may be added rich evidence pertaining to settlement pattern of the period brought to light by extensive exploratory work in certain parts of Uttar Pradesh and Haryana. These data warrant some observations about the material culture of the PGW period.

Structural activity of the PGW culture is largely confined to wattle and daub huts and mud houses. Unbaked (mud) bricks were also recovered at

Hastinapur. A baked brick too was found in a pit at Hastinapur (Lal 1954–55). Its use for structural activity has, however, not been suggested. Large-sized baked bricks, perhaps for ritualistic purposes, were found at Jakhera (Sahi 1994). At Bhagwanpura structural evidence of a 13-room, baked-brick house has come to light (Joshi 1993). Whether the house was constructed by the PGW people is not beyond doubt, in view of the absence of evidence of such a house complex from any other PGW site. There is a greater likelihood of the PGW folk reusing the house constructed and occupied by the Late Harappan people earlier.The Late Harappan folk probably also lived side by side with the PGW people for quite some time.

Besides the residential complex, Jakhera has yielded evidence of some kind of bund and a 60 m long water channel—a unique evidence of its kind (Sahi 1994: 147). This structural feature was found on the western slope of the mound and could have been longer. One more channel besides this one was also traced. This evidence bespeaks some kind of water resource management of the PGW community. Roads and lanes paved with potsherds and also a mud brick platform with unevenly laid bricks are other architectural features that came to light here. The platform was associated with a fire altar. Other fire pits with a terracotta hooded snake, a handmade crude figurine and a bowl were also unearthed at Jakhera. Many of these houses have multiple hearths, said to be community hearths, such as the ones found at Atranjikhera (Gaur 1983). Jakhera has yielded storage bins (both square and roundish) suggesting surplus production necessitating storage of grains and other food products.

Jakhera seems to represent an evolved stage of PGW culture, somewhat closer to an urban phase. It is also reflected in the cultural material of this period. Objects include gold ornaments, a gold foil and beads of semi-precious stones (numbering 106). Copper bracelets, bangles, beads and other pieces of ornaments; antimony rod, nail parer, tooth pick and copper dish along with indeterminate pieces (totalling 85 objects) were recovered from Jakhera. Ivory objects include a comb, a decorated dagger-shaped pendant and buttons. These objects contrast in shape with the finds from other PGW sites. This could be explained by suggesting that either Jakhera represents a late phase of the PGW culture or else it was an urban centre having a set of satellite settlements around it.

The PGW economy was based on agriculture and animal husbandry. Many of the animal bones are charred and bear cut marks. We come across the bones of cattle, sheep and pigs. Hastinapur has yielded horse bones too. Fish bones as well as fish-hooks are indicative of fishing. Rice, wheat, barley (wheat showing up for the first time) were the main crops cultivated during the PGW period.

Jakhera has yielded geometric appliances of stone. Weights of semi-precious stones (chert and jasper) were found at Hastinapur (Lal 1954–55: pls. 5 and 11). Other objects include bone points, arrowheads, sockets, stone blades, balls, whetstones, grinders, pestles and querns, terracotta beads, discs, balls, animal figurines and terracotta bangles. Needles, pins, etc. were objects of domestic use.

Iron was used in a regular way by the PGW people. At a few sites there is evidence of beginning of iron in pre-PGW levels, such as at Jakhera and Kausambi. There is also evidence of bits of iron at Noh in Bharatpur (Rajasthan). But proper use of iron in a noticeable way may generally be attributed to the PGW people (except Jakhera where it starts earlier in the proto-PGW level). As discussed above, the PGW has a distribution which indicates movement in time and space. In the earlier phases of the PGW culture, as found in the Bikaner region or in Saraswati valley at sites like Bhagwanpura and others, there is no evidence of iron. On the other hand, at sites in the Ganga-Yamuna doab iron appears from the earliest levels of the PGW culture, as at Atranjikhera, Alamgirpur and other sites. There is every reason to believe that the technology of iron was acquired in the passage from the Indo-Gangetic divide to the Ganga-Yamuna doab. Though this is not the right place to go into the details of the origin and dispersal of iron in India, it may be suggested that iron was recognized as a separate metal (as suggested by the bits of iron in the pre-PGW level at Noh) and experimented with (as at Jakhera). The pre-PGW BRW at Atranjikhera does not yield iron, thereby indicating that its use was not a regular one during this period. However, even the earliest layers of PGW have yielded iron at Atranjikhera, Alamgirpur, Allahpur and other sites of the region.

The use of iron during PGW period was primarily for war or hunting. One comes across a good number of arrowheads, spearheads, points, blades, daggers and lances. Almost every site has yielded these hunting/war tools. In addition, there are clamps, sockets, rods, pins, chisels, rings, adzes, axes, borers and scrapers, which are most useful in carpentry and woodwork. Jakhera has also brought forth agricultural implements like sickles, plough-shares and hoes; such implements have hardly been reported from other PGW sites. Iron was utilized for war and hunting as well as for making chariots and carts which must have been an essential part of warfare and transport. Carpentry was a respectable profession of the period, if literary evidence is any guide. The buildings of the period hardly required iron objects. Pins, rods and clamps found at most of the sites and classified as building material must have been more likely to have been used, as suggested above, in chariots or carts meant for use by the elite of the time. Thus iron at this stage hardly played a role in economic activities. Barring the rare specimens like sickle and ploughshare and hoe at Jakhera, agricultural implements have not been reported from other sites. Needless to argue, iron technology played but a minor role in economic growth, as has frequently been argued by scholars (Ghosh 1973; Chakrabarti 1994). Consolidation of power over the newly acquired land and people comes at a later stage. It is at this stage that iron technology is harnessed for purposes leading to growth and prosperity.

Settlement Pattern

Not enough data has come forth in recent years to revolutionize our ideas of the cultural dimensions of the PGW culture. However, extensive exploratory work in certain parts of the distribution zone of PGW sites does provide new insights into the settlement pattern of the culture. Archaeology has borrowed the geographical model of interpretation of certain aspects of life of man, i.e., spatial distribution and locational positioning of settlements. Such models have helped in the cultural reconstructions of past societies in a big way. In our area of study, though the data is not exhaustive, some idea may be had about the life of common man. Investigations by archaeologists in small areas have brought forth evidence of a new kind. Makkhan Lal (1984) undertook exploration of Kanpur district, Brahemdutt (1980) in Haryana, Erdosy (1985) around Kausambi and Mughal (1980) in Bahawalpur state of Pakistan. One can easily deduce a pattern in the distribution of settlements on the basis of this data. In each of these areas there are three or four categories of habitational sites, viz., small, medium and extensive.

Makkhan Lal located forty-six sites in Kanpur district. Out of these forty sites occupied below two hectares of area, two were between 2 and 2.99 ha, three were between 3 and 3.99 ha and only one site was between 4 and 4.99 ha. George Erdosy explored the area around Kausambi and brought to light 16 PGW bearing sites. One site occupied 1 hectare area and nine were between 1 and 1.99 ha, five were between 2 and 2.99 ha. Only one site was between 5 and 9.99 ha. In Haryana, Brahemdutt located thirty-four sites. Twenty-three sites were below the size of 3400 sq m in extent and nine were above this size. In Cholistan (Bahawalpur state of Pakistan) Mughal located fourteen PGW sites. The site at Satwali was very extensive and measured 13.7 ha in extent, three were below 1 ha, seven range between 1.1 and 2.1 ha and the remaining three between 3 and 4 ha.

This evidence suggests that during the PGW period there were important large-sized centres in each area. These centres were supported by certain medium-sized habitations referred to as satellite settlements. There were a number of small villages to support the larger settlements. Several such villages probably formed one larger unit of administration. The *Arthasastra* clearly refers to such administrative units that existed during the Mauryan period or even in pre-Mauryan India.

Archaeological reconstructions generally ignore the fact that the nature of cultural material will be conditioned by the type of settlement. An extensive politico-cultural centre should display more sophistication in the nature of findings compared to smaller village settlements. If we take a count of the *de luxe* pottery of its age (i.e., PGW in this case) the number should be higher with better specimens at important centres compared to the habitations of lesser significance. Thus even a single cultural component like pottery may tell us a lot about the nature and type of the settlements. Although differences in material culture remains might be related to chronological factors, still in contemporaneous situations and in divergent geographical units the village-town dichotomy should have played a key role.

The other factor of great significance here is the nature of the settlement itself: Why at all sites came up in distant regions? They must have served some specific functional requirements, viz., mineral needs of the society. There are PGW sites in Kumaon-Garhwal area that have come to light in recent years. We know that this area is rich in minerals including metal ore deposits. Stones, both ordinary and precious and semi-precious, and flora and fauna of exclusive nature were found in these areas. There is little doubt that these difficult terrains were inhabited primarily to meet the urgent needs of the society. This view is supported by the analysis undertaken by Agrawal in Kumaon. The site of Uleni in upper Ramganga basin (Almora district, Kumaon) has yielded slag heaps and iron objects. It has been C^{14} dated to 1022–826 BC (calibrated). The PGW culture flourished during this very period. To meet the requirement of minerals the culture extended up to these hills (Thapli and Purola in Garhwal region). This, in the view of Agrawal (1995: 84), was the source of iron ore for PGW folk. Thus the date and smelting evidence of iron at Uleni is very signficant (Tripathi and Mishra 1977). To arrive at definite conclusions about aspects of cultural reconstruction a resource zone study is called for. Meanwhile suffice it to state that a thorough examination of cultural material with new approaches is bound to yield encouraging results in bringing alive the life pattern of ancient societies. What is called for at this juncture is a critical and analytical approach to examine the excavated material. It is through such an approach that we will be able to provide the proverbial flesh and blood to the skeleton, as envisaged decades back by Subbarao.

REFERENCES

Agrawal, D.P. 1982. *The Archaeology of India*. London: Curzon Press.

Agrawal, D.P., Kusumgar, S., Yadava, M.G., Gogte, V.D., Kharakwal, J., and Pant, M. 1995. Was Kumaon the Source of Early Iron in North India? *Man and Environment* 20: 81–85.

Banerjee, N.R. 1969. Brief Report of Excavation at Ahichchhatra, in *Indian Archaeology—A Review, 1964–65*. New Delhi: Archaeological Survey of India, pp. 39–42.

Brahamdutt. 1980. Settlements of Painted Grey Ware Culture in Haryana. Unpublished Ph.D. Thesis. Kurukshetra: Kurukshetra University.

Chakrabarti, D.K., and Lahiri, N. 1994. The Iron Age in India: The Beginning and Consequences. *Puratattva* 24: 12–32.

Chowdhury, K.A. 1983. The Plant Remains, in *Excavations at Atranjikhera*, R.C. Gaur, ed. Delhi: Motilal Banarasidass, pp. 457–60.

Deshpande, M.N. 1965. Comments on A. Ghosh's paper on 'Indus Civilization: Its Origins, Authors, Extent and Chronology', in *Indian Prehistory*, V.N. Misra and M.S. Mate, eds. Pune: Deccan College, pp.127–29.

Dikshit, K.N. 1971. Harappa Culture in Western Uttar Pradesh. *Bulletin of National Museum* 2: 21–38. New Delhi.

—1973. The Allahpur Evidence and Painted Grey Ware Chronology, in *Radiocarbon and Indian Archaeology*, D.P. Agrawal and A. Ghosh, eds. Bombay. Tata Institute of Fundamental Research, pp.148–53.

—1979. The Ochre Coloured Ware Settlements in Ganga-Yamuna Doab, in *Essays in Indian Protohistory*. D.P. Agrawal and D.K. Chakrabarty, eds. Delhi: B.R. Publishing Corporation, pp. 285–99.

Erdosy, G. 1985. Settlement Archaeology of Kausambi Region. *Man and Environment* 9: 66–76.

Gaur, R.C. 1969. The Painted Grey Ware at Atranjikhera: An Assessment, in *Potteries in Ancient India*, B.P. Sinha, ed. Patna: Patna University, pp.185–87.

—1983. *Excavations at Atranjikhera*. Delhi: Motilal Banarasidass.

—., ed. 1994. *Painted Grey Ware*. Jaipur: Publication Scheme.

—1995. *Excavations at Lal Qila*. Jaipur: Publication Scheme.

Ghosh, A., and Panigrahi, K.C. 1945. The Pottery of Ahichchhatra. *Ancient India* 1: 37–59.

Ghosh, A. 1973. *The City in Early Historic India*. Simla: Indian Institute of Advanced Study.

Hegde, K.T.M. 1987. The Scientific Basis of Three Ancient Ceramics, in *Archaeology and History: Essays in Memory of Shri A. Ghosh*, B.M. Pande and B.D. Chattopadhyay, eds. Delhi: Agam Kala Prakashan, pp. 376–82.

Joshi, J.P. 1993. *Excavations at Bhagawanpura 1975–76 and Other Explorations and Excavations 1975–81 in Haryana, Jammu and Kashmir and Punjab*. New Delhi: Archaeological Survey of India, Memoir no. 81.

Lal, B.B. 1951. Further Copper Hoards from the Gangetic Basin and a Review of the Problem. *Ancient India* 7: 20–39.

—1954–55. Excavations at Hastinapur and Other Explorations in the Upper Ganga and Sutlej Basins (1950–52). *Ancient India* 10–11: 5–151.

—1969. Inaugural Address, in *Potteries in Ancient India*, B.P. Sinha, ed. Patna: Patna University, pp. 3–8.

—1971–72. A Note on the Excavation at Saipai. *Puratattva* 5: 46–49.

—1993. *Excavations at Sringaverpura (1977–86)*, vol. I. New Delhi: Archaeological Survey of India.

Lal, B.B. (Dr.) 1971–72. The Ochre-Coloured Pottery—A Geochronological Study. *Puratattva* 5: 49–58.

Lal, Makkhan. 1984. *Settlement History and Rise of Civilization in Ganga-Yamuna Doab*. New Delhi: B.R. Publishing Corporation.

Nautiyal.K.P., Khanduri, B.M., Nautiyal, V., and Pharswan, Y.S. 1996. Excavations at Purola: An Important PGW-cum-Vedic Ritual Site, in *Spectrum of Indian Culture*: Prof. S.B. Deo Felicitation Volume. C. Margabandhu and K.S. Ramachandran, eds. Delhi: Agam Kala Prakashan, pp.115–27.

Sahi, M.D.N. 1994. *Aspects of Indian Archaeology*. Jaipur: Publication Scheme.

—1996. Painted Grey Ware: Its Origin, Direction of Dispersal and Significance, in *Spectrum of Indian Culture*: Prof. S.B. Deo Felicitation Volume, C.Margabandhu and K.S. Ramachandran, eds. New Delhi: Agam Kala Prakashan, pp.105–12.

Sana Ullah, Khan Bahadur Mohammad. 1934–35. *Annual Reports of Archaeological Survey of India 1934–35*: 87–90.

Saran, Ballabh. 1969. Technology of the Painted Grey Ware, in *Potteries in Ancient India* B.P. Sinha, ed. Patna: Patna University, pp. 124–28.

Sharma, Y.D. 1961. Copper Hoards and Ochre Coloured Ware in Ganga Basin, in *Summaries of Papers of International Conference on Asian Archaeology*. New Delhi: Archaeological Survey of India.

Subbarao, B. 1958. *The Personality of India*, sec. edn. Vadodara: M.S.University of Baroda.

Suraj Bhan. 1971–72. Comments, in 'Proceedings of the Seminar on OCP and a Brief Report on Siswal'. *Puratattva* 5: 16–21 and 44–46 respectively.

Thapar, B.K. 1970. The Aryans: A Reappraisal of the Problem, in *India's Contribution to the World Thought and Culture* (Vivekananda Commemoration Volume), Lokesh Chandra, S.P. Gupta, Devendra Swarup and S.R. Goel, eds. Chennai: Vivekanand Rock Memorial Committee, pp. 147–64.

Tripathi, Vibha. 1976. *Painted Grey Ware—An Iron Age Culture of Northern India*. New Delhi: Concept Publishing House.

—1990. Early Historical Archaeology of India and Radiocarbon Dating, in *Proceedings of the 2nd International Symposium on C^{14} and Archaeology*, W.G. Mook and H.T. Waterbolk, eds. PACT 29, the Netherlands, pp. 289–303.

—1990–91. Macro Level Study of Painted Grey Ware Culture, *Pragdhara* (Journal of U.P. State Archaeological Organization), 1: 59–64.

—1992–93. Painted Grey Ware at Vaisali (?): a Note. *Bharati* 19 (pts. I, II): 87–90.

—1997a. Painted Grey Ware: the Ceramic and Cultural Dimensions, in *Ancient Ceramics—Historical Enquiries and Scientific Approaches,* P.C. Pant and V. Jaiswal, eds.

Delhi: Agam Kala Prakashan, pp. 63–76.
—1997b. Stages of the Painted Grey Ware Culture, in *Indian Prehistory—1980*, V.D. Misra and J.N. Pal, eds. Allahabad: University of Allahabad, pp. 318–322.
Wahal, L.M. 1971–72. Comments, in 'Proceedings of the Seminar on OCP'. *Puratattva* 5: 12–13.
Wheeler, R.E.M. 1959. *Early India and Pakistan*. London: Thames and Hudson.

10 ❖ Historical Archaeology in India

M.K. DHAVALIKAR

THE beginning of the historical period in India is generally placed in *c.* 600 BC because the great religious leaders, the Buddha and Mahavira whose historicity has been established, lived in that period. However, it is highly likely that this date may go back further into antiquity if the events recorded in our Epics and the Puranas can be corroborated by archaeological evidence. This is now in the range of possibility because it is generally agreed that the Painted Grey Ware (PGW) culture, dated to *c.* 1000–600 BC, represents the culture of the *Mahabharata* (*MB*) period. There is circumstantial evidence to corroborate the shifting of the capital Hastinapur to Kausambi because of flood in the Ganga which is recorded in the Puranas (Lal 1954–55). It is the general belief that the MB war did take place. Even when Hieun Tsang visited the Kurukshetra region, he was told by the local people that a great war was fought there in the ancient past (Watters 1904–05: vol. I, 314–15). It is also significant that the PGW has been found at most of the MB sites. Further work is bound to throw light on the problem and the potentiality is exciting.

There is a possibility of the beginning of the historical period going back to the Vedic period in the middle of the second millennium BC, for some of the tribes mentioned in the *Rigveda* (*RV*) are also referred to in inscriptions in West Asia and Egypt. H.K. Deb (1948a) has identified four of the tribes mentioned in the *RV* which were allied against Sudas with those figuring in Egyptian documents of about 1200 BC. He has suggested that the Vedic Tarksya can be identified with Egyptian Tearkon. Similarly, the Shekelesh is identified with the Greek Sikelos, and Sigru, Teresh and Wesesh with Vedic Turvasa, Ekwesh with Vedic Yaksha and Pelset with

Pulastya. It may be noted in this context that the Puranas have preserved the tradition that the Turvasas were of foreign origin as they are said to have descended from the Yavanas (*MB*, I, 85). There are more names in West Asian inscriptions of the second millennium BC such as Dushratta (Dasarath), Raman (Rama), Shattruhana (Satrughna) and so on (Akhtar 1978–79). What all this means so far as the Aryan problem is concerned, is difficult to say; but it raises the possibility of our ancient literature having some historical substratum in it and it cannot therefore be discarded lightly.

CULTURE SEQUENCES

Archaeological research began officially in India from 1861 with the establishment of the Archaeological Survey of India (ASI), although interest in Indology had started much earlier when Sir William Jones founded the Asiatic Society at Calcutta in 1784. Alexander Cunningham was appointed to head the Survey, but he was not supposed to carry out excavations and was asked only to record standing monuments. His successor, James Burgess did some digging at Mathura solely for recovering sculptures. The era of systematic excavation commenced with the appointment of John Marshall in 1902 by Lord Curzon, the then Viceroy. Cunningham had already recorded several Buddhist sites in northern India following the itineraries of Fa Hien and Hieun Tsang whose testimony came in handy for Marshall who concentrated on early historical sites such as Taxila, Sravasti, Pataliputra, etc. Even the spectacular and epoch-making discovery of the Indus civilization was accidental for the excavation at Mohenjodaro was taken up for uncovering the Kushana stupa at the site.

Marshall returned to England in 1928 and the Survey lapsed into inactivity because of heavy financial cuts during the Depression of the 1930s. The appointment of Wheeler in 1944 brought in a whiff of fresh air for he introduced latest techniques of excavations and explorations. In a brief stint of four years (1944–48), he carried out four large excavations, published their full reports and trained a whole generation of Indian archaeologists who have been at the helm of affairs in the post-independence period. He planned his excavation meticulously and carried it out like a military expedition. But his most noteworthy contribution was that he taught his pupils to build up culture sequences for different regions and as a result we now have well-established culture sequences for different parts of the country (for an early but still useful account of historical sites, see Y.D.

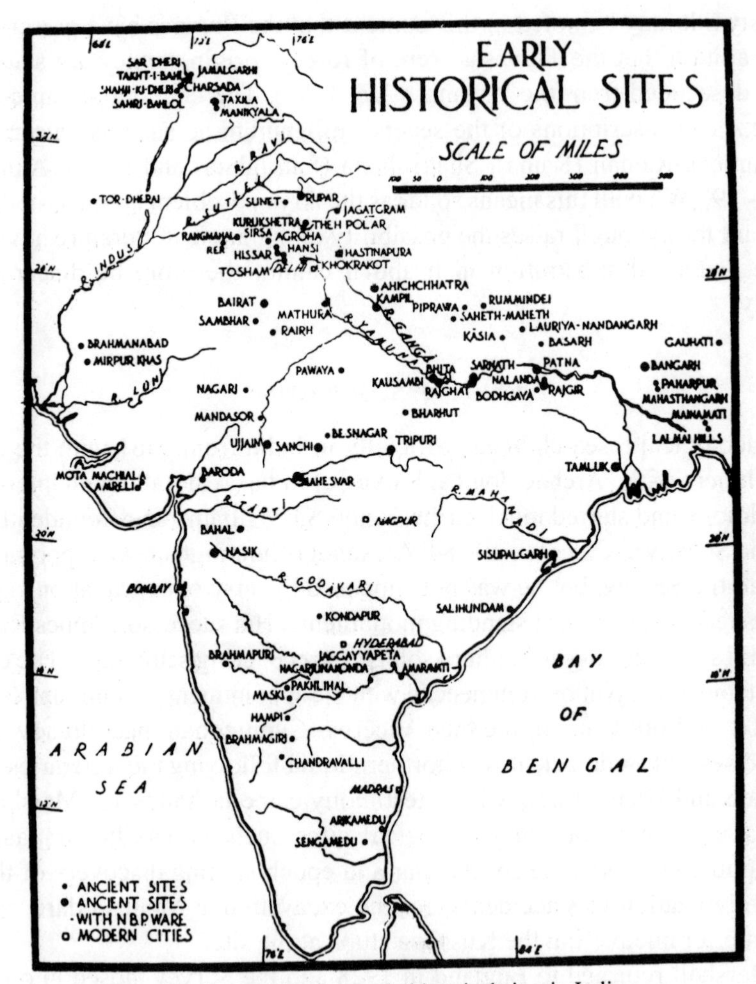

Fig. 1. Map showing early historical sites in India.
(After Y.D. Sharma 1953)

Sharma 1953). The map in Fig. 1 shows the distribution of major early historic sites in the subcontinent.

North India

In north India, the historical period begins with the habitation which had been dated to the sixth century BC. At several sites in the Punjab and Haryana the occupation starts with the Harappan and, after a hiatus of about half a millennium, the PGW people arrive on the scene as at Rupar. The historical past covers a long span of about 2400 years from the sixth century BC to eighteenth century AD. It has been divided by archaeologists into Early Historical (*c.* 600 BC–AD 600), Late Historical (AD 600–1200) and Medieval (AD 1200–1800) periods. The Early Historical period is sub-divided into pre-Maurya to Kushana (600 BC–AD 300) or Sunga-Kushana-Gupta (200 BC–AD 600) sub-periods, depending upon the evidence at a particular site. The main reason for this is the occurrence of Northern Black Polished Ware (NBP) in northern India in the pre-Mauryan, Mauryan and Sunga levels from the sixth century to second century BC. But it is necessary that further sub-divisions of this period are properly determined by a minute study of characteristic artefacts such as coins and terracottas which have some dating value.

Punjab and Haryana constitute the homeland of Vedic Aryans which was watered by the rivers Saraswati and Drishadvati as also the Satadru (Sutlej), and was referred to in ancient literature as Brahmarshi *desa*. This was the land of the Aryan tribes, the Bharatas and the Purus being the chief ones among them. It is one of the most fertile regions in the country and was obviously an area of attraction from very early times and the same holds good today. Several sites have been excavated in this area among which the most noteworthy are Rupar (Rupnagar district), Sanghol (Ludhiana district) and Sugh (Ambala district), all in the Punjab. It is now clear that there is an overlap between the PGW and NBP periods. Sometimes the Sunga period can be identified because of Sunga terracottas as at Sanghol (ancient Sanghapura) (*IAR 1968–69*: 25–26) but the Kushana-Gupta levels have been lumped together (Period V). At Sugh (ancient Srughna) Period I yielded late PGW and NBP (*c.* 500–100 BC) and Period II covers the Sunga-Kushana levels but the excavator has prolonged it up to AD 500, although there is nothing that can be identified as Gupta (*IAR 1964–65*: 35–36). It may be noted that several sites in this region were deserted after the Kushana period only to be occupied in the mediaeval times. Some sites, however, continued to be occupied in the Gupta period, as for instance Rupar and Sunet. The latter (ancient Suneta) was a very important centre of trade and commerce as the 30,000 coin moulds would indicate.

Rupar (Fig. 2)

The culture sequence in Punjab is very well signified by the excavation at Rupar. The ancient site, located on the left bank of the Sutlej, was excavated by Y.D. Sharma (1956–57) of Archaeological Survey of India in 1952–55. It revealed a sequence of six cultural periods starting from the

Fig. 2. Sequence of cultural periods at Rupar: Period I (*c.* 2000–1400 BC); Period II (*c.* 1000–700 BC); Period III (*c.* 600–200 BC); Period IV (*c.* 200 BC–AD 600); Period V (*c.* 800–AD 1000); Period VI (*c.* 1300–AD 1700). (After Y.D. Sharma 1953).

Harappan (I) followed by PGW after a hiatus of about 7–8 centuries. The succeeding early historic period is assigned to *c.* 600–200 BC which is characterised by NBP and plain red wares. It also yielded punch-marked and uninscribed coins, besides an ivory seal inscribed with Mauryan Brahmi characters. Since the excavation was of a restricted nature, no complete house plans were recovered. The structures were built of fired bricks and slabs of *kankar* stone. Mention should be made of the retaining wall of an oval-shaped water reservoir. Period IV (200 BC–AD 700) covers the Sunga-

Kushana-Gupta epochs and is subdivided accordingly on the basis of the evidence of terracotta figurines among which the most remarkable is a lady playing *vina* which belongs to the Gupta period. The footed cup and a ladle, both of silver, appear to be of classical origin. Besides there were several sealings of the Gupta period. The site was deserted for a brief period around AD 700 and then reoccupied. This inference is based on the evidence of coins of Toramana. But it is highly likely that the site was deserted after Period V (200 BC–AD 600) and inhabited again in medieval times (AD 1300–1600).

Haryana

The culture sequence of Punjab recurs at most of the sites in Haryana, but for historical period the continuous evidence of habitation is furnished by Thaneswar (Kurukshetra district) which was excavated by B.M. Pande of the Archaeological Survey of India in 1988–89. The site is located on the banks of the Saraswati where extensive mounds known as Harsha-ka-Tila can be seen. Of these, the Karan-ka-Qila was the township and the 'Bahari' was the outer fort. Here the habitation starts in Kushana times from the beginning of the Christian era and continues through the Gupta, post-Gupta, Rajput and the medieval periods. It is highly likely that the habitation may have started much earlier, as a few PGW sherds picked up on the surface would indicate and also considering that Kurukshetra was the locale of the MB war and, being associated with Krishna, is a sacred place in the country. The excavation brought to light a maze of structures of different periods; parts of houses along streets and lanes, sometimes brick paved, and provided with drains and *tandoors*.

A complete sequence of cultures is to be found at Delhi which has been continuously inhabited from the Harappan times to the present day, and the antiquity may now go back to the Stone Age as the discovery of stone artefacts from the Ridge area would show. The excavations at Purana Qila which is located in the heart of the city have yielded evidence of occupation from the PGW period (*IAR 1954–55*: 13–14) which supports the identification of the place with Indraprastha of *MB*. It is followed by NBP (600–200 BC), whereas the Sunga habitation could be distinguished by the typical terracotta plaques. Rubble structures belong to this phase but the burnt brick ones are of the Saka-Kushana times. The pottery is a red ware and was stamped with auspicious symbols such as *srivatsa, swastika*, etc. The Gupta period structures were built of bricks from earlier buildings. The succeeding post-Gupta, Rajput, Sultanate and Mughal periods are also represented. A Chinese porcelain bowl of the Mughal period was found bearing an inscription dated AD 1465–87 (*IAR 1969–70*; *1971–72*: 7–8, *1972–73*: 8–9).

Rajasthan

As in Punjab, in Rajasthan also the habitation began from the pre-Harappan times. Most of the pre-Harappan and Harappan settlements were located in the Saraswati basin (now known as Ghaggar) and the Drishadvati (now Chautang), and were deserted after the shift in the hydrological regime. At some places the habitation took place in the PGW period in the dried up bed of the river as at Sardargarh (Sri Ganganagar district). However, in spite of the arid environment, habitation took place in the area east of the Aravallis. Of the few excavations in Rajasthan in the post-independence period, two deserve special mention viz., Jodhpura (Jaipur district) and Noh (Bharatpur district) as they have revealed evidence of cultures from the OCP period onwards. Of the five cultural periods, identical at both sites, the first is OCP, and the second is Black-and-Red Ware which marks the Iron Age (*c.*1400–1100 BC); and Period III is characterised by PGW. The historical period starts with Period IV marked by NBP, which is followed by Sunga-Kushana (V) after which the sites were deserted. The same evidence recurs at Noh (*IAR 1963–64*: 28–29; *1964–65*: 34–35).

A vast majority of the sites in Rajasthan were deserted after the Kushana period in the fourth century. Among the few which continued to be occupied in the Gupta period, mention should be made of Rangmahal. Located in the dry bed of the Saraswati, it was excavated by the Swedish archaeologist Hanna Rydh (1953) in 1952–54. The black-on-red painted pottery has proved to be of the Kushana and early Gupta times (first to fifth centuries AD). It is a distinctive ceramic, now known as the Rangmahal ware, very sturdy and of fine fabric. Globular jars and *handi*s are the main forms and some of them have a rusticated lower portion having moulded designs, whereas applique and incised patterns adorn the upper part. Bowls and basins are mostly moulded. Eight structural phases have been distinguished; in the fifth phase was a wall having a small niche probably for keeping a deity. Evidence shows that walls were decorated with paintings. A structure identified as a temple was unearthed at Bairat, ancient Viratanagar, in Jaipur district (*IAR 1962–63*: 31) but more interesting are the fragments of Mauryan pillars from an earlier excavation.

Uttar Pradesh

U.P. is the largest state in the country having numerous pilgrimage

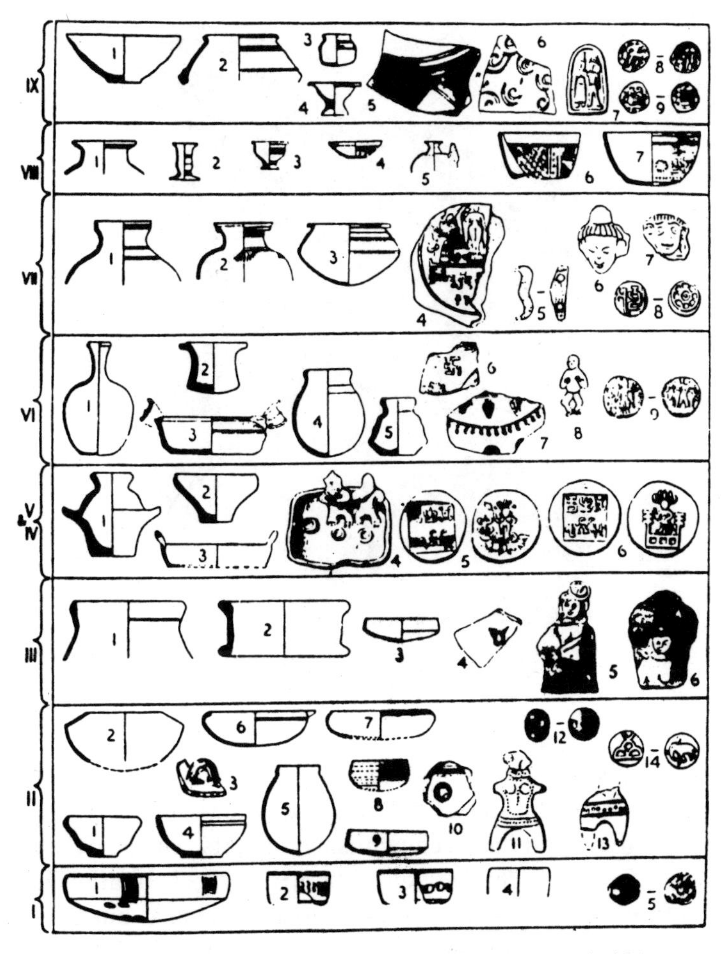

Fig. 3. Sequence of cultural periods at Ahichchhatra: Period I (pre-NBP Ware); Period II (*c.* 300–200 BC); Period III (*c.* AD 200–100); Period VI (*c.* AD 100–350); Period VII (*c.* AD 350–750); Period VIII (*c.* AD 750–850); Period IX (*c.* AD 850–1100). (After Y.D. Sharma 1953).

centres, most of which have a hoary antiquity. It is drained by the Ganga and the Yamuna, the two most scared rivers and hence Wheeler is justified in his observation that "the Indus has given India its civilization and the Ganga, its faith". There are many historical sites in the state, but most of the excavations were just a touch-and-go affair. Marshall, however, had carried out a few large-scale excavations. An important excavation is that of Ahichchhatra (present Ramnagar, Bareilly district), which has been iden-

Fig. 4. Flood deposits at Hastinapur.
(After B.B. Lal 1954–55)

tified as the capital of the Uttara Panchalas (Fig. 3). It was excavated on a large scale by K.N. Dikshit of the Archaeological Survey of India from 1940–44 and the report has been published in parts. The PGW was found here for the first time, but mixed with NBP. The habitation has been divided into nine periods, from pre-Mauryan to Gupta, but they appear more to represent structural phases (Ghosh and Panigrahi 1946).

The site has yielded a large number of terracottas of exquisite beauty and a few almost life-size specimens such as those of Ganga and Yamuna which once adorned a Gupta temple (Agrawala 1947–48).

Of the numerous excavations in U.P., two stand out on account of their scale and evidence. The first is that of Hastinapur (Meerut district) by B.B. Lal (1954–55) where the sequence starts with OCP (Period I, pre-1200 BC), followed by PGW habitation (*c.* 1100–800 BC) which was destroyed by a flood. According to Lal, this evidence corroborates the Puranic legend which states that the capital at Hastinapur was shifted because of floods to Kausambi during the time of Nichaksu, fifth in line from Janamejaya (Fig. 4). It is therefore argued that the PGW culture represents the MB period.

After the flood the capital seems to have been deserted for a couple of centuries and was occupied again in Period III (sixth to third centuries BC). It is characterised by a *de luxe* ware known as the NBP. It is perhaps the finest pottery produced in India, and has a thin black slip but there are varieties of grey, red, silver and gold, and even painted NBP is reported. As the very name signifies, it is essentially a pottery of northern India but has a very wide distribution in terms of time and space. Its main focus, however, is the middle Ganga basin, and the area around ancient Pataliputra (Patna), probably its original home. It has a very wide span from the seventh century BC to mid-first century BC. Attempts have been made to identify the Aryans as the makers of this pottery because of the superiority of Aryan culture and their high skill (Roy in *Potteries in Ancient India* edited by B.P. Sinha, 1969: 167–73) and it is maintained that only they could have produced such a technically brilliant pottery. The pottery was first found in the excavations at Sarnath (*Annual Report of the Archaeological Survey of India* 1904–5: 59) and Bhita by John Marshall where it occurred in pre-Mauryan levels (*Annual Report of the Archaeological Survey of India* 1909–10: 37, 80–81) and later at Taxila in Bhir mound in the levels underlying those yielding a coin of Alexander the Great as also two coin hoards which could be dated to *c.* 300 BC. Marshall first mistook it as a variety of the Greek black ware of the fourth to third centuries BC but was not sure whether it was imported or locally made. But the pottery occurred at Taxila much below the Greek levels and was thus older than the Greek pottery. Till 1977 some 415 NBP sites were reported and the number must have doubled by now.

The most controversial aspect of NBP is its mirror-like polish which is still an enigma. According to Sana Ullah (*Ancient India* 4: 59 ff), it is due to 13% ferrous oxide whereas others explain it as due to the formation of ferrous lime and ferrous magnesia silicates or because of oxide of iron, and its lustre may be a sort of glaze for which powdered glass may have been used (Hegde 1962). Bharadwaj's investigations (in *Potteries in Ancient Times* edited by B.P. Sinha, 1969: 188–92) led him to conclude that the black colour of the slip is the result of carbon. There is thus no unanimity so far as the technology of NBP is concerned.

The variety of forms in NBP is limited (Fig. 5). The most common shapes are straight-sided bowls and dishes with incurved rims. Knobbed lids, spouted vessels and saucers are very rare. The pottery must have been very expensive and highly prized as is evident from the copper riveting joining broken parts of a vessel found at Rupar. Painted NBP has been

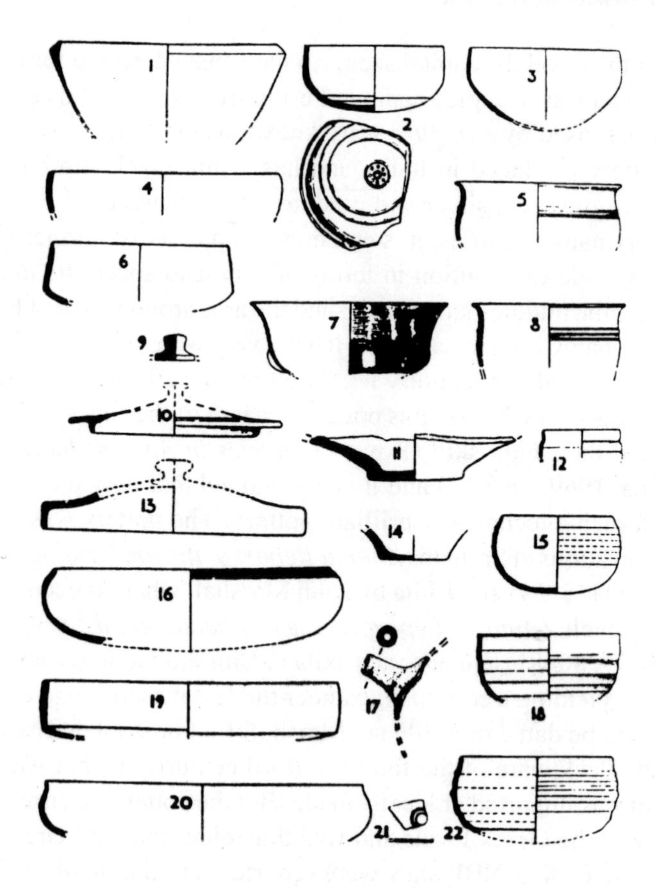

Fig. 5. Representative types in Northern Black Polished Ware.
(After Y.D. Sharma 1953)

reported from Sravasti, Kausambi and a few other sites in eastern U.P.

The NBP has a very wide distribution in India. It is found almost all over the country save the extreme south. The northernmost sites are Udergram in Swat valley (Pakistan) and Charsada near Peshawar. In the south it is found at Amaravati (A.P); and also found widely from Prabhas Patan (Gujarat) in the west to Tamluk and Chandraketugarh in the east. It has also been reported from Tilaurakot and Banjarahi (Nepal) and from Anuradhapura in Sri Lanka.

The date of NBP is not free from controversy. At Taxila, Marshall dated it to 500–200 BC and at several sites in the Ganga valley it was placed in 600–200 BC, but Lal (1993) has now assigned the beginning to the seventh century BC on the basis of evidence from Sringaverpur (U.P.). At some sites in Bihar it lingers up to the middle of the first century BC (Roy 1986: 89 ff). The entire duration of NBP can be divided into three phases; the first would be the beginning in the Kausambi-Patna region in the seventh to sixth centuries BC; the second covers the Maurya epoch from the fifth to the second centuries BC when it spreads all over the Maurya empire and which is the phase of its zenith; and the decline begins from the downfall of the Mauryan empire from the second century BC. After the middle of the first century BC, it totally goes out of vogue.

It is the NBP which marks the beginning of the historical period all over northern India and hence in the cultural sequence the first period is dated to the sixth to second centuries BC, followed by Sunga-Kushana-Gupta epochs. It has been observed that the Kushana levels reflect prosperity, whereas the Gupta strata mark decline (Sharma 1987). As a matter of fact at several sites in the middle Ganga basin, the Gupta levels are absent as at Hastinapur, but as one enters the lower Ganga basin Gupta period is present in the archaeological record as at Kausambi. Again at a vast majority of sites, there is no trace of post-Gupta habitation, and that they are occupied again in the medieval period only. This is a very enigmatic phenomenon which deserves careful consideration.

An important but the most controversial excavation is that of Kausambi which was conducted by the late G.R. Sharma (1960; 1969) and his colleagues at Allahabad University. Here the sequence starts with the OCP culture, followed by BSW (black slipped ware), BR (black-and-red) and burnished grey ware. Period III (605–45) is characterised by PGW which is found mixed with NBP, but is degenerate. This was the time when Kausambi became the capital of the Vatsa Mahajanapada and it was a flourishing city even in Buddha's time. It figures frequently in our ancient literature. The beginning of the historical period also marks the beginning of structural activity at the site. The city was protected by a massive fortification which Sharma dated to a very early period but it has been shown that it is much later (Ghosh 1989: vol. II, 212–13). The original mud rampart was faced with brick revetment later in the Kushana times. It was provided with gateways, bastions and guard-rooms and so on. There was a channel (21.3 m wide) between the eastern gateway and the tower which could be crossed by a drawbridge. The evidence of drawbridge has also been noted at Satanikota in Andhra Pradesh.

One of the structures at Kausambi was identified by Sharma as *asyena-chiti* of the *Agni-chayana* where a human sacrifice was performed. It was built in the form of an eagle in the second century BC but the identification has not been accepted. Similarly the stone built palace has been identified as that of king Udayan and was supposed to have been burnt by Menander, in the second century BC. The arches in the structure have been shown to be medieval in date and not Kushana as was argued by the excavator (Soundara Rajan 1979–80). But the Buddhist monastic complex inside the walled city which was built by Anathapindaka for Buddha corroborates the literary evidence. An inscribed terracotta lamp and an inscribed *Ayagapata* refer to it as *Ghositarama*.

Period IV (45 BC–AD 580) roughly covers the Saka-Kushana-Gupta epochs. The excavation has yielded a wealth of antiquities among which the most noteworthy are the terracottas. There is no evidence of post-Gupta habitation.

It is unfortunate that one of the most extensive and important sites in the country should have met such a fate. Everything about it is controversial; every interpretation of Sharma has been rightly challenged, but only after his death.

Bihar

Quite a few sites have been excavated in Bihar in the post-independence period. There is no evidence of OCP and PGW in Bihar; they are replaced by BSW and BR wares. The culture sequence in general is as follows: I—Neolithic, II—Chalcolithic, III—Iron Age, IV—NBP, V—Kushana, VI—Gupta, and VII—Pala. The historical period thus starts with the NBP of which Bihar is the home. It is associated with BR ware, red ware and a black ware. A majority of sites were occupied during the NBP and the Sunga-Kushana epochs e.g., Maner (Patna district), Senuwar (Rohtas district), Chirand (Saran district) and so on. But the two sites which are most important for the historical period are Vaishali and Pataliputra (Patna). They were both excavated earlier in the pre-independence era and also in the post-independence period. The most important feature of Vaishali, the capital of the Lichchhavis, is that it has been described in ancient literature as divided into three parts, one each for the Brahmins, the Kshatriyas and the Vaisyas, and had three walls, two of which have been traced. This reminds one of the division of Harappan towns such as Kalibangan and Harappa (Dhavalikar 1994: 164 ff). Different localities mentioned in literature have been identified: Vaishali (Raja Vishal-ka-Gadh), Vanijyagrama (Bania), Kundagrama (Basokund) and Kollaga (Koluha). Later excavation by K. Deva and V. Mishra (1961) has revealed a fourfold sequence of culture starting with I (500–150 BC) marked by NBP and BR wares. All the different varieties of NBP such as steel blue, silvery, golden, etc. occur. This period has been divided into two sub-phases on the basis of the quantity of BR ware. Period II (300 BC–AD 100) marks the flowering of the culture as is evident from terracotta figurines, and punch-marked and cast coins. NBP becomes rare and BR ware is absent, but the red and buff wares are abundant. The most interesting are votive stone discs of semi- precious stones like jasper, which are carved with a mother goddess, a winged lion, pipal tree and floral designs. The following two are the Kushana (AD 100–300) and Gupta periods (AD 300–600). Later excavations by A.S. Altekar and S.R. Roy at Raja Vishal-ka-Gadh surprisingly yielded evidence of the Sunga-Kushana period. The exquisite silver and gold jewellery belongs to the Kushana times. Their excavation (*IAR 1957–58*: 10–11; *1958–59*: 12) of a tank and a stupa deserve a special mention. The tank (49.60 × 19.80 m), locally known as Kharauna-Pokhra, is believed to be the ancient Abhisheka-Pushkarini in which only the Lichchhavi kings bathed. (The Mohenjodaro bath may have been similarly used.) It is pre-Sunga in date whereas the stupa was built in *c.* 600 BC.

There are several sites in Bihar of great potentiality among which Champa (Bhagalpur), the capital of Anga, has been excavated. Here the habitation goes back to BR ware phase followed by NBP, Kushana, Gupta and Medieval periods (*IAR 1971–72–73*, *1982–83*: 15–16). Rajgir (ancient Rajagriha), the pre-Mauryan capital, is noted for its massive cyclopean wall running on the hilltop with a circuit of 25 km (Ghosh 1951), and the Jivikamravana, the Buddhist monastery built by Jivaka, the court physician for Buddha. The excavation yielded evidence of habitation during the NBP, Sunga and Kushana periods, and elliptical structures (*IAR 1958–59*: 13).

Bengal

The culture sequence in Bengal is not much different but the only noteworthy feature is that the habitation at most of the sites was continuous from the NBP phase to the medieval times. There are several sites in Bengal but only a few have been dug, that too on a small scale. Chandraketugarh (24 Parganas district), a very extensive ancient site, has been sporadically excavated for several seasons, but on a small scale every year, and the evidence therefore is not clear. The occupation has been divided into ten cultural periods starting from pre-NBP (I), NBP (II), but the succeeding III to VI periods represent Sunga-Kushana epochs, followed by Gupta (VII) and (VIII) post-Gupta and Pala periods. Only a well-planned, long-term

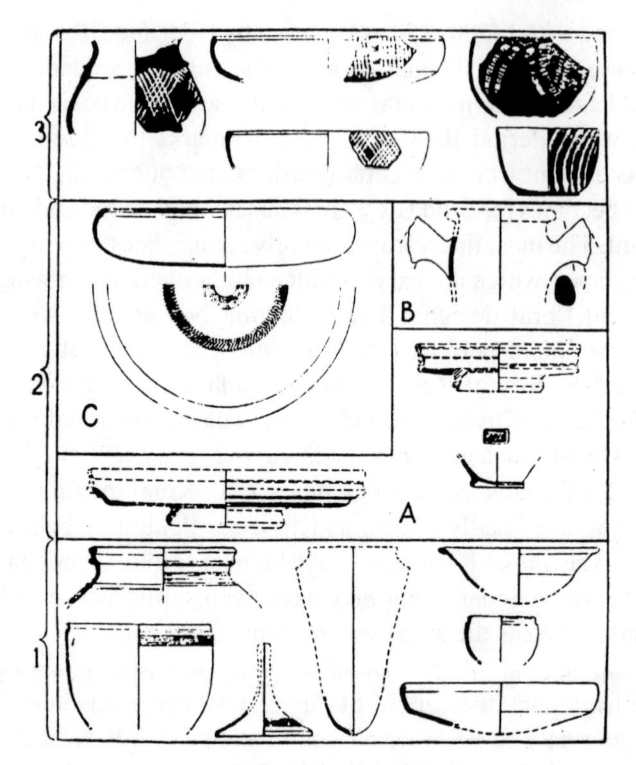

Fig. 6. Pottery sequence in South India. (1) Black and Red Ware; (2A) Arretine Ware; (2B) Amphora; (2C) Rouletted Ware; (3) Andhra Ware. (After Y.D. Sharma 1953)

horizontal excavation will prove rewarding, otherwise the site is likely to be destroyed by sporadic digging.

Rouletted Ware (Fig. 6)

Rouletted ware (RW) occurs at most of the sites in Bengal. It is a very distinctive ceramic which was first noticed at Arikamedu (Wheeler 1946: 45 ff). It is made of extremely fine, well-levigated clay and fired grey and was treated with a thin slip. It looks almost like a variety of BR ware and has a high polish. Usually dishes with incurved rims constitute the dominant form. Their noteworthy feature is that on the interior in the centre they are decorated with two or three concentric bands of rouletted pattern which are produced by a rotating toothed wheel; on the exterior are grooves. According to Wheeler (ibid.: 45), this is not an Indian feature and may be regarded as an importation from the Mediterranean region and it is there-

Fig. 7. Aerial view of Sisupalgarh.
(After B.B. Lal 1949)

fore taken as Roman pottery (Deshpande, in *Potteries in Ancient India*, edited by B.P. Sinha, 1969: 275 ff). This view will now have to be revised in the light of evidence from several sites where the pottery occurs in much earlier levels, even before the beginning of trade with the Roman empire. At Chandraketugarh it is reported from the beginning of habitation which goes back to the Mauryan period in the third century BC or even earlier. Moreover, the trace element analysis of the mineral contents has shown that the RW from different sites in the country was made in the Tamluk-Chandraketugarh region in Bengal whence it was sent to other centres (Gogte 1997). It is therefore highly likely that the ware is an Indian invention from where it went to the Mediterranean region.

Orissa

Very few sites have been excavated in Orissa and, among these, the only noteworthy excavation is that of Sisupalgarh in Puri district which was done by B.B. Lal in 1949. A squarish fort, with 9 m high walls having towers and gateways, exists at the site, and the ancient site is located in it (Fig. 7). According to a local legend, the fort was built by Sisupala of the

Kesari dynasty. The site identified as Kharavela's capital, Kalinganagara, was occupied from the third century BC to the fourth century AD. The habitation has been divided into three cultural periods of which the first (*c*. 300–200 BC) is characterised by red pottery. This is followed by II-A—Early Middle period (200 BC–AD 100)—when BR and RW appear; but the most distinctive pottery is what has been labelled as the 'Knobbed ware'. It is grey or greyish black in colour and the dominant form is a bowl having a knob in the centre of the base. A number of iron objects and terracotta ear pendants occur. The mud rampart strengthened with brick revetmentbelongs to this period. The gateway was constructed of large lateritic blocks. Period II B—Late Middle period (AD 100–200)—is the transitional phase which marks degeneration in pottery. Further deterioration takes place in Period III (AD 200–350).

An interesting feature of the ancient site is formed by the monolithic pillars still standing. They are about 4.5 m high and are carved with medallions. Some of them have sockets at the top which indicate that they once supported a superstructure.

Most of the sites in Orissa were occupied up to the fourth century AD as in other parts of the country; but a few were occupied even in the medieval period. The excavation at Khalakatapatna (Puri district) has revealed a single culture habitation of the twelfth to fourteenth centuries AD, as is evident from the Chinese celadon ware and glazed pottery of Arab origin as also Chinese coins which point to trade with China (*IAR* 1964–65: 59). More work on coastal sites in Orissa is necessary especially for medieval archaeology.

Northeast India

Assam is almost a *terra incognita*, at least archaeologically. It was generally held that civilisation reached Assam with Samudragupta's (AD 355–70) conquest and it is supported by the earliest Hindu temple at Dah Parbatiya in Tezpur district. In the seventh century Hiuen Tsiang (AD 629–45) saw many temples of Devas at Pragjyotishpur, some of which lie buried in the heart of the city of Guwahati. Accidentally a few were encountered in the construction work at the site (Dhavalikar 1972). The boat burials in Assam also deserve attention (Dhavalikar 1972). In Meghalaya the remains of a fortified town were discovered at Vadagkugiri and also the traces of habitation of the Pala-Sena times (eighth to twelfth centuries AD), whereas medieval remains have been reported from Naksaparvat in Arunachal Pradesh (Sharma 1995).

Madhya Pradesh

Several sites have been excavated in Madhya Pradesh and the evidence indicates that many of the sites in the Malwa region were occupied from the NBP period (sixth to fifth centuries BC) till the end of the Satavahana-Kshatrapa rule, whereas in the eastern part habitation continued in the Gupta period as well. Perhaps the most important excavations are those at Ujjain and Maheshwar. Ujjain, the fabled capital of legendary king Vikramaditya, was excavated by N.R. Banerjee of ASI in 1955–58. His fourfold sequence begins with Period I (700–500 BC) characterised by BR ware. The rampart and the moat belong to this period, but were breached in Period II (500–200 BC) on the river side by floods and were therefore repaired by constructing buttress walls. But they were damaged again by floods during this period. A single PGW sherd found at the site may have come from the early levels of Period I. Period II (500–200 BC) marks the NBP phase and was quite prosperous as the wealth of antiquities show. Period III covers a long span of some twelve centuries (from 200 BC–AD 1000). However, in the later excavations at the site this period has been sub-divided into three phases; A, 200 BC—AD 500; B, 500–AD 900; C, AD 900–1300 (Banerjee in Ghosh 1989: vol. II, 449). Since the full report of the excavation has not been published, it is not clear how this division has been arrived at.

Maheshwar

Maheshwar, identified with ancient Mahishmati, was excavated by H.D. Sankalia in 1952–53 to test the veracity of Puranic myths and the Aryan problem (Sankalia et al. 1958). Here the historical period starts from Period IV (400 BC–100 BC). The site was occupied by the Chalcolithic people who deserted it around 1400 BC and it remained unoccupied for a thousand years. NBP and punch-marked coins occur in Period IV and so also a brick stupa with circumambulatory path. Bulk of the pottery is a non-descript red ware of daily use. Period V (100 BC–AD 100) seems to be an overlapping phase in which the BR ware is absent, whereas R.P.W occurs in Period VI (AD 100–500) along with mother and child (*ankadhatri*) terracottas. After this again the site was abandoned for over a millennium. Traces of medieval period (sixteenth to seventeenth centuries) have been noticed at the site.

There are several sites in Madhya Pradesh which were occupied in the Gupta period. Tumain (ancient Tumbavana, district Guna), has yielded evidence of occupation from 500 BC up to twelfth century AD (*IAR 1972–72*; 27–28; *1972–73*: 15–16) and the same sequence repeats at Tripuri (district Jabalpur) (*IAR* 1966–67: 17–19) and Malhar (district Bilaspur) where in addition a stone Sivalinga bearing an inscription allegedly mentioning the name of Menander was found.

Gujarat

In Gujarat, the ancient sites were occupied in the historical period from the fifth to fourth centuries BC and many of them were abandoned in the fourth century AD after the downfall of the Western Kshatrapas. This is evident from excavations at Nagara in Kaira district (Mehta 1968). In the fourfold sequence of cultures, the first is dated to sixth to fifth centuries BC and is characterised by BR ware. Rice cultivation became possible because of a dam built by the people. Period II is not much different; Periods I and II appear to constitute one phase. Period III, characterised by RPW, lasts till the ninth century AD, but on what grounds is not clear. This tendency of prolonging the early historic period is to be noticed in Gujarat as at Valabhi, Shamlaji and other sites probably because of the excavators' desire to include the Maitraka period in it.

Almost at every site in Gujarat the RPW is found in levels dated from first to fifth centuries AD with a margin of century each on either site. It is a *de luxe* ceramic, the original focus of which is Gujarat, particularly Saurashtra, but occurs at many sites in western India and rarely in other regions. It is of a very fine fabric and is treated with a red slip which is very smooth and bears a high polish. The commonest form is what is known as 'sprinkler' having a graceful oval profile, a ring base, and a high slender neck with a narrow flaring mouth. In addition, there is a spout on the shoulder. The bronze copy of this vessel has been found in the Kolhapur hoard (Khandalwala 1960). The pottery is supposed to be of Roman origin (Subba Rao 1958: 46–47), whereas Rao (1966: 53–59) argues for an indigenous origin.

Maharashtra

All the excavations in Maharashtra save that at Brahamapuri (Kolhapur) were carried out in the post-independence period. The most noteworthy among these are those at Nevasa, Prakash and Adam. Most of the sites in Maharashtra were occupied from the Satavahana period (from the second century BC) or slightly earlier in the third century BC when Mauryan rule was established here. Wherever the Chalcolithic habitation took place, the sites were deserted towards the end of the second millennium BC and remained unoccupied for a thousand years. At Prakash (district Dhulia), however, there is an Iron Age deposit (Period II) which has been assigned to 800 BC–200 BC, followed by period III (second century BC to sixth century AD) which is characterised by RPW. Period IV (sixth to eleventh centuries AD) has yielded a drab grey pottery and a mica dusted brown ware (Thapar 1965–66). Prakash is thus a rare example where the post-Satavahana occupation has been found.

Several sites in the state have yielded evidence of Roman contact as at Nasik, Nevasa and Ter (district Osmanabad). The habitations start in the third to second centuries BC. and are later distinguished by Roman artefacts such as amphorae, clay bullae, etc. in the first to second centuries AD. The most important is the bronze hoard from Kolhapur which contains several Roman bronze objects (Khandalwala 1960) (Fig. 8). This phase has been labelled as the Indo-Roman period as at Nevasa (Sankalia et al. 1960) (Fig. 9). After the third to fourth centuries the sites are deserted and are occupied only in the Mughal-Maratha period (AD 1600–1800).

A noteworthy excavation in recent years is that at Adam by Amarendra Nath (1989–90). Here the sequence starts from pre-pottery phase (I), Chalcolithic (II), Iron Age (III) and the historical period (IV) from 500 BC –150 BC. But the most prosperous seems to be the last one (Period V) dated to 150 BC–AD 200 when the site was fortified by a mud rampart and a moat. Several coins of the Bhadras, the Mitras, the Satavahanas and the Maharathis were found. A significant find is a clay sealing inscribed with Asaka *Janapada*—Ashmaka republic. It may be mentioned that there are some sites in Vidarbha such as Paunar (Deo and Dhavalikar 1968) and Arambha where evidence of Vakataka period is available.

Karnataka

Culture sequence in Karnataka is more or less the same as in Maharashtra, starting with the Mauryan rule in the third century BC and ending in the second to third centuries AD after the Satavahana domination. Wheeler's (1947–48) excavation at Brahmagiri revealed a threefold sequence starting with Neolithic (I); Megalithic (II) and ending at what he called the Andhra period (III) which is the same as the Satavahana. Two important Satavahana sites which deserve a special mention are Sannati (Gulbarga district) and Vadgaon-Madhavpur (Belgaum district). The former, referred to as Ahimahikaya in an inscription found at the site, is a compact Satavahana township with a massive brick fortification wall. Its importance can be gauged from the location of an Asokan edict and some stupas (Howell 1995). The other site, Vadgaon-Madhavpur was a very

Fig. 8. Roman bronze jar from Kolhapur (Brahmapuri). (After H.D. Sankalia and M.G. Dikshit 1952)

extensive settlement (40 ha) on the outskirts of the present city of Belgaum. It is a single culture Satavahana township (third century BC to second century AD) with spacious brick built residential structures, a granary, and an apsidal shrine. It yielded punch-marked and Satavahana coins and Satavahana terracottas. It is significant that a Vajapeya sacrifice was performed here in the first century BC by a Brahmin of Kashyapa *gotra* as a stone inscription from the site testifies (Sundara 1981).

A very large scale excavation is presently underway at Hampi (ancient Vijayanagar) where several structures have been unearthed (Fritz et al. 1984).

Andhra Pradesh

As in Karnataka, in Andhra Pradesh also the habitation in the historical period began with the Mauryan domination in the third century BC but the most flourishing was the Satavahana period because around 150 BC the Satavahanas shifted their capital from Pratishthan (Paithan in Maharashtra) to Dhanyakataka (Dharanikota in district Guntur). Far more important is

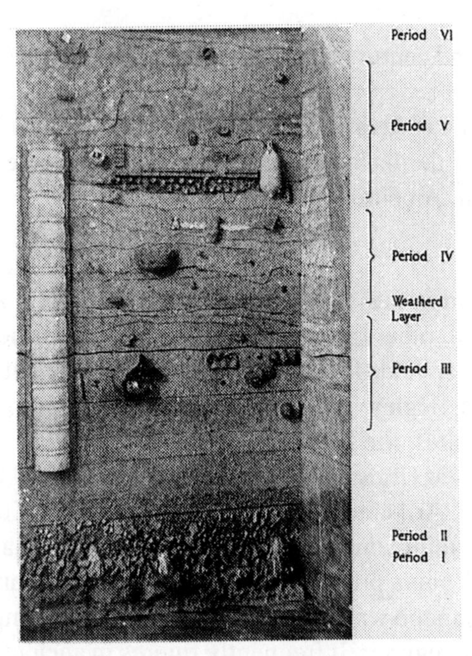

Fig. 9. Sequence of cultural periods at Nevasa: Period I (Early Palaeolithic); Period II (Middle Palaeolithic); Period III (Chalcolithic); Period IV (Early Historic); Period V (Indo-Roman); Period VI (Muslim-Maratha). (After H.D. Sankalia et al. 1960)

the nearby Amaravati site, celebrated for its ornate *Mahastupa* and Asokan edicts, where the habitation is said to have continued up to the eleventh century AD (*IAR 1973–74*: 4–5). Another site of importance is Peddaveggi (district West Godavari) which has been identified as ancient Vengi, the capital of the Salankayanas, the Vishnukundins and the Eastern Chalukyas. It was also occupied from the third to the eleventh centuries AD (*IAR 1984–85*: 7–8; *1986–87*: 13–22). Actually the habitation may have started earlier as the find of a Roman intaglio suggests, but the entire occupation has been clubbed into one single cultural period sub-divided into three phases: Ia—Salankayana (fourth to fifth centuries AD), Ib—Vishnukundin (fifth to sixth centuries AD) and Ic—Eastern Chalukyan.

The ruins of the Satavahana capital at Dharanikota are very extensive. The excavation revealed a high embankment-cum-wharf abutting a deeply cut navigation channel which was connected to the main river Krishna for leading the boats. Six phases of construction of the wall have been discerned and dated to second century BC to third century AD (*IAR 1962–63*: 3; *1963–64*: 12; *1964–65*: 3).

The large scale excavation at Nagarjunakonda (district Guntur) which was the capital of the Ikshvakus in the third to fourth centuries AD was a salvage operation. An entire ancient city was dug up.

Tamil Nadu

In Tamil Nadu, the only well studied sites are Arikamedu and Kaveripattinam, all others are just small digs. At the former site the habitation starts (Wheeler et al. 1946) in the first century BC but the recent excavations by Vimla Begley (1983) indicate that it may go to a still earlier period. At some sites, the beginning of settled life goes back to even the third century BC as at Uraiyur (district Tiruchirapalli) and Gutturmala (district Dharmapuri). Arikamedu, identified as 'Poduce' of classical writers, was an ancient trading emporium—a port town—and has yielded excellent evidence of Roman presence in the form of pottery and Roman coins.

Kaveripattinam too was a port and was known as Pumpuhar during the Pallava and Chola regimes. It frequently figures in ancient Tamil literature and is the Kaberis of Ptolemy. Two cultural periods have been distinguished, viz., I—Early Historic from third century BC to fifth century AD and II—Early Medieval from ninth to twelfth centuries AD. The former is characterised by BR ware and the latter by Chinese Celadon and other ceramics (Soundara Rajan 1994). Among the important structures unearthed mention should be made of a brick built wharf, an inlet channel and a Buddhist monastic complex, all of Period I.

Kerala

Kerala was occupied by the Megalithic people, and in spite of a reference to the Keralaputas in Asokan edicts and allusions in the classical literature to *Templum Augusti*, no traces of early habitation have come to light. Muziris, near Calicut (Kozhikode) where the temple of Augustus is supposed to have been located, was subjected to excavation which yielded some dull red pottery, a few porcelain pipes and glass beads belonging to the thirteenth to sixteenth centuries AD (*IAR 1969–70*: 10). Even Soundara Rajan's excavation near Cranganore revealed only Chera period (ninth to eleventh centuries AD) remains (*IAR 1969–70*: 13–15).

SECOND URBANISATION

It has now been clearly established that the beginning of the historical period in the sixth century BC also marks the rise of urbanisation. After the decline of the Indus cities from 2000 BC, almost the entire subcontinent was dotted by village cultures with pockets of hunter-gatherers in some areas. It was thus far held that the advent of iron was the prime mover of urbanisation (Kosambi 1965: 108) but recent archaeological evidence indicates that iron appears in India in the second half of the second millennium BC, and it took almost half a millennium for urbanisation to occur. The main cause seems to be that the entire second and the first half of the following millennium BC were a period of adverse environment characterised by frequent droughts almost all over the Old World and hence has been referred to as 'Dark Age' (Bell 1970). The environment began to improve by the middle of the first millennium which made the second urbanisation possible.

It appears that the technology of iron was fully developed in the sixth century BC. This was the period of great religious leaders like the Buddha and Mahavira, and small states were emerging in different parts of the country, more particularly in northern India. Of these, sixteen were great republican states—*mahajanapadas*—among which that of Magadha was gradually becoming dominant. The capital cities of many of these republican states have been subjected to excavation and the evidence shows that they had attained the urban status by the sixth century BC for the simple reason that they fulfil most of the criteria of ubranisation listed by Gordon V. Childe (1979). They are as follows:

1. Size
2. Specialised classes of skilled workers
3. Centralisation of surplus
4. Monumental architecture
5. A ruling class
6. Knowledge of writing
7. Sophisticated art style
8. Long distance trade
9. Exact and predictive sciences regulating the cycle of agricultural operations
10. Social organisation based on residence rather than kinship

This is a fairly exhaustive list and it will be seen that all these criteria are fulfilled in ample measure by many towns and cities of the early historical period. Childe has employed the term revolution to describe the change that took place in early rural farming cultures which attained the urban status. The early agriculturists, living in fertile river basins, began to produce surplus food on which could subsist a class of skilled workers and specialised craftsmen. This, in turn, led to development of barter and exchange, first into inter-regional and later into long distance trade. Population increased fast and villages, especially larger ones became big agglomerations—towns and cities. Food surplus and trade brought prosperity never witnessed before. With the development of trade, it became necessary to invent a system of recording. This is how scripts developed. A currency system was earlier thought to be *sine qua non* of urbanisation but since it has been found that there existed large towns such as Catal Huyuk (Turkey) and Jericho (Israel) in prehistoric times where no writing system or currency existed, these two are now not taken as criteria for urbanisation.

It is now agreed that the chief characteristics of urbanisation include a large population, a strong agricultural base, developed trade, growth of skilled craftsmen and so on, but behind it all lies the centralisd power structure. This will be reflected generally in monumental architecture such as forts, palaces, irrigation works, etc. Literary evidence furnishes the names of kings along with their lineages who ruled the *janapadas*, and there are several fortified towns of the early historical period such as Rajgir (Cyclopean wall), Pataliputra (palisade and palace), Kausambi (fortification wall), etc. The growth in agrarian production due to the introduction of plough agriculture led to increase in population and settlements (Erdosy 1988; Makkhan Lal 1984). Pataliputra was then the largest city in South Asia, spread over an area of 22 ha., with a population of some 2,70,000 souls (Allchin 1993: 69). The Mauryan state was administered by an efficient bureaucracy which was armed with coercive power to implement laws of the state rigourously, as Kautilya in his *Arthasastra* has prescribed. Megasthenes too gives an account of the administrative system of the Mauryas, but it is at variance with that of Kautilya. This disparity is probably due to what Megasthenes actually saw whereas Kautilya states what an ideal administrative system should be.

For the smooth functioning of government, maintenance of records, especially taxes, land records, etc. is very necessary. The earliest evidence of writing in the country, barring the Indus script which is as yet undeciphered, belongs to the period of Asoka (272–32 BC) whose edicts reveal a developed system of writing. Recent excavations at Anuradhapura (Sri Lanka) have yielded inscribed potsherds which are radiocarbon dated to 600–500 BC (Deraniyagala 1990). It is therefore highly likely that the antiquity of Brahmi script may go back to the sixth century BC. In this connection it would be pertinent to draw attention to B.B. Lal's (1960) study of graffiti on megalithic pottery consisting of symbols, many of which (80%) are to be found in the Indus script. This suggests that the origin of Brahmi may ultimately be traced in the Indus script. Similarly the introduction of coinage also has to be assigned to the sixth to fifth centuries BC (Dhavalikar 1975).

Urbanism brings in its wake sophistication, and a sophisticated art style is supposed to be a characteristic feature of urbanisation. A Ghosh, who has made a very intensive study of the urbanisation in the early historical period, is convinced that "No spirit of artistic activity . . . is noticeable immediately with the start of the early historical period though there might have been proliferation of argillaceous art. There is no definitely pre-Mauryan sculpture, whether in native tradition, such as the later *Yaksa* figures, or in imitation of foreign style such as the pillar capitals of Asoka" (Ghosh 1973: 27–28).

This observation is no doubt valid but up to a limited extent. First, the potter's art cannot be rejected out of hand because in India the terracotta art made tremendous progress and goes hand in hand with stone sculpture. Secondly, some stone sculpture also existed in pre-Mauryan times (Gupta 1980). There is a strong possibility that some of the Asokan pillars may be pre-Mauryan. This is evident from his own edicts—Pillar Edict VII, and Minor Rock Edict, Sahasram and Rupnath versions—in which he orders that they be engraved on rocks and pillars wherever they existed (Mookerjee 1972: 87–88; Irwin 1976). Another evidence of sophisticated art is available in the form of discs and ringstones which are most daintily carved with various motifs. They have mostly turned up at north Indian sites and till now over 70 specimens have been reported (Gupta 1980:). They generally occur in the early historical levels and may belong to the Mauryan and pre-Mauryan times.

Perhaps the most important criterion of urbanisation is long distance trade. According to Ghosh (1973: 28), there is no evidence of any extensive trade with outside countries. This is also partially true if we mean by long distance trade only foreign trade. But if we take the long distances involved in different regions, even the internal trade is nothing short of long distance trade as it covered thousands of kilometres, as for instance from Pataliputra to Taxila or to Amaravati in the south. Some trade also existed with Iran after Sindh and Punjab were annexed to the Achaemenid empire by Darius (522–486 BC). The evidence of silver bent bars from Taxila—the double Sigloi—which have been identified as the *Satamana* of Panini, suggest trading contact. Later still, around the Christian era, trade with Roman empire was in a flourishing state (Warmington 1927).

It will thus be seen that urbanisation in India was ushered in the sixth century BC from the beginning of the early historical period. It probably originated in the Ganga valley between Pataliputra and Kausambi and then spread in course of time all over the Indo-Gangetic plains and even to central India. Later still it reaches western India and the Deccan in the fourth to third centuries BC and the south. The growth of urbanisation has been traced in two (Gupta 1974) or three phases (Chakrabarti 1974 and 1984–85; Erdosy 1993: 104). This developmental model, however, is not acceptable to many (Ghosh 1973; Sinha 1979–80). Be that as it may, there is hardly any doubt that India enjoyed prosperity in the early historical period (600 BC–AD 600). This however, was not peculiar to India, but was more or less the case in many parts of the Old World. This was an age of empires in Greece, Rome, Persia, China and India. A major factor responsible for this growth seems to be a favourable environment. Kautilya (*Arthasastra* II, 24, 116) gives rainfall in different regions and it is clear that it was more than at present. Moreover, it has been found that in many cases the mud ramparts were embankments for flood protection (Mate 1968). This is one important factor which contributed to the prosperity of the early historical period.

SECOND DEURBANISATION

Archeological evidence from different parts of the country shows that the Kushana levels in the north and the Satavahana levels in the west and the Deccan are well represented, but the Gupta and post-Gupta epochs are poorly represented in the north, more particularly in the upper Ganga basin, whereas in western India and the Deccan they are almost absent. It appears that a vast majority of sites were deserted after the third century. In the lower Ganga basin, however, the occupation continued in the Gupta and post-Gupta periods. Many urban centres betray evidence of decline in the Gupta and post-Gupta epochs. This phase can be described as 'second deurbanisation' for which the cessation of long distance trade, over exploitation of resources and the rise of feudalism are supposed to have been responsible (Sharma 1987). But it appears that a very important factor responsible for this degeneration was the adverse environment. We have some literary evidence to indicate that the period was marked by frequent droughts and famines; Varahamihira had predicted it and Hieun Tsang's testimony corroborates it (Dhavalikar 1989–90).

Further supportive evidence is furnished by the Nile flood records (Dhavalikar 1997). It may be noted that this phenomenon was not confined to India only but recurred even in the west. After the decline of the Roman empire, in the fifth century, even Europe was passing through troubled times, and slightly later in the seventh century West Asia witnessed the rise of Islam and the consequent turmoil. It was a period of stress and strain almost everywhere in the Old World.

Feudalism has been cited as one of the important causes of the degeneration that set in during the Gupta and post-Gupta times (Sharma 1965) but it seems more to be the consequence than the cause. When there was no trade worth the name, neither internal nor external, there was almost total absence of coinage and the state officers received their salaries in the form of land grants (Watters 1904–05: vol. I, 340); rulers began to make donations to religious establishments (*brahma-deya*) and educational institutions (*agrahara*) in the form of land grants. Consequently people began to migrate from towns and cities to rural areas where grant lands were situated. Merchants and traders had no occupation in cities and artisans had lost patronage; they applied to government for permission to purchase lands. Thus migrations began on a large scale, which resulted in depopulation and the consequent deurbanisation, several new villages came into being and vast stretches of virgin lands were brought under cultivation, but agrarian production did not increase because of frequent droughts. There was a slight recovery between AD 1000–1400 but again the entire medieval period is also marked by economic decline (Raichaudhury and Habib 1982) and the same is corroborated by archaeological evidence.

This brief survey of historical archaeology in India brings into sharp focus the important lacunae in our knowledge. Our sources of ancient history are very meagre and archaeology will doubtless contribute to the resolution of some of the issues. Perhaps the chief issue is that of the hiatus from the fourth century up to the tenth century or even up to the fifteenth century in some areas. More intensive work is required to obtain evidence for this period. We have seen that adverse environment forced people to migrate to mofussil regions and land grants created several new villages; it is therefore necessary to explore these places which occur in inscriptions and copperplate charters. This is rural archaeology which we must now do. For this scientific aids such as laser techniques and equipments will be of great help. More emphasis should be laid on the recovery of biological material which will throw light on economy.

A glaring lacuna in our knowledge of historical archaeology is that the entire millennium or more from the sixth century BC to the sixth century AD is clubbed into one single early historical period. In fact this was the formative period in Indian history when the very ethos of our culture was being moulded. It is, therefore, necessary that in our future work we should try to distinguish different cultural sub-phases as pre-Mauryan, Mauryan, Sunga, Kushana, Satavahana, and Gupta. It is possible to do so by studying artefacts intensively. A careful examination of terracotta figurines will go a long way in determining the various cultural phases. A. Ghosh (1989: vol. I, 135 ff) has suggested the division of early historical period into three phases: (1) 600–300 BC, (2) 300–50 BC, and (3) 50 BC–AD 300. This scheme covers the pre-Mauryan to Kushana times. Ghosh has also given the characteristic features of each phase. But we are sure that it is possible to distinguish between the pre-Mauryan, Mauryan, Sunga, Satavahana, Kushana and Gupta phases by an intensive study of artefacts, as has been done at Mathura (Joshi 1989). Minute changes in the development of artefacts will go a long way in determining these phases.

Finally, it is pertinent to emphasise that we need to carry out large-scale excavations such as Marshall's work at Taxila for resolving the vexing issues in historical archaeology. Till now historical levels at an ancient site were treated as a hindrance as the main objective was to reach the lowermost protohistoric strata; so the former had to be removed without much consideration. This tendency has to be curbed. Culture sequences for different regions was a desideratum when Wheeler came in 1944. In fact even then he had exhorted his pupils that we now have a timetable, and let us have some trains. But alas! those trains have not yet arrived.

REFERENCES

Agrawala, V.S. 1947–48. Terracotta Figurines from Ahichchhatra. *Ancient India* 4: 104–79.

Akhtar, J.D. 1978–79. Indo-Aryan Rulers of Ancient West Asia and their Documents. *Puratattva* 10: 66–69.

Allchin, F.R. 1993. *The Archaeology of Early Historic South Asia: The Emergence of Cities and States*, Cambridge: Cambridge University Press.

Altekar, A.S., and Misra, V.N. 1959. *Report on Kumrahar Excavations (1951–55)*. Patna: K.P. Jayaswal Research Institute.

Amarendra Nath. 1989-90. Archaeology of the Wardha-Wainganga Divide. *Puratattva* 20: 93–98.

Begley, Vimla. 1983. Arikamedu Reconsidered. *American Journal of Archeology* 87: 461–81.

Begley, Vimla and de Puma, R.D. 1991. *Rome and India: Ancient Sea Trade*. Madison: University of Wisconsin Press.

Bell, Barbara. 1970. The Oldest Records of the Nile Floods. *Geographical Journal* 136: 569–73.

Chakrabarti, D.K. 1972–73. Concept of Urban Growth and the Indian Context. *Puratattva* 6: 27–32.

—1974. Theoretical Aspects of Early Indian Urban Growth. *Puratattva* 7: 87–89.

Chattopadhyaya, B.D. 1974. Trade and Urban Centres in Early Mediaeval India. *Indian Historical Review* I(2): 203–19.

—1975–76. Indian Archaeology and the Epic Traditions. *Puratattva* 8: 67–72.

Childe, Gordon V. 1979. The Urban Revolution. Reprinted in G.L. Possehl, ed., *Ancient Cities of the Indus*. New Delhi: Vikas Publishing House.

—1948a. Vedic India and the Middle East. *Journal of the Asiatic Society of Bengal* 14: 121–43.

—1948b. Vedic India and Minoan Men. *Journal of the Asiatic Society of Bengal* 14: 137–43.

Deraniyagala, S.U. 1990. Radiocarbon Dating of Early Brahmi Script in Sri Lanka 600-500 BC. *Ancient Ceylon:* 149–68.

Deo, S.B., and Dhavalikar, M.K. 1968. *Paunar Excavation*. Nagpur: Nagpur University.

Deva, K., and Misra, V. 1961. *Vaishali Excavations 1950*. Vaishali: Vaishali Sangh.

Dhavalikar, M.K. 1972. Archaeology of Gauhati. *Bulletin of the Deccan College Research Institute* 31–32: 137–49.

—1973. *Masterpieces of Indian Terracottas*. Mumbai: Taraporewala.

Dhavalikar, M.K., and Jamkhedkar, A.P. 1989–90. The Kshetrapala Shrine at Kandhar. *Puratattva* 20: 99–106.

Dikshit, M.G. 1955. *Tripuri* (*1952*), Nagpur.

—1968. Rotary Querns in India, in V.D. Rao, ed., *Dr. A.G. Pawar Volume*, pp. 25–46.

—1969. *History of Indian Glass*. Mumbai: University of Bombay.

Erdosy, G. 1988. *Urbanization in Early Historical India*. Oxford: British Archaeological Reports.

Fritz, J.M., Michell, G., and Nagaraja Rao, M.S. 1984. *Where Kings and Gods Meet—The Royal Center at Vijaynagar, India*. Tucson: University of Arizona Press.

Gaur, R.C. 1944, ed. *The Painted Grey Ware: Proceedings of the Seminar*. Jaipur: Publication Scheme.

Ghosh, A. 1951. Rajgir. *Ancient India* 7: 66–78.

—1973. *The City in Early Historical India*. Simla: Indian Institute of Advanced Study.

—, ed. 1989. *Encyclopaedia of Indian Archaeology*, 2 vols., New Delhi: Munshiram Manoharlal Publishers.

Ghosh, A. and Panigrahi, K.C. 1946. The Pottery of Ahichchatra. *Ancient India* 4: 35–79.

Ghosh, N.C. 1986. *Excavations at Satanikota 1977–80*. New Delhi: Archaeological Survey of India.

Gogte, V.D. 1997. The Chandraketugarh-Tamluk Region of Bengal: Source of Early Historic Rouletted Ware from India and Southeast Asia. *Man and Environment* 22: 69–85.

Gupta, S.P. 1974. Two Urbanizations of India—A Study in their Social Structure. *Puratattva* 7: 53–60.

—1980. *Roots of Indian Art*. New Delhi: B.R Publishing Corporation.

Hertel, H. 1976. The Excavation at Sonkh, in *German Scholars in India* II: 66–99.

Hegde, K.T.M. 1962. Technical Studies in NBP Ware. *Antiquity* 11: 159–61.

Howell, J.R. 1995. *Excavations at Sannathi* (*1986–89*). New Delhi: Archaeological Survey of India.

Indian Archaeology—A Review. Annual Publication of Archaeological Survey of India, New Delhi.

Irwin, John. 1976. Asokan Pillars-Symbolism. *Burlington Magazine* 18: 734–53.

Joshi, M.C. 1989. Mathura: An Ancient Settlement, in Doris Srinivasan, ed., *Mathura—The Cultural Heritage*. New Delhi: American Institute of Indian Studies, pp. 165–70.

Kosambi, D.D. 1965. *The Culture and Civilization of India*. London: Routledge & Kegan Paul.

Khandalawala, Karl. 1960. Brahmapuri. *Lalit Kala* 7: 29–75.

Lal, B.B. 1949. Sisupalgarh 1948: An Early Historical Fort in Eastern India. *Ancient India* 5: 62–105.

—1954–55. Excavation at Hastinapura and Other Explorations in the Upper Ganga and the Sutlej Basins. *Ancient India* 10–11: 5–151.

—1960. From the Megalithic to the Harappa—Tracing Back the Graffiti on the Pottery. *Ancient India* 16: 4–24.

—1979–80. Are the Defences of Kausambi as Old as 1025 BC? *Puratattva* 11: 88–95.

—1993. *Excavations at Sringaverapura (1977–86)*, vol. 1. New Delhi: Archaeological Survey of India.

Legge, J. 1991. *A Record of Buddhist Kingdoms*, New Delhi: Munshiram Manoharlal Publishers.

Makkhan Lal, 1984. *Settlement History and Rise of Civilization in the Ganga-Yamuna Doab from 1500 BC–300 AD*, New Delhi: B.R. Publishing Corporation.

Mani, B.R. 1991–92. Excavations at Lalkot 1991–92 and Further Explorations in Delhi. *Puratattva* 22: 75–87.

Margabandhu, C. 1985. *Archaeology of the Satavahana Kshatrapa Times*. New Delhi: Sandeep Prakashan.

Marshall, John. 1951. *Taxila*, 3 vols., Cambridge: Cambridge University Press.

Mate, M.S. 1969–70. Early Historic Fortifications in the Ganga Valley. *Puratattva* 3: 58–69.

Mate, M.S., and Dhavalikar, M.K. 1968. Excavation at Pandharpur. *Bulletin of the Deccan College Research Institute* 29: 76–117.

Mehta, R.N. 1968. *Excavation at Nagara*. Vadodara: M.S. University of Baroda.

—1988. *Champaner—A Mediaeval Capital*. Vadodara: Heritage Trust.

Mookerji, R.K. 1972. *Asoka*, third edn. Delhi: Motilal Banarsidass.

Narain, A.K. and Roy, T.N. 1967. *Excavations at Prahladpur*. Varanasi: Banaras Hindu University,

—1976. *Excavation at Rajghat*, part I. Varanasi: Banaras Hindu University.

Nanavati, J.M., and Mehta, R.N. 1971. *Somnath 1956*. Vadodara: M.S. University of Baroda.

Nautiyal, K.P., and Khanduri, B.M. 1988–89. Excavation of a Vedic Altar at Purola, Uttar Kashi, Central Himalayas.*Puratattva* 19: 68–69.

Pande, B.M. 1966. Ring Wells in Ancient India. *Bulletin of the Deccan College Research Institute* 25: 207–20.

—1988–89. Archaeology of Thanewsar: A Brief Report on the Excavations at Harsha-ka-Tila. *Puratattva* 19: 1–5.

Prasad, A.K. 1980–81. Excavation at Taradih. *Puratattva* 12: 138–39.

Ramachandran, T.N. 1953. Asvamedha Site near Kalsi. *Journal of Oriental Research* 21: 1–31.

Rao, S.R. 1966. *Excavation at Amreli: A Kshatrapa-Gupta Town*. Vadodara: Baroda Museum and Picture Gallery.

Raychaudhury, T., and Habib, I. 1982. *Cambridge Economic History of India*, vol. I, *c*. 1250–1750. Cambridge: Cambridge University Press.

Roy, T.N. 1986. *A Study of Northern Black Polished Ware Culture of India.* New Delhi: Ramanand Vidya Bhavan.
Rydh, Hannah. 1959. *Rang Mahal.* Lund: CWK Gleerup Publishers.
Sankalia, H.D., and Dikshit, M.G. 1952. *Excavations at Brahmapuri (Kolhapur).* Pune: Deccan College.
Sankalia, H.D., Subbarao, B., and Deo, S.B. 1958. *Excavations at Maheshwar and Navdatoli (1952–53).* Pune: Deccan College and Vadodara: M.S. University of Baroda.
Sankalia, H.D., Deo S.B., Ansari, Z.D., and Ehrhardt, S. 1960. *From History to Prehistory at Nevasa (1954–56).* Pune: Deccan College.
Sarkar, H., and Misra, B.N. 1972. *Nagarjunakonda.* New Delhi: Archaeological Survey of India.
Sharma, A.K. 1995. *Evidence of Early Cultures in Northeast India.* New Delhi: Aryan Books International.
Sharma, G.R. 1960. *Excavations at Kausambi 1957–59.* Allahabad: University of Allahabad.
—1969. *Excavations at Kausambi 1949–50.* New Delhi: Archaeological Survey of India.
—1980. *History to Prehistory—Archaeology of the Ganga Valley and the Vindhyas.* Allahabad: Kausambi Museum.
Sharma, R.S. 1987. *Urban Decay in India* c. 300–c 1000 New Delhi: Munshiram Manoharlal Publishers.
Sharma, Y.D. 1953. Exploration of Historical Sites. *Ancient India* 9: 116–69.
—1955–56. Past Patterns of Living as Revealed by Excavations at Rupar. *Lalit Kala* 1–2: 21–29.
Sinha, B.P., ed. 1969. *Potteries in Ancient India.* Patna: Patna University.
Sinha, B.P., and Narain, L.A. 1970. *Pataliputra Excavations 1955–56.* Patna: Directorate of Archaeology & Museums.
Sinha, B.P., and Roy, S.K. 1962. *Vaishali Excavations (1958–62).* Patna.
Sinha, K.K. 1967. *Excavations at Sravasti (1959).* Varanasi: Banaras Hindu University.
Singh, P. 1994. *Excavations at Narhan (1984–89).* Varanasi: Banaras Hindu University.
Soundara Rajan, K.V. 1979–80. Use of Arch in Kushana Palace at Kausambi. *Puratattva* 11: 96–102.
—1994. *Kaveripattinam Excavations 1963–73.* New Delhi: Archaeological Survey of India.
Srivastava, K.M. 1996. *Excavations at Piprahwa and Ganwaria.* New Delhi: Archaeological Survey of India.
—*Baroda Through the Ages.* Vadodara: M.S. University of Baroda.
Sundara, A. 1981. Vadgaon-Madhavpur (Belgaum) in Karnataka, in M.S. Nagaraja Rao, ed., *Madhu—Sri M.N. Deshpande Felicitation Volume*, New Delhi: Agam Kala Prakashan, pp. 87–98.
Thakur, V.K. 1981. *Urbanization in Ancient India.* New Delhi: Abhinav Publications.
Thapar, B.K. 1967. Prakash 1955. *Ancient India* 20: 5–167.
Tripathi, Vibha. 1976. *The Painted Grey Ware—An Iron Age Culture of Northern India.* New Delhi: Concept Publishing Company.
Warmington, E.H. 1927. *The Commerce Between Roman Empire and India*, Cambridge: Cambridge University Press, reprint, 1995, New Delhi, Munshiram Manoharlal Publishers.
Watters, T. 1904–05. *On Yuan Chwang's Travels in India,* 2 vols., London: Royal Asiatic Society, reprint, 1996, New Delhi: Munshiram Manoharlal Publishers.
Wheeler, R.E.M. 1947–48. Brahmagiri and Chandravalli. *Ancient India* 4: 181–310.
Wheeler, R.E.M. and K. Deva. 1946. Arikamedu—An Indo-Roman Trading Station on the East Coast. *Ancient India* 2: 17–124.

11 ❖ Medieval Archaeology in India

M.S. MATE

INTRODUCTION

'Medieval' Defined

THE title of the paper begs a question: what is 'medieval' in the Indian context? The term, in its literal sense, would mean a period between the 'ancient' and the 'modern'. This periodisation of Indian history was based on the European model, but was more a superficial than a substantial copy. For, in the European context each of the three periods had a distinctive socio-economic order as its basis—'the ancient' represented the period of all-pervasive Holy Roman Empire while the 'modern' represented the scientifically oriented, industrial age. The medieval period in contrast was the age of feudalism, of small but all-powerful landlords wielding political and economic power over the entire society. There was nothing in India's ancient past comparable to the Roman Empire nor was feudalism all-pervasive and all-powerful as in Europe. In fact there was very little difference between the socio-economic structures of the ancient and medieval periods. However, by 1100 AD a new political and cultural force burst on the Indian scene and altered the way of life of a large part of the subcontinent. Islamic invaders brought with them a religion, a language and a culture that had profound effects on the Indian society. Hence nineteenth century historians termed the period between 1100–1800 AD as the 'Islamic Period'. It was soon realised that such a designation was inadequate as the entire southern portion of the peninsula was beyond the pale of Islamic rule for a large part of this period. Hence the more inclusive but less apt term 'medieval' has now been adopted to designate these seven centuries.

Previous Work

Indian archaeologists have so far focussed their attention almost exclusively on the ancient, pre-Islamic period. Almost everyone was, and today is, engaged in the search for the 'early, ' 'earlier' and 'earliest' man and his culture. This preference is best illustrated by the number of sites explored and excavated by the Archaeological Survey of India, the Archaeology Departments of various states, universities and research institutes. The following chart speaks for itself:

	No. of sites excavated	Medieval sites
1985–86	33	3
1986–87	36	3
1987–88	40	3
1988–89	45	2
1889–90	30	1

The above statistics is derived from *Indian Archaeology—A Review* (*IAR*), the official annual publication of the ASI. The 2 or 3 sites excavated during this period were the same, Daulatabad in Maharashtra, Fatehpur Sikri in Uttar Pradesh and Hampi (Vijayanagar) in Karnataka. While there is something to be said in favour of continuous work at a given site, it is not clear why no new medieval sites were discovered, selected or excavated (see Paddayya 1990; Aruni 1998). Prior to this period only Champaner in Gujarat was subjected to extensive excavations and explorations (Mehta 1979 and 1988). There was the inevitable cutting of 'medieval' layers during the course of vertical digs at some sites like Mangalkot (West Bengal), Thaneshvar-Harsh Ka Tila (Haryana), Jhimjhimia-Kalistan (Bihar) and Ambari (Assam) (*IAR* 1987–88); Erich (Uttar Pradesh), Barabati Fort (Orissa), Gormati-ni-Khan (Gujarat) (*IAR* 1989–90). But beyond reporting the occurrence of some structural remains (wall fragments) and a few sherds of glazed/Chinese celadon ware, nothing of a distinctive nature has been indicated. Much more detailed discussion on two sites viz., Mangalkot (Ray 1990: 131 ff) and Thaneshvar (Pande 1990: 141 ff) is now available. However, identification of antiquities of an exclusively 'medieval' nature still eludes archaeologists.

The only major activity relating to the medieval period was recording and conservation of some monuments. This task was performed quite admirably by the Archaeological Survey of India, and some State Governments like those of the erstwhile princely states of Hyderabad or Mysore. One thus gets well-documented and well-produced reports on the monuments of Agra (Smith 1901) or Bijapur (Cousens 1916) or the Chalukyan temples of Karnataka (Cousens 1926). Monuments like the Taj Mahal at Agra, the Mughal forts at Agra and Delhi, the Gol Ghumat at Bijapur or the temple gopuras of South India have been very well preserved.

However, neither the official agencies like the Archaeological Survey of India nor non-official ones like universities and research institutions have crossed the narrow limits of recording and conservation except on rather rare occasions.

Several factors appear to have led to this inhibition towards the medieval period. This period was recent, considered fit for historians to discuss. Perhaps the vast amount of contemporary literature and documents available for study created a feeling that archaeological studies of the medieval period were superfluous. It was rarely realised that archaeology provided a tool useful not merely for verification of these records but for discovering newer facts about the daily life of the kings and their subjects.

Secondly, in almost all universities where archaeology is being offered as a subject of study medieval studies are invariably bracketed with 'ancient' Indian culture. By doing so the medieval period was automatically excluded from the purview of the discipline of archaeology. One of the major reasons for this bias was the training of early archaeologists. Almost all of them, Indian as well as foreign, were Sanskritists. Whereas any understanding of the medieval period would require knowledge of the Persian language and culture, as they have deeply influenced the languages and culture of medieval India. Unfortunately, these two branches stand neglected even today. The neglect of this period by archaeologists inevitably followed. Of late the emphasis of archaeological investigations has shifted and it has almost become a branch of anthropology!

SOURCES

The preliminary studies, before archaeological survey, explorations or excavations are undertaken, are of necessity library studies. A large amount of material in the form of literary works and official records of this period is extant. Many have been published and a much greater number (especially records) are to be found in archival collections. Literary works—travelogues, memoirs, etc.—have served the pioneering studies for the ancient period. The account of Megasthenes of ancient Pataliputra or the account of Hiuen Tsiang, which literally served as a guide to Cunningham, can be cited as examples. In the case of the medieval period, one has to take into consideration a much vaster amount. There are autobiographies, biographies, histories, travellers' and merchants' accounts, administrative documents and records. Some of the better known ones can be cited. Babur, the first Mughal ruler, has left an autobiography (Talbot 1909); one of his successors, Jehangir himself wrote or caused to be written memoirs of his reign (Elliot and Dowson 1867, vol. VI: 244 ff). Abul Fazal has left a comprehensive, almost encyclopaedic, account of the reign of Akbar (Blochmann 1873). Much earlier Alberuni had written an encyclopaedia (although he did not name it as such) on India, Indian society and its culture (Sachau 1993). Historical accounts like Tabakat-i-Nasiri of Minhaj Siraj dealing with the period prior to 1259 or the ones left by Zia-ud-Barni (Elliot and Dowson 1867, vol. III: 93 ff) or Ferishta (Briggs 1981) present a comprehensive, though not always impartial, picture of medieval rulers and society. Accounts of numerous foreign travellers starting with Marco Polo (Komroff 1929), Ibn Batuta (Gibbs 1992) and coming down to likes of Abder Razzak and Nicoli Conti (Major 1974) are extant and supplement these historical accounts. There are literary works of a poetical and fictional nature like 'Yusuf wa Zelekha' or 'Shirin-Farhad', stories of the *Panchatantra* (Anvar-i-Suhayli), translations of the *Mahabharat* (Razm-nama) in Persian (Losty 1982: 121, 136). The archives of palaces like Bikaner or Hyderabad have preserved valuable documents.

Most of these are in Persian; a few are in Arabic, whereas those of individuals like Conti are in their native language viz., Italian. Translations in other languages—especially in English (and some in Hindi)—are no doubt available (Elliot and Dowson 1867; Rizvi 1956). However, these are more often than not translations of portions considered to be important by the concerned scholars. Hence recourse to original works is absolutely necessary. Unfortunately, there is a sad neglect of the studies of Persian, thereby depriving an investigator of medieval archaeology access to a valuable source.

Some of the other difficulties in using this source can be mentioned. Often there is exaggeration; accounts of only those aspects which the author felt were important have been recorded and sometimes imagination gets better of sound factual statements. An account of the second capital of Muhammad bin Tughluq speaks of an ideally planned township, with quarters for various classes of population, each self-sufficient and segregated from each other, but the structural remains exposed during explorations and excavations do not show such arrangements (Husain 1963). Both Ibn Batuta and Abder Razak (Gibbs 1922: 227; Major 1974) were so enamoured of the pleasure-houses of Daulatabad and Vijayanagar and have waxed so eloquent about the beauties parading there that one would get the impression that the cities were nothing but an immense flesh-market! Abder Razak also probably confuses between Bijapur, the capital of the Adil Shahis, and Vijayanagar, the capital of the Arividu kings, when he mentions the tomb of Muhammad Shah as forming part of the third fortified enclosure of the latter place. The reference obviously is to the tomb of Muhammad Adil Shah—the famous Gol Ghumat at Bijapur. But one should not paint all accounts with the same brush. The account of Ibn Batuta mentions the use of leather ladders to approach the top of the hill of Devagiri (Daulatabad), the sides of which had been scarped sheer. This indicates that the subterranean passage that now gives access to the top of the hill was not then in existence or was incomplete. This statement therefore is of great assistance in determining the chronological evolution of the magnificent fortress. Accounts left by Rafi al din Shirazi of the Firuzabad on the Bhima have been found to be factual by Michell and Eaton (1992: 19) on close survey of the extant remains. This would indicate that literary sources, though not entirely reliable, cannot be altogether neglected.

Epigraphy has served as an important source for the ancient period. It continues to play that role in the medieval period but its utility is limited to the southern part of the peninsula, where inscriptions in the old manner, consisting of dynastic lists, details of office-bearers, of grantees, etc. are meticulously mentioned; those of the Vijayanagar rulers and Nayaks of Madura follow this pattern. But the epigraphs of the Muslim rulers are of a different nature; these are to be found on tombs and mosques and are dedicatory in nature or are quotations from sacred texts of the Muslims. In those regions where the rulers had multi-lingual populations, epigraphs were cut in Persian and the local language. Some are even trilingual, an inscription of the Bijapur rulers being in three languages—Persian, Marathi and Kannada. The contents of the inscriptions of the Islamic rulers imposes limitations on their utility for archaeological studies.

Coins of this period are useful for historians in reconstructing the economic history of the period but are not of much use to the archaeologist.

Miniature paintings of the period are of real assistance, but their utility has not been fully realised nor has this source been fully exploited as yet. Mughal miniatures of the early phase almost exclusively and in a majority of cases of the late phase as well were manuscript illustrations and as such depicted real-life events like court-scenes, constructions of forts and buildings, occasions in the royal family like circumcision of a child or the weighing of a prince. The great attention to details and exactitude in rendering them make these paintings mines of information on contemporary life. Even minor details like the cow-head used as a water-chute or the lock on a door have not escaped the attention of the painters. The best use of these renderings has been made by Qaisar (1988) and Chattopadhya (1990) in their treatises on the art of building under the Mughals. Paintings of other schools like the Pahari school depict the ethos of rural India in a highly pleasing and informative manner. Paintings of the Bhagavat Purana exemplify this. (Rajasthani Ragamala paintings depict court-life of the period in all its splendour.) South Indian artists appear to have followed their ancient tradition of wall-paintings and those from temples like those at Anegundi or Kumbhakonam supply many details of contemporary life—buildings, costumes, ornaments and so on. Late medieval wall-paintings often depict European soldiers with their canon, etc. The paintings of Daulatabad and Dharur fort in the *Shah Jahan-Nama* of Inayat Khan (Begley and Desai 1990: 42) are so realistic as to be mistaken for photographs.

METHODOLOGY

In the Field

Methods of study of an archaeological site of the medieval period are largely dictated by the nature of the remains on such sites. One hardly comes across well-marked or clearly identifiable mounds of debris at these sites. Medieval, especially Islamic townships, were generally spread over a very wide area. Most of the important structures like mosques, tombs and places had around them wide open areas, generally well-laid out gardens. In the case of Hindu townships, a tendency to grow around more important or more frequented temples is noticeable. These temples were, however, located quite apart from each other as in the case of Bhuvaneshwar in Orissa. This resulted in the township being spread over vast areas. The dwellings of ordinary people and markets were located around such monumental features resulting in isolated clusters within the town.

Another peculiarity of most medieval sites was fortifications. These range from comparatively simple but strong town-walls provided with bastions and gates to complex systems consisting of multiple lines, loop-lines, salients, gates, barbicans, ditches and glacis. These were altered and expanded often, complicating the layout of the original township. Instances of such cities are too numerous and too well known to require any mention.

This tendency of the horizontal growth of medieval townships presents a real archaeological problem, especially to the Indian archaeologist, who generally takes excavation as the ultimate in archaeology and who is generally trained to tackle thick deposits requiring vertical digs Horizontal excavations, whenever carried out, dealt with coherent as opposed to scattered sites. Debris of the medieval period never behave in the manner the archaeologist is taught to expect. They are never very thick and vertical stratification is usually impossible to determine. Then, spatially proximate mounds may not be proximate in respect of time or culture. What assumes importance is the ability to 'read' the large areas over which the ruins are spread. The good old Cunningham 'leg work' and 'observation' replace everything else. Surface surveys supported by accurate contour maps become the main thrust of archaeological investigations of a medieval site. Aerial photography is an imperative, it should precede work on the ground.

The next step would be to mark out a few salient features like standing structures or their ruins, streets and indications of water-supply lines or larger tanks and wells. Study of standing structures would reveal the stylistic peculiarities they might have and enable the investigator to determine the age or the authorship or both (Fig.1). Identification of streets would be of much more importance as this would mark out different habitational areas or wards which would then be explored or excavated for tale-tell artefacts and placed in their proper chronological and cultural brackets. Medieval water-supply lines were almost always underground but their progress is dotted with small minaret-like structures which are 'air-shafts' allowing bubbles to escape and thus ensure free flow. If these are marked on a map, they reveal the points of both intake and off-take, the former being a large well or dam and the latter being the site of a public fountain or more often that of a palace or garden. Apart from pin-pointing such structural items, they give valuable glimpses into medieval hydraulic technology. This aspect is a peculiarity of townships established or enlarged by Islamic rulers (Mate and Pathy 1993: 46–49).

Apart from careful survey, recording, etc. newer methods of interpretation of data and deductive pattern of reasoning are necessary in dealing with a medieval site. An example would make this point clear.

Daulatabad was known as Devagiri, the capital of the powerful Yadava rulers of the Deccan, before 1315 i.e., before the Khalji Sultans appropriated it in their empire. Digs at various spots revealed the existence, right up to the lowest levels, of Chinese celadon ware and polychrome glass bangles,

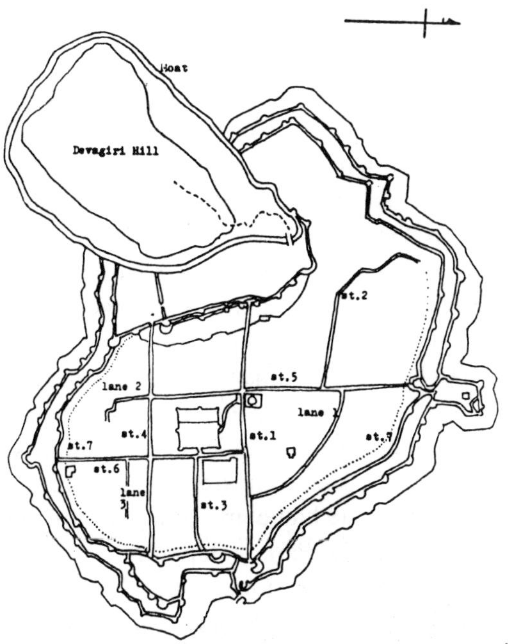

Fig. 1. Plan of excavated streets, Mahakot area, Daulatabad

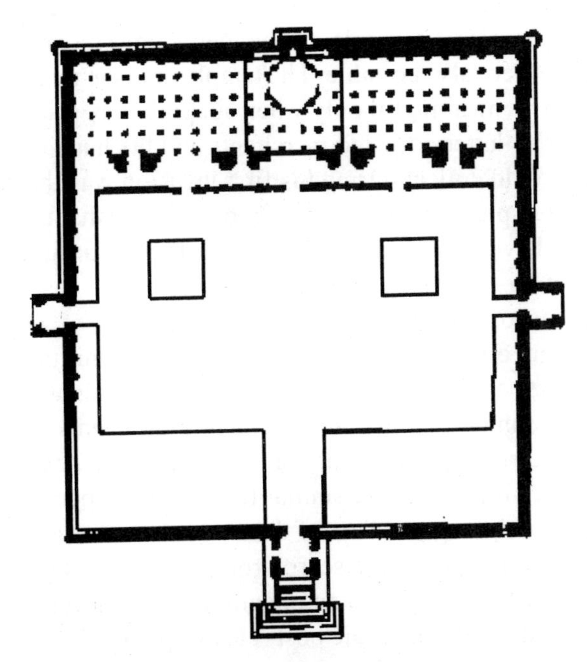

Fig. 2. Plan of Jami Mosque/Hindmata Mandir, Daulatabad

which are associated with the Islamic rule i.e., 1325–50 onwards. In other words, no material remains of the Yadava period, pre-1300 period, were to be found. This led to speculation in some quarters that after all this might not have been the spot where the Yadava capital was located. However, tradition was firm in this belief. A solution to the riddle had to be found.

It came in the form of a structure standing intact today and a number of stone pieces uncovered through excavations. The huge building today called 'Hindmata Mandir' was erected by Mubarak Khalji in 1317–18 as the Jami mosque (Fig.2). Since that date no material changes have occurred in the building. It is built almost entirely of pillars, beams, brackets, bases, etc. that once belonged to Hindu and Jaina temples. The present author and his colleagues carefully counted them and then compared these with the number of parts making up various types of temples in this region used in the twelfth and thirteenth centuries. It became apparent from this comparison that the parts used in the Jami mosque had come from two fairly large and about twelve medium-sized temples. Parts belonging to a Shikhar, ceilings of temples, and a highly ornate door-frame either found during explorations or uncovered through excavations not only confirmed this guess but also made it obvious that the larger temples belonged to a particular style, known as the Bhumija, that was prevalent in the region during the period of tenth to fourteenth centuries. From this, further deductions regarding the nature of the township were also possible. The temples and the tanks in their front portions would be meaningful only when supported by priests, attendants and pilgrims. The latter attracted merchants and the huge booty that Ala-ud-din Khalji could collect during his first invasion was the accumulated wealth of this temple-market centre. A good idea of what the township of Devagiri must have been was thus obtained through an interpretation—through deduction—of a standing structure (Fig. 3).

The chronology of the gradual development of Devagiri into Daulatabad, from a religious-commercial centre to a military stronghold, could be reconstructed evolved through a careful examination of standing or partially standing structures and rock-cut monuments cut in the hill. There are five fairly large rock-cut halls with squat, square pillars, in the upper part of the hill; these were similar to the Yadava period caves found at many places in the region. Two of the caves were, it was observed, cut almost in half while cutting the scarp around the hill. The scarp and the moat are contemporary and form an integral part of a scheme of defences. Thus, these could be placed in the post-Yadava period.

These are just two examples of what can be achieved by closer obser-

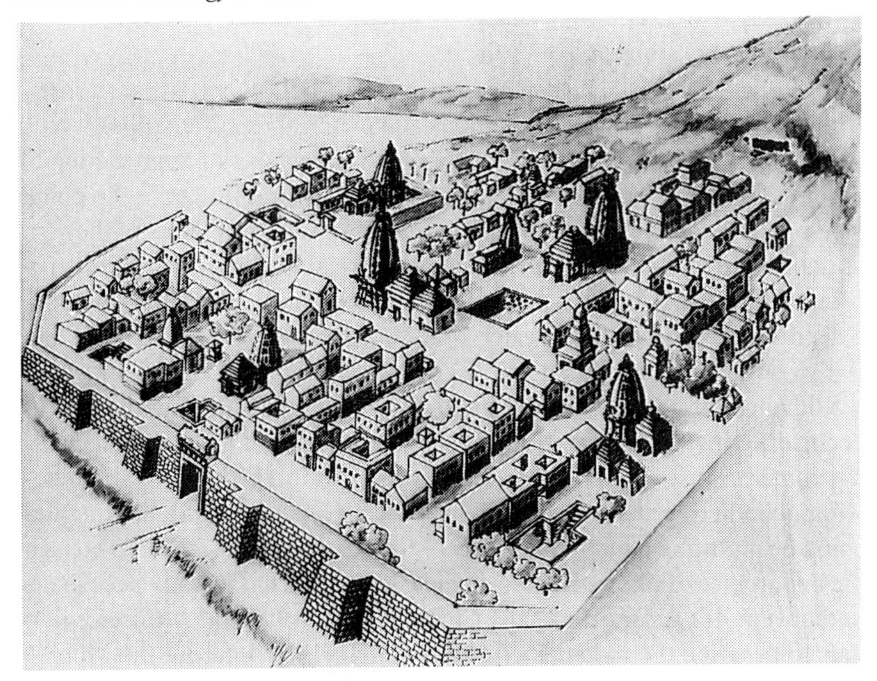

Fig. 3. Conjectural reconstruction of Yadava Devagiri

vation, recording and selective digs. The conclusions are deduced from these features read with similar features elsewhere as well as information from literary sources.

The ruined township of Firuzabad on the Bhima has been surveyed by Michell (Michell and Eaton 1992) and his colleagues and their surveys give a good idea as to the origin, layout and eventual desertion of the town. However, due to the very short period of time that it was occupied, the process of evolution or development could not be observed. The attention of the authors was almost exclusively centered on architectural monuments and hence no antiquities have been recovered, which is a distinct loss. For, given a specific life-span for the town, its antiquities would have helped in fixing a precise date, especially for minor antiquities or pottery, that could eventually assist in fixing the upper and lower chronological limits of a stratum.

Discoveries of Ming pottery—almost intact—at Ahmednagar in Maharashtra (Gadre 1986: 78–88, M.XV–XIX) are undoubtedly significant but being out of context cannot serve as a guide to future investigators.

Library Studies: Paintings

Library studies, both before and after the field-work, are necessary. Comparison with literary descriptions and pictorial representations would assist in better understanding of the problems and a better appreciation of the remains uncovered. A couple of examples would illustrate the point. Literary data specifies the upper and lower chronological limits of the construction and utilisation of the palace-complex at Fatehpur Sikri, thus enabling an archaeologist to evolve a chronological-cultural framework Occurrence of a cow-head water-chute in a tank at Daulatabad was initially confusing as it was an adjunct of a Hindu temple. This single piece would have raised doubts regarding the authorship of the waterworks. Its occurrence in Mughal paintings, in the background of an encampment of the emperor, made it very clear that it was used by the Mughal architects without bothering about its previous religious connotation. Such examples could be multiplied, but the mention of the above two cases would convey the importance of library backup studies. Reference has already been made to the work of Qaisar (1988) and Chattopadhya (1990) that utilises paintings to describe the methods of construction adopted during the Mughal period.

PROBLEMS

The need to have clear-cut understanding of the problems involved, of having a well-defined objective, before any archaeological investigation is undertaken, can hardly be overemphasised. These could be particular to a given site or of such a nature that they are common to medieval sites in general. Of course many fresh problems would crop up in the process of investigations either in the library or in the field. They will have to be tackled as and when they arise. A few can be mentioned, which of necessity are of a general nature and common to most if not all medieval sites.

From a purely archaeological point of view, identification of characteristic remains (structures, antiquities, etc.) is yet to be evolved. In the case of monumental architecture, the true arch (and the dome based on the same principle) has been treated as a distinctive feature (Figs. 4 and 5). However, there are some other features like rubble and timber masonry which typically use brick at those places wherever a right angle is required (e.g., window frames, door-frames, etc.). This practice is current in the Deccan even now. Brick masonry was the most common method in the preceding periods as revealed by a number of excavations.

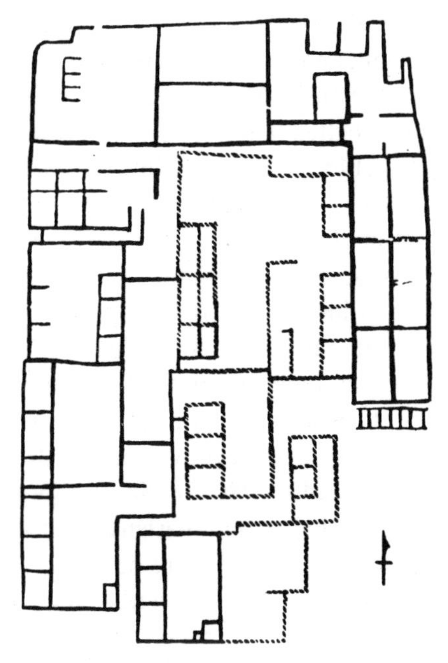

Fig. 4. Plan of excavated structures, Area C, Daulatabad

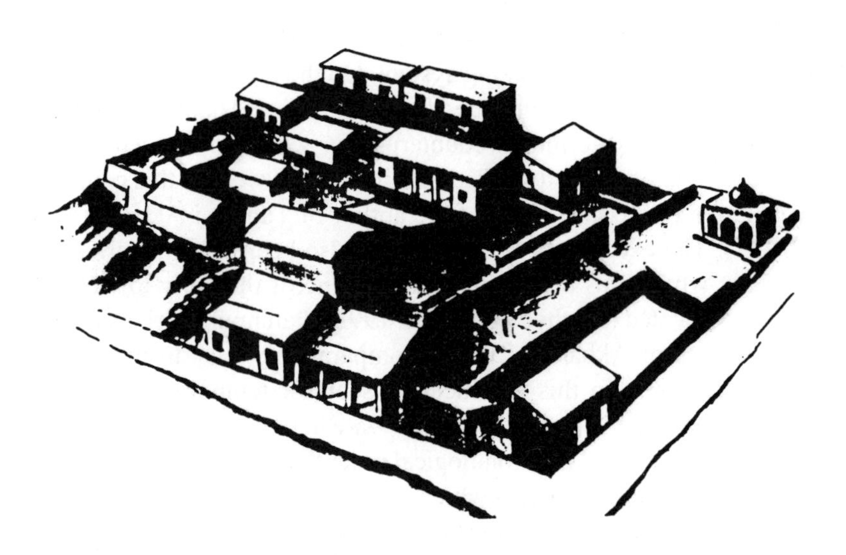

Fig. 5. Conjectural reconstruction of area C, Daulatabad

Next comes pottery, which is generally very crude. Even here the globular pots with a short spout and thick pans are typical of the medieval sites in the Deccan. One has to find out if the same is valid in other parts. Far more distinctive is the so called 'Chinese celadon' ware—fine, thin glazed pottery—with designs in blue or green. A few sherds with Chinese characters on them were discovered at Daulatabad but in the absence of comparative materials (at least published ones) their provenance, date, etc. could not be determined. It is generally presumed that it was introduced by the Islamic rulers, but the point of time is hardly clear. The find of Ming-period porcelain of Chinese origin in Ahmednagar (Maharashtra) has already been noted. However, these pots were found in the cellar of a house and as such had no stratigraphic context, nor were any other objects that would establish the precise date or the provenance of these objects recorded by the scholar concerned (Gadre 1986: 78–88, Pl. XV–XIV). Polychrome glass-bangles are another variety of antiquarian remains that need a detailed study. The so-called Chinese celadon ware has been tentatively assigned by earlier archaeologists to the 'Islamic Period'—the period between 1350 and AD 1650.

Mehta has conducted surveys of some townships in Gujarat and has undertaken extensive excavations at the site of Champaner (Mehta 1979). He has attempted to address himself to the larger problem of town planning during this period. His observations are not without interest: "The town was planned as a series of fortifications, one overlooking the other. Each fortification had its own planning system. On the ground the central place was assigned to the Jami mosque. This is a typical Islamic concept that also seems to have the Indian counterpart in which in the centre of the town the temple of the deity is kept. A little to the west of this centre was the royal area or Hissar-i-Khas of the author of Tabkat-i-Akban" (Mehta 1979: 141). The excavators at Hampi have also been able to mark out the palace area which was proximate to the shrine of the deity to which the rulers were devoted (Michell and Eaton 1992). Fatehpur Sikri was famous for the palaces of Akbar and it was comparatively easy to mark out its important features. In this instance the seats of temporal and spiritual power—the palace and the Jami mosque—are not quite close to each other. But the former preceded in chronological order the latter in a clear departure from orthodox Islamic precepts which enjoin that the mosque should come first and the palaces later. Excavations conducted at the site have brought to light the bazaar-street flanked by rows of shops on either side, water-supply system and a rather unusual and slightly queer enclosure. It is roughly square on plan and along the four walls are rows of latrines—without a trace of privacy. For whom were these common latrines built? At Daulatabad and Hampi similar latrines were found but each one was enclosed within walls ensuring complete privacy. The one at Fatehpur Sikri has not been properly explained by the excavators. Perhaps it was attached to the Zenana apartments and used only by the female folk; still its uncommon arrangement rankles. But this of course is a side observation.

Studies in medieval technology have been till now undertaken by historians only. Based upon contemporary texts and documents, the nature of technology of minor crafts and trades, and metallurgy and manufacture of guns and the geared wheel have been discussed. It has been argued that many of the innovations were introduced by craftsmen coming from West Asia, especially Persia. The most efficient means of water raising viz., the Persian wheel, as the name suggests, was one such innovation. Mughal paintings depict this contrivance (Fig.6). Archaeological studies indicate that raising of water to levels much higher than the source was an essential feature of medieval palaces and gardens. Hydraulic engineering—building of dams and distribution of water through canals—has not been fully explained in spite of very perceptive studies in this direction (Iqtidar 1986; Wadhwan 1988; Ravindra Kumar 1990). Archaeologists would have to seek the cooperation of engineers in the particular branch. Buchanan has enumerated a method of storing and releasing of water current in South India during the eighteenth and nineteenth centuries (Buchanan 1807, I: 1–5). The method is too primitive and cumbersome. It would be useful in the case of small bunds but not for larger dams. Water was supplied to most urban centres in medieval Deccan (Mate and Pathy 1993: 43–44; *Gazetteers of the Bombay Presidency 1883, 1885*). Most of these systems are now defunct but exhibit a very sound knowledge of hydraulic engineering on the part of the engineers of the medieval period. From where they obtained it and who they were need to be investigated.

Many other problems, technological but having a bearing on social and economic structures of the society, could be fruitfully investigated. Mention can be made of one such problem here. Again reverting to Daulatabad, the site with which the present author is more familiar, the defensive elements—scarps, moat and ramparts—pose interesting questions.

It is realised hardly ever that the fortifications have social and economic relevance. Apart from imparting security to the king or the officials and the surrounding areas these massive diggings and constructions served another important purpose. They represent a huge effort in manpower. It is

Fig. 6. Mughal miniature depicting Persian wheel

worth finding out as to how many man-hours must have been required to bring these things into existence. Our observations at Daulatabad were highly instructive. The cutting of the vertical scarp around the hill, the digging of the deep moat at the foot of the hill and the two moats beyond the Mahakot and Amberkot lines, and the construction of bastions, ramparts, loop-lines, gates and the bunds across the moats, all considered together, represent a colossal effort in terms of manpower and man-hours spent

Fig. 7. Seige of the fort of Daulatabad, 1530 AD.
After Begley and Desai (1990)

(Fig.7). These were to be constantly kept in repair, thereby requiring additional man-hours all the year round. The houses in the Mahakot area were built of rubble or dressed stone which needed quarrying: additional man-hours. From where was this man-power obtained? The most obvious answer seems to be: through forced labour, that is, 'veth-bigar'. The problem faced by the medieval rulers was simple: they needed fortifications; more important, they had to keep a large population out of mischief—the people who had nothing to do during some months of the year as agriculture needed their services during certain months but not the year round. In order to keep them busy and also to feed them, these gigantic works were in all probability undertaken. This insight into medieval military architecture has been gained only through constant observation of the amount of labour required to remove the stones from the small trenches we had taken. The issue can be clinched only when careful measurements are taken and the cubic meters are calculated and matched with the amount of work one person can put up during a day. This work is projected and would be taken in hand soon. There are numerous references in medieval Marathi literature to forced labour and one of the saint poets, Chokha Mela, lost his life while building a mud rampart around Mangalwedha in Sholapur district. However, it was never before realised that archaeology could provide concrete evidence in that respect. It would also be possible to calculate the population involved. This is a line of investigation that has come up only because of the application of the archaeological approach to a medieval site.

Finally, attempts have got to be made by the archaeologists to convey the knowledge they obtain to the people at large in a manner that is less technical, use less of jargon and present their reconstructions of the past dwellings and towns, howsoever tentative they might be.

REFERENCES

Aruni, S.K. 1998. History and Culture of Surapura Samsthana, North Karnataka, AD 1650–1858. Unpublished Ph.D. thesis. Pune: University of Pune.

Begley, W.F., and Desai, Z.A. 1990. *The Shah Jahan-Nama of Inayat Khan*. New Delhi: Oxford University Press.

Blochmann, H. 1873. *Ain-i-Akbari* by Abul Fazl Allami, 3 vols., Calcutta: Asiatic Society, reprint, 1978, New Delhi, Oriental Book Reprint Corporation.

Briggs, J. 1981. *History of the Rise of Mahomedan Power in India*, 4 vols., translation of Ferishta. New Delhi: Oriental Book Reprint Corporation.

Chattopadhya, Ratnabali. 1990. Mughal Paintings as a Source of History: Certain Methodological Problems, in *Historical Archaeology in India*, A. Ray and S. Mukherjee, eds. pp. 131–40, New Delhi.

Cousens, H. 1916. *Bijapur and its Architectural Remains*, Mumbai.

—1926. *Chalukyan Architecture of the Canarese Districts*. Calcutta.

Elliot, H.M. and Dowson John. 1867. *The History of India as Told by its Own Historians*, 8 vols., London.

Fritz, J.M. and Michell, G. 1991. *City of Victory: Vijayanagar*, New York.

Gadre, Pramod. 1986. *Cultural Archaeology of Ahmadnagar*. Delhi.

Gazetteers of the Bombay Presidency, 1883–85, Districts of Ahmednagar, Bijapur, Nasik and Pune, Mumbai.

Gibbs, H.A.R., 1992. *Ibn Batuta-Travels in Asia and Africa, 1325–54*, New Delhi: Oriental Books Reprint Corporation.

Habib, Irfan. 1969. Presidential Address to the Medieval History Section, in *Proceedings of the Indian History Congress*, Varanasi, pp. 131–61.

—1979. Technology and Barriers to Social Change in Mughal India, *Indian Historical Review*, 1: 55–158.

—1986. Capacity of Technological Change in Mughal India, in *Technology of Ancient and Medieval India*, A. Ray and S.K. Bagchi, ed. pp. 1–14, Delhi.

Husain M. 1963. *Tughluq Dynasty*. Calcutta: Thacker Spink.

Indian Archaeology—A Review, Annual Publication of the Archaeological Survey of India, New Delhi.

Iqtidar Alam Khan. 1986. (with Ravindra Kumar) Manasagar Dam of Amber, in *Technology of Ancient and Medieval India*. A. Ray and S.K. Bagchi, ed. Delhi: Sundeep Prakashan, pp. 25–40.

Komroff, M. 1926. *Travels of Marco Polo*, New York.

Losty, J. 1982. *The Art of the Book in India*, London.

Major, R.H. 1974. *India in the Fifteenth Century*, Delhi.

Mate, M.S., and Pathy, T.V. 1993. *Daulatabad: Report*, Pune and Aurangabad.

Mehta, R.N. 1979. *Medieval Archaeology*. Delhi: Ajanta Publications.

—1988. *Champaner—a Medieval Capital*, Vadodara: Heritage Trust.

Michell, G. and Eaton, Richard. 1992. *Firuzabad—A Palace City of the Deccan*, Oxford.

Paddayya, K. 1990. Towards the Archaeology of the Medieval Shorapur Doab, Deccan. *Islamic Culture* 44: 75–112.

Pande, B.M. 1990. Archaeology of Thaneshvar: A Brief Report on the Excavation at Harsha Ka Tila, in *Historical Archaeology in India*, A. Ray and S. Mukherjee, ed. New Delhi: Books & Books. pp. 141–54.

Qaisar, Ahsan Jan. 1988. *Building Construction in Mughal India—The Evidence from Paintings*. New Delhi: Oxford University Press.

Ravindra Kumar. 1990. Irrigation Technology in Medieval India, in *Proceedings of the Indian History Congress*, Gorakhpur, p. 850.

Ray, Amita. 1990. Archaeology of Mangalkot, in *Historical Archaeology in India*, A.Ray and S. Mukherjee, ed. New Delhi: Books & Books. pp. 131–40.

Rizvi, S.A.A. 1956. *Aditurk Kalin Bharat* (Hindi). Aligarh: Aligarh Muslim University.

Sachau, E.C., ed. 1992. *Alberuni's India*, 2 vols., Delhi: Munshiram Manoharlal Publishers.

Smith, E.W. 1901. *Mughal Colour Decoration of Agra*, Allahabad.

Talbot, F.G., 1909. *Memoirs of Babur—Emperor of India*, London.

Wadhawan, Prachee. 1988. Satapula—A Lesser Known Monument of the Fourteenth Century in *Proceedings of the Indian History Congress*, Dharwar, p. 684.

12 ❖ Rock Art of India

V.H. SONAWANE

FOR a long time, the existence of rock art in India was an enigma and even its very antiquity was questioned. Though its study crossed the threshold of archaeology rather late, it is now regarded as one of the prime sources of study. A cursory glance at the panorama of rock art is enough to reveal its diversity in time and space. In a way, rock art is mostly a reflection of the human mind to a changing environment and culture. From times immemorial, such creative works of human origin have been controlled by his feelings of visual space and reflect how man perceived the world. Extensive painted galleries prepared in the hollows of rock shelters and engravings executed on stone, bone and ostrich egg shells stand as mute testimony to this bygone art. An attempt can therefore be made to reconstruct the lifestyle of the people of different cultural periods with the integrated study of these extant works of art.

HISTORY OF ROCK ART RESEARCH

Rock paintings in India were first recorded by the pioneering discoveries made in 1867 by Archibald Carllyle in the forested region of the Kaimur ranges in Mirzapur district, Uttar Pradesh. These paintings were discovered about twelve years prior to the discovery of Altamira cave paintings in Spain. Though Carllyle did not publish any account of his discovery, he had left his notes with a friend and these were published by Vincent A. Smith (1906). Carllyle assigned these paintings to the prehistoric period. John Cockburn, a contemporary of Carllyle, studied these rock paintings systematically and produced tracings of several of them. However, he failed to recognize their prehistoric antiquity. In 1899, he published an account of all his discoveries. In this, he compared them with those found in Australia, South Africa, North and South America (Cockburn 1899). Percy Brown, who visited the painted shelters at Singanpur in Raigarh district of Madhya Pradesh in 1914, recognized their importance and included them as prehistoric art in his book on Indian paintings (Brown 1917).

The rock engravings of South India were first brought to light only after the visit of F. Fawcett to Kupgallu in 1892. Fawcett is better known for his discovery of Edakal cave (Fawcett 1901). Prior to this, rock bruisings were reported by H. Knox from Bellary district of Karnataka. Subsequently, more rock bruisings were reported from this area by F.R. Allchin (1963: 161), A. Sundara (1974), K. Paddayya (1968: 294–98) and N. Chandramouli (1995).

In 1921, Manoranjan Ghosh brought to light a group of painted rock shelters at Adamgarh near Hoshangabad (Ghosh 1932). In 1930's, D.H. Gordon tried to tackle the chronological problems of rock art by observing the superimposition of paintings, their style and technological contents. He worked basically on the rock paintings of Pachmarhi confined to the Mahadeo hills of central India. Unfortunately, he could not visualize a long autochthonous development of the Indian rock art in its original setting. Nevertheless, he was the first antiquarian to write extensively on the thematic elements shown in the rock paintings. A chapter dealing with rock art in his book became a widely read introduction to rock art in Indian archaeology (Gordon 1958).

Since then, more than 5,000 painted shelters have been reported from different parts of the Indian subcontinent. These spectacular discoveries brought a new momentum to rock art studies. V.S. Wakankar, who recognized its archaeological potential, was the driving force behind these recent large scale discoveries. He had discovered several hundred painted rock shelters mainly in central India and attempted a broad survey of the rock art sites of the whole country (Wakankar 1975a; 1987; 1992; Wakankar and Brooks 1976). Wakankar had employed an appropriate guideline to determine the chronology of the paintings based on their themes, style, superimposition and the archaeological context in historical perspective. The most outstanding contribution of Wakankar to the field of rock art was the discovery of Bhimbetka in 1957. It is one of the most splendid rock art sites known to the world. This site has now become synonymous with rock art in India. Among the prominent contemporary researchers of rock art are S.K. Pandey (1975; 1993), Shankar Tiwari (1975), Jagdish Gupta (1967),

R.K. Varma (1964), A. Sundara (1984), Erwin Neumayer (1983; 1993) and Yashodhar Mathpal (1984; 1995) who have contributed comprehensively to develop a possible link between rock art and archaeological data in order to ascertain its antiquity in terms of historical relevance.

The rock art studies in India, as they stand today, are devoid of the application of any scientific or technological base. However, strides are being made by young researchers to develop a multidisciplinary approach for its systematic investigation focusing on regional studies. The most active among these are K.K. Chakravarty of the Museum of Man, Bhopal, Giriraj Kumar of Dayalbagh Institute, Agra Somnath Chakraverty of Calcutta University, Rakesh Tewari (1990) of U.P. State Archaeological Organization, S. Pradhan of Sambalpur University, N. Chandramouli of Telugu University, Murarilal Sharma of Government P.G. College, Kotputali, Jeewan Kharakwal of the Institute of Rajasthan Studies, Udaipur, K. Rajan of Tamil University, Thanjavur, B.L. Malla of Indira Gandhi National Centre for the Arts, New Delhi, besides Gajendra Tyagi, R.K. Pancholi, Meenakshi Pathak and Sudha Malaiya. The foreign scholars of post-independence period include R.R.R. Brooks (U.S.A.), Erwin Neumayer (Austria), R.G. Bednarik (Australia) and Michel Lorblanchet (France). They have made substantial contributions to promote rock art research in India.

SALIENT FEATURES

Distribution and Nature of Rock Art

The vast corpus of rock art in India is confined to sandstone and granite pockets, stretching from the southern parts of Kerala to the high altitudes of the Ladakh and Zanskar valleys in the north and from Gujarat in the west to Orissa, Assam and Manipur in the east (Fig. 1). However, the largest concentration is confined to the Vindhyan ranges of Madhya Pradesh and its Kaimurean extensions into Uttar Pradesh. Equally important paintings and engravings were reported from southern Deccan in the extensive granite wilderness of the Krishna-Tungabhadra doab.

In the sandstone region of central India, rock paintings were found on the walls or ceilings of shelters and sometimes in cliff wall cavities as well or at any other suitable places where they could withstand the effects of different weathering agencies. Bhimbetka, Jaora, Kathotia, Firengi, Kharwai, Gupha Maser, Lakhajoar, Adamgarh and Pachmarhi are the important localities representing rock art sites of this nuclear region. The geomorphological setting of the rock art sites of south India is strikingly

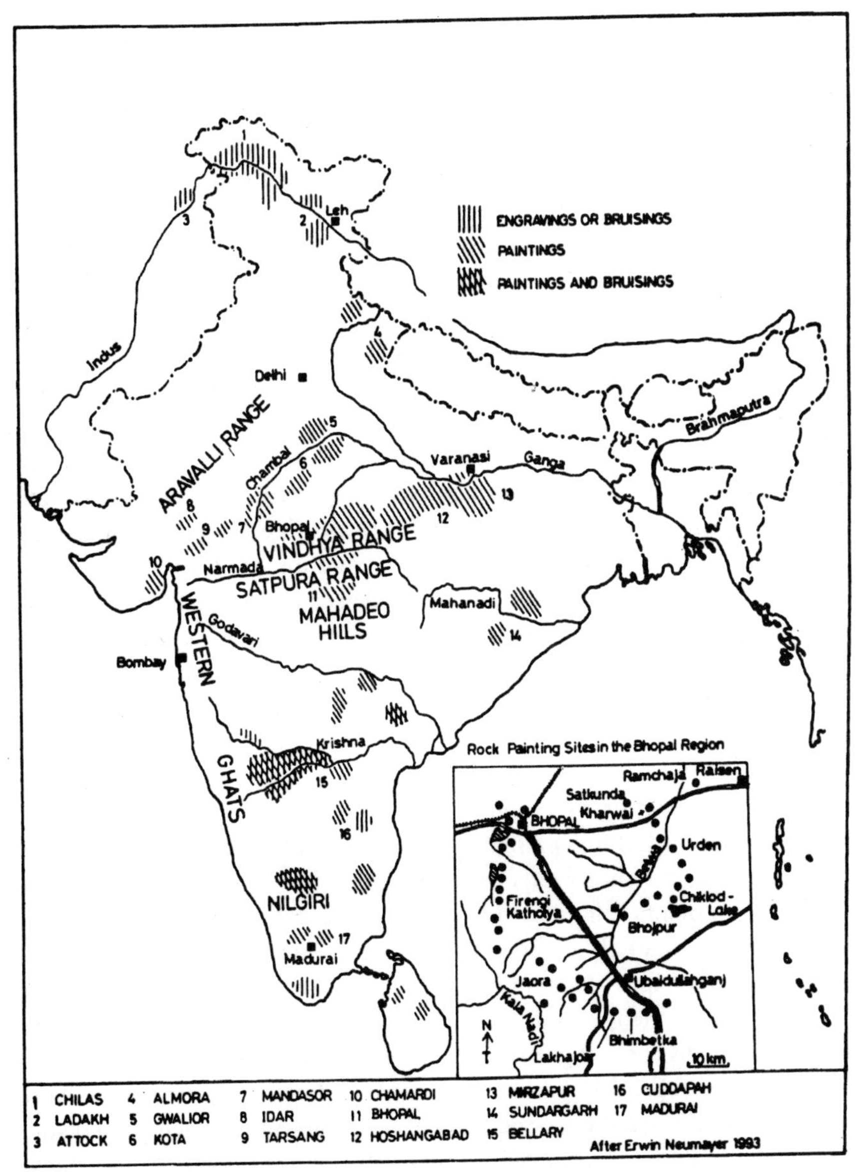

Fig. 1. Map showing the major rock art regions of India

different from that of central India. To a large extent, the rock art of south India is represented by rock bruising. Incidentally, there are cases of paintings also. The paintings are generally found on the shelter walls of projected ceilings hoods and invariably in niches developed by natural weathering. Among the several south Indian sites, the better known are

Kupgallu, Maski, Piklihal, Edakal cave, Tekkalakota and Badami.

So far as rock paintings are concerned, they are found in various states of preservation depending upon their location. Many of these paintings have partially faded away because of the destructive action of natural and human agencies. The paintings on granite surface are not very durable. As a result, only those paintings which are located in well-protected spots or hollows maintaining environmental balance are well preserved. The great mass of rock paintings show a predilection towards the red colour in several shades ranging from rather dark violet to yellowish brick red. The red pigment, in most cases, was acquired from red haematite nodules, called *geru*, containing iron oxide found in lateritic formations. The next most frequently used colour was white. It would have been obtained either from calcium carbonate nodule (*kankar*) or kaoline clayey deposits. Occasionally, some of the earliest paintings were depicted in green and yellow, employing mineralized chalcedony of the respective colours. Though most of the paintings were monochrome, there were instances of bichrome and polychrome drawings too. The authors of these paintings had exploited the natural resources available within the proximity of the rock art sites for colour pigments. At places, the rock floors of shelters show scooped out circular depression often retaining the traces of paints. Such 'cupmarks' were intended for preparing colours for painting the rock.

Unfortunately, no serious attempts have so far been made by scholars to use various scientific methods for studying these pigments. It has been proposed that the authors painted the pictures either by securing the paint by diluting the colour in water or by tempera. The use of fibrous material derived from plants cannot be ruled out in the creation of some of the rock paintings. They had also used dry colour technique using crayons or employed stencil or spray technique. Drawing by means other than colour are also recorded on the rock surfaces. These include engravings and carvings better specified as bruisings or petroglyphs. In the Indian context, bruisings constitute the second important component of rock art. Bruisings were executed either by rubbing or pecking of rough granite surface. As a result, the intended picture in white appears clearly against the dull brown background of the rock. Such bruised works of art can withstand all weathering agencies even on unprotected rock surfaces and survive for a prolonged period of time.

Besides rock paintings and bruisings, portable artefacts carved on stone, bone and ostrich egg shell pieces, though very meagre in number, form an additional source of information. These early forms of applied art reflecting an aesthetic taste in the archaeological context are of extreme importance in the absence of absolute dating evidence.

Chronology

Although rock art was discovered in India quite early, the knowledge of its existence had little influence on archaeological research until the last two or three decades (Mathpal 1992). Recent attempts to find the chronological indicators for rock art from associated artefacts through excavations have helped to some extent to establish the antiquity of some of these paintings. Such paintings, in the absence of absolute chronometric dating, are taken into consideration to formulate tentative stylistic criteria for establishing the chronological sequence of Indian rock art as a broad-based working hypothesis. Besides, the rock paintings themselves are useful in establishing the relative chronology on the basis of their thematic content, superimposition, style and context. Therefore, one could use these different parameters for chrono-cultural classification of our vast and diverse rock art treasures.

In many shelters, rock pictures are very often found painted one over the other. In such cases, building up a relative chronology of the picture becomes quite easy by observing the overlapping of paints. Here, one has to note the stylistic features of the successive paintings as well as the use of colour. Thus, by correlating the relevant chronology with chronologically relative features, one can unravel the age or cultural phase of the rock pictures effectively. Indian rock pictures are numerous and extremely narrative having diverse details. A thematic analysis can therefore establish a wide-ranging picture of the technological and social conditions under which they were created. The correlation of such paintings with archaeologically known data will bring us closer to a technologically well-defined periodization of Indian history. For convenience, the pictures drawn before the introduction of the Brahmi script, are considered as prehistoric and are divided into two distinct groups: those of hunter and gatherers and those of agriculturists, representing the food-gathering and food-producing societies, respectively. Pictures showing neither domesticated/ridden animals nor giving any clue of the use of metal weapons obviously belong to a class of society which did not possess these innovations. Such early pictures show that the hunting and gathering groups fashioned microlith-barbed weapons like spears and arrows and account for the developed microlithic technology current of India from the late Upper Palaeolithic to the Mesolithic period.

Unlike the pictures of hunters and gatherers, the paintings of people practising animal domestication depict humped cattle, goat and sheep. In this category, we also find yoked oxen, two-wheeled bullock cart and many other features of an agriculture-based settled lifestyle (Neumayer 1991). In central India, particularly, they resemble the Chalcolithic pottery designs found on the Malwa ware. None of the south Indian bruisings can be compared with any of the Mesolithic paintings. It seems that all bruisings were done once agriculture and animal domestication were well established. The main subject of the bruisings and paintings of this period are cattle.

On the contrary, rock paintings of the historical period are characterized by the appearance of inscriptions along with painted compositions. The presence of Brahmi and Shanka writings, besides depiction of religious icons and symbols of Brahmanical and Buddhist faiths, war scenes or processions showing horse and elephant riders armed with swords and shields and mythological and contemporary narrations are the predominant depictions of the historical period. Very often there is a predilection for white colour in later paintings of this period.

The periodization of Indian rock paintings is thus supported by a chronological framework based on the observation of overlapping rock pictures belonging to different stylistic groups. The dating is further based on the thematic analysis of pictures showing patterns of subsistence, tool technology and technological innovations. Unfortunately, unlike parts of Europe, datable finds such as carbed or engraved artefacts from archaeological strata are lacking in India which would have enabled the comparison of rock paintings with the designs found on such artefacts. As in India, most rock art around the world has not been securely dated so far; however, with the advent of the AMS (Accelerator Mass Spectrometry) dating through pigment analysis at least a few paintings of selected areas can be dated to confirm their chronological classification.

Earliest Rock Art Expressions

In the Indian context, the antiquity of rock art dates back to the Upper Palaeolithic period: however, the evidence begins with the haematite and quartz crystals found in the Acheulean deposits of the Lower Palaeolithic period. One such haematite specimen was found on the exposed floor of locality V at Hunsgi (Karnataka) and bears a worn facet with distinctive striation marks suggesting that it had been used as a crayon to colour or mark a rock surface (Bednarik 1990). The excavator believes that these small haematite nodules might have been brought to the spot from some distance since this material does not occur in its natural state around the site. He further states that these red ochre nodules must have been used for body decoration and similar purposes (Paddayya 1984: 365). Interesting evidence also comes from Singi Talav (Rajasthan) where, from the base of the Lower Palaeolithic deposit, six small quartz crystals had been recovered. They measured 7 to 25 mm in length and are therefore too small to have been used as tools and were almost entirely unmodified. Like the Hunsgi haematite nodules, they had been brought to the site deliberately and were apparently collected for their visual qualities (Bednarik 1994: 356–57a). Although regarded as a tentative inference, one cannot rule out the possible functional reality involving an aesthetic sense among our early ancestors.

Such an early beginning for rock art is further substantiated by the discovery of petroglyphs found at the site of Bhimbetka. Bednarik has reported two petroglyphs from the excavated Auditorium rock shelter (III F-24). These consisted of a large circular scooped out cupule and a pecked meandering line running parallel to its periphery. Their stratigraphic position within the habitation deposit suggests that they were made during the Acheulean period. He considered them as the oldest known rock art in the world (Bednarik 1994: 356–57a; Bednarik et al. 1991: 34). More recently, Giriraj Kumar has reported nearly 500 cupules at a place called Daraki-Chattan near Bhanpura in Chambal valley and assigned them to the Palaeolithic period based on the occurrence of the Acheulean and Middle Palaeolithic implements on the same cave floor (Kumar 1996).

It is quite possible to infer that some of the symmetrically formed and beautiful looking bifaces often encountered in the lithic assemblages of the Lower Palaeolithic period reflect the artistic ability of the tool makers and served as either art or religious objects. Two such circular discoid stone artefacts of non-utilitarian character, one found from Bhimbetka III F-24 and the other from Maihar (Madhya Pradesh), have provided possible relevant evidence in this regard (Bednarik 1992). The anthropomorphs forming part of the Copper Hoards and numerous ethnographic analogies would corroborate this assumption.

Upper Palaeolithic Phase

Though there is no dispute about the historicity of the Mesolithic rock paintings, it is quite likely, as Wakankar believed, that some of the early depictions in rock paintings painted in green colour do belong to the Upper Palaeolithic phase of Indian prehistory. The possible basis for this supposition is that faceted green earth (what he calls terra verta) have been found in the Upper Palaeolithic deposits of one of the excavated rock shelters (III A-28) at Bhimbetka (Wakankar 1975b: 19; 1983). There is some dispute however about the chronological position of the green paintings. Some researchers have remarked that green paintings were preceded by red paintings (Tyagi 1992: 304). Here, emphasis has to be given to the style rather than the colour of paintings. Though red colour is most frequently found in the paintings of the earliest style in the region around Bhopal, there are instances of paintings drawn in green and a few even in yellow. These paintings show a strictly codified repertoire in their style and use of space as if they were part of a widely understood communication system. They are distinguished from later paintings by a very high degree of craftsmanship and a characteristic uniformity. The quality of application of the pigment in the form of fine and controlled lines seen in these early paintings symbolize the beginning of known or surviving rock art in India. Basically, the Upper Palaeolithic paintings can be broadly subdivided into two phases, pre-figurative and figurative or non-iconic and iconic representations, on the basis of their thematic styles.

Closer inspection of global rock art sites shows that pre-figurative rock art precedes the figurative one in most cases. The pre-figurative art consists of a fairly restricted range of elements or form constants, which are found in numerous variants or which may be built into elaborate "mazes" or geometric arrangements. The basic elements of all archaic rock art are dominated by curvilinear motifs, such as concentric circles, spirals and their variations and intermediate forms including geometric motifs (Bednarik 1994b). Indian rock art is no exception to this widely accepted phenomenon. The paintings consisting of geometric patterns or intricate designs form the most conspicuous feature of this earlier style (Neumayer 1993: 43). In several paintings these intricate designs often identified as 'Labyrinthian', are composed of rhombic meanders and honeycomb patterns along with their multiple derivatives and cover a large space of virgin rock shelter surface (Fig. 2). None of these are superimposed on any of the earlier paintings (Tyagi 1992: 304–06).

Chronologically, pre-figurative or non-iconic symbolic motifs are followed by figurative or iconic representations. This has been attested at some places where 'S' types green paintings depicting dynamic dancing human figures have been observed superimposed on the intricate designs of earlier paintings drawn in red ochre (Fig. 3). The striking feature of this later style consists of human forms which are transformed to perfect 'S'

Fig. 2. Pre-figurative rock paintings

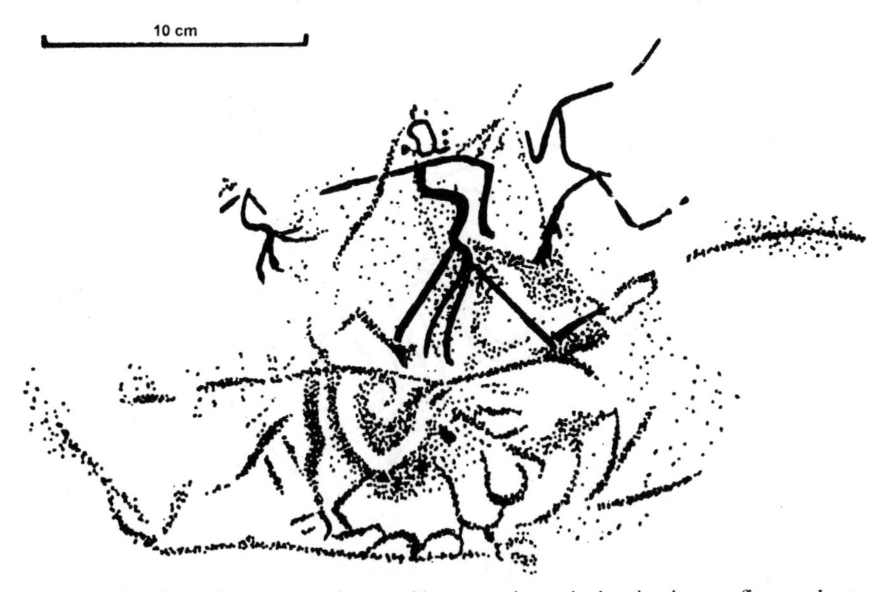

Fig. 3. Red intricate designs superimposed by green dynamic dancing human figures, Jaora

Fig. 4. Dynamic dancing human figures painted in green colour, Lakhajour

shapes (Fig. 4). These paintings do not depict any activities except dancing and hunting scenes and are known for their vigorous dynamism which is unparalleled in later rock art (Fig. 5). In this regard, the authenticity of a green painting depicting an ostrich noticed recently by S.K. Pandey at one of the sites in Central India might resolve the earlier controversy (personal communication from S.K. Pandey). In several rock shelters the intricate designs are found as body decoration of some animal figures (fig. 6). Here, among other designs, the spiral rhomboid is a recurring motif on the large and uncommon depiction of wild boar, elephant, rhinoceros and deer. These large figures are identified as 'deified animals' (Misra 1985: 120). It seems

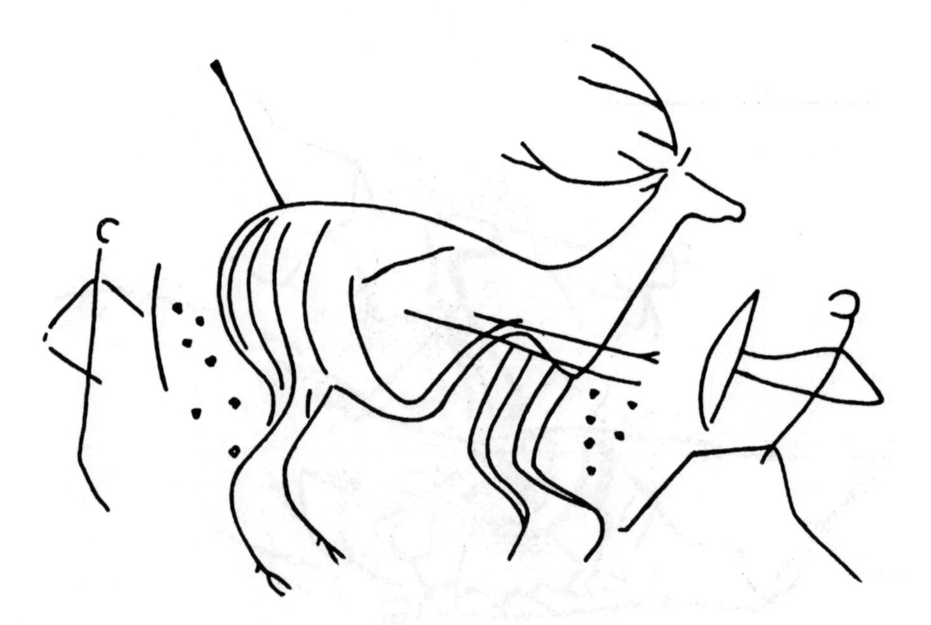

Fig. 5. Hunting scene, Putli Karar

Fig. 6. Deified animals

this early tradition continued to some extent even during the Mesolithic period and therefore sometimes becomes difficult to demarcate precisely.

Other Forms

Apart from rock paintings, interesting evidence pertaining to ostrich egg-shells, bones and stones comes from a few sites of this period. In this regard, an engraved portable artefact of applied art is reported from Patne (Maharashtra). Out of several ostrich egg shell pieces recovered from the Upper Palaeolithic levels here, one had distinct simple geometric pattern forming a criss-cross hatching between two parallel lines. A somewhat similar engraved design is also seen on the lower part of the same egg shell

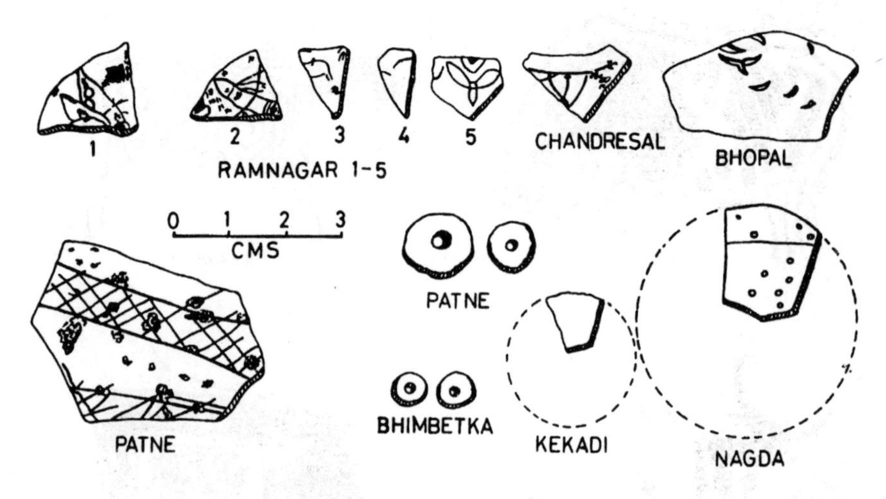

Fig. 7. Decorated ostrich egg-shell objects

fragment (Fig. 7). This has been dated to 25,000 BP based on C^{14} dates of the ostrich egg-shell samples from the same strata (Sali 1974: 157). The authenticity of the engraving found on the ostrich egg shell pieces reported from Bhopal, Ramnagar and Chandresal has been questioned by scholars (Bednarik 1993; 24; 1994; 359a; Neumayer 1990: 27), though they have furnished very early dates ranging from 40,000 to 25,000 BP (Kumar et al. 1988).

Ostrich egg shells were also effectively exploited for making ornamental beads. Two such perforated disc beads were reported from Patne. Two more heads of this category were found at Bhimbetka in Shelter III A-28 excavated by Wakankar. All of them were recovered from the stratified archaeological deposits of the Upper Palaeolithic period. In this context, recent discovery of an ostrich egg shell bead manufacturing site in Narmada valley at Khaparkheda by S.B. Ota and Sheila Mishra is very interesting (Ota: personal communication). Apart from these, barrel-shaped bone beads and grooved animal teeth (bovid) pendants were found from one of the Kurnool caves (Bila Surgam III) of Andhra Pradesh (Murty and Reddy 1975). The Upper Palaeolithic cave site of Muchchatala Chintamanu Gavi has furnished a TL date of *c.* 19,000 BP from where one such bone bead was obtained (Murty 1974). All these specimens show facilities of attachment to a string and they constitute the earliest known evidence of ornamentation in India.

In this context, a carved bone artefact recovered from cemented gravel

Fig. 8. Bone object, Belan valley

Fig. 9. Engraved chert core, Chandravati

layer III of Lohanda Nala in the Belan valley (Uttar Pradesh) is worth recalling (Fig. 8). The specimen is about 8 cm long, 1.5 to 2.5 cm broad and about 1 cm thick. It had generated two divergent feelings among scholars, viz., whether to call it a figure of mother-goddess or an object similar to that of a harpoon (Gupta 1979–80; Bednarik 1993: 34–35); however, it is now regarded as a well made bone harpoon which has suffered extensive damage in the very coarse sediment matrix. Its presence does provide cogent evidence of a highly sophisticated tradition of bone working during this period even in India. The stratum in which this artefact was embedded contains evidence of an Upper Palaeolithic blade and burin industry and has been dated to 25,000 BP on the basis of c–14 dating of freshwater shells (Mishra 1977: 49).

A solitary object found from Chandravati (Rajasthan) in the form of an engraved core is highly significant in this context. The design engraved on the simi-rectangular patinated cortex of the chert nodule appears to be like a spiral rhomboid (Fig. 9). The disign consists of a pair of parallel lines moving clockwise from the center forming two intertwining spiraling arms. One of these arms bears a series of short diagonal lines whereas the other one has been left plain to render a foreground and background effect. The engraver has taken care to make these infinitesimal yet distinguishable marks. This precisely indicates the specific intention of the artist to ensure that the significance and visual effect of the engraved design should not go unnoticed. The design was engraved on the nodule prior to its use as a core (Sonawane 1995–96). Identical designs have been found painted in earlier rock paintings at Mahadev Hills, Cheel Dant, Bhimbetka, Kathotiya and several other places in India which are identified as examples of prefigurative rock art. A striking parallel exists even in the Upper Palaeolithic art of Mezin, a site in Crimea (south Russia) where similar designs have been found on the mammoth ivory female figurines as well as ivory bracelet of Late Pleistocene period (Clark 1977).

Unfortunately, the earliest paintings representing geometric patterns, because of close similarity of the design engraved on the Chandravati core, has been attributed to the Mesolithic phase (Sonawane 1992). However, the Chandravati specimen is not actually dated, since it forms a part of the surface assemblage. It is merely assumed to be Mesolithic and acknowledged that the engraving on the object predates its use as core (Bednarik 1993: 34). Tyagi's only objection to Wakankar's observation is that green paintings representing 'S' shaped dynamic dancing human figures are not the earliest painting (Tyagi 1992: 310). In the light of new evidences, both

Fig. 10. Hunters carrying arrows set with microliths, Kharwai

from Chandravati and elsewhere, it appears that the pattern of design engraved on the chandravati core is of the Upper Palaeolithic tradition (Sonawane 1996). In view of the above situation, rock paintings representing purely geometric patterns as pre-figurative or non-iconic art forms and succeeding figurative or iconic depictions painted either in red or green, animated human and animal figures need to be seriously considered as the earliest depictions belonging to the Upper Palaeolithic period. The existence of these early paintings has been consolidated by other contemporary surviving art objects as a parallel or simultaneous development at par with the rest of the world.

Mesolithic Phase

The wide spectrum of rock art of the Mesolithic phase is full of varied descriptive details. It is suprisingly uniform in style and content all over India. There is a remarkable divergence in the degree of abstraction between the depiction of human and animal forms. While animals are depicted quite naturalistically, the human forms are reduced to stick-like figures in a stylistic manner. Sometimes, humans are shown wearing masks or elaborate head dress. this difference between human and animal depictions is

Fig. 11. Transverse microlith set on the shaft, Lakhajour

Fig. 12. Hunter carrying a net filled with hunt, Jaora

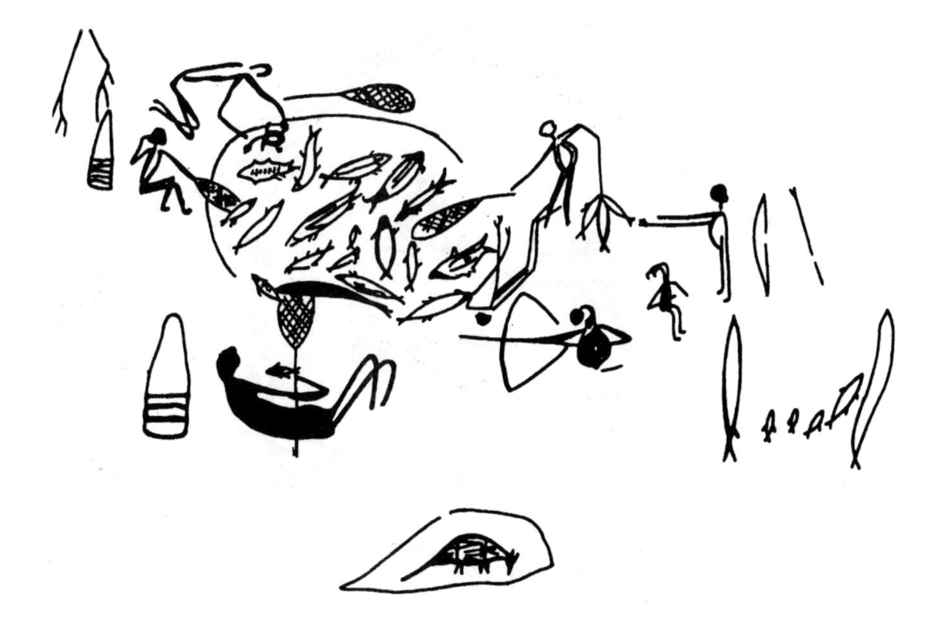

Fig. 13. Fishing scene, Lakhajour

Fig. 14. Women engaged in catching rats, Jaora

most visible in hunting scenes. Again, in contrast to fragile male figures, the female form is always static with a plum square body. Since animals and women are quite bulky, there was enough room for body decoration. Most of the intricate design patterns like the spiral or honeycomb are seen

Fig. 15. A family in a hut-like structure, Lakhajour

in such paintings and thus show continuity with the earlier tradition. There is no clear demarcation between body pattern and "X-Ray depictions". Both appear at places side by isde within a single composition. Mesolithic paintings give a remarkably detailed account of the various activities, recording minute details of the intended message. The hunting scenes which predominate in the rock art of this period show a variety of game animals, both big and small, being hunted with spears and arrows tipped and barbed with microliths (Figs. 10–11). They also furnish fairly detailed description of a variety of traps used for capturing game, shooting arrows at prey, transporting the kill (Fig. 12), butchering, fishing with net traps (Fig. 13), catching rats by pushing digging sticks into the burrow (Fig. 14), as well as the collection of fruits, honey and other subsistence practices. Apart from these, there are paintings which depict other activities such as dancing, singing, playing with musucal instruments (Neumayer 1992–93), drinking and eating inside a roofed house (Fig. 15). A large number of paintings show subjects which may be classed as religious or cultic. Here, we find mythical stories depicting huge deified animals chasing diminutive human beings. Scenes narrating magical cures or medical treatments signify a deeper meaning in their creation. The most touching is the scene of a child burial where family members are shown mourning over the death (Fig.

Fig. 16. Paintings depicting magical cures, medical treatment and burial scene

16).

Compared to the rock paintings, Mesolithic engravings are few and far between, with whatever is known being in the form of mere scratches, figures of animals or abstract patterns. In Orissa (Pradhan 1995) and Bihar (Chakraverty 1996), such engravings were invariable filled in with colours. The continuity in the tradition of engravings as mode of expression is further supported by discovery of bone objects recovered from the Mesolithic deposits in the rock shelter III A-28 of the Bhimbetka complex (Wakankar 1975b). The engraving consists of simple straight or zig-zag lines and irregular parallelogrammatic designs. Apart from this, the evidence of bone and antler rings used as ornamental ear rings and components of a necklace from Sarai Nahar Rai and Mahadaha (Uttar Pradesh) supply additional information on the aesthetic taste developed by these Mesolithic communities (Pal 1994).

Neolithic and Chalcolithic Phases

An abrupt change is seen in style and theme between the rock art of the hunter gatherers and that of the early agriculturalists. The earliest pictures of this period featuring domesticated animals are stylistically well demar-

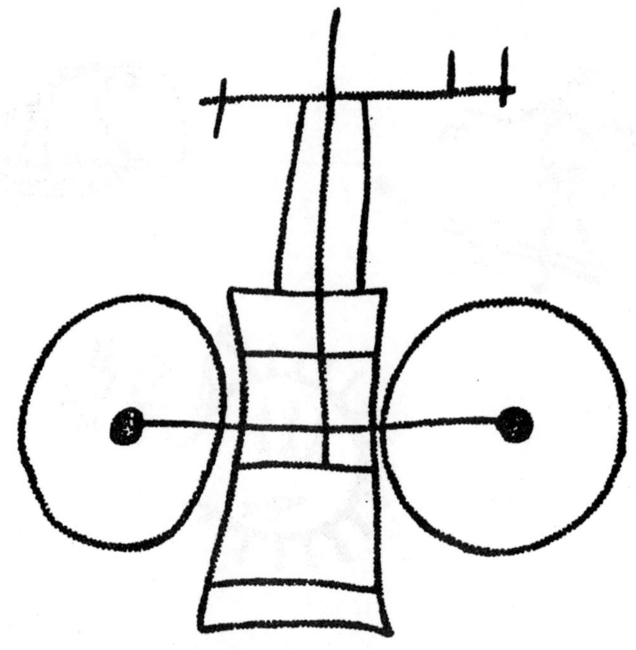

Fig. 17. Rock bruising of a cart, Kupgallu

cated from the pictures of the preceding periods. The dynamic art of the hunters and gatherers gets replaced by a progressively stiff and static art of the agriculturalists and cattle keepers whose thematic spectrum is extremely limited and confined to the depiction of long-horned humped cattle; however, where hunting scenes are painted, they give a good idea about the weapons used during this period. Although the most common weapons were bows and arrows, the appearance of metal arrow-heads, spears and axes herald a fast changing technology. The complexity of this available technology is best represented by depiction of the chariots. Several large Chalcolithic pictures show processions, accompanied by acrobats, boxers, load carriers and musicians. In several such scenes, chariots and their crew are prominently depicted sowing an advanced state of social stratification. Agriculture, the economic foundation of this period, is hardly shown in the painting except those found at Chaturbhujnath Nala and Lakhajoar, where paintings of ploughing farmers are seen. All the chalcolithic pictures of central India represent very much a man's world, in which women were depicted very peripherally. Similar tendencies are also visible in the Neolithic/Chalcolithic pictures of south India where women appear very subservient to ithypallic men. There are also instances of scenes depicting

Fig. 18. Rock bruising of long-horned bulls, Kupgallu

heterosexual intercourse in different postures.

Depictions of bullock carts are quite frequent as the common vehicle for transportation. A cart bruising from Kapgallu resembles the terracotta toy cart models reported from several Chalcolithic sites and is worth recalling (Fig. 17). There are several indications that chariots were drawn by horses and in paintings they also appear as mounts. Compared to this, elephant riders are very few.

Elegant long–horned bulls are a special feature of Neolithic/Chalcolithic pictures in south India, taking the position of an icon. One interesting depiction comes from Kapgallu where four typical bulls are arrayed at the periphery of a circle (Fig. 18). In other pictures, they are placed on a T–shaped pedestal. Besides this, there are several bruisings of large implements. Compared to the size of the accompanying human figures, they are drawn excessively large. These engravings of implements are often placed at prominent points on the granite hills indicating their use as standards or cultic weapons. Likewise, depictions of endless knots recall the design pattern engraved (Sundara 1996) on the copper tablets found at Mohenjodaro. Of these, several rock art sites are situated in the vicinity Megalithic burials. Obviously, some of the paintings and bruisings can be related to

Fig. 19. Hunting scene engraved on a stone slab, Burzahom

Fig. 20. Balarama, Krishna and Vinadhar Shiva, Tikula

Fig. 21. Classical paintings, Badami

Fig. 22. Stupa paintings, Gambhirpura

Fig. 23. Sailing boats, Chamardi

burial practices (Rajan 1991). One such painting shows a dead person within the burial inventory of a stone circle in Benakal forest.

In the same spirit, rock engravings found in the Karakoram region and Himalays, particularly in the upper course of the river Indus and its tributaries in Ladakh and Zanskar, show hunters with bows and arrows stalking ibex, deer and bovids (Frankfort et al. 1992). These compare well with the hunting scenes engraved on the stone slab (Fig. 19) recovered from the rectangular structure belonging to the Neolithic phase II at Burzahom showing the hunting of a deer by two armed persons (Pande 1971). Another slab found in the same context has an abstract design identified as a tectiform or trap, representing a hut with a thatched domed roof (Pande 1972).

The obvious advantages of dating the rock art of this cultural phase is the availability of reliable stratified archaeological data in the form of contemporary protohistoric art forms.

Historical Period

So far as the rock art of historical period is concerned, it is characterized by the presence of writings of Brahmi, Sankha nad even Nagari scripts, besides the introduction of religious icons and symbols of various prevailing faiths. The depiction of Krishna, Balarama and vinadhar Shiva (Fig. 20) at Tikula near Gwalior (Neumayer 1992–93), Ganesha and Yaksha at Bhimbetka, Lajja Gauri at Chintakunta (Andhra Pradesh), Buddha at Satdhara near Sanchi, stupas showing structural and decorative details at Satdhara, Kotra near Narsinghgarh, Gambhirpura, near Idar (Fig. 21) (Sonawane 1992–93), Dharmachakra on a pillar, Bodhi tree and Triratna symbol besides the story of Shravan Kumar at Chibbarnala near Bhanpura, suggest the depth of penetration of a codified and uniform system of religious beliefs throughout the country. Similar depictions mostly in the form of petroglyphs have been found further north in Ladakh and Chilas (Pakistan) narrating Buddhist themes along with Kharoshti and Brahmi inscriptions (Orofino 1990; Dani 1983: 43–58).

Apart from distinct religious or cultic narrations, rock art of the historical period is dominated by heavily caparisoned horses and elephants often with riders depicting battle scenes, with soldiers engaged in fighting with metal weapons such as spears, swords and shields, daggers and occasionally bows and arrows. Sometimes soldiers are shown wearing armour. There are also royal processions depicting royal personages standing under canopies. In addition, there are pictures representing many aspects of the contemporary life of the people residing both in plains and forests, together with a variety of animals, birds and plants confined to the regions of rock art distribution. The aesthetic sophistication of some of these paintings, particularly those from Badami (Fig. 22) and Mahadev Hills, is comparable with the famous Fresco painting of classical Indian art and some show close parallels with the Kushana and Gupta sculptural styles in their descriptive details. In this regard, the rock painting of sailing boats found at Chamardi (Fig. 23) near Bhavnagar in Gujarat depicting sea-going vessels current on the west coast of Saurashtra is unique (Sonawane 1996: 72–72). Apart from these, there are several examples of traditionally accepted themes and styles marked by monotonous depictions showing a decline in artistic standards. Geometric and floral patterns, signs, symbols, etc., which are distinctly different from earlier paintings, show strong stylistic and thematic analogies with modern pictures found in houses in the tribal belts.

CONCLUSION

The data provided in the preceding pages not only reveals the antiquity and development of rock art in India but also enriches our understanding of the way of life of the people of different cultural periods. These works of art can tell about the contemporary flora, fauna, hunting, gathering and other subsistence tactics, use of a variety of stone and metal implements, and social and religious aspects. The origin of rock art is still open to speculation, but one should not overlook the decorative value of such forms of expression. Though many of these are highly abstract, at least a few of them can be regarded as symbolic; there are some which are rich in descriptive details.

The motif engraved on the Chandravati core and its variations found elsewhere in numerous early rock paintings clearly denote some religious connotations in prehistoric art (Sonawane 1995–96). In this regard, the evidence obtained from the Upper Palaeolithic site of Baghor I (Son Valley, Madhya Pradesh) offers an important convincing clue (Kenoyer et al. 1983). The pictures of 'deified animals' often decorated with 'spiral' patterns are linked with the mythological stories prevalent among the tribals.

Symbols are often considered to be material representations of immaterial concepts. There is no visually obvious association between the symbol and the entity which it represents. Typical non-iconic art is far more likely to be symbolic than iconic art. The latter is only symbolic when the depiction of the object refers to an abstract concept (Bednarik 1994: 1974). The depiction of 'deified' animals is the best example to illustrate this ideological concept. Therefore, most of the graphic representations found in the Indian rock art served as expressions of the metaphysical beliefs of their authors. Hence, it is the reflection of human culture on the whole which the authors had experienced, observed and believed in as members of the society. However, knowing the weakness of archaeological interpretation, Kenoyer has rightly pointed out that, traditionally speaking, objects or patterns on objects with no definite of identifiable utilitarian function are, by default, symbolic in function (Kenoyer 1987). The most obvious examples of this type of interpretation is formed by rock paintings and carved objects; therefore, one has to be very cautious while interpreting any work related to rock art. At the same time there is definite need for regional studies in rock art and the peculiarities of a microregion should not be overlooked in a holistic macro-level study.

ACKNOWLEDGEMENTS

I am grateful to Mr. Erwin Neumayer, Dr. Giriraj Kumar and Dr. J.N. Pal for allowing me to use their line drawings and photographs of rock paintings and art objects, besides mine, to illustrate the text.

REFERENCES

Allchin, F.R. 1963. *Neolithic Cattle-Keepers of South India: A Study of the Deccan Ashmounds.* Cambridge: Cambridge University Press.

Bednarik, R.G. 1990. An Acheulean Haematite Pebble with Striations. *Rock Art Research* 7 (1): 75.

—1992. The Palaeolithic Art of Asia, in *Ancient Images, Ancient Thought: The Archaeology of Indology,* S.Goldsmith, S. Garvie, D Selin and J. Smith eds. Calgary: University of Calgary, pp. 383–90.

—1993. Palaeolithic Art in India. *Man and Environment* 18(2): 33–40.

—1994a. The Pleistocene Art of Asia. *Journal of World Prehistory* 8 (4): 351–75.

—1994b. Art Origins. *Anthropos* 89: 169–80.

Bednarik, R.G., Kumar, G., and Tyagi, G.S. 1991. Petroglyphs from Central India. *Rock Art Research* 8 (1): 33–35.

Brown, P. 1917. *Indian Painting.* Calcutta: YMCA Publishing House.

Chakraverty, Somnath. 1996. ISCO—Rock Art Site in Hazaribagh District: An Ethno-Archaeological Profile, in *Recent Perspectives on Prehistoric Art in India and Allied Subjects*, R.K. Sharma and K.K. Tripathi, eds. New Delhi: Aryan Books International, pp. 74–99.

Chandramouli, N. 1995. Petroglyphs from Naidupalli, Andhra Pradesh. *Purakala* 6 (1–2): 29–34.

Clark, G. 1977. *World Prehistory in New Perspective.* Cambridge: Cambridge University Press, p. 102, Fig. 39.

Cockburn, J. 1899. Cave Drawings in the Kaimur Range, North West Provinces. *Journal of the Royal Asiatic Society of Great Britain* 51: 89–97.

Dani, A.H. 1983. *Human Records on Karakorum Highway,* Islamabad.

Fawcett, F. 1901. Notes on the Rock Carvings in the Edakal Cave, Wynaad. *The Indian Antiquary* 30: 409–521.

Francfort, H.P., Klodzinski, D. and Mascle, G. 1992. Archaic Petroglyphs of Ladakh and Zanskar, in *Rock Art in the Old World,* M. Lorblanchet, ed., New Delhi, pp. 147–92.

Ghosh, M. 1932. Rock Printings and Other Antiquities of Prehistoric and Later Times. Calcutta, Archaeological Survey of India, Memoir no. 24.

Gordon, D.H. 1958. *The Prehistoric Background of Indian Culture*, Mumbai, reprint, 1997, New Delhi: Munshiram Manoharlal Publishers.

Gupta, J. 1967. *Pragaitihasik Bharatiya Chitrakala* (Hindi), New Delhi.

Gupta, S.P. 1979–80. The Alleged Upper Palaeolithic Bone Mother Goddess From Belan. *Puratattva* 11: 116.

Kenoyer, J.M. 1987. Ritual Artefacts of Prehistoric Hunter–Gatherers in South Asia, Paper presented at the 16th Annual Conference of South Asia, Madison, Wisconsin.

Kenoyer, J.M., Clark, J.D., Pal, J.N., and Sharma, G.R. 1983. An Upper Palaeolithic Shrine in India? *Antiquity* 54: 88–94.

Kumar, Giriraj. 1996. Daraki–Chattan: A Palaeolithic Cupule Site in India. *Rock Art Research* 13 (1): 38–46.

Kumar, Giriraj, Narvare, Geeta, and Pancholi, Ramesh. 1988. Engraved Ostrich Egg-Shell Objects: New Evidence of Upper Palaeolithic Art in India. *Rock Art Research* 5 (1): 43–53.

Mathpal, Yashodhar. 1984. *Prehistoric Rock Paintings of Bhimbetka, Central India.* New Delhi: Abhinav Publications.

—1992. Rock Art Studies in India, in *Rock Art in the Old World*, M. Lorblanchet, ed. New Delhi, pp. 207–14.

—1995. *Rock Art in Kumaon Himalaya.* New Delhi: Aryan Book International.

Misra, V.D. 1977. *Some Aspects of Indian Archaeology,* Allahabad: Prabhat Prakashan.

Misra, V.N. 1985. Mesolithic Industries in India, in *Recent Advances in Indo-Pacific Prehistory*, V.N. Misra and Peter Bellwood, eds. New Delhi: Oxford & IBH Publishing Co., pp. 111–22.

Murty, M.L.K. 1974. A Late Pleistocene Cave Site in Southern India. *Proceedings of the American Philosophical Society* 118 (2): 196–230.

Murty, M.L.K. and Reddy, K.T. 1975. The Significance of Lithic Finds in the Cave Areas of Kurnool, India. *Asian Perspectives* 18 (2): 214–26.

Neumayer, Erwin. 1983 *Prehistoric Indian Rock Paintings.* New Delhi: Oxford University Press.

—1990. A Note on Ostriches in India. *Man and Environment* 15 (1): 25–28.

—1991. Wheeled Vehicles and Mounted Animals in Prehistoric Indian Rock Art. *Man and Environment* 26 (2): 39–70.

—1992–93a. On the Identification of Bhakti Deities in Rock Pictures. *Puratattva* 23: 53–60.

—1992–93b. Music and Musical Instruments in Indian Rock Art. *Puratattva* 23: 69–83.

—1993. *Lines on Stone: The Prehistoric Rock Art of India.* New Delhi: Manohar Publications.

Orofino, G. 1990. A Note on Some Tibetan Petroglyphs of the Ladakh Area. *East and West* 40 (1–4): 173–200.

Paddayya, K. 1968. *Pre- and Protohistoric Investigations in Shorapur Doab.* Ph.D. Thesis. Pune: University of Pune.

—1984. India, in *Neue Forschuqen Zur Altsteinzeit*, H. Mueller–Karpe, ed. Munich: C.H.

Beck Verlag, pp. 345–403.

Pal, J.N. 1994. Mesolithic Settlements in the Ganga Plain. *Man and Environment* 19 (1–2): 91–101.

Pande, B.M. 1971. Neolithic Hunting Scene on a Stone Slab From Burzahom, Kashmir. *Asian Perspectives* 14: 134–38.

—1972. A Neolithic Tectiform from Burzahom, Dist. Srinagar, Kashmir. *Journal of Indian Anthropological Society* 7: 175–177.

Pandey, S.K. 1975. Indian Rock Paintings: A Study in Symbology. *Marg* 28(4): 35–46.

—1992. *Indian Rock Art*. New Delhi: Aryan Books International.

Pradhan, S. 1995. Rock Art of Orissa: A Study of Regional Style. *Purakala* 6 (1–2): 5–15.

Rajan, K. 1991. Archaeology of Dharmapuri District, Tamil Nadu. *Man and Environment* 16 (1): 37–47.

Sali, S.A. 1974. Upper Palaeolithic Research Since Independence. *Bulletin of the Deccan College Research Institute.* 34 (1–4): 147–60.

Smith, V.A. 1906. Pigmy Flints. *The Indian Antiquary* 6: 185–95.

Sonawane, V.H. 1992. Significance of the Chandravati Engraved Core in the Light of Prehistoric Art of India, in *Rock Art in the Old World,* M. Lorblanchet, ed. New Delhi, pp. 273–83.

—1992–93. Stupas: A Rare Depiction in Rock Paintings of Gujarat, India. *Puratattva* 23: 66–69.

—1995–96. Symbolism of the Engraved Design on the Mesolithic Core of Chandravati. *Pragdhara* 6: 33–39.

—1996a. Rock Paintings of Gujarat, in *Recent Prespectives on Prehistoric Art in India and Allied Subjects*, R.K. Sharma and K.K. Tripathi, eds. New Delhi, pp. 66–73.

—1996b. Engraved Core from Chandravati, Rajasthan: A Second Thought. Paper Presented at the Third RASI Congress held at Kotputli.

Sundara, A. 1974. Further Notices of Rock Paintings in Hire Benakal. *Journal of Indian History* 52(1): 21–32.

—1984. Some Selected Rock Paintings from North Karnataka, in *Rock Art of India*, K.K. Chakravarty, ed. New Delhi: Arnold Heinemann, pp. 137–48.

—1996. An Engraved Geometrical Design from Gudnapura: From Harappa to Sonda (16th–17th century), in *Recent Perspectives on Prehistoric Art in India and Allied Subjects*, R.K. Sharma and K.K. Tripathi, eds. New Delhi, pp. 41–45.

Tewari, Rakesh. 1990. *Rock Paintings of Mirzapur*, Lucknow.

Tiwari, Shankar. 1975. Jaora: The Shelter of the Largest Rock Painting in India. *Prachya Pratibha* 3 (2): 93–96.

Tyagi, G.S. 1992. Decorative Intricate Patterns in Indian Rock Art, in *Rock Art in the Old World*, M.Lorblanchet, ed. New Delhi, pp. 303–17.

Varma, R.K. 1964. Stone Age Culture of Mirzapur. Ph.D. Thesis, Allahabad: University of Allahabad.

Wakankar, V.S. 1975a. Prehistoric Cave Paintings. *Marg* 28 (4): 17–34.

—1975b. Bhimbetka: The Prehistoric Paradise. *Prachya-Pratibha* 3 (2): 7–29.

—1983. The Oldest Works of Art? *Science Today* 20: 43–48.

—1984. Rock Art of India, in *Archaeology and History: Essays in Memory of Shri A. Ghose*, B.M. Pande and B.D. Chattopadhyaya, eds., New Delhi, pp. 583–97.

—1992. Rock Painting in India, In *Rock Art in the Old World*, M. Lorblanchet, ed. New Delhi, pp. 319–36.

Wakankar, V.S. and Brooks, R.R.R. 1976. *Stone Age Paintings in India,* Mumbai: Tarapsrewala.

13 ❖ Contributions of Science to Indian Archaeology

D.P. AGRAWAL

INTRODUCTION

INDIA is a land of contrasts: today both nuclear technology and bullock cart are used, and I think it is quite sensible too. India is a country with a hoary past and traditions that go back to millennia. This has allowed a traditional system of knowledge to develop which is perhaps more important than what we have copied from the western science. In a way we use western science and technology to unravel our past with its rich knowledge systems.

Archaeological techniques only provide us with remains which are silent. To make them speak we have to use scientific techniques (Mueller 1979; Rahman 1984; Sen and Chaudhuri 1985; *World Archaeology,* volumes 19(2), 19(3), 20(3), 21(1), 24(2), 25(1), 28(1)). Archaeology thus acquires the character of a detective job. And today we have virtually non-destructive techniques available as they require only nanogram amounts of sample. In India now a variety of techniques are available which are as good as in the West but not all of them are being used for archaeology. For example, India has SEM, Ion Probe, Mass Spectrometers, radiocarbon dating (LSS, GP, AMS), TL, fission track, palaeomagnetism, U/Th, neutron activation, atomic absorption spectrometry, sensitive molecular biology techniques, etc. In fact, you name the technique, India has it.

In this paper, I propose to discuss what has been achieved in India through the application of scientific techniques; what is being done globally; and what needs to be done in India. At the outset I must confess that it is not humanly possible for one person to survey all the studies that have been carried out in India using a variety of scientific techniques. If I miss somebody's important work in the brief space allotted to me, I will blame it only to my oversight or ignorance.

The main institutions where techniques relevant to archaeology are available/or being used in India are the following:

—Archaeological Survey of India, Delhi.
—Birbal Sahni Institute of Palaeobotany, Lucknow.
—Bhabha Atomic Research Centre, Mumbai.
—Centre for Molecular Biology, Hyderabad.
—Deccan College, Pune.
—National Geographical Research Institute, Hyderabad.
—National Museum, Delhi.
—Physical Research Laboratory, Ahmedabad.
—Wadia Institute of Himalayan Geology, Dehradun.

MAIN APPLICATIONS

I review here applications of science and technology to Indian archaeology under the following categories:

Theory
Prospecting
Ceramics
Metals
Stone artifacts
Rock art
Paleoanthropology
Marine archaeology
Plants and animals
Chronologies
Palaeoenvironment

Theory

There are many schools of theoretical archaeology (Clarke 1968, 1972) today, though none of them seems to be popular in India. Lamberg-Karlovsky's book (1989), *Archaeological Thought in America* gives a very balanced account of the various contending schools of theoretical archaeology. This volume is the best source of references for various schools, besides Paddayya's book (1990).

I have included theory in this note as I think that it is high time we systematised the fundamentals of archaeology as a discipline. In Lamberg-Karlovsky's (1989: 14) words, "The scope of archaeology's ambition is enormous and there is no surprise that tensions should exist, healthy ones, in search of a seamless totality."

Except for Sankalia's book on New Archaeology (1977) and Paddayya's, *The New Archaeology and Aftermath* (1990), no other major works have been published in India. Dilip Chakrabarti's (1997) recent book, *Colonial Indology*, is a landmark in Indian theoretical writings. It boldly deals with the racial prejudices of western scholars in discussing India's past. He says, ". . . the most pressing need is certainly to go beyond the bagful of colonial theories . . . and try to build up an image of themselves in which every member of their nation state can participate, irrespective of their regional, caste, tribal, religious, sectarian and a whole host of other affiliations . . ."(Chakrabarti 1997). Paddayya seems to endorse Dilip Chakrabarti's view, "Almost all existing reviews devoted to the examination of processual and post-processual trends emanate from the Anglo-American world and are, therefore, rarely free from regional and personal biases. A stage has come when workers in other parts of the world need to undertake independent evaluations of these developments in the discipline and relate them to archaeological research in their respective regions" (Paddayya 1990: Author's Note).

Dilip Chakrabarti's earlier book, *Theoretical Issues in Indian Archaeology* (1988) has, in fact, not much to do with theoretical issues. It only deals with three levels of preoccupation of Indian archaeology: (1) there are some changing foci of thought in the background of the archaeological activities in different periods; (2) attention on such themes as the study of prehistory, food production, urbanisation, etc.; and (3) the more technical issues like agriculture, metallurgy and trade.

Some thinking has now also been directed to the study of the nature of the Harappan state. Kenoyer (1994: 71) says, "Recent discussions on the nature of early state societies have led some scholars to suggest that the early urban phenomenon of the Indus Civilisation should not be characterised as a state level society . . . Harappan socio-political organisation was quite different from Mesopotamian or Egyptian states, but that it should nevertheless be considered a state level society." Concluding this interesting article, Kenoyer says, "I would support the concept of a Harappan state that was characterised by different levels of integration, encompassing the largest geographical area, would have competing classes of elite. . . . The largest cities may have been relatively independent, possibly organised as city states, with direct political control only over local settlements and lands. . . . Instead of some social group with absolute control, the rulers of dominant members in the various cities would have included merchants, ritual specialists and individuals who controlled resources such as land, livestock, and raw materials" (ibid., 77).

Olivier Guillaume pleads for scientific rigour in his *Analysis of Reasonings in Archaeology* (1990) which is basically an examination of Tarn's and Narain's views about the Indo-Greeks. The theoretical framework of his study is logicist analysis, as defined by J.C. Gardin in his *Archaeological Constructs—An Aspect of Theoretical Archaeology*. Guillaume asks, ". . . is history to be an area in which it is possible and desirable to introduce a certain measure of scientific exactness"? Dilip Chakrabarti, however, is very critical of this work and says, "From the continental point of view A.K.Narain's visualisation of the historical position of the Indo-Greeks was no doubt right; it had nothing to do with what Guillaume characterises as 'Indian nationalism' freshly victorious in 1957" (Chakrabarti 1997: 19).

Through my studies (Agrawal 1990, 1992a, 1994, 1996) on the concept of time, I am also trying to work out a seamless holistic theory of archaeology, though no full-fledged theory has emerged so far. There are quite a few other articles written from a theoretical angle.

Prospecting

Locating the right sites is the beginning of an archaeological exploration (Brandt et al. 1992).

A variety of geophysical instruments have been used both for archaeological and palaeoenvironmental explorations. Geophysical probes were used for locating submerged sites, e.g. Kaveripatnam. Both resistivity and proton magnetometer surveys have been made. Under the leadership of S.R. Rao a Marine Archaeology wing has been located at Goa. They are using sophisticated under-water techniques to explore and record archaeological finds in Dwarka region (Rao 1987a, 1987b).

Remote sensing techniques are much in use now. Comparing the relative merits of remote sensing and aerial photography, Cox says, "Aerial photographs may not show the full extent of a site due to unfavourable environmental conditions at the time of photography, whereas the superior spectral range of the MSS imagery may be able to supplement aerial photographic data. When stored and presented in a neat digitally mapped format, these data seem extremely believable and 'correct', having apparently enormous advantages over the 'old fashioned' desk and stereoscope air photo interpretation or the prospect of months of possibly unproductive field survey" (Cox 1992: 248).

Landsat and high resolution satellite photography have been used for the Harappan site of Lothal (Gujarat) and palaeochannels of the lost Saraswati. As the palaeochannels of the river Yamuna reach the Ganga, they are associated with progressively younger archaeological sites. It is gratifying to note that now younger workers have also started using remote sensing techniques in Indian archaeology (Deo and Joglekar 1996; Balaji et al. 1996).

Much progress has recently taken place in such techniques. Hunt reports, "The benefit of GIS as the methodological basis for catchment analysis include overcoming the limitations of shape and form, ability and accuracy of recreating the physiographic categories utilised in analysis, and, more importantly, having the ability to conduct more thorough analyses of the relationships between an array of physiographic attributes" (Hunt 1992: 306).

Ceramics

To unravel the temperature of firing, the technique used in producing a slip, a decoration, a colour, is the task of ceramic technologist. *World Archaeology* (vol. 21 (1), 1989) brought out a special issue on ceramic technology in which a variety of technological studies have been discussed, but none from India. In this issue, Barbetti and Hein (pp. 51–70) discuss the use of paleomagnetic techniques for high resolution dating of some Thai kilns. Optical petrology, trace impurity patterns, SEM studies, etc. have been discussed in this volume. Of course there are other major works on ceramic technology (Matson 1966; Olin and Aland 1982) but none in India.

Ceramics have been loosely described in terms of dishes, jars and bowls. Only Dales (1986, 1991) has used scientific criteria to define morphological categories of Harappan pottery.

We had tried to calibrate degree of vitrification using SEM to determine firing temperatures. Archaeological Survey of India and the Baroda University have identified the NBPW gloss as euhedral crystals of magnetic oxide of iron on a background of glass-like structureless material.

About the Painted Grey Ware of India, Hegde (1975) says, "It appears therefore that the potters were experimenting. They first used red ochre as the painting medium to decorate the Painted Grey Ware. In the second stage, they ground it with clay to produce the black slip on the Black Slipped

Ware. In the third stage, they ground it with clay and sajjimatti to produce the lustrous slip-glaze on the Northern Black Polished Ware. All the three wares were baked in a reducing atmosphere. The NBP Ware was their highest achievement which, according to Wheeler, is as distinctive in the Indian subcontinent as is terra sigillata on European sites."

Nicholson and Paterson have carried out some basic studies on the effects of firing on ceramics. "It was partially with the aim of better understanding the relationship between firings and fabric colour that the writers undertook fieldwork at Deir el-Gharbi, near Ballas in Upper Egypt" (Nicholson and Patterson 1989: 71). They conclude, "The evidence from the two firings would suggest that the peak temperature aimed for the load as a whole is approximately 850 degrees centigrade, which means that the lowermost vessels are probably subjected to temperatures as high as 900 degress and in some cases 1,000 degrees" (Nicholson and Patterson 1989: 84).

Metal Technology

Much of civilisational process owes itself to the use of metals in place of earlier stone tools. Copper is known from the fifth millennium BC. In its native form, it is readily available and has been used for thousands of years. Oxide and carbonate ores (malachite, azurite, etc.) were easy to smelt but the main ore was in the form of sulphide ores (pyrites) which was quite difficult to smelt. Pure copper was soft and malleable and to make it hard it had to be beaten but such work makes it brittle. Eventually it was discovered that a small amount of other metals if added to copper make it harder without sacrificing its ductility. Arsenic and tin were used to improve its hardness and ductility.

Discussing alloying practices used in Southeast Asia, Bennett (1989: 347) says, "The arsenic was probably derived from the smelting of arsenical sulphides and, whether or not the use of such ores was deliberate, the presence of arsenic at levels of up to 5.3 per cent is significant. . . . In an area which has shown no evidence of the use of tin at this time, the production of arsenical bronzes would have been advantageous." Similarly, arsenic alloying in the Copper Hoard artefacts could be due to the presence of impurities in the ore itself.

Zinc smelting is now firmly dated to *c.* 300 BC in Rajasthan, though elsewhere in the world zinc appears only by the second or third century AD. Copper is known from the pre-Harappan levels of Mehergarh from the fourth millennium BC context. Copper is in abundance in the Harappan and

Copper Hoard cultures (Agrawal 1969, 1971, 1982). We find that in India:

1. Tin alloying range is 3% to 12%
2. Arsenic alloying range is 1% to 7%
3. Lead was occasionally added for better fusibility.
4. Metallographic studies show use of: cold and hot work; annealing; close and open casting; and cire perdue e.g. dancing girl from Kulli.
5. Trace impurity pattern studies by Agrawal (1971) show that the Khetri belt was used both by the authors of the Harappan and Chalcolithic cultures.
6. The Copper Hoards were derived from Bihar mines.
7. Alloying patterns indicate that: (a) Harappans used both tin and arsenic; (b) Chalcolithic cultures used only tin; and (c) Copper Hoards used only arsenic.

Iron was used much later by man as it was more difficult to smelt and the furnaces required much higher temperatures. As a result, iron appears late, towards the end of the second millennium BC (Photos 1989), and in India in early first millennium BC (Tripathi and Tripathi 1994).

Now considerable work has been done on early iron metallurgy, yet we do not know if meteoric iron was used in India or not. Earlier many workers identified meteoric iron just only on the basis of presence of nickel. Recent work, however, shows that it is not that simple. Photos says, "It emerges that the determination of the meteoritic origin of a nickel-rich iron does not depend on a single chemical analysis of nickel and cobalt but on a combination of chemical, electron microprobe, and metallographic examinations"(Photos 1989: 418).

Stone Artefacts

Flaking mechanics and cognition: Stone Age artefacts have always fascinated prehistorians. A lot of scholars have tried to master the techniques of flaking used by early humans. But now the emphasis is on the correlation between technological and neuro-biological evolution. I have worked on this aspect with very interesting results (Agrawal: in press). In recent years, very stimulating discussions are going on among the anthropologists and other scientists (Bronowsky 1977; Davidson and Noble 1993; Deacon 1992; Falk 1991; McGrew 1992; Ingold and Gibson 1993; Jared 1992; Pinker 1994; Reynolds 1993; Sagan and Druyan 1992; Toth and Schick 1993; Wynn 1993) about the relationship between cognition, tool technology, language and evolution. McGrew even suggested that quite a few tools attributed to early hominids may belong to chimps instead (McGrew 1992).

Recently, archaeologists are looking beyond the tools towards their maker and his cognitive processes. Hassan says, "One of the primary features of this notion is the emphasis on a cognitive substratum for the production of artifacts following base and transformational rules. The approach provides a basis for ordering artifacts in a manner that facilitates interpreting the sources for similarity or variability between assemblages. The concepts of a token design, a prototype, and design schemata as a model for describing assemblages in terms of a few and fundamental designs provide an alternative to traditional 'types'" (Hassan 1988: 292).

Many groups have experimented with replication of stone tool types, though very little systematic study has been carried out.

On the basis of studies in mechanics of flaking, Agrawal (in press) has suggested a correlation between:

Homo habilis—Oldowan technique
Homo erectus—Levallois technique
Homo sapiens—Crested ridge technique.

In our paper (Agrawal and Kusumgar, in press), we had said, "But we don't believe in the anthropocentric views of human uniqueness or greatness. The language instinct makes humans unique in the same sense as the elephant's trunk makes the animal unique. May be whales with their large brains and complicated song systems are capable of conducting philosophical discussions. May be one day we will like to explore what they are talking about. Humans are unique in the sense of not only being gifted with the unique language instinct but perhaps also with some capability for innovating techniques which again may not be unrelated with the language instinct.

"We concede that language and speech capability confer many evolutionary advantages on the hominids, including planning, reflection, theoretically instructing the juniors about the dangers of the wild. Language is crucial for proper social interaction and to manipulate other group members, as well as time.

"But here we have tried to plead that the new artefact innovating process was the strongest stimulus, and also a feedback process, to brain evolution, especially of its language centres and instincts. Evolution of brain is manifested by several parameters: growth in size and weight; encephali-sation quotient; complexity of the cortical brain and sulci in speech areas (Broca's and Wernicke's). We suggest that a study of techniques of tools and their contexts can give us an index of both his capability to empirically comprehend flaking mechanics and the manual dexterity needed to fabricate the required artefacts. Such a study may also help us to delineate evolution in terms of a quantified, calibrated technique evolution index. Humans may be no better than whales and dolphins in brain power, and may be, even in the power for deep philosophical reflection! But humans stand apart from other animals by virtue of the complex material world that they have created. So the material world, tools and other artefacts that they have created were a powerful stimulus, also a feedback, to the evolution of human brain, mainly to its language and co-ordination areas."

Microwear: The other well studied aspect is deducing the use tools were put to by studying the traces of microwear. Very little work on microwear studies of artifacts has been done in India, though pioneered by P.C.Pant, S.P.Gupta and Prakash Sinha quite some time back.

There is considerable divergence between the approaches to microwear studies of the western schools and the Russian workers. Phillips specifically went to Russia to learn about the two systems of studies on traceology. She says, "The visit offered an opportunity to compare current West European and American approaches to microwear research with those of the Russian specialists" (Phillips 1988: 349). She further says, "In the first place, the longevity and long-term staffing of the laboratory (in Russia) by the same researchers has enabled a fine background of knowledge and information to be built up"(Ibid., 354).

Further, Phillips remarks, "A second point to note is the central role of experimentation and replication of artifacts and structures in the laboratory's methodology. All western researchers conduct experiments, but these are necessarily on a smaller and shorter-term scale."

The last point Phillips makes is, "A third point is the attempt by the Leningrad researchers to study the totality of artifacts and structures recovered from a particular site; as has been described above, the tools can be classified into groups, with sample artifacts being subjected to microscopic identification for confirmation of their function" (Phillips 1988).

It is obvious that there is vast scope to conduct microwear research in India using the Russian integrated approach.

Rock Art

Indian rock art studies are generally confined to stylistic comparisons. Only recently we have collected some samples for AMS dating of rock paintings. We need to use physical and chemical techniques to study pigments, binders; oxalate, silica and carbonate laminae; and microbiological techniques to analyse blood and other organic remains (Agrawal and

Kharakwal 1994). All these techniques are available in the country but have hardly been used for this purpose.

Parameters for Chronostratigraphy: For this purpose we need to use independent parameters such as:

1. Changes in the use of inorganic pigments;
2. Changes in the use of organic pigments;
3. Variations in the use of binders;
4. Changes in colour schemes;
5. Changes in style;
6. Changes in the thematic contents;
7. Changes in the flora and fauna depicted;
8. Chemical weathering: patina, oxalate layers, sinter lamina, desert varnish, silica skins and such coatings.

What I am emphasising is that we have to establish independent stratigraphies based on each of these individual parameters. The criterion of validity for an acceptable chronostratigraphy should be a concordance among the majority of such parameters which are independent variables. Such a convergent stratigraphy will finally have to be validated by physical and chemical methods of dating. We are assuming that most of the parameters will be changing in different phases though it is not always necessary. For example, some of the pigments—both inorganic and organic—may be common between two or more phases. But such a non-variability of some parameters should not invalidate convergent chronostratigraphy.

All this will require considerable sophisticated chemical analysis. For example, the ochre used between different phases may belong to different mines and therefore will show changes in minor and trace element composition. For example, in the black pigments used at Lakhudyar rock shelter (Almora) we found 5.73 ppm iron and 12.1 ppm cobalt. In the same rock shelter the red pigment gave 320 ppm iron and 13.4 ppm cobalt. Similarly, the blood may belong to different human blood groups or different animal species. If they used beeswax, resin, honey and glue of different origins, it could be reflected in trace element composition, or one could try to identify specific organic compounds up to nanogram levels. Even the plant fibres used may belong to different species. For such analyses besides the botanical techniques to identify plant material, one could use gas chromatography, electrophoresis, C-H-N analysers and so on.

In this connection, the recent articles that have appeared in the special biomolecular archaeology issue of *World Archaeology* (vol. 25, 1993) will prove very relevant. Cattaeneo et al. (*World Archaeology* vol. 25, 1993: 29–43) have identified blood residues on stone artifacts and have also carried out some artificial experiments. They used specific and sensitive enzyme-linked immuno solvent assays (ELISA) in monoclonal skeleton and cattle bone, and have produced positive identifications as far back as the early Bronze Age. Urinalysis test strips were also used to suggest blood might be present in some samples. Their studies have shown that blood components can survive. The proteins used in archaeological work are mainly haemoglobin, immunoglobin G (IgG) and albumin. They suggest that haemoglobin being an abundant molecule could be a better target antigen than albumin and immunoglobin for the application of our ELISA monoclonal antibodies. This line of analysis could prove very useful for identifying blood in ancient rock paintings. Loy (1993: 44–63) has studied stone artifacts for identifying blood and hair on some stone artifacts. In this one can use both colorimetric and immunological methods. The Ames Hemastix is a colorimetric peroxidase based test developed for clinical urinalysis, used in blood residue analysis, which indicates the presence of haemoglobin and myoglobin. In this particular work they have used the following four methods:

(i) Radioimmunoassay;
(ii) Isoelectric focusing (an electrophoretic method);
(iii) Haemoglobin crystallisation of proteins; and
(iv) DNA analysis.

Comparison of the pI (Isoelectric points) values of separated proteins using isoelectric focusing led to the identification of the blood of bison on the stone tools. By using DNA analysis they could identify these species even from 30,000 year old tissue extracts from extinct species of *Bison priscus*. Some of these tests have lower detection limits in the range of less than 100 nanogram to as little as 1 picogram, whereas AMS radiocarbon dating requires about 50 microgram of carbon or about 100 microgram of blood. Evershed (1993: 74–93) has used lipids for the identification of ancient organic residues. He has used gas chromatograph mass spectrometric techniques for elucidation of the generic origins of ancient resins, tars, pitches and bitumen and beeswax used in ancient times. Use of beeswax and resin is suspected in the Kumaon rock art also. We thus see that a whole lot of the latest sophisticated biomolecular techniques have become available for a possible use in the study of organic residues in Indian rock paintings. Such techniques are also available at the Centre For

Cellular and Molecular Biology, Hyderabad, Institute Of Immunology, Delhi and Molecular Biology Division at TIFR, Mumbai.

Absolute and Relative Dating: The biggest revolution in rock art dating has been brought about by AMS C^{14} dating technique. We need not go into the details of the technique here as considerable literature exists on the subject. With this technique one can date miniscule amounts of carbon found in the form of organic pigments, adhesives or binders. The Co^2 in the composition of the oxalate laminations can also be dated. The main consideration has to be that the carbon sampled for dating has to be coeval with the paintings. Unfortunately, it is not always easy to determine. In some caves, e.g., Malanginek in South Australia, they have been able to date petroglyphs, as they were covered by sinter laminae ($CaCo^3$) which can be dated by C^{14} and U/Th techniques. Bednarik reports two organic pigments from the central Indian rock shelters which can be C^{14} dated, though none of the Indian rock art examples have so far been dated. But elsewhere, the rock art dates are now going back to 43,000 BP. These are probably the oldest rock art dates in the world so far. Valladas et al. (1992: 68–70) report the first AMS dates from Altamira, El Castillo and Niaux paintings. They find that stylistically similar bisons date to 13 and 14 Kyr, whereas stylistically different bisons also give a 13 Kyr date, and therefore style alone is not an adequate criterion. As minute samples of rock art are difficult to extract, a laser technique has been developed which can convert minute amounts of carbon into Co^2 by using kryptonion laser. Charcoal, beeswax, organic fibres and dye can be used for AMS dating. Watchman has suggested that even the paint was sprayed through the mouth and thus saliva could be used for AMS dating as it also contains proteins. Watchman puts a lot of emphasis on the dating of calcium oxalate (whewellite) which is formed by a reaction of organic acids in rain water with dust and through biological activity e.g., fungi produce calcium oxalate.

Similarly, transparent silica skins, less than 1 mm thick, are formed by silica deposition from the seeping water on sandstone and quartzite. Some trace amounts of organic particles or algal matter get encapsulated in the microlaminations which can be AMS dated. Thus AMS dating has opened up vast new potentialities for dating rock paintings. In India no AMS dating facilities are so far available, but we are expecting to get some beam time for AMS dating next year when the Accelerator Mass Spectrometer (AMS) becomes critical at the Institute of Physics at Bhuvaneshwar. Bednarik writes, "Using primarily the micro-waves on individual crystal cleavage faces that had been exposed when the petroglyphs were fashioned, I noted the differential wear of the feldspars and the quartz components. I could establish a dual calibration curve". He found a good concordance between the relative dates of glaciated striae and relative degree of microerosion. There is, however, controversy about the use of cation-ratios on rock varnish. This is based on the differential dissolution of K and Ca as compared to Ti—with time the ratio increases. Of course, these curves have to be calibrated by AMS dating of cellulose plant material found in the rock varnishes.

The amino acid dating technique on the other hand has not proved so successful, mainly because of the difficulty of obtaining reliably contemporary amino acid samples from the binding material of the paintings. Besides, the method depends upon the accurate knowledge of the climatic conditions prevailing at the time the paintings were made.

We thus see that a variety of new techniques are beckoning us to place our rock art studies on a firmer substratum and evolve regional chronostratigraphies based on physical and chemical techniques. Of course, application of new techniques can initially lead to considerable confusion unless great care is taken in collecting and recording samples to be dated. It will be necessary to chalk out a national programme so that some rigorous guidelines can be prescribed and enforced.

Palaeopathology and Palaeoanthropology

Palaeoanthropology has made great strides all over the globe, and to some extent in India too. The only problem is that we hardly have any early hominid remains, except the Narmada skull. Most of the studies, therefore, are confined to Mesolithic and Harappan skeletal material. Most of the progress in this field can be attributed to one individual—K.A.R. Kennedy (1984, 1984a; Kennedy et al. 1986, 1992), though others have also contributed (see review by Walimbe and Tavares in this volume).

Lukacs (1994: 153), writing about the osteological paradox and the Indus Civilisation, says, "Gender differences in frialty and in LEH (linear enamel hypoplasis) prevalence in Harappa are interpreted in the context of a broad database for LEH among developing and western societies. LEH prevalence is associated with the prevalence of illness and under-nutrition in many groups. At Harappa, gender differences in LEH prevalence are suggestive of the practice of son preference/daughter neglect, a cultural norm common today among the people of north India."

Hemphill et al. (1991: 174) say, ". . . these data suggest that Harappan phase individuals . . . bear closest affinities to populations from the West . . .

Peoples to the West interacted with those in the Indus Valley during this and the preceding proto-Elamitic periods and thus may have influenced the development of the Harappan civilisation".

Kennedy who studied the Harappan skeletal remains found evidence of thalassemia in the Harappan populations. From his studies the famous Mohenjodaro massacre has turned out to be only accidental deaths (Kennedy 1984: 433).

Kennedy reported considerable heterogeneity in the Harappan populations as also reflected by diverse burial customs. Their multivariate and principal component analyses show two distinct discontinuities from Neolithic to the dawn of Christian era, thus refuting Renfrew's Neolithic hypothesis. Food habits have also been inferred from teeth remains by Kennedy and Lukacs.

The Narmada skull discovered by Sonakia has been identified as archaic *Homo sapiens*. It is strange that in a country where millions of stone tools have been reported, no hominids have been found. It perhaps reflects some snag in our prehistoric research strategies. Mohan Singh of Chandigarh has reported some early hominid teeth from the Siwaliks but there is not much unanimity about their identification.

Kennedy (1986, 1992) has also reported on the skeletal remains of Sarai Nahar Rai and Mahadaha, and discussed the affinities of the Indian Mesolithic skeletal remains (1984: 29–58). They report a "Parallel morphological development of facial size and cranial robusticity, and large tooth size which is characteristic of prehistoric populations of hunters and gatherers . . ." (Kennedy et al. 1986: 43). They find similar adaptations in the Mahadaha skeletal remains (Kennedy et al. 1992: 307). The human skeletal remains of Bagor and Tilwara in Rajasthan were described by Lukacs et al. (1982) in an earlier publication.

In recent years a variety of molecular biology techniques are being used in archaeology, "It is clear from the above overview that substantial scope exists for the use of lipids in archaeological investigations . . . Notable successes include elucidation of the generic origins of ancient resins, tars, pitches, and bitumen based on analyses of their biomarker components" (Evershed 1993: 90).

Kenneth D. Thomas (1993: 7) summarises the famous work of geneticists, Cavalli-Sforza et al. "They suggest that successful innovations, whether biological or cultural, lead to local population growth and to outward movement of populations carrying those innovations with them. It is claimed that these patterns of outward migration can be traced by gradients of genetic frequencies, and Cavalli-Sforza et al. have produced a series of genetic maps (based on principal component values calculated from all available gene frequencies) for the major continents, showing their 'genetic geography'. The resulting gene maps show one or (in some cases) more regions in which gradients map out as patterns of concentric rings focused on areas which could be the centres from which population dispersal happened in the past."

Loy (1993: 56) refers to the sophistication of the techniques which have become almost non-destructive: "The various biomolecular tests employed have lower detection limits in the range of less than 100 nanogram to as little as 1 picogram. The AMS radiocarbon dating sample requires at least 50 microgram of carbon contained in roughly 100 micrograms of blood residue and consumed the bulk of the removed residue. . . . The species of animal being butchered was bison."

Marine Archaeology

S.R. Rao (1987a, b) for the first time has used underwater techniques for archaeological excavations near Dwaraka and now other universities are following suit. He has claimed the discovery of the legendary site of Dwaraka and has dated it to *c.*1400 BC. He has used Miniranger, which is an electronically positioned fixing system. But old sextants are still in use whenever electronic systems go out of order. They have also made use of echosounder and side scan sonar for underwater surveys. They have also employed oceanographic magnetometer to measure magnetic intensity of earth's magnetic field. The techniques used do not yet have the sophistication of the western ships for marine archaeology but a beginning has been made. It would be much more important to explore Harappan shipwrecks so that we may have a chance to decipher the Indus script. Recently a Harappan shipwreck has been reported from the Gulf of Oman. The problem of the mythical Dwaraka can never be solved for pre-literate periods, as it is for Mahabharata and Ramayana related sites.

Study of Plants and Animals

Plants: Thanks to the efforts of K.A. Chowdhury, Vishnu-Mittre, K.S. Saraswat, M.D. Kajale and other workers, we have a fair knowledge of the plants domesticated during the protohistoric phase (for a review study, see Kajale 1991). The following types of plant were used by different cultures: Harappan culture: Use of silk, flax, cotton, wheat and barley in Gujarat; also rice. At Rojdi three different millets were used in the three phases.

Neolithic Culture: Various millets reported. No systematic study of plant domestication has been undertaken so far.

Cerealia type pollen has been reported from 7000–8000 BP levels from the Rajasthan lakes, but no cereal grains as such have been reported by Singh et al. This raises the possibility of the beginning of agriculture in India in early Holocene.

Animals: Quite extensive studies have been carried out in India on animal remains from archaeological sites (for a review study, see Thomas and Joglekar 1995). We will only briefly mention some important aspects in this article.

World Archaeology (1996) brought out a special issue on Zooarchaeology. In this issue K.D.Thomas's editorial article, "Zooarchaeology: past, present and future", is very perceptive and relevant to India too. In his editorial note, Thomas (1996: 3) says, "Some of the papers in this issue illustrate the fruitful results of an unblinkered approach involving combinations of older and newer paradigms. O'Connor's general review urging a broadening of approach by zooarchaeologists; Halsted's consideration of pastoralism or herding in small-scale societies; Reid's analysis of power structures and the redistribution of cattle resources; and Crabtree's analysis of production and consumption systems in an early complex society, all demonstrate the potential value of combining traditional systems and interpretations of animal assemblages with appropriate ethnographic, social or political models. The cognitive and societal interpretation of animal remains is taken further in the papers by Bond and Holt, where the ritual and symbolic significance of animals is addressed in two very different case studies."

Clason (1975) edited a pioneering work in archaeozoology in which, besides western scientists, many Indian scientists like Murthy, Thomas, Alur and Paddayya also contributed their papers.

So far there is no unanimity about horse remains from the Harappan levels. Horse-like remains from Banawali and Lothal have been reported but with wild onager still thriving in that region, it is difficult to distinguish it from true horse. Only Meadow, Alur and Thomas have tried to work out systematic criteria of domestication of animals. It appears goat and sheep were domesticated first. Meadow claims that at Mehrgarh, sheep, goat and cattle were herded from 6000 BC. Thomas and his colleagues at the Deccan College, Pune, Chattopadhyaya of Allahabad University, and Richard Meadow (1991) of Harvard University have contributed very significantly to archaeozoological studies in India and Pakistan.

From Neolithic Burzahom (*c.* 2500 BC) have been reported the first regular dog burials. The evidence shows that the meat eaten during the Neolithic and Bronze Age India consisted of beef, pork, venison and mutton.

I found Chattopadhyaya's (1996) recent article, "Subsistence and mortuary practices in the Mesolithic Ganges Valley" most stimulating. He has asked some unconventional questions, "so the above analysis shows that the results from Mahadaha and Damdama do not truly match any of the three ideal site categories, i.e., hunting camp, kill-butchery site and base camp" (ibid., 472).

He gives a more convincing explanation of geometric and non-geometric microlithic sites: "Most of the sites are close to oxbow lakes and the streams issuing from them . . . They fall into two categories: non-geometric microliths (172 sites) and geometric microliths (22 sites). The sites with geometric microliths are generally larger. These two site categories should not necessarily be viewed as chronologically distinct as has been hypothesised. Rather, they might indicate sites of varying size and function used by the same groups." (ibid., 464). He further argues, ". . . Mahadaha provides fairly good evidence for the existence of corporate group rights over productive, reliable but restricted resources legitimised by lineal descent from the dead"(ibid., 473).

Chattopadhayaya thus shows the way zooarchaeological material should be interpreted. Most of the time the articles on animal remains present only technical morphological descriptions. In contrast, Chattopdhayaya's note shows what a bright creative scientist can infer from the bones.

Rissmann (1986: 257–77) has inferred from tooth cement rings that Oriyo (Gujarat) was a dry season cattle camp.

Chronology

In India a variety of dating techniques have been used: C^{14} (GP/LSS/AMS), TL, fission track, palaeomagnetism, U/Th, etc. have been used both for archaeological and Quaternary sites (Agrawal and Yadava 1995; Agrawal et al. 1981). A few thousand C^{14} dates are now available.

Vertebrate chronology: Palaeomagnetic and fission track dating has firmly placed the appearance of Villafranchian fauna (*Equus sivalensis, Cervus kashmiriensis, Elephas hysudricus*, etc.) to 2.4 myr (for summary, see Agrawal 1992b).

Palao environment

Agrawal (1992) provides a brief account and useful references about this aspect.

Pollen: Numerous pollen profiles are available from the lakes of Rajasthan, Kumaon, Kashmir, Ladakh, Sikkim, Nilgiris, etc. Quantitative palaeoclimatic estimates are available for Rajasthan.

Diatoms: Data are available from Kashmir, Orissa and the marine sites.

Charophytes: This work has been done mainly in Kashmir and Punjab.

Palaeopedologic and mineral magnetic studies have been carried out on loess and sand dune profiles of Kashmir and Rajasthan.

We may summarise the important results: (1) Geomagnetic reversals and climatic changes coincide in Kashmir; (2) Deglaciation in the Kashmir valley starts *c.* 20,000 BP when it was still Last Glacial Maximum (LGM) in the north.

Microvertebrates appear only during the glacial periods.

Stable Isotopes: Carbon and oxygen isotopes have been used for palaeoclimatic reconstruction in Kashmir lake deposits and loess profiles (for references, see Agrawal 1992).

Thus we see that scientific techniques have contributed a great deal to Indian archaeology, though a lot more needs to be done to exploit the full potential of the latest techniques. Amongst the developing countries, India has a unique advantage of possessing most of the latest technologies. Now it is up to the archaeologists to use them fully for their cause.

REFERENCES

Agrawal D.P. 1969. The Copper Hoards Problem: A Technological Angle. *Asian Perspectives* 12: 113–19.

—1971. *The Copper Bronze Age in India*. New Delhi: Munshiram Manoharlal Publishers.

—1982. The Indian Bronze Age Cultures and their Metal Technology, in F. Wendorf and A.E. Close, eds. *Advances in World Archaeology*, vol. 1. New York: Academic Press, pp. 213–64.

—1992a. The Other Dimensions of Archaeology, in G.L. Possehl, ed. *South Asian Archaeology Studies*, pp. 101–10. New Delhi: Oxford & IBH Publishing Co.

—1992b. *Man and Environment in India Through Ages*, Books & Books, New Delhi.

—1994. Archaeology and the Concept of Time, in Asko Parpola and Pettari Koskikallio ed. *South Asian Archaeology 1993*. Helsinki: Soumalainen Tiedeakatemia, pp. 35–42.

—1996. Geological and Archaeological Time: Some Concepts and Their Implications, in Kapila Vatsyayan ed. *Concepts of Time: Ancient and Modern*. New Delhi: Indira Gandhi National Centre for the Arts and Sterling Publishers, pp. 127–31.

Agrawal D.P., and Kusumgar, S. In press. Tool Making and Language in Human Evolution. *Europea*.

Agrawal D.P., Bhandari, N., Lal, B.B., and Singhvi, A.K. 1981. Thermoluminescence Dating of Pottery from Sringaverapura: A Ramayana Site. *Proceedings of the Indian Acad-*

emy of Sciences 90(2): 161–72.

Agrawal, D.P., and Kharakwal, J.S. 1994. Use of Scientific Techniques in Indian Rock Art Studies. *Purakala* 5 (1–2): 67–69.

Agrawal, D.P., and Yadava, M.G. 1995. *Dating the Human Past*. Pune: ISPQS.

Balaji, K., Suresh, L.S., Raghuswamy, V., and Gautam, N.C. 1996. The Use of Remote Sensing in Monitoring Changes in and Around Archaeological Monuments—A Case Study from Hyderabad, A.P. *Man and Environment* 21(2): 63–70.

Barbetti, Mike and Hein, Don. 1989. Palaeomagnetism and High-Resolution Dating of Ceramic Kilns in Thailand: A Progress Report. *World Archaeology* 21(1): 51–70.

Bennett, Anna. 1989. The Contribution of Metallurgical Studies to South-East Asian Archaeology.*World Archaeology* 20(31): 329–51.

Brandt, Roel, Groenewoudt, Bert J., and Kvamme, Kenneth L. 1992. An Experiment in Archaeological Site Location: Modelling in the Netherlands Using GIS Techniques. *World Archaeology* 24(2): 268–82.

Bronowski, J. 1977. *A Sense of the Future*. Cambridge (Mass.): MIT.

Chakrabarti, D.K. 1988. *Theoretical Issues in Indian Archaeology*. New Delhi: Munshiram Manoharlal Publishers.

—1997. *Colonial Indology*. New Delhi: Munshiram Manoharlal Publishers.

Chattopadhyaya, Umesh C. 1996. Settlement Pattern and the Spatial Organisation of Subsistence and Mortuary Practices in the Mesolithic Ganges Valley, North-Central India. *World Archaeology* 27(3): 461–76.

Clarke, David L. 1968. *Analytical Archaeology*. London: Methuen.

—1972. *Models in Archaeology*. London: Methuen.

Clason, A.T., 1974. *Archaeozoological Studies*. Amsterdam: North-Holland Publishing Company.

Cox, Chris. 1992. Satellite Imagery, Aerial Photography and Wetland Archaeology. *World Archaeology* 24(2): 249–67.

Dales, George F. 1986. *Excavations at Mohenjodaro, Pakistan: the Pottery*. Philadelphia: University Museum.

Davidson I., and Noble, W. 1993. Tools and Language in Human Evolution, in K. Gibson and T. Ingold eds. *Tools, Language and Cognition in Human Evolution*. Cambridge: Cambridge University Press, pp. 363–88.

Deacon, T.W. 1992. Primate Brains and Senses: Human Brain, in S.Jones, R. Martin and D. Pilbeam eds. *Human Evolution*. Cambridge: Cambridge University Press, pp. 109–36.

Deo, S.G., and Joglekar, P.P. 1996. Satellite Remote Sensing in Archaeology. *Man and Environment* 21(2): 59–70.

Diamond, Jared. 1992. *The Rise And Fall of the Third Chimpanzee*. London: Vintage.

Evershed, Richard P. 1993. Biomolecular Archaeology and Lipids. *World Archaeology* 25(1): 74–93.

Falk, Dean. 1991. Implications of the Evolution of Writing for the Origin of Language, in J. Wind, P. Lieberman and B. Chiarelli eds. *Language Origins: A Multi-Disciplinary Approach*, pp. 245–51. Dordrecht: Kluwer Academic Publishers.

Gibson, Kathleen R., and Ingold, Tim ed. 1993. Tools, Language and Cognition, in *Human Evolution*, Cambridge: Cambridge University Press.

Guillaume, Olivier. 1990. *Analysis of Reasonings in Archaeology*. New Delhi: Oxford University Press.

Hassan, Fekri A. 1988. Prolegomena to a Grammatical Theory of Lithic Artifacts. *World*

Archaeology 19(3): 281–96.

Hegde K.T.M. 1975. The Painted Grey Ware of India. *Antiquity* 49: 187–90.

Hemphill, Brian E., Lukacs, John R. and Kennedy, K.A.R. 1991. Biological Adaptations and Affinities of Bronze Age Harappans, in R.H. Meadow, ed. *Harappa Excavations: 1986–90*. Madison: Prehistory Press, pp. 137–82.

Hunt, Eleazer D. 1992. Up-Grading Site-Catchment Analyses with the Use of GIS: Investigating the Settlement Patterns of Horticulturalists. *World Archaeology* 24(2): 283–309.

Kajale, M.D. 1991. Current Status of Indian Palaeoethnobotany: Introduced and Indigenous Food-Plants with a Discussion of the Historical and Evolutionary Developments of Indian Agriculture and Agricultural Systems in General, in Jane M. Renfrew ed. *New Light on Early Farming: Recent Developments in Palaeoethnobotany*. Edinburgh: Edinburgh University Press, pp. 155–89.

Kennedy, K.A.R. 1984. Trauma and Disease in the Ancient Harappans, in B.B. Lal and S.P., Gupta, eds. *Frontiers of Indus Civilisation*. New Delhi: Books & Books, pp. 425–36.

—1984a. Biological Adaptations and Affinities of Mesolithic South Asians, in Lukacs, J.R., ed. *The People of South Asia*. London: Plenum Press, pp. 29–57.

Kennedy, K.A.R., Lowell, N.C., and Burrow, C.B. 1986. *Mesolithic Human Remains from Gangetic Plain: Sarai Nahar Rai*. Ithaca: Cornell University.

Kennedy, K.A.R., Lukacs, J.R., Pastor, R.F., Johnston, T.L., Lowell, N.C., Pal, J.N., Hemphill, B.E., and Burrow, C.B. 1992. *Human Skeletal Remains from Mahadaha: A Gangetic Mesolithic Site*. Ithaca: Cornell University.

Kenoyer, Jonathan Mark. 1994. The Harappan State, Was It or Wasn't It? in J.M. Kenoyer ed. *From Sumer to Meluhha*. Madison: University of Wisconsin, pp. 71–80.

Lamberg-Karlovsky, C.C. 1989. *Archaeological Thought in America*. Cambridge: Cambridge University Press.

Loy, Thomas H. 1993. The Artifact as Site: An Example of the Biomolecular Analysis of Organic Residues on Prehistoric Tools. *World Archaeology* 25: 44–63.

Lukacs, John R. ed. 1984. *The People of South Asia*, London: Plenum Press.

—1994. The Osteological Paradox and the Indus Civilization: Problems Inferring Health from Human Skeletons at Harappa, in J.M. Kenoyer ed. *Sumer to Meluhha*. Madison: University of Wisconsin, pp. 143–56.

Lukacs, J.R., Misra, V.N., and Kennedy, K.A.R. 1982. *Bagor and Tilwara: Late Mesolithic Cultures of Northewest India*, vol. 1: *Human Skeltal Remains*. Pune: Deccan College.

Matson, F.R. 1966. *Ceramics and Man*. London, Methuen.

McGrew, William C. 1992. *Chimpanzee Material Culture: Implications for Human Evolution*, Cambridge: Cambridge University Press.

Meadow, Richard H. 1991a. Faunal Remains and Urbanism at Harappa, in R.H. Meadow ed. *Harappa Excavations: 1986–90*. Madison: Prehistory Press, pp. 89–106.

Mueller, James W. 1979. *Sampling in Archaeology*. Tucson: University of Arizona.

Nicholson, Paul T. and Patterson, Helen. 1989. Ceramic Technology in Upper Egypt: A Study of Pottery Firing. *World Archaeology* 21(1): 71–86.

Olin, Jacqueline S. and Franklin, Alan D., eds. 1982. *Archaeological Ceramics*. Washington: Smithsonian Institution Press.

Paddayya, K. 1990. *The New Archaeology And Aftermath*. Pune: Ravish Publishers.

Phillips, Patricia. 1988. Traceology (Microwear) Studies in the USSR. *World Archaeology* 19(3): 349–56.

Photos, E. 1989. The Question of Meteoritic Versus Smelted Nickel-rich Iron: Archaeological Evidence and Experimental Results. *World Archaeology* 20(3):

Pinker, Steven. 1994. *The Language Instinct*. New York: William Morrow.

Rahman, A. ed. 1984. *Science And Technology in Indian Culture*: A *Historical Perspective*. New Delhi: National Institute of Science, Technology & Development Studies.

Rao, S.R. 1987a. Marine Archaeological Explorations off Dwaraka, Northwest Coast of India, *Journal of Marine Sciences* 16: 22–30.

—1987b. Progress and Prospect of Marine Archaeology in India, Goa: *First Indian Conference on Marine Archaeology of Indian Ocean Countries*, Dona Paula, Goa: National Institute of Oceanography.

Reynolds, Peter C. 1993. The Complimentation Theory of Language and Tool Use, in K. Gibson and T. Ingold, eds. *Tools, Language and Cognition in Human Evolution*. Cambridge: Cambridge University Press, pp. 407–28.

Rissman, Paul C. 1986. Seasonal Aspects of Man/Cattle Interaction in Bronze Age India. *Journal of Ethnobiology* 6(4): 257–77.

Sagan, Carl and Druyan Ann. 1992. *Shadows of Forgotten Ancestors*. London: Arrow.

Sankalia, H.D. 1977. *New Archaeology: Its Scope and Application to India*. Lucknow: Ethnographic and Folk Culture Society.

Sen, S.N. and Mamata Chaudhuri. 1985. *Ancient Glass and India*. New Delhi: Indian National Science Academy.

Thomas, Kenneth D. 1993. Molecular Biology and Archaeology: A Prospectus for Interdisciplinary Research. *World Archaeology* 25(1): 1–17.

—1996. Zooarchaeology: Past, Present and Future. *World Archaeology* 28(1): 1–4.

Thomas, P.K. and Joglekar, P.P. 1995. Faunal Studies in Archaeology, in S. Wadia, R. Korisettar and V.S. Kale, ed. *Quaternary Environments and Geoarchaeology of India*, Bangalore: Geological Society of India, pp. 496–514.

Toth, Nicholas and Schick Kathy. 1993. Early Stone Age Industries and Inferences and Language and Cognition, in K. Gibson and T. Ingold, ed. *Tools, Language and Cognition in Human Evolution*, Cambridge: Cambridge University Press, pp. 346–62.

Tripathi, Vibha and Tripathi, Amit. 1994. Iron Working in Ancient India: an Ethnoarchaeological Study, in J.M. Kenoyer, ed. *From Sumer to Meluhha*. Madison: University of Wisconsin, pp. 241–52.

Valladas, H. et al.. 1992. Direct Dates for Prehistoric Paintings at Altamira, El Castello and Niaux. *Nature* 357: 68–70.

World Archaeology, 1987. Special issue, Rock Art, vol. 19, no. 2.

World Archaeology, 1988. Special issue:, New Directions in Palaeolithic Archaeology, vol. 19, no. 3.

World Archaeology, 1989. Special issue, Archaeometallurgy, vol. 20, no. 3.

World Archaeology, 1989. Special issue, Ceramic Technology, vol. 21, no. 1.

World Archaeology, 1992. Special issue, Analytical Field Survey, vol. 24, no. 2.

World Archaeology, 1993. Special issue, Biomolecular Archaeology, vol. 25, no. 1.

World Archaeology, 1996. Special issue, Zooarchaeology. vol. 28 (1).

Wynn, Thomas. 1993. Layers of Thinking in Tool Behaviour, in K. Gibson and T. Ingold ed. *Tools, Language and Cognition in Human Evolution*. Cambridge: Cambridge University Press, pp. 389–406.

14 ❖ The Monsoon Background and the Evolution of Prehistoric Cultures of India

R. KORISETTAR and S.N. RAJAGURU

INTRODUCTION

THE global palaeoclimatic record, derived from oxygen isotopic analysis of the deep sea sediment cores, betrays alternation of warmer and cooler stages during the Quaternary (the last 2.5 million years of earth's history). These changes appear more pronounced and intense since the Middle Pleistocene (after 0.7 Myr). 22 Oxygen Isotope Stages represent 9–10 full glacial-interglacial cycles during the last 1 million years (Bowen 1978; Shackleton 1975; Kukla 1977). Late Quaternary (the last 125 Kyr) stratigraphy and radiocarbon dating of lake levels in Africa have corrected the misconception that glacials in the middle and northern latitudes were accompanied by a wet climate in the tropics. In fact the high lake levels corresponded with the Early Holocene interglacial and proved that climate of the tropics was both drier and cooler during the Last Glacial Maximum (21–18 Kyr). Considerable evidence has accumulated pointing to the fact that vegetation changes in the tropics took place in response to glacial and interglacial cycles. The expansion of tropical savannas and the opening of tropical forests occurred during the Last Glacial Maximum, under decreased monsoon conditions. In addition to multidisciplinary scientific investigations on the Quaternary palaeoclimate the geoarchaeological investigations (in western and central India) have provided reasonably good and potential records of the palaeomonsoon and the associated evidence of human occupation.

The monsoon is one of the most attractive natural phenomena not only for climatologists and meteorologists but also archaeologists the world over. It shows not only remarkable intra-seasonal changes but also year to year and secular variations. The extent of its impact on the ecodiversity and food production is of fundamental importance. Palaeoclimatic studies have shown that the Indian monsoon responded to the global changes and reveal an inverse correlation with glaciations—during cold glacial periods the monsoon was weak and it was strong during interglacial warm periods.

The Indian civilization is to a large extent shaped by the Indian Ocean Monsoon which is characterized by circulation of the prevailing moisture bound winds between summer and winter seasons, causing rainfall over the South Asian landmass. The Southwest monsoon sets in around the beginning of June and lasts till mid-September and is followed by the winter Northeast monsoon which covers the eastern half of the subcontinent. The monsoon circulation is a major source of freshwater in much of southern Asia. It plays a vital role in shaping the agricultural economy of the people living in the alluvial plains and deserts, and exerts absolute control on the availability of food resources to the hunting-gathering tribal populations occupying the hills and forests of the subcontinent.

The Southwest monsoon rainfall (75–80% of the annual total rainfall) is higher than that of the winter. Although the monsoon systems all over the world are interconnected, the Indian monsoon betrays individuality in being able to build its circulation between the Himalayas and the Indian Ocean. There are two branches of the Southwest monsoon: (a) the Bay of Bengal branch arriving earlier and (b) the Arabian Sea branch arriving later. A shift in the heat belt occurs in October (causing moderately hot conditions over the Deccan), this shift takes place from Rajasthan-Punjab to the equator effecting the dominance of Northeast winds. The Northeast monsoon is characterized by frequent cyclonic storms arising in the Bay of Bengal. These storms are low pressure systems in which the associated wind rotates in an anti-clockwise direction in the Northern Hemisphere. During the Southwest monsoon the cyclonic storms forming over the Bay of Bengal (to the north of eighteen degrees latitude) move in a northwesterly direction causing heavy rainfall along its transect. Cyclonic depressions in the Bay during active Southwest monsoon season result in strengthening of the Arabian Sea monsoon current and cause heavy rainfall over the Western Ghats, largely due to orographic ascent of moisture-laden winds. During intramonsoonal breaks the low pressure monsoon trough shifts towards the Himalayas, causing rainfall over north India (Rakhecha and Pisharoty 1996; also see Naidu 1998).

Details of the monsoon meteorology are beyond the scope of this paper, but one is struck by the intensity of research on the dynamics of the Indian monsoon and its place in global climatology. The rise and fall of pressure between the West Pacific Ocean and East Pacific Ocean in the Southern Hemisphere is known as Southern Oscillation. This is linked with the variations in the east-west circulation in the tropics. There is close association between the Indian monsoon circulation and large scale oscillation in surface pressure in the Southern Hemisphere and with the elevation of the Tibetan plateau in the Transhimalayan region. The impact of the tropical easterly jet (TEJ), the existence of monsoon trough over north India, the permanent snow cover on Tibet and obstruction of the advance of polar cold winds by the Himalayas are major factors causing monsoon over India. During the last 4,500 years the Indian monsoon is periodically experiencing the impact of El Nino, and as such falls in the ambit of El Nino and Southern Oscillation (referred to as ENSO) (Deodhar 1988).

The total average annual rainfall over India at present is said to be 117 cm. The southwest monsoon does not cover Kashmir, the southern tip of the peninsula and the east coast. Within its reach the southwest monsoon progresses with decreasing quantum of rainfall across the mainland. Orographic obstructions on its path render heavy to very heavy rainfall in the Western Ghats, west coast and the Burma mountains; the Deccan plateau is a rain-shadow zone; and the air mass inversion between lower shallow moist current and upper drier air mass causes least rainfall in the Thar desert (Deodhar 1988). The varied rainfall and diverse physiographic configurations have created a variety of habitats supporting endemic sets of plants and animal species, and were subject to human colonization from the Palaeolithic times onwards. Changes in climate regimes and human interference have caused modification of the ecosystems/habitats.

The emergence of orographic landforms across the Asian landmass and the thermal contrast between land and sea have controlled the timing and intensity of the monsoon rainfall. The Western Ghats, Himalayas and the Burma mountains cause the ascent of the monsoon currents and thus help higher precipitation in the orographic belts and low rainfall on their leeward. Furthermore the Himalayas and the Tibetan plateau on the northern side of the subcontinent anchor the onset of monsoon over South Asia. The Indian monsoon circulation covers a very large sector between the East African Rift Valley in Africa and the Tibetan plateau.

Tibetan Plateau: Key to the Indian Monsoon System

The uplift of the Tibetan plateau has played an important role in the early establishment of the monsoon over South Asia. The plateau occupies an area of 2 million sq km and lies at an average elevation of 5,000 m amsl on the northeastern part of the Indian subcontinent. Though much of it is a monotonous plain it is surrounded by some of the world's well-known peaks, including the Mount Everest. The formation of this plateau is of much scientific interest in understanding the climate of South Asia. The permanent snow cover on it has been at the pivot of the prevailing monsoon circulation over the region. The monsoon circulation was established following the rise of the Tibetan plateau to its maximum elevation which resulted in the disruption of west-east air flow across the Northern Hemisphere and initiated the monsoon driven wind across India and consequent increase in precipitation along the Himalayas. Further, higher chemical erosion in the Himalayan plateau triggered a draw-down of carbon dioxide and the consequent global cooling (Searle 1995; Xu 1993).

The rise of Tibet helped the initiation of the Indian Ocean monsoon circulation between East Africa and the South Asian region under the influence of thermal contrast between land and sea. In summer the plateau anchors a heat low over the subcontinental landmass and affects the onset of the strongest monsoon inflow in the form of Southwest monsoon. Thus the Tibetan plateau in the north and the Indian ocean in the south help generate monsoon circulation that feeds the major water courses which were the nerve centres of the early phase of the Indian civilization.

Antiquity of Uplift and Initiation of Monsoon

The uplift of Tibetan plateau is interlinked with the processes leading to the collision of Asian and Indian landmasses. The timing of this collision is placed at 54–49 Myr. Since the collision the plateau grew in elevation and crustal thickness. It reached its maximum sustainable elevation of about 5,000 m and reversed its trend around 14 Myr ago, and has since been collapsing. The timing of this event has been made possible by Ar/Ar dating of muscovites growing along the north-south faults; this age is considerably older than what was previously thought, i.e., 8 Myr ago. Based on this date it was argued that the collapsing trend of the plateau was coeval with climate change and the resultant strengthening of the Indian monsoon circulation (Searle 1995). The new age (the minimum age of the maximum uplift of the Plateau) pushes the antiquity of the monsoon circulation further back by 7 Myr.

The terrestrial record of a series of palaeosols in the Siwaliks of Pakistan, attests to the prevalence of monsoon climate well in the Miocene (Retallack 1995). The stable isotopic analysis of pedogenic carbonates from the palaeosols of Late Miocene age also attest to the influence of monsoon conditions on soil formation (Quade and Cerling 1995).

Upland and Lowland Laterites: Evidence of Monsoon

The western sector of peninsular India preserves evidence of Late Tertiary monsoon in the form of ferricrete capped soil profiles commonly referred to as laterite. The laterite is the most common soil (both fossil and developing) in western peninsular India, especially between the elevated basalt mesas of the Western Ghats and the west coast lowlands of Konkan and Kanara (covering Maharashtra and Karnataka). In Konkan and the adjoining high mesa tops of the Western Ghats the laterite has developed on the Deccan Trap which has an age of 60–65 Myr. Southwards in Karnataka it has developed over the pre-Deccan Trap basement of the Archaean and Proterozoic age, as well as occasional outcrops of Mio-Pliocene age sediments (Widdowson and Gunnel, in press).

The lowland laterites occur as clusters of plateaus. Plateau elevations show a remarkable uniformity in height from Maharashtra to Kerala and show systematic variations in elevation from west to east with a consistent slope towards the sea (Widdowson and Gunnel, in press). The lowland laterites are of significance in understanding the geological and geomorphic processes as well as the seasonal monsoon circulation. The latter feature was already prevalent over this area, giving rise to lateritic formations in the Late Tertiary period.

Laterites on the uplifted Western Ghats crest and towards east are much older in age (Kumar 1986). Typical deep lateritic profiles (with lithomarge, mottled and pallid zones, and indurated crust at the top) occur on the crest of the Ghats, for instance, at Mahabaleshwar in Maharashtra. Such profiles developed on a peneplaned surface at near sea-level under equatorial hot humid conditions when the Indian plate was closer to the equator (Sahasrabudhe and Rajaguru 1990). During the lateritic phase the existence of tropical woodland ecosystem can be envisaged.

The coastal lowlands along the western seaboard evolved geomorphologically in response to the scarp retreat of the Western Ghats during the Neogene, followed by an extensive phase of lateritisation which developed upon a pediment surface when climatic and tectonic conditions were conducive for deep weathering. The lowlands are a low relief pediment formed under relative tectonic stability. Present monsoonal rainfall is very heavy with an average of 5,000 mm at the foot of the Ghats and offers the ideal tropical conditions for continuation of lateritization from Miocene through Pliocene to the major part of Quaternary. Prevalence of tropical climate throughout the Cenozoic is attested by palaeobotanical (Meher-Homji 1989) and palaeoweathering (Bruckner and Bruhn 1992) data. Evidence for hot humid seasonal circulation with greater intensity of rainfall has also been dated to at least 8 Myr ago (Prell and Niitsuma 1989).

Massive lithic calcretes, with relief inversion (rihizoliths and nodules), on laterites and ferricretes of Later Tertiary age in upland western Deccan evidence the initiation of semi-arid monsoonal conditions in the Late Neogene and Early Pleistocene, in conformity with the onset of global cooling around the beginning of the Pleistocene (2.5 Myr ago) (Rajaguru 1997a).

PALAEOMONSOON RECORD

The Palaeomonsoon: Fluvial Proxy Records

In recent years, investigation of proxy records of the Quaternary palaeomonsoon has gained much emphasis in Indian prehistoric research. It was R.V. Joshi who identified the fluvial deposits as potential indicators of monsoon precipitation (Joshi 1970). Additional Quaternary research during the last couple of decades has recognized the potential of fluvial records, which have formed in response to hydrological changes under the influence of fluctuating palaeomonsoon. A good dating control essential for the reconstruction of the frequency of palaeoclimate changes, especially for the terrestrial environment where the proxy records are seldom continuous and long, has also been achieved. While all the archaeological material is landbased, its association with datable material is crucial for establishing the relationship between culture change and climate change in the past.

Aside from the traditional stratigraphic dating and relative dating based on chemical changes such as fluorine to phosphate ratios in bones from Quaternary sites (Kshirsagar 1993), quite a few radiometric dating techniques with increasing time depth have been successfully employed in the Quaternary studies of India (Korisettar and Rajaguru 1998). However, owing to natural constraints dating of sites older than the Late Pleistocene (between 40 and 10 Kyr ago) is infrequent and as yet lacks a secure footing. The Holocene situations have an impressive radiocarbon timeframe. Since the dating is within the Late Quaternary, the land-sea correlation has been possible for a diverse variety of sedimentary environments in western and central India. This has led to a major departure from using archaeological material as an aid to dating Quaternary sequences. Radiometric dating has enabled integration of archaeological and environmental data for delineating man-environment relationships and palaeoecology.

The Middle Pleistocene Monsoon Records

In Gujarat Quaternary deposits have been documented from marine, fluvial and aeolian environments (Chamyal and Merh 1995). The marine sequences are confined to the littoral zones of Kachchh and Saurashtra. The fluvial and aeolian sequences are best exposed in the Sabarmati, Mahi and Narmada valleys dating back to the Middle Pleistocene. Miliolites are the conspicuous littoral and aeolian formations and represent transgressive and regressive phases of the sea during the late Middle to Late Pleistocene. Beach rocks, raised mud flats, raised beaches and inland ridges represent a Holocene transgressive sea. The *ranns* of Kachchh also represent a Holocene fluvio-transitional environment.

Lele (1972) and Marathe (1981) have established the relationship between sea-level changes and the Stone Age occupation in Saurashtra. During the mid-Quaternary the rivers were flowing 10–15 m below the present bed levels and the Lower Palaeolithic occupation took place at this time. The fluvial gravel containing Acheulian tools was buried under the sediments of a major transgressive phase of the sea, represented by miliolite M-I, occurring at an elevation of 40-60 m amsl. This phase was followed by channel incision (3–5 below the present bed of the rivers) at the time of a low sea-level. The gravel overlying M-I contain Middle Palaeolithic tools. These gravels are in turn overlain by miliolite M-II representing yet another phase of transgressive sea. Th-U dating places the Lower Palaeolithic at around 190 Kyr ago and the Middle Palaeolithic around 56 Kyr ago (Baskaran et al. 1989; Patel and Bhat 1996).

The occurrence of Acheulian artefacts on a fossil terra rosa (red soil) developed over a clacarinite (miliolite limestone—M-I) appears to have formed during a low sea-level phase during Middle Pleistocene, at Gopnath in the Bhavnagar district, Gujarat. This is in turn capped by miliolite (M-II), which is unconformably overlain by a aeolianite of terminal Pleistocene age. This red soil is ascribed to the humid phase of the Last Interglacial. The sea-level during this phase was 5 m higher than the present (Bruckner et al. 1987).

A composite lithostratigraphy of the Mahi sequence reveals a succession of six units with intervening conglomerates and a series of buried soils. The red palaeosol is equated with the Oxygen Isotope Stage 5e and is considered a marker bed because of its ubiquitous presence in the alluvial sequences of south Gujarat. Detailed pedogenic analysis of buried soils in the Mahi valley has resulted in identification of cyclic changes in climate between arid and humid phases of varying intensity during the last 300 Kyr (Pant and Chamyal 1990; Khadkikar et al. 1996).

In north central India, in the Son and Belan valleys, sedimentary sequences have been dated from Middle Pleistocene to Holocene. Three successive formations—(a) Sihawal, (b) Patpara and (c) Baghor Formations— have been designated (Williams and Clarke 1995). The central Narmada basin shows a sequence of four formations associated with a Palaeolithic succession. They are (a) Shobpur Formation, (b) Narsinghpur Formation (Early Acheulian), (c) Devakachar Formation (Late Acheulian), and (d) Jhalon Formation (Middle and Upper Palaeolithic) (Acharyya and Basu 1993). More recently, Tiwari and Bhai (1997) have worked out a sequence of seven formations. The basal two formations, Pilikarar and Dhansi Formations, have been tentatively dated to the Neogene and Early Pleistocene respectively on the basis of degree of oxidation and reversed magnetic polarity stratigraphy. The Pilikarar sediments show high degree of latosolic weathering under relatively humid conditions. Occurrence of hominid remains and typical Middle Pleistocene fauna such as *Bos namadicus* and *Equus namadicus*, typical of the Middle Pleistocene, in the highly calcretised members of the Surajkund Formation are suggestive of adaptation to semi-arid conditions (Sonakia and Basu 1998).

Late Quaternary fluvial sediments in the central Narmada valley have also preserved excellent records of prehistoric sites as well as lenses of volcanic ash which are dated to 75 Kyr both by geochemical fingerprinting with the Youngest Toba Tuff and by isothermal plateau fission-track dating (Shane et al. 1995; Westgate et al. 1998). By and large the climate was semi-arid almost throughout the Late Quaternary. Geoarchaeological studies of a semi-primary Middle Palaeolithic site preserved in the alluvial sediments of the Narmada at Samnapur in Narsinghpur district have revealed the effects of debris flow/soil creep on the occupation horizon following the ash fall event and the consequent dry phase (Ahsan 1993). Climatic inferences in terms of fluctuating monsoon conditions are yet to be properly deciphered from these areas.

A new beginning has been made in the 1990s to recognize potential fluvial deposits having implications for monsoon reconstructions. Investigations by Rajaguru and Kale (1985), Kale and Rajaguru (1987) and Mishra et al. (1996) have identified aggradational and erosional sequences in the Late Quaternary alluvia of the upland rivers in Maharashtra (Western Ghats), the source region of the Godavari, Pravara, Bhima and Krishna river systems. Further work is called for in the river basins of peninsular India from the perspective of the palaeomonsoon and the fluvial response.

Climate continued to remain semi-arid monsoonic in upland Maharashtra and western Rajasthan till the end of the Middle Pleistocene. This is indicated by calcretes and vertisols preserved in the alluvial, lacustral and aeolian sediments. Ephemeral stream processes, debris flow deposits, colluvial unweathered or weakly weathered deposits interfingering with alluvial and aeolian sediments also suggest relatively dry climate around 300–400 Kyr ago. During this time the global climate was characterized by glacial aridity and Acheulian occupation appears to have been an adaptation to such an environment (Rajaguru 1997a; Misra and Rajaguru 1987; Misra 1995; Wasson et al. 1984, 1983).

The prevalence of semi-arid monsoonic conditions prior to the ash fall tephra, dated to 75 Kyr ago, is attested by the occurrence of calcretised vertic soils below the ash horizon in the Upland Deccan region (western Maharashtra) (Rajaguru 1997a). The Kukdi tephra is of Toba origin and is related to the last high magnitude eruption of 75 Kyr ago. This Youngest Toba Tuff also marks the onset of the Last Glacial phase (Shane et al. 1995; Westgate et al. 1998). Earlier Mishra et al. 1995 had dated this tephra to 0.6 Myr ago and had used the evidence of Acheulian artefacts in support of this Middle Pleistocene age. Despite this discordance, the tephra serves as a marker in Quaternary stratigraphy and also has environmental significance.

The Last Interglacial climate (about 125 Kyr ago) was warmer and wetter than the present interglacial (Holocene, the last 10,000 years) in higher latitude regions of the world. A unique calcic soil horizon has been encountered in the Thar desert at Didwana buried in the classic sand dune at 16R and associated with the Middle Palaeolithic artefacts (Singhvi et al. 1982). This calcic palaeosol represents a relatively wet interlude in the largely semi-arid phase of climate.

Late Quaternary: Late Pleistocene-Holocene Monsoon Records

Though the marine cores show a high frequency of warmer and cooler episodes (see below) during the Middle Pleistocene comparable evidence is as yet not revealed either in the alluvial or aeolian stratigraphy in western and peninsular India. For the period from about 100 Kyr ago to 13–14 Kyr ago there are well preserved proxy records of palaeoclimate in northern Deccan and elsewhere in northwest India.

Multidisciplinary studies on the lakes, playas and dune formation around Didwana (Nagaur district, Rajasthan) have helped in establishing the antiquity of dune forming processes and estimating the rate of accumulation as well (Allchin and Goudie 1974; Allchin et al. 1978). The antiquity of dunes goes back to 100 Kyr ago and the major dune field of the Thar seems to have formed between 15 and 12 Kyr ago (Dhir et al. 1994). Whereas Wasson (1995) on the basis of TL and radiocarbon dates estimated that peak of dune construction was prior to 16 Kyr ago and that dune construction was slight by 8 Kyr ago, with implications for strengthening of the monsoon by mid-Holocene times.

Evidence of climatic fluctuations is also reflected in the Nilgiri peat (Sukumar et al. 1993) and the Didwana lake in the Thar desert of India (Singh et al. 1972, 1974; Wasson et al. 1983, 1984). Such changes in lake levels in both the hemispheres can now be shown as uniform and synchronous events (Wasson 1995). Sukumar et al. (1993) analyzed the peat bogs of the Nilgiris for variation in the C3 and C4 vegetation. A shift from C3 (forest/grassland) to C4 vegetation took place during 6 and 3, 5 Kyr due to lowering of rainfall and lower carbon dioxide. C4 vegetation is typical of arid climate (the carbon isotopic ratio varying between –15% and –11%) and C3 (the carbon isotopic ratio between –26% and –28%) that of humid climate. C4 vegetation explains the expansion of savanna ecosystem on the Nilgiris.

That the Pleistocene-Holocene transition (14–19 Kyr ago) witnessed rapid switches in climate is clearly reflected in the alluvial sequences. Episodic and strong gravel aggradation occurred in the Godavari and Bhima river valleys in response to intensification of summer monsoon in the Western Ghats. The most distinctive evidence of a dramatic switch to aridity during Late Pleistocene is seen in the form of filled up gorges through which the Pushpawati and Mula rivers flow, at Chilewadi and Bote respectively. The Chilewadi evidence is intriguing as this catchment lies in the high rainfall Western Ghats. This is an instance of aggradation punctuating a long period of quietitude, earlier recorded by Mishra and Rajaguru (1993). Sadakata et al. (1993) have provided a radiocarbon framework which shows two groups of dates clustering prior to and after the Last Glacial Maximum.

Mishra et al. (1996) have documented evidence for fluvial response to global climatic changes during the Pleistocene-Holocene transition. They have also shown that different sectors of the river respond differently to a particular phase of climatic change, which is again governed by the nature of the catchment. They found that aggradation was dominant during Late

Pleistocene in the region west of 75 degrees longitude, whereas in the region towards its east aggradation was dominant during the Early Holocene (prior to 7 Kyr ago) (for details see Mishra et al. 1996; Rajaguru 1997a and b).

At Nevasa, Chandoli and Sashtewadi gravels dated to 13–14 Kyr ago, show an unconformable relationship with the underlying silty alluvium of the Late Pleistocene. The gravels betray maturity as revealed by the degree of rounding and lithology, as compared with the older gravels of 25–14 Kyr ago. Mishra et al. (1996) have interpreted these gravels as representing the initiation of a channel incision phase of the Pleistocene-Holocene transition. This, according to the authors, is comparable to the evidence of deglaciation from the Himalayas (Singh and Agrawal 1976).

Contrasting fluvial responses to climate change are recorded for the period between 12 and 10 Kyr ago. While at Inamgaon flood plain aggradation was going on at 12 Kyr, silty aggradation at Gargoan and erosion to the modern bed level was reached at Asla around 10 Kyr ago. Evidence of Early Holocene floods is interpreted by the evidence of burial of microlithic sites at Ranjegaon and Shaksal Pimpri.

The thermoluminescence dates (TL) obtained for Rajasthan aeolian sediments and radiocarbon dates for molluscan shells from the alluvial deposits containing archaeological material suggest that wind blown (aeolian) sedimentation was the strongest during the transition from Late Pleistocene to Holocene. Choking of alluvial streams took place in response to arid phase aggradation of the terminal Pleistocene. During the 40–25 Kyr period channel incision and stabilization of alluvial fill surfaces with vertisol formation upon them took place; the rainfall was relatively higher than during the post-25 Kyr period. Between 22 Kyr and 16 Kyr the climate was distinctly dry, in conformity with the Last Glacial Maximum. This aggradational phase is represented by poorly sorted gravels with a large component of transported carbonates, interlayering with floodplain deposits which are predominantly silty in northern Deccan.

An erosional buried red soil in the Sabarmati alluvial sequence is TL dated to 50 and 30 Kyr ago and the development of gypcrete within the aeolian profile at Kavas (Barmer district, Rajasthan) are a couple of examples of climatic amelioration during the otherwise dry climatic phase of the Late Pleistocene (Sareen et al. 1992; Singhvi et al. 1982).

The Palaeomonsoon Records in the Indian Ocean

The marine pollen diagram from the Arabian Sea off the east coast of Africa, shows periodic fluctuation in monsoon conditions that correlated with glacial climatic changes as indicated by Oxygen Isotope Stages. Glacial periods were arid because of decreased monsoon flow and during early interglacial stages the Southwest monsoon flow was intense resulting in the rise of lake levels in the tropics (Van Campo et al. 1982). An increase in rainfall between 10 and 5 Kyr ago was also recorded from lakes in Australia and India. Temperate regions of Australia and China have shown records of major fluctuations in lake levels in response to the onset of glacial aridity during the Last Glacial Maximum, during 25–16 Kyr ago. At the end of the Ice Age, 10 Kyr ago, these lakes were restored to levels a little higher than today (Bowler et al. 1995).

Although a large number of surface and subsurface sediments from the Arabian Sea have been analyzed for reconstructing palaeomonsoon fluctuations over the Indian region, this research is generally confined to the period of the Last Glacial Maximum and the latest interglacial. Duplessy (1982) inferred that climate was very arid about 22–18 Kyr ago and the Asian summer monsoon was weaker during the LGM than it is today, whereas the winter monsoon was stronger. The palynological study of marine cores off the southwest coast of India has revealed two phases of the monsoon. The low mangrove pollen frequency is dated to between 22 and 18 Kyr ago, a dry climatic phase, followed by a humid phase at the early post-glacial period (Van Campo 1986). Mineralogical study of the Arabian Sea shelf sediments has also shown aridity around 11 Kyr ago (Nigam and Hashimi 1995).

Another significant development in the Indian Ocean region is the reconstruction of palaeoclimatic changes for the Middle and Late Pleistocene from the deep sea (DSDP sites) and the continental shelf cores off the eastern coast of India. These cores show marked fluctuation in the population of planktonic foraminifera *Globorotalia menardii* (deep sea species), *Globigerina bulloides, Globigerinita glutinata, Globigernoides ruber, Globogerina falconensis*, etc. (tropical and subtropical shallow marine species) and pteropods (see A.D. Singh 1998, for a recent summary). These species' productivity is sensitive to changes in sea surface temperature, intensity of upwelling and monsoon strength and therefore the cyclic variation in the abundance of the foraminifera and pterodos at these sites is a good record of temperature changes during the Pleistocene. At least three glacial-interglacial cycles from the Upper Pleistocene to Holocene have been identified in these cores (Sarkar and Guha 1993).

The strength of the Southwest monsoon winds, upwelling in the Arabian Sea and precipitation are strongly interrelated. The upwelled waters are characterized by cooler temperature supporting the productivity of planktonic fauna. The Northeast monsoon winds in winter suppress upwelling and lower the productivity. Hence upwelling index from the Arabian Sea cores is a good indicator of monsoon conditions. Weak monsoon prevailed during 5,000 and 3,500 years before the present, and this coincided with the onset of arid climate of glacial strength over much of the tropics (Naidu 1995, 1997).

Continental shelf cores from the eastern Arabian Sea and the Oman region have been analyzed for high resolution reconstruction of oceanographic and climatic changes during the Late Quaternary. Detailed micropalaeontological and sedimentological study of several gravity cores off Kerala shelf of the Arabian Sea have been carried out by A.D. Singh (1998). While planktonic foraminifera are commonly used for climatic reconstructions, pteropods are found to be equally suited for this purpose. The pteropods constitute one of the main carbonate components among a variety of micro-organisms in the shelf sediments of the eastern Arabian Sea. Like foraminifera pteropod assemblages also respond to upwelling changes which are related to fluctuation in the monsoon intensity. Therefore conjunctive quantitative analyses of foraminifera and pteropod assemblages were examined by A.D. Singh as evidence for the fluctuations in the upwelling intensity and associated changes in the monsoonal strength. Minimum upwelling and weaker monsoon occurred around 23–18 Kyr ago. Marked increase in both these took place during 18–15 Kyr ago, followed by a weak monsoon and weaker upwelling around 15–12 Kyr ago. The monsoon intensified again between 12 and 10 Kyr ago. Since 5 Kyr the monsoon intensity has lowered. This reconstruction is in general agreement with the results of earlier studies of other scholars (mentioned above) in the north Indian Ocean.

Lake and Off-Shore Palynology

Palynological studies have been carried out in the lakes of Rajasthan, Uttar Pradesh, Kashmir, Ladakh, Kathmandu and Sikkim. In the Kashmir valley pollen analysis suggests a cooler period around 10,000 years BP, followed by a gradual warming between 7,000 and 4,000 years BP. Pollen studies in the Ladakh region indicate that during the last 30,000 years the climate was dry and cold. There were, however, brief periods, when warm climate lasting 200 to 300 years existed. About 1,000 years ago there was a transition from moist to relative dry conditions in the western Himalayas (see Srinivasan 1998 for an overview).

Rajasthan is one of the few regions in India where interdisciplinary prehistoric and palaeoclimatic research has been carried out in order to provide climate/environmental background to prehistoric cultures. A large number of playas and lakes in this region have provided pollen profiles facilitating the reconstruction of changing vegetation and the corresponding rainfall regimes. The saline lakes of Lunkaransar, Didwana and Sambar were some of the lakes first studied for this purpose. Gurdeep Singh and his colleagues (Singh et al. 1974, 1990; G. Singh 1988) carried out detailed palynological research on these lake sediments and inferred higher rainfall regimes during Early Holocene and attributed to them the prosperity of the Indus Civilization (2500–1900 BC). Terminal Pleistocene was characterized by hyper arid conditions followed by warm and wet conditions between 10,000 and 6,000 BP. Aridity around 4,000 BP was recorded by the dry phase of the lakes. Similar vegetation change between arboreal and herbaceous ecosystems is observed from the Nal Sarovar pollen spectrum (also see Sharma and Chauhan 1991; Kajale and Deotare 1997).

Bryson and Swain (1981) utilized the pollen spectra from these lakes and estimated a rainfall that was twice the present between 5,000 and 1,500 BP Later Swain et al. (1983) interpreted the pollen record in terms of 500 mm per annum of rainfall between 10,500 and 3,500 years BP followed by a dry phase leading to increasing salinity of the lakes.

The playas like Bap-Malar (district Jodhpur) and Kanod (district Jaisalmer) originated within the structural depressions around 14–15 Kyr ago. They carried brackish water between 8 and 6 Kyr ago and nearly dried up around 5 Kyr ago (Kajale and Deotare 1997). These playas in western arid parts of Rajasthan seem to have dried up at least a thousand years earlier than the playas in the eastern parts of the Thar desert (Deotare et al. 1998). Similar multidisciplinary investigations in the Nal Sarovar in Gujarat (Prasad et al. 1997) show that the lake was almost dry around 6 Kyr ago, carried enough water between 4 and 3 Kyr and again dried up after 3 Kyr. In general these lake records betray regional variation in hydrological changes during Early to Mid-Holocene times and that the rainfall was not higher than the present even during relatively wet phase of the Holocene.

A change in the vegetation was recorded by Caratini by analyzing the pollen grains from two cores from the inner shelf of the Arabian Sea off the mouth of the Kalinadi (Caratini et al. 1994). A decline in the evergreen, deciduous and mangrove forest species in favour of savanna vegetation was observed from 3,200 years ago. This was interpreted as the beginning of a less humid phase under a weaker monsoon.

In sum one can observe a convergence of evidences, from marine, lacustral and terrestrial records, relating to frequency and intensity of monsoonal fluctuations during the Late Quaternary. The climate of sub-tropical India during the Last Glacial Maximum at 18 Kyr ago reveals a global unity, though the Kashmir evidence is indicative of an early deglaciation; the rest of the subcontinent and the Indian Ocean region were relatively dry. Evidence from sand dunes, desert lakes, alluvial sequences and off-shore cores clearly converges to indicate drier conditions between 25 and 18 Kyr, between 16 and 12 Kyr, and again around 9 Kyr ago.

HUMAN ADAPTATIONS

The Middle and Late Pleistocene Adaptations in India

Although the Lower Palaeolithic evidence in the majority of cases comes from Middle Pleistocene contexts, it is still not possible to assign the Lower Palaeolithic occupations to a particular glacial or interglacial or oxygen isotopic stage. There is a general lack of climate sensitive biotic material associated with the stone tool assemblages of this period. The present evidence points to a gross picture of savanna ecosystems and human adaptations to drier climate. Site specific geoarchaeological studies and geochronology are few in number. Moreover the Palaeolithic record is quite unevenly distributed in time and space in the subcontinent (Rendell and Dennell 1985; Dennel and Rendell 1991; Acharyya and Basu 1993; Shane et al. 1995; Mishra et al. 1995; Westgate et al. 1998). A large majority of sites are surface or plow-zone situations, lacking in complementary data for a palaeoenvironmental and palaeogeographic reconstruction. To date excavated Lower Palaeolithic sites are very few in India (Corvinus 1982; Misra 1985; Paddayya 1982; Kenoyer and Pal 1982; Pant and Jayaswal 1991; Bose et al. 1958; Sharma and Clark 1983).

The evidence for Lower Palaeolithic occupation on the east coast of the Peninsula is better than that of the west coast. The absence of Lower Palaeolithic artefacts in Todd's collection and evidence of a single chopper from the Manori cemented river gravel leaves much of the material as surface occurrences (Guzder 1980). Although Goudeller and Korisettar (1993) have made a substantial claim for the Acheulian occupation of the west coast, the evidence again comes from the surface of fluvial gravels in the Dudhsagar and Mandai river valleys of Goa. A quartz chopper assemblage is also reported from Kerala and a couple of bifaces from coastal Karnataka (Rajendran 1990). Guzder (1980) treats the Lower Palaeolithic assemblages from Borande on the Vaitarna, and from Malvan together with the collection made by others (Todd 1939; Malik 1963; Joshi and Bopardikar 1972) as representing a 'regional cultural group' and it is difficult to establish detailed stratigraphy on individual sites as the majority are surface occurrences. During the last three decades Lower Palaeolithic occurrences in the basal conglomerates have been reported from different sectors of the east coast (see Reddy 1994, for a summary), though significant data pertaining to Quaternary stratigraphy and climate is not forthcoming. The region south of the Kaveri continues to draw a blank in regard to Lower Palaeolithic occupation.

In the sub-Himalayan region the Upper Siwalik strata are now known to yield Lower Palaeolithic evidence (Mohapatra 1976; Verma 1991). Sharma (1995) mentions the discovery of Early Palaeolithic tools from below a tuffaceous bed dated to 2.5 Myr ago in the Upper Siwalik beds. Although such an early date is doubted, it certainly deserves serious attention of both geologists and prehistorians to establish the context and nature of industry in Ladakh. In recent years more evidence of indubitable local provenance is known from this area (Ota 1992). These artefacts have been made from locally occurring fine-grained volcanics and cherty tuffs. One site is located in the Indus valley at Alchi village and another is a rock-shelter at Hunder Dok in the Shyok valley (Sharma 1995). Kashmir valley draws a blank in terms of Lower Palaeolithic occupation and the situation is no better than in 1947 (Krishnaswami 1947). Joshi et al. (1974) found evidence of only one glaciation at a lower altitude of 7,000 ft around Pahlgam and collected some suspected Palaeolithic artefacts, adding to the earlier collection made by Sankalia (1971), but later surveys have not produced additional evidence anywhere in Kashmir. This is one of the best investigated regions in India, both for geological and climatic history of the Cenozoic period (Agrawal et al. 1989). In eastern India Early Quaternary deposits are represented by ferruginous conglomerates with occasional Palaeolithic material.

The Middle Palaeolithic in India is known from a variety of contexts from western, central and southern India. Early research placed this culture in the second gravel conglomerate in the alluvial sequence of peninsular India (Sankalia 1974). Now surface, cave and buried contexts with a higher site integrity are known from Rajasthan, Madhya Pradesh and the Deccan (Allchin and Allchin 1982); there is better dating control too (Mishra et al. 1989, 1993; Rajaguru and Mishra 1997). The Middle Palaeolithic covers the time span from about 140 Kyr to 40 Kyr.

At Ranjani and Chandoli in the Bhima basin the Middle Palaeolithic artefacts are associated with a poorly sorted fluvial gravel indicative of a period when the river was aggrading due to low discharge and high sediment load in a climate more arid than now (Mishra and Ghate 1989; Rajaguru and Mishra 1997). Similar occurrences of Middle Palaeolithic artefacts are reported from the Tapi basin at Dahivel, Amoda, Badne (district Dhule, Maharashtra) by Sali (1990). At Lakhmapur in the Kaladgi basin, north Karnataka, the surface Middle Palaeolithic sites in the piedmont context are associated with the spring tufa (Korisettar et al., in preparation). The arid climate of this period might represent the onset of the Last Glaciation, around 80 Kyr ago. In general the Middle Palaeolithic sites are rarely buried with Quaternary sequences in the peninsular region; this possibly indicates the dominantly erosive mode of the streams in the Deccan. They are common on the surface with rubble and fan gravels and generally lie away from the streams but close to the quarries or sources of raw material.

In Rajasthan the Middle Palaeolithic witnessed a relatively wet climate and appears to date to the Last Interglacial wet climate. The Luni evidence has a TL date of greater than 100 Kyr (A.K. Singhvi: personal communication). In the Jaisalmer region, close to the core of arid Rajasthan, Middle Palaeolithic sites have been reported. Mishra et al. (1993) are of the opinion that the Middle Palaeolithic communities exploited the resources in such areas during wet phases of the Late Quaternary. At Jetpur in the Bhadar valley (Gujarat) the Middle Palaeolithic horizon underlies a 2 m thick miliolite formation, dated to around 56 Kyr ago.

The Upper Palaeolithic phase dates from around 40 to 10 Kyr ago. The evidence is mostly known from the Deccan and north central India (Murty 1979; Raju 1985). A group of rock-shelters in central India have provided a sequence of human occupation from the Acheulian to the Upper Palaeolithic through Middle Palaeolithic (Joshi 1978; Misra 1985). The Kurnool caves have yielded faunal and lithic assemblages (Murty 1974; Reddy 1977). The Upper Palaeolithic material is found in the Late Pleistocene alluvium, such as at Sangamner, Nevasa, Inamgaon; in the colluvial deposits at Patne (Sali 1974, 1989; Mishra 1995; Sharma and Clark 1983); as surface scatters in the vicinity of raw material (Paddayya 1970). In the Narmada and Son valleys the evidence comes from within the silty alluvium, whereas in the Tarafeni valley (West Bengal) the evidence comes from a clayey alluvium within which a calcrete has formed (Basak et al. 1998).

Microlithic artefacts date from the Upper Palaeolithic in western

Maharashtra (at Dharagoan on the Godavari) and central India (at Mehtakheri on the Narmada). These are in the Late Pleistocene gravels in which the artefacts are associated with mollusc shells yielding radiocarbon dates of 28 and 30 Kyr respectively. Radiocarbon dates for the Late Pleistocene gravel are clustered into two groups: (a) 25 and 20–19 Kyr, and (b) 12–10 Kyr. The first two correspond well with the Last Glacial Maximum and the last with the Younger Dryas and represent aggradational response to arid conditions.

In the Thar desert Upper Palaeolithic artefacts occur on the stabilized dune surfaces, within buried calcisols, in fossil playas and in cemented gravels, suggestive of contemporary climatic conditions at the time of human occupation. TL dates place the Upper Palaeolithic at Didwana around 35 Kyr ago, an adaptation to a slightly wetter condition that prevailed around 35–40 Kyr ago, when playas were carrying more water and dune building activity was interrupted by fluvial activity, further suggestive of a wetter climate. There are no sites assignable to the Last Glacial Maximum in the Thar; however, between 13 and 7 Kyr ago the monsoon dynamism became intense with periodic switches between dry and wet phases. This is clearly documented in the dune profiles, showing alternating bands of evaporites and organic rich clays in the playas of Didwana and by the development of calcisols on dunes and sandsheets. The Mesolithic communities colonized most parts of the desert during this time.

Interpretation

While the Siwalik and deep sea records and the lowland west coast laterite extend the monsoon records to the Mio-Pliocene period, the palaeomonsoon reconstructions for the rest of the region are best only for the Late Quaternary.

The physiographic configuration of India controls the movement of both the Southwest and Northeast monsoons, during summer and winter respectively. The internal topographic subdivisions do not necessarily coincide with natural ecosystems, the characteristics of which are strongly influenced by the monsoon flow. The orographic barriers in the proximal area of the flow from the Arabian Sea to the Himalayas and vice versa. Accordingly a network of ecosystems are formed, including deciduous woodlands, tropical evergreen forests, savanna, semi-arid to arid scrub lands, arid sand deserts and periglacial loessic landforms, in response to long term changes in climate.

The uplift of Western Ghats effectively changed the peninsular ecosystem from tropical woodland (Early Tertiary) to a network of savanna ecosystems between the west coast and the plateau along with the establishment of allochthonous river systems in peninsular India. The savanna ecosystem became well-defined in the rocky triangle between the Western and Eastern Ghats. This orographic configuration resulted in a progressive decrease in the intensity of rainfall along the path of the Southwest monsoon, the basic element controlling the habitability of the area. Obviously the structure of food resources between the coastal, upland and plateau ecosystems was very different, the key controlling factor would have been the secular variation in the intensity of Southwest monsoon across the peninsular region.

Owing to heavy to very heavy Southwest rainfall in the Western Ghats this zone presents a good example of biodiversity, between the mouth of the Tapi in the north and the southern tip of India (Menon and Bawa 1997). Damage to the biodiversity of the Western Ghats by human interference is being assessed. During the last 4,000 years human interference has steadily increased, more so under the impact of the post-Industrial Revolution developmental programmes and the demographic pressure necessitating expansion of agricultural land.

A close look at the archaeological and palaeontological evidence from the riverine deposits in southern and central India reveals an assemblage of fossil ungulates in the proximity of Lower Palaeolithic sites, and attests to the prevalence of savanna habitats and riverine gallery forests. Fossil fauna, such as *Bos, Sus, Elephas, Equus, Hexaprotodon, Stegodon* and *Cervus* from Middle and Late Pleistocene contexts in India are suggestive of the prevalent savanna and woodland ecosystems (Badam 1984; Misra 1989: Appendix I). Although the evidence for Palaeolithic colonization is present in a variety of ecosystems in the subcontinent, it was the adaptive capability of the colonizing groups that gave character to their lifeways.

The distribution pattern of Palaeolithic sites is indicative of the preference for savanna habitats. Radiometric dating either by K-Ar or Ar-Ar method of the Lower Palaeolithic occupation has been controversial owing to discordant dates produced by isothermal plateau fission track dating and geochemical finger printing of the volcanic ash from Bori (Mishra et al. 1995, 1997; Shane et al. 1995; Westgate et al. 1998). However, geochemical dates by U-series method suggest a Middle Pleistocene age.

Recent palynological and isotopic research, as outlined above, also clearly reveals that vegetation changes were not primarily controlled by temperature changes, as generally believed, but also by periodic changes in the intensity of precipitation and monsoon upwelling. Such vegetation changes have implications for fragmentation of habitats and forest area as well as differentiation of animal and plant species.

Therefore one needs to understand the extent of damage to the forest area under long term climatic changes. As indicated by palynological studies the montane evergreen forest of the Western Ghats might have given way to the expanded grasslands under the arid climate of the Last Glacial Maximum (25–18 Kyr ago). The expansion of grasslands as a corollary could have affected biological species endemic to a particular habitat/ ecosystem. And the impact of climate on habitat change was determined by the intensity of climate during each phase of wet and dry climatic phases.

Increased continentality and low sea-levels during glacial epochs, as envisaged by Rajaguru and Kale (1985) and Kale and Rajaguru (1987), is a significant factor affecting the ecosystems across the continental area. During the Last Glacial Maximum the sea-level was lower by at least 100 m. This must have resulted in the shifting of Southwest rainfall belts away from the continental region. As evidenced by off-shore research, during these periods the Northeast monsoon was stronger, and perhaps covered a larger area than at present (interglacial period). The present reach of both the monsoons has to be viewed as an interglacial high sea level ecopara-meter.

Evidence for a prolonged dry period in the subtropical regions of India appears to have had an overriding influence on the ecodiversity and human adaptations to savanna ecosystems. During the Last Interglacial period prevailing wetter conditions in the Thar (Rajasthan) and Saurashtra peninsula (Gujarat) supported the Middle Palaeolithic adaptation, while in other areas it was an adaptation to savanna and woodland ecosystems.

The Late Pleistocene aridity is well documented all over India: in Kashmir loess deposition was dominant (Agrawal et al. 1989; Bronger and Heinkele 1995); dune formation in Rajasthan; aggradation and loess deposition in Gujarat; colluvial cone formation developed over alluvial and lacustral deposits in northeast India (Manipur and Garo hills) (Thokchom 1987; Medhi 1981) and aggradational and colluvial deposition in peninsular India. The formation of calcrete in the present humid tropical region of West Bengal (Basak et al. 1998), in terms of rainfall, is significant, for it indicates decrease in the rainfall during the later Pleistocene. This is further attested by the fossil evidence of grassland fauna, like *Axis axis, Antelope cervicapra* and *Bos namadicus*. In Tripura extensive development of calcrete in the alluvial deposits is documented in the Late Pleistocene context (Ramesh 1989).

If Late Quaternary palaeoclimatic inferences are any guide, it should be possible to extrapolate the same to the rest of the Quaternary. Multidisciplinary palaeoclimate studies carried out on continental and offshore deposits in southern India are suggestive of variation in vegetation cover of the Western Ghats between tropical evergreen and savanna ecosystems. While the evergreen forests were associated with stable humid conditions, the spread of savanna vegetation took place during arid to semi-arid transitions.

On the basis of our current knowledge of Pleistocene stratigraphy across the subcontinent one notices an apparent similarity of geomorphic processes operating throughout the Pleistocene under the influence of fluctuating monsoon. The regional environments fluctuated in accordance with these changes between savanna and woodland ecosystems affecting human occupation of the areas. The lithological successions suggest that during the Middle Pleistocene bedrock erosion and pedimentation were the dominant processes leading to the formation of debris flow, rubble and colluvial deposits and fan gravels prior to human occupation. Towards the close of the Middle Pleistocene some of these materials were incorporated into alluvial systems, leading to the formation of present patterns of drainage in the Late Quaternary.

In the coastal region, particularly along the west coast, the rise in sea-level was extremely rapid during the Pleistocene-Holocene transition (Kale and Rajaguru 1985). Oceanographic research off the west coast of India revealed a still stand at 11 Kyr, with a sea-level still 80 m below the present which rapidly rose to a level higher than the present around 6 Kyr ago (Hashimi et al. 1995) and gradually reached the present level (Ghate 1988).

Holocene Adaptations

The archaeological cultures of the Holocene present a picture of multilineal evolution. A series of overlapping cultures have defined their areas in time and space across the subcontinent. While the northwest witnesses vibrant developments leading to the emergence of the First Urbanization in the region between Baluchistan in the west and the Aravallis in the east, around the middle of third millennium BC, the rest of the subcontinent witnessed a tardy growth of hunting-gathering economies and their transformation into food-producing economies leading to the Second Urbanization in the fifth century BC in the Ganga valley and its spread into the Deccan in the early part of Christian era. Radiocarbon dating has facilitated the identification of regional continuities, parallel developments and geographical as well as temporal gaps in the evolution of Holocene cultures. The oldest of the Holocene cultures, i.e., Mesolithic survived into the Neolithic-Chalcolithic and Iron Age of south India.

Undoubtedly the number and density of Mesolithic sites in India is far greater than those of the Palaeolithic. Although the earliest vestiges of the Mesolithic culture in the northwestern part of the subcontinent (Mehrgarh in Pakistan) are dated to the Early Holocene, its manifestations are clearly seen across the northern plains since about 5000–6000 years ago and much later in the Deccan. In addition to colonizing the previously known habitats new areas were occupied such as the Ganga plains, the rocky uplands of Gujarat, the western and the southeast coast of India, the rock-shelters and caves of central India. Among the couple of thousand sites the excavated sites are Tilwara (Misra 1971), Bagor (Misra 1973), Langhnaj (Karve-Corvinus and Kennedy 1964), Sarai Nahar Rai (G.R. Sharma 1973), Adamgarh (Joshi 1978), Mahadaha (Sharma et al. 1980), Damdama (Varma 1986) and Muchchatla Chinatmanu Gavi (Murty 1974, 1981).

The Neolithic culture can be broadly grouped on a regional basis into four complexes: (a) Northern Neolithic, (b) the Southern Neolithic, (c) the Eastern Neolithic, and (d) the Ganga Valley Neolithic. They range in time from the beginning of the fourth millennium to mid-second millennium and betray regional adaptations to the prevalent environment. In central India and northern Deccan a distinctive Neolithic phase is as yet unknown. However, regular agricultural settlements in these regions are known to appear in the later part of the third millennium BC and in the post-Harappan period (Allchin and Allchin 1982; Murty 1989; Dhavalikar 1989, 1990, 1994).

Interpretation

Early Holocene was a period of climatic amelioration as well as abrupt changes in the intensity of rainfall. Between 6 and 4 Kyr ago the Thar desert received higher rainfall both during summer and winter: playas carried fresh water, the dunes were stabilized and the stream activity was strong in the northern part of the Thar desert. Mesolithic cultures continued to flourish in the region as a whole and the stream banks sheltered the Harappan settlements. The semi-arid savanna ecosystems across the subcontinent continued to support hunting-gathering and fishing, and favoured transition to food-producing economy in the mid-Holocene; perhaps human groups were adapting themselves to a decreasing monsoon regime.

The widespread occurrence of Mesolithic sites in India appears to coincide with the climatic phase characterized by monsoon recovery after the dry spell between 9000 and 8000 years ago. These Mesolithic communities continued to inhabit the region colonized by them and survived the vagaries of monsoonal conditions by developing adaptive capabilities. Delineation of processes responsible for expansion of agricultural economies in the Neolithic and Chalcolithic stages is beyond the scope of the present paper. Beginning of agriculture in the different regions was initially governed by the rainfall regimes and the adoption of suitable introduced and indigenous crops, as well as domestication of cattle, sheep and goats. Sheep and goats possess greater adaptive capability than cattle. Sheep-goat pastoralism is more viable in low rainfall areas.

In northern Deccan farming was adopted around 3.5 Kyr ago. The first farmers settled along the streams exploiting the alluvial strips along the floodplains. However a conspicuous hiatus occurs in the archaeological record of western India (Dhavalikar 1992). This gap is attributed to the onset of severe dry conditions by Dhavalikar (1992), as envisaged by Krishnamurthy et al. (1981). There is supporting evidence for this inference from geological, isotopic, micropalaeontological and palynological analyses, as shown above. The upwelling indices from the Indian Ocean decline further indicating decrease in the monsoon rainfall. Interesting evidence of decreasing lake levels around this period is also reported from Ethiopia and Tibet (Gillesie et al. 1983; Gasse and van Campo 1994). Other meteorological parameters such as abrupt change in solar radiation, temperature, and southeasterly winds are cited as good evidence of an abrupt switch in climate causing higher frequency of floods. On the other hand there is evidence of continuation of stabilization of dunes and soil formation on these surfaces. In fact the summer monsoon was weaker between 3.5 and 3 Kyr ago, the peak of farming activity in the western Deccan. The intensity of monsoon was at its minimum during the period between 4,000 and 1,500 BP (Late Holocene) as compared with the Mid-Holocene (8,000 to 4,000 BP). Great floods occurred between 4,000 and 1,500 BP. (Naidu 1995). Kale et al. (1997) have documented well-dated evidence for a 2,000-year-old flood on the Narmada in central India. On the other hand the Late Holocene witnessed extreme dynamism of the monsoon and this period also witnessed widespread adoption of agriculture in the Deccan and central India revealing both waxing and waning phases.

At this stage it is not possible to identify a single factor playing a determinant role in the shaping of the cultural complexity of the Holocene Indian subcontinent, but a combination of physiographic, hydrological, edaphic and seasonal, and cultural factors can safely be envisaged, especially in respect of the introduction of a variety of cereals for agriculture. Wheat, barley, rice, *ragi*, *jowar*, etc. form the staple foods of the human population living in various regions of the subcontinent.

Wheat and barley are weedy grasses with lesser adaptive capability. They prosper in areas of disturbed soils such as on hill slopes in the areas of winter rainfall. These plants were domesticated in the region stretching between the eastern Mediterranean and the western borderlands of the Indian subcontinent. This region receives rainfall during the winter that naturally supports their cultivation, and they were adopted by the Harappans in the northern sector of the Harappan domain. Whereas in the southern sector (particularly Gujarat), which is covered by the summer monsoon, *ragi* and *jowar* were introduced for cultivation by the Harappans right in the beginning of the third millennium BC (Possehl 1992).

Ragi and sorghum are generally summer sown, rainfed crops particularly suited to monsoon seasonality. They are capable of high productivity in areas marginal for wheat and barley. Archaeoethnobotanical research has revealed that none of these cereals are native to the land and were introduced into these cultures owing to their adaptive capability to the mosaic of climatic regimes across the subcontinent. Cultural processes were primarily responsible for their availability in the Neolithic and Bronze Age contexts. The archaeological evidence shows difference in the timing and spacing of adoption of these cereals in the different Neolithic zones of India.

While evidence of rice cultivation goes back to the middle of the second millennium BC at Koldihwa in the Ganga valley (there is uncertainty regarding its earlier dating), it is also known from Lothal in Gujarat in the Harappan context; it was introduced in the south beginning in the Megalithic period (Kajale 1991). Since the Early Historic period one observes a continuing expansion of rice cultivation under intensive agriculture in the semi-arid regions. The effective management of rainfed reservoirs across the major river systems has enabled the growth of economic prosperity. Despite this technological control the El Nino years cause drought conditions. However, by virtue of its ability to build itself the monsoon recovers and restores normalcy in about 3–4 years, this being the mainstay of India's agricultural stability and cultural complexity. Regularity of the monsoon is crucial to agricultural prosperity and stable demography of the Indian civilization.

In conclusion it can be stated that the available multidisciplinary data on the palaeomonsoon reveals a global unity in the monsoon function. The Southwest monsoon was weak during the Last Glacial Maximum and rapidly fluctuated during the Pleistocene-Holocene transition. Further multidisciplinary studies aided by the application of AMS (accelerator mass spectrometer) radiocarbon chronology would facilitate a better understanding of the monsoon and its effects on the lifeways of both past and present societies in India.

REFERENCES

Acharyya, S.K., and Basu, P.K. 1993. Toba Ash on the Indian Subcontinent and its Implications for Correlation of Late Pleistocene Alluvium. *Quaternary Research* 40: 10–19.

Agrawal, D.P., Dodia, R., Kotlia, B.S., Razdan H., and Sahni, A. 1989. Plio-Pleistocene Geologic and Climatic Record of the Kashmir Valley: A Review and New Data. *Palaeogeography, Palaeoclimatology and Palaeoecology* 73: 267–86.

Ahsan, S.M.K. 1993. A Study of Site Formation Processes in the Sub-Humid Environment of Central India with Special Reference to Samnapur Palaeolithic Site (Madhya Pradesh). Ph.D. Dissertation. Pune: University of Pune.

Allchin, B., and Allchin, F.R. 1982. *The Rise of Civilization in India and Pakistan*. Cambridge: Cambridge University Press.

Allchin, B., and Goudie, A. 1974. Pushkar: Prehistory and Climatic Change in Western India. *World Archaeology* 5(3): 359–68.

Allchin, B., Goudie, A., and Hegde, K.T.M. 1978. *The Prehistory and Paleogeography of the Great Indian Desert*. London: Academic Press.

Badam, G.L. 1984. The Pleistocene Faunal Succession, in R.O. White, ed. *The Evolution of East Asian Environment*. Hong Kong: University of Hong Kong, pp. 746–75.

Basak, B., Badam, G.L., Kshirsagar, A., and Rajaguru, S.N. 1998. Late Quaternary Environment, Palaeontology and Culture of the Tarafeni Valley, Midnapur District, West Bengal: A Preliminary Study. *Journal of the Geological Society of India* 51 (6): 731-40.

Baskaran, M., Rajagopalan, G., and Somayajulu, B.L.K. 1989. 230Th/234U and 14C Dating of Quaternary Carbonate Deposits of Saurashtra, India. *Chemical Geology* (Isotope Geoscience Section) 13: 505–14.

Bose, N.K., Sen D., and Ray, G. 1958. Geological and Cultural Evidence of the Stone Age in Mayurbhanj. *Man in India* 38(1): 49–55.

Bowen, D.Q. 1978. *Quaternary Geology*. Oxford: Pergamon Press.

Broekker, W. 1996. Glacial Climate in the Tropics. *Science* 272: 1902–04.

Bowler, J.M., Jones, R., and Zhisheng, An. 1995. Climate Change in the Western Pacific: its Implications for Green House Scenarios, in S. Wadia, R. Korisettar and V.S. Kale, ed., *Quaternary Environments and Geoarchaeology of India*. Bangalore: Geological Society of India, pp. 1–21.

Bronger, A., and Heinkele, T. 1995. Loess-Paleosol Sequences as Witness of Palaeoclimatic Records?: the Kashmir Valley as an Example, in S. Wadia, R. Korisettar and V.S. Kale, ed., *Quaternary Environments and Geoarchaeology of India*. Bangalore: Geo-

logical Society of India, pp. 109–23.
Bruckner, H. 1987. Miliolite Occurrences off Kathiawar, Peninsular (Gujarat) India. *Journal of Archaeological Science* 13: 135–45.
Bruckner, H., and Bruhn, N. 1992. Aspects of Weathering and Pene-planation in Southern India. *Zeitschrift fur Geomorphologie* (Supplement Band) 91: 43–66.
Bryson, R.A., and Swain, A.M. 1981. Holocene Variation of Monsoon in Rajasthan. *Quaternary Research* 16: 35–45.
Caratini, C.B.I., Fontugne, M., Morzadec-Kerfourn, M.T., Pascal, J.P., and Tissot, C. 1994. A Less Humid Climate Since *ca.* 3500 yr. BP from Marine Cores off Karwar, Western India. *Palaeogeography, Palaeoclimatology and Palaeoecology* 109: 371–84.
Chamyal, L.S., and Merh, S.S. 1995. The Quaternary Formations of Gujarat, in S. Wadia, R. Korisettar and V.S. Kale, ed., *Quaternary Environments and Geoarchaeology of India*. Bangalore: Geological Society of India, pp. 246–57.
Corvinus, G. 1981 and 1983. *A Survey of the Pravara River System in Western Maharashtra, India*, 2 vols. Tubingen: Institut fur Urgeschichte.
Dennell, R.W., Rendell, H.M. and De Terra Paterson. 1991. The Soan Flake Industry: A New Perspective from the Soan Valley, Northern Pakistan. *Man and Environment* 16(2): 91–99.
Deodhar, H. 1988. *Understanding Monsoons*. Mumbai: Nehru Centre.
Deotare, B.C., Kajale, M.D., Kshirsagar, A.A., and Rajaguru, S.N. 1998. Geoarchaeological and Palaeoenvironmental Studies Around Bap-Malar Playa, District Jodhpur, Rajasthan. *Current Science* 75(3): 316–20.
Dhavalikar, M. K. 1989. Human Ecology in Western India in the Second Millennium BC. *Man and Environment* 14(1): 83–90.
—1990. *The First Farmers of the Deccan*. Pune: Ravish Publishers.
—1994. Early Farming Communities of Central India. *Man and Environment* 19 (1–2): 159–68.
—1992. *Culture-Environment Interface: A Historical Perspective*. Presidential Address, Archaeology and Anthropology Section, Indian Science Congress, 52nd Session, New Delhi, February 21–23, 1992.
Dhir, R.P., Rajaguru, S.N., and Singhvi, A.K. 1994. Desert Quaternary Formations and their Morphostratigraphy: Implications for the Evolutionary History of the Thar. *Journal of the Geological Society of India* 43: 435–47.
Duplessy, J.C. 1982. Glacial and Interglacial Contrasts in the Northern Indian Ocean. *Nature* 295: 494–98.
Gasse, F., and van Campo, E. 1994. Abrupt Post-Glacial Climate Events in West Asia and North African Monsoon Domains. *Earth and Planetary Science Letters* 126: 435–56.
Ghate, S. 1988. Sea Level Fluctuations in North Konkan with Special Reference to Sopara. *Current Science* 57: 1317–20.
Gillespie, R., Street-Perrot, F.A., and Switzur, R. 1983. Post-glacial Arid Episodes in Ethiopia: Implications for Climate Prediction. *Nature* 306: 680–83.
Goudeller, L.D., and Korisettar, R. 1993. The First Discovery of Acheulian Bifaces in Goa: Implications for the Archaeology of the West Coast of India. *Man and Environment* 18 (1): 35–42.
Guzder, S. 1980. *Quaternary Environments and Stone Age Cultures of the Konkan, Coastal Maharashtra, India*. Pune: Deccan College.
Hashimi, N.H., Nigam, R., Nair R.R., and Rajagopalan, G. 1995. Holocene Sea Level Fluctuations off Western Indian Continental Margin: an Update. *Journal of the Geological*

Society of India 46: 157–232.

Joshi, R.V. 1970. The Characteristics of Pleistocene Climatic Events in Indian Subcontinent, Land of Monsoon Climate. *Indian Antiquary* 4(1–4): 53–63.

—1978. *Stone Age Cultures of Central India: Report of the Excavations of Rock-Shelters at Adamgarh, Madhya Pradesh*. Pune: Deccan College.

Joshi, R.V., and Bopardikar, B.P. 1972. Stone Age Cultures of Konkan (Coastal Maharashtra), in S.B. Deo, ed., *Archaeological Congress and Seminar Papers*. Nagpur: Nagpur University, pp. 42–52.

Joshi, R.V., Rajaguru, S.N., Pappu, R.S., and Bopardikar, B.P. 1974. Quaternary Glaciation and Palaeolithic Sites in the Liddar Valley (Jammu and Kashmir). *World Archaeology* 5(3): 369–79.

Kajale, M.D. 1991. Current Status of Indian Palaeoethnobotany: Introduced and Indigenous Food-Plants with a Discussion of the Historical and Evolutionary Developments of Indian Agriculture and Agricultural Systems in General, in Jane M. Renfrew, ed., New Light on Early Farming: Recent Developments in *Palaeoethnobotany*. Edinburgh: Edinburgh University Press, pp. 155–89.

Kajale, M.D., and Deotare, B.C. 1997. Late Quaternary Environmental Studies on Saline Lakes in Western Rajasthan: A Summarized View. *Journal of Quaternary Research* 12(5): 405–12.

Kale, V.S. and Rajaguru, S.N. 1987. Late Quaternary Alluvial History of the North-Western Deccan Upland Region. *Nature* 325: 612–14.

Kale, V.S., Mishra, Sheila, and Baker, V.R. 1997. A 2000-Year Palaeoflood Record from Sakarghat on Narmada, Central India, *Journal of the Geological Society of India* 50(3): 283–88.

Karve-Corvinus, G., and Kennedy, K.A.R. 1964. Preliminary Report on Langhnaj Excavation 1963, *Bulletin of the Deccan College Research Institute* 24: 44–57.

Khadkikar, A.S., Chamyal, L.S., Malik, J.N., Maurya, D.M., and Merh, S.S. 1996. Arid-Humid Cycles in Mainland Gujarat over the past 300 Ka: Evidence from the Mahi River Basin. India. *Journal of Geological Society of India* 47, 3: 383–88.

Kenoyer, J.M., and Pal, J.N. 1982. Report on the Excavation and Analysis of an Upper Acheulian Assemblage from Sihawal II, in G.R. Sharma and J.D. Clark, ed. *Palaeoenvironment and Prehistory in the Middle Son Valley*. Allahabad: Abinash Prakashan, pp. 23–38.

Korisettar, R., and Rajaguru, S.N. 1998. Quaternary Stratigraphy, Palaeoclimate and the Lower Palaeolithic Evidence of India, in M.D. Petraglia and R. Korisettar, ed., *Early Human Behaviour in the Global Context: The Rise and Diversity of the Lower Palaeolithic Period*. London: Routledge, pp. 304–42.

Korisettar, R., Petraglia, M.D., Schuldenrein, J., and LaPorta, P. (in preparation). Geoarchaeology of the Lakhmapur Lower Palaeolithic site, Karnataka.

Korisettar, R., Venkatesan, T.R., Mishra, Sheila, Rajaguru, S.N., Somayajulu, B.L.K., Tandon, S.K., Gogte, V.D., Ganjoo, R.K., and Kale, V.S. 1989a. Discovery of a Tephra Bed in the Quaternary Alluvial Stratigraphy of Pune District (Maharashtra), Peninsular. *Current Science* 58, 10: 564–67.

Korisettar, R., Mishra, Sheila, Rajaguru, S.N., Gogte, V.D., Ganjoo, R.K., Venkatesan, T.R., Tandon, S.K., Somayajulu, B.L.K., and Kale, V.S. 1989b. Age of Bori Volcanic Ash and Acheulian Culture of the Kukdi Valley. *Bulletin of the Deccan College Research Institute* 49: 564–67.

Krishnamurthy, R.V., Agrawal, D.P., Misra, V.N., and Rajaguru, S.N. 1981. Palaeoclimatic

Inferences from the Behaviour of Radiocarbon Dates of Carbonates from Sand Dunes of Rajasthan. *Proceedings of the Indian Academy of Sciences* (*Earth and Planetary Sciences*) 90 (2): 155–60.

Krishnaswami, V.D. 1947. Stone Age India. *Ancient India* 3: 11–57.

Kshirsagar, A. 1993. The Role of Fluorine in the Chronometric Dating of Indian Stone Age Cultures. *Man and Environment* 18: 23–32.

Kukla, G.J. 1977. Pleistocene Land-Sea Correlations: I Europe. *Earth Science Review* 13: 307–74.

Kumar, A. 1986. Palaeolatitutes and the Age of Indian Laterites. *Paleogeography, Paleoclimatology, Paleoecology* 53: 231–37.

Lele, V.S. 1972. Late Quaternary Studies on the Bhadar Valley Saurashtra. Ph.D. Dissertation. Pune: University of Pune.

Malik, S.C. 1963. Studies in the Prehistory of Western India with Special Reference to Gujarat. Ph.D. Dissertation. Vadodara: M.S. University of Baroda.

Marathe, A.R. 1981. Geoarchaeology of the Hiran Valley, India. Pune: Deccan College.

Medhi, D.K. 1981. Quaternary History of the Garo Hills, Meghalaya. Ph.D. Dissertation. Pune: University of Pune.

Meher-Homji, V.M. 1989. History of Vegetation of Peninsular India. *Man and Environment* 13: 1–10.

Menon, S., and Bawa, Kamaljit S. 1997. Application of Geographic Information Systems, Remote Sensing, and a Landscape Ecology Approach to Biodiversity Conservation in the Western Ghats. *Current Science* 73 (2): 134–45.

Mishra, S. 1995. Prehistoric and Quaternary Studies at Nevasa: The Last Forty Years, in S. Wadia, R. Korisettar and V.S. Kale, eds., *Quaternary Environments and Geoarchaeology of India*. Bangalore: Geological Society of India, pp. 324–32.

Mishra, S., and Ghate, S. 1989. Middle Palaeolithic Site of Ranjani. *Man and Environment* 15: 23–27.

Mishra, S., and Rajaguru, S.N. 1993. Quaternary Deposits at Bhedaghat, near Jabalpur, Madhya Pradesh. *Man and Environment* 18: 7–12.

Mishra, S., Kshirsagar, A., and Rajaguru, S.N. 1988. Relative Dating of the Quaternary Record from Upland Western Maharashtra, in M. Patel and N. Desai, ed., *National Seminar on Recent Quaternary Studies in India*. Vadodara: M.S. University of Baroda, pp. 267–78.

Mishra, S., Rajaguru, S.N., and Ghate, S. 1993. Stone Age Jaisalmer: Implications for Human Adaptation to Deserts. *Bulletin of the Deccan College Research Institute* 53: 260–68.

Mishra, S., Venkatesan, T.R., Rajaguru, S.N., and Somayajulu, B.L.K. 1995. Earliest Acheulian Industry from Peninsular India. *Current Anthropology* 36(5): 847–51.

Mishra, S., Rajaguru, S.N., Naik, Sonali, Ghate, Savita, and Kshirsagar, A. 1996. Climate Change During the Pleistocene/Holocene Transition in Upland Western Maharashtra, Western India, in *Proceedings of Seminar on Quaternary Environment and Society*, Baker Sedget, Israel, 7–12 July 1996.

Misra, V.N. 1971. Two Late Mesolithic Sites in Rajasthan: A Brief Review of Investigations. *Journal of Poona University* (*Humanities*) 35: 59–77.

—1973. Bagor: A Mesolithic Settlement in Northwest India. *World Archaeology* 5 (1): 92–110.

—1985. The Acheulian Industry of Rock Shelter IIIF-23 at Bhimbetka, Central India, in *Recent Advances in Indo-Pacific Prehistory*. V.N. Misra and P. Bellwood, ed. New

Delhi: Oxford & IBH Publishing Co., pp. 35–47.
—1989. Stone Age India. *Man and Environment* 14 (1): 17–64.
—1995. Geoarchaeology of the Thar Desert, in S. Wadia, R. Korisettar and V.S. Kale, ed., *Quaternary Environments and Geoarchaeology of India*. Bangalore: Geological Society of India, pp. 210–30.
Misra, V.N., and Rajaguru, S.N. 1987. Palaeoenvironment and Prehistory of the Thar Desert, Rajasthan, India, in K. Frifelt and P. Sorensen, ed., *South Asian Archaeology 1985*, Scandinavian Institute of Asian Studies. London: Curzon Press, pp. 296–320.
Mohapatra, G.C. 1976. Geotectonic Developments, Sub-Himalayan Lithic Complex and Post-Siwalik Sediments, in A.K. Ghosh, ed., *Perspectives in Paleeoanthropology*, Calcutta: Firma K.L. Mukhopadhay, pp. 31–59.
Murty, M.L.K. 1974. A Late Pleistocene Cave Site in Southern India. *Proceedings of the American Philosophical Society* 118 (2): 196–230.
—1979. Recent Research on the Upper Palaeolithic Phase in India. *Journal of Field Archaeology* 6: 301-20.
—1981. Hunter-gatherer Ecosystems and Archaeological Patterns of Subsistence Behaviour on the Southeast Coast of India: An Ethnographic Model. *World Archaeology* 13 (1): 47–58.
—1989. Pre-Iron Age Settlements in South India: An Ecological Perspective. *Man and Environment* 14(1): 65–82.
Naidu, P.D. 1995. Onset of an Arid Climate at 3.5 Ka in Tropics: Evidence from Monsoon Upwelling Index. *Current Science* 71: 715–18.
—1997. Rapid Climatic Shifts and its Influence on Ancient Civilizations: Evidence from Marine Records, in D. Balasubramaniam and N. Appaji Rao, ed., *The Indian Heritage*. Hyderabad: University Press, pp. 69–77.
—1998. Driving Forces of Indian Summer Monsoon on Milankovitch and Sub-Milankovitch Time Scales: A Review. *Journal of the Geological Society of India* 52: 257–72.
Nigam, R., and Hashimi, N.H. 1995. Marine Sediments and Palaeo Climatic Variations Since the Late Pleistocene: An Overview for the Arabian Sea, in S. Wadia, R. Korisettar, V.S. Kale, ed., *Quaternary Environments and Geoarchaeology of India*. Bangalore: Geological Society of India, pp. 380–90.
Ota, S.B. 1992. Ladakh Evidence of Stone Age Culture. *Himalaya Today* III (3–4): 359–68.
Paddayya, K. 1970. The Blade Tool Industry of Shorapur Doab. *Indian Antiquary* (Third Series) 4 (1–4): 165–90.
—1982. *The Acheulian Culture of the Hunsgi Valley (Peninsular India): A Settlement System Perspective*. Pune: Deccan College.
Pant, P.C., and Jayaswal, V. 1991. *Paisra: The Stone Age Settlement of Bihar*. Delhi: Agam Kala Prakashan.
Pant, R.K., and Chamyal, L.S. 1990. Quaternary Sedimentation Pattern and Terrain Evolution in the Mahi River Basin, Gujarat, India. *Proceedings of the Indian National Science Academy* 56A: 501–11.
Patel, M.P., and Bhat, N. 1996. Evidence of Palaeoclimatic Fluctuations in Miliolite Rocks of Saurashtra, Western India. *Journal of the Geological Society of India* 45: 191–200.
Pappu, R.S., and Deo, S.G. 1994. *Man-Land Relationships During Palaeolithic Times in the Kaladgi Basin, Karnataka*. Pune: Deccan College.
Possehl, G. L. 1992. The Harappan Civilization in Gujarat: The Sorath and the Sindhi Harappans. *The Eastern Anthropologist* 45 (1–2): 117–54.
Prasad, S., Kusumgar, S., and Gupta, S.K. 1997. A Mid- to Late Holocene Record of

Palaeoclimatic Changes from Nal Sarovar: A Palaeodesert Margin Lake in Western India. *Journal of Quaternary Science* 12: 153–59.

Prell, W.L., and Van Campo, E. 1986. Coherent Response of Arabian Sea Upwelling and Pollen Transport to Late Quaternary Monsoonal Winds. *Nature* 322: 526–28.

Prell, W.L., and Niitsuma, L. 1989. Introduction, Background and Major Objectives for ODP Leg 117 (Western Arabian Sea) in Search of Ancient Monsoons, in *Proceedings of the Ocean Oil Drilling Program, Initial Reports*. Texas: College Station, pp. 5–9.

Quade, J., and Cerling, T.E. 1995. Expansion of C4 Grasses in the Late Miocene of Northern Pakistan: Evidence from Stable Isotopes in Palaeosols. *Paleogeography, Paleoclimatology, Paleoecology* 115: 91–116.

Rajaguru, S.N. 1970. Studies in the Late Pleistocene Stratigraphy of the Mula-Mutha Valley. Ph.D. Dissertation. Pune: University of Pune.

—1997a. Climatic Changes in Western India During the Quaternary: a Palaeopedological Approach. DST—Project Completion Report (Unpublished).

—1997b. Quaternary Palaeoclimate of Northern Deccan, India. Paper presented at the Seminar on Deccan Heritage during the 63rd Meeting of the Indian National Science Academy, National Geophysical Research Institute, Hyderabad, September 29–31, 1997.

Rajaguru, S.N., and Kale, V.S. 1985. Changes in Fluvial Regime of Western Maharashtra Upland Rivers During Late Quaternary. *Journal of the Geological Society of India* 26 (1): 16–27.

Rajaguru, S.N., and Mishra, S. 1997. Late Quaternary Climatic Changes in India: a Geoarchaeological Approach. *Bulletin of the Indo-Pacific Prehistory Association* 16: 27–32.

Rajendran, P. 1990. The Mesolithic Cultures of Karnataka, Kerala and Tamil Nadu, in A. Sundara, ed., *Archaeology in Karnataka*. Mysore: Directorate of Archaeology and Museums, pp. 48-57.

Raju, D.R. 1985. The Upper Palaeolithic Industries of the Cuddapah District, Andhra Pradesh, in *Recent Advances in Indo-Pacific Prehistory*. V.N. Misra and P. Bellwood, New Delhi: Oxford & IBH Publishing Co., pp. 147–56.

Rakhecha, P.R., and Pisharoty, P.R. 1996. Heavy Rainfall During Monsoon Season: Point and Spatial Distribution. *Current Science* 71 (3): 179–86.

Ramesh, J. 1989. A Study of Geomorphology, Quaternary Geology and Associated Cultural Remains of West Tripura District, Tripura. Ph.D. Dissertation, Gauhati: Gauhati University.

Reddy, K.T. 1977. Billasurgam: an Upper Palaeolithic Cave Site in South India. *Asian Perspectives* 20 (2): 206–27.

—1994. Coastal Ecology and Archaeology: Evidence from the East Coast of India. *Man and Environment* 19: 43–55.

Rendell, H.M., Dennell, R.W., and Halim, M.A. 1989. *Pleistocene and Palaeolithic Investigations in the Soan Valley, Northern Pakistan, British Archeological Mission of Pakistan,* F.R. Allchin, B. Allchin, and S.M. Ashfaque, eds. Oxford: BAR International Series no. 544.

Retallack, G.J. 1995. Palaeosols of the Siwalik Group as a 15 Myr Record of South Asian Monsoon, in S.Wadia, R. Korisettar and V.S. Kale, ed., *Quaternary Environments and Geoarchaeology of India*. Bangalore: Geological Society of India, pp. 36–51.

Sadakata, N., Maemoko, H., Rajaguru, S.N., Mishra, S., and Fujiwara, K., 1995. Late Quaternary Environmental Change in Tropical-Subtropical Northwest Deccan Upland India, in *Proceedings of the International Symposium on Palaeoenvironmental Change*

in Tropical-Subtropical Monsoon Asia. Hiroshima: Hiroshima University, pp. 43–56.
Sahasrabudhe, Y., and Rajaguru, S.N. 1990. The Laterites of Maharashtra State. *Bulletin of the Deccan College Research Institute* 49: 357–70.
Sali, S.A. 1974. The Upper Palaeolithic Since Independence. *Bulletin of the Deccan College Research Institute* 34: 147–160.
—1989. *The Upper Palaeolithic and Mesolithic Cultures of Maharashtra*. Pune: Deccan College.
Sankalia, H.D. 1965. *Excavations at Langhnaj: 1944–63*, part I. Pune: Deccan College.
—1971. New Evidence of Early Man in Kashmir. *Current Anthropology* 11(4): 558–62.
—1974. *Prehistory and Protohistory of India and Pakistan*. Pune: Deccan College.
Sareen, B.K., Someshwara Rao, M., Tandon, S.K., and Singhvi, A.K. 1992. A Tentative Chronological Framework for the Quaternary Deposits of the Sabarmati Basin of Semi-arid Western India Using Thermoluminescence: Extended Abstract, in *International Symposium on Evolution of Deserts*. Ahmedabad: Physical Research Laboratory, pp. 117–18.
Sareen, B.K., and Tandon, S.K. 1995. Petrology, Micromorphology and Granulometry of Mid- to Late Quaternary Continental Deposits of the Semi-Arid Sabarmati Basin, Western India, in S. Wadia, R. Korisettar and V.S. Kale, ed. *Quaternary Environments and Geoarchaeology of India*. Bangalore: Geological Society of India, pp. 258–76.
Sarkar, A., and Guha, A.K. 1993. Palaeoceanographic Implications of Planktonic Formainiferal Abundance at DSDP Sites 219–20 and 241: An Approach Based on Paleontologic Time Series. *Journal of the Geological Society of India* 41 (5): 397–416.
Searle, M. 1995. The Rise and Fall of Tibet. *Nature* 374: 17–18.
Shackleton, N.J. 1975. The Stratigraphic Record of Deep-Sea Cores and its Implications for the Assessment of Glacials, Linterglacial Stadials and Interstadials in the Mid-Pleistocene, in K.W. Butzer and G.L. Isaac, eds., *After the Australopithecines*. The Hague: Mouton Publishers, pp. 1–124.
Shane, Phil, Westgate, J., Williams, M, and Korisettar, R. 1995. New Geochemical Evidence for the Youngest Toba Tuff in India. *Quaternary Research* 44: 200–04.
Sharma, G.R. 1973. Mesolithic Lake Cultures in the Ganga Valley. *Proceedings of the Prehistoric Society* 39: 129–46.
Sharma, G.R., and Clark, J.D., eds., 1983. *Palaeoenvironment and Prehistory in the Middle Son Valley, Madhya Pradesh, North Central India*. Allahabad: Abinash Prakashan.
Sharma, G.R., Mishra, V.D., Mandal, D., Misra, B.B., and Pal, J.N. 1980. *Beginnings of Agriculture (Epipalaeolithic to Neolithic): Excavations at Chopani-Mando, Mahadaha and Mahagara*. Allahabad: Abinash Prakashan.
Sharma, J.C. 1977. Palaeolithic Tools from Pleistocene Deposits in Punjab. *Current Anthropology* 18: 94–95.
Sharma, K.K. 1995. Quaternary Stratigraphy and Prehistory of the Upper Indus Valley, Ladakh, in S. Wadia, R. Korisettar and V.S. Kale, ed., *Quaternary Environments and Geoarchaeology of India*. Bangalore: Geological Society of India, pp. 98–108.
Sharma, C., and Chauhan, M.S. 1991. Palaeovegetation and Palaeoenvironmental Inferences from the Quaternary Palynostratigraphy from the Western Indian Plains. *Man and Environment* 16: 65–71.
Singh, A.D. 1998. Late Quaternary Oceanographic Changes in the Eastern Arabian Sea: Evidence from Planktonic Foraminifera and Pteropods. *Journal of the Geological Society of India* 52 (2): 203–12.

Singh, G. 1988. History of Arid Land Vegetation and Climate: Global Perspective. *Biological Reviews* 63: 159–95.

Singh, G., and Agrawal, D.P. 1976. Radiocarbon Evidence in North-Western Himalaya, India. *Nature* 260: 232.

Singh, G., Wasson, R.J., and Agrawal, D.P. 1990. Vegetational and Seasonal Climatic Changes Since the Last Full Glacial in the Thar Desert, Northwestern India. *Review of Palaeobotany and Palynology* 64: 351–58.

Singh, G., Joshi, R.D., and Singh, A.B. 1972. Stratigraphic and Radiocarbon Evidence for the Age and Development of Three Salt Lake Deposits in Rajasthan, India. *Quaternary Research* 2: 496.

Singh, G., Joshi, R.D., Chopra, S.K., and Singh, A.B. 1974. Late Quaternary History and Climate of the Thar Desert, India. *Philosophical Transactions of the Royal Society of London* 276: 467–501.

Singhvi, A.K., Sharma, Y.D., and Agrawal, D.P. 1982. Thermoluminescence Dating of Sand Dunes in Rajasthan. *Nature* 295: 313.

Singhvi, A.K., Bronger, A., Pant, R.K., and Sauer, W. 1987. Thermoluminescence Dating and its Implications on the Chronostratigraphy of Loess-Palaeosol-Sequences in the Kashmir Valley (India). *Chemical Geology* (*Isotope Geoscience Section*) 65: 45–56.

Sirocko, F., Garbo-Schoenberg, D., McIntyre, A., and Molfino, B. 1996. Teleconnections Between the Subtropical Monsoon and High Latitude Climates During the Last Deglaciation. *Science* 272: 526–29.

Sonakia, A., and Biswas, S. 1998. Antiquity of the Narmada *Homo Erectus*, the Early Man in India. *Current Science* 75 (4): 391–93.

Soundara Rajan, K.V. 1958. Studies in the Stone Age of Nagarjunakonda and its Neighbourhood. *Ancient India* 14: 49–113.

Srinivasan, J. 1998. The Monsoon—Past, Present and Future. *Current Science* 74 (3): 187–89.

Sukumar, R., Ramesh, R., Pant, R.K., and Rajagopalan, G. 1993. A Delta C-13 Record of Late Quaternary Climate Change from Tropical Peats in Southern India. *Nature* 364: 703.

Sundaram, R.M., Rakshit, P., and Pareek, K. 1996. Regional Stratigraphy of Quaternary Deposits in Parts of Thar Desert, Rajasthan. *Journal of the Geological Society of India* 48: 203–10.

Thockchom, A. Singh 1987. Quaternary Studies in the Manipur Valley. Ph.D. Dissertation. Pune: University of Pune.

Tiwari, M.P. and Bhai, H.Y. 1997. Quaternary Stratigraphy of the Narmada Valley, in *Quaternary Geology in the Narmada Valley: a Multidisciplinary Approach*, Special Publication no. 46. Calcutta: Geological Survey of India, pp. 33-63.

Todd, K.R.U. 1932. Prehistoric Man Around Bombay. *Proceedings of the Prehistoric Society of East Anglia* 9: 35–42.

—1939. Palaeolithic Industries of Bombay. *Journal of the Royal Anthropological Institute* LXIX: 257–72.

—1950. Microlithic Industries of Bombay. *Ancient India* 6: 4–16.

Van Campo, E. 1986. Monsoon Fluctuation in Two 20,000 yr BP Oxygen Isotope-Pollen Records of Southwest India. *Quaternary Research* 26(3): 376–88.

Van Campo, E., Duplessy, J.C. and Rossignol-Strick, M. 1982. Climatic Conditions Deduced from a 150 Kyr Oxygen Isotope-Pollen Record from the Arabian Sea.*Nature* 296: 56–59.

Varma, R.K. 1986. *The Mesolithic Age in Mirzapur*. Allahabad: Paramjyoti Prakashan.

Verma, B.C. 1991. Siwalik Stone Age Culture. *Current Science* 61(8): 496.

Wasson, R.J. 1995. The Asian Monsoon During the Late Quaternary, in S. Wadia, R. Korisettar and V.S. Kale, ed., *Quaternary Environments and Geoarchaeology of India*, Bangalore: Geological Society of India, pp. 22–35.

Wasson, R.J., Smith G.I., and Agrawal, D.P. 1984. Late Quaternary Sediments, Minerals and Inferred Geochemical History of Didwana Lake, India. *Paleogeography, Palaeoclimatoloty and Palaeoecology* 46: 345–72.

Wasson, R.J., Rajaguru, S.N., Misra, V.N., Agrawal, D.P., Dhir, R.P., Singhvi, A.K., and Rao, K.K. 1983. Late Quaternary Stratigraphy and Palaeoclimatology of the Thar Dunefield. *Zeitschrift fur Geomorphologie* (*Supplement*) 45: 117–25.

Westgate, J.A., Shane, P., Pearce, N. J.G., Perkins, W.T., Korisettar, R., Chesner, C.S., Williams, M.A.J., and Acharyya, S.K., 1998. All Toba Tephra Occurrences Across Peninsular India Belong to 75, 000 Years Eruption.*Quaternary Research* 50: 107–12.

Williams, M.A.J., and Clarke, M.F. 1995. Quaternary Geology and Prehistoric Environments in the Son and Belan Valleys, North Central India, in S. Wadia, R. Korisettar and V.S. Kale, ed., *Quaternary Environments and Geoarchaeology of India*. Bangalore: Geological Society of India, pp. 282–308.

Widdowson, M., and Gunnel, Y. In press. Tertiary Lateritisation Along the Konkan and Kanara Coastal Lowlands of Western Peninsular India.

Xu, Quiqui. 1993. The Appearance of the Himalayas and its Relation to Global Climatic Events, in N.K. Jablonsky, ed., *Evolving Landscapes and Evolving Biotas of East Asia Since the Mid-Tertiary*. Hong Kong: Centre for East Asian Studies, pp. 115–22.

15 ❖ Studies in Harappan Technology: A Review

K. KRISHNAN

TECHNOLOGY may be defined as the conscious processing of raw materials in an organized way to produce a desired and functionally oriented object. To understand it fully, a wide spectrum of parameters need to be studied. It is not wrong to state that the biological and cognitive evolution of the human species was accompanied by a series of technological developments. Studies in animal behaviour, especially those of chimpanzees, have revealed that they have a tendency to use various materials in their natural forms for achieving goals such as food procurement and defence. Similarly, we have ample evidence to state that the pre-*sapiens* man was well-versed with the processing of raw materials such as stone, wood, and bone to meet different needs. Later, the transformation of hunter-gatherers to agriculturalists led to the conceptualization of storage of surplus production. This, in turn, necessitated the requirement of a raw material which could be altered to a desired shape. Consequently, the easily available raw material, i.e., clay, was chosen and used. These farming settlements slowly evolved into rural centres, and in course of time, some of the latter developed into urban centres. The use of metals started with such rural communities and immediately the advantages of metal over other materials were realized. Of all the metals, copper was the first to be extracted successfully.

Studying technological progress and understanding various aspects of technology requires an interdisciplinary approach. There is archaeological evidence to reconstruct the various stages of production right from procurement of the raw material. The archaeological data does not help us read the cognitive part of human beings that led to these inventions; however, while studying the evolution of technology some progress can perhaps be made in evaluating its impacts on the respective society which may ultimately help one to modestly appreciate the ancient mind.

This paper reviews the studies in technology of selected materials in the Indian subcontinent ranging in age from the early (pre-Harappan) farming communities to the end of the Harappan Civilization.

CERAMIC TECHNOLOGY

Though the term 'ceramics' covers a wide range of materials prepared by the heating of clay, in this context I confine myself to reviewing studies on pottery, terracotta objects, glazed materials, stoneware and faience objects during the first urbanization of the Indian subcontinent.

Pottery Production

The earliest evidence of pottery in the subcontinent comes from the Neolithic phase where surplus production of food led to the concept of storage; however, it was not until the succeeding Chalcolithic phase that a large variety of pottery came into use. Neolithic pottery types were mostly hand made, some of them having mat or basket impressions, whereas Chalcolithic pottery was mainly wheel-thrown with specialized surface treatment in the form of slip/wash. In addition to this surface coating, many vessels bear decorations in the form of paintings, rustication, incised and applique designs. Furthermore, in addition to the handmade and wheel-made vessels, there also exist examples of vessels made by moulding and coiling.

The studies on pottery may be classified into two broad categories: (1) conventional archaeological studies and (2) scientific analyses using physico-chemical methods.

Conventional archaeological studies on ceramics are a part of excavation reports. These mostly concentrate on typological variations in pottery forms and decorations. This has helped archaeologists to pose questions concerning evolution of shapes, paintings, migration, invasion, cultural transitions, regionality, etc. (Rao 1963, Bisht 1984, Joshi 1972, Shinde and Kar 1992, Soundara Rajan 1962, Sonawane and Ajithprasad 1994); however, these cultural phenomena are not yet convincingly defined. Some excavation reports have also incorporated isolated physico-chemical analyses of pottery or its production related raw-materials. The earliest attempts on this line were chemical analyses from Harappa by Sana Ullah (Vats

1974: 468), from Mohenjo-daro by Sana Ullah and Hamid (Marshall 1931: 689–90), and from Rangpur (Rao 1963: 133–37) and Lothal (Rao 1985: 461–74) by Lal.

The earliest examples of pottery production in the subcontinent come from Mehrgarh (Period IB/IIA). At Mehrgarh, Vandiver (Jarrige et al. 1995–99: 648–61) cites the use of baskets as moulds for preparing pottery during the initial stages of the settlement. It is also observed that the coarse wares and early fine wares were manufactured using the method of sequential slab construction. Moreover, it appears that from the early phase itself pottery production was standardized and refined. Thus, Mehrgarh has given clues pertaining to the earlier stages of pottery production.

The introduction of wheel-thrown pottery technology was the next major innovation and has resulted in the appearance of a wide variety of pot types. Allchin and Allchin (1968: 288–91) suspect that the flat-based and round-based pots were produced by throwing on different types of wheels—former attributed to a foot wheel and the latter to a spun wheel. Recent ethnographic surveys and many experimental reconstructions of Harappan shapes have, however, suggested that these pottery types could have been produced in many other ways.

The production of pottery involves various stages, such as:

1. collection of the clay forming the raw material,
2. preparation of the clay,
3. shaping the vessels,
4. drying of the vessels to leather hard stage,
5. application of slip and decorations on them, and
6. baking.

To take an example, the excavation of a workshop at Nausharo has yielded a good deal of evidence of pottery manufacture (Mery 1994). There is, however, no clue regarding refining of the clay at this workshop as it did not yield any unprepared clay or other materials which could be used for tempering. The fine-grained clay paste analyzed from this workshop revealed only its mineralogy and grain size. The presence of fired clay moulds indicated that moulding was one of the techniques used for shaping vessels. The technique of wheel throwing is marked by the presence of a fragmentary clay ball, in the shape of a flat base truncated cone having fine parallel striations on the sides and a small depression at the top. Tools such as flint blades with polished edges along with scraps of clay are indicative of vessel trimming during the leather hard stage in order to make the thickness of its walls uniform. It appears that the luting of parts produced individually (in order to give rise to complex shapes) was done in the leather hard stage. Application of slip and its decoration with incisions or paintings were also done during the leather hard stage.

Mackay (1937: pl. XXIII.2, 1938: 172) has reconstructed a pottery kiln from Mohenjo-daro. Dales (1974: 3–22) also refers to kilns identified from Mohenjo-daro, Harappa, Chanhu-daro and Balakot. The excavations at Nageswar in Gujarat have revealed an interesting structure belonging to Phase B from Layer 4 of Trench III which became a topic of debate among the excavators. In the excavation report, this is mentioned as a fire altar (Hegde et al.1990: 13) along with an alternate interpretation of the same as a pottery kiln (Hegde et al.1990: 6). This structure at Nageswar is a circular pit 165 cm in diameter having a long channel, measuring 170 × 50 cms, and also provided with a conical clay mould in the centre. During the excavation this circular chamber was found filled with ash and reed-impressed as well as vitrified clay lumps. This circular chamber had double-lined walls suggesting its subsequent restoration. The clay wall of the pit was fused in its southern and eastern parts, thereby indicating a very high temperature. Exploration in this area had also yielded a fired pottery mould, a terracotta dabber, and a lot of vitrified potsherds and clay lumps. These are typical manufacturing indicators usually found in association with pottery kilns. This structure from Nageswar is similar to pottery kilns reported from Harappa, Mohenjo-daro and Balakot. In the light of all this evidence the view that the 'fire altar' of Nageswar is actually a 'pottery kiln' seems correct.

Specific studies on Harappan pottery technology have also been carried out using physico-chemical methods with a view to understanding the paste-texture (Krishnan 1986, Krishnan and Hegde 1987, Panjwani 1989, Chandler 1994, Krishnan 1997 and Krishnan, in press). These emphasize fabric characterization based on the mineralogy of non-plastic inclusions, their shape, size and grain size distribution patterns. Krishnan (1997, in press) has correlated these results with the cultural phenomena by integrating information from ethnographic experiments and petrographic analyses (Rao 1991, Krishnan and Rao 1994, Shah 1994). These have helped in defining how different processes of clay paste preparation by potters are translated into the microstructure of the final product. The variation in the patterns thus formed, are accounted for by inter-workshop and intra-workshop differences. The reasons for such variations include differences in the provenance of the raw material, seasonality, market demand, mental template and individuality of the potter. These works have helped in explaining why microstructural fabric groups differ from specific archaeological categories (Krishnan, in press).

Physico-chemical analyses have also helped in understanding the level of specialization in Harappan pottery production (Krishnan 1997, in press). For example, the production of coarse wares during the Mature Harappan period can be cited in order to appreciate the level of this specialization. Petrographically, coarse wares fall into distinct fabric groups. Here, it has been observed that minerals with either low thermal expansion values or close to that of clay, form the non-plastic inclusions in these wares; thus, stress due to repeated heating and cooling is avoided, ensuring longer durability periods for these vessels. Evidence of such specialization, however, occurs mostly during the Mature Harappan phase. By contrast, in the subsequent phases potters seem to have moved toward non-specialization. This may have been the result of the general change in the cultural trend represented by the 'localization phenomena'. A case study on pottery of various phases from Banawali, Haryana, indicates that the Mature Harappan pottery displays maximum care and consistency in the preparation of the clay paste as compared with the pre- and Late Harappan pottery. This phenomenon is proposed as constituting a cycle of development of pottery technology leading from a non-specialized stage to a specialized stage and, finally, to a non-specialized stage again. It is, therefore, possible that during the Mature Harappan period pottery specialization had reached a point where workshops were making only certain types of pottery, while in later periods workshops would have made a larger variety of shapes. Moreover, as an important craft specialization, pottery making would have been one of the major segments of the economy of prehistoric societies. Inferences have also been drawn about different traditions of pottery manufacture such as the 'handicraft style' and 'industrial style' through typo-technological study of Micaceous Red Ware, a fabric type found in association with the Harappan pottery in Saurashtra (Herman and Krishnan 1994, Dimri 1994).

Different types of surface treatment found on the Harappan pottery have also attracted the attention of investigators. Starr (1941) studied the stylistic aspects of the decorations on Harappan pottery and Plenderleith (Marshall 1931: 692) has carried out microscopic observations on Reserved Slip Ware. Analysis of pigments and slips on Harappan pottery from Gujarat (Krishnan 1992) and technology of the surface treatment of Reserved Slip Ware (Krishnan and Freestone, in press) are some of the other works in this direction. For example, two types of black pigment have been identified on Harappan Red Ware, namely, manganese-rich black pigment and iron-rich black pigment. It appears that crushed manganiferrous ore was mixed with very fine quality clay to prepare the pigment (Krishnan 1992). The surface pattern on "glazed" Reserved Slip Ware was produced by overlaying slips of contrasting iron content. The lower, iron-rich slip was produced by mixing an iron-rich pigment with a fine fraction of the body clay or with the pale slip. The firing temperatures of this pottery is determined to be of the 850°–1000°C range. The special features of "glazed" Reserved Slip Ware are due to careful preparation and control of the slip coats, an essentially non-intrusive method of partial removal of the upper slip, and a relatively strong reduction firing. During the course of firing, the body and upper slip turned white to grey, whereas the lower iron rich slip turned black. Given the nature of the surface coats, it is suggested that the term "glossy" Reserved Slip Ware is probably preferable to the continued use of the term "glaze" (Krishnan and Freestone, in press).

Experimental reconstructions have also been done to understand the production technology of many Harappan ceramics (Rao 1991, Kenoyer 1994, Roux 1994, Courty and Roux 1995). These studies have given us information about the types of manufacturing indicators, the treatment required for processing raw clay, for shaping various vessel forms on a wheel or by other methods and also the temperature range required for the production of good quality ceramics. Based upon both experimental reconstruction and micromorphological analysis Courty and Roux (1995) argue that the technological analysis of archaeological ceramics should be reassessed in view of the recognition of the complex nature of forming processes as described in the ethnographic literature. In this study, these two workers propose that the majority of vessels of the Harappan period were initially formed by coiling and then shaped on a wheel. In this category they also include the majority of contemporary vessels from Mesopotamia and Iran dating back to the third millennium BC. This proposition is based on certain micromorphological observations.

Observations made by the present author on certain vessels have indicated that changes occur in the micromorphology of vessels produced in the same workshop from time to time even while using the same technique. This change in micromorphology becomes more significant as one moves from one workshop to another. These changes are due to intra-workshop and inter-workshop differences, seasonality, and the mental templates of the craftsmen. This makes one feel that to establish such propositions a number of case studies are required. While doing this exercise the regional variations in ceramic production also need to be well understood. This will hopefully enable one to define the possible micromorphological features resulting from simple wheel throwing and coiling followed by wheel throwing, respectively.

Stoneware Bangle Production Technology

Stoneware bangles constitute another important artefact type that one encounters in the Harappan context. Two categories of these have been distinguished on the basis of colour, one being terracotta red and the other grey-black. A lot of work pertaining to the manufacture of stoneware bangles at Mohenjo-daro has been carried out by Vidale and others (Halim and Vidale 1984, Blackman and Vidale 1993). The process involves initially the fabrication of small firing containers or saggers in which two to three bangles were inserted and sealed with special lids. These saggers were then piled one above the other, forming small pillar like arrangement of 5 or 6 containers and coated with a thin layer of chaff tempered coarse clay. This set was inserted in a second larger sagger which was then sealed with a lid. This whole system was carefully closed with more chaff-tempered clay. The final closing was done by applying three oval sheets of highly refined clay around the mouth of the sagger. This container was kept in a kiln for firing. A bed of coarse terracotta rings arranged in small pieces, was laid over the grid, separating the bottom of the saggars from the floor of the kiln and thus providing better air circulation. Firing was done in a reducing atmosphere (Vidale 1990). Shneider (1984) suggested that these objects were formed in moulds and fired at temperatures between 1000° and 1100°C.

However, experiments conducted by Kenoyer (1994) at Harappa have demonstrated the employment of a much better technique which is perhaps more economical. According to Kenoyer's experiment, clay cylinders were first thrown on a fast wheel. These cylinders were segmented with pointed tools which resulted in bangle blanks. They were then trimmed with a stone blade and removed using a cord. Once removed, the bangle was placed around a dry clay pillar on a wheel. Final trimming of bangles with a stone blade was followed by burnishing of the exterior possibly with an agate bead/pebble. The interior of the bangle was also burnished using the same material. Firing of these bangles was done in reducing atmosphere using a system of double closed containers coated with chaff-tempered clay. The bangles thus produced had identical colour. The significance of this kind of study is that it gives an insight into the type of kilns that may have been used as well as the firing procedures.

Terracotta Object Production Technology

In addition to the above, a number of terracotta objects have been recovered from archaeological excavations. Their production is more or less similar to that of pottery, both in the treatment given to the raw material and firing. The main difference probably lies in the shaping of the objects, some of which were made using moulds. Some complex forms such as human and animal figurines and toy-cart frames may have been made in pieces and later luted together. Trimming of the surface to make it even was also practised.

Faience Technology

With regard to the production of faience, it appears that a multiple step grinding and fritting process of manufacture was used to make the finely ground uniform blue green and other coloured bodies. It is also observed that Harappan faience is denser and stronger than its contemporary faience from Mesopotamia and Egypt (McCarthy and Vandiver 1991). The glassy matrix and external glaze of these objects were achieved using the efflorescence technique, where an object is made from quartz paste containing pigments and double salts. The surface of the objects developed glaze when fired between 800° and 1200° C.

METAL TECHNOLOGY

The tradition of using metals in the subcontinent for various purposes has been indicated by the large number of metal objects recovered from different settlements through archaeological excavations. The first metal that appears to have been used by the pre-urban (pre-Harappan) communities is copper, the earliest evidence of metal objects coming from Mehrgarh II A around the beginning of the fourth millennium BC. This find includes a copper ring, a bead and a small ingot. According to Jarrige (1984), however, metallurgy was a limited activity during this phase at Mehrgarh.

With the establishment of urban centres during the Harappan period, along with increased social complexity, development of redistribution systems, advanced levels of technology and fine workmanship in the Indus and Saraswati basins, a variety of metal objects produced through different technologies appear. These can be broadly grouped into tools, weapons, utensils, ornaments and art objects of religious and cultural significance. Besides copper, the other metals known to the Harappan people include gold, silver, lead, tin and nickel.

Gold

Gold was essentially used for making ornaments. These include beads, armlets, brooches, pendants and also ornaments used on head-dresses and clothes. Lal has analyzed two gold pendants from Lothal (Lal 1985: 665), one of these being yellow and the other light yellow in colour. The former had a composition of 66.65% gold and 33.45% silver, while the latter contained 58.52% gold and 41.48% silver. Lal identifies this as electrum (an alloy of gold and silver), as the proportion of the latter metal ranges from 30% to 40%. Chemists, who have analyzed these objects, do not seem to believe in the alluvial origin of the metal. The absence of lead is considered to rule out the possibility of deliberate alloying of silver with gold. Instead, the use of native electrum for preparing these pendants is proposed (Lal 1985: 665).

Attempts have been made to postulate contacts with south India, based on the occurrence of steatite disc beads and carnelian beads characteristic of the Harappan settlements in the Neolithic sites near the gold mining area of Kolar. Hegde (1991), however, points out that in the early stages of our history, gold was generally obtained from placer deposits in alluvial formations. As gold has a high specific gravity of 19.3, it is deposited by rivers near the junction of hills and plains. The gold dust acquired from these deposits is concentrated and then melted in small crucibles at a temperature of 1065° C. The molten metal is then allowed to cool down and beaten to form sheets. A variety of ornaments were produced from these metal sheets.

Silver

Silver was also used for making ornaments by embossing it on conch shells. Marshall (1931) states that silver objects were more common than gold objects at Mohenjo-daro in contrast to Mesopotamia or Egypt where silver finds are rare. Besides ornaments, a variety of vessels were also made using silver. The source of silver is unknown; however, Hamid (Marshall 1931) has suggested that most of the silver was extracted from galena.

Copper

Copper was the main metal used by the Harappans. It was alloyed for better fusibility, strength, hardness and also for complicated casting. Although many attempts have been made to study the Harappan technology of extracting, alloying and fabricating copper artefacts (Sana Ullah 1931,

Lal 1962–63, Agrawal 1971 and 1984, Lal 1979 and 1985, Seshadri 1994), much more work needs to be done. Sana Ullah (Marshal 1931) has identified crude copper, refined copper, arsenial bronze and tin bronze at Mohenjo-daro. Agrawal (1984) states that almost 70% of the analyzed copper artefacts from the Harappan sites indicate no alloying. Marshall (1931) has reported oxide ore from the DK area of Mohenjo-daro. Similarly, small fragments of chrysocolla and chalcopyrite have been recovered from Harappa (Dales and Kenoyer 1990). From the chemical composition of finished objects, Agrawal (1971) suggests that native copper and oxide ores were used at Harappa and Mohenjo-daro for making objects. He also mentions the use of sulphide ores by the Harappans (Agrawal 1984). Nevertheless, questions regarding the source of Harappan copper are still unanswered. It is also not clear whether the Harappans themselves were involved in the mining activity or they brought ores or refined metals to their settlements to make different artefacts.

If one assumes that the ore deposit exploited by the Harappans should be within reasonable geographical proximity to their settlements where evidences of cultural interactions are seen, four major areas come under consideration. These source areas are Baluchistan (Shah Ballaul, Rohat, Raskuk and the Kojak Amran range), Afghanistan (Kalihzeri and Shah Maksud), the inland mountain ranges of modern Oman and the Aravalli ranges. Sana Ullah (Vats 1974: 379) states that the Baluchistan copper ores contain lead, arsenic and nickel whereas in Afghanistan the copper veins contain nickel and arsenic. Connections between Oman and the Indus region are evident from the presence of Harappan artefacts in Oman (Cleuziou 1984). The copper deposits in the Aravalli ranges have been studied by Agrawal (1971), Hegde and Ericson (1985) and Rao (1985). The presence of zinc, manganese, iron, lead, nickel, bismuth and arsenic has been observed in these deposits.

The presence of a few Harappan artefacts has been recorded from sites in Baluchistan and Afghanistan. However, due to the lack of detailed analytical reports one cannot presume that these mining areas were used by the Harappan people or by those people who supplied the raw material or metal to them. The earliest evidence of copper smelting is reported from the Aravalli Range by Hegde and Ericson (1985), but linking the authorship of this smelting operation to any cultural group becomes difficult as the aforesaid report contains no description of the associated archaeological assemblage or any chronometric date. Nevertheless, Hegde and Ericson (1985) tend to believe that it belongs to the third millennium BC. Agrawal

(1984) cites that the antiquity of Khetri workings has been traced to the Mauryan times which is supported by a radiocarbon date (TF-1117, 360± 105 BC) for the Dariba mines. There is also evidence of mine exploitation in Rajasthan during the Early Historic period. Two radiocarbon dates from timbers of ancient zinc mines at Zawar Mala—2120± 60 BP (from a haulage scaffold) and 1920± 50 BP (from a launder) (Craddock et al.1983)—confirm the existence of mining activity in this region during the Early Historic period.

Many Harappan sites in Gujarat have yielded a considerable number of copper objects. Of these, two celts along with a chisel (Nagwada—Harappan); five bangles and one pendant (Kuntasi—Harappan); a bangle (Pithad—Late Harappan) and one axe (Somnath—Late Harappan) have been analyzed by Seshadri (1994: 89). Many copper objects from Rangpur and Lothal have also been analyzed by Lal (in Rao 1963 and Rao 1985). The presence of arsenic was noticed in the celts from Nagwada, one bangle from Kuntasi, the bangle from Pithad, the axe from Somnath, and one celt and one bangle from Rangpur (Seshadri 1984: 89, Lal in Rao 1963: 153). Arsenic is not reported from any of the objects from Lothal (Lal 1985: 654–60). Tin was present in a few samples from Lothal, many samples from Rangpur, two samples from Nagwada, all samples from Kuntasi, one from Pithad and one from Somnath. Of the above-mentioned objects, only one contained a significant amount of arsenic (one axe from Nagwada having 2.72%). The rest of the objects have less than 1% arsenic. The presence of tin in these samples varies from 0.6% to 22.57%. At this point, it should be noted that the amount of tin in these samples (except for six samples) does not fall in the optimum range required for calling it a proper alloy. A question, therefore, arises while interpreting these analytical results in terms of alloying. Can one attribute these variations of composition to the craftsman's incomplete knowledge of metallurgy or could it be a result of recycling processes? During an ethnographic study Lahiri (1995) has observed that such compositional variations, especially in alloys, can occur as a result of recycling. This is significant as one cannot rule out the fact that copper was one of the most precious metals for the Harappans; and the stages involved in extracting it beginning with the procurement of raw material were complex. Hence the chances of recycling of the metal objects during the Harappan period cannot be dismissed. Most of the evidences of metal working at excavated sites appear to be related to melting. Along with the melting of pure metal some amount of recycling also could have taken place.

It is these drastic compositional variations of different elements in the metal objects and the absence of trace elements from various ore sources that have made it difficult for archaeologists to pinpoint the source of copper. Although the Khetri ore belts have a close geographical proximity to many Harappan sites, further detailed exploration in this area along with trace element analysis is required to ascertain whether this ore source was exploited by the Harappans.

Although a number of Harappan sites have been subjected to detailed investigations, not much evidence is available to reconstruct the metal technology right from its first stage. The evidence needed to establish metal working in any settlement is in the form of crushed ore pieces, furnaces for smelting, smelting slag and other accessory materials such as moulds, hammers, stakes, melting crucibles, anvils, etc. Besides this, a processing centre would also yield unfinished, partly finished and finished metal objects along with the industrial waste. It may not be possible to get all this evidence at one site, but at least some indicators of metal processing would enable one to derive information on its processing. Plano-convex, disc-shaped ingots have been reported from Mohenjo-daro (Marshall 1931, Mackay 1938), Chanhu-daro (Mackay 1943) and Lothal (Rao 1979). The presence of these ingots when coupled with the absence of smelting indicators supports the view that the metal was imported to the Harappan sites in its ingot form and there are crucibles indicating the process of melting from Mohenjo-daro (Sana Ullah in Marshall 1931: 485), Harappa (Vats 1940: 471), Lothal (Lal in Rao 1985: 661) and Dholavira (Bisht 1997: personal communication). Vats has mentioned that the contents of the crucible from Harappa indicate bronze melting, whereas the same from Mohenjo-daro, according to Sana Ullah, is for the remelting of crude copper for refining. Lal has not reported any traces of copper or slag from the crucible at Lothal and the crucibles from Dholavira are yet to be analyzed. We also have examples of certain kilns that have been attributed to copper metallurgy by the excavators from Mohenjo-daro (Mackay 1938: 49–50, 452), Harappa (Vats 1940: 470–73) and Lothal (Rao 1979: 522); however, further research is required to confirm whether these kilns were used for copper processing.

Agrawal mentions that the axes and other flat objects obtained from the Harappan sites indicate the use of open flat moulds for casting (Agrawal 1984). Although open stone moulds have been reported from some Harappan sites, their descriptions are not satisfactory enough to call them moulds used for metal casting. An observation made during an ethnographic field survey in a coppersmith's workshop at Dariawad in Rajasthan (along with K.K. Bhan and Nikita Mehta 1996) suggests that sand moulds could have been used for casting flat metal objects; however, such sand moulds are broken immediately after the process and they tend to be easily destroyed by natural agencies. Agrawal (1984) also suggests that those objects having thin flat sections could have been chiselled out from sheets of copper. Metallographic studies have revealed that cold hammering was done to increase the hardness of an artefact and further the defects encountered during excess cold hammering were overcome by annealing. The vessel forms were shaped either by beating the metal sheet from inside into a depression or by beating it externally on a dome-shaped wooden anvil or by both. These processes have been termed as *sinking* and *raising*. In our aforesaid ethnographic survey (along with K.K. Bhan and Nikita Mehta 1996), we have noticed that a similar technique is being employed by the coppersmiths of Dariawad in making metallic crucibles. The metal sheet was kept on the ring portion of an iron anvil and beaten into the depression. Agrawal (1984) suggests that lapping, pouring molten bronze over cleaned parts and rivetting were probably the techniques used by the Harappans for joining. Finally, not much is known about the finishing of copper, as the tendency of copper to undergo corrosion invariably erases the evidence of finishing.

From the foregoing studies it would appear that the Harappans possessed a good working knowledge of metallurgy. Although a lot of effort has been put into the investigation of their metallurgy, we are still faced with many questions. Most of these pertain to the sources of raw material, various stages of processing and the mechanisms that had spread knowledge of metal working among the Harappan sites. It may be possible to infer certain stages of production through a series of experiments followed by scientific analyses. This may help us to understand how each process is reflected in the product or the waste resulting from its manufacture.

STUDIES ON OTHER MATERIALS

In addition to the above, studies on other materials such as lithics, shells, steatite, etc. have been carried out and these have given some insights into the technological and socio-cultural processes of the Harappans.

Lithic Technology

The lithic repertoire of the Harappans included blades and flakes, which formed the components of cutting tools, drills and stones used in lapidary, stone weights and stone blocks used in building activities. The lithic industries have also played a major role in other craft activities of the Harappan people such as wood-working, shell-working, ceramic production and metallurgy. Polished, dressed and undressed stones were employed as building materials in some of the urban centres of the Harappan period. Detailed studies have been undertaken to investigate the bead manufacturing processes of the Harappan period, using ethnographic models (Kenoyer et al.1991, Kenoyer et al.1994). Kenoyer and others believe that the indirect percussion technique observed at Cambay, where they carried out their ethnographic experiments, was probably used for initial chipping while the final chipping was carried out using the punch technique during the Harappan times for the manufacture of beads. Attempts have also been carried out to study the lithic tool technology of the Harappans (Pelegrin 1994). This study has indicated that the Harappan flint knappers employed traditional techniques in the manufacture and retouch of tools. These techniques date back to at least the Neolithic period. Recent excavations at Datrana, Gujarat have yielded a copper punch, which was probably used by the Harappan stone-knappers (Ajithprasad 1995: personal communication). However, no systematic study has been carried out on the quarrying, dressing and polishing of the stone blocks used as building materials and ornamental pillars. This is an area which requires attention in future research.

Shell Technology

The shell objects produced by the Harappans included bangles, beads, pendants, inlays and ladles (Bhan and Kenoyer 1984). The Harappans selected several shell species, namely *Turbinella pyrum*, *Chicoreus ramosus*, *Fasciolaria trapezium*, *Lambis truncata*, *Tivela damaoids*, etc. for working (Bhan et al.1994). Three distinct areas were apparently used for procuring the shell raw materials, namely, the western coast (Karachi and Makran region), the eastern coast (Gulf of Kutch and Gulf of Khambat) and the coast of Oman. Bhan and others (1994) also cite the hypothesis of Kenoyer, in which he postulates the existence of " a complex hierarchy of interaction spheres and trade systems within the greater Indus Valley region". This hypothesis was formulated on the basis of the distribution of different species originating from these source areas and the nature of shell manufacturing indicators at specific Harappan sites. This kind of integrated work has given an insight into the factors that contributed to the formation of settlements in different geographical areas and organizational aspects of the craft.

Steatite Technology

The Harappans also had the infrastructure to use talcose steatite or soapstone for making different materials. These soft rocks are common in the metamorphic formations in Baluchistan, the Aravalli range and the Deccan plateau. This material was used for producing beads, pendants, inlay, inscribed seals and tablets, amulets and even sculptures. Not many studies have been carried out on the technology of steatite materials. From the analysis of steatite micro-beads from Zekhda (Hegde et al.1982) it appears that the steatite materials were probably baked at 900° to 1000° C to make them hard. From his preliminary examination of the specimens from Mehrgarh and Nausharo Vidale (1989) suggests a manufacturing cycle for steatite beads. This involved the preparation of long cylindrical blanks, their partial smoothening and perforation. These cylindrical blanks would have been cut into different beads. As there are different types and sizes of steatite beads, the study of their manufacture can be one of the interesting areas for future researchers.

In the above pages studies on the technological processes concerning in the manufacture of selected items by the Harappan people have been reviewed. Although items like agriculture, irrigation, transportation, architecture, domestication of animals, etc. fall under the broad category of technology, it is not possible to cover all these aspects in one article.

The existing studies in technology are generally confined to identifying different stages of manufacture of specific products. Very few attempts have been made to view the impact of technology on the cultural milieu. This kind of correlation is possible only when information from social anthropology, economic anthropology, cultural anthropology and ethnography are properly integrated. Socio-cultural phenomena such as trade, migration and invasion can be interpreted only through this integrated effort.

REFERENCES

Agrawal, D.P. 1971. *The Copper Bronze Age in India*. New Delhi: Munshiram Manoharlal Publishers.

—1984. Metal Technology of the Harappans, in *Frontiers of the Indus Civilization*, B.B. Lal and S.P. Gupta, eds. New Delhi: Books & Books, pp. 163–67.

Allchin, B., and Allchin, F.R. 1968. *The Birth of Indian Civilization*. New Delhi: Penguin Books.

Bhan, K.K., and Kenoyer, J.M. 1984. Nageswar: A Mature Harappan Shell Working Site on the Gulf of Kutch. *Journal of the Oriental Institute* 34 (1–2): 67–80.

Bhan, K.K., Vidale, M., and Kenoyer., J.M. 1994. Harappan Technology: Theoretical and Methodological Issues. *Man and Environment* 19 (1-2): 141–57.

Bisht, R.S. 1984. Structural Remains and Town Planning of Banawali, in *Frontiers of the Indus Civilization,* B.B. Lal and S.P. Gupta, eds. New Delhi: Books & Books, pp. 89–124.

Blackman, J.M., and Vidale, M. 1993. The Production and Distribution of Stoneware Bangles at Mohenjo-daro and Harappa as Monitored by Characterization Studies, in *South Asian Archaeology 1989*, C. Jarrige, ed. Madison: Prehistory Press, pp. 37–44.

Chandler, G.M. 1994. Petrographic Analysis of Some Early Harappan Ceramics from Bugti Region, Baluchistan, in *South Asian Archaeology 1993*, A. Parpola and P. Koskikallio, ed. Helsinki: Suomalainen Tiedeakatemia, pp. 147–55.

Cleuziou, S. 1984. Oman Peninsula and its Relations Eastwards During the Third Millennium, in *Frontiers of the Indus Civilization,* B.B. Lal and S.P. Gupta, eds. New Delhi: Books & Books, pp. 371–94.

Courty, M.A., and Roux, V. 1995. Identification of Wheel Throwing on the Basis of Ceramic Surface Features and Microfabrics. *Journal of Archaeological Science* 22: 17–50.

Craddock, P.T., Gurjar, L.K., and Hegde, K.T.M. 1983. Zinc Production in Medieval India. *World Archaeology* 15 (2): 211–17.

Dales, G.F. 1974. Excavation at Balakot, Pakistan. *Journal of Field Archaeology* 1 (1-2): 3–22.

Dales, G.F. and J.M. Kenoyer. 1990. Excavation at Harappa—1988. *Pakistan Archaeology* 24: 68–176.

Dimri, Kiran. 1994. Ceramic Variability at Vagad With Special Emphasis to Micaceous Red Ware—A Petrographic Approach. M.A. Dissertation, Unpublished. Vadodara: M.S. University of Baroda.

Halim, A., and Vidale, M. 1984. Kilns, Bangles and Coated Vessels: Ceramic Production in Closed Containers at Mohenjo-daro, in *Interim Reports,* vol. 2, M. Jansen and G. Urban, eds. Aachen: IsMEO/RWTH, pp. 63–67.

Hegde, K.T.M. 1991. An Ancient Affair. *The India Magazine—Her People and Culture* 12 (December): 166–67.

Hegde, K.T.M., Karanth, R.V., and Sychanthavong, S.P. 1982. On the Composition and Technology of Harappan Microbeads, in *Harappan Civilization: A Contemporary Perspective,* G.L: Possehl, ed., New Delhi: Oxford & IBH Publishing Co., pp. 239–44.

Hegde, K.T.M., and Ericson, J.E. 1985. Ancient Indian Copper Smelting Furnaces, in *Furnaces and Smelting Technology in Antiquity*, P.T. Craddock and M.J. Hughes, eds. British Museum Occasional Papers no. 48. London: British Museum Research Laboratory, pp. 59–70.

Hegde, K.T.M., Bhan, K.K., Sonawane, V.H., Krishnan, K., and Shah, D.R. 1990. *Excavation at Nageswar, Gujarat: A Harappan Shell Working Site on the Gulf of Kutch.* Maharaja Sayajirao University Archaeology Series no. 18. Vadodara: M.S. University of Baroda.

Herman, C.F., and Krishnan, K. 1994. Micaceous Red Ware: A Gujarat Proto-Historic Cultural Complex or just Ceramics? in *South Asian Archaeology 1993,* vol. 1, A. Parpola and P. Koskikallio, eds. Helsinki: Suomalainen Tiedeakatemia, pp. 225–43.

Jarrige, J.F. 1984. Towns and Villages of Hills and Plain, in *Frontiers of the Indus Civilization*, B.B. Lal and S.P. Gupta, eds. New Delhi: Books & Books, pp. 289–300.

Joshi, J.P. 1972. Exploration in Kutch and Excavation at Surkotada and New Light on Harappan Migration. *Journal of the Oriental Institute of Baroda* 22: 98–144.

Kenoyer, J.M. 1994. Experimental Studies of the Indus Valley Technology at Harappa, in *South Asian Archaeology 1993*, vol. 1, A. Parpola and P. Koskikallio, eds. Helsinki: Suomalainen Tiedeakatemia, pp. 345–62.

Kenoyer, J.M., Vidale, M., and Bhan, K.K. 1991. Contemporary Stone Bead Making in Khambhat, India: Patterns of Craft Specialization and Organization of Production as Reflected in the Archaeological Record. *World Archaeology* 23 (1): 44–63.

—1994. Carnelian Bead Production in Khambat, India: An Ethnoarchaeological Study in *Living Traditions: Studies in Ethnoarchaeology of South Asia*, B. Allchin, ed. New Delhi: Oxford & IBH Publishing Co., pp. 281–306.

Krishnan, K. 1986. Chemical and Petrological Studies in Ancient Indian Pottery. Ph. D. thesis, Vadodara: M.S. University of Baroda.

—1992. An Analysis of Decorative Pigments and Slips on Harappan Pottery from Gujarat. *South Asian Studies* 8: 125–32.

—1997. Scientific Analysis of Pottery and Their Cultural Implications, in *Ancient Ceramics: Historical Enquiries and Scientific Approaches*, P.C. Pant and V. Jayaswal, eds. New Delhi: Agam Kala Prakashan, pp. 177–96.

Krishnan, K. (in press) Thin-section Analysis of Some Harappan Pottery from Gujarat, in *Proceedings of the Seminar on Gujarat Harappans 1993*, G.L. Possehl and V. Shinde, eds. Pune: Deccan College.

Krishnan, K., and Hegde, K.T.M. 1988. Chemical and Petrographic Studies in Pottery of Harappa Culture in Gujarat. *Journal of the M.S. University of Baroda (Humanities)* 35–36, 1 (1986–87): 27–56.

Krishnan, K., and Rao, Veena. 1994. A Study of Clay Paste Preparation Through Textural Analysis. *South Asian Studies* 10: 113–17.

Krishnan, K., and Freestone, I.C. (in press) Technology of the "Glazed" Reserved Slip Ware.

Lal, B.B. 1985. Report on Pottery from Lothal, in *Lothal: A Harappan Port Town (1955–62)* vol. 2, S.R. Rao, ed. New Delhi: Archaeological Survey of India, pp. 461–74.

—1985. Report on the Chemical Analysis and Examination of Metallic and Other Objects from Lothal, in *Lothal: A Harappan Port Town (1955–62)*, vol. 2, S.R. Rao, ed. New Delhi: Archaeological Survey of India, pp. 651–66.

Lahiri, N. 1995. Indian Metal and Metal-Related Artefacts as Cultural Signifiers: an Ethnographic Perspective. *World Archaeology* 27 (1): 116–32.

Mackay, E.J.H. 1937. *Further Excavations at Mohenjo-daro*, vol. I, New Delhi: Government of India, reprint, 1998, New Delhi: Munshiram Manoharlal Publishers.

Mackay, E.J.H. 1938. *Further Excavations at Mohenjo-daro*, vol. II, New Delhi: Government of India, reprint, 1998, New Delhi: Munshiram Manoharlal Publishers.

Mackay, E.J.H. 1943. *Chanhu-daro Excavations 1935–36*, New Haven: American Oriental Society.

Marshall, J. 1931. *Mohenjo-daro and the Indus Civilization*, vols. I, II and III. London: Arthur Probsthain.

McCarthy, B., and Vandiver, P. 1991. Ancient High Strength Ceramics: Fritted Faience Bracelet Manufacture at Harappa (Pakistan), ca. 2300–1800 BC, in *Material Issues in Art and Archaeology* vol. 2, P.B. Vandiver, J. Druzik and G.S. Wheeler, eds. Pittsburgh: Material Research Society, pp. 495–510.

Mery, S. 1994. Excavation of an Indus Potter's Workshop at Nausharo (Baluchistan), Period II. in *South Asian Archaeology 1993,* vol. 2, A. Parpola and P. Koskikallio, eds. Helsinki: Suomalainen Tiedeakatemia, pp. 471–82.

Pelegrin, J. 1994. Lithic Technology in Harappan Times, in *South Asian Archaeology 1993* vol. 2, A. Parpola and P. Koskikallio, eds. Helsinki: Suomalainen Tiedeakatemia, pp. 587–98.

Panjwani, P.A. 1989. Petrography of Harappan Pottery from Lothal. *Man and Environment* 13: 83–86.

Rao, S.R. 1963. Excavation at Rangpur and Other Explorations in Gujarat. *Ancient India* 18–19: 5–207.

—1979. *Lothal: a Harappan Port Town (1955–62),* vol. 1, New Delhi: Archaeological Survey of India.

—1985. *Lothal: a Harappan Port Town (1955–62),* vol. 2, New Delhi: Archaeological Survey of India.

Rao, Veena. 1991. Harappan Pottery Manufacture: A Preliminary Ethnographic Investigation. M.A. Dissertation. Vadodara: M.S. University of Baroda.

Roux, V. 1994. The Wheel Throwing Technique: Definition and Identification on the Basis of Ceramic Surface Features. *Man and Environment* 19(1–2): 275–84.

Schneider, G. 1984. Chemical Analysis of Stone Ware Bangles and Related Materials from Mohenjo-daro, in *Interim Reports* vol. 2, M. Jansen and G. Urban eds. Rome: IsMEO/ Aachen: RWTH, pp. 73–78.

Seshadri, Rajam. 1994. The Metal Technology of the Harappans and the Copper Hoard Culture—A Comparative Study. Ph.D. thesis. Vadodara: M.S. University of Baroda.

Shah, Kajal. 1994. Textural Differences in Ceramic Thin-Sections and Their Relationship with Technology. M.A. Dissertation. Vadodara: M.S. University of Baroda.

Shinde, V.S., and Kar, S.B. 1992. "Padri Ware": A New Painted Ceramic Found in the Harappan Levels at Padri in Gujarat. *Man and Environment* 17 (2): 105–10.

Sonawane, V.H., and Ajithprasad, P. 1994. Harappa Culture and Gujarat. *Man and Environment* 19 (1–2): 129–39.

Soundara Rajan, K.V. 1962. Community Movement in Protohistoric India—An Archaeological Perspective. *Journal of Oriental Institute* 12 (1): 74–75.

Starr, R.F.S. 1941. *Indus Valley Painted Pottery.* Princeton: Princeton University Press.

Vandiver, P.B. 1995-96. The Production Technology of Early Pottery at Mehrgarh, in *Mehrgarh Field Reports 1974–1985—From Neolithic Times to the Indus Civilization,* C. Jarrige, J.F. Jarrige, R.H. Meadow and G. Quivron, eds., The Department of Culture and Tourism, Government of Sindh, Pakistan. pp. 648–61.

Vats, M.S. 1998. *Excavation at Harappa,* 2 vols., reprint, New Delhi: Munshiram Manoharlal Publishers.

Vidale, M. 1989. Early Harappan Steatite, Faience and Paste Beads in a Necklace from Mehrgarh-Nausharo (Pakistan). *East and West* 39 (1–4): 291–300.

—1990. Stoneware Industry of the Indus Civilization: An Evolutionary Dead-End in the History of Ceramic Technology, in *Ceramics and Civilization,* D. Kingery, ed. Westerville, Ohio: American Ceramic Society, pp. 231–54.

16 ❖ Human Skeletal Biology: Scope, Development and Present Status of Research in India

S.R. WALIMBE and A. TAVARES

ORIGIN AND SCOPE OF HUMAN SKELETAL BIOLOGY

ANTHROPOLOGY, the science of man, was established as a scientific discipline in the early sixteenth and seventeenth centuries. Physical anthropology, a sub-discipline of anthropology, in its early stages, was considered to be primarily a technique concerned with the study of humankind, its origin, evolution and place in the animal kingdom. During the search for our ancestors, many fossil remains were discovered which led to the development of various schools of thought, each advocating its own hypothesis as to who our direct ancestors were. Mere analytical descriptions, classifications and metric comparisons of the fossils were not enough, however, to understand the events and processes of human evolution. With the development of new investigative tools and techniques, during the last few decades, significant additions were made to the scientific knowledge, and, palaeoanthropology, the study of primate and human development, as an interdisciplinary science was born.

Palaeoanthropologists studied the fossil record with a view to ascertaining and establishing human antiquity and tracing the evolutionary progress from the time we first diverged from the apes, our close relatives. This exercise necessitated development in many of the techniques employed to map the features of the then contemporary humans and the past ancestors. Among the anthropologists, dealing with skeletal and living human groups, questions were raised about the genetic, ecological and technological components in influencing the diversity existing among our species, *Homo sapiens*. This led to a whole generation of publications on comparative studies about extinct and extant humans. The traditional physical anthropologists studied extant human groups and attempted to classify them on the basis of their phenotypic features like skin colour, hair colour, hair texture and various other bodily characteristics. Those working on skeletal populations tried to classify their study sample on the basis of phenotypic variations, i.e., physical characterizations like face or head shape, e.g. whether they were dolichocephalic (long headed) or brachycephalic (broad headed). Unfortunately, the comparative studies which dealt with living populations gave rise to a host of racial ideas, particularly employed during World War II. The usage of the term 'race' for social or economic discrimination aroused anti-Semitic feelings, most notably during the War. To discourage this sort of thinking and put an end to comparative studies being used for such ends, in 1951 the UNESCO re-evaluated the concept of race on a scientific footing (UNESCO 1952) and stated that the present human population belongs to one species, *Homo sapiens sapiens*, despite the differences that are viewed macroscopically. However, though the UNESCO made serious efforts to suppress the concept of 'racism' (i.e., establishing superiority of one race over the other), identification of "racial element" continued to be the focus of attention in anthropological research for at least three decades thereafter.

In the archaeological context 'racial' similarities or differences in two skeletal populations were used to emphasize either cultural contact or changes in the material culture. Such examples are found in the Indian context also (Sewell and Guha 1931; Guha and Basu 1938). This was the trend of the early twentieth century when theories of invasion, migration and 'mixing of blood' were the answers to diversity or 'discrepancies' noted in the skeletal record. In other words, anthropological research was guided by archaeological needs and the anthropological evidence was used primarily to complement archaeological hypotheses of cultural migration or diffusion.

Nevertheless, the skeletal variations were gradually regarded as the net result of a highly complex process of genetic and non-genetic factors. This conceptual change necessitated reevaluation of the skeletal data and the earlier hypotheses needed to be reframed. These fresh studies led to a better understanding of the ability of the humans to adapt to new environments by adopting appropriate cultural strategies and responding biologically within the plausible phenotypic range, as determined by genotype.

The earlier approach, which was descriptive and limited to racial classification, was inadequate to deal with the questions related to human adaptation. The techniques employed for racial categorization continued, with better standardization, but these no longer constituted a mere appendix to the archaeological reports. Skeletal remains were looked not as isolated pieces of evidence, but by placing the skeletal material into an assigned cultural context, anthropologists could trace the evolutionary routes of the human form in time and also establish the movement of populations from different areas with improvements in technology.

Skeletal biology has thus come a long way from the mere descriptive and classificatory analysis of dry bones to a stage where the dead can speak volumes. Today, anthropologists involved in the study of archaeological populations are referred to as not just "physical anthropologists" but as "skeletal biologists". The recent literature refers to this science as "osteobiography" (derived from the Greek *osteon* = bone, Greek *bios* = life, mode of life, Greek *graphia* from *graphein* = to write), meaning a study of skeletons to extract information on the life histories of their occupants. In osteobiographic analysis an attempt is made to answer five basic questions: "who was there?", "how did they look like?" "where did they come from?" (originally and over time), "what happened to them?", and "what can be said about their way of life?". Skeletal evidence employing such a processual approach could be used effectively in archaeology to understand *why, where, when* and *how* of changes in ancient lifeways.

The story of biological evolution of man in the Indian sub-continent and its relevance to the understanding of the cultural evolutionary process must be evaluated in this perspective.

THE PREHISTORIC SKELETAL RECORD IN THE INDIAN SUBCONTINENT

While the fossil record to trace the evolutionary routes of *Homo sapiens* is scanty, the Indian subcontinent provides an excellent spectrum of human skeletal evidence covering the last 20,000 years.

Research on the ancient human skeletal remains was, however, negligible in India till the 1950s. The discoveries of human skeletons figured merely as appendices to the main reports of the sites excavated. Though more attention is being paid now to this evidence, conditions are far from satisfactory even today. Excavation reports for more than 300 sites record recovery of human burials (Kennedy and Caldwell 1984). However, detailed anthropological reports are available only for about 40 skeletal series. Evidence recovered from other sites is either lost for ever or still awaits careful anthropological scrutiny.

The reasons for overlooking human skeletal evidence are many. The general lack of awareness regarding the research potential of the data on the part of excavators was, and continues to be, one of the major reasons for the slow progress of the discipline in India. While the archaeological evidence of burials was always sought for, since physical anthropologists were very rarely involved in actual excavations, no adequate post-excavation care was rendered to the bones. In many cases fragmentary bones were often overlooked or not meticulously collected in the field. Many of the excavators never bothered to have their collections studied by the experts. Research orientations in the subject of anthropology itself are also largely responsible for this unfortunate situation. The principal research focus and training facilities in physical anthropology remained primarily confined to analyses and comparisons of bodily features (like somatoscopy, somatometry, serology, dermatoglyphics, etc.) of the present-day populations. Even today no anthropology department in India offers adequate training in human skeletal biology. Lack of training facilities, lack of laboratory and library facilities, and, more importantly, lack of job opportunities in this branch probably resulted in restricting the discipline to just a few scholars, who find it impossible to examine the vast array of human skeletal data available in India.

Whenever the skeletal material reached the laboratories, as stated earlier, it was studied to infer their 'ethnic' or 'racial' identity. Nevertheless, there were some scholars who sought to analyze the osseous remains and interpret them in the cultural context they were discovered. Table 1 lists the major human skeletal series excavated and studied so far in the Indian subcontinent. The following review is broadly based on the sources mentioned in Table 1. Figures 1–4 and 6 give approximate locations of the sites mentioned in the text.

Table.1. **List of Major Archaeological Human Skeletal Series Excavated and Studied so far in the Indian Subcontinent**

Site	*Important Anthropological Reference(s)*
1	*2*
Early Holocene and later Mesolithic Communities	
Baghai Khor	Kennedy (1990a)
Bagor	Lukacs et al. (1982)
Bata Domba Lena	Kennedy et al. (1986a)
Bellan Bandi Palassa	Kennedy (1965); Deraniyagala and Kennedy 1972)

1	*2*
Bhimbetka	Kennedy (personal communications)
Hathnora	Sonakia (1985a/b), Kennedy et al. 1991)
Langhnaj	Ehrhardt and Kennedy (1965)
Mahadaha	Kennedy et al. (1992)
Damdama	Kennedy (Personal communications)
Sarai Nahar Rai	Kennedy et al. (1986b)
Harappan and Gandharan Grave Cultures	
Harappa	Gupta, Dutta and Basu (1962), Dutta (1984)
Kalibangan	Sharma (1970, 1972)
Lothal	Chatterjee and Kumar (1963b)
Mohenjo-Daro	Sewell and Guha (1931); Guha and Basu 1938)
Mehrgarh	Lukacs (1983, 1885); Lukacs and Hemphill (1991)
Nal	Sewell and Guha (1929)
Rupar	Dutta et al. (1987)
Sarai Khola	Bernhard (1969); Lukacs et al. (1989)
Timargarh	Bernhard (1967, 1968); Lukacs and Pastor (1988)
Neolithic-Chalcolithic Cultures	
Agripalli	Walimbe (in prep.)
Apegaon	Lukacs (1980)
Bagor	Lukacs et al. (1982)
Banahali	Walimbe (in prep.)
Brahmagiri	Sarkar (1960, 1972)
Budihal	Walimbe and Paddayya (in press)
Burzahom	Basu and Pal (1980)
Chandoli	Malhotra (1965a)
Chinnamarur	Walimbe (in prep.)
Daimabad	Walimbe (1986)
Hullikallu	Walimbe (1993a)
Ieej	Walimbe (1993b)
Inamgaon	Lukacs and Walimbe (1986)
Kaothe	Walimbe (1990)
Nagarjunakonda	Gupta, Basu and Dutta (1970)
Nevasa	Kennedy and Malhotra (19656)
Piklihal	Ayer (1960), Sarkar (1972), Malhotra (1968)
Ramapuram	Walimbe (in prep.)
Tekkalakota	Malhotra (1965b)
T. Narasipur	Malhotra (1971)
Walki	Mushrif and Walimbe (1998)

1	*2*
Megalithic-Iron Age and Early Historic Cultures	
Adittanallur	Chatterjee and Gupta (1963)
Banahalli	Walimbe (in prep.)
Bhagi Mohari	Walimbe (1988)
Brahmagiri	Sarkar (1960, 1972)
Khapa	Rao (1970)
Khairwada	Walimbe (1988)
Kodumanal	Walimbe (in prep.)
Mahurjhari	Kennedy (Personal communications), Rao (1973)
Maski	Sarkar (1972)
Nagarjunakonda	Gupta, Basu and Dutta (1970)
Naikund	Lukacs et al. (1982)
Nevasa	Kennedy and Malhotra (1966)
Padri	Walimbe and Shinde (1995)
Pomparippu	Lukacs and Kennedy (1981)
Raigir	Kennedy (1965a, 1990b)
Raipur	Walimbe (1993d)
S.Pappinayakanpatti	Walimbe and Selvakumar (1998)
Yelleswaram	Gupta and Dutta (1962), Sarkar (1972)

Specimens of Late Miocene and Uncertain Antiquity

The fossil record of the evolution of *Homo sapiens* in the Indian subcontinent is rather scanty. The earliest fossil found, thought to be closer to the *Homo* line, is that of the genus *Ramapithecus* at Haritalyangar in the Siwaliks, and is dated to around eight to twelve million years. This genus is now linked with the earlier taxon *Sivapithecus*, but controversies exist about its phyletic relations with the extant great apes and the Plio-Pleistocene hominoids (Andrew and Cronin 1982; Sankhyan 1988). This genus is primarily represented by well preserved dental remains as well as a few facial and post-cranial bones from the Potwar region.

The other important fossil in the Indian subcontinent is the skull found at Hathnora on the river Narmada, 40 km northeast of Hoshangabad, Madhya Pradesh (Sonakia 1985a). This fossil was recovered from the Pleistocene alluvium in association with stone artifacts like heavy handaxes, cleavers and scrapers. This skull is represented by completely preserved right half of the skull cap with part of the left parietal attached. No facial bone has been recovered. The individual concerned appears to have been fairly old, robust with an erect posture and a fairly well-developed brain. The general robusticity, the thick and projecting supra-orbital torus and its occipital protuberance are akin to the classic Neanderthal group, while slight sagittal keeling, widely placed mastoids and its less cranial capacity (1200 cc) bring it closer to the *Homo erectus* of Java, China, Tanzania and Kenya. Nevertheless it is often taken to be much closer to Java man (Sonakia 1985b). There are others, however, who group it under '*Archaic Homo sapiens*' on the basis of the cultural material found associated with it (Badam 1989; Badam et al. 1986). This hypothesis has been tested through comparisons with *Homo erectus* metric/morphological traits which showed that only 43% of these traits are present in the Narmada specimen. Further investigations and comparisons of each morphological trait with those of the Middle and Late Pleistocene fossils from Africa, Europe and Asia, prove that the Narmada specimen is *Homo sapiens* and not 'evolved' *Homo erectus* or "archaic" *Homo sapiens*. Moreover, these terms no longer hold any taxonomic significance in the newer trends witnessed in palaeoanthropology (Kennedy et al. 1991).

The recent discovery of the right hominid clavicle from the conglomerate bed at Hathnora (Sankhyan 1998), of an adult individual, is noteworthy because of its robust features and short length. The short and stocky hominid represented by this post-cranial element is reported to be different from African *Homo erectus* as well as from the Neanderthals and western 'archaic' *Homo sapiens*.

The fossil gap between *Ramapithecus* and the Narmada specimens is, however, much too wide to give a continuous picture of the stages in the evolution of *Homo sapiens* in India with respect to its position in the worldwide scheme of evolution.

The Mesolithic Phase

The Indian Mesolithic (10,000–7,000 BP) is characterized by microlithic tools of geometric and non-geometric shapes. Brown suggested the term Mesolithic in 1892 to define the transition period from food-gathering to food-producing societies (cited in Kennedy 1984a). The Indian Mesolithic appears to be a period of intense population expansion and cultural innovation as indicated by the varied ecological settings occupied by man—ranging from the loessic hills of Gujarat to the islands off the coast of Mumbai (Bombay), atop fossil sand dunes along the Chennai (Madras) coast, in both open air and cave habitats in the dry jungles of Sri Lanka, in the rock shelters of the Vindhyas and on the shores of the lakes of the Gangetic plains (Fig.1).

The fossil hominid remains from Batadomba Lena and Beli Lena caves

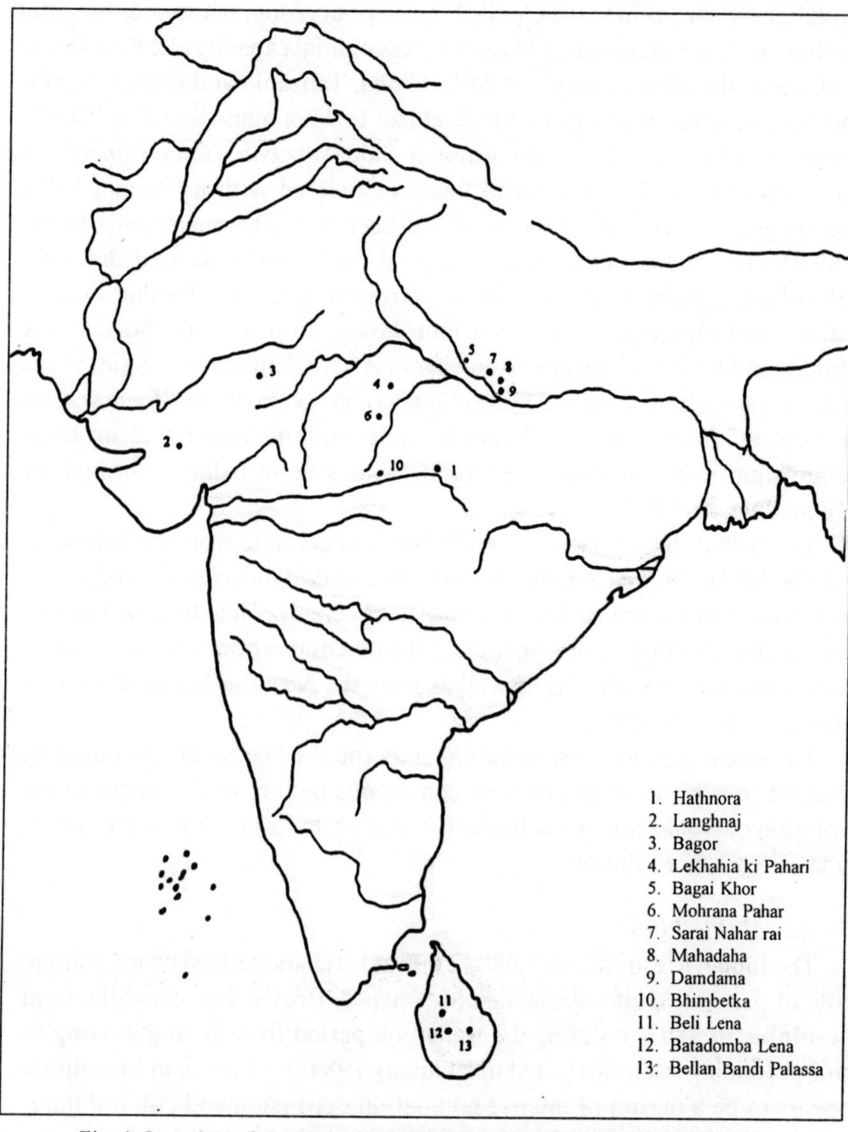

Fig. 1. Location of the Hathnora hominid fossil find and Mesolithic sites with human skeletal remains

in Sri Lanka contribute in several significant ways to a broader knowledge of human evolution in South Asia. The skeletal evidence enables us to extend the antiquity of the settlement of Sri Lanka by *Homo sapiens* to the Upper Pleistocene. The skeletal-bearing deposits from Batadomba Lena have a radiocarbon date of *c.* 16,000 years BP, while the archaeological evidence dates the occupation of the cave to *c.* 28,500 years BP. These data modified earlier views concerning the relatively recent, Holocene, migration of human populations to the island (Kennedy 1973, 1980), and support P.E.P. Deraniyagala's (1962) contention that settlement of Sri Lanka took place in the Pleistocene. Pleistocene fossils, except for the Narmada skull and some human remains in the lowermost level at Batadomba lena Cave, are by and large unknown in the Indian subcontinent.

The dating of the Beli Lena human remains to *c.* 12,000 years BP suggests relative continuity of occupation of the south-central portion of Sri Lanka from terminal to post-Pleistocene times when, around 6,500 years BP, human habitation appears at Bellan Bandi Palassa.

The Mesolithic specimens from Batadomba Lena, Beli Lena and Bellan Bandi Palassa are characterized by robust cranial and post-cranial features (Kennedy 1965b; Kennedy et al. 1986a). Considerable homogeneity is evident among them. Some of these similarities may have a genetic basis, indicating close biological affinity between the Upper Pleistocene and post-Pleistocene populations of the island. Continuity of morphometric variables within an indigenous population over a temporal span of some 10,000 years is not surprising given the geographical circumstances that Sri Lanka was an island of relative isolation until the fifth century BC, when it was settled by peoples from the Indian mainland. However, to a considerable extent, morphological similarities in these populations may be attributed to parallelisms arising within the ancient populations as a consequence of similar adaptive responses to similar ecological settings or to ontogenetic responses to similar socio-cultural conditions, or even to random effects.

The earliest reported discovery in India of human skeletons associated with the Mesolithic cultural phase was at Morahana Pahar, Uttar Pradesh (Kennedy 1980). The Mesolithic sites of Sarai Nahar Rai and Mahadaha (Pratapgarh district) on the Gangetic plains of Uttar Pradesh, give the most ancient representatives of anatomically modern *Homo sapiens* known till now from India. The radiocarbon dates associated with the specimens indicate an age of 10,000 to 12,000 years BP. The Gangetic skeletal specimens are separated by four to eight millennia from later Mesolithic specimens from Bagor (Bhilwara district, Rajastan), Lekhahia ki Pahari (Mirzapur district, Uttar Pradesh), and Langhnaj (Ahmedabad district, Gujarat) that have yielded radiocarbon focal dates of 5,800 BP, 4,290 BP, and 3,925 BP, respectively. The Sri Lankan site of Bellan Bandi Palassa has been dated to 6,500 + 700 BP on the basis of thermoluminescence of fired rock crystal that was associated with one of the skeletons.

The Sarai Nahar Rai and Mahadaha skeletons, which have been studied in the light of the recent trends in palaeoanthropology, have yielded important information concerning the course of human biological evolution in the Indian subcontinent (Kennedy et al. 1986b, 1992). These skeletons are characterized by large and muscular robust skulls, tall stature and large teeth, slowly leading to reduction in body size in later Mesolithic times. The explanation offered for these differences in populations belonging to different time periods, is the ever present evolutionary mechanism of adaptation. The successful biological adaptation of the Mesolithic populations and the exploitation of new ecological settings, which has been well documented by the archaeological record, attests to the development of fairly sophisticated socio-economic strategies well before the advent of the food-producing communities (Kennedy et al. 1986b). These trends towards decreased cranial robusticity, reduction of body and tooth size to skeletal gracility has been observed in the course of hominid evolution over a period of 10,000 years (Wolpoff 1980). These changes are due to factors like natural selection which makes the human body more adaptive to village and urban lifeways which entail increased carbohydrate intake and a decrease in protein intake. Tooth size reduction is also indicative of dietary change. The progress of dental reduction over time has been closely linked to the rate of technological development and increased efficiency of food producing techniques. The people with the smallest teeth in the world are said to be those whose remote ancestors first developed a complex technology (Brace 1978). Consequently, according to further observations, the smallest teeth appear among South Asian populations living today in the northern and northwestern portions of the subcontinent, whereas large teeth survive in Peninsular India and Sri Lanka (Kennedy 1984a). For example, the Sarai Nahar Rai skeletal population exhibits large teeth which are said to be adaptive for a pre-agricultural, pre-pastoral society, whereas the subsequent Neolithic skeletal population of the same area exhibits smaller dentition which is suited to the diet of an agricultural society. The pattern of dental variation among the present-day Indian populations is also closely correlated to differing levels of technological development, subsistence pattern and methods of food preparation (Walimbe and Kulkarni 1993).

The Harappan and Gandhara Grave Phases

The Harappan phase has an extensive human skeletal series (Fig.2) and has a well-documented record of cultural identity. The Harappan civi-

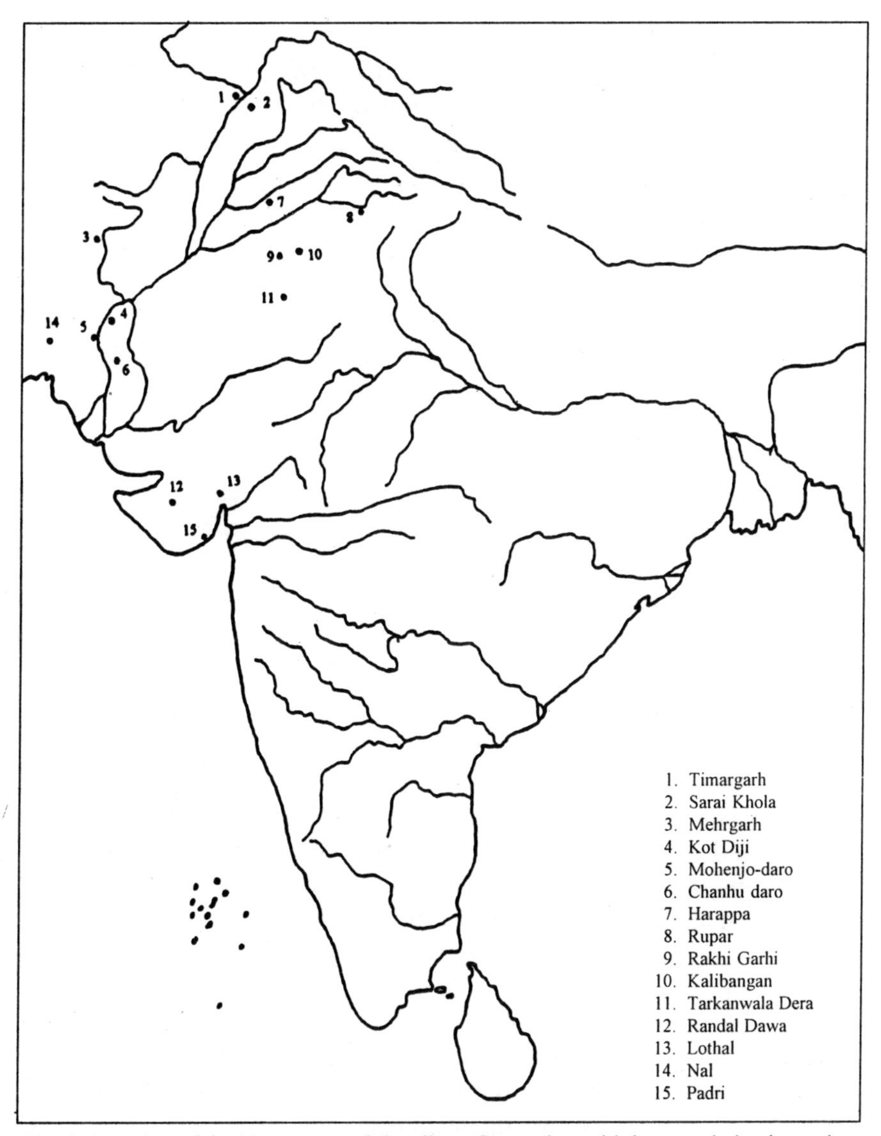

Fig. 2. Location of the Harappan and Gandhara Grave sites with human skeletal remains

lization arose towards the end of the third millennium BC in the Indus basin and flourished there for nearly a thousand years. Besides Harappa itself, there are other sites yielding human skeletal remains; some of them are located outside the confines of the Indus valley proper. These represent the Mature Harappan phase, like Rupar (Punjab), Rakhi Garhi (Haryana), Kalibangan and Tarkanwala Dera (Rajasthan), Lothal and Randal Dawa

(Gujarat), Mohenjo-daro and Chanhu-daro (Sind). This culture thus covers a wide geographical area extending from Baluchistan in the west to beyond Delhi into the interfluve in the east and from the eastern foot of the Sulaiman mountain range in the north to the Tapti estuary in the south. The Harappan culture was highly urbanized and self-sufficient; it supported a huge population which adopted a variety of occupations. They had well planned cities with public buildings, fortification walls, granaries and standardization of weights and measures. All these reflect a highly developed socio-political and religious society depending on farming and domestication of cattle as well as other animals. The public buildings and granaries signify a well ordered and disciplined society.

On the basis of certain cranial measurements it has been shown that despite the skeletal material coming from three different deposits at Harappa, the skeletons belong to a single morphologically homogeneous series, contrary to their previous classification into morphological "races" and "sub-races". The Harappan population is stated to have close affinity with the Tepe Hissar (Iran) and Sakkara (Egypt) population belonging to the same period but having diverse geographical and cultural settings (Dutta 1984). However, it should be noted that comparisons based on a limited number of measurements are not always conclusive. Certain differences do exist in facial features, and these differences though small are of immense value, specially when trying to place the Harappan population in the biological taxon. These differences would suggest that the Harappans occupied a distinct unique status. This uniqueness need not indicate that the Harappans came from elsewhere. Sites like Mehrgarh, documenting human skeletal remains which are still being analyzed, and cultural features such as ceramics of non-Harappan character found at Kot Diji, which records a pre-Harappan phase, make it clear that the Indus valley was inhabited by food producing communities before the advent of the Harappans (Lukacs, personal communications). It would seem reasonable to conclude that there might have been biological links and genetic continuities between the pre-Harappans and the Harappans, considering the uniqueness of the Harappan physique with regard to the reference population groups and the cultural sequence in this region.

Nevertheless, the Harappan archaeological record has preserved evidence of trade interaction with the people from Iran and Mesopotamia, based on items such as beads, pottery types and styles, seals, etc. (Chakrabarti 1993). Besides, interaction between the agro-based urban Harappans and the hunter-gatherers from the surrounding areas has also been documented. An example of such interaction has been reported between the contemporary Mesolithic nomadic hunter-gathers/pastoralists of Langhnaj and the technologically more developed, sedentary agriculturists at the Harappan sites of Lothal and/or Kalibangan (Lukacs and Pal 1992).

The Harappan civilization which came to an abrupt end at *c.* 1700 BC has mystified many scholars giving rise to various hypotheses, such as invasions, massacre (as at Mohenjo-daro) and even climatic changes. From the perspective of physical anthropology this problem may be considered in two ways: the claim for a "foreign" phenotypic element in the later phases of the Harappan culture and the so-called "massacre" evidence at Mohenjo-daro.

The skeletal collection recovered from the excavations at Harappa has been restudied anthropologically to assess their racial affinities and to verify the hypothesis attributing the termination of the Harappan culture to a "foreign" racial element in the mature Harappan phase (Guha and Basu 1938). The foreign racial element, i.e., people who looked slightly different from those staying at the site earlier, was obviously supposed to have represented other non-Harappan invaders (labelled as "Aryans"). The recent reinvestigation of the Harappan skeletal series concludes that the population of Harappa does not exhibit any significant phenotypic diversity over different levels of habitation and probably belongs to a single homogeneous unit (Kennedy 1982). The variation in size and form is taken to be in the acceptable range and be better understood as normal range of physical variability present in most urban populations, past and present, or, it can also be attributed to the gradual bodily adaptations to the changes in subsistence pattern and settlement style. Any heterogeneity that exists in the Harappan sample may be explained by continuous immigration of rural people to these urban centers.

The mature Harappan civilization lasted till about 1500 BC when the Indo-Aryan invaders are said to have put an end to it. The 'Massacre theory' found 'ardent' proponents in Marshall (1931), Mackay (1938), Guha and Basu (1938) and Wheeler (1960, second ed.). The post-mortem modifications were interpreted as trauma marks, as signs of massacre (Guha and Basu 1938). Further the ideas of invasion and migration of people forced the data itself to be analyzed within a given model confirming the hypothesis (of "Aryan" invasion) put forward by archaeologists based on stylistic changes observed in the pottery.

Conclusions regarding the traumatic end of the inhabitants of Mohenjo-daro had been drawn based on the disorderly disposal of the skeletons. At Mohenjo-daro the evidence of death of a group of people has been recovered. These skeletons, unlike those found in other Harappan sites, were found in the residential area or streets of this ancient city. There is no evidence of a cemetery so far found at the site. Some of these skeletons were found in contorted positions and groupings that cannot suggest anything but unceremonial burials. Many skeletons are either disarticulated or incomplete. Even at Harappa quite a few skeletons were discovered in a confused mass in a tightly packed heap lying in a narrow trench, quite unlike other regular burials. Earlier anthropologists and archaeologists suggested plague or famine as causes of death. It was also suggested that these individuals had been slain by raiders while attempting to escape from the city during a military attack by the Aryans (cited in Dales 1964: 37). Excavators, thrilled by the disorderly disposal of dead bodies and with the support of skeletal evidence, indicated that the massacre was a specific event in the Late Harappan phase at Mohenjo-daro when armed foreign invaders destroyed the city and liquidated its citizens. Several other factors, including absence of a formal mortuary area at the site, were taken as supporting evidence for this massacre and the massacre idea was immediately considered as proof of the invasion of the subcontinent by the Aryans.

Archaeological assessment of the massacre theory remained debatable for a long time. The main blow to this theory came when it was proved that these skeletons did not represent a single archaeological time frame (cited Kennedy 1984b). In other words, if at all the event had occurred, it was not the case of a single tragedy. Moreover, there was no material evidence to substantiate the supposed invasion and massacre. There was no evidence of burnt fortress, arrowheads, weapons, pieces of armour, smashed chariots and bodies of invaders and defenders. The skeletons of the 'massacred' set of persons were found in the residential area and not in the area of fortified citadel where one would reasonably expect the final defense of this thriving capital city to have been made. There is no unconditional proof of an armed conquest and destruction on the supposed scale of Aryan invasion. On the contrary, it is very clearly documented by material evidence that in their later stages, the Harappan cities had suffered a considerable decline in material prosperity (Possehl 1993). To some extent pressure from floods and climatic changes may have been responsible for this decline. If the Indo-Aryans were a factor in this last phase, their hostility could only have accelerated the end of this remarkable civilization. But in reality there remains a grave doubt whether these invaders could be connected at all with the collapse of the Harappan culture. And, most important, any conclusions about traumatic stress should rest on indisputable skeletal evidence. The skeletal material when taken up for palaeopathological restudy (Kennedy 1984b, 1994) provided fresh insights. Its critical reassessment in the light of the new methodological approaches in the field of forensic anthropology and palaeopathology very clearly indicated that all the so-called wound marks (except in one of the 24 reported cases) appear to be only erosional in origin or are cases of successful healing of lesions, unrelated to circumstances and places of burial. And the lone evidence cannot be used to prove the massacre thesis. The proposition of a traumatic end of the Harappan population (Mohenjo-daro in particular) is based essentially on archaeological evidence of disorderly disposal of the dead rather than on the skeletal evidence of trauma. If the pathological evidence does not support the massacre theory, then the problem of interpreting the disarray of skeletons becomes still more complicated. The haphazard mode of disposal of dead might have had some social implications rather than solely pathological (Walimbe 1993c).

Assessment of the biological continuum and affinities between the pre-Harappan and Harappan populations have always been a matter of prime interest to archaeologists as well as skeletal biologists. A recent study (Hemphill et al. 1991) suggests that there existed two phases of biological discontinuity within the Indus valley from the Neolithic times to the Christian era. The first is said to occur between 6000 and 4500 BC which is reflected in the strong differences irrespective of the occupational continuity between the Neolithic and Chalcolithic inhabitants of Mehrgarh. The second discontinuity exists between the inhabitants of Harappa, Chalcolithic Mehrgarh and post-Harappan Timargarha on the one hand, and the Early Iron Age (better known as the Gandhara Grave culture) inhabitants of Sarai Khola, on the other, between 800 and 200 BC.

The Gandhara Grave culture of northwest Pakistan is known mainly from the grave goods and refers to a pattern of living in the hill zones of Gandhara, Swat valley. People were equipped with bronze and iron tools and weapons. Timargarha and Sarai Khola, the two main cemetery sites of this culture, have an antiquity of 1400–850 BC and 260 BC, respectively (Bernhard 1967, 1968, 1969). Though originating in the Bronze Age and continuing into the Iron Age, the culture represents a different story and is said to be connected with movement of people having strong links with northern Iran and Central Asia (Dani 1967, 1968). It is fundamentally different from the Indus civilization and also has little relationship with the

Baluchi village culture. While the Indus civilization was rooted in the intense cultivation of the fertile soil of the main Indus valley, the Baluchi village culture grew along the land routes that connected the Indus zone with the main centers of civilization in Western Asia. Plain pottery tradition (gray and red ware), as opposed to the painted pottery of the Indus civilization, marks the introduction of a completely new tradition in Pakistan.

Skeletal remains from Sarai Khola are still being scrutinized anthropologically. Biological affinities of the Timargarha population are also not conclusively stated. It is stated that the population of Timargarha was closely connected with the southern migration of foreign people into the Indian subcontinent which began in the second millennium BC. These 'Iron Age' inhabitants of Pakistan are believed to have closer affinities with the eastern Mediterranean people than with the populations of the Indian subcontinent (Bernhard 1967: 382).

The Neolithic Phase

Contemporary with the Harappan civilization in India is the Neolithic phase which covers a wide time span from 3,000 to 1,000 BC. Sites yielding skeletal material from this cultural phase cover a wide geographic area spreading from Burzahom (Kashmir) in the north to Assam and other sites in the northeast, right up to the south at sites like Utnur, Nagarjunakonda, Palavoy, Hulikallu and Ieej in Andhra Pradesh, Tekkalakota, T.Narasipur and Budihal in Karnataka, and Paiyampalli in Tamil Nadu (Fig.3).

The site of Burzahom shows some 'non-Neolithic' features. It is devoid of a stone blade industry which is otherwise characteristic of the Neolithic sites in India. The cultural material from Burzahom consists of stone axes, ringstones, a single copper arrowhead, and a range of bone tools. The economy was primarily based on hunting and gathering. The South Indian Neolithic culture extends from around 2,500 BC to 1,000 BC. The inhabitants of this culture occupied areas in and around the hills overlooking the plains. However, not many skeletal remains are available from the Southern Neolithic culture except at some sites like Tekkalakota, Piklihal and T.Narasipur. Not much of anthropological information is available about the Neolithic skeletal series, except for the comments on their origin and biological affinities.

The cultural material of Burzahom shows some links with the Neolithic cultures of north and northwest China and Central Asia. But the human skeletal remains show biological affinity to the mature Harappan skulls

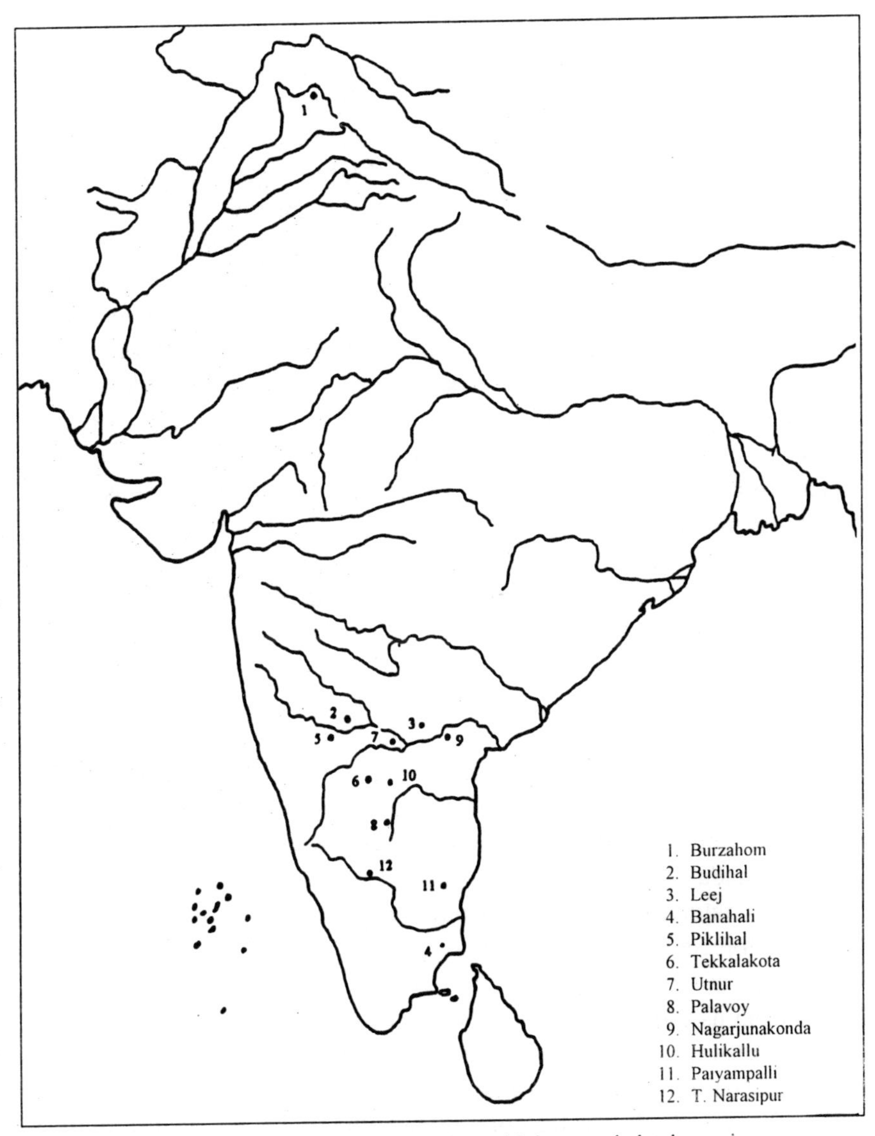

Fig. 3. Location of the Neolithic sites with human skeletal remains

from Cemetery R-37, suggesting some ethnic continuity between the Harappan and Burzahom series in spite of cultural differences (Basu and Pal 1980).

Regarding the origin of the Southern Neolithic culture, it has been postulated that the Iranian Plateau was the center from where it was derived (Allchin 1963, Jain 1979). However, the metric and morphological features of the skeletal material from Tekkalakota show certain similarities with that of Mohenjo-daro, Cemetery R-37, Bellan Bandi Palassa (Sri Lanka), Nal, Sialkot and Lothal (Malhotra 1965a). When the Tekkalakota specimens are compared with those of Neolithic Burzahom, the latter show closer affinity to the skeletons from the Mature Harappan than to the Tekkalakota specimens (Basu and Pal 1980). The Burzahom skeletal characteristics that exhibit similarities with the Mature Harappan material are the long and narrow heads (dolichocephaly), low receding forehead, and a sturdy physique with a tall to medium stature. These features suggest some ethnic continuity between the two cultures separated by a temporal span. At the same time, the variations between the Burzahom and Tekkalakota specimens could be attributed to regional differences. Nothing more can be said at this stage as the sample size is small and so far only the Tekkalakota and Piklihal specimens have been compared with those from the Harappan sites.

Archaeological evidence suggests trade between the Neolithic inhabitants of southern India and their contemporary populations like the Chalcolithic inhabitants of central India and the Deccan plateau. More specifically, the Jorwe phase of the Deccan Chalcolithic indicates trade between sites as far as T.Narasipur and Tekkalakota (Dhavalikar 1988; Nagaraja Rao and Malhotra 1965). Biologically too the Southern Neolithic specimens show close affinity with the Chalcolithic specimens from Nevasa and Chandoli. These studies are based on cranio-morphometry and non-metric traits and serve to establish a biological continuum in the area south of the Narmada.

Unfortunately, the skeletons from the Southern Neolithic sites have not been subjected to a rigorous palaeodemographic analysis that has been adopted for studying the skeletal database from the Mesolithic of the Gangetic plains and the Harappan and succeeding Chalcolithic phases. The Neolithic sites represent a mixed hunter-gatherer and incipient agro-based subsistence pattern. A detailed analysis of the skeletons from the Southern Neolithic sites could therefore provide a valuable source of information regarding bodily, morphological and pathological adaptations in relation to mixed economic strategies. It would be of much interest then to compare their body features with those of the Harappans who practised intensified agriculture and had a well-established food exchange network. The recent anthropological study of the Budihal skeletal series (Walimbe and Paddayya *in press*) is one good example in this direction. This study comments on some kind of physiological stress on these early agro-pastoral communities and emphasizes the need for a fresh anthropological appraisal of the entire Neolithic skeletal series.

The Chalcolithic Phase

The Chalcolithic phase flourished between 2000 BC.and 700 BC and marks the beginning of sedentary life. In central India, Navdatoli and Kayatha (Madhya Pradesh) and Ahar and Bagor (Rajasthan) are some of the sites preserving Chalcolithic levels of occupation. In the Deccan, the first Chalcolithic settlement was discovered at Jorwe in 1950 and since then over 200 sites of this culture have been found (Fig.4). Systematic excavations at many of these sites have revealed many interesting features of these early farmers.

The Chalcolithic culture is primarily characterized by the use of copper and stone technology and a settled lifestyle based on plant agriculture and pastoralism. Though many of the excavated Chalcolithic sites have revealed the presence of a well-formed trade network with regional exchange centres such as Prakash, Daimabad and Inamgaon (Dhavalikar 1988), the trade activities might not have been as extensive as those of the Harappan phase. They were all rural settlements which did not develop into urban centres like those of Harappa and Mohenjo-daro. Nevertheless, the Chalcolithic sites have yielded evidence of a well-organized social life. This culture is characterized by a wheel-made black-on-red painted pottery, and had a well-developed blade/flake industry of siliceous stones such as chalcedony and chert. Copper was known to the Chalcolithic people but was used on a restricted scale. The food economy was based on a combination of agricultural products and animal foods (both domestic and wild). The people lived in either rectangular or round huts and the use of pit dwellings is also attested (Dhavalikar 1988).

The Chalcolithic people occupied the entire Maharashtra region except some parts of Vidarbha and the Konkan. Sites of this culture appear to be heavily concentrated in the Tapi valley (Prakash, Savalda and Kaothe in Dhulia district; Bahal and Tekwada in Jalgaon district), less in the Godavari-Pravara valleys (Jorwe, Nasik, Nevasa and Daimabad) and sporadic in the Bhima valley (Chandoli, Walki and Inamgaon in Pune district).

The Chalcolithic sites of the Deccan provide rich evidence of ceremonial human burials, which come from the habitational levels rather than a conventional cemetery. Almost every excavated Chalcolithic site has yielded evidence of human burials. However, many of these burials are symbolic and osseous remains have not survived. Nevertheless, some of these sites

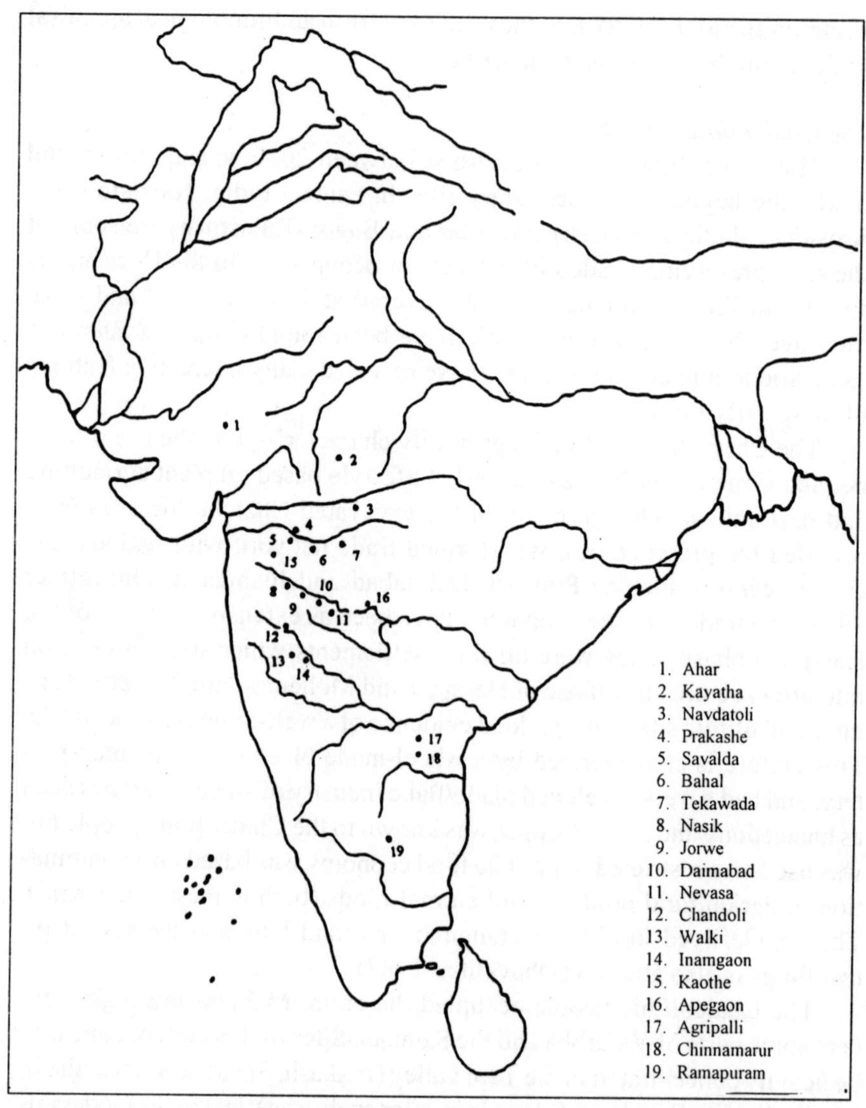

Fig. 4. Location of the Chalcolithic sites with human skeletal remains

have yielded excellently preserved human skeletons. The Deccan Chalcolithic human skeletal series, recovered primarily from five Chalcolithic sites, viz. Nevasa, Chandoli, Inamgaon, Daimabad and Kaothe, is one of the largest human skeletal series in the Indian subcontinent (Kennedy and Malhotra 1965; Malhotra 1965b; Lukacs and Walimbe 1986; Walimbe 1986, 1990). This series is characterized by the over-representation of sub-adult segment which accounts for almost 70% of the collection—an exceptionally rare situation in any part of the world. The presence of sub-adults in large numbers has been attributed to the differential preservation in burial urns which provided a protective cover to delicate bones against the pressure of surrounding earth. The under-representation of the adolescents and adults has been attributed to exposure, disposal and cremation or other alternative burial practices (Lukacs and Badam 1981; Malhotra 1965b). However, it cannot be said that the burial practices of this cultural phase were different from those of the Mesolithic phase, because Mahadaha and Damdama have given evidence of child and infant skeletons respectively (Lukacs and Pal 1992). The large number of sub-adults, belonging to a well-knit temporal, cultural and regional unit, is a definite boon for biocultural studies in India. Moreover, the rural base of the culture without much of trade activity (and not much of external biocultural influence) provides a sort of "controlled" laboratory situation for undertaking demographic and pathological analyses, which have provided valuable insights into the biological adaptive strategies of these early farmers in response to the changing ecosystems.

The use of multivariate analysis and other statistical tests have facilitated more precise comments on the biological homogeneity of these early farmers. When the adult specimens are compared, relative homogeneity is evident in cranial and facial features. The most obvious reason offered is the close geographical, temporal and cultural proximity between the sites (Lukacs and Walimbe 1984).

Though extensive craniometric data is available for this skeletal series, it is not employed for conventional racial or typological analysis but a functional analysis of this data has led to a better understanding of the microevolutionary trends in craniofacial morphology.

The adult Chalcolithic specimens are characterized by long to moderately long cranium, with weak musculature resulting in a gracile appearance. Receding to vertical forehead with faintly developed glabello-superciliary region, square to horizontal orbits, broad nose with depressed root, medium to low upper facial height, moderate cheek bones, and slight alveolar prognathism, are important facial features. The post-cranial elements also exhibit less rugocity. The mean stature is 172.48 cm and 167.13 cm for males and females, respectively. There is a relatively low degree of sexual dimorphism, females tend to be more robust than expected and males somewhat gracile, in both cranial and post-cranial features.

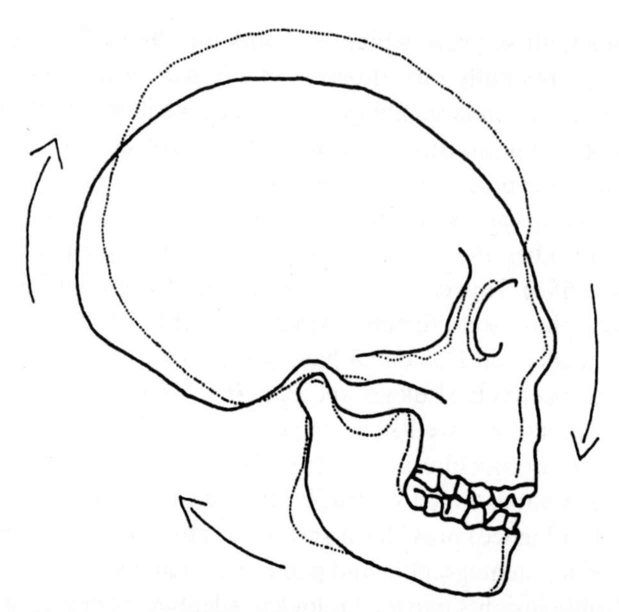

Fig. 5. Cranial changes during the transition from the pre-agricultural stage (indicated by continuous line) to agricultural stage (indicated by dotted line). (After D.L. Martin et al. 1984).

The earlier Mesolithic hunting-gathering populations, especially of the Gangetic region, were characterized by sturdily built, large, muscular and dolichocranial skulls, tall stature and large teeth. The mean cranial index of the Mesolithic populations falls under dolichocrany (long-headed). The Chalcolithic specimens are long- or medium-headed (dolichocrany or mesocrany), but a tendency towards broad-head (brachycrany) is seen especially in the later period. Other changes noticeable in Chalcolithic populations, when compared with their Mesolithic predecessors, are a progressive decrease in robusticity, a rotation of the facial region to a position more inferior to the cranium and a relative increase in cranial height and decrease in cranial length (Fig.5).

Various morphometric features of these early farmers have been discussed in bio-cultural perspective. The overall gracile appearance of the Chalcolithic population, in comparison with the Mesolithic predecessors, can be attributed to factors like natural selection involving a settled life-style, increased carbohydrate intake and a decrease in protein intake.

It has been documented that human populations undergoing starvation and protein malnutrition have a smaller body size and stature than populations with adequate nutrition (Stini 1969, 1975, Larson 1984). In addition to nutritional stress, it has also been postulated that the Deccan

Chalcolithic populations had experienced severe physiological stress (increased disease-nutrition stress) (Walimbe and Tavares 1996).

In prehistoric South Asia decrease in stature and skeletal robusticity occurs with the onset of food production and coincides with the reduction in the sexual dimorphism (robusticity difference in male and female) (Kennedy 1975a, 1984c). There appears to be a reduction in the functional demand placed on the post-cranial skeleton (reduced mechanical stress) in agriculturally settled populations. It has been hypothesized that in hunting-gathering subsistence strategies there is more functional demand on males than females. On the other hand, work demand placed on males and females is more or less equal in agricultural activities. Also it has been argued (Stini 1969) that males are more affected under stress while the female metabolic system is better able to buffer nutritional insults.

The appearance of brachycrany (broad head) in the later phases at archaeological sites (as at Harappa) had often been interpreted as indicative of an 'intruder population' replacing earlier dolichocranial (long headed) inhabitants. While the genetic and regional influence in determining the phenotype cannot be ignored, changes in cranio-facial morphology could be better explained non-genetically, as resulting from the differential functional demand placed on the body in the changed lifestyle of the early farming societies and their sophisticated food preparation techniques (Walimbe 1998, Walimbe and Tavares 1996).

As stated earlier, tooth size reduction is indicative of dietary change. The dental size of Chalcolithic populations suggests mixed food economy and indicates a trend in size reduction in comparison with the Mesolithic dentition (Walimbe and Kulkarni 1993).

The smaller dentition and consequently smaller jaws releases pressure on the masticatory muscles, and thus a progressive tendency towards a vertical facial angle (orthognathus) is evident in agricultural populations. In the prognathus facial appearance, to counterbalance weight of the skull posteriorly, the neck muscles of the occipital region are more pronounced, as in the Mesolithic or earlier fossils. The gracility of the occipital bone (nuchal area) in the later farming communities is the outcome of modifications in the facial region; the cranio-facial modifications lead to decrease in cranial length, thereby increasing the value of cranial index.

The drastic change in the climate around *c.* 1000 BC, leading to increasing aridity, has been given as an explanation for the decline in health during the later Chalcolithic period (Dhavalikar 1988; Dhavalikar et al. 1988). It has also been hypothesized that there was an increase in population pressure in the later phases leading to general mal- or under-nourishment, higher morbidity, and decrease in life expectancy. The climatic changes coupled with the problems of increasing population pressure probably might have resulted in the decline of the culture. In later phases the stressful conditions forced these early farming communities to resort gradually to sheep/goat pastoralism leading to a semi-nomadic existence. The Chalcolithic culture, unlike the Harappan culture, died off as a village culture.

The Iron Age Megalithic Cultural Phase

Coming next in the line of archaeological cultural strata is the skeletal material from the Megalithic sites (Fig.6). Anthropological information is limited in quantity due to the relatively small size of the collection and also because only crania are often represented. It has been stated that the Megalithic population belonged to a single racial stock. Such assumptions were based on metrical data. Wherever variation was noticed, it was ascribed to 'divergent ethnic characters' or interaction between two races. However, a reexamination of the skeletal material has led to the conclusion that variability of physical characteristics is a conspicuous feature of the biological nature of the Megalithic population (Kennedy 1975b). It is an established fact that since the terminal Pleistocene population groups underwent an evolutionary process whereby the cranial vault gained in its breadth dimension in relation to its length, resulting in gradual increase in brachycrany over dolichocrany, though some people retained their dolichocranic feature. Besides genetic reasoning, these changes have also been attributed to non-genetic pressures such as infant cradling practices, pathological factors and other effects of the cultural and non-cultural environment, along with dietary habits. With regard to the Megalithic population in India, specimens from Adittanallur, Ramgarh, Sanur, Ranchi, Savandurga and Pomparippu are represented by the dolichocranic head form, whereas specimens from Brahmagiri, Nagarjunakonda and Yelleswaram represent the brachycranic head form. These two categories have often led writers to assume that the specimens from the latter group of sites belong to an 'intruder population' replacing the earlier dolichocranic Neolithic inhabitants of the area (cited in Kennedy 1975b). The existence of cairn burials in north India and among some of the living tribal populations also casts doubt about the 'sudden invasion' of new people. It does, however, seem unscientific to assume that an aboriginal dolichocranic population was suddenly uprooted by a broad-headed population arriving from

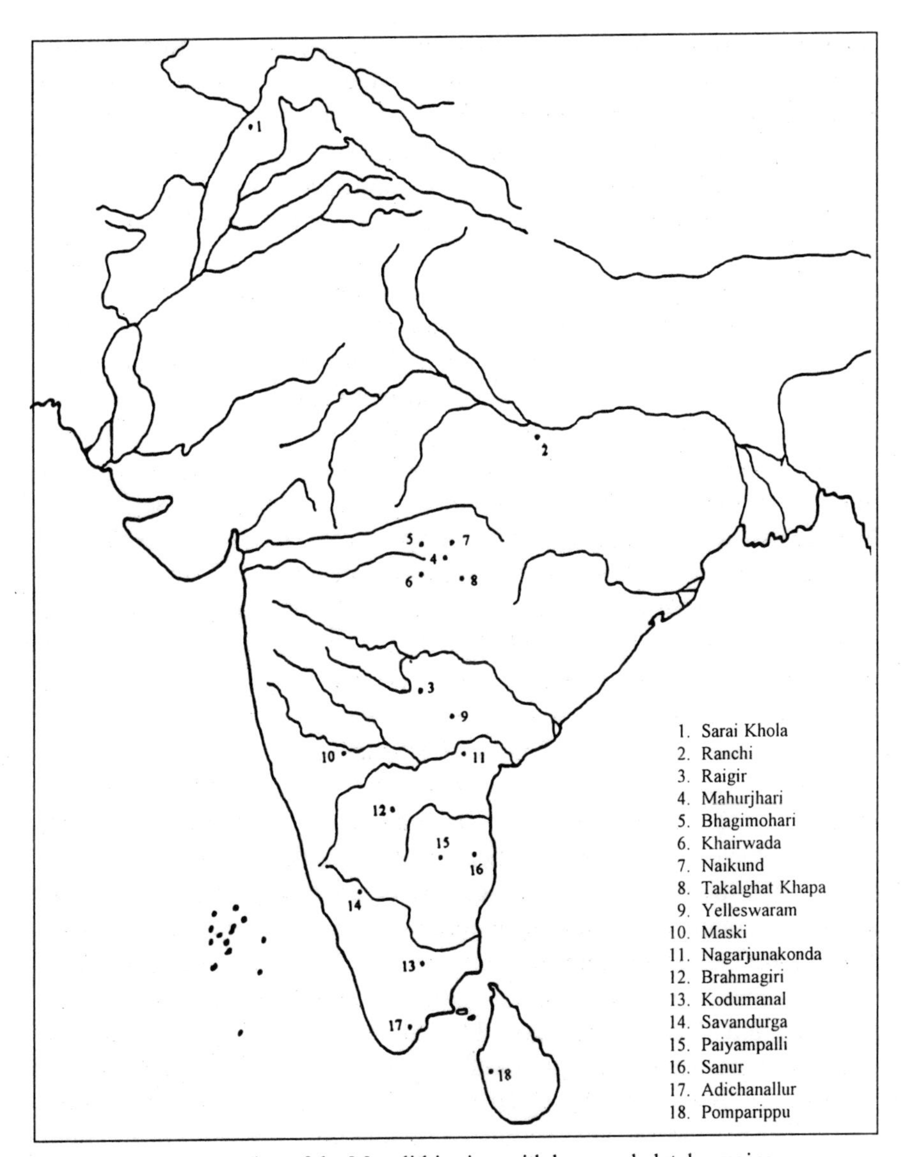

Fig. 6. Location of the Megalithic sites with human skeletal remains

outside the continent. Brachycrany is encountered, though in smaller proportions, in the skeletal record from several Harappan and Neolithic-Chalcolithic sites. With a history of brachycrany present in different cultures, recognizable from widely separated geographical regions, it would seem inconceivable to think that a sudden catastrophic event like the invasion of new people into the Indian subcontinent could replace the existing population (Kennedy 1975b). From the anthropological studies thus far carried out, it can safely be said that the Megalithic population does not represent a single racial element but was phenotypically variable with respect to a broad spectrum of physical characteristics. The living people of Peninsular India constitute a biological continuum with their Megalithic predecessors, as represented by the broad range of phenotypic characteristics.

With the exception of a few Iron age sites which have yielded cultural remains from habitation area (like Maski, Paiyampalli, Takalghat, Raipur, Bhagimohari), it has been impossible to ascertain the dietary patterns of this cultural stage. Though the recent excavations at Raipur and Bhagimohari have yielded agricultural evidence (Deglurkar and Lad 1992), skeletal and dental pathology has so far been the only indirect method of assessing the diet and subsistence pattern, as attempted on the Mahurjhari series from Nagpur district. There has always been a controversy regarding the subsistence economy of the Iron Age settlers, whether or not they practised agriculture. Dental evidence from the site of Mahurjhari however suggested a mixed economy (Lukacs 1981; Deo 1985). Based on the 'tooth reduction' hypothesis discussed earlier, the dental size of Mahurjhari population falls in line with the Mesolithic site of Mahadaha and the Chalcolithic site of Inamgaon, whereas Sarai Khola, an Iron age site in northern Pakistan, reflects smaller tooth size (Lukacs et al. 1989). The site of Sarai Khola is located near the Indus flood plain where agricultural subsistence practices are said to have a much greater antiquity than in Peninsular India (Hemphill et al. 1991). Intensification of agriculture is said to lead to certain growth disruptions, high frequency of infection and certain dental pathologies. Agriculture-based communities are said to exhibit a high prevalence of dental caries, enamel hypoplasia, dental calculus, pulp exposure, dental crowding and alveolar resorption. The caries rate at the two Iron age sites spatially apart, Sarai Khola and Mahurjhari, is low when compared with those ancient populations known to have an agricultural base but above the hunter-gatherer range. This is thus consistent with a subsistence pattern based on mixed economy, where agriculture and hunting and collecting played important roles (Lukacs et al. 1989).

GENERAL OBSERVATIONS

The aim of this paper has been to present a brief review of the research undertaken by human skeletal biologists over the last fifty years on the archaeological skeletal evidence as part of their efforts to understand the biological and cultural history of peoples in the context of changing environment. The discipline of skeletal biology like any other developing disciplines has undergone the descriptive and classificatory stages of development. The earlier approach of classifying the populations "racially" on the basis of their bodily features is no longer considered adequate to understand the variations evident in skeletal remains and to trace the progress of human evolution and adaptation. The "biocultural perspective" introduced in recent times in the analyses of skeletal populations enables the researchers to evaluate populations within their environmental settings and the effects of human activities on the environment. Processes in biology like adaptation, growth, nutrition and their effects on dry bones were utilized to solve and explain the cultural changes that past populations underwent. The integration of anthropological and archaeological data led to the development of the sub-discipline of palaeodemography and its further specialized branch called palaeopathology.

Previously, palaeoanthropological research was focused only on complete adult crania, the primary objective of such studies was to draw conclusions regarding the possible ethnic identity of the population. Infant and sub-adult bones were usually discarded, so also were the post-cranial bones, as these elements do not possess racially diagnostic features. The immediate impact of the changed research perspective is the inclusion of immature and fragmentary bones in the anthropological scrutiny. A significant component of the archaeological human skeletal series in the Indian subcontinent is constituted by the sub-adult segment, a condition not very common in other parts of the world. The presence of sub-adults in large numbers may be attributed to some extent to the differential preservation in burial urns which provided a protective cover to delicate bones against the pressure of surrounding soil sediments. The finding of sub-adults, belonging to a well-knit temporal, cultural and regional zone, is a definite boon to biocultural studies in India. Children in the growing age group are more sensitive to any adverse genetic, nutritional, epidemiological and environmental factors and metabolic upsets, in general. Researchers have now realized the potential of sub-adult skeletons, since an individual's history of illness in the delicate period can be read more easily in sub-adults than in mature adult bones and can be taken as a sensitive indicator of the effects of subsistence change. Moreover, the rural base of the Neolithic and Chalcolithic cultures without much of trade activity (and not much of external biocultural influence) provides a sort of "controlled" laboratory situation for undertaking a demographic and pathological analysis, which incidentally provides valuable insights into the biological adaptive strategies of the ancient pastoral groups in response to the changing ecosystems.

A number of techniques and perspectives have emerged during the last two decades to help skeletal biologists in testing propositions and hypotheses about the relative quality of hunter-gatherer's and farmer's health and nutrition, more specifically, the effects of an increase in the population densities and the less nutritious diet of the farmers as compared to that of the hunter-gatherers.

As has been elaborated earlier, the hunting-gathering way of life probably brought with it a dramatically low density dispersal leading to the exploitation of new areas in a variety of ecological settings and an advancement in technology to cope with the new environment (see Cohen 1977). The stability of the food resource base for many hunting-gathering communities is evidenced in the skeletal record in the form of relatively high ages at the time of death as compared to the lower ages evidenced in the later farming-herding communities. A combination of factors appears to be responsible for this. The high incidence of pathologies noticed in the skeletal record of the early farming-herding communities of India may be due to a nutritionally poor diet which consisted mostly of cereals and/or root crops. Moreover, hunter-gatherers probably ate both meat and forest products whereas the agriculturists had a narrow choice of food with nothing to supplement their diet if and when their crops failed. For example, the evidenced nutritional stress in the Deccan Chalcolithic populations (Lukacs et al. 1986, Walimbe and Gambhir 1994, Walimbe and Lukacs 1992, Walimbe and Tavares 1996, Tavares 1998) was probably caused by the deficiency of nutrients in staple crops, periodic famines evidenced by archaeological data, food shortages and high infection rates due to population growth.

Integral and synergistic effects of malnutrition and disease, coupled with low acquired resistance for a disease, appear on the skeleton as a pathological lesion or anomaly and can be used as indicators of physiological stress. General or cumulative stress is reflected in higher mortality rates, decreased ages at death, retarded body growth, reduced robusticity and stature, and reduced sexual dimorphism. Increased dental crowding and dental asymmetry can be indicative of severe or chronic stress. Periodic indicators of stress provide information on the age at which stress episodes occurred. Two common examples of such periodic stress indicators are Harris lines, i.e., disruption in linear bone growth, and enamel hypoplasia, i.e., disruption in tooth enamel matrix formation. Some diseases leave more specific indicators of stress on bone and teeth. Infectious diseases, nutritional deficiencies, traumatic and degenerative lesions are classified in this category. Porotic hyperostosis, cribra orbitalia (vitamin C deficiency) and iron deficiency anemia indicate nutritional stress. Specific infectious diseases, such as treponema (yaws/syphilis), tuberculosis and leprosy, or non-specific infectious lesions like periosteal reactions, osteomyelitis (inflammation of bone) can be diagnosed. Traumatic lesions such as fractures, dislocations and artificially induced deformities are caused by physical force or by contact with blunt or sharp objects. Degenerative conditions like osteoarthritis (joint disease) and vertebral osteophytosis (vertebral lipping) are common in old individuals. Dental pathologies like caries, attrition, alveolar resorption (abscess in jaw bone), tartar accumulation and premature tooth loss, all reflect dietary habits. Incidence of these pathologies have been documented in some populations, indicating high research potential of the Indian skeletal evidence.

The skeletal record that exhibits such pathologies gives us a lucid picture of the population's behaviour—their subsistence economy, structure of settlements, warfare, division of labour, social class structure and even trade networks. Although the etiology of a lesion may be multiple and its exact cause unknown, it is possible to reconstruct the history of stress for a given population by taking into account the various other lesions that may have affected the rest of the population.

Such a detailed osteological study demands a multidisciplinary approach and seeks help from other physical sciences. Advanced macroscopic and microscopic analysis (SEM) of the bone have contributed a lot to the understanding of lesions and the complexity of human adaptation. Radiographs and photographs of bone are non-destructive ways of analyzing bones. Chemical analysis on dry bone has provided new insights into the dynamics of bone tissue in health, disease and nutrition. Trace element and isotopic analysis have forwarded a better understanding of skeletal pathologies not visible by gross analysis. The most investigated and studied has been the Strontium-Calcium ratio, which highlights the cereal versus meat intake by humans. The Sr/Ca ratio has also supplied information on the pattern of dietary supplementation and age of weaning of infants. Change in the weaning age is said to indicate a shift in the subsistence base and is also important to project estimates for population growth rate.

A significant boon to the subject is expected from the advances in molecular biology, specially sequencing of mitochondrial DNA, for understanding the process of peopling of India from the protohistoric times. Efforts in this direction have been made at the Deccan College, Pune, in collaboration with the leading molecular laboratories in India and abroad.

Though the interpretive phase in the discipline has already commenced, there is a long way to go. National level efforts are required to overcome its serious lacunae and drawbacks. For example, proper co-ordination between various anthropology/archaeology museums and excavating agencies would help create a good database of archaeological human skeletal material, which is the prerequisite for research on skeletal biology. The subject demands a more intimate interaction between archaeologists and skeletal biologists. The osseous remains should be collected with great care: not only should adult crania be recorded but every post-cranial and sub-adult or infant bone, fragmentary or complete, should be adequately attended to and be made available to skeletal biologists. Since physical anthropologists rarely participate in excavations adequate care is not give to delicate pathological bones. Since such bones are often fragmentary, they are often overlooked or not meticulously collected in the field. Similarly, interaction between medical practitioners and palaeopathologists is expected. There is a lack of clinical database with a good cross-section of the population of a particular region and community.

Lack of adequate training facilities, limited exposure of students to the skeletal remains and inadequate literature limits the growth of this interesting field of research in the subcontinent.

The Indian skeletal record, covering a vast time span, can be used to carry out meaningful research and would help skeletal biologists as well as archaeologists to understand the interaction between ancient populations and their habitats, the shift from a hunting-gathering lifestyle to a settled way of life. The subject of human skeletal biology has come a long way from the classification of the fossils of 'ancient man' and grouping them into 'ethnic classes' to studying the skeletal record as an entity in itself, which has a wide scope for providing answers regarding the continuous biocultural adaptation of ancient populations of the subcontinent.

REFERENCES

Allchin, F.R. 1963. *Neolithic Cattle-Keepers of South India: A Study of the Deccan Ashmounds*. Cambridge: Cambridge University Press.

Andrew, P., and Cronin, J. 1982. The Relationship of Sivapithecus and Ramapithecus and the Evolution of the Orang-utan. *Nature* 297: 541–46.

Ayer, A.A. 1960. Report on Human Remains Excavated at Piklihal Near Mudgal, in F.R. Allchin, ed. *Piklihal Excavations*, Hyderabad: Andhra Pradesh Government Archaeology Department, pp. 143–54.

Badam, G.L. 1989. Observations on Fossil Hominid Site at Hathnora, M.P., India, in A. Sahani and R.Gaur, eds. *Perspectives in Human Evolution.* New Delhi: Renaissance Publishing House, pp. 153–72.

Badam, G.L., Ganjoo, R.K., Salahuddin, and Rajaguru, S.N. 1986. Evaluation of the Fossil Hominid: the Maker of Late Acheulian Tools at Hathnora, M.P., India. *Current Science* 55(3): 143–45.

Basu, A., and Pal, A. 1980. *Human Remains from Burzahom.* Calcutta: Anthropological Survey of India.

Bernhard, W. 1967. Human Skeletal Remains from the Cemetery of Timargarha, in A.H. Dani ed. *Timargarha and the Gandhara Grave Culture*, Special Volume of *Ancient Pakistan* 3: 289–407.

Bernhard, W. 1968. Human Skeletal Remains from the Bronze and Early Iron Age Cemetery of Timargarha (Dir State, West Pakistan). *Proceedings of 8th International Congress of Anthropological and Ethnological Sciences,* 2: 144–54, Tokyo.

Bernhard, W. 1969. Preliminary Report on the Human Skeletal Remains From the Prehistoric Cemetery of Sarai Khola. *Pakistan Archaeology* 6: 100–116.

Brace, C. L. 1978. Tooth Reduction in the Orient. *Asian Perspectives* 19: 203–19.

Chakrabarti D.K. 1993. 'Long Barrel Cylinder' Beads and the Issue of Pre-Sargonic Contact Between the Harappan Civilization and Mesopotamia, in G.L.Possehl ed. *Harappan Civilization: A Recent Perspective*, sec. ed. New Delhi: American Institute of Indian Studies, pp. 265–70.

Chatterjee, B.K., and Gupta, P. 1963. *Report on the Adittanalur Skulls.* Calcutta: Anthropological Survey of India.

Chatterjee, B.K., and Kumar, G.D. 1963. Racial Elements in Post-Harappan Skeletal Remains at Lothal, in B. Ratnam ed. *Anthropology on the March.* Madras: Social Sciences Association, pp. 104–10.

Cohen, M.N. 1977. *The Food Crisis in Prehistory: Overpopulation and the Origin of Agriculture.* New Haven: Yale University Press.

Dales, G.F. 1964. The Mythical Massacre at Mohenjodaro. *Expedition* 6(3): 37–43.

Dani, A.H. ed. 1967. Timargarha and the Gandhara Grave Culture. *Ancient Pakistan* 3: 1–407.

—1968. Gandhara Grave Complex in West Pakistan. *Asian Perspectives* 8(1): 164–65.

Deglurkar, G.B., and Lad Gouri. 1992. *Megalithic Raipur: 1985–90.* Pune: Deccan College.

Deo, S.B. 1985. The Megaliths: Their Culture, Ecology, Economy and Technology, in S.B. Deo and K. Paddayya eds. *Recent Advances in Indian Archaeology.* Pune: Deccan College, pp. 89–99.

Deraniyagala, P.E.P. 1962. The Extinct Hominoidea of Ceylon. *Anthropological Annals of the Vidyodaya University of Ceylon* 52–62.

Deraniyagala, S., and Kennedy, K.A.R. 1972. Bellan-Bandi Palassa 1970: A Mesolithic Burial Site in Ceylon. *Ancient Ceylon* 2: 18–47.

Dhavalikar, M.K. 1988. *First Farmers of the Deccan.* Pune: Ravish Publishers.

Dhavalikar, M.K., Sankalia, H.D., and Ansari, Z.D. eds. 1988. *Excavations at Inamgaon:* vol I: part I and II. Pune: Deccan College.

Dutta, P.C. 1984. *The Bronze Age Harappans*. Calcutta: Anthropological Survey of India.
Dutta, P.C., Pal, A., Gupta, P., and Dutta, B.C. 1987. *Ancient Human Remains from Rupar*. Calcutta: Anthropological Survey of India.
Ehrhardt, S., and Kennedy, K.A.R. 1965. *Excavations at Langhnaj: 1944–63*, part III: *The Human Remains*. Pune: Deccan College.
Guha, B.S., and Basu, P.C. 1938. Report on the Human Remains Excavated at Mohenjodaro in 1928–29, in J.H. Mackay ed. *Further Excavations at Mohenjodaro*, New Delhi: Government of India, reprinted, 1998. New Delhi: Munshiram Manoharlal Publishers, pp. 613–38.
Gupta, P., and Dutta, P.C. 1962. Human Remains Excavated From Megaliths at Yelleswaram (Andhra Pradesh). *Man in India* 42: 19–34.
—1970. *Ancient Human Remains*: part I: A *Study of the Nagarjunakonda Skeletons*. Memoirs of Anthropological Survey of India 20: 1–33.
Gupta, P.C., Dutta, P.C., and Basu, A. 1962. *Human Skeletal Remains from Harappa*. Memoirs of the Anthropological Survey of India 9.
Hemphill, B.E., Lukacs, J.R., and Kennedy, K.A.R. 1991. Biological Adaptations and Affinities of Bronze Age Harappans, in R.H. Meadow ed. *Harappan Excavation 1986–90*: *A Multidisciplinary Approach to Third Millennium Urbanism*. Madison: Prehistory Press, pp.137–82.
Jain, K.C. 1979. *Prehistory and Protohistory of India*. New Delhi: Agam Kala Prakashan.
Kennedy, K.A.R. 1965a. Megalithic Calvariae From Raigir, Andhra Pradesh. *Anthropologist* 11: 1–24.
—1965b. Human Skeletal Material from Ceylon, with an Analysis of the Island's Prehistoric and Contemporary Populations. *Bulletin of the British Museum (Natural History)* 11: 135–213.
—1973. The Paleodemography of Ceylon: A Study of the Biological Continuum of a Population from Prehistoric to Historic Times, in A.K. Ghosh ed. *Perspectives in Palaeoanthropology*. Calcutta: Firma K.L. Mukhopadhyay, pp. 95–112.
—1975a. Biological Adaptations of Prehistoric South Asian Populations to Different and Changing Ecological Settings, in E.S. Watts, F.E. Johnston and G.W. Lasker eds. *Biosocial Interrelations in Population Adaptation*,. The Hague: Mouton Publishers, pp. 65–90.
—1975b. *The Physical Anthropology of the Megalithic Builders of South India and Sri Lanka*. Canberra: Australian National University.
—1980. Prehistoric Skeletal Record of Man in South Asia. *Annual Review of Anthropology* 9: 391–432.
—1982. Paleodemographic Perspectives of Social Structural Change in Harappan Society, in S. Pastner and L. Flam eds. *Anthropology in Pakistan: Recent Socio-Cultural and Archaeological Perspectives*, South Asia Occasional Papers and Theses, Ithaca: Cornell University, pp. 211–18.
—1984a. Biological Adaptations and Affinities of Mesolithic South Asians, in J.R. Lukacs ed. *The People of South Asia: The Biological Anthropology of India, Pakistan and Nepal*, New York: Plenum Press, pp. 29–57.
—1984b. Trauma and Disease in the Ancient Harappans: Recent Assessments of the Skeletal Record, in B.B. Lal and S.P. Gupta eds. *Frontiers of the Indus Civilization*. New Delhi: Books & Books, pp. 425–36.
—1984c. Growth, Nutrition and Pathology in Changing Paleodemographic Setting in South Asia, in M.N. Cohen and G.J. Armelagos eds. *Paleopathology at the Origins of Agri-*

culture. New York: Academic Press, pp. 169–192.
—1990a. Porotic Hyperostosis on Human Remains from Mesolithic Baghai Khor. *Bulletin of the Deccan College Research Institute* 49: 183–98.
—1990b. Skeletons in the Closet: Recent Recovery of Lost Human Remains from Iron Age Raigir, Andhra Pradesh. *South Asian Studies* 6: 201–26.
—1994. Identification of Sacrificial and Massacre Victims in Archaeological Sites: The Skeletal Evidence. *Man and Environment* 19(1–2): 247–51.
Kennedy, K.A.R., and Caldwell, P. 1984. South Asian Prehistoric Human Skeletal Remains and Burial Practices, in J.R. Lukacs ed. *The People of South Asia: The Biological Anthropology of India, Pakistan and Nepal*. New York: Plenum Press, pp. 159–97.
Kennedy, K.A.R., Disotell, T., Roertgen, W.J., Chiment, J., and Sherry, J. 1986a. Biological Anthropology of Upper Pleistocene Hominids From Sri Lanka: Batadomba Lena and Beli Lena Caves. *Ancient Ceylon* 6: 68–168.
Kennedy, K.A.R., Lovell, N.C., and Burrow, C.B. 1986b. *Mesolithic Human Remains from the Gangetic Plain: Sarai Nahar Rai*. South Asian Occasional Papers and Theses, Ithaca: Cornell University.
Kennedy, K.A.R., Lukacs, J.R., Pastor, R.F., Johnston, T.L., Lovell, N.C., Pal, J.N., Hemphill, B.E., and Burrow, C.B. 1992. *Human Skeletal Remains from Mahadaha: A Gangetic Mesolithic Site*. South Asia Program. Ithaca: Cornell University.
Kennedy, K.A.R., and Malhotra, K.C. 1965. *Human Skeletal Remains from Chalcolithic and Indo-Roman Levels from Nevasa: An Anthropometric and Comparative Analysis*. Pune: Deccan College.
Kennedy, K.A.R., Sonakia, A., Clement, J., and Verma, K.K. 1991. Is the Narmada Hominid an Indian *Homo Erectus? American Journal of Physical Anthropology* 86: 475–96.
Larsen, C.S. 1984. Health and Disease in Prehistoric Georgia: The Transition to Agriculture, in M.N. Cohen and G.J. Armelagos eds. *Paleopathology at the Origins of Agriculture*. New York: Academic Press, pp. 367–92.
Lukacs, J.R. 1976. Dental Anthropology and Biological Affinities of an Iron Age Population from Pomparripu, Sri Lanka, in K.A.R. Kennedy and G.L. Possehl, eds. *Ecological Background of South Asian Prehistory*. Occasional Paper no. 5, South Asia Program. Ithaca: Cornell University, pp. 197–215.
—1980. The Apegaon Mandible: Morphology and Pathology. *Bulletin of the Deccan College Research Institute* 40: 88–95.
—1981. Dental Anthropology and Nutritional Patterns of South Asian Megalithic Builders: The Evidence from Iron Age Mahurjhari. *Proceedings of the American Philosophical Society* 125(3): 220–37.
—1983. Dental Anthropology and the Origins of Two Iron Age Populations from Northern Pakistan. *Homo* 34: 1–15.
—1985. Dental Pathology and Tooth Size at Early Mesolithic Mehrgarh: An Anthropological Assessment, in J. Schotsman and M. Taddei eds. *South Asian Archaeology 1983*. Naples: Instituto Universitario Orientale, pp. 121–50.
Lukacs, J.R., and Badam, G.L. 1981. Paleodemography of Post-Harappan Inamgaon: A Preliminary Report. *Journal of the Indian Anthropological Society* 16: 59–74.
Lukacs, J.R., Bogorad, R.K., Walimbe, S.R., and Dunbar, D.C. 1986. Paleopathology at Inamgaon: A Post-Harappan Agrarian Village in Western India. *Proceedings of the American Philosophical Society* 130(3): 289–311.
Lukacs, J.R., and Hemphill, B.E. 1991. The Dental Anthropology of Prehistoric Baluchistan:

A Morphometric Approach to the Peopling of South Asia, in M.A. Kelley and C.S. Larsen eds. *Advances in Dental Anthropology*. New York: Alan R.Liss, pp. 77–119.

Lukacs, J.R., and Kennedy, K.A.R. 1981. Biological Anthropology of Human Remains from Pomparippu, in V. Begley, J.R. Lukacs, and K.A.R. Kennedy eds. *Excavations of Iron Age Burials at Pomparippu, 1970*. Special Volume of *Ancient Ceylon*, pp. 97–130.

Lukacs, J.R., Kennedy, K.A.R., and Burrow, C. 1982. Note on Human Skeletal Specimen From Naikund, in S.B. Deo and A.P. Jamkhedkar eds. *Naikund Excavations 1978–80*. Mumbai: State Department of Archaeology, pp. 49–51.

Lukacs, J.R., and Minderman, L.L. 1989. Dental Pathology and Agricultural Intensification from Neolithic to Chalcolithic Periods at Mehrgarh (Baluchistan, Pakistan), in C. Jarrige ed. *South Asian Archaeology*. Madison: Prehistory Press, pp. 167–79.

Lukacs, J.R., Misra, V.N., and Kennedy, K.A.R. 1982. *Bagor and Tilwara: Late Mesolithic Cultures of Northwest India*, vol. I: *The Human Skeletal Remains*. Pune: Deccan College.

Lukacs, J.R., and Pal, J.N. 1992. Dental Anthropology of Mesolithic Hunter-gatherers: A Preliminary Report of the Mahadaha and Sarai Nahar Rai Dentitions. *Man and Environment* 17(2): 45–55.

Lukacs, J.R., and Pastor, R.F. 1988. Activity-induced Patterns of Dental Abrasion in Prehistoric Pakistan: Evidence from Mehrgarh and Harappa. *American Journal of Physical Anthropology* 76: 377–98.

Lukacs, J.R., Schulz, M., and Hemphill, B.E. 1989. Dental Pathology and Dietary Patterns in Iron Age Northern Pakistan, in K. Frifelt and P. Sorenson eds. *South Asian Archaeology 1985*. London: Curzon Press, pp. 475–96.

Lukacs, J.R., and Walimbe, S.R. 1984. Paleodemography at Inamgaon: an Early Farming Village in Western India, in J.R. Lukacs ed. *The People of South Asia: The Biological Anthropology of India, Pakistan and Nepal*. New York; Plenum Press, pp. 105–32.

Lukacs, J.R., and Walimbe, S.R. 1986. *Excavations at Inamgaon*, vol II: *The Physical Anthropology of Human Skeletal Remains*, part I: *An Osteographic Analysis*. Pune: Deccan College.

Mackay, E.J.H. ed. 1938. *Further Excavations at Mohenjo-daro*. New Delhi: Government of India, reprint, 1998. New Delhi: Munshiram Manoharlal Publishers.

Malhotra, K.C. 1965a. Human Skeletal Remains from Neolithic Tekkalakota, in M.S. Nagaraja Rao and K.C. Malhotra eds. *The Stone Age Hill Dwellers of Tekkalakota*. Pune: Deccan College, pp.109–62.

—1965b. Human Skeletal Remains from Chandoli, in S.B. Deo and Z.D. Ansari eds. *Chalcolithic Chandoli*. Pune: Deccan College, pp. 143–84.

—1968. Further Observations on the Human Skeletal Remains from Neolithic Piklihal. *Anthropologist* 14: 99–111.

—1971. Report on the Human Skeleton from the Burial, in M. Seshadri ed. *Report on the Excavations at T. Narasipur*. Bangalore: Karnataka Archaeology Department, pp. 79–104.

Marshall, J. 1931. *Mohenjodaro and the Indus Civilization*. London: Arthur Probsthain.

Martin, L.M., Armelagos, G.J., and Van, Gerven, D.P. 1984. The Effects of Socio-Economic Change in Prehistoric Africa: Sudanese Nubia as a Case Study, in M.N. Cohen and G.J. Armelagos eds. *Paleopathology at the Origins of Agriculture*. New York: Academic Press, pp. 193–214.

Mushrif, Veena, and Walimbe, S.R. 1998. Human Skeletal Remains from Chalcolithic Walki. in U.P.Arora ed. *Reconstructing History: Essays in Honour of Professor V.C.Srivastava*. Varanasi: Banaras Hindu University.

Nagaraja Rao, M.S., and Malhotra, K.C. 1965. *The Stone Age Hill Dwellers of Tekkalakota*. Pune: Deccan College.

Possehl, G.L. ed. 1993. *Harappan Civilization: A Contemporary Perspective*. New Delhi: Oxford & IBH Publishing Co.

Rao, V.V. 1970. Skeletal Remains from Takalghat and Khapa Excavation, in S.B. Deo ed. *Excavations at Takalghat and Khapa, 1968–69*. Nagpur: Nagpur University, pp. 60–77.

—1973. Skeletal Remains from Mahurjhari, in S.B. Deo ed. *Mahurjhari Excavations 1970–72*. Nagpur: Nagpur University, pp. 63–76.

Sankhyan, A.R. 1988. Latest Occurrence of Sivapithecus in Indian Siwaliks and Phyletic Implications, in K.L. Bhowmik ed. *Current Anthropological and Archaeological Perspectives*, vol. I: *Man*. New Delhi: Inter-India Publications, pp. 57–88.

Sarkar, S.S. 1960. Human Skeletal Remains from Brahmagiri. *Bulletin of the Department of Anthropology* 9: 5–26.

—1972. *Ancient Races of the Deccan*, New Delhi: Munshiram Manoharlal Publishers.

Sewell, R.B.S. and Guha, B.S. 1929. *Report on the Bones Excavated at Nal*. Memoirs of Archaeological Survey of India 35: 56–86.

Sewell, R.B.S., and Guha, B.S. 1931. Human Remains, in J. Marshall ed. *Mohenjodaro and the Indus Civilization*. vol. II. London: Arthur Probsthain, pp. 599–642.

Sharma, A.K.. 1970. Kalibangan Human Skeletal Remains: An Osteoarchaeological Approach. *Journal of Oriental Institute*, Baroda 19: 109–13.

—1972. Harappan Cemetery at Kalibangan: A Demographic Survey. *Proceedings of 4th Indian Archaeological Society Congress*, Nagpur, pp. 113–16.

Sonakia, A. 1985a. Skull Cap of an Early Man from the Narmada Valley Alluvium (Pleistocene) of Central India. *American Anthropologist* 87(3): 612–16.

—1985b. Early Homo from Narmada Valley, India, in E. Delson ed. *Ancestors: The Hard Evidence*. New York: Alan R. Riss, pp. 334–38.

Stini, W.A. 1969. Nutritional Stress and Growth: Sex Difference in Adaptive Response. *American Journal of Physical Anthropology* 31: 417–26.

—1975. Adaptive Strategies of Human Populations Under Nutritional Stress, in E.S.Watts, F.E. Johnston and G.W. Lasker eds. *Biosocial Interrelations in Population Adaptation*. The Hague: Mouton Publishers, pp. 19–41.

Tavares, A. 1998. Paleopathology: Its Implications in the Archaeological Record. Unpublished Ph.D. thesis. Pune: University of Pune.

UNESCO. 1952. *What is Race?* Paris: UNESCO.

Walimbe, S.R. 1986. Paleodemography of Protohistoric Daimabad, in S.A. Sali ed. *Daimabad 1976–79*. New Delhi: Archaeological Survey of India, pp. 641–740.

—1988. Human Skeletal Evidence from Megalithic Vidarbha. *Puratattava* 18: 61–71.

—1990. Human Skeletal Remains, in M.K. Dhavalikar, V.S. Shinde and Shubhangana Atre eds. *Excavations at Kaothe*. Pune: Deccan College, pp. 111–231.

—1993a. A Report on Adult Human Skeleton from Neolithic Leej (A.P.). *Bulletin of Andhra Pradesh Archaeology Department*.

—1993b. An Anthropometric and Comparative Analysis of the Human Skeletal Remains from the Chalcolithic Levels of Hulikallu (A.P.). *Bulletin of Andhra Pradesh Archaeology Department*.

—1993c. The Aryans: The Physical Anthropological Approach, in S.B.Deo and S.Kamath eds. *The Aryan Problem*. Pune: Bharatiya Itihas Sankalan Samiti, pp. 97–104.

—1993d. Human Skeletal Remains From Megalithic Raipur. *Bulletin of the Deccan College Research Institute* 50: 667–78.

Walimbe, S.R. 1998. Bio-cultural Adaptations in Cranial Morphology Among the Early Farming Chalcolithic Populations of the Deccan Plateau, in M.K. Bhasin and S.L. Malik eds. *Contemporary Studies in Human Ecology: Human Factor, Resource Management and Development*. New Delhi: Indian Society for Human Ecology, pp. 25–40.

Walimbe, S.R., and Gambhir, P.B. 1994. *Long Bone Growth in Infants and Children: Assessment of the Nutritional Status*. Mangalore: Mujumdar Publications.

Walimbe, S.R., and Kulkarni, S.S. 1993. *Biological Adaptations in Human Dentition: An Odontometric Study on Living and Archaeological Populations in India*. Pune: Deccan College.

Walimbe, S.R., and Lukacs, J.R. 1992. Dental Pathology at the Origins of Agriculture: Evidence from Chalcolithic Population of the Deccan Plateau, in J.R. Lukacs ed. *Culture, Ecology and Dental Anthropology*. New Delhi: Kamala Raj Enterprises, pp. 117–32.

Walimbe, S.R., and Paddayya, K. In press. Human Skeletal Remains from the Neolithic Ashmound Site at Budihal, Gulbarga District, Karnataka. *Bulletin of the Deccan College Research Institute*.

Walimbe, S.R., and Selvakumar, V. 1998. Anthropological Investigations on an Iron Age Adult Male Skeleton from S. Pappinayakkanpatti, Madurai district, Tamil Nadu. *Journal of Human Evolution* 9(1): 19–34.

Walimbe, S.R. and Shinde, V.S. 1995. Anthropometric Data on the Adult Skeleton from Medieval Padri. *Man and Environment* 20: 43–55.

Walimbe, S.R., and Tavares, A. 1996. Evolving Trends in Skeletal Biology in the Indian Subcontinent: A Case Study on the Incipient Agricultural Populations of Deccan Plateau, in S. Wadia, R. Korisettar and V.S. Kale eds. *Quaternary Environments and Geoarchaeology of India*. Bangalore: Geological Society of India, pp. 515–29.

Wheeler, R.E.M. 1968. *The Indus Civilization*, third ed. Cambridge: Cambridge University Press.

Wolpoff, M.H. 1971. Metric Trends in Hominid Dental Evolution. *Studies in Anthropology* 2: 1–244.

Zuckerman, S. 1930. The Adichanallur Skulls. *Bulletin of Madras Government Museum* 2: 1–24.

17 ❖ Physical Dating Methods in South Asian Archaeology: A Brief Review

S. KUSUMGAR and M.G. YADAVA

INTRODUCTION

THE use of a large number of dating techniques has now provided us with absolute time-frames for the origin of the universe, our solar system, the origin of life and the origin of man. Today we know that the universe is not infinitely old; it is only a few orders of magnitude older than the human beings. The universe is estimated to be about 15 billion years old and the earliest hominids have now proved to be more than 4 million years old.

Soon after Independence, Pandit Nehru and Homi Bhabha did realise the importance of developing physical dating methods for defining the chronology of India's remote past. In the mid-50's Williard Libby discovered that a radioactive form of carbon can be used for dating objects of organic origin. It was creditable indeed that this new and sophisticated technique of measuring very weak radioactivity was installed as early as 1962 at TIFR, Mumbai, by D. Lal who had the privilege of working with Libby in the US. In fact, Lal also employed this technology of measuring weak radioactivity, by using a variety of isotopes, to study various geophysical processes. A national programme of dating the Indian archaeological sites was undertaken by D.P. Agrawal and the senior author at the Radiocarbon Laboratory of TIFR since its inception in 1962. By now, the Radiocarbon Laboratory of TIFR, which later on shifted to Physical Research Laboratory, Ahmedabad, has produced about 3,000 C^{14} measurements. Later on, another ^{14}C laboratory became operational at Birbal Sahni Institute of Palaeobotany, Lucknow. Many of the sites in Pakistan have also been dated by foreign laboratories. In the 70's another method of dating was developed by measuring thermoluminescence (TL) emitted by pottery, terracottas and bricks. Most of the Stone Age was still out of the range of C^{14} dating. Therefore, some other techniques based on U-Th, K-Ar and fission track were also developed and used to a limited extent to date the Quaternary events as also the early part of Stone Age.

The Radiocarbon Laboratory at Mumbai did bring archaeologists and scientists together. It was hoped that this interaction between the laboratories and field archaeologists would lead to much wider and more profound applications of a variety of scientific techniques to resolve archaeological problems. But the gulf between the two Cultures is too deep to have been bridged by a radiocarbon laboratory. The archaeologist still does not like to go into the nitty-gritty of the problems of calibration or contamination of samples, nor does he want to know about the basic limitations of the physical dating methods.

Today India can boast of having the latest technology in a variety of fields. This technology has a great potential for resolving outstanding archaeological problems, but it is yet to be used for this purpose. Basically, it is due to the old mindset, the divide between the two Cultures, which does not allow a fruitful interaction between scientists and archaeologists. But we do hope that now with several young archaeologists coming from science background, there will be a change in this attitude and we may soon be able to see more fruitful interaction between the scientific laboratories and archaeological institutions.

The Technique

We will only briefly explain the principles and limitations of C^{14} dating technique here; for other dating methods and a more detailed treatment of the radiocarbon method we would like the readers to refer to our popular book, *Dating the Human Past* (Agrawal and Yadava 1995).

In nature, generally, we have chemical elements which are stable, but there are some which are unstable because of some extra neutrons in their nucleus or such other reasons. Radiocarbon (carbon-14) is similar to stable carbon (C^{12}) in all other respects except that it has two extra neutrons in its nucleus which make it unstable and liable to change with time. Such unstable elements are called 'radioactive' because in course of time they decay or give out a part of themselves by way of some radiation (alpha, beta particles or gamma-rays). Carbon-14 gives out an electron (beta-particles) and becomes stable nitrogen (N^{14}).

For each radioactive species there is an immutable rate of spontaneous decay which is unaffected by any other agency. Carbon-14, when isolated, decays by 1% every 83 years which means that in 5730 years a given amount will be reduced to half, after 11460 years to a quarter and so on. In modern plants and animals the ratio of radioactive to non-radioactive carbon atoms is approximately one to a million million (carbon-14/carbon-12 = $1/8\times10^{11}$). Once a plant or an animal dies, it does not get any replacement of carbon through photosynthesis or food intake and, therefore, as time goes on, the concentration ratio keeps going down. In this natural carbon cycle, therefore, plants get their food intake (and therefore carbon) through the assimilation of carbon dioxide through photosynthesis. Plants are consumed by animals and humans and thus all life forms are labelled by carbon-14. In the laboratory one measures the residual radiocarbon in organic remains. As one knows the half-life (5730 years) and can also measure the residual radiocarbon, one can easily calculate the age.

Calibration of Carbon-14 Dates

Ideally, the real and measured ages should be the same, but in reality they are not so. As one goes beyond 500 BC, the carbon-14 ages tend to become consistently younger and, between 500 BC and 1300 AD, the ages are overestimated. Such discrepancy can be measured by dating tree-rings of a known age. One can use trees like bristlecone pine and sequoia which live for thousands of years, or one can use tree trunks from bogs which have been dendrochronologically dated and thus are related to each other. This way one can go back to about 8000 BC.

As a result of the work done by several laboratories, the main calibration curves tend to agree among themselves. This has made it possible to have an internationally accepted calibration curve which can now be used by all laboratories and users (see Appendix 5, Agrawal and Yadava 1995).

How to Calculate Error

If the age is 4000 ± 100 BP, the probability that the true lies within the given ranges is as follows:

one sigma error = 4100–3900 BP Probability = 68.3%
two sigma error = 4200–3800 BP Probability = 95.5%
three sigma error = 4300–3700 BP Probability = 99.7%

Besides these probabilistic errors, there are other systematic errors.

Accelerator Mass Spectrometry (AMS) Technique

In accelerator mass spectrometry, one measures the actual number of carbon-14 atoms present, not the very small number that radioactively decay during the measurement time. The greatest advantage of AMS dating is the sample size. Routinely 1 mg of carbon is sufficient for AMS techniques. It leads to a precision of ± 50 years or better for 1 mg amount of sample. As little as 100 micrograms of carbon has been dated recently.

Contamination

In tropical and sub-tropical countries like India, the thickness of the soil (archaeological debris) over the sample works as a buffer to prevent contamination by younger carbon. Bones from open sites are not useful for carbon dating as there is no collagen left in tropical sites. Caves and rock shelters minimise bone contamination. Sampling from the periphery of a mound should be avoided.

DATING APPLICATIONS

We propose to discuss the application of physical dating techniques in Indian archaeological studies using the conventional categories of Stone Age, Neolithic, Harappan, Chalcolithic and Megalithic periods. In addition, we have obtained C^{14} dates for some rock art sites (Table 1C), Painted Grey Ware sites (Table 8), Northern Black Polished Ware sites and early Iron Age sites (Table 9), and also dates from various old workings of gold, copper, zinc, etc. (Table 6). It may be noted that in all the tables the "BP" (before present) radiocarbon dates are based on the half-life value of 5568 years (and not 5730 years). The calibrated dates are expressed in terms of "BC/AD". But in the text, to avoid any confusion, only BC/AD terms have been used, though the discussion and interpretations are based on calibrated dates.

The present paper does not claim to analyse the implications of all the dates but we have tried to provide a compilation in a manner which should appear meaningful to the archaeologists. For C^{14} dates bearing TF (TIFR) or PRL (Physical Research Laboratory) numbers we may have some additional information in the sample sheets provided by the excavators; for all other dates, the readers desirous of further information should address inquiries to the respective excavators themselves.

Stone Age (Tables 1a, 1b and 1c)

The earliest stone tools belonging to *Homo habilis* are dated to 2.4 Myr and are expected to go further back (Semaw et al. 1997). *Homo erectus* has been dated to 1.6 Myr in Africa. The only early K-Ar date in India has been reported from Bori, near Pune and goes back to 1.38 Myr. It is a volcanic material overlying an Acheulian assemblage (Korisettar et al. 1989)[1]. Baskaran et al. (1989) have used U-Th dating technique on the Quaternary carbonate deposits of Saurashtra. They have reported two groups of such carbonate deposits: Group I has a range of 50–70 Kyr and Group II, 75–115 Kyr. Circumstantially, these dates have been used to define the chronology of the underlying Acheulian assemblage.

There are a few C^{14} dates for the Middle Palaeolithic sites but they are generally too young to be taken into account. For example, PRL-293, PRL-13, BS1-163 (Table 1a) are on shell material. At this range, a little contamination can make them look as if they are within the C^{14} dating range. We dated two wood samples from Mula dam (TF-217, 345, Table 1a). Both were beyond the limit of C^{14} range. One TL date for Didwana gives the range 144–350 Kyr. Similarly, TF-1002 from Dhom dam gives a date of greater than 35 Kyr and is thus beyond the range of C^{14} dating method.

In Kashmir (Kusumgar et al. 1985) fission track dating technique has been used to date the Matuyama/Gauss magnetic reversal boundary to about 2.3 Myr. This is close to the globally accepted value of 2.4 Myr for this event. Its importance lies in the fact that this date marks the lower boundary of the Villafranchian fauna in South Asia.

Table 1a. **Dates for Palaeolithic Sites**
all BP ages are based on 5568 yr half-life of radiocarbon.
Calibrated ages are given in BC.

Site	*Sample no.*	*Dates (BP)*	*Calib. Dates*	*Culture*	*Material*
1	*2*	*3*	*4*	*5*	*6*
BHIMBETKA	PRL-787	15370+570 -530 BP	None	Middle Palaeolithic	Charcoal
BHIMBETKA	PRL-789	17670+490 -460 BP	None	Middle Palaeolithic	Charcoal
BHIMBETKA	PRL-788	17230+480 -440 BP	None	Middle Palaeolithic	Charcoal
DHAMNER	PRL-143	10130±250 BP	None	Middle Palaeolithic	Shell
DHOM DAM	TF-1004	38470+8940 -4125 BP	None	Middle Palaeolithic	Unknown
DIDWANA	PRL-911	26210+211 -1670 BP	None	Middle/ lower Palaeolithic	Organic Matter

1	*2*	*3*	*4*	*5*	*6*
GERWA WELL	PRL-710	26090+800 -720 BP	None	Middle Palaeolithic	Calcium Carbonate
KALDEVAN-HALLI	PRL-79	1560±120 BP	463, 478 530 cal.BC	Middle Palaeolithic	Shell
MULA DAM	TF-217	>39000 BP	None	Middle Palaeolithic	Wood
MULA DAM	TF-345	31075+5550 -3254 BP	None	Middle Palaeolithic	Wood
NANDIPALLI	PRL-293	23670+690 -640 BP	None	Middle Palaeolithic	Shell
NANDUR MADMESHWAR	BS-163	26600±430 BP	None	Middle Palaeolithic	Shell
PRABHAS PATAN	PRL-30	20825+6670 -540 BP	None	Middle Palaeolithic	Shell

Table 1b. Dates for Mesolithic Sites

All BP ages are based on 5568 yr half-life of radiocarbon.

Calibrated ages are given in BC/AD.

Site	*Sample no.*	*Dates (BP)*	*Calib. Dates*	*Culture*	*Material*
1	*2*	*3*	*4*	*5*	*6*
BHIMBETKA	PRL-317	2490±100 BP	762, 678 662, 627 600 cal.BC	Microliths	Charcoal
BHIMBETKA	PRL-18	2650±125 BP	813 cal.BC	Microliths	Charcoal
CHAULDARI	BS-617	1350±100 BP	663 cal.AD	Shell Midden	Charred or Uncharred Marine Shells
CHENNUR	BS-79	>40,000 BP	None	Microliths	Shell
INAMGAON	BS-146	11700±150 BP	None	Microliths	Shell
LANGHNAJ	TF-744	3875±105 BP	2452, 2427 2395, 2374 2366 cal.BC	Microliths	Bone Inorganic Fraction
LEKHAHIA	TF-342	180±110 BP	1673, 1753 1796, 1994 1950 cal.BC	Phase 4, Microliths and Pottery	Charcoal
LEKHAHIA	TF-417	3560±105 BP	1908 cal.BC	Lekhahia I, Phase 3, Microliths and Pottery	Bone
LEKHAHIA	TF-419	4240±110 BP	2895 cal.BC	Lekhahia I, Phase 1, Microliths	Bone

1	*2*	*3*	*4*	*5*	*6*
MAHADAHA	BS-137	2880±250 BP	1044 cal.BC	Mesolithic	Charred bone carbonate
MAHADAHA	BS-138	3840±130 BP	2315 cal.BC	Mesolithic	Charred bone carbonate
MAHADAHA	BS-136	4010±120 BP	2569, 2538 2503 cal.BC	Mesolithic	Charred bone carbonate
MANTAI	BM-2341	3550±70 BP	1895 cal.BC	Microliths	Charcoal
MANTAI	BM-2340	3520±45 BP	1883 cal.BC	Microliths	Charcoal
NIRGUDSAR	BS-43	39000±3200 BP	None	Microliths	Wood
ORIYO TIMBO	PRL-888/9	4720±160 BP	3510, 3396 3388 cal.BC	Period I, Microliths	Charcoal
ORIYO TIMBO	PRL-886	4160±170 BP	2870, 2806 2774, 2720 2702 cal.BC	Period I, Microliths	Charcoal
ORIYO TIMBO	PRL-876	4080±160 BP	2850, 2845 2652, 2647 2612, cal.BC	Period I, Microliths	Charcoal
PAISRA	BS-675	7420±110 BP	6223, 6195 6187 cal.BC	Mesolithic	Charcoal
PATIRAJA-WELA SITE	PRL-107	4500±170 BP	3307, 3255 3177, 3163 3134, 3112 3110 cal.BC	Microliths	Shells
SARAI NAHAR RAI	TF-1356/59	2860±120 BP	1021 cal.BC	Microliths	Charred and semi-charred bone
SARAI NAHAR RAI	TF-1104	10050±110 BP	None	Microliths	Human bone Inorganic

Table 1c. **Dates for Stone Age Sites with Rock Art**
All BP ages are based on 5568 yr half-life of radiocarbon.
Calibrated ages are given in BC.

Site	*Sample no.*	*Dates (BP)*	*Calib. Dates*	*Culture*	*Material*
1	*2*	*3*	*4*	*5*	*6*
TENMALAI	BS-646	4420±110 BP	3040 cal.BC	Microliths	Wood and Charcoal Paintings
TENMALAI	BS-630	5210±110 BP	4032, 4026 4001 cal.BC	Microliths	Wood and Charcoal Paintings
TENMALAI	BS-525	4971±115 BP	3780, 3731 3728 cal.BC	Microliths	Wood and Charcoal Paintings

Neolithic Cultures (Tables 2a, 2b, 2c and 2d)

In India the Neolithic is generally equated with the beginning of agriculture and polished stone axes. It may not however be true for all the sites. There is circumstantial evidence from the lakes of Didwana, Sambhar and Lunkaransar in Rajasthan that agriculture may have started 7–8 Kyr ago in that region. This evidence is in the form of Cerealia type pollen and finely comminuted pieces of charcoal indicative of large scale burning and clearance.

Tables 2a, 2b, 2c and 2d list the dates for various Neolithic sites in Kashmir, Pakistan and Iranian plateau, peninsular India, and eastern India and Gangetic doab respectively.

In Kashmir Burzahom and Gufkral were excavated by the Archaeological Survey of India. The earliest dates for Burzahom go back to 2600 BC. Table 2b includes dates for Mehrgarh in Pakistan, belonging to periods 1A, B, and 2A, B. Mehrgarh period 1A goes back beyond 8000 BC. Thus, in the Indian subcontinent the oldest dates for the Neolithic should go back to this period. It must be noted that Mehrgarh shows a transition from late Stone Age to early agriculture; finally, blossoming into the Harappa culture. The Peninsular Indian Neolithic goes back to 2200 BC. at Terdal and Tekkalakota. Chirand, a Neolithic site in Bihar, is dated to about 2000 BC. The Vindhyan Neolithic (Table 2d) goes back to 3300 BC.

Table 2a. **Dates for the Neolithic Sites of Kashmir**
All BP ages are based on 5568 yr half-life of radiocarbon.
Calibrated ages are given in BC.

Site	*Sample no.*	*Dates (BP)*	*Calib. Dates*	*Culture*	*Material*
1	*2*	*3*	*4*	*5*	*6*
BURZAHOM	TF-123	4055±110 BP	2586 cal.BC	Period IA Neolithic	Charcoal
BURZAHOM	TF-13	3690±125 BP	2130, 2074 2045 cal.BC	Period IA Neolithic	Charcoal
BURZAHOM	TF-127	3935±110 BP	2465 cal.BC	Period IB Neolithic	Charcoal
BURZAHOM	TF-14	3860±340 BP	2343 cal.BC	Neolithic	Charcoal
BURZAHOM	TF-129	3670±90 BP	2114, 2086 2039 cal.BC	Neolithic	Charcoal
BURZAHOM	TF-15	3390±105 BP	1730, 1729 1689 cal.BC	Period IB Neolithic	Burnt Organic Material

1	*2*	*3*	*4*	*5*	*6*
BURZAHOM	TF-10	2580±100 BP	797 cal.BC	Neolithic	Charcoal
BURZAHOM	TF-128	4205±115 BP	2881, 2797 2783 cal.BC	Period IB Neolithic	Charcoal
GUFKRAL	BS-359	3864±115 BP	2347 cal.BC	Period IB Neolithic	Wood Charcoal
GUFKRAL	BS-356	3466±105 BP	1860, 1847 1770 cal.BC	Period IB, Neolithic	Wood Charcoal
GUFKRAL	BS-370	2709±105 BP	842 cal.BC	Period IC, Neolithic	Wood Charcoal
GUFKRAL	BS-371	3466±95 BP	1860, 1847 1770 cal.BC	Period IC, Neolithic	Wood Charcoal
GUFKRAL	BS-358	3039±105 BP	1313 cal.BC	Period IA, Aceramic Neolithic	Wood Charcoal
GUFKRAL	BS-360	3243±95 BP	1519 cal.BC	Period IC, Neolithic	Wood Charcoal
GUFKRAL	BS-357	3369±105 BP	1681 cal.BC	IB Period Neolithic	Wood Charcoal

Table 2b. **Dates for the Neolithic Sites in Pakistan and Iranian Plateau**
All BP ages are based on 5568 yr half-life of radiocarbon.
Calibrated ages are given in BC.

Site	*Sample no.*	*Dates (BP)*	*Calib. Dates*	*Culture*	*Material*
1	*2*	*3*	*4*	*5*	*6*
MEHRGARH	BETA-2690	3590±60 BP	1997 cal.BC	Period IV	Unknown
MEHRGARH	BETA-1719	13340±125 BP	14, 191-13 789 cal.BC 2e, 14, 381-13, 567 cal.BC centre 3990 cal.BC	Period IB	Unknown
MEHRGARH	BETA-1721	9385±120 BP	1 8827-8818 8591-8542 8539-8335 8305-8261 cal.BC (2) 8949-8090 cal.BC; center 8420 cal.BC	Period IA	Unknown

1	2	3	4	5	6
MEHRGARH	LV-993	6110±90 BP	5190, 5058 cal.BC	Period IB	Unknown
MEHRGARH	BETA-2686	5860±70 BP	4777 cal.BC	Period IA	Unknown
MEHRGARH	BETA-2688	5490±70 BP	4350 cal.BC	Period IIA	Unknown
MEHRGARH	LY-1945	5360±310 BP	4235 cal.BC	Period IIB	Unknown
MEHRGARH	BETA-7315	5620±100 BP	4465 cal.BC	Period IIA	Unknown
MEHRGARH	BETA-2689	6500±78 BP	5474, 5435 5426 cal.BC	Period III	Unknown
MEHRGARH	LV-994	6290±70 BP	5238 cal.BC	Period IB	Unknown
MEHRGARH	LY-1946	33000±3000 BP	None	Period IB	Charcoal
MEHRGARH	BETA-1408	6925±80 BP	5749 cal.BC	Period IA	Unknown
MEHRGARH	BETA-1407	7115±290 BP	5980 cal.BC	Period IA	Unknown
MEHRGARH	BETA-1720	7115±120 BP	5980 cal.BC	Period IIB	Unknown
MEHRGARH	LY-1950	8440±250 BP	(1) 7694-7651 7648-7239 7223-7200 7180-7141 7119-7096 cal.BC; (2) 8008-6758 6739-6719 cal.BC; center 7490 cal.BC	Period IB	Unknown
MEHRGARH	LV-906	5950±65 BP	4894, 4883 4845 cal.BC	Period IB	Unknown
MEHRGARH	LV-907	6020±80 BP	4937, 4917 4907 cal.BC	Period IB	Unknown
MEHRGARH	LV-909	5940±55 BP	4892, 4887 4841 cal.BC	Period IB	Unknown
MEHRGARH	LY-1948	5720±730 BP	4653, 4648 4581 cal.BC	Period IA	Charcoal
MEHRGARH	LV-908	6090±70 BP	5046, 5019 5004 cal.BC	Period IB	Unknown
MEHRGARH	LY-1949	5530±180 BP	4360 cal.BC	Period IA	Charcoal
MEHRGARH	BETA-	5400±90 BP	4318, 4285 4246 cal.BC	Period IIA	Unknown
MEHRGARH	LY-1947	5830±190 BP	4725 cal.BC	Period IA	Charcoal

1	*2*	*3*	*4*	*5*	*6*
MEHRGARH*	LY-1528	4190±140 BP	2877, 2800 2780, 2712 2708 cal.BC	Period IV	Charcoal
MEHRGARH	LY-1529	3960±140 BP	2470 cal.BC	Period VI	Charcoal
MEHRGARH	LV-910	5880±100 BP	4782 cal.BC	Period IB	Unknown
MEHRGARH	LY-1527	3570±150 BP	1923 cal.BC	Period VII	Charcoal
MEHRGARH	BETA-7316	5990±120 BP	4931, 4928 4901 cal.BC	Period IA	Unknown
REHMAN DHERI	PRL-675	4400±110 BP	3034 cal.BC	Period I Kechi Beg	Charcoal
REHMAN DHERI	PRL-676	4520±110 BP	3331, 3226 3185, 3155 3143 cal.BC	Period I Kechi Beg	Charcoal
REHMAN DHERI	WIS-1698	4190±70 BP	2877, 2800 2780, 2712 2708 cal.BC	Period I Kechi Beg	Unknown
REHMAN DHERI	WIS-1697	4300±70 BP	2915 cal.BC	Period I Kechi Beg	Unknown
SAID QALA	DIC-22	3620±220 BP	2018, 2002 1980 cal.BC	Occupation no.1 (Damb Sadaat III)	Charcoal
SAID QALA	DIC-20	3710±90 BP	2135, 2052 2050 cal.BC	Occupation no. 1 (Damb Sadaat II)	Charcoal
SAID QALA	DIC-18	3800±220 BP	2278, 2234 2209 cal.BC	Occupation no. 3 (Damb Sadaat II)	Charcoal
SARAIKHOLA	BM-1934R	4470±150 BP	3263, 3246 3102 cal.BC	Period I Neolithic	Charcoal
SARAIKHOLA	BM-1939R	4530±160 BP	3334, 3219 3189, 3152 3148 cal.BC	Period I Neolithic	Charcoal
SARAIKHOLA	BM-1940R	4600±200 BP	3360 cal.BC	Period I Neolithic	Charcoal
SARAIKHOLA	BM-1935R	4370±250 BP	3023, 2994 2928 cal.BC	Period I Neolithic	Charcoal
SHAHR-I-SOKHTA	P-2077	3950±60 BP	2468 cal.BC	Shahr-i-Sokhta II, Phase 5, proto-Urban	Charcoal
SHAHR-I-SOKHTA	R-627	4020±50 BP	2573, 2535 2506 cal.BC	Shahr-i-Sokhta II, Phase 5-6, proto-Urban	Charcoal
SHAHR-I-SOKHTA	R-634	4050±50 BP	2584 cal.BC	Shahr-i-Sokhta II,	Charcoal

1	*2*	*3*	*4*	*5*	*6*
				Phase 6, proto-Urban	
SHAHR-I-SOKHTA	P-2542	3990±60 BP	2559, 2544 2495 cal.BC	Shahr-i-Sokhta II, Phase 5-6, proto-Urban	Charcoal
SHAHR-I-SOKHTA	P-2543	4200±60 BP	2880, 2798 2782 cal.BC	Shahr-i-Sokhta I, Phase 9-10, proto-Urban	Charcoal
SHAHR-I-SOKHTA	TUNC-24	3943±70 BP	2466 cal.BC	Shahr-i-Sokhta III, Phase 3-4	Charcoal
SHAHR-I-SOKHTA	R-623	4050±50 BP	2584 cal.BC	Shahr-i-Sokhta II, Phase 5-6, proto-Urban	Charcoal
SHAHR-I-SOKHTA	TUNC-27	3890±90 BP	2455, 2416 2405 cal.BC	Shahr-i-Sokhta III, Phase 3-4 proto-State	Charcoal
SHAHR-I-SOKHTA	R-405A	3960±50 BP	2470 cal.BC	Shahr-i-Sokhta II, Phase 5-6 proto-Urban	Charcoal
SHAHR-I-SOKHTA	TUNC-22	3829±61 BP	2298 cal.BC	Shahr-i-Sokhta III, Phase 3-4, proto-Urban	Charcoal
SHAHR-I-SOKHTA	R-629	4200±50 BP	2880, 2798 2782 cal.BC	Shahr-i-Sokhta I, Phase-8-9, Archaic	Charcoal
SHAHR-I-SOKHTA	P-2081B	4150±70 BP	2867, 2808 2772, 2723 2699 cal.BC	Shahr-i-Sokhta II, Phase 6, proto-Urban	Charcoal
SHAHR-I-SOKHTA	TUNC-26	4115±72 BP	2859, 2819 2692, 2686 2661, 2635 2625 cal.BC	Shahr-i-Sokhta III, Phase 3-4, proto-State	Charcoal
SHAHR-I-SOKHTA	P-2084	4110±60 BP	2587, 2821 2691, 2689 2660, 2637 2623 cal.BC	Shahr-i-Sokhta II, Phase 6, proto-Urban	Charcoal

1	*2*	*3*	*4*	*5*	*6*
SHAHR-I-SOKHTA	R-632	4100±50 BP	2855, 2824 2657, 2640 2619 cal.BC	Shahr-i-Sokhta II, Phase 6, proto-Urban	Charcoal
SHAHR-I-SOKHTA	P-2071	3970±60 BP	2483 cal.BC	Shahr-i-Sokhta IV, Phase 0, post-Urban	Charcoal
SHAHR-I-SOKHTA	TUNC-21	4065±65 BP	2598 cal.BC	Shahr-i-Sokhta III, Phase 3-4, proto-State	Charcoal

Table 2c. **Dates for the Neolithic Sites of South India**
All BP ages are based on 5568 yr half-life of radiocarbon.
Calibrated ages are given in BC.

Site	*Sample no.*	*Dates (BP)*	*Calib Dates*	*Culture*	*Material*
1	*2*	*3*	*4*	*5*	*6*
HALLUR	TF-576	3280±105 BP	1570, 1528 cal.BC	Period IB Late Neolithic	Charcoal
HALLUR	TF-580	3560±105 BP	1908 cal.BC	Period IA Early Neolithic	Charcoal
HALLUR	TF-586	3055±95 BP	1379, 1343 1319 cal.BC	Period IB Late Neolithic	Charcoal
HALLUR	TF-575	2895±100 BP	1065 cal.BC	Period II Neolithic/ Iron Age overlap	Charcoal
PAIYAM-PALLI	TF-349	3340±100 BP	1643 cal.BC	Neolithic/ Megalithic transition	Charcoal
PAIYAM-PALLI	TF-833	3215±210 BP	1513 cal.BC	Late Southern Neolithic	Charcoal
PAIYAM-PALLI	TF-827	3570±105 BP	1923 cal.BC	Neolithic/ Megalithic transition	Charcoal
PALAVOY	TF-700	3390±95 BP	1730, 1729 1689 cal.BC	Neolithic/ Megalithic transition	Charcoal

1	2	3	4	5	6
PALAVOY	TF-701	3805±100 BP	2281 cal.BC	Early Southern Neolithic	Charcoal
POLAKONDA	BS-98	3255±120 BP	1522 cal.BC	Southern Neolithic	Wood
POLAKONDA	BS-97	2045±90 BP	83 cal.BC	Megalithic Period	Wood Charcoal
SANGANA-KALLU	TF-354	3440±100 BP	1746 cal.BC	Middle Southern Neolithic	Charcoal
SANGANA-KALLU	TF-359 1697	3400±100 BP	1733, 1721 cal.BC	Middle Southern Neolithic	Charcoal
SANGANA-KALLU	TF-355	3435±100 BP	1745 cal.BC	Late Southern Neolithic	Charcoal
SATANIKOTA	BS-204	8960±120 BP	None	Megalithic	Charcoal
SATANIKOTA	BS-203	7520±140 BP	66410 cal.BC	Megalithic	Charcoal
T.NARASIPUR	TF-412	3645±105 BP	2033 cal.BC	Southern Neolithic	Charcoal
T.NARASIPUR	TF-413	3345±105 BP	1672 cal.BC	Southern Neolithic	Charcoal
TEKKALA-KOTA	TF-237	3465±105 BP	1859, 1848 1769 cal.BC	Neolithic Period	Charcoal
TEKKALA-KOTA	TF-239	3395±105 BP	1732, 1725 1692 cal. BC	Neolithic Period	Charcoal
TEKKALA-KOTA	TF-266	3625±100 BP	2023, 1998 1983 cal.BC	Neolithic Period	Charcoal
TEKKALA-KOTA	TF-262	3460±135 BP	1851, 1850 1761 cal.BC	Neolithic Period	Charcoal
TERDAL	TF-684	3775±95 BP	2200 cal.BC	Southern Neolithic	Charcoal
TERDAL	TF-683	3615±120 BP	2014, 2016 1976 cal.BC	Southern Neolithic	Charcoal
UTNUR	TF-168	3875±110 BP	2452, 2427 2395, 2374 2366 cal.BC	Period IIIA Neolithic	Charcoal
UTNUR	BM-54	4120±150 BP	2860, 2817 2693, 2684 2662, 2633 2626 cal.BC	Period I, Neolithic	Charcoal
UTNUR	TF-167	3890±110 BP	2455, 2416 2405 cal.BC	Period IIA, Neolithic	Charcoal

Table 2d. **Dates for the Neolithic Sites of Gangetic Valley and Eastern India**
All BP ages are based on 5568 yr half-life of radiocarbon.
Calibrated ages are given in BC/AD.

Site	*Sample no.*	*Dates (BP)*	*Calib. Dates*	*Culture*	*Material*
1	*2*	*3*	*4*	*5*	*6*
CHIRAND	TF-1032	3600±150 BP	1961 cal.BC	Period I, Neolithic	Charcoal
CHIRAND	TF-446	1930±105 BP	72 cal.BC	Northern Black Polished Ware Period	Charcoal
CHIRAND	TF-1035	3125±100 BP	1418 cal.BC	Period I Neolithic	Charcoal
CHIRAND	TF-1031	3525±135 BP	1884 cal.BC	Period I, Neolithic	Charcoal
CHIRAND	TF-1126	2290±120 BP	391 cal.BC	Period I, Neolithic	Charcoal
CHIRAND	TF-1125	3365±150 BP	1679 cal.BC	Period I, Neolithic	Charcoal
CHIRAND	TF-1127	3230±95 BP	1516 cal.BC	Period I, Neolithic	Charcoal
CHIRAND	TF-1034	3420±110 BP	1740 cal.BC	Period I, Neolithic	Charcoal
CHIRAND	TF-1036	2485±120 BP	761, 681 659, 596 633, 577 561 cal.BC	Period I, Neolithic	Charcoal
CHIRAND	TF-1033	3390±110 BP	1730, 1729 1689 cal.BC	Period I, Neolithic	Charcoal
CHIRAND	TF-334	2715±120 BP	890, 845 cal.BC	Period I, Neolithic	Charcoal
CHIRAND	BS-129	4540±110 BP	3338, 3213 3203 cal.BC	Period III Neolithic	Charcoal
KOLDIHWA	PRL-224	8280±210 BP	None	Neolithic	Charcoal
KOLDIHWA	PRL-56	820±100 BP	1225 cal.AD	Chalcolithic	Charcoal
KOLDIHWA	PRL-227	2050±110 BP	92 cal.BC	Chalcolithic	Charcoal
KOLDIHWA	PRL-101	6295±180 BP	5240 cal.BC	Neolithic	Charcoal
KOLDIHWA	PRL-100	7180±230 BP	6075, 6059 6043, 6018 6001 cal.BC	Neolithic	Charcoal
KOLDIHWA	PRL-102	2380±105 BP	405 cal.BC	Chalcolithic	Charcoal
KOLDIHWA	PRL-99	2900±150 BP	1092 cal.BC	Chalcolithic	Charcoal
KOLDIHWA	PRL-223	3300±120 BP	1607, 1554 1544 cal.BC	Neolithic	Charcoal

1	2	3	4	5	6
KUNJHUN	BETA-6414	4010±110 BP	2569, 2538 2503 cal.BC	Vindhyan Neolithic	Unknown
KUNJHUN	BETA-6415	4660±180 BP	3360 cal.BC	Vindhyan Neolithic	Unknown
KUNJHUN	BETA-4879	3120±70 BP	1414 cal.BC	Vindhyan Neolithic	Unknown
MAHAGARA	PRL-409	3260±150 BP	1523 cal.BC	Neolithic	Charcoal
MAHAGARA	BS-128	3330±100 BP	1628 cal.BC	Neolithic	Charcoal
MAHAGARA	PRL-407	3300±100 BP	1607, 1554 1544 cal.BC	Neolithic	Charcoal
MARAKDOLA	BS-42	660±95 BP	1287 cal.BC	Neolithic	Charcoal
NAMPHUK	PRL-539	19310±920 BP	None	Neolithic	Charcoal

Harappan Culture (Table 3)

Table 3 gives radiocarbon dates for pre-Harappan and Harappan sites in India and Pakistan. It may be noted that even the calibrated dates from Harappa generally do not go beyond 2500 BC. Only the pre-Harappan/Kotdijian dates go beyond *c.* 2500 BC. The dates for the Kulli culture also suggest a timespread between 2500 and 2200 BC. A large number of Harappan and pre-Harappan sites in Pakistan have been dated by foreign labs. The site of Kalibangan also shows a spread between 2400 and 2000 BC. Lothal is dated to 2200–2000 BC. Rojdi also gives a similar timespread, though a couple of radiocarbon dates go back to *c.* 2500 BC. At Surkotda most of the dates fall around 2000 BC.

Table 3. **Dates for pre-Harappan and Harappan Sites of India and Pakistan**
All BP ages are based on 5568 yr half-life of radiocarbon.
Calibrated ages are given in BC.

Site	*Sample no.*	*Dates (BP)*	*Calib. Dates*	*Culture*	*Material*
1	*2*	*3*	*4*	*5*	*6*
HARAPPA	WIS-2145	4020±60 BP	2573, 2535 2506 cal.BC	Urban Harappan	Charcoal
HARAPPA	WIS-2074	3700±60 BP	2133, 2067 2047 cal.BC	Urban Harappan Hearth	Charcoal
HARAPPA	WIS-2142	4135±65 BP	2863, 2812 2742, 2776 2696, 2677 2666 cal.BC	Transitional Early Harappan/ Urban	Carbonized wood

1	*2*	*3*	*4*	*5*	*6*
				Harappan Hearth	
HARAPPA	QL-4380	3950±80 BP	2468 cal.BC	Transitional Early Urban Harappan Hearth	Charcoal
HARAPPA	QL-4377	3770±100 BP	2198, 2151 2149 cal.BC	Transitional Early/Urban Harappan Hearth	Charcoal
HARAPPA	QL-4378	3850±50 BP	2334 cal.BC	Urban Harappan Charcoal Kiln	Charcoal
HARAPPA	Ql-4372	3890±40 BP	2455, 2416 2405 cal.BC	Early Harappan Hearth/pit	Charcoal
HARAPPA	QL-4374	3800±50 BP	2278, 2234 2209 cal.BC	Urban Harappan, Charcoal in front of kiln	Charcoal
HARAPPA	WIS-2144	3720±100 BP	2138 cal.BC	Urban Harappan	Charcoal
HARAPPA	WIS-2075	3830±60 BP	2299 cal.BC	Urban Harappan floor level	Charcoal
HARAPPA	QL-4376	3810±50 BP	2283 cal.BC	Urban Harappan kiln	Charcoal
HARAPPA	QL-4373	3960±30 BP	2470 cal.BC	Early Harappan kiln	Charcoal
HARAPPA	QL-4375	3920±40 BP	2462 cal.BC	Early Harappan Hearth pit	Charcoal
HARAPPA	WIS-2043	3770±70 BP	2268, 2263 2203, 2147 2146 cal.BC	Urban Harappan Upper level	Charcoal wood
HARAPPA	WIS-2141	3920±70 BP	2462 cal.BC	Urban Harappan	Carbonized wood
HARAPPA	BETA-33873	4540±85 BP	3338, 3213 3203 cal.BC	Early Harappan	Charcoal
HARAPPA	WIS-2143	3825±60 BP	2293 cal.BC	Urban Harappan Hearth	Charcoal

1	2	3	4	5	6
HARAPPA	BETA-33874	4540±180 BP	3338, 3213 3203 cal.BC	Urban Harappan Charcoal in front of klin	Charcoal
HARAPPA	WIS-2139	3820±60 BP	2288 cal.BC	Urban Harappan Hearth	Carbonized wood
HARAPPA	WIS-2053	3920±210 BP	2469 cal.BC	Urban Harappan Upper level	Unknown
HARAPPA	WIS-2140	4290±70 BP	2913 cal.BC	Urban Harappan	Charcoal
HARAPPA	QL-4483	3784±30 BP		Urban phase Harappan	Charcoal
HARAPPA	QL-4486	3785±45 BP		pre-Urban Urban phase Transition (late)	Charcoal
HARAPPA	QL-4485	3863±45 BP		pre-Urban/ Urban phase Transition-late	Charcoal
HARAPPA	QL-4487	3816±25 BP		Urban phase Harappan	Charcoal
HARAPPA	QL-4484	3730±30 BP		Urban phase Harappan	Charcoal
HARAPPA	QL-4488	3750±40 BP		Urban phase Harappan	Charcoal
HATHIAL WEST	BM-1949R	3980±140 BP	2554, 2548 2491 cal.BC	Late early Harappan Late Kot Dijian	Charcoal
HATHALA	P-1813	4040±160 BP	2580 cal.BC	Early Harappan; Kot Dijian	Charcoal
HATHIAL WEST	BM-1948R	3820±120 BP	2288 cal.BC	Late early Harappan; Late Kot Dijian	Charcoal
HISHAM	WIS-1703	3720±80 BP	2138 cal.BC	Mature Harappan	Unknown
JHANG	BM-2201R	4260±110 BP	2903 cal.BC	Early Kot Dijian	Charcoal
JHANG	BM-2200R	4010±250 BP	2569, 2538 2503 cal.BC	Late Kot Dijian	Charcoal
ISLAM CHOWKI	BM-2403	3840±110 BP	2315 cal.BC	Late Kot Dijian	Charcoal

1	*2*	*3*	*4*	*5*	*6*
ISLAM CHOWKI	BM-1941R	3910±460 BP	2459 cal.BC	Late Kot Dijian	Charcoal
ISLAM CHOWKI	OXA-1004	4010±120 BP	2569, 2538 2503 cal.BC	Late Kot Dijian	Charred goatdung
ISLAM CHOWKI	OXA-1005	4160±100 BP	2870, 2806 2774, 2720 2702 cal.BC	Kot Dijian	Charcoal
JHUKAR	P-2476	4630±300 BP	3371 cal.BC	Mature Harappan from an oven	Charcoal
NAUSHARO	BETA-18844	4010±80 BP	2569, 2538 2503 cal.BC	Period IC Mehrgarh VII	Unknown
NAUSHARO	BETA-18842	4030±170 BP	2576, 2531 2510 cal.BC	Period IC Mehrgarh VII	Unknown
NAUSHARO	BETA-18845	4040±170 BP	2580 cal.BC	Period III, Mature Harappan	Unknown
NAUSHARO	BETA-18843	4070±170 BP	2598 cal.BC	Period IB Mehrgarh VII	Unknown
NIAI BUTHI	P-478	3740±64 BP	2181, 2166 2142 cal.BC	Period II Kulli	Unknown
NINDOWARI	TF-862	3900±105 BP	2457 cal.BC	Period II, or III, Kulli	Charcoal
NINDOWARI	TF-862(BS)	3840±235 BP	2315 cal.BC	Period II or III, Kulli	Charcoal
RANA GHUNDAI	P-2149	4600±60 BP	3360 cal.BC	Period IIIA and burned seeds	Charcoal
RANA GHUNDAI	P-2148	5580±60 BP	4456, 4417 4403 cal.BC	Period I, or Pre-period	Charcoal
REHMAN-DHERI	WIS-1699	4180±70 BP	2875, 2802 2778, 2715 2706 cal.BC	Early Harappan Period II, Early Kot Dijian n.a	Unknown
REHMAN-DHERI	PRL-673	3900±130 BP	2475 cal.BC	Late early Harappan; Period III Late Kot Dijian	Charcoal
REHMAN-DHERI	BM-2062R	3810±150 BP	2283 cal.BC	Late early Harappan; Period III	Charcoal

1	*2*	*3*	*4*	*5*	*6*
				Late Kot Dijian	
REHMAN-DHERI	BM-2062R	3960±110 BP	2470 cal.BC	Late early Harappan; Period III Late Kot Dijian	Charcoal
REHMAN DHERI	PRL-674	4000±150 BP	2564, 2541 2499 cal.BC	Early Harappan; Period II, Early Kot Dijian	Charcoal
REHMAN-DHERI	WIS-1701	3850±70 BP	2334 cal.BC	Late early Harappan; Period III Late Kot Dijian	Unknown
REHMAN-DHERI	WIS-1700	4070±90 BP	2598 cal.BC	Early Harappan; Period II, Early Kot Dijian	Unknown
SARAI KHOLA	BM-1946R	3920±130 BP	24662 cal.BC	Late Early Harappan; Period IB, Late Kot Dijian	Charcoal
SARAI KHOLA	BM-1945R	4020±120 BP	2573, 2535 2506 cal.BC	Late Early Harappan; Period IB, Late Kot Dijian	Charcoal
SARAI KHOLA	BM-1936R	4120±250 BP	2860, 2817 2693, 2684 2662, 2663 2626 cal.BC	Early Harappan Period IIA Early Kot Dijian	Charcoal
SARAI KHOLA	BM-±938R	4030±120 BP	2576, 2531 2510 cal.BC	Early Harappan Period IIA Early Kot Dijian	Charcoal
SARAI KHOLA	BM-1944R	4270±220 BP	2909 cal.BC	Early Harappan Period IIA Early Kot Dijian	Charcoal

1	*2*	*3*	*4*	*5*	*6*
SARAI KHOLA	BM-1943R	3920±120 BP	2576, 2531, 2510 cal.BC	Early Harappan Period IIB Late Kot Dijian	Charcoal
SARAI KHOLA	BM-1942R	4130±120 BP	2862, 2814 2738, 2728 2696, 2679 2665, 2630 cal.BC	Early Harappan; Period IIA Early Kot Dijian	Charcoal
SHAHR-I-SOKHTA	R-900	3730±50 BP	2140 cal.BC	Shahr-i-Sokhta IV, Phase 1, post-Urban	Charcoal
SHAHR-I-SOKHTA	P-2073	3840±60 BP	2315 cal.BC	Shahr-i-Sokhta IV Phase 1, post-Urban	Charcoal
SHAHR-I-SOKHTA	R-899A	3800±150 BP	2278, 2234 2209 cal.BC	Shahr-i-Sokhta III IV Phase 1 post-Urban	Charcoal
SHAHR-I-SOKHTA	P-2072	3750±160 BP	2191, 2161 2145 cal.BC	Shahr-i-Sokhta IV Phase 0, post-Urban	Charcoal
SHAHR-I-SOKHTA	P-2070	4070±160 BP	2598 cal.BC	Shahr-i-Sokhta IV Phase 1, post-Urban	Charcoal
SHAHR-I-SOKHTA	P-2082	4020±170 BP	2573, 2535 2506 cal.BC	Shahr-i-Sokhta II Phase 6, post-Urban	Charcoal
SHAHR-I-SOKHTA	R-425	3950±150 BP	24668 cal.BC	Shahr-i-Sokhta IV post-Urban	Charcoal
SHAHR-I-SOKHTA	P-2068	4220±160 BP	2885, 2794 27866 cal.BC	Shahr-i-Sokhta IV Phase 1, post-Urban	Charcoal
SHAHR-I-SOKHTA	P-2071	3970±160 BP	2483 cal.BC	Shahr-i-Sokhta IV Phase 0, post-Urban	Charcoal

1	*2*	*3*	*4*	*5*	*6*
TARAKAI QILA	BM-1691	3510±160 BP	1880, 1830 1829 cal.BC	Late Early Harappan Late Kot Dijian	Charcoal
TARAKAI QILA	BM-1692	3680±50 BP	2123, 2080 2042 cal.BC	Late Early Harappan Late Kot Dijian	Charcoal
TARAKAI QILA	BM-1694	3770±90 BP 2149	2198, 2151 cal.BC	Late Early Harappan Late Kot Dijian	Charcoal
TARAKAI QILA	BM-1695	4060±120 BP	2587 cal.BC	Late Early Harappan Late Kot Dijian	Charcoal
TARAKAI QILA	BM-1690 Harappan	3640±180 BP	2032 cal.BC	Late Early Late Kot Dijian	Charcoal
TARAKAI QILA	BM-1693	3810±160 BP	2283 cal.BC	Late Early Harappan Late Kot Dijian	Charcoal
HULAS	PRL-1031	3840±110 BP	2315 cal.BC	Early Late Harappan	Charcoal
HULAS	PRL-1032	4380±150 BP	3028, 2985 2930 cal.BC	Early Late Harappan	As above
KALIBANGAN	TF-152	3615±85 BP	2014, 2006 1976 cal.BC	Period II Urban Harappan	Charcoal
KALIBANGAN	TF-145	3895±100 BP	2456, 2412 2408 cal.BC	Period II Urban Harappan	Charcoal
KALIBANGAN	TF-157	4120±110 BP	2860, 2817 2693, 2684 2662, 2633 2626 cal.BC	Period I Early Harappan	Charcoal
KALIBANGAN	TF-161	3930±100 BP	24664 cal.BC	Period I, Early Harappan	Charcoal
KALIBANGAN	TF-147	3865±100 BP	2450, 2348 cal.BC	Period II Urban Harappan	Charcoal
KALIBANGAN	TF-143	3510±110 BP	1880, 1830 1829 cal.BC	Period II Urban Harappan	Wood

1	*2*	*3*	*4*	*5*	*6*
KALIBANGAN	TF-163	3910±100 BP	2459 cal.BC	Period II Urban Harappan	Charcoal
KALIBANGAN	TF-150	3740±100 BP	2181, 2166 2142 cal.BC	Period II Urban Harappan	Charcoal
KALIBANGAN	TF-25	3930±110 BP	2464 cal.BC	Period II Urban Harappan charred	Charcoal mixed with bone
KALIBANGAN	TF-244	3250±90 BP	1521 cal.BC	Period II Urban Harappan	Charcoal
KALIBANGAN	TF-139	3775±100 BP	2200 cal.BC	Period II Urban Harappan	Charcoal
KALIBANGAN	TF-151	3800±100 BP	2278, 2234 2209 cal.BC	Period II Urban Harappan	Charcoal
KALIBANGAN	TF-241	4090±90 BP	2853, 2882 2655, 2644 2615 cal.BC	Period I Early Harappan	Charcoal
KALIBANGAN	TF-155	4195±115 BP	2879, 2799 2781, 2711 2709 cal.BC	Period I Early Harappan	Charcoal
KALIBANGAN	TF-947	3765±85 BP	2197, 2154 2148 cal.BC	Period II, Urban Harappan	Wood Charcoal
KALIBANGAN	TF-162	3940±100 BP	2466 cal.BC	Period I, Early Harappan	Charcoal
KALIBANGAN	TF-138	3075±100 BP	1391, 1334 1327 cal.BC	Pariod II Urban Harappan	Charcoal
KALIBANGAN	TF-605	3810±105 BP	2283 cal.BC	Period II, Urban Harappan	Charcoal
KALIBANGAN	TF-153	3910±110 BP	2459 cal.BC	Period II, Urban Harappan	Charcoal
KALIBANGAN	TF-439	6507±125 BP	5475, 5431 5429 cal.BC	Period I, Early Harappan	Unknown
KALIBANGAN	TF-946	3605±100 BP	1968 cal.BC	Period II, Urban Harappan	Wood Charcoal

1	2	3	4	5	6
KALIBANGAN	TF-948	3815±100 BC	2286 cal.BC	Period II, Urban Harappan	Wood Charcoal
KALIBANGAN	TF-942	4055±110 BP	25866 cal.BC	Period II, Urban Harappan	Charcoal
KALIBANGAN	TF-142	3635±100 BP	2030, 1990 cal.BC	Period II, Urban Harappan	Charcoal
KALIBANGAN	TF-141	3705±110 BP	2134, 2059 2048 cal.BC	Period II, Urban Harappan	Charcoal
KALIBANGAN	TF-160	4060±100 BP	2587 cal.BC	Period II, Urban Harappan	Charcoal
KALIBANGAN	TF-149	3675±140 BP	2118, 2083 2041 cal.BC	Period II, Urban Harappan	Charcoal
KALIBANGAN	TF-156	3740±105 BP	2181, 2166 2142 cal.BC	Period I, Early Harappan	Charcoal
KALIBANGAN	TF-152 (BS)	3570±125 BP	1923 cal.BC	Period II, Urban Harappan	Charcoal
KALIBANGAN	TF-163 (BS)	3925±125 BP	2462 cal.BC	Period II, Urban Harappan	Charcoal
KALIBANGAN	TF-439 (BS)	6507±125 BP	5475, 5431 5429 cal.BC	Period I, Early Harappan	Unknown
KALIBANGAN	TF-240	3610±110 BP	2010, 1973 cal.BC	Period I, Early Harappan	Charcoal
KALIBANGAN	P-481	3879±72 BP	2453, 2424 2398 cal.BC	Period II, Urban Harappan	Charcoal
KALIBANGAN	TF-165	3800±100 BP	2278, 2334 2209 cal.BC	Period I, Early Harappan	Charcoal
KALIBANGAN	TF-957	2355±200 BP	401 cal.BC	Period I, Early Harappan	Wood
KALIBANGAN	TF-607	3930±120 BP	2464 cal.BC	Period II, Urban Harappan	Charred wheat

1	*2*	*3*	*4*	*5*	*6*
KALIBANGAN	TF-156 (BS)	4010±165 BP	2570, 2537 2503 cal.BC	Period I, Early Harappan	Charcoal
KALIBANGAN	TF-154	3665±110 BP	2105, 2088 2038 cal.BC	Period I, Urban Harappan	Charcoal
KALIBANGAN	TF-608	3910±110 BP	2459 Cal.BC	Period II, Urban Harappan	Charred Wheat
KALIBANGAN	TF-149 (BS)	3585±120 BP	1942 cal.BC	Period II, Urban Harappan	Charcoal
KALIBANGAN	PRL-1282	3470±140 BP	1866, 1846 1772 cal.BC	Rojdi B, 46L Harappan	Charcoal
KUNTASI	PRL-1371	3650±140 BP	2014 cal.BC	Sorath Harappan	Charcoal
KUNTASI	PRL-1370	3710±160 BP	2135, 2052 2050 cal.BC	Sorath Harappan	Charcoal
LOTHAL	TF-135	3405±125 BP	1735, 1717 1701 cal.BC	Period IIA Lothal A, Urban Harappan	Charcoal
LOTHAL	TF-29	3740±110 BP	2181, 2166 2142 cal.BC	Period IVA Lothal A, Urban Harappan	Charcoal
LOTHAL	TF-23	3705±105 BP	2134, 2059 2048 cal.BC	Period VA Lothal B post-Urban Harappan	Charcoal
LOTHAL	TF-26	3830±120 BP	2299 cal.BC	Period IIIB Lothal A, Urban Harappan	Charcoal
LOTHAL	TF-136	3915±130 BP	2461 cal.BC	Period IA Lothal A, Urban Harappan	Charcoal
LOTHAL	TF-19	3650±135 BP	2034 cal.BC	Period VA Lothal B, post-Urban Harappan	Charcoal
LOTHAL	TF-133	3740±110 BP	2328 cal.BC	Period IIA Lothal A, Urban Harappan	Charcoal

1	*2*	*3*	*4*	*5*	*6*
LOTHAL	TF-22	3845±110 BP	2328 cal.BC	Period IIIB Lothal A, Urban Harappan	Charcoal
LOTHAL	TF-27	3840±110 BP	2315 cal.BC	Period IIIB Lothal A, Urban Harappan	Charcoal
MALVAN	TF-1084	2675±90 BP	826 cal.BC	post-Urban Harappan	Charcoal
MITATHAL	PRL-290	3820±130 BP	2288 cal.BC	Period I, Urban Phase	Charcoal
MITATHAL	PRL-292	4210±210 BP	2883, 2796 2784 cal.BC	Period IIB, Punjab, post-Urban Phase, BARA Ware	Charcoal
MITATHAL	PRL-291	3600±110 BP	1961 cal.BC	Period IIA, Urbàn Phase	Charcoal
NAGWADA	A-4555	3700±80 BP	2133, 2067 2047 cal.BC	Late Sorath Harappan	Unknown
ROJDI	PRL-1091	4150±110 BP	2867, 2808 2772, 2723 2699 cal.BC	Rojdi A, 45K, Urban Harappan	Charcoal
ROJDI	TF-199	3590±100 BP	1947 cal.BC	Period I, Phase B, Harappan	Charcoal
ROJDI	PRL-1093	3920±110 BP	24662 cal.BC	Rojdi A, 45K, Harappan	Charcoal
ROJDI	PRL-1083	3875±120 BP	2452, 2427 2395, 2374 2366 cal.BC	Rojdi B, 45K, Harappan	Charcoal
ROJDI	PRL-1089	3870±120 BP	2451, 2433 2392, 2384 2356 cal.BC	Rojdi A, 45 K, Harappan	Charcoal
ROJDI	TF-200	3810±110 BP	2283 cal.BC	Period I, Phase B, Harappan	Unknown
ROJDI	PRL-1081	2360±210 BP	402 cal.BC	Rojdi C, 78 J, post-Urban Harappan	Charcoal

1	*2*	*3*	*4*	*5*	*6*
ROJDI	PRL-1085	4020±110 BP	2573, 2535 2506 cal.BC	Rojdi A,45K Harappan	Charcoal
ROJDI	PRL-1087	4010±110 BP	2569, 2538, 2503 cal.BC	Rojdi A, 45K Harappan	Charcoal
ROJDI	PRL-1284	3810±100 BP	2283 cal.BC	Rojdi A, 46L Harappan	Charcoal
ROJDI	BETA-61767	3570±60 BP	1973, 1872, 1840, 1811, 1809, 1780; 2113, 2087, 2038-1742 cal.BC	Late Sorath Harappan, Rojdi C	Charcoal
ROJDI	PRL-1281	3520±110 BP	1883 cal.BC	Rojdi B, 46L Harappan	Charcoal
ROJDI	PRL-1084	3700±150 BP	2133, 2067, 2047 cal.BC	Rojdi c, 76I post-Urban Harappan	Charcoal
ROJDI	PRL-1088	3770±120 BP	2198, 2151, 2149 cal.BC	Rojdi B, 45K Harappan	Charcoal
ROJDI	PRL-1283	3980±100 BP	2554, 2548, 2491 cal.BC	Rojdi A, 46L Harappan	Charcoal
ROJDI	BETA-61768	3520±60 BP	1, 1913-1745, 2, 2013-2007, 1977-1682 cal.BC	Late Sorath Harappan Rojdi C	Charcoal
SANGHOL	PRL-TL-10	None	None	Period I, Late Harappan	Soil in Asssocia-tion with Period I Pottery
SURKOTADA	TF-1295	3780±95 BP	2202 cal.BC	Period IB,	Charcoal
SURKOTADA	TF-1311	3625±90 BP	2023, 1998 1983 cal.BC	Period IC, Urban Harappan	Charcoal
SURKOTADA	TF-1301	3840±130 BP	2315 cal.BC	Period IA	Charcoal
SURKOTADA	TF-1304/9	3645±90 BP	2033 cal.BC	Period IA	Charcoal
SURKOTADA	TF-1310	3810±95 BP	2283 cal.BC	Period IA, Upper level	Charcoal
SURKOTADA	TF-1305	3890±95 BP	2455, 2416 2405 cal.BC	Period IA Earliest Levels	Charcoal

1	*2*	*3*	*4*	*5*	*6*
SURKOTADA	PRL-85	4140±130 BP	2865, 2810 2747, 2725 2697, 2674 2668 cal.BC	Period IA Mid-Levels	Charcoal
SURKOTADA	TF-1307	3510±105 BP	1880, 1830 1829 cal.BC	Period IC Urban Harappan	Charcoal
SURKOTADA	TF-1294	3620±95 BP	2018, 2002 1980 cal.BC	Period IC Urban Harappan	Charcoal
SURKOTADA	TF-1297	3635±95 BP	2030, 1990 cal.BC	Period IC Urban Harappan	Charcoal

Chalcolithic Cultures (Tables 4a, 4b, 4c and 4d)

Table 4a, gives C^{14} dates for Chalcolithic sites in Pakistan, mainly from Pirak, ranging from 1500–800 BC. Table 4b gives dates for the Indian Chalcolithic sites belonging to the Jodhpura, Lustrous Red Ware (LRW), pre-Prabhas, Bara, Malwa, Jorwe, Daimabad and Savalda cultures. The Jodhpura culture is associated with a typical copper artifact assemblage in Rajasthan. It is dated to about 3000 BC. The Lustrous Red Ware dates from Oriyo Timbo tend to go even beyond 3000 BC (PRL-1425, 1426).

Prabhas Patan had earlier given C^{14} dates going back to *c.* 3000 BC. It appears that in Gujarat one is dealing with an indigenous culture which is pre-Harappan. On the whole, C^{14} dates now suggest that in the northwestern part of the suBcontinent there is a Neolithic emerging out of local cultures, which in some areas developed into the urban Harappan culture. Table 4c gives radiocarbon dates for the Chalcolithic cultures of eastern India. The dates range from *c.* 1800–900 BC Table 4d covers the central Indian and Deccan Chalcolithic sites of Chandoli, Daimabad, Dangwada, Eran, Inamgaon, Kheda, Navdatoli, Nevasa and Sonegaon. Most of these sites have Jorwe and Malwa culture habitations. Though some of the calibrated dates go back to *c.* 3000 BC, the general time spread seems to be confined to 2000–1500 BC and for Jorwe culture it is 1500–1000 BC. There are a few dates for Daimabad culture suggesting a time spread between 1800 and 1700 BC.

Table 4a. **Dates for Chalcolithic Sites in Pakistan**
All BP ages are based on 5568 yr half-life of radiocarbon.
Calibrated ages are given in BC.

Site	*Sample no.*	*Dates (BP)*	*Calib. Dates*	*Culture*	*Material*
1	*2*	*3*	*4*	*5*	*6*
SIBRI	BETA-2691	3220±60 BP	1541 cal.BC	Mehrgarh VIIC or Later	Unknown
PIRAK	PRL-388	2730±110 BP	897 cal.BC	Chalcolithic	Charcoal
PIRAK	PRL-390	2730±100 BP	897 cal.BC	Chalcolithic	Charcoal
PIRAK	PRL-389	2590±100 BP	799 cal.BC	Chalcolithic	Charcoal
PIRAK	PRL-391	2730±100 BP	897 cal.BC	Chalcolithic	Charcoal
PIRAK	LY-1641	4080±290 BP	2250, 2245 2652, 2647 2617 cal.BC	Period I	Charcoal
PIRAK	TF-1202	2940±80 BP	1159, 1142 1138 cal.BC	Period II	Charcoal
PIRAK	LY-1642	3150±150 BP	1428, cal.BC	Period II	Charcoal
PIRAK	LY-1640	3410±140 BP	1737, 1713 1706 cal.BC	Period II	Charcoal
PIRAK	LY-1643	2970±140 BP	1255, 1240 1221 cal.BC	Period II	Charcoal

Table 4b. **Dates for Chalcolithic Sites of Gujarat, Rajasthan and Punjab**
All BP ages are based on 5568 yr half-life of radiocarbon.
Calibrated ages are given in BC.

Site	*Sample no.*	*Dates (BP)*	*Calib. Dates*	*Culture*	*Material*
1	*2*	*3*	*4*	*5*	*6*
JODHPURA	PRL-275	4360±160 BP	3018, 3001 2926 cal.BC	Ganeshwar/ Jodhpura Culture	Charcoal
JODHPURA	PRL-278	4060±10 BP	2578 cal.BC	Ganeshwar/ Jodhpura culture	Charcoal
JODHPURA	PRL-277	2610±110 BP	803 cal.BC	Ganeshwar/ Jodhpura culture	Charcoal
ORIYO TIMBO	PRL-1424	3750±130 BP	2191, 2161 2145 cal.BC	Period II, Lustrous Red Ware	Charcoal

1	2	3	4	5	6
ORIYO TIMBO	PRL-1425	5010±170 BP	3706 cal.BC	Period II, Lustrous Red Ware	Charcoal
ORIYO TIMBO	PTL-1427	3240±110 BP	1519 cal.BC	Period II, Lustrous Red Ware	Charcoal
ORIYO TIMBO	PRL-1426	4250±160 BP	2897 cal.BC	Period II, Lustrous Red Ware	Charcoal
PRABHAS PATAN	PRL-20	3340±105 BP	1643 cal.BC	Period III, Lustrous Red Ware	Charcoal
PRABHAS PATAN	TF-1287	4280±105 BP	2911 cal.BC	Period I, pre-Prabhas	Shell
PRABHAS PATAN	PRL-91	3860±165 BP	2343 cal.BC	Period III, Lustrous Red Ware	Charcoal
PRABHAS PATAN	TF-1284	3465±95 BP	1859, 1848 1769 cal.BC	Period II, Prabhas	Charcoal
PRABHAS PATAN	PRL-90	4240±110 BP	2892 cal.BC	Period I, pre-Prabhas	Charcoal
PRABHAS PATAN	PRL-19	3100±160 BP	1406 cal.BC	Period III, Lustrous Red Ware	Charcoal
PRABHAS PATAN	TF-1286	3595±90 BP	1953 cal.BC	Period II, Prabhas	Charcoal
PRABHAS PATAN	PRL-92	3830±95 BP	2299 cal.BC	Period II, Prabhas	Charcoal
SANGHOL	PRL-510	3550±150 BP	1895 cal.BC	Period I, post-Urban Bara culture	Charcoal
SANGHOL	PRL-511	3740±60 BP	2181, 2166 2142 cal.BC	Period I, post-Urban Bara culture	Charcoal
SANGHOL	PRL-509	3570±150 BP	1923 cal.BC	Period I, post-Urban Bara culture	Charcoal
SANGHOL	PRL-513	3540±150 BP	1888 cal.BC	Period I, post-Urban Bara culture	Charcoal
SANGHOL	PRL-512	3350±110 BP	1673 cal.BC	Period I, post-Urban Bara culture	Charcoal

Table 4c. **Dates for Chalcolithic Sites of Eastern India**
All BP ages are based on 5568 yr half-life of radiocarbon.
Calibrated ages are given in BC.

Site	*Sample no.*	*Dates (BP)*	*Calib. Dates*	*Culture*	*Material*
1	*2*	*3*	*4*	*5*	*6*
CHIRAND	TF-1030	3430±110 BP	1740 cal.BC	Period II, Chalcolithic	Charcoal
CHIRAND	TF-444	2590±105 BP	799 cal.BC	Period II, Chalcolithic	Charcoal
CHIRAND	TF-1028	3390±90 BP	1730, 1729 1689 cal.BC	Period II, Chalcolithic	Charcoal
CHIRAND	TF-1029	2915±85 BP	1121, 1119, 1104 cal.BC	Period II, Chalcolithic	Wood Charcoal
CHIRAND	TF-445	3500±100 BP	1877, 1824 1824, 1793 1787 cal.BC	Period II, Chalcolithic	Wood
MAHISDAL	TF-391	3235±105 BP	1517 cal.BC	Early Chalcolithic	Charcoal
MAHISDAL	TF-392	2950±105 BP	1211, 1180 1165 cal.BC	Early Chalcolithic	Charcoal
MAHISDAL	TF-390	2725±100 BP	894, 875 850 cal.BC	Late Chalcolithic	Charred Rice

Table 4d. **Dates for Chalcolithic Sites of Central India and Deccan**
All BP ages are based on 5568 yr half-life of radiocarbon.
Calibrated ages are given in BC.

Site	*Sample no.*	*Dates (BP)*	*Calib. Dates*	*Culture*	*Material*
1	*2*	*3*	*4*	*5*	*6*
CHANDOLI	TF-43	2905±100	1096 cal.BC	Jorwe	Charcoal
CHANDOLI	P-474	3099±185 BP	140 cal.BC	Jorwe	Charcoal
CHANDOLI	TF-42	3035±115 BP	131 cal.BC	Jorwe	Charcoal
CHANDOLI	P-472	3157±68 BP	143 cal.BC	Jorwe	Charcoal
CHANDOLI	P-473	3184±68 BP	144 cal.BC	Jorwe	Charcoal
DAIMABAD	PRL-419	2980±110 BP	1258, 1235 1226 III, cal.BC	Period Daimabad culture	Charcoal
DAIMABAD	BS-177	3460±100 BP	1851, 1850 1761 cal.BC	Period III, Daimabad culture	Charcoal
DAIMABAD	BS-178	2950±100 BP	1211, 1180 1165 cal.BC	Period V, Jorwe	Charcoal

1	2	3	4	5	6
DAIMABAD	PRL-655	3490±110 BP	1875, 1838 1818, 1800 1782 cal.BC	Period III, Daimabad culture	Charcoal
DAIMABAD	PRL-429	3390±150 BP	1730, 1729 1689 cal.BC	Period I, Savalda	Charcoal
DAIMABAD	PRL-428	3400±110 BP	1733, 1721 1697 cal.BC	Period III, Daimabad culture	Charcoal
DAIMABAD	BS-176	3590±90 BP	1947 cal.BC	Period I, Savalda	Charcoal
DAIMABAD	BS-181	2990±100 BP	1261 cal.BC	Period IV Malwa	Charcoal
DAIMABAD	PRL-412	3250±110 BP	1521 cal.BC	Period IV Malwa	Charcoal
DAIMABAD	BS-179	2970±100 BP	1255, 1240 1221 cal.BC	Period V Jorwe	Charcoal
DAIMABAD	PRL-654	3460±100 BP	1851, 1850, 1761 cal.BC	Period I, Savalda	Charcoal
DAIMABAD	PRL-411	3230±100 BP	1561 cal.BC	Period IV/V Malwa/ Jorwe overlap	Charcoal
DAIMABAD	PRL-656	3050±150 BP	1376, 1346 1318 cal.BC	Period V, Jorwe	Charcoal
DAIMABAD	BS-182	3130±90 BP	1420 cal.BC	Period III, Daimabad culture	Charcoal
DANGWADA	PRL-690	3400±150 BP	1733, 1721 1697 cal.BC	Malwa Period	Charred Rice
DANGWADA	PRL-686	3110±140 BP	1411 cal.BC	Malwa Period	Charcoal
DANGWADA	PRL-687	3810±140 BP	2283 cal.BC	Malwa Period	Charred Grain
DANGWADA	PRL-691	3200±120 BP	1506, 1475 1465 cal.BC	Malwa Period	Charcoal
DANGWADA	PRL-692	2900±140 BP	1092 cal.BC	Malwa Period	Charred Wheat
DANGWADA	PRL-693	3280±100 BP	1570, 1528, cal.BC	Malwa Period	Charcoal
ERAN	TF-327	3280±100 BP	1570, 1528, cal.BC	Period I, Malwa	Charcoal
ERAN	P-526	3136±68 BP	1422 cal.BC	Period I, Malwa	Charcoal
ERAN	TF-331	3355±90 BP	1675 cal.BC	Period I, Malwa	Charcoal
ERAN	TF-324	3130±105 BP	1420 cal.BC	Period I, Malwa	Charcoal

1	*2*	*3*	*4*	*5*	*6*
ERAN	TF-326	2905±105 BP	1096 cal.BC	Period I, Malwa	Charcoal
ERAN	P-528	2878±65 BP	1042 cal.BC	Period I, Malwa	Charcoal
ERAN	P-527	2515±58 BP	786 cal.BC	Period II, Iron ?	Charcoal
ERAN	TF-330	3220±100 BP	1514 cal.BC	Period I, Malwa	Charcoal
ERAN	P-525	3193±69 BP	1496, 1485, 1455 cal.BC	Period I, Malwa	Charcoal
ERAN	TF-329	3300±105 BP	1607, 1554 1544 cal.BC	Period I, Malwa	Charcoal
INAMGAON	BS-486	3020±100 BP	1299, 1276 1269 cal.BC	Period III, Late Jorwe	Unknown
INAMGAON	BS-489	3020±100 BP	1299, 1276 1269 cal.BC	Period III, Jorwe	Unknown
INAMGAON	BS-463	2980±110 BP	1258, 1235 1226 cal.BC	Period III, Jorwe	Unknown
INAMGAON	BS-277	3078±100 BP	1393, 1332 1328 cal.BC	Period I, Malwa	Unknown
INAMGAON	BS-263	3310±130 BP	1614 cal.BC	Period I, Malwa	Unknown
INAMGAON	TF-1085	3295±105 BP	1603, 1558 1538 cal.BC	Period II Early Jorwe	Charcoal
INAMGAON	PRL-93	3020±105 BP	1299, 1276 1269 cal.BC	Period III, Late Jorwe	Charcoal
INAMGAON	TF-1330	3090±100 BP	1400 cal.BC	Period III, Late Jorwe	Charcoal
INAMGAON	PRL-94	3020±115 BP	1299, 1276 1269 cal.BC	Period III, Late Jorwe	Charcoal
INAMGAON	BS-502	3050±100 BP	1376, 1346 1318, BC	Period Late Jorwe	Unknown
INAMGAON	TF-923	2890±170 BP	1057 cal.BC	Period III, Late Jorwe	Charcoal
KHED	PRL-221	3040±90 BP	1314 cal.BC	Jorwe	Charcoal
KHED	PRL-220	2900±160 BP	1092 cal.BC	Jorwe	Charcoal
NAVDATOLI	P-205	3294±125 BP	1602, 1559 1536 cal.BC	Phase 4, Malwa, Jorwe Coarse red,	Burnt Wheat
NAVDATOLI	P-475	3455±70 BP	1754 cal.BC	Phase I, Malwa, Bichrome, Ahar	Charcoal

1	2	3	4	5	6
NAVDATOLI	P-476	4125±69 BP	2861, 2815 2733, 2729 2694, 2681 2664, 2632 2681 cal.BC	Phase II, Malwa, Late Jorwe, Bichrome	Charcoal
NAVDATOLI	P-202	3503±128 BP	1878, 1833 1826, 1791 1789 cal.BC	Phase II, Malwa, Late Jorwe, Bichrome	Charcoal
NAVDATOLI	P-204	3449±127 BP	1749 cal.BC	Phase II, Malwa, Jorwe, cream-slipped	Charcoal
NAVDATOLI	TF-59	3380±105 BP	1685 cal.BC	Phase I, Malwa, Biochrome, Ahar	Charcoal
NAVDATOLI	P-201	3492±128 BP	3032, 2962 2942 cal.BC	Phase I, Malwa, Bichrome, Ahar	Charcoal
NAVDATOLI	P-200	3457±127 BP	1757 cal.BC	Phase I, Malwa, Biochrome, Ahar	Charcoal
NEVASA	P-181	3106±122 BP	1409 cal.BC	Period III, Jorwe	Charcoal
NEVASA	TF-40	3110±110 BP	1411 cal.BC	Period III, Jorwe	Charcoal
NEVASA	P-184	2545±115 BP	790 cal.BC	Period III, Jorwe	Charcoal
SONEGAON	TF-384	3415±105 BP	1783 cal.BC	Period I, Blotchy grey ware	Charcoal
SONEGAON	TF-383	3185±100 BP	1448 cal.BC	Period II, Jorwe	Charcoal
SONEGAON	TF-379	3150±90 BP	1428 cal.BC	Period II, Jorwe	Charred Grain
SONEGAON	TF-380	3230±105 BP	1516 cal.BC	Period II, Jorwe	Charcoal
SONEGAON	TF-382	3195±100 BP	1499, 1482 1458 cal.BC	Period II, Jorwe	Charred Wheat

Megalithic Phase (Tables 5a and 5b)

Tables 5a and b give radiocarbon dates for the Megalithic sites of the Gangetic zone and peninsular India, respectively. The dates from the Gangetic area indicate that the beginning of Megalithic culture goes back to *c.* 2000 BC. In peninsular India *c.* 1000 BC probably marks the transition between the Neolithic and Megalithic phases.

Table 5a. **Dates for Megalithic Sites in the Gangetic Zone**
All BP ages are based on 5568 yr half-life of radiocarbon.
Calibrated ages are given in BC.

Site	*Sample no.*	*Dates (BP)*	*Calib. Dates*	*Culture*	*Material*
1	*2*	*3*	*4*	*5*	*6*
KAKORIA	TF-183	200±95 AD	1666, 1790 1949, 1952 cal.BC	Megalithic	Charcoal
KAKORIA	TF-179	195±90 AD	1668, 1783 1791, 1948 1953 cal.BC	Megalithic	Charcoal
KOTIA	TF-319	2135±100 BC	182 cal.BC	Megalithic	Charcoal

Table 5b. **Dates for Megalithic Sites in Peninsular India**
All BP ages are based on 5568 yr half-life of radiocarbon.
Calibrated ages are given in BC/AD.

Site	*Sample no.*	*Dates (BP)*	*Calib. Dates*	*Culture*	*Material*
1	*2*	*3*	*4*	*5*	*6*
HALINGALI	TF-685	1970±95 BP	22 cal.BC	Megalithic, Neolithic	Charcoal
HALLUR	TF-570	2970±105 BP	1255, 1240 1221 cal.BC	Period II Neolithic/ Iron Age Overlap	Charcoal
HALLUR	TF-573	2820±100 BP	993 cal.BC	Period II, Neolithic/ Iron Age Overlap	Charcoal
HATHINIA HILL	TF-109	30 ± 90 BP	1955 cal.BC	Megalithic	Charcoal
KORKAI	TF-987	2680±90 BP	828 cal.BC	Megalithic, Ancient port	Wood

1	2	3	4	5	6
NAIKUND	BS-94	2495±105 BP	763, 675 665, 620 604 cal.BC	Megalithic	Charcoal
NAIKUND	BS-92	2455±100 BP	753, 704, 533 cal.BC	Megalithic	Charcoal
PAIYAMPALLI	TF-828	2100±95 BP	151, 149, 117 cal.BC	Megalithic	Charcoal
PAIYAMPALLI	TF-824	785±90 BP	1256 cal.BC	Megalithic	Charcoal
PAIYAMPALLI	TF-823	2515±100 BP	786 cal.BC	Megalithic	Charred Grain
PAIYAMPALLI	TF-825	695±95 BP	1280 cal.AD	Megalithic	Charcoal
T.NARASIPUR	TF-414	220±90 BP	1660 cal.AD	Megalithic period	Charcoal
TOGARAPALLI	PRL-134	2180±100 BP	340, 322, 203 cal.BC	Megalithic	Charcoal
TOGARAPALLI	PRL-135	2150±110 BP	192 cal.BC	Megalithic	Charcoal
VEERAPURAM	PRL-727	2090±140 BP	110 cal.BC	Megalithic	Charcoal
VEERAPURAM	PRL-730	3150±140 BP	1428 cal.BC	Megalithic	Charcoal
VEERAPURAM	PRL-725	1780±140 BP	239 cal.AD	Megalithic	Charcoal
VEERAPURAM	PRL-728	2870±140 BP	1035 cal.BC	Megalithic	Charcoal

Ancient Metal Working Sites

Table 6 gives radiocarbon dates for some copper, gold, silver and zinc mines from different parts of India. Radiocarbon dates suggest that the exploitation of Kolar Gold Mine goes back to 600 BC. The earliest evidence of copper mining comes from Rajpura Dariba (Rajasthan), giving a date of *c.* 1300 BC. The Zawar zinc mines have given dates which go back *c.* 400 BC As zinc is very volatile it was not smelted in the west till the Roman times. When mixed with copper it produced brass. The date of 400 BC. from Zawar mines is the earliest recorded evidence for zinc smelting through distillation technique in the whole world.

Copper is known from the Harappan sites and even some pre-Harappan sites like Mehrgarh but the old workings have not been studied in detail. Therefore we do not have dates going back to 3000 BC or so. Tables 7a and 7b give C^{14} dates from important early historic sites.

Table 6. **Dates from Early Metal Working Sites in India**
All BP ages are based on 5568 yr half-life of radiocarbon.
Calibrated ages are given in BC/AD.

Site	*Sample no.*	*Dates (BP)*	*Calib. Dates*	*Culture*	*Material*
1	*2*	*3*	*4*	*5*	*6*
CHIGAR GUNTA MINE	PRL-1188	1050±100 BP	991 cal.AD	Gold mine	Charcoal
CHIGAR GUNTA MINE	PRL-1187	1270±100 BP	716, 743 757 cal.AD	Gold Mine	Charcoal
INGALDHAL COPPER MINES	BM-2364	1810±35 BP	221 cal.AD	Copper Mine	Wood
INGALDHAL COPPER MINES	PRL-252	1680±100 BP	381 cal.BC	Copper Mine	Wood
INGALDHAL COPPER MINES	PRL-1097	2010±110 BP	10 cal.BC	Copper Mine	Wood
KOLAR MINE	TF-1199	1260±85 BP	725, 735 766 cal.AD	Gold Mine	Charcoal
KOLAR MINE	TF-879	1460±110 BP	605 cal.AD	Mine	Wood
KOLAR MINE	MO-352	1460±160 BP	605 cal.AD	Gold Mine	Carbona-ceous Material from bonfire
MAILARAM	TF-373	520±90 BP	1414 cal.AD	Copper Mine	Charcoal
DARIBA MINES	TF-1117	2245±100 BP	372 cal.BC	Mine	Wood
DARIBA SMELTING AREA	BM-2492	1940±70 BP	66 cal.BC	Lead/Silver zinc smelting	Charcoal
DARIBA SMELTING AREA	BM-2490	2340±60 BP	399 cal.BC	Lead/Silver zinc smelting	Charcoal
DARIBA SMELTING AREA	BM-2491	2170±45 BP	331, 329, 200 cal.BC	Lead/Silver zinc smelting	Charcoal
KHODARBIA MINE	PRL-927	Modern	None	Mine	Wood
KUMBARIA	TF-1222	880±85 BP	1166 cal.AD	Copper Mine	Charcoal
KUMBARIA	TF-1221	520±90 BP	1414 cal.AD	Copper Mine	Charcoal
KUMBARIA	PRL-549	670±110 BP	1285 cal.AD	Copper Mine	Charcoal
RAJPUR DARIBA	PRL-928	2390±140 BP	407 cal.BC	Old Mine Shaft	Wood
RAJPURA DARIBA	PRL-210	3040±150 BP	1314 cal.BC	Copper Mine	Wood
RAJPURA DARIBA	PRL-208A	2140±100 BP	186 cal.BC	Copper Mine	Wood

1	*2*	*3*	*4*	*5*	*6*
RAJPURA DARIBA	PRL-209	1790±120 BP	233 cal.AD	Copper Mine	Wood
ZAWAR LEAD SLAG HEAP	BM-2484	100±45 BP	1885, 1912 1955 cal.AD	Smelting	Charcoal
ZAWAR MALA MINE	BM-2065	Modern	None	Zinc Mine	Charcoal
ZAWAR MALA MINE	BM-2578	500±50 BP		Zinc Smelting	Charcoal
ZAWAR MALA MINE	BM-2482	2150±110 BP	192 cal.BC	Smelting	Wood
ZAWAR MALA MINE	PRL-934	730±130 BP	1272 cal.AD	Zinc Mine	Charcoal
ZAWAR MALA MINE	PRL-935	820±130 BP	1225 cal.AD	Zinc Mine	Charcoal
ZAWAR MALA MINE	PRL-932	2410±100 BP	410 cal.BC	Zinc Mine	Charcoal
ZAWAR MALA MINE	BM-2017	Modern	None	Zinc Mine	Charcoal
ZAWAR MALA MINE	BM-2243	80±60 BP	1898, 1902 1955 cal.AD	Zinc Mine	Charcoal
ZAWAR MALA MINE	BM-2381	Modern	None	Smelting	Charcoal
ZAWAR MALA MINE	BM-2338	170±50 BP	1676, 1747 1799, 1942 1922 cal.AD	Zinc Mine	Wood
ZAWAR MALA MINE	BM-2148	2120±60 BP	196 cal.BC	Zinc Mine	Wood
ZAWAR MALA MINE	BM-2222	10±40 BP	1955 cal.AD	Zinc Mine	Charcoal
ZAWAR MALA MINE	BM-2223	230±60 BP	1657 cal.AD	Zinc Mine	Charcoal
ZAWAR MALA MINE	BM-2381	2360±50 BP	1676, 1747 1799, 1942 1955 cal.AD	Zinc Mine	Wood
ZAWAR MALA MINE	PRL-933	1940±140 BP	666 cal.BC	Zinc Mine	Charcoal
ZAWAR MALA MINE	PRL-298	Modern	None	Lead Smelting	Carbon
ZAWAR MALA MINE	BM-2149	1920±50 BP	77 cal.AD	Zinc Mine	Wood
ZAWAR SMELTING AREA	BM-2486	200±35 BP	1666, 1790 1949, 1952 cal.AD	Smelting	Charcoal

1	*2*	*3*	*4*	*5*	*6*
ZAWAR SMELTING AREA	BM-2485	1950±60 BP	58 cal.AD	Smelting	Charcoal
ZAWAR SMELTING AREA	BM-2487	1930±80 BP	72 cal.AD	Smelting	Charcoal
ZAWAR SMELTING AREA	BM-2488	1370±80 BP	657 cal.AD	Smelting	Charcoal

Table 7a. **Dates for Early Historic Sites in India**
All BP ages are based on 5568 yr half-life of radiocarbon.
Calibrated ages are given in BC/AD.

Site	*Sample no.*	*Dates (BP)*	*Calib. Dates*	*Culture*	*Material*
1	*2*	*3*	*4*	*5*	*6*
BUTKARA-II	R-194	2425±40 BP	512 cal.BC	Pre-Buddhist Necropolis	Burnt Human bone
DHARNIKOTA	TF-247	2275±95 BP	385 cal.BC	Early Historic	Charcoal
DHARNIKOTA	TF-246	2355±95 BP	401 cal.BC	Early Historic	Charcoal
DHARNIKOTA	TF-248	2095±100 BP	113 cal.BC fortification	Satavahana	Charcoal
DHULIKATTA	BS-118	1910±95 BP	82 cal.AD	Historic Period	Wood Charcoal
DHULIKATTA	BS-117	1965±90 BP	25 cal.AD	Historic Period	Wood Charcoal
DHULIKATTA	BS-119	2210±100 BP	1681 cal.BC	Historic Period	Wood Charcoal
DUMAKHAD	PRL-1074	1360±90 BP	660 cal.AD	Early Historic levels	Charcoal
DUMAKHAD	PRL-1073	590±90 BP	1322, 1340 1392 cal.AD	Historic Levels	Charcoal
ERAN	P-529	3868±72 BP	2451, 2440 2391, 2388, 2352 cal.BC	Period II, Iron	Charcoal
KAKARAHTA	PRL-1051	2870±120 BP	1035 cal.BC	Maurya-Sunga	Charcoal
KAKARAHTA	PRL-1054	2310±110 BP	405 cal.BC	Maurya-Sunga	Charcoal

1	2	3	4	5	6
KANCHI PURAM	PRL-22	2360±120 BP	402 cal.BC	Early Historic	Charcoal
KANCHI-PURAM	PRL-785	8551±15 BP	1191 cal.BC	Black and red ware	Charcoal
KANCHI-PURAM	TF-1216	2085±90 BP	107 cal.BC	Early Historic	Charcoal
KANCHI-PURAM	TF-1115	2480±110 BP	760, 648 656, 638 592, 586 550 cal.BC	Palisades	Wood
KANTARODAI	P-2515	2990±660 BP	1261 cal.BC	Late pre-Rouletted ware	Charcoal
KANTARODAI	P-2526	2090±50 BP	110 cal.BC	Phase 1, Ceramics	Charcoal
KANTARODAI	P-2524	2340±50 BP	399 cal.BC	Pre-Roule-tted ware	Charcoal
KANTARODAI	P-2529	2350±200 BP	400 cal.BC	Late pre-rouletted ware	Charcoal
KANTARODAI	P-2517	2250±50 BP	374 cal.BC		Charcoal
KANTARODAI	P-2521	2020±50 BP	36 cal.BC	Rouletted ware	Charcoal
KANTARODAI	P-2514	2250±60 BP	374 cal.BC	Pre-Roule-tted ware	Charcoal
KANTARODAI	P-2518	2290±50 BP	391 cal.BC	Rouletted ware	Charcoal
KANTARODAI	P-2528	2370±60 BP	403 cal.BC	Phase 1, Ceramics	Charcoal
KANTARODAI	P-2520	2180±60 BP	340, 322, 203 cal.BC	Rouletted ware	Charcoal
KANTARODAI	P-2522	2110±60 BP	160, 138, 124, cal.BC	Phase 2, Ceramics	Charcoal
KANTARODAI	P-2523	2060±50 BP	96 cal.BC	Phase 1, Ceramics	Charcoal
KARLACAVE	TF-185	2180±95 BP	340, 322, 203, cal.BC	Buddhist cave	Wood
KARLA CAVE	BM-92	2240±150 BP	370 cal.BC	Buddhist cave	Wood from chaitya hall
KARLA CAVE	TF-171	2075±100 BP	103 cal.BC	Buddhist cave	Wood
KAUSAMBI	TF-94	1945±90 BP	62 cal.AD	Period IV, Early Historic	Charcoal
KAUSAMBI	TF-97	1640±105 BP	411 cal.AD	Period IV, Early Historic	Charcoal

1	*2*	*3*	*4*	*5*	*6*
KAUSAMBI	TF-98	1470±90 BP	600 cal.AD	Period IV, Early Historic	Charcoal
KAUSAMBI	TF-95	1840±115 BP	140 cal.AD	Period IV, Early Historic	Charcoal
KAUSAMBI	TF-96	2005±95 BP	5 cal.BC	Period IV, Early Historic	Charcoal
KAUSAMBI	TF-93	1655±105 BP	401 cal.AD	Period IV, Early Historic	Charcoal
MANTAI	BM-2588	1690±50 BP	348, 367 371, cal.BC.	Early Historic	Charcoal
MANTAI	BM-2587	1700±50 BP	343 cal.AD	Early Historic	Charcoal
MANTAI	BM-2589	1810±50 BP	221 cal.AD	Early Historic	Charcoal
NARHAN	BS-582	2200±100 BP	353, 306 236, cal.BC.	Sunga-Kushana Period IV	Unknown
NEVASA	TF-38	1755±105 BP	252, 308, 311, cal.BC.	Period V, Indo-Roman	Charcoal
NEVASA	P-183	1846±106 BP	136 cal.AD	Period IV, Satyavahana	Charred grain
NEVASA	TF-41	1675±96 BP	386 cal.AD	Period IV, Early Historic	Charred grain
NEVASA	TF-39	1860±100 BP	128 cal.AD	Period IV, Early Historic	Charred grain
PAIYAMPALLI	TF-350	2265±100 BP	381 cal.BC	post Megalithic	Charred grain
PAIYAMPALLI	TF-169	2005±95 BP	5 cal.BC	Early Historic Palisades	Wood
PIPRAHWA	PRL-324	2170±130 BP	331, 329 200, cal.BC.	pre-Mauryan Period	Charcoal
PIPRAHWA	PRL-323	2290±100 BP	391 cal.BC	pre-Mauryan Period	Charcoal
PIPRAHWA	PRL-322	2250±100 BP	374 cal.BC	Sunga-Kushana period	Charred Rice
SEMTHAN	PRL-959	1730±130 BP	261, 288 327, cal.BC.	Indo-Greek Period III	Charcoal

Table 7b. **Dates for Certain Early Historic Sites in India and Pakistan**
All BP ages are based on 5568 yr half-life of radiocarbon.
Calibrated ages are given in BC/AD.

Site	*Sample no.*	*Dates (BP)*	*Calib. Dates*	*Culture*	*Material*
1	*2*	*3*	*4*	*5*	*6*
CAKHANSUR	HV-190	700±80 BP	1279 cal.AD	Historical	Sheep Dung
CHANDRA-KETUGARH	TF-367	660±90 BP	1287 cal.AD	Historical Deposits	Shell, Inorganic fraction
CHARSADA	MSU-XXX	1990±120 BP	8 cal.AD	Room with coins of Kanishka	Charcoal
CHARSADA	UW-78	1940±70 BP	66 cal.AD	Room with coins of Kanishka	Charcoal
CHARSADA	UW-77	2155±60 BP	194 cal.BC	Room with coins of Kanishka	Charcoal
HATIKRA	PRL-1194	1480±90 BP	596 cal.AD	Iron Age	Charcoal
HATIKRA	PRL-1190	1310±90 BP	677 cal.AD	Iron Age	Charcoal
HATIKRA	PRL-1189	1400±90 BP	6647 cal.AD	Iron Age	Charcoal
HATIKRA	PRL-1193	1540±130 BP	539 cal.AD	Iron Age	Charcoal
HATIKRA	PRL-1191	2870±120 BP	1035 cal.BC	Iron Age	Charcoal
DWARKA	TF-173	310±90 BP	1528, 1554 1633 cal.AD	Historic Period	Charcoal
SEMTHAN	PRL-959	1730±130 BP	261, 288 327 cal.AD	Indo-Greek Period III	Charcoal

Painted Grey Ware Sites, and Northern Black Polished Ware and Early Iron Age Sites (Tables 8, 9a and 9b)

Now 21 radiocarbon dates are available for Painted Grey Ware sites and it is clear that their time spread is between 800 and 400 BC (Table 8). The Northern Black Polished Ware sites are covered between 600 and 300 BC, though some of the dates seem to go back a little earlier. The dates from Pirak suggest the advent of iron in the beginning of the first millennium BC (Table 9a).

Table 9b gives radiocarbon for Black and Red Ware. At Sohgaura the Chalcolithic dates go back *c.* 1400 BC but otherwise the Black and Red Ware is confined between 800 and 300 BC. Probably it does not have a very diagnostic cultural value. It is found with different types of cultural assemblages. Hatikara presents some early first millennium dates for the beginning of iron.

Table 8. **Dates for Painted Grey Ware Culture Site**
All BP ages are based on 5568 yr half-life of radiocarbon.
Calibrated ages are given in BC/AD.

Site	*Sample no.*	*Dates (BP)*	*Calib. Dates*	*Culture*	*Material*
1	*2*	*3*	*4*	*5*	*6*
HASTINAPUR	TF-90	2270±110 BP	383 cal.BC	Uppermost Painted Grey Ware, Period II,	Charcoal
HASTINAPUR	TF-112	2260±95 BP	379 cal.BC	Upper most Painted Grey Ware, Period II	Charcoal
HASTINAPUR	UCLA-684	1800±100 BP	227 cal.AD	Painted Grey Ware Period II probably an intrusive burial ?	Bone Collagen
HASTINAPUR	TF-85	2385±125 BP	406 cal.BC	Late Painted Grey Ware, Period II	Charcoal
HASTINAPUR	TF-83	2220±110 BP	362, 282, 258, cal.BC	Uppermost Painted Grey Ware, Period II	Charcoal
HASTINAPUR	TF-91	2450±120 BP	752, 709, 530, cal.BC	Late Painted Grey Ware, Period II	Charcoal
HULAS	PRL-HLS-TL-1	None	None	Period II, Painted Grey Ware, late phase	Soils in association with Period II
KHALAUA	PRL-67	2450±155 BP	752, 709 530, cal.BC	Painted Grey Ware	Charcoal
KHALAUA	TF-1228	2420±95 BP	484, 437 424, cal.BC	Painted Grey Ware	Charcoal
KHALAUA	PRL-68	2370±170 BP	403 cal.BC	Painted Grey Ware	Charcoal
NOH	TF-1144	2370±85 BP	403 cal.BC	Painted Grey Ware	Charcoal
NOH	TF-994	2560±100 BP	793 cal.BC	Painted Grey Ware	Charcoal
NOH	UCLA-703A	2480±250 BP	760, 684 656, 638 592, 586 550 cal.BC	Painted Grey Ware	Charcoal

1	2	3	4	5	6
NOH	UCLA-703B	2690±220 BP	833 cal.BC	Painted Grey Ware	Charcoal
NOH	TF-993	2600±145 BP	801 cal.BC	Painted Grey Ware	Charcoal
SONKH MOUND MATHURA	I-6277	2570±85 BP	795 cal.BC	Painted Grey Ware	Charcoal
SONPUR	TF-376	2510±105 BP	767 cal.BC	pre-Northern Black Polished Ware	Charred rice
THAPLI	PRL-732	2070±120 BP	101 cal.BC	Painted Grey Ware	Charcoal
THAPLI	PRL-731	2030±140 BP	43 cal.BC	Painted Grey Ware	Charcoal
TILAURAKOT	TF-737	2235±95 BP	368, 273 268, cal.BC	Painted Grey Ware	Charcoal
JODHPURA	PRL-212	2270±100 BP	383 cal.BC	Black & Red Ware/Painted Grey Ware overlap	Charcoal

Table 9a. **Dates for NBP Ware and Early Iron Sites in India and Pakistan**
All BP ages are based on 5568 yr half-life of radiocarbon.
Calibrated ages are given in BC/AD.

Site	*Sample no.*	*Dates (BP)*	*Calib. Dates*	*Culture*	*Material*
1	*2*	*3*	*4*	*5*	*6*
ATRANJI KHERA	TF-283	2150±105 BP	192 cal.BC	Northern Black Polished Ware, Period IV	Charcoal
ATRANJI KHERA	BM-193	2040±150 BP	50 cal.BC	Painted Grey Ware/ Northern Black Polished Ware overlap	Charcoal
ATRANJI KHERA	TF-415	2450±200 BP	752, 709 530, cal.BC	Period II, Black and Red Ware	Charcoal

1	*2*	*3*	*4*	*5*	*6*
ATRANJI KHERA	TF-289	2550±105 BP	791 cal.BC	Period II, Black and Red Ware	Charcoal
ATRANJI KHERA	TF-194	2410±85 BP	410 cal.BC	Painted Grey Ware, Period III	Charcoal
ATRANJI KHERA	TF-291	2415±100 BP	512 cal.BC	Painted Grey Ware, Period III	Charcoal
ATRANJI KHERA	BM-194	2420±150 BP	484, 437 424, cal.BC	Painted Grey Ware/ Northern cal.BC Black Polished Ware overlap	Charcoal
ATRANJI KHERA	TF-191	2890±105 BP	1057 cal.BC	Painted Grey Ware, Period III,	Charcoal
ATRANJI KHERA	TF-287	1605±95 BP	427 cal.BC	Painted Grey Ware, Period III	Charcoal
ATRANJI KHERA	TF-284	2180±95 BP	340, 322 203, cal.BC	Northern Black Polished Ware, Period IV	Charcoal
ATRANJI KHERA	TF-195	1845±95 BP	137 cal.BC	Post-Northern Black Polished Ware, Period IV	Charcoal
ATRANJI KHERA	UW-XXXX	2407±150 BP	489 cal.BC	Painted Grey Ware/ Northern Black Polished Ware overlap	Unknowwn
ATRANJI KHERA	OXFORD-TL-111 -C1	2280 BC	None	Ochre-Colored Pottery Period I	Pottery
ATRANJI KHERA	OXFORD -TL-111 -B4	1670 BC	None	Ochre-Colored Pottery, Period I	Pottery

1	2	3	4	5	6
ATRANJI KHERA	OXFORD -TL-111 -B5	1170 BC	None	Ochre-Colored Pottery, Period I	Pottery
ATRANJI KHERA	OXFORD -TL-111 -C2	1250 BC	None	Ochre-Colored Pottery, Period I	Pottery
ATRANJI KHERA	OXFORD -TL-111 -C3	2130 BC	None	Ochre-Colored Pottery, Period I	Pottery
HASTINAPUR	TF-88	2225±110 BP	364, 279 261, cal.BC	Lowest Northern Black Polished Ware, Period III	Charcoal
HASTINAPUR	TF-80/82	1940±110 BP	66 cal.AD	Uppermost Northern Black Polished Ware, Period III	Charcoal
HASTINAPUR	TF-81	2015±95 BP	32 cal.BC	Uppermost Northern Black Polished Ware, Period III	Charcoal
HETIMPUR	TF-176	2000±100 BP	1 cal. BC	Northern Black Polished Ware Period	Charcoal
HETIMPUR	TF-177	1820±100 BP	214 cal.AD	Northern Black Polished Ware Period	Charcoal
HILI 1	SM-1239	3940±213 BP	2466 cal.BC	Hili 1, Jamdat Nasr	Unknown
HILI 1	SM-1236	3603±213 BP	1965 cal.BC	Hili 1, Jamdat Nasr	Unknown
HILI 1	SM-1238	3606±213 BP	1970 cal.BC	Hili 1, Jamdat Nasr	Unknown

1	*2*	*3*	*4*	*5*	*6*
HILI 1	SM-1237	3715±217 BP	2136 cal.BC	Hili 1, Jamdat Nasr	Unknown
HILI 8	MC-2264	3840±100 BP	2315 ca.BC	Hili 8, IIIE Akkadian	Unknown
HILI 8	MC-2263	3950±90 BP	2468 cal.BC	Hili 8, IIIF Akkadian/ Ur III/Indus Pottery	Unknown
HILI 8	MC-2267	4400±100 BP	3034 cal.BC	Hili 8, IA Building III, Early Dynastic II	Unknown
HILI 8	MC-2260	3430±90 BP	1743 cal.BC	Hili 8, IIIA-B, Early Dynastic II	Unknown
HILI 8	MC-2261	3710±90 BP	2135, 2052 2050 cal.BC	Hili 8, IIIF Akkadian/ Ur III/Indus pottery	Unknown
HILI 8	MC-2262	3690±90 BP	2130, 2074 2045 cal.BC	Hili 8, IIIF Akkadian/ Ur III/Indus pottery	Unknown
HILI 8	MC-2265	3900±100 BP	2457 cal.BC	Hili 8, IIIE Akkadian	Unknown
KAUSAMBI	TF-225	2285±105 BP	390 cal.BC	Mid-level, mid-Northern Black Polished Ware, Period III	Charcoal
KAUSAMBI	TF-105	2220±110 BP	362, 282 258, cal.BC	Late level mid-Northern Black Polished Ware, Period III	Charcoal
KAUSAMBI	TF-103	2295±105 BP	391 cal.BC	Mid-level, Late Northern Black Polished Ware, Period III	Charcoal

1	*2*	*3*	*4*	*5*	*6*
KAUSAMBI	TF-219	2325±100 BP	396 cal.BC	Mid-level, mid-Northern Black Polished Ware, Period III	Charcoal
KAUSAMBI	TF-221	2385±100 BP	406 cal.BC	Early level, mid-Northern Black Polished Ware, Period III	Charcoal
KAUSAMBI	TF-226	2110±95 BP	160, 138, cal.BC	Late level mid-Northern Black Polished Ware, Rampart II	Charcoal
KAUSAMBI	TF-100	2160±95 BP	196 cal.BC	Mid-level, mid-Northern Black Polished Ware, Period III	Charcoal
KAUSAMBI	TF-104	2150±105 BP	192 cal.BC	Late level, mid-Northern Black Polished Ware, Period III	Charcoal
KAYATHA	TF-674	2350±95 BP	400 cal.BC	Northern Black Polished Ware with some Painted Grey Ware	Charcoal
KAYATHA	TF-394	2380±95 BP	405 cal.BC	Northern Black Polished Ware, with some Painted Grey Ware	Charcoal
KHAIRADIH	PRL-1050	2060±150 BP	96 cal.BC	Northern Black Polished Ware	Charcoal

1	*2*	*3*	*4*	*5*	*6*
MANJHI	PRL-980	1930±140 BP	72 cal.AD	Late Northern Black Polished Ware	Charcoal
MANJHI	PRL-983	2350±140 BP	400 cal.AD	Early Northern Black Polished Ware	Charcoal
MATHURA	PRL-343	2150±100 BP	192 cal.BC	Late Northern Black Polished Ware	Charcoal
MATHURA	PRL0340	2390±150 BP	407 cal.BC	Painted Grey Ware/ Northern Black Polished Ware overlap	Charcoal
MATHURA	PRL-333	2490±140 BP	762, 678 662, 627, 600, cal.BC	Late Northern Black Polished Ware	Charcoal
MATHURA	TF-338	2280±100 BP	387 cal.BC	Late Northern Black Polished Ware	Charcoal
MATHURA	TF-342	2180±160 BP	340, 322 203, cal.BC	Early Northern Black Polished Ware overlap	Charcoal
MATHURA	TF-339	2380±100 BP	405 cal.BC	Post Northern Black Polished Ware	Charcoal
MATHURA	TF-337	2340±100 BP	399 cal.BC	Mid-Northern Black Polished Ware	Charcoal
MATHURA	TF-336	2540±90 BP	786 cal.BC	Mid-Northern Black Polished Ware	Charcoal
MATHURA	TF-334	2600±150 BP	801 cal.BC	Early Northern Black Polished Ware	Charcoal

1	2	3	4	5	6
NARHAN	BS-563	2240±100 BP	370 cal.BC	Northern Black Polished Ware Period III	Unknown
NARHAN	BS-564	2200±100 BP	353, 306 236, cal.BC	Northern Black Polished Ware Period III	Unknown
NARHAN	BS-581	2100±100 BP	151, 149 117, cal.BC	Northern Black Polished Ware	Unknown
RAJGHAT	TF-293	2370±105 BP	403 cal.BC	Northern Black Polished Ware	Charcoal
RUPAR	TF-209	2365±100 BP	403 cal.BC	Northern Black Polished Ware	Charred Wood
RUPAR	TF-213	2275±100 BP	385 cal.BC	Northern Black Polished Ware	Charred Wood
SEMTHAN	PRL-946	1880±120 BP	118 cal.AD	Northern Black Polished Ware Period II	Charcoal
SEMTHAN	PRL-945	2280±110 BP	387 cal.BC	Northern Black Polished Ware Period II	Charcoal
SEMTHAN	PRL-941	2200±140 BP	353, 306 236, cal.BC	Northern Black Polished Ware Period II	Charcoal
SOHGAURA	PRL-182A	2130±90 BP	177 cal.BC	Northern Black Polished Ware Period III	Charcoal

1	*2*	*3*	*4*	*5*	*6*
SOHGAURA	PRL-183	2466±105 BP	756, 692 541, cal.BC	Northern Black Polished Ware Period III	Charcoal
SOHGAURA	PRL-182B	2290±400 BP	391 cal.BC	Northern Black Polished Ware Period III	Charcoal
PIRAK	LY-1643	2970±140 BP	1255, 1240 1221 cal.BC	Northern Black Polished Ware Period II	Charcoal

Table 9b. **Dates for Black and Red Ware Sites**
All BP ages are based on 5568 yr half-life of radiocarbon.
Calibrated ages are given in BC/AD.

Site	*Sample no.*	*Dates (BP)*	*Calib. Dates*	*Culture*	*Material*
1	*2*	*3*	*4*	*5*	*6*
CHIRAND	TF-336	2640±95 BP	809 cal.BC	Black & Red Ware Period Iron	Charcoal
KHAIRADIH	PRL-1049	2890±150 BP	484, 437 424, cal.BC	Black & Red Ware	Charcoal
KILAYUR	TF-207	2200±100 BP	353, 306 236 cal.BC	Black & Red Ware	Wood
MAHISDAL	TF-389	2565±105 BP	794 cal.BC	Early Iron Age	Charcoal
RAJGHAT	TF-294	2190±85 BP	348, 316 207 cal.BC	Black & Red Ware	Charcoal
RAJGHAT	TF-292	2350±95 BP	400 cal.BC	Black-slipped Ware	Charcoal
SOHGAURA	PRL-178	3190±110 BP	1491, 1489 1451 cal.BC	Black & Red Ware Chalcolithic	Charcoal
SOHGAURA	PRL-179	3090±130 BP	1400 cal.BC	Black & Red Ware, Chalcolithic	Charcoal
SRINGAVER PURA	PRL-669	2620±130 BP	805 cal.BC	Black & Red Ware	Charcoal
UJJAIN	TF-407	1990±100 BP	8 cal.ad	Black & Red Ware	Charcoal

NOTE

1. The editors would like to draw the attention of readers to the controversy about the dating of tephra formation at Bori. Recent geochemical studies have revealed that the ash was correlated with the youngest Toba ash eruptions dated to about 74 Kyr (Shane et al. 1995). At the same time there are also some fission-track and Ar/Ar dates ranging between 640 and 680 Kyr (Mishra et al. 1995).

ACKNOWLEDGEMENTS

The authors gratefully acknowledge that some radiocarbon dates have been used from Possehl (1994) and Lal(1997), mainly for their archaeological coordinates. We are thankful to Prof. D.P. Agrawal for disussions.

REFERENCES

Agrawal, D.P., and Yadava, M.G. 1995. *Dating the Human Past.* Pune: Indian Society for Prehistoric and Quaternary Studies.

Baskaran, M., Rajagopalan, G., and Somayajulu, B.L.K. 1989. $Th^{230}/U^{234}/C^{14}$ Dating of the Quaternary Carbonate Deposits of Saurashtra, India, *Chemical Geology* (Isotope Geoscience Section) 79: 65-82.

Kusumgar, S., Bhandari, N., and Agrawal, D.P. 1985. Fission Track Ages of the Romishi Lower Karewas, in *Climate and Geology of Kashmir: The Last Four Million Years,* ed., D.P. Agrawal, S. Kusumgar and R.V. Krishnamurthy eds. New Delhi: Today and Tomorrow's Printers and Publishers, pp. 245–47.

Lal, B.B. 1997. *The Earliest Civilisation of South Asia.* New Delhi: Aryan Books International.

Mishra, S., Venkatesan, T.R., Rajaguru, S.N., and Somayajulu, B.L.K. 1995. Earliest Acheulian Industry from Peninsular India. *Current Anthropology* 36: 847–51.

Possehl, G.L. 1994. *Radiometric Dates for South Asian Archaeology.* Publisher not given.

Korisettar, R., Venkatesan, T.R., Mishra, S., Rajaguru, S.N., Somayajulu, B.L.K., Tandon, S.K., Gogte, V.D., Ganjoo, R.K., and Kale, V.S. 1989. Discovery of a Tephra Bed in the Quaternary Alluvial Sediments of Pune District (Maharashtra), Peninsular India. *Current Science* 58: 564–67.

Semaw S., Renne, P., Harris, J.W.K., Feibel, C.S., Berner, R.L., Fesseha, N., and Mowbray, K. 1997. 2.5 Million-Year-Old Stone Tools from Gona, Ethiopia. *Nature*, 385: 333–36.

Shane, P., Westgate, J., Williams, M., and Korisettar, R. 1995. New Geochemical Evidence for the Youngest Toba Tuff in India. *Quaternary Research* 44: 200–204.